ALL GLORY TO ŚRĪ GURU AND GAURĀṄGA

# ŚRĪMAD BHĀGAVATAM

of

KṚṢṆA-DVAIPĀYANA VYĀSA

येऽन्येऽरविन्दाक्ष विमुक्तमानिन-
स्त्वय्यस्तभावादविशुद्धबुद्धयः ।
आरुह्य कृच्छ्रेण परं पदं ततः
पतन्त्यधोऽनादृतयुष्मदङ्घ्रयः ॥३२॥

*ye 'nye 'ravindākṣa vimukta-māninas*
*tvayy asta-bhāvād aviśuddha-buddhayaḥ*
*āruhya kṛcchreṇa paraṁ padaṁ tataḥ*
*patanty adho 'nādṛta-yuṣmad-aṅghrayaḥ*

(p. 172)

## BOOKS by
## His Divine Grace
## A. C. Bhaktivedanta Swami Prabhupāda

Bhagavad-gītā As It Is
Śrīmad-Bhāgavatam, cantos 1-10 (12 vols.)
Śrī Caitanya-caritāmṛta (17 vols.)
Teachings of Lord Caitanya
The Nectar of Devotion
The Nectar of Instruction
Śrī Īśopaniṣad
Easy Journey to Other Planets
Kṛṣṇa Consciousness: The Topmost Yoga System
Kṛṣṇa, The Supreme Personality of Godhead (3 vols.)
Perfect Questions, Perfect Answers
Teachings of Lord Kapila, the Son of Devahūti
Transcendental Teachings of Prahlāda Mahārāja
Dialectic Spiritualism—A Vedic View of Western Philosophy
Teachings of Queen Kuntī
Kṛṣṇa, the Reservoir of Pleasure
The Science of Self-Realization
The Path of Perfection
Search for Liberation
Life Comes from Life
The Perfection of Yoga
Beyond Birth and Death
On the Way to Kṛṣṇa
Geetār-gan (Bengali)
Vairāgya-vidyā (Bengali)
Buddhi-yoga (Bengali)
Bhakti-ratna-bolī (Bengali)
Rāja-vidyā: The King of Knowledge
Elevation to Kṛṣṇa Consciousness
Kṛṣṇa Consciousness: The Matchless Gift
Back to Godhead magazine (founder)

*A complete catalog is available upon request.*

Bhaktivedanta Book Trust
Hare Krishna Land
Juhu, Bombay-400 049

Bhaktivedanta Book Trust
1A, Rainey Park
Calcutta-700 019

# ŚRĪMAD BHĀGAVATAM

## Tenth Canto
## "The Summum Bonum"
## (Part One—Chapters 1–13)

*With the Original Sanskrit Text, Its Roman Transliteration, Synonyms, Translation and Elaborate Purports*

*by*

His Divine Grace
A.C. Bhaktivedanta Swami Prabhupāda
Founder-*Ācārya* of the International Society for Krishna Consciousness

THE BHAKTIVEDANTA BOOK TRUST
Los Angeles · London · Stockholm · Bombay · Sydney

Readers interested in the subject matter of this book are invited by the International Society for Krishna Consciousness to correspond with its Secretary at either of the following addresses:

International Society for Krishna Consciousness
Hare Krishna Land
Juhu, Bombay-400 049

Bhaktivedanta Book Trust
Hare Krishna Land
Juhu, Bombay-400 049

First Indian Printing 1992 / 2000 Copies
Second Indian Printing 1995 / 2000 Copies
Third Indian Printing 1997 / 2000 Copies
Fourth Indian Printing 1998 / 2000 Copies


Printed in India
at Rekha Printers Pvt. Ltd., New Delhi-110 020

*Library of Congress Cataloging in Publication Data (Revised)*

Purāṇas. Bhāgavatapurāṇa. English and Sanskrit.
Śrīmad-Bhāgavatam: with the original Sanskrit text, its roman transliteration, synonyms, translation and elaborate purports.

In English and Sanskrit.
Translation of: Bhāgavatapurāṇa
Includes index.
Contents: 1st canto. Creation— 2nd canto. The cosmic manifestation— 3rd canto. The status quo (2 v)— 4th canto. The creation of the fourth order (2 v)— 5th canto. The creative impetus— 6th canto. Prescribed duties for mankind— 7th canto. The science of God— 8th canto. Withdrawal of the cosmic creations— 9th canto. Liberation— 10th canto. The summum bonum (4 v)— 11th canto. General history (2 v)— 12th canto. The age of deterioration.
Cantos 10 (v 2-4), 11 and 12 by Hridayananda dāsa Goswami, completing the great work of His Divine Grace A. C. Bhaktivedanta Swami Prabhupāda; Sanskrit editing by Gopīparāṇadhana dāsa Adhikārī.
1. Purāṇas. Bhāgavatapurāṇa—Criticism, interpretation, etc. I. Bhaktivedanta Swami, A. C., 1896-1977. II. Title.
BL1140.4.B432E5 1987 294.5'925 87-25585
ISBN 0-89213-261-2 (v. 12)

# Table of Contents

## CHAPTER NINE
# Mother Yaśodā Binds Lord Kṛṣṇa

## CHAPTER TEN
# Deliverance of the Yamala-arjuna Trees

## CHAPTER ELEVEN
# The Childhood Pastimes of Kṛṣṇa

CHAPTER TWELVE

## The Killing of the Demon Aghāsura 615



CHAPTER THIRTEEN

## The Stealing of the Boys and Calves by Brahmā 657

# Appendixes

# Preface

We must know the present need of human society. And what is that need? Human society is no longer bounded by geographical limits to particular countries or communities. Human society is broader than in the Middle Ages, and the world tendency is toward one state or one human society. The ideals of spiritual communism, according to *Śrīmad-Bhāgavatam,* are based more or less on the oneness of the entire human society, nay, of the entire energy of living beings. The need is felt by great thinkers to make this a successful ideology. *Śrīmad-Bhāgavatam* will fill this need in human society. It begins, therefore, with an aphorism of Vedānta philosophy, *janmādy asya yataḥ,* to establish the ideal of a common cause.

Human society, at the present moment, is not in the darkness of oblivion. It has made rapid progress in the fields of material comforts, education and economic development throughout the entire world. But there is a pinprick somewhere in the social body at large, and therefore there are large-scale quarrels, even over less important issues. There is need of a clue as to how humanity can become one in peace, friendship and prosperity with a common cause. *Śrīmad-Bhāgavatam* will fill this need, for it is a cultural presentation for the respiritualization of the entire human society.

*Śrīmad-Bhāgavatam* should be introduced also in the schools and colleges, for it is recommended by the great student-devotee Prahlāda Mahārāja in order to change the demoniac face of society.

*kaumāra ācaret prājño*
*dharmān bhāgavatān iha*
*durlabhaṁ mānuṣaṁ janma*
*tad apy adhruvam artha-dam*
(*Bhāg.* 7.6.1)

Disparity in human society is due to lack of principles in a godless civilization. There is God, or the Almighty One, from whom everything emanates, by whom everything is maintained and in whom everything is merged to rest. Material science has tried to find the ultimate source of creation very insufficiently, but it is a fact that there is one ultimate source of everything that be. This ultimate source is explained rationally and authoritatively in the beautiful *Bhāgavatam,* or *Śrīmad-Bhāgavatam.*

*Śrīmad-Bhāgavatam* is the transcendental science not only for knowing the ultimate source of everything but also for knowing our relation with Him and our duty toward perfection of the human society on the basis of this perfect knowledge. It is powerful reading matter in the Sanskrit language, and it is now rendered into English elaborately so that simply by a careful reading one will know God perfectly well, so much so that the reader will be sufficiently educated to defend himself from the onslaught of atheists. Over and above this, the reader will be able to convert others to accepting God as a concrete principle.

*Śrīmad-Bhāgavatam* begins with the definition of the ultimate source. It is a bona fide commentary on the *Vedānta-sūtra* by the same author, Śrīla Vyāsadeva, and gradually it develops into nine cantos up to the highest state of God realization. The only qualification one needs to study this great book of transcendental knowledge is to proceed step by step cautiously and not jump forward haphazardly as with an ordinary book. It should be gone through chapter by chapter, one after another. The reading matter is so arranged with the original Sanskrit text, its English transliteration, synonyms, translation and purports so that one is sure to become a God-realized soul at the end of finishing the first nine cantos.

The Tenth Canto is distinct from the first nine cantos because it deals directly with the transcendental activities of the Personality of Godhead, Śrī Kṛṣṇa. One will be unable to capture the effects of the Tenth Canto without going through the first nine cantos. The book is complete in twelve cantos, each independent, but it is good for all to read them in small installments one after another.

I must admit my frailties in presenting *Śrīmad-Bhāgavatam,* but still I am hopeful of its good reception by the thinkers and leaders of society on the strength of the following statement of *Śrīmad-Bhāgavatam* (1.5.11):

*tad-vāg-visargo janatāgha-viplavo*
*yasmin prati-ślokam abaddhavaty api*

*nāmāny anantasya yaśo 'ṅkitāni yac*
*chṛṇvanti gāyanti gṛṇanti sādhavaḥ*

"On the other hand, that literature which is full of descriptions of the transcendental glories of the name, fame, form and pastimes of the unlimited Supreme Lord is a transcendental creation meant for bringing about a revolution in the impious life of a misdirected civilization. Such transcendental literature, even though irregularly composed, is heard, sung and accepted by purified men who are thoroughly honest."

*Oṁ tat sat*

A. C. Bhaktivedanta Swami

# Introduction

"This *Bhāgavata Purāṇa* is as brilliant as the sun, and it has arisen just after the departure of Lord Kṛṣṇa to His own abode, accompanied by religion, knowledge, etc. Persons who have lost their vision due to the dense darkness of ignorance in the age of Kali shall get light from this *Purāṇa*." (*Śrīmad-Bhāgavatam* 1.3.43)

The timeless wisdom of India is expressed in the *Vedas*, ancient Sanskrit texts that touch upon all fields of human knowledge. Originally preserved through oral tradition, the *Vedas* were first put into writing five thousand years ago by Śrīla Vyāsadeva, the "literary incarnation of God." After compiling the *Vedas*, Vyāsadeva set forth their essence in the aphorisms known as *Vedānta-sūtras*. *Śrīmad-Bhāgavatam* (*Bhāgavata Purāṇa*) is Vyāsadeva's commentary on his own *Vedānta-sūtras*. It was written in the maturity of his spiritual life under the direction of Nārada Muni, his spiritual master. Referred to as "the ripened fruit of the tree of Vedic literature," *Śrīmad-Bhāgavatam* is the most complete and authoritative exposition of Vedic knowledge.

After compiling the *Bhāgavatam*, Vyāsa imparted the synopsis of it to his son, the sage Śukadeva Gosvāmī. Śukadeva Gosvāmī subsequently recited the entire *Bhāgavatam* to Mahārāja Parīkṣit in an assembly of learned saints on the bank of the Ganges at Hastināpura (now Delhi). Mahārāja Parīkṣit was the emperor of the world and was a great *rājarṣi* (saintly king). Having received a warning that he would die within a week, he renounced his entire kingdom and retired to the bank of the Ganges to fast until death and receive spiritual enlightenment. The *Bhāgavatam* begins with Emperor Parīkṣit's sober inquiry to Śukadeva Gosvāmī: "You are the spiritual master of great saints and devotees. I am therefore begging you to show the way of perfection for all persons, and especially for one who is about to die. Please let me know what a man should hear, chant, remember and worship, and also what he should not do. Please explain all this to me."

Śukadeva Gosvāmī's answer to this question, and numerous other questions posed by Mahārāja Parīkṣit, concerning everything from the nature of the self to the origin of the universe, held the assembled sages in rapt attention continuously for the seven days leading up to the king's death. The sage Sūta Gosvāmī, who was present in that assembly when Śukadeva Gosvāmī first recited *Śrīmad-Bhāgavatam,* later repeated the *Bhāgavatam* before a gathering of sages in the forest of Naimiṣāraṇya. Those sages, concerned about the spiritual welfare of the people in general, had gathered to perform a long, continuous chain of sacrifices to counteract the degrading influence of the incipient age of Kali. In response to the sages' request that he speak the essence of Vedic wisdom, Sūta Gosvāmī repeated from memory the entire eighteen thousand verses of *Śrīmad-Bhāgavatam,* as spoken by Śukadeva Gosvāmī to Mahārāja Parīkṣit.

The reader of *Śrīmad-Bhāgavatam* hears Sūta Gosvāmī relate the questions of Mahārāja Parīkṣit and the answers of Śukadeva Gosvāmī. Also, Sūta Gosvāmī sometimes responds directly to questions put by Śaunaka Ṛṣi, the spokesman for the sages gathered at Naimiṣāraṇya. One therefore simultaneously hears two dialogues: one between Mahārāja Parīkṣit and Śukadeva Gosvāmī on the bank of the Ganges, and another at Naimiṣāraṇya between Sūta Gosvāmī and the sages at Naimiṣāraṇya forest, headed by Śaunaka Ṛṣi. Furthermore, while instructing King Parīkṣit, Śukadeva Gosvāmī often relates historical episodes and gives accounts of lengthy philosophical discussions between such great souls as Nārada Muni and Vasudeva. With this understanding of the history of the *Bhāgavatam,* the reader will easily be able to follow its intermingling of dialogues and events from various sources. Since philosophical wisdom, not chronological order, is most important in the text, one need only be attentive to the subject matter of *Śrīmad-Bhāgavatam* to appreciate fully its profound message.

The translators of this edition compare the *Bhāgavatam* to sugar candy—wherever you taste it, you will find it equally sweet and relishable. Therefore, to taste the sweetness of the *Bhāgavatam,* one may begin by reading any of its volumes. After such an introductory taste, however, the serious reader is best advised to go back to the First Canto and then proceed through the *Bhāgavatam,* canto after canto, in its natural order.

This edition of the *Bhāgavatam* is the first complete English translation of this important text with an elaborate commentary, and it is the first widely available to the English-speaking public. The first twelve volumes (Canto One through Canto Ten, Part One) are the product of the scholarly and devotional effort of His Divine Grace A. C. Bhaktivedanta Swami Prabhupāda, the founder-*ācārya* of the International

Society for Krishna Consciousness and the world's most distinguished teacher of Indian religious and philosophical thought. His consummate Sanskrit scholarship and intimate familiarity with Vedic culture and thought as well as the modern way of life combine to reveal to the West a magnificent exposition of this important classic. After the departure of Śrīla Prabhupāda from this world in 1977, his monumental work of translating and annotating *Śrīmad-Bhāgavatam* has been continued by his disciples Hridayananda dāsa Goswami and Gopīparāṇadhana dāsa.

Readers will find this work of value for many reasons. For those interested in the classical roots of Indian civilization, it serves as a vast reservoir of detailed information on virtually every one of its aspects. For students of comparative philosophy and religion, the *Bhāgavatam* offers a penetrating view into the meaning of India's profound spiritual heritage. To sociologists and anthropologists, the *Bhāgavatam* reveals the practical workings of a peaceful and scientifically organized Vedic culture, whose institutions were integrated on the basis of a highly developed spiritual world view. Students of literature will discover the *Bhāgavatam* to be a masterpiece of majestic poetry. For students of psychology, the text provides important perspectives on the nature of consciousness, human behavior and the philosophical study of identity. Finally, to those seeking spiritual insight, the *Bhāgavatam* offers simple and practical guidance for attainment of the highest self-knowledge and realization of the Absolute Truth. The entire multivolume text, presented by the Bhaktivedanta Book Trust, promises to occupy a significant place in the intellectual, cultural and spiritual life of modern man for a long time to come.

—The Publishers

# SUMMARY OF THE TENTH CANTO

A short description of each chapter of this Tenth Canto is as follows. The First Chapter, which has sixty-nine verses, describes Mahārāja Parīkṣit's eagerness to learn about the incarnation of Lord Kṛṣṇa, and it also tells how Kaṁsa killed the six sons of Devakī because of his fear of being killed by her eighth child. The Second Chapter contains forty-two verses, describing the entrance of the Supreme Personality of Godhead, Kṛṣṇa, into the womb of Devakī to fulfill His mission of killing Kaṁsa. When Lord Kṛṣṇa was within Devakī's womb, all the demigods, headed by Brahmā, offered prayers to the Lord. The Third Chapter contains fifty-three verses. This chapter describes the appearance of Lord Kṛṣṇa as He is. The Lord's father and mother, understanding the Lord's appearance, offered prayers. Fearing Kaṁsa, the Lord's father brought the child from Mathurā to Gokula Vṛndāvana. The Fourth Chapter contains forty-six verses, which tell of a prophecy by the goddess Caṇḍikā. After consulting demoniac friends, Kaṁsa began killing all the children born at that time, since he thought this would be to his benefit.

The Fifth Chapter contains thirty-two verses, describing how Nanda Mahārāja performed the birth ceremony of Kṛṣṇa and then went to Mathurā, where he met Vasudeva. The Sixth Chapter contains forty-four verses. In this chapter, Nanda Mahārāja, following the advice of his friend Vasudeva, returns to Gokula and on the way sees the dead body of the Pūtanā demoness and is astonished at her having been killed by Kṛṣṇa. The Seventh Chapter, which contains thirty-seven verses, describes Mahārāja Parīkṣit's enthusiasm to hear about the boyhood pastimes of Lord Kṛṣṇa, who killed Śakaṭāsura and Tṛṇāvartāsura and showed within His mouth the entire cosmic manifestation. In the Eighth Chapter there are fifty-two verses, which describe Gargamuni's performing the name-giving ceremony of Kṛṣṇa and Balarāma and how Kṛṣṇa and Balarāma performed playful childish activities, crawling on the ground, trying to walk with Their small legs, and stealing butter and breaking the pots. This chapter also describes the vision of the universal form.

The Ninth Chapter, which has twenty-three verses, describes how Kṛṣṇa disturbed His mother while she was churning butter. Because she left Kṛṣṇa to see to the stove, where the milk was boiling, and did not allow Him to suck her breast, Kṛṣṇa was very angry and broke a pot of yogurt. To chastise her naughty child, mother Yaśodā wanted to bind Him with rope, but every time she tried she failed because of a shortage of rope when the time came to knot it. In the Tenth Chapter there are forty-three verses. This chapter describes how Kṛṣṇa, as Dāmodara, caused the twin Yamalārjuna trees to fall and how the two demigods within the trees were delivered by the mercy of Kṛṣṇa. In the Eleventh Chapter there are fifty-nine verses. This chapter describes how Nanda Mahārāja released Kṛṣṇa from the ropes, how Kṛṣṇa showed His mercy to a fruit seller while exchanging grains for fruit, and how Nanda Mahārāja and others decided to leave Gokula for Vṛndāvana, where Kṛṣṇa killed Vatsāsura and Bakāsura.

Chapter Twelve contains forty-four verses, describing Kṛṣṇa's pastimes with the cowherd boys in the forest and the killing of the demon named Aghāsura. Chapter Thirteen contains sixty-four verses, describing how Brahmā stole Kṛṣṇa's calves and His friends, the cowherd boys. Kṛṣṇa expanded His pastimes for one year, representing Himself as the calves and boys in forms exactly like their own. In this way He bewildered Brahmā, who at last surrendered when his illusion was over. The Fourteenth Chapter contains sixty-one verses. In this chapter, Brahmā offers prayers to Kṛṣṇa after fully understanding Him to be the Supreme Personality of Godhead. The Fifteenth Chapter contains fifty-two verses. This chapter describes how Kṛṣṇa entered Tālavana Forest with Balārama, how Balārama killed Dhenukāsura, and how Kṛṣṇa protected the cowherd boys and cows from the poisonous effects of Kāliya.

The Sixteenth Chapter contains sixty-seven verses. This chapter describes the chastisement of Kāliya by Kṛṣṇa, and it also describes the prayers offered by Kāliya's wives. In the Seventeenth Chapter there are twenty-five verses. This chapter describes why Kāliya entered the River Yamunā after leaving his home, Nāgālaya, one of the *dvīpas,* which according to some corresponds to the Fiji Islands. This chapter also describes how Garuḍa was cursed by Saubhari Ṛṣi, how the cowherd boys, Kṛṣṇa's friends, were enlivened when Kṛṣṇa emerged from the Yamunā, and how Kṛṣṇa stopped the forest fire and saved the sleeping inhabitants of Vraja.

The Eighteenth Chapter contains thirty-two verses, giving a description of Kṛṣṇa and Balarāma, Their picnics within the forest, the climate of Vṛndāvana in the summer and the spring, and Lord Balarāma's killing of Pralambāsura. Chapter Nineteen contains sixteen verses, describing Kṛṣṇa's entering the forest known as Muñjāraṇya, saving the cowherd boys and cows from the forest fire, and bringing them to Bhāṇḍīravana. Chapter Twenty contains forty-nine verses. This chapter describes the enjoyment of Balarāma and Kṛṣṇa in the forest with the cowherd boys during the rainy season, and it gives various instructions through analogies concerning the rainy season and autumn.

Chapter Twenty-one contains twenty verses, describing how Kṛṣṇa entered the forest of Vṛndāvana in the autumn, playing His flute, and how He attracted the *gopīs*, who were singing His glories. The Twenty-second Chapter contains thirty-eight verses, describing how the *gopīs* prayed to the goddess Kātyāyanī to obtain Kṛṣṇa as their husband and how Kṛṣṇa later stole the garments of the *gopīs* while the *gopīs* were bathing in the Yamunā. The Twenty-third Chapter contains fifty-two verses, describing how the cowherd boys, being very hungry, followed Kṛṣṇa's directions by begging some food for Him and themselves from *brāhmaṇas* engaged in performing *yajñas.* The *brāhmaṇas* refused to give food to Kṛṣṇa and Balarāma, although the boys begged for it, but the wives of the *brāhmaṇas* agreed, and therefore Kṛṣṇa bestowed His mercy upon them.

The Twenty-fourth Chapter contains thirty-eight verses, describing how Kṛṣṇa defied King Indra, despite Indra's position of prestige, by stopping the *indra-yajña* and instead worshiping Govardhana. The Twenty-fifth Chapter contains thirty-three verses. As described in this chapter, because the *indra-yajña* was stopped, King Indra was very angry, and to kill the inhabitants of Vṛndāvana, Vraja, he flooded the entire area with rain. Kṛṣṇa, however, accepted King Indra's challenge by lifting Govardhana Hill as an umbrella to protect Vṛndāvana and all the cows. The Twenty-sixth Chapter contains twenty-five verses, describing how Nanda Mahārāja, seeing the extraordinary activities of Kṛṣṇa, was struck with wonder and how he thus narrated for all the cowherd men the whole story of Kṛṣṇa's opulence, as foretold by Gargamuni. Chapter Twenty-seven, which contains twenty-eight verses, describes how King Indra, upon seeing Kṛṣṇa's unlimited power, worshiped Lord Kṛṣṇa, who was fully washed with milk supplied by the *surabhi* and who thus became known as Govinda. The Twenty-eighth Chapter contains seventeen verses. In this chapter Kṛṣṇa saves His father, Nanda Mahārāja, from the custody of Varuṇa and shows the cowherd men how Vaikuṇṭhaloka is situated.

The Twenty-ninth Chapter contains forty-eight verses, describing how Kṛṣṇa talked to the *gopīs* before performing the *rāsa-līlā* and how, after the beginning of the *rāsa-līlā*, Kṛṣṇa disappeared from the scene. Chapter Thirty contains forty-four verses, describing how the *gopīs*, being separated from Kṛṣṇa, went mad and began to wander in the forest in search of Him. The *gopīs* met Śrīmatī Rādhārāṇī, the daughter of King Vṛṣabhānu, and they all wandered on the bank of the Yamunā searching for Kṛṣṇa. Chapter Thirty-one contains nineteen verses, describing how the bereaved *gopīs* waited in great anxiety to meet Kṛṣṇa. Chapter Thirty-two contains twenty-two verses. In this chapter, Kṛṣṇa appears among the *gopīs*, who are fully satisfied in ecstatic love for Him. Chapter Thirty-three contains thirty-nine verses. In this chapter Kṛṣṇa appears in multiforms in the midst of the *gopīs*, with whom He dances in the *rāsa* dance. Then they all bathe in the River Yamunā. Also in this chapter, Śukadeva mitigates the doubts of Parīkṣit concerning the performance of the *rāsa-līlā*.

Chapter Thirty-four contains thirty-two verses. This chapter describes how Nanda Mahārāja, Kṛṣṇa's father, was swallowed by a big python, who had been a demigod named Vidyādhara but was cursed by Aṅgirā Ṛṣi. Kṛṣṇa rescued His father and saved this demigod simultaneously. Chapter Thirty-five contains twenty-six verses. This chapter describes how Kṛṣṇa went to the pasturing grounds with the cows and how the *gopīs* sang in separation from Him.

Chapter Thirty-six contains forty verses. This chapter describes Kṛṣṇa's killing of Ariṣṭāsura. It also describes Nārada's disclosure to Kaṁsa that both Rāma and Kṛṣṇa were sons of Vasudeva. Because of this disclosure, Kaṁsa arranged to kill both Rāma and Kṛṣṇa. He sent his assistant Keśī to Vṛndāvana, and later he sent Akrūra to bring Rāma and Kṛṣṇa to Mathurā. Chapter Thirty-seven contains thirty-three verses. In this chapter Kṛṣṇa kills the Keśī demon, Nārada worships Kṛṣṇa by narrating His future activities, and Kṛṣṇa kills the demon named Vyomāsura. Chapter Thirty-eight contains forty-three verses. This chapter describes how Akrūra went to Vṛndāvana and how he was received by Rāma-Kṛṣṇa and Nanda Mahārāja. Chapter Thirty-nine contains fifty-seven verses. This chapter describes how Rāma and Kṛṣṇa, having been invited by Kaṁsa, started for Mathurā. While They were ready on the chariot, the *gopīs* began to cry, and Kṛṣṇa sent His messenger to pacify them. Thus He was able to travel toward Mathurā. On the way, Akrūra was shown the entire Viṣṇuloka within the water of the Yamunā.

Chapter Forty contains thirty verses, in which the prayers of Akrūra are described. Chapter Forty-one, which contains fifty-two verses, describes the entrance of Rāma and Kṛṣṇa into the city of Mathurā, where the ladies were very jubilant to see these two brothers. Kṛṣṇa killed a washerman, glorified Sudāmā and gave Sudāmā His benediction. Chapter Forty-two, which contains thirty-eight verses, describes how Kṛṣṇa delivered Kubjā and how He broke Kaṁsa's gigantic bow and killed its caretakers. Thus Kaṁsa and Kṛṣṇa met. Chapter Forty-three contains forty verses. Outside the sporting arena of Kaṁsa, Kṛṣṇa killed an elephant named Kuvalayāpīḍa. Then He entered the arena and spoke with Cāṇūra. Chapter Forty-four, which contains fifty-one verses, describes how Kṛṣṇa and Balarāma killed the wrestlers named Cāṇūra and Muṣṭika and thereafter killed Kaṁsa and his eight brothers. Kṛṣṇa, however, pacified Kaṁsa's wives and His own father and mother, Vasudeva and Devakī.

Chapter Forty-five contains fifty verses. This chapter describes how Kṛṣṇa pacified His father and mother and celebrated the enthronement of His grandfather Ugrasena. After promising the inhabitants of Vṛndāvana that He would return very soon, Kṛṣṇa underwent ritualistic ceremonies as a *kṣatriya*. He took the vow of *brahmacarya* and lived in the *guru-kula*, where He studied regularly. By killing the demon named Pañcajana, He received a conchshell named Pāñcajanya. Kṛṣṇa rescued the son of His *guru* from the custody of Yamarāja and returned them. After thus offering *guru-dakṣiṇā* to repay His teacher, Lord Kṛṣṇa returned to Mathurā-purī. Chapter Forty-six contains forty-nine verses. As described in this chapter, Kṛṣṇa sent Uddhava to Vṛndāvana to pacify His father and mother, Nanda Mahārāja and Yaśodā. Chapter Forty-seven contains sixty-nine verses, describing how Uddhava, following Kṛṣṇa's order, went to pacify the *gopīs* and then returned to Mathurā. Thus Uddhava appreciated the ecstatic love felt for Kṛṣṇa by the inhabitants of Vṛndāvana.

Chapter Forty-eight contains thirty-six verses. This chapter describes how Kṛṣṇa fulfilled the desire of Kubjā by going to her house and enjoying her. Kṛṣṇa then went to the home of Akrūra. Satisfied by Akrūra's prayers, Kṛṣṇa praised him very much and sent him to Hastināpura to gather information about the Pāṇḍavas. Chapter Forty-nine contains thirty-one verses. As described in this chapter, Akrūra, following Kṛṣṇa's orders, went to Hastināpura, where he met Vidura and Kuntī and heard from them about Dhṛtarāṣṭra's mistreatment of the Pāṇḍavas. Informed of the Pāṇḍavas' faith in Kṛṣṇa, Akrūra advised Dhṛtarāṣṭra, and after understanding Dhṛtarāṣṭra's mind, he returned to Mathurā, where he described everything about the situation in Hastināpura.

Chapter Fifty contains fifty-seven verses. In this chapter, Jarāsandha, having heard that his son-in-law Kaṁsa was killed, attacked Mathurā to kill Rāma and Kṛṣṇa but was defeated seventeen times. When Jarāsandha was about to attack for the eighteenth time, Kālayavana, having been advised by Nārada, also attacked Mathurā. Thus the Yādava dynasty entered a fort in the midst of the water and lived there by mystic power. After giving full protection to the Yādava dynasty and conferring with Lord Baladeva, Lord Kṛṣṇa emerged from Dvārakā. Chapter Fifty-one, which contains sixty-three verses, describes how Mucukunda killed Kālayavana simply by glancing upon him.

Chapter Fifty-two contains forty-four verses. In this chapter, Mucukunda offers prayers to Kṛṣṇa, and then Kṛṣṇa kills all the soldiers of Kālayavana and returns to Dvārakā with their booty. When Jarāsandha attacked Mathurā again, Rāma and Kṛṣṇa, as if afraid of him, fled to the top of a mountain, to which Jarāsandha then set fire. Unseen by Jarāsandha, Kṛṣṇa and Balarāma jumped from the mountain and entered Dvārakā, which was surrounded by the sea. Jarāsandha, thinking that Kṛṣṇa and Balarāma had been killed, returned with his soldiers to his own country, and Kṛṣṇa continued to live in Dvārakā. Rukmiṇī, the daughter of Vidarbha, was very much attracted to Kṛṣṇa, and she sent Kṛṣṇa a letter through a *brāhmaṇa*. Chapter Fifty-three contains fifty-seven verses. Following Rukmiṇī's request, Kṛṣṇa went to the city of Vidarbha and kidnapped her in the presence of such enemies as Jarāsandha. Chapter Fifty-four contains sixty verses. As described in this chapter, Kṛṣṇa defeated all the opposing princes and disfigured Rukmiṇī's brother Rukmī. Then Kṛṣṇa returned with Rukmiṇī to Dvārakā, where they were united in a regular marriage. Rukmī, however, remained in a place known as Bhojakaṭa, being angry at his brother-in-law, Kṛṣṇa. Chapter Fifty-five, containing forty verses, describes the birth of Pradyumna, how Pradyumna was kidnapped by Śambarāsura, and how Pradyumna later killed Śambarāsura and returned to Dvārakā with his wife, Ratidevī.

Chapter Fifty-six contains forty-five verses. As described in this chapter, King Satrājit, by the mercy of the sun-god, received a jewel called Syamantaka. Later, when this jewel was stolen, Satrājit unnecessarily became doubtful of Kṛṣṇa, but Kṛṣṇa, to vindicate His position, retrieved the jewel, along with the daughter of Jāmbavān. Kṛṣṇa later married Satrājit's daughter and received a full dowry. As described in Chapter Fifty-seven, which contains forty-two verses, both Balarāma and Kṛṣṇa went to Hastināpura, having heard about the fire in the shellac house of the Pāṇḍavas. After Satrājit was killed by Śatadhanvā at the instigation of Akrūra and Kṛtavarmā, Balarāma and Kṛṣṇa returned to Dvārakā. Śatadhanvā left the Syamantaka jewel with Akrūra and fled to the forest. Thus although Kṛṣṇa killed Śatadhanvā, He was unable to retrieve the jewel. Finally the jewel was discovered and awarded to Akrūra. Chapter Fifty-eight contains fifty-eight verses. After the Pāṇḍavas finished living incognito in the forest, Kṛṣṇa went to Indraprastha to see them. He then married five wives, headed by Kālindī. After Kṛṣṇa and Arjuna set fire to the Khāṇḍava Forest, Arjuna received the Gāṇḍīva bow. The demon Maya Dānava constructed an assembly house for the Pāṇḍavas, and Duryodhana was very much aggrieved.

Chapter Fifty-nine contains forty-five verses. In this chapter, Kṛṣṇa, at the request of Indra, kills the demon Narakāsura, the son of the earth personified, along with the demon's associates, headed by Mura. The earth personified offers prayers to Kṛṣṇa and returns to Him all the paraphernalia that Narakāsura has stolen. Kṛṣṇa then bestows fearlessness upon the son of Narakāsura and marries the sixteen thousand princesses whom the demon kidnapped. Also in this chapter, Kṛṣṇa takes away the *pārijāta* plant from the heavenly planets, and the foolishness of Indra and others is described.

Chapter Sixty contains fifty-nine verses. In this chapter, Kṛṣṇa makes Rukmiṇī angry with His joking words. Kṛṣṇa pacifies Rukmiṇī, and there is a lover's quarrel between them. Chapter Sixty-one contains forty verses. This chapter contains a description of the sons and grandsons of Kṛṣṇa. At the time of Aniruddha's marriage, Balarāma kills Rukmī and breaks the teeth of the King of Kaliṅga.

Chapter Sixty-two contains thirty-three verses. This chapter begins the discourse concerning the abduction of Ūṣā, the daughter of Bāṇāsura, and the amorous pastimes between Ūṣā and Aniruddha. It also describes a fight between Aniruddha and Bāṇāsura and how Bāṇāsura seized Aniruddha with a snake-noose. Chapter Sixty-three, which contains fifty-three verses, describes how the strength of Lord Śiva was defeated in a battle between Bāṇāsura and the Yādavas. The Raudra-jvara, having been defeated by the Vaiṣṇava-jvara, offered prayers to Kṛṣṇa. Kṛṣṇa severed all but four of Bāṇa's one thousand arms and thus showed him mercy. Kṛṣṇa then returned to Dvārakā with Ūṣā and Aniruddha.

Chapter Sixty-four contains forty-four verses. In this chapter, Kṛṣṇa liberates King Nṛga, the son of Ikṣvāku, from a curse and instructs all kings by explaining the fault in misappropriating the property of a *brāhmaṇa.* In connection with the deliverance of King Nṛga, there are instructions for the Yādavas, who were puffed up with pride due to wealth, opulence, enjoyment and so on.

Chapter Sixty-five contains thirty-four verses. As described in this chapter, Lord Baladeva, desiring to see His friends and relatives, went to Gokula. In the months of Caitra and Vaiśākha, in the groves by the Yamunā, Lord Balarāma performed the *rāsa-rasotsava* and *yamunā-karṣaṇa līlās* in the association of His *gopīs.*

As described in Chapter Sixty-six, which contains forty-three verses, Kṛṣṇa went to Kāśī and then killed Pauṇḍraka, as well as his friend the King of Kāśī, Sudakṣiṇa and others. Chapter Sixty-seven, which contains twenty-eight verses, describes how Lord Baladeva, while enjoying with many young girls on Raivataka Mountain, vanquished the extremely mischievous ape Dvivida, who was the brother of Mainda and a friend of Narakāsura's.

Chapter Sixty-eight has fifty-four verses. As described in this chapter, when Sāmba, the son of Jāmbavatī, kidnapped Lakṣmaṇā, the daughter of Duryodhana, he was captured in a fight with the Kauravas. In order to free him and establish peace, Lord Baladeva went to Hastināpura as a well-wisher. The Kauravas, however, were uncooperative, and upon seeing their arrogance, Lord Baladeva began pulling their city of

Hastināpura with His plow. The Kauravas, headed by Duryodhana, offered prayers to Lord Baladeva, who then returned to Dvārakā with Sāmba and Lakṣmaṇā.

Chapter Sixty-nine contains forty-five verses. As described in this chapter, Kṛṣṇa exhibited His householder life with His sixteen thousand wives. Even the great sage Nārada was astonished at how Kṛṣṇa, having expanded Himself into sixteen thousand forms, was conducting His householder life. Thus Nārada offered prayers to Lord Kṛṣṇa, and Kṛṣṇa was very much pleased with him.

Chapter Seventy, which contains forty-seven verses, describes how Kṛṣṇa exhibited His daily ritualistic ceremonies and how He released the kings arrested by Jarāsandha. While Lord Kṛṣṇa was receiving a messenger sent by these kings, Nārada came to see Kṛṣṇa and told Him news of the Pāṇḍavas. Nārada informed Kṛṣṇa that the Pāṇḍavas desired to perform a *rājasūya* sacrifice, and Kṛṣṇa agreed to attend it, but He first asked for Uddhava's decision about whether to give preference to killing King Jarāsandha or performing the *rājasūya-yajña.* Chapter Seventy-one contains forty-five verses, describing the happiness of the Pāṇḍavas when Kṛṣṇa went to Indraprastha. By the inconceivable desire of Kṛṣṇa, Jarāsandha would be killed, and the *rājasūya-yajña* would be performed by Mahārāja Yudhiṣṭhira.

Chapter Seventy-two contains forty-six verses. By agreeing to perform the *rājasūya-yajña,* Kṛṣṇa gave Mahārāja Yudhiṣṭhira great pleasure. This chapter also describes the killing of Jarāsandha, the enthroning of his son, and the release of the kings whom Jarāsandha had arrested. Chapter Seventy-three contains thirty-five verses. After Lord Kṛṣṇa released the kings and restored their royal power, He was worshiped by Sahadeva, the son of Jarāsandha, and then He returned to Indraprastha with Bhīma and Arjuna. Chapter Seventy-four contains fifty-four verses. Mahārāja Yudhiṣṭhira offered prayers to Kṛṣṇa and offered Him the first worship in the *rājasūya-yajña.* To honor the Lord in this way is the foremost duty of every man, but this was intolerable to Śiśupāla, the King of Cedi. Śiśupāla began to blaspheme Kṛṣṇa, who thus severed the King's head from his body and awarded him the salvation called *sārūpya-mukti.* After the conclusion of the *rājasūya* sacrifice, Kṛṣṇa returned to Dvārakā with His queens. Chapter Seventy-five contains forty verses. As described in this chapter, Mahārāja Yudhiṣṭhira, after the *rājasūya-yajña*, performed the final ritualistic bathing ceremonies. Duryodhana was bewildered in the palace constructed by Maya Dānava, and thus he felt insulted.

Chapter Seventy-six contains thirty-three verses, describing how Śālva, one of the kings Kṛṣṇa defeated when He kidnapped Rukmiṇī, decided to rid the entire world of the Yādavas. To defeat the Yādavas, Śālva worshiped Lord Śiva, who rewarded him with an aerial car named Saubha. When Śālva fought with the Vṛṣṇis, Pradyumna smashed the car designed by Maya Dānava, but he was attacked by Śālva's brother, whose name was Dyumān. Beaten unconscious by Dyumān's club, Pradyumna was carried some distance away from the warfield by his charioteer, but later he lamented having been removed from the battlefield. Chapter Seventy-seven contains thirty-seven verses. In this chapter, Pradyumna recovers from his injuries and begins fighting with Śālva. When Kṛṣṇa returned to Dvārakā from Indraprastha, He immediately went to the battlefield where Śālva and Pradyumna were fighting. There He killed Śālva, although Śālva was powerfully equipped with illusory weapons.

Chapter Seventy-eight contains forty verses. As described in this chapter, a friend of Śālva's named Dantavakra and Dantavakra's brother Vidūratha were killed by Śrī Kṛṣṇa. Instead of taking part in the fighting between the Kauravas and the Pāṇḍavas, Baladeva, who had been staying at Dvārakā-purī, went touring holy places. Because of the misbehavior of Romaharṣaṇa, Baladeva killed him at Naimiṣāraṇya and appointed his son Ugraśravā, Sūta Gosvāmī, the speaker of *Śrīmad-Bhāgavatam*, to continue the discourses on the *Purāṇas*. Chapter Seventy-nine contains thirty-four verses. This chapter describes how the *brāhmaṇas* of Naimiṣāraṇya advised Baladeva to atone for the death of Romaharṣaṇa. After killing a demon named Balvala, Baladeva traveled and bathed in holy places until He at last came to the Battlefield of Kurukṣetra, where Bhīma and Duryodhana were fighting. Then He returned to Dvārakā and went again to Naimiṣāraṇya, where He instructed the *ṛṣis*. Then He left with His wife Revatī.

Chapter Eighty, which contains forty-five verses, describes how Sudāmā Vipra, a friend of Kṛṣṇa's, approached Kṛṣṇa for money and was worshiped by Kṛṣṇa, who reminisced with him about their boyhood at the *guru-kula*. Chapter Eighty-one contains forty-one verses. This chapter describes the friendly talks between Kṛṣṇa and His friend

Sudāmā. Kṛṣṇa very gladly accepted a gift of flat rice from Sudāmā Vipra. When Sudāmā Vipra returned home, he saw that everything there was wonderfully opulent, and he praised the friendship of the Supreme Personality of Godhead. With the gifts of the Lord, he enjoyed material opulence, and later he was promoted back home, back to Godhead.

Chapter Eighty-two contains forty-eight verses. This chapter describes how the Yādavas went to Kurukṣetra because of a solar eclipse and how other kings spoke to them of Kṛṣṇa. At this meeting, Kṛṣṇa satisfied Nanda Mahārāja and the residents of Vṛndāvana, who had also come there. Chapter Eighty-three contains forty-three verses, describing how the women assembed at Kurukṣetra engaged in topics of Śrī Kṛṣṇa and how Draupadī asked all Kṛṣṇa's queens about how they had married Him. Chapter Eighty-four contains seventy-one verses. As described in this chapter, when great sages went to see Kṛṣṇa at Kurukṣetra, Kṛṣṇa took this opportunity to praise them. Because Vasudeva desired to perform a great sacrifice on this occasion, the sages advised him regarding worship of Kṛṣṇa, the Supreme Personality of Godhead. After the *yajña* was performed, all who were present dispersed to their respective abodes. Chapter Eighty-five contains fifty-nine verses. At the request of His father and mother, Kṛṣṇa, by His mercy, returned their dead sons, all of whom were liberated. Chapter Eighty-six contains fifty-nine verses. This chapter describes how Arjuna kidnapped Subhadrā with a great fight. It also describes how Kṛṣṇa went to Mithilā to favor His devotee Bahulāśva and stay at the house of Śrutadeva and advise them about spiritual advancement.

Chapter Eighty-seven contains fifty verses, describing the prayers offered to Nārāyaṇa by the *Vedas.* Chapter Eighty-eight contains forty verses. This chapter describes how Vaiṣṇavas become transcendental by worshiping Lord Viṣṇu and then return home, back to Godhead. By worship of demigods, one may get material power, but this chapter describes how an ordinary living being in the material world can be favored by Lord Śrī Kṛṣṇa, and it establishes Lord Viṣṇu's supremacy above Lord Brahmā and Lord Śiva. Chapter Eighty-nine contains sixty-five verses, disclosing who is the best among the material deities. Although Viṣṇu is among the three deities—Brahmā, Viṣṇu and Maheśvara—He is transcendental and supreme. In this chapter we also find a description of how Kṛṣṇa and Arjuna went to Mahākāla-pura to deliver the son of a Dvārakā *brāhmaṇa* and how Arjuna was astonished. Chapter Ninety contains fifty verses. This chapter summarizes Kṛṣṇa's *līlās* and presents the logic of *madhureṇa samāpayet*, establishing that everything ends well in transcendental bliss.

**His Divine Grace**
**A. C. Bhaktivedanta Swami Prabhupāda**
*Founder-Ācārya of the International Society for Krishna Consciousness*

PLATE ONE: Upon hearing the omen foretelling his death, the envious and sinful Kaṁsa caught hold of Devakī's hair and took up his sword to sever her head from her body. *(p. 60)*

PLATE TWO: Having instructed His father and mother, the Supreme Personality of Godhead, Kṛṣṇa, transformed Himself into His original form as a small human child. (*p. 265*)

PLATE THREE: The magnanimous Nanda Mahārāja, overjoyed upon the birth of his son, arranged for a Vedic birth ceremony to be celebrated by the residents of Gokula. (*p. 320*)

PLATE FOUR: All of a sudden Kṛṣṇa threw His legs upward and struck the cart, and although His legs were as soft as newly-grown leaves, the cart turned over violently and collapsed. (*pp. 395-96*)

PLATE FIVE: The whirlwind demon carried Kṛṣṇa very high into the sky, but Kṛṣṇa suddenly became heavier than the demon and stopped his ascent. To the demon, the child felt as heavy as a mountain. (*pp. 415-16*)

PLATE SIX: Sometimes Kṛṣṇa and Balarāma would sneak into the storeroom, steal yogurt and butter, and feed it to the monkeys. On one such occasion mother Yaśodā caught Them in the act. (*p. 463*)

PLATE SEVEN: When Kṛṣṇa opened His mouth wide, mother Yaśodā saw within His mouth the entire creation—all moving and nonmoving entities, outer space and all directions, and all the planetary systems. (*p. 471*)

PLATE EIGHT: Child Kṛṣṇa fled from mother Yaśodā as if very much afraid. Finally, because of her great love for Him, Kṛṣṇa allowed her to capture Him. (*pp. 502-3*)

PLATE NINE: Sometimes Nanda Mahārāja would ask Kṛṣṇa to bring him his wooden slippers, and Kṛṣṇa, apparently with great difficulty, would put the slippers on His head and take them to His father. (*p. 574*)

PLATE TEN: When Kṛṣṇa came before the fruit vendor, she filled His hands with ripe fruits, and her fruit basket was immediately filled with jewels and gold. (*pp. 575–76*)

PLATE ELEVEN: The cowherd boys were afraid to see the huge demon in the form of a duck with a sharp beak. His name was Bakāsura, and having come to the reservoir, he immediately swallowed Kṛṣṇa. (*p. 603*)

PLATE TWELVE: The demon Aghāsura assumed the form of a huge, eight-mile-long python. He spread his mouth like a big mountain cave and lay down on the road, expecting to swallow Kṛṣṇa and His friends. (*p. 629*)

PLATE THIRTEEN: At a pleasant spot on the bank of the Yamunā, Kṛṣṇa and His friends opened their baskets of food and began eating in great transcendental pleasure. (*p. 664*)

PLATE FOURTEEN: While Lord Brahmā looked on, all the calves and the boys tending them immediately transformed into Viṣṇu forms, with complexions the color of bluish rainclouds and garments made of yellow silk. (*p. 705*)

PLATE FIFTEEN: With his mind fully concentrated and his body trembling, Lord Brahmā very humbly began offering praise to Lord Kṛṣṇa with faltering words. (*p. 734*)

## CHAPTER ONE

# The Advent of Lord Kṛṣṇa: Introduction

The summary of the First Chapter is as follows. This chapter describes how Kaṁsa, frightened by hearing an omen about his being killed by the eighth son of Devakī, killed Devakī's sons one after another.

When Śukadeva Gosvāmī finished describing the dynasty of Yadu, as well as the dynasties of the moon-god and sun-god, Mahārāja Parīkṣit requested him to describe Lord Kṛṣṇa, who appeared with Baladeva in the Yadu dynasty, and how Kṛṣṇa performed His activities within this world. Kṛṣṇa is transcendental, the King said, and therefore to understand His activities is the occupation of liberated persons. Hearing of *kṛṣṇa-līlā* is the boat by which to achieve the ultimate goal of life. Except for an animal killer or one who is following a policy of suicide, every intelligent person must strive to understand Kṛṣṇa and His activities.

Kṛṣṇa was the only worshipable Deity for the Pāṇḍavas. When Mahārāja Parīkṣit was in the womb of his mother, Uttarā, Kṛṣṇa saved him from the attack of the *brahma-śastra*. Now Mahārāja Parīkṣit asked Śukadeva Goṣvāmī how His Lordship Baladeva, the son of Rohiṇī, could have appeared in the womb of Devakī. Why did Kṛṣṇa transfer Himself from Mathurā to Vṛndāvana, King Parīkṣit asked, and how did He live there with His family members? What did Kṛṣṇa do in Mathurā and Vṛndāvana, and why did He kill His maternal uncle Kaṁsa? For how many years did Kṛṣṇa reside in Dvārakā, and how many queens did He have? Mahārāja Parīkṣit asked Śukadeva Gosvamī all these questions. He also requested Śukadeva Gosvāmī to describe other activities of Kṛṣṇa about which he could not inquire.

When Śukadeva Gosvāmī began to speak about Kṛṣṇa consciousness, Mahārāja Parīkṣit forgot the fatigue brought about by his fasting. Enthusiastic to describe Kṛṣṇa, Śukadeva Gosvāmī said, "Like the waters of the Ganges, descriptions of the activities of Kṛṣṇa can purify the entire universe. The speaker, the inquirer and the audience all become purified."

Once when the entire world was overburdened by the increasing military power of demons in the form of kings, mother earth assumed the shape of a cow and approached Lord Brahmā for relief. Sympathetic to mother earth's lamentation, Brahmā, accompanied by Lord Śiva and other demigods, took the cow-shaped mother earth to the shore of the milk ocean, where he offered prayers to please Lord Viṣṇu, who lay there on an island in transcendental ecstasy. Brahmā thereafter understood the advice of Mahā-Viṣṇu, who informed him that He would appear on the surface of the earth to mitigate the burden created by the demons. The demigods, along with their wives, should appear there as associates of Lord Kṛṣṇa in the family of Yadu to increase the sons and grandsons in that dynasty. By the will of Lord Kṛṣṇa, Anantadeva would appear first, as Balarāma, and Kṛṣṇa's potency, *yogamāyā*, would also appear. Brahmā informed mother earth about all this, and then he returned to his own abode.

After marrying Devakī, Vasudeva was returning home with her on a chariot driven by Kaṁsa, her brother, when an ominous voice addressed Kaṁsa, warning him that Devakī's eighth son would kill him. Upon hearing this omen, Kaṁsa was immediately ready to kill Devakī, but Vasudeva diplomatically began to instruct him. Vasudeva stressed that it would not be good for Kaṁsa to kill his younger sister, especially at the time of her marriage. Anyone who possesses a material body must die, Vasudeva advised him. Every living entity lives in a body for some time and then transmigrates to another body, but one is unfortunately misled into accepting the body as the soul. If a person under this mistaken conception wants to kill another body, he is condemned as hellish.

Because Kaṁsa was not satisfied by Vasudeva's instructions, Vasudeva devised a plan. He offered to bring Kaṁsa all of Devakī's children so that Kaṁsa could kill them. Why then should Kaṁsa kill Devakī now? Kaṁsa was satisfied by this proposal. In due course of time, when Devakī gave birth to a child, Vasudeva brought the newborn baby to Kaṁsa, who, upon seeing Vasudeva's magnanimity, was struck with wonder. When Vasudeva gave Kaṁsa the child, Kaṁsa, showing some intelligence, said that since he was to be killed by the eighth child, why should he kill the first? Although Vasudeva did not trust him, Kaṁsa requested Vasudeva to take the child back. Later, however, after Nārada approached Kaṁsa and disclosed to him that the demigods were appearing in the Yadu and

Vṛṣṇi dynasties and conspiring to kill him, Kaṁsa decided to kill all the children born in these families, and he also decided that any child born from the womb of Devakī must be killed. Thus he arrested and imprisoned both Devakī and Vasudeva and killed six of their sons, one after another. Nārada had also informed Kaṁsa that in his previous birth Kaṁsa was Kālanemi, a demon killed by Viṣṇu. Consequently, Kaṁsa became a great enemy to all the descendants of the *yadu-vaṁśa*, the Yadu dynasty. He even arrested and imprisoned his own father, Ugrasena, for Kaṁsa wanted to enjoy the kingdom alone.

Kṛṣṇa has threefold pastimes—the Vraja-līlā, Māthura-līlā and Dvārakā-līlā. As already mentioned, in the Tenth Canto of *Śrīmad-Bhāgavatam* there are ninety chapters, which describe all these *līlās*. The first four chapters describe Brahmā's prayers for the relief of the earth's burden, and they also describe the appearance of the Supreme Personality of Godhead. Chapters Five through Thirty-nine recount Kṛṣṇa's pastimes in Vṛndāvana. The Fortieth Chapter describes how Kṛṣṇa enjoyed in the water of the Yamunā and how Akrūra offered prayers. Chapters Forty-one through Fifty-one, eleven chapters, tell of Kṛṣṇa's pastimes in Māthura, and Chapters Fifty-two through Ninety, thirty-nine chapters, relate Kṛṣṇa's pastimes in Dvārakā.

Chapters Twenty-nine through Thirty-three describe Kṛṣṇa's dancing with the *gopīs*, known as the *rāsa-līlā*. Therefore these five chapters are known as *rāsa-pañcādhyāya*. The Forty-seventh Chapter of the Tenth Canto is a description known as the *bhramara-gītā*.

## TEXT 1

श्रीराजोवाच

कथितो वंशविस्तारो भवता सोमसूर्ययोः ।
राज्ञां चोभयवंश्यानां चरितं परमाद्भुतम् ॥ १ ॥

*śrī-rājovāca*
*kathito vaṁśa-vistāro*
*bhavatā soma-sūryayoḥ*
*rājñāṁ cobhaya-vaṁśyānāṁ*
*caritaṁ paramādbhutam*

*śrī-rājā uvāca*—King Parīkṣit said; *kathitaḥ*—has already been described; *vaṁśa-vistāraḥ*—a broad description of the dynasties; *bhavatā*—by Your Lordship; *soma-sūryayoḥ*—of the moon-god and the sun-god; *rājñām*—of the kings; *ca*—and; *ubhaya*—both; *vaṁśyānām*—of the members of the dynasties; *caritam*—the character; *parama*—exalted; *adbhutam*—and wonderful.

## TRANSLATION

**King Parīkṣit said: My dear lord, you have elaborately described the dynasties of both the moon-god and the sun-god, with the exalted and wonderful character of their kings.**

## PURPORT

At the end of the Ninth Canto, Twenty-fourth Chapter, Śukadeva Gosvāmī summarized the activities of Kṛṣṇa. He spoke of how Kṛṣṇa had personally appeared to reduce the burden on the earth, how He had manifested His pastimes as a householder, and how, soon after His birth, He had transferred Himself to His Vrajabhūmi-līlā. Parīkṣit Mahārāja, being naturally a devotee of Kṛṣṇa, wanted to hear more about Lord Kṛṣṇa. Therefore, to encourage Śukadeva Gosvāmī to continue speaking about Kṛṣṇa and give further details, he thanked Śukadeva Gosvāmī for having described the activities of Kṛṣṇa in brief. Śukadeva Gosvāmī had said:

*jāto gataḥ pitṛ-gṛhād vrajam edhitārtho*
*hatvā ripūn suta-śatāni kṛtorudāraḥ*
*utpādya teṣu puruṣaḥ kratubhiḥ samīje*
*ātmānam ātma-nigamaṁ prathayañ janeṣu*

"The Supreme Personality of Godhead, Śrī Kṛṣṇa, known as *līlā-puruṣottama*, appeared as the son of Vasudeva but immediately left His father's home and went to Vṛndāvana to expand His loving relationships with His confidential devotees. In Vṛndāvana the Lord killed many demons, and afterward He returned to Dvārakā, where according to Vedic principles He married many wives who were the best of women, begot through them hundreds of sons, and performed sacrifices for

His own worship to establish the principles of householder life." (*Bhāg.* 9.24.66)

The Yadu dynasty belonged to the family descending from Soma, the moon-god. Although the planetary systems are so arranged that the sun comes first, before the moon, Parīkṣit Mahārāja gave more respect to the dynasty of the moon-god, the *soma-vaṁśa,* because in the Yādava dynasty, descending from the moon, Kṛṣṇa had appeared. There are two different *kṣatriya* families of the royal order, one descending from the king of the moon planet and the other descending from the king of the sun. Whenever the Supreme Personality of Godhead appears, He generally appears in a *kṣatriya* family because He comes to establish religious principles and the life of righteousness. According to the Vedic system, the *kṣatriya* family is the protector of the human race. When the Supreme Personality of Godhead appeared as Lord Rāmacandra, He appeared in the *sūrya-vaṁśa,* the family descending from the sun-god, and when He appeared as Lord Kṛṣṇa, He did so in the Yadu dynasty, or *yadu-vaṁśa,* whose descent was from the moon-god. In the Ninth Canto, Twenty-fourth Chapter, of *Śrīmad-Bhāgavatam,* there is a long list of the kings of the *yadu-vaṁśa.* All the kings in both the *soma-vaṁśa* and *sūrya-vaṁśa* were great and powerful, and Mahārāja Parīkṣit praised them very highly (*rājñāṁ cobhaya-vaṁśyānāṁ caritaṁ paramād-bhutam*). Nonetheless, he wanted to hear more about the *soma-vaṁśa* because that was the dynasty in which Kṛṣṇa had appeared.

The supreme abode of the Personality of Godhead, Kṛṣṇa, is described in *Brahma-saṁhitā* as the abode of *cintāmaṇi: cintāmaṇi-prakara-sadmasu kalpavṛkṣa-lakṣāvṛteṣu surabhīr abhipālayantam.* The Vṛndāvana-dhāma on this earth is a replica of that same abode. As stated in *Bhagavad-gītā* (8.20), in the spiritual sky there is another, eternal nature, transcendental to manifested and unmanifested matter. The manifested world can be seen in the form of many stars and planets such as the sun and moon, but beyond this is the unmanifested, which is imperceptible to those who are embodied. And beyond this unmanifested matter is the spiritual kingdom, which is described in *Bhagavad-gītā* as supreme and eternal. That kingdom is never annihilated. Although material nature is subject to repeated creation and annihilation, that spiritual nature remains as it is eternally. In the Tenth Canto of *Śrīmad-Bhāgavatam,* that spiritual nature, the spiritual world, is described as

Vṛndāvana, Goloka Vṛndāvana or Vraja-dhāma. The elaborate description of the above-mentioned *śloka* from the Ninth Canto—*jāto gataḥ pitṛ-gṛhād*—will be found here, in the Tenth Canto.

## TEXT 2

यदोश्च धर्मशीलस्य नितरां मुनिसत्तम ।
तत्रांशेनावतीर्णस्य विष्णोर्वीर्याणि शंस नः ॥ २ ॥

*yadoś ca dharma-śīlasya*
*nitarāṁ muni-sattama*
*tatrāṁśenāvatīrṇasya*
*viṣṇor vīryāṇi śaṁsa naḥ*

*yadoḥ*—of Yadu or the Yadu dynasty; *ca*—also; *dharma-śīlasya*—who were strictly attached to religious principles; *nitarām*—highly qualified; *muni-sattama*—O best of all *munis,* king of the *munis* (Śukadeva Gosvāmī); *tatra*—in that dynasty; *aṁśena*—with His plenary expansion Baladeva; *avatīrṇasya*—who appeared as an incarnation; *viṣṇoḥ*—of Lord Viṣṇu; *vīryāṇi*—the glorious activities; *śaṁsa*—kindly describe; *naḥ*—unto us.

## TRANSLATION

**O best of munis, you have also described the descendants of Yadu, who were very pious and strictly adherent to religious principles. Now, if you will, kindly describe the wonderful, glorious activities of Lord Viṣṇu, or Kṛṣṇa, who appeared in that Yadu dynasty with Baladeva, His plenary expansion.**

## PURPORT

The *Brahma-saṁhitā* (5.1) explains that Kṛṣṇa is the origin of the *viṣṇu-tattva.*

*īśvaraḥ paramaḥ kṛṣṇaḥ*
*sac-cid-ānanda-vigrahaḥ*
*anādir ādir govindaḥ*
*sarva-kāraṇa-kāraṇam*

"Kṛṣṇa, who is known as Govinda, is the supreme controller. He has an eternal, blissful, spiritual body. He is the origin of all. He has no other origin, for He is the prime cause of all causes."

*yasyaika-niśvasita-kālam athāvalambya*
*jīvanti loma-vilajā jagad-aṇḍa-nāthāḥ*
*viṣṇur mahān sa iha yasya kalā-viśeṣo*
*govindam ādi-puruṣaṁ tam ahaṁ bhajāmi*

"The Brahmās, the heads of the innumerable universes, live only for the duration of one breath of Mahā-Viṣṇu. I worship Govinda, the original Lord, of whom Mahā-Viṣṇu is but a portion of a plenary portion." (Bs. 5.48)

Govinda, Kṛṣṇa, is the original Personality of Godhead. *Kṛṣṇas tu bhagavān svayam.* Even Lord Mahā-Viṣṇu, who by His breathing creates many millions upon millions of universes, is Lord Kṛṣṇa's *kalā-viśeṣa,* or plenary portion of a plenary portion. Mahā-Viṣṇu is a plenary expansion of Saṅkarṣaṇa, who is a plenary expansion of Nārāyaṇa. Nārāyaṇa is a plenary expansion of the *catur-vyūha,* and the *catur-vyūha* are plenary expansions of Baladeva, the first manifestation of Kṛṣṇa. Therefore when Kṛṣṇa appeared with Baladeva, all the *viṣṇu-tattvas* appeared with Him.

Mahārāja Parīkṣit requested Śukadeva Gosvāmī to describe Kṛṣṇa and His glorious activities. Another meaning may be derived from this verse as follows. Although Śukadeva Gosvāmī was the greatest *muni,* he could describe Kṛṣṇa only partially (*aṁśena*), for no one can describe Kṛṣṇa fully. It is said that Anantadeva has thousands of heads, but although He tries to describe Kṛṣṇa with thousands of tongues, His descriptions are still incomplete.

## TEXT 3

अवतीर्य यदोर्वंशे भगवान् भूतभावनः ।
कृतवान् यानि विश्वात्मा तानि नो वद विस्तरात् ॥ ३ ॥

*avatīrya yador vaṁśe*
*bhagavān bhūta-bhāvanaḥ*

*kṛtavān yāni viśvātmā*
*tāni no vada vistarāt*

*avatīrya*—after descending; *yadoḥ vaṁśe*—in the dynasty of Yadu; *bhagavān*—the Supreme Personality of Godhead; *bhūta-bhāvanaḥ*—who is the cause of the cosmic manifestation; *kṛtavān*—executed; *yāni*—whatever (activities); *viśva-ātmā*—the Supersoul of the entire universe; *tāni*—all of those (activities); *naḥ*—unto us; *vada*—kindly say; *vistarāt*—elaborately.

## TRANSLATION

**The Supersoul, the Supreme Personality of Godhead, Śrī Kṛṣṇa, the cause of the cosmic manifestation, appeared in the dynasty of Yadu. Please tell me elaborately about His glorious activities and character, from the beginning to the end of His life.**

## PURPORT

In this verse the words *kṛtavān yāni* indicate that all the different activities Kṛṣṇa performed while present on earth are beneficial to human society. If religionists, philosophers and people in general simply hear the activities of Kṛṣṇa, they will be liberated. We have described several times that there are two kinds of *kṛṣṇa-kathā*, represented by *Bhagavad-gītā*, spoken personally by Kṛṣṇa about Himself, and *Śrīmad-Bhāgavatam*, spoken by Śukadeva Gosvāmī about the glories of Kṛṣṇa. Anyone who becomes even slightly interested in *kṛṣṇa-kathā* is liberated. *Kīrtanād eva kṛṣṇasya mukta-saṅgaḥ paraṁ vrajet* (*Bhāg*. 12.3.51). Simply by chanting or repeating *kṛṣṇa-kathā*, one is liberated from the contamination of Kali-yuga. Caitanya Mahāprabhu therefore advised, *yāre dekha, tāre kaha 'kṛṣṇa'-upadeśa* (Cc. *Madhya* 7.128). This is the mission of Kṛṣṇa consciousness: to hear about Kṛṣṇa and thus be liberated from material bondage.

## TEXT 4

निवृत्ततर्षैरुपगीयमानाद्
भवौषधाच्छ्रोत्रमनोऽभिरामात् ।

क उत्तमश्लोकगुणानुवादात्
पुमान् विरज्येत विना पशुघ्नात् ॥ ४ ॥

*nivṛtta-tarṣair upagīyamānād*
*bhavauṣadhāc chrotra-mano-'bhirāmāt*
*ka uttamaśloka-guṇānuvādāt*
*pumān virajyeta vinā paśughnāt*

*nivṛtta*—released from; *tarṣaiḥ*—lust or material activities; *upagīyamānāt*—which is described or sung; *bhava-auṣadhāt*—which is the right medicine for the material disease; *śrotra*—the process of aural reception; *manaḥ*—the subject matter of thought for the mind; *abhirāmāt*—from the pleasing vibrations from such glorification; *kaḥ*—who; *uttamaśloka*—of the Supreme Personality of Godhead; *guṇa-anuvādāt*—from describing such activities; *pumān*—a person; *virajyeta*—can keep himself aloof; *vinā*—except; *paśu-ghnāt*—either a butcher or one who is killing his own personal existence.

## TRANSLATION

**Glorification of the Supreme Personality of Godhead is performed in the paramparā system; that is, it is conveyed from spiritual master to disciple. Such glorification is relished by those no longer interested in the false, temporary glorification of this cosmic manifestation. Descriptions of the Lord are the right medicine for the conditioned soul undergoing repeated birth and death. Therefore, who will cease hearing such glorification of the Lord except a butcher or one who is killing his own self?**

## PURPORT

In India it is the practice among the general populace to hear about Kṛṣṇa, either from *Bhagavad-gītā* or from *Śrīmad-Bhāgavatam*, in order to gain relief from the disease of repeated birth and death. Although India is now fallen, when there is a message that someone will speak about *Bhagavad-gītā* or *Śrīmad-Bhāgavatam*, thousands of people still gather to hear. This verse indicates, however, that such recitation of *Bhagavad-gītā* and *Śrīmad-Bhāgavatam* must be done by persons completely freed from material desires (*nivṛtta-tarṣaiḥ*). Everyone within this material world, beginning from Brahmā down to the insignificant ant, is full of material desires for sense enjoyment, and everyone is busy in sense gratification, but when thus engaged one cannot fully understand the value of *kṛṣṇa-kathā,* either in the form of *Bhagavad-gītā* or in *Śrīmad-Bhāgavatam.*

If we hear the glories of the Supreme Personality of Godhead from liberated persons, this hearing will certainly free us from the bondage of material activities, but hearing *Śrīmad-Bhāgavatam* spoken by a professional reciter cannot actually help us achieve liberation. *Kṛṣṇa-kathā* is very simple. In *Bhagavad-gītā* it is said that Kṛṣṇa is the Supreme Personality of Godhead. As He Himself explains, *mattaḥ parataraṁ nānyat kiñcid asti dhanañjaya:* "O Arjuna, there is no truth superior to Me." (Bg. 7.7) Simply by understanding this fact—that Kṛṣṇa is the Supreme Personality of Godhead—one can become a liberated person. But, especially in this age, because people are interested in hearing *Bhagavad-gītā* from unscrupulous persons who depart from the simple presentation of *Bhagavad-gītā* and distort it for their personal satisfaction, they fail to derive the real benefit. There are big scholars, politicians, philosophers and scientists who speak on *Bhagavad-gītā* in their own polluted way, and people in general hear from them, being uninterested in hearing the glories of the Supreme Personality of Godhead from a devotee. A devotee is one who has no other motive for reciting *Bhagavad-gītā* and *Śrīmad-Bhāgavatam* than to serve the Lord. Śrī Caitanya Mahāprabhu has therefore advised us to hear the glories of the Lord from a realized person (*bhāgavata paro diya bhāgavata sthane*). Unless one is personally a realized soul in the science of Kṛṣṇa consciousness, a neophyte should not approach him to hear about the Lord, for this is strictly forbidden by Śrīla Sanātana Gosvāmī, who quotes from the *Padma Purāṇa:*

*avaiṣṇava-mukhodgīrṇaṁ*
*pūtaṁ hari-kathāmṛtam*
*śravaṇaṁ naiva kartavyaṁ*
*sarpocchiṣṭaṁ yathā payaḥ*

One should avoid hearing from a person not situated in Vaiṣṇava behavior. A Vaiṣṇava is *nivṛtta-tṛṣṇa;* that is, he has no material purpose, for his only purpose is to preach Kṛṣṇa consciousness. So-called scholars, philosophers and politicians exploit the importance of *Bhagavad-gītā* by distorting its meaning for their own purposes. Therefore this verse warns that *kṛṣṇa-kathā* should be recited by a person who is *nivṛtta-tṛṣṇa.* Śukadeva Gosvāmī epitomizes the proper reciter for *Śrīmad-Bhāgavatam,* and Parīkṣit Mahārāja, who purposefully left his kingdom and family prior to meeting death, epitomizes the person fit to hear it. A qualified reciter of *Śrīmad-Bhāgavatam* gives the right medicine (*bhavauṣadhi*) for the conditioned souls. The Kṛṣṇa consciousness movement is therefore trying to train qualified preachers to recite *Śrīmad-Bhāgavatam* and *Bhagavad-gītā* throughout the entire world, so that people in general in all parts of the world may take advantage of this movement and thus be relieved of the threefold miseries of material existence.

The instructions of *Bhagavad-gītā* and the descriptions of *Śrīmad-Bhāgavatam* are so pleasing that almost anyone suffering from the threefold miseries of material existence will desire to hear the glories of the Lord from these books and thus benefit on the path of liberation. Two classes of men, however, will never be interested in hearing the message of *Bhagavad-gītā* and *Śrīmad-Bhāgavatam*—those who are determined to commit suicide and those determined to kill cows and other animals for the satisfaction of their own tongues. Although such persons may make a show of hearing *Śrīmad-Bhāgavatam* at a *Bhāgavata-saptāha,* this is but another creation of the *karmīs,* who cannot derive any benefit from such a performance. The word *paśu-ghnāt* is important in this connection. *Paśu-ghna* means "butcher." Persons fond of performing ritualistic ceremonies for elevation to the higher planetary systems must offer sacrifices (*yajñas*) by killing animals. Lord Buddhadeva therefore rejected the authority of the *Vedas* because his mission was to stop animal sacrifices, which are recommended in Vedic ritualistic ceremonies.

*nindasi yajña-vidher ahaha śruti-jātaṁ*
*sa-daya-hṛdaya darśita-paśu-ghātam*
*keśava dhṛta-buddha-śarīra jaya jagadīśa hare*
(*Gīta-govinda*)

Even though animal sacrifices are sanctioned in Vedic ceremonies, men who kill animals for such ceremonies are considered butchers. Butchers cannot be interested in Kṛṣṇa consciousness, for they are already materially allured. Their only interest lies in developing comforts for the temporary body.

*bhogaiśvarya-prasaktānāṁ*
*tayāpahṛta-cetasām*
*vyavasāyātmikā buddhiḥ*
*samādhau na vidhīyate*

"In the minds of those who are too attached to sense enjoyment and material opulence, and who are bewildered by such things, the resolute determination of devotional service to the Supreme Lord does not take place." (Bg. 2.44) Śrīla Narottama dāsa Ṭhākura says:

*manuṣya-janama pāiyā, rādhā-kṛṣṇa nā bhajiyā,*
*jāniyā śuniyā viṣa khāinu*

Anyone who is not Kṛṣṇa conscious and who therefore does not engage in the service of the Lord is also *paśu-ghna,* for he is willingly drinking poison. Such a person cannot be interested in *kṛṣṇa-kathā* because he still has a desire for material sense gratification; he is not *nivṛtta-tṛṣṇa.* As it is said, *traivargikās te puruṣā vimukhā hari-medhasaḥ.* Those interested in *trivarga*—that is, in *dharma, artha* and *kāma*—are religious for the sake of achieving a material position with which to gain better facilities for sense gratification. Such persons are killing themselves by willingly keeping themselves in the cycle of birth and death. They cannot be interested in Kṛṣṇa consciousness.

For *kṛṣṇa-kathā,* topics about Kṛṣṇa consciousness, there must be a speaker and a hearer, both of whom can be interested in Kṛṣṇa consciousness if they are no longer interested in material topics. One can actually see how this attitude automatically develops in persons who are Kṛṣṇa conscious. Although the devotees of the Kṛṣṇa consciousness movement are quite young men, they no longer read materialistic newspapers, magazines and so on, for they are no longer interested in such topics (*nivṛtta-tarṣaiḥ*). They completely give up the bodily understanding of life. For topics concerning Uttamaśloka, the Supreme Personality of Godhead, the spiritual master speaks, and the disciple hears with attention. Unless both of them are free from material desires, they cannot be interested in topics of Kṛṣṇa consciousness. The spiritual master and disciple do not need to understand anything more than Kṛṣṇa because simply by understanding Kṛṣṇa and talking about Kṛṣṇa, one becomes a perfectly learned person (*yasmin vijñāte sarvam evaṁ vijñātaṁ bhavati*). The Lord sits within everyone's heart, and by the grace of the Lord the devotee receives instructions directly from the Lord Himself, who says in *Bhagavad-gītā* (15.15):

*sarvasya cahaṁ hṛdi sanniviṣṭo*
*mattaḥ smṛtir jñānam apohanaṁ ca*
*vedaiś ca sarvair aham eva vedyo*
*vedānta-kṛd veda-vid eva cāham*

"I am seated in everyone's heart, and from Me come remembrance, knowledge and forgetfulness. By all the *Vedas*, I am to be known; indeed, I am the compiler of *Vedānta*, and I am the knower of the *Vedas*." Kṛṣṇa consciousness is so exalted that one who is perfectly situated in Kṛṣṇa consciousness, under the direction of the spiritual master, is fully satisfied by reading *kṛṣṇa-kathā* as found in *Śrīmad-Bhāgavatam*, *Bhagavad-gītā* and similar Vedic literatures. Since merely talking about Kṛṣṇa is so pleasing, we can simply imagine how pleasing it is to render service to Kṛṣṇa.

When discourses on *kṛṣṇa-kathā* take place between a liberated spiritual master and his disciple, others also sometimes take advantage of hearing these topics and also benefit. These topics are the medicine to stop the repetition of birth and death. The cycle of repeated birth and death, by which one takes on different bodies again and again, is called *bhava* or *bhava-roga*. If anyone, willingly or unwillingly, hears *kṛṣṇa-kathā*, his *bhava-roga*, the disease of birth and death, will certainly stop. Therefore *kṛṣṇa-kathā* is called *bhavauṣadha*, the remedy to stop the repetition of birth and death. *Karmīs*, or persons attached to material sense enjoyment, generally cannot give up their material desires, but *kṛṣṇa-kathā* is such a potent medicine that if one is induced to hear *kṛṣṇa-kīrtana*, he will certainly be freed from this disease. A practical example is Dhruva Mahārāja, who at the end of his *tapasya* was fully satisfied. When the Lord wanted to give Dhruva a benediction, Dhruva refused it. *Svāmin kṛtārtho 'smi varaṁ na yāce.* "My dear Lord," he said, "I am fully satisfied. I do not ask for any benediction for material sense gratification." We actually see that even young boys and girls in the Kṛṣṇa consciousness movement have given up their long practice of bad habits like illicit sex, meat-eating, intoxication and gambling. Because Kṛṣṇa consciousness is so potent that it gives them full satisfaction, they are no longer interested in material sense gratification.

## TEXTS 5–7

पितामहा मे समरेऽमरञ्जयै-
र्देवव्रताद्यातिरथैस्तिमिङ्गिलैः ।
दुरत्ययं कौरवसैन्यसागरं
कृत्वातरन् वत्सपदं स्म यत्प्लवाः ॥ ५ ॥
द्रौण्यस्त्रविप्लुष्टमिदं मदङ्गं
सन्तानबीजं कुरुपाण्डवानाम् ।
जुगोप कुक्षिं गत आत्तचक्रो
मातुश्च मे यः शरणं गतायाः ॥ ६ ॥
वीर्याणि तस्याखिलदेहभाजा-
मन्तर्बहिः पूरुषकालरूपैः ।
प्रयच्छतो मृत्युमुतामृतं च
मायामनुष्यस्य वदस्व विद्वन् ॥ ७ ॥

*pitāmahā me samare 'marañjayair*
*devavratādyātirathais timiṅgilaiḥ*
*duratyayaṁ kaurava-sainya-sāgaraṁ*
*kṛtvātaran vatsa-padaṁ sma yat-plavāḥ*

*drauṇy-astra-vipluṣṭam idaṁ mad-aṅgaṁ*
*santāna-bījaṁ kuru-pāṇḍavānām*
*jugopa kukṣiṁ gata ātta-cakro*
*mātuś ca me yaḥ śaraṇaṁ gatāyāḥ*

*vīryāṇi tasyākhila-deha-bhājām*
*antar bahiḥ pūruṣa-kāla-rūpaiḥ*
*prayacchato mṛtyum utāmṛtaṁ ca*
*māyā-manuṣyasya vadasva vidvan*

*pitāmahāḥ*—my grandfathers, the five Pāṇḍavas (Yudhiṣṭhira, Bhīma, Arjuna, Nakula and Sahadeva); *me*—my; *samare*—on the Battlefield of Kurukṣetra; *amaraṁ-jayaiḥ*—with fighters who could gain victory over the demigods on the battlefield; *devavrata-ādya*—Bhīṣmadeva and others; *atirathaiḥ*—great commanders in chief; *timiṅgilaiḥ*—resembling great *timiṅgila* fish, which can easily eat large sharks; *duratyayam*—very difficult to cross; *kaurava-sainya-sāgaram*—the ocean of the assembled soldiers of the Kauravas; *kṛtvā*—considering such an ocean; *ataran*—crossed it; *vatsa-padam*—exactly as one steps over a small hoofprint of a calf; *sma*—in the past; *yat-plavāḥ*—the shelter of the boat of Kṛṣṇa's lotus feet; *drauṇi*—of Aśvatthāmā; *astra*—by the *brahmāstra; vipluṣṭam*—being attacked and burned; *idam*—this; *mat-aṅgam*—my body; *santāna-bījam*—the only seed left, the last descendant of the family; *kuru-pāṇḍavānām*—of the Kurus and the Pāṇḍavas (because no one but me lived after the Battle of Kurukṣetra); *jugopa*—gave protection; *kukṣim*—within the womb; *gataḥ*—being placed; *ātta-cakraḥ*—taking in hand the disc; *mātuḥ*—of my mother; *ca*—also; *me*—my; *yaḥ*—the Lord who; *śaraṇam*—the shelter; *gatāyāḥ*—who had taken; *vīryāṇi*—the glorification of the transcendental characteristics; *tasya*—of Him (the Supreme Personality of Godhead); *akhila-deha-bhājām*—of all the materially embodied living entities; *antaḥ bahiḥ*—inside and outside; *pūruṣa*—of the Supreme Person; *kāla-rūpaiḥ*—in the forms of eternal time; *prayacchataḥ*—who is the giver; *mṛtyum*—of death; *uta*—it is so said; *amṛtam ca*—and eternal life; *māyā-manuṣyasya*—of the Lord, who appeared as an ordinary human being by His own potency; *vadasva*—kindly describe; *vidvan*—O learned speaker (Śukadeva Gosvāmī).

## TRANSLATION

**Taking the boat of Kṛṣṇa's lotus feet, my grandfather Arjuna and others crossed the ocean of the Battlefield of Kurukṣetra, in which such commanders as Bhīṣmadeva resembed great fish that**

**could very easily have swallowed them. By the mercy of Lord Kṛṣṇa, my grandfathers crossed this ocean, which was very difficult to cross, as easily as one steps over the hoofprint of a calf. Because my mother surrendered unto Lord Kṛṣṇa's lotus feet, the Lord, Sudarśana-cakra in hand, entered her womb and saved my body, the body of the last remaining descendant of the Kurus and the Pāṇḍavas, which was almost destroyed by the fiery weapon of Aśvatthāmā. Lord Śrī Kṛṣṇa, appearing within and outside of all materially embodied living beings by His own potency in the forms of eternal time—that is, as Paramātmā and as virāṭ-rūpa—gave liberation to everyone, either as cruel death or as life. Kindly enlighten me by describing His transcendental characteristics.**

## PURPORT

As stated in *Śrīmad-Bhāgavatam* (10.14.58):

*samāśritā ye pada-pallava-plavaṁ*
*mahat-padaṁ puṇya-yaśo murāreḥ*
*bhavāmbudhir vatsa-padaṁ paraṁ padaṁ*
*padaṁ padaṁ yad vipadāṁ na teṣām*

"For one who has accepted the boat of the lotus feet of the Lord, who is the shelter of the cosmic manifestation and is famous as Murāri, or the enemy of the Mura demon, the ocean of the material world is like the water contained in a calf's hoofprint. His goal is *paraṁ padam*, or Vaikuṇṭha, the place where there are no material miseries, not the place where there is danger at every step."

One who seeks shelter at the lotus feet of Lord Kṛṣṇa is immediately protected by the Lord. As the Lord promises in *Bhagavad-gītā* (18.66), *ahaṁ tvāṁ sarva-pāpebhyo mokṣayiṣyāmi mā śucaḥ:* "I shall deliver you from all sinful reactions. Do not fear." By taking shelter of Lord Kṛṣṇa, one comes under the safest protection. Thus when the Pāṇḍavas took shelter at the lotus feet of Kṛṣṇa, all of them were on the safe side of the Battlefield of Kurukṣetra. Parīkṣit Mahārāja, therefore, felt obliged to think of Kṛṣṇa in the last days of his life. This is the ideal result of Kṛṣṇa consciousness: *ante nārāyaṇa-smṛtiḥ.* If at the time of death one can remember Kṛṣṇa, one's life is successful. Parīkṣit Mahārāja, therefore, because of his many obligations to Kṛṣṇa, intelligently decided to think of Kṛṣṇa constantly during the last days of his life. Kṛṣṇa had saved the Pāṇḍavas, Mahārāja Parīkṣit's grandfathers, on the Battlefield of Kurukṣetra, and Kṛṣṇa had saved Mahārāja Parīkṣit himself when he was attacked by the *brahmāstra* of Aśvatthāmā. Kṛṣṇa acted as the friend and worshipable Deity of the Pāṇḍava family. Moreover, apart from Lord Kṛṣṇa's personal contact with the Pāṇḍavas, Kṛṣṇa is the Supersoul of all living entities, and He gives everyone liberation, even if one is not a pure devotee. Kaṁsa, for example, was not at all a devotee, yet Kṛṣṇa, after killing him, gave him salvation. Kṛṣṇa consciousness is beneficial to everyone, whether one is a pure devotee or a nondevotee. This is the glory of Kṛṣṇa consciousness. Considering this, who will not take shelter at the lotus feet of Kṛṣṇa. Kṛṣṇa is described in this verse as *māyā-manuṣya* because He descends exactly like a human being. He is not obliged to come here, like *karmīs*, or ordinary living beings; rather, He appears by His own internal energy (*sambhavāmy ātma-māyayā*) just to show favor to the fallen conditioned souls. Kṛṣṇa is always situated in His original position as *sac-cid-ānanda-vigraha*, and anyone who renders service to Him is also situated in his original, spiritual identity (*svarūpeṇa vyavasthitiḥ*). This is the highest perfection of human life.

## TEXT 8

**रोहिण्यास्तनयः प्रोक्तो रामः सङ्कर्षणस्त्वया ।**
**देवक्या गर्भसम्बन्धः कुतो देहान्तरं विना ॥ ८ ॥**

*rohiṇyās tanayaḥ prokto*
*rāmaḥ saṅkarṣaṇas tvayā*
*devakyā garbha-sambandhaḥ*
*kuto dehāntaraṁ vinā*

*rohiṇyāḥ*—of Rohiṇīdevī, the mother of Baladeva; *tanayaḥ*—the son; *proktaḥ*—is well known; *rāmaḥ*—Balarāma; *saṅkarṣaṇaḥ*—Balarāma is none other than Saṅkarṣaṇa, the first Deity in the quadruple group (Saṅkarṣaṇa, Aniruddha, Pradyumna and Vāsudeva); *tvayā*—by you (it is so said); *devakyāḥ*—of Devakī, the mother of Kṛṣṇa;

*garbha-sambandhaḥ*—connected with the womb; *kutaḥ*—how; *deha-antaram*—transferring bodies; *vinā*—without.

## TRANSLATION

**My dear Śukadeva Gosvāmī, you have already explained that Saṅkarṣaṇa, who belongs to the second quadruple, appeared as the son of Rohiṇī named Balarāma. If Balarāma was not transferred from one body to another, how is it possible that He was first in the womb of Devakī and then in the womb of Rohiṇī? Kindly explain this to me.**

## PURPORT

Here is a question particularly directed at understanding Balarāma, who is Saṅkarṣaṇa Himself. Balarāma is well known as the son of Rohiṇī, yet it is also known that He was the son of Devakī. Parīkṣit Mahārāja wanted to understand the mystery of Balarāma's being the son of both Devakī and Rohiṇī.

## TEXT 9

कस्मान्मुकुन्दो भगवान् पितुर्गेहाद् व्रजं गतः ।
क्व वासं ज्ञातिभिः सार्धं कृतवान् सात्वतांपतिः ॥ ९ ॥

*kasmān mukundo bhagavān*
*pitur gehād vrajaṁ gataḥ*
*kva vāsaṁ jñātibhiḥ sārdhaṁ*
*kṛtavān sātvatāṁ patiḥ*

*kasmāt*—why; *mukundaḥ*—Kṛṣṇa, who can award liberation to everyone; *bhagavān*—the Supreme Personality of Godhead; *pituḥ*—of His father (Vasudeva); *gehāt*—from the house; *vrajam*—to Vraja-dhāma, Vrajabhūmi; *gataḥ*—went; *kva*—where; *vāsam*—placed Himself to live; *jñātibhiḥ*—His relatives; *sārdham*—with; *kṛtavān*—did so; *sātvatām patiḥ*—the master of all Vaiṣṇava devotees.

## TRANSLATION

**Why did Kṛṣṇa, the Supreme Personality of Godhead, leave the house of His father, Vasudeva, and transfer Himself to the house**

**of Nanda in Vṛndāvana? Where did the Lord, the master of the Yadu dynasty, live with His relatives in Vṛndāvana?**

## PURPORT

These are inquiries about the itinerary of Kṛṣṇa. Just after His birth in the house of Vasudeva in Mathurā, Kṛṣṇa transferred Himself to Gokula, on the other side of the Yamunā, and after some days He moved with His father, mother and other relatives to Nanda-grāma, Vṛndāvana. Mahārāja Parīkṣit was very much eager to hear about Kṛṣṇa's activities in Vṛndāvana. This entire canto of *Śrīmad-Bhāgavatam* is full of activities performed in Vṛndāvana and Dvārakā. The first forty chapters describe Kṛṣṇa's Vṛndāvana affairs, and the next fifty describe Kṛṣṇa's activities in Dvārakā. Mahārāja Parīkṣit, to fulfill his desire to hear about Kṛṣṇa, requested Śukadeva Gosvāmī to describe these activities in full detail.

## TEXT 10

व्रजे वसन् किमकरोन्मधुपुर्यां च केशवः ।
भ्रातरं चावधीत् कंसं मातुरद्धातदर्हणम् ॥१०॥

*vraje vasan kim akaron*
*madhupuryāṁ ca keśavaḥ*
*bhrātaraṁ cāvadhīt kaṁsaṁ*
*mātur addhātad-arhaṇam*

*vraje*—at Vṛndāvana; *vasan*—while residing; *kim akarot*—what did He do; *madhupuryām*—in Mathurā; *ca*—and; *keśavaḥ*—Kṛṣṇa, the killer of Keśi; *bhrātaram*—the brother; *ca*—and; *avadhīt*—killed; *kaṁsam*—Kaṁsa; *mātuḥ*—of His mother; *addhā*—directly; *a-tat-arhaṇam*—which was not at all sanctioned by the *śāstras.*

## TRANSLATION

**Lord Kṛṣṇa lived both in Vṛndāvana and in Mathurā. What did He do there? Why did He kill Kaṁsa, His mother's brother? Such killing is not at all sanctioned in the śāstras.**

## PURPORT

One's maternal uncle, the brother of one's mother, is on the level of one's father. When a maternal uncle has no son, his nephew legally inherits his property. Therefore, why did Kṛṣṇa directly kill Kaṁsa, the brother of His mother? Mahārāja Parīkṣit was very much inquisitive about the facts in this regard.

## TEXT 11

**देहं मानुषमाश्रित्य कति वर्षाणि वृष्णिभिः ।**
**यदुपुर्यां सहावात्सीत् पत्न्यः कत्यभवन् प्रभोः ॥११॥**

*deham mānuṣam āśritya*
*kati varṣāṇi vṛṣṇibhiḥ*
*yadu-puryāṁ sahāvātsīt*
*patnyaḥ katy abhavan prabhoḥ*

*deham*—body; *mānuṣam*—exactly like a man; *āśritya*—accepting; *kati varṣāṇi*—how many years; *vṛṣṇibhiḥ*—in the company of the Vṛṣṇis, those who were born in the Vṛṣṇi family; *yadu-puryām*—in Dvārakā, in the residential quarters of the Yadus; *saha*—with; *avātsīt*—the Lord lived; *patnyaḥ*—wives; *kati*—how many; *abhavan*—were there; *prabhoḥ*—of the Lord.

## TRANSLATION

**Kṛṣṇa, the Supreme Personality of Godhead, has no material body, yet He appears as a human being. For how many years did He live with the descendants of Vṛṣṇi? How many wives did He marry, and for how many years did He live in Dvārakā?**

## PURPORT

In many places the Supreme Personality of Godhead is described as *sac-cid-ānanda-vigraha*, possessing a spiritual, blissful body. His bodily feature is *narākṛti*, that is, exactly like that of a human being. Here the same idea is repeated in the words *mānuṣam āśritya*, which indicate that He accepts a body exactly like that of a man. Everywhere it is confirmed that Kṛṣṇa is never *nirākāra*, or formless. He has His form, exactly like that of a human being. There is no doubt about this.

## TEXT 12

**एतदन्यच्च सर्वं मे मुने कृष्णविचेष्टितम् ।**
**वक्तुमर्हसि सर्वज्ञ श्रद्दधानाय विस्तृतम् ॥१२॥**

*etad anyac ca sarvaṁ me*
*mune kṛṣṇa-viceṣṭitam*
*vaktum arhasi sarvajña*
*śraddadhānāya vistṛtam*

*etat*—all these details; *anyat ca*—and others also; *sarvam*—everything; *me*—unto me; *mune*—O great sage; *kṛṣṇa-viceṣṭitam*—the activities of Lord Kṛṣṇa; *vaktum*—to describe; *arhasi*—you are able; *sarva-jña*—because you know everything; *śraddadhānāya*—because I am not envious but have all faith in Him; *vistṛtam*—in full detail.

## TRANSLATION

**O great sage, who know everything about Kṛṣṇa, please describe in detail all the activities of which I have inquired and also those of which I have not, for I have full faith and am very eager to hear of them.**

## TEXT 13

**नैषातिदुःसहा क्षुन्मां त्यक्तोदमपि बाधते ।**
**पिबन्तं त्वन्मुखाम्भोजच्युतं हरिकथामृतम् ॥१३॥**

*naiṣātiduḥsahā kṣun māṁ*
*tyaktodam api bādhate*
*pibantaṁ tvan-mukhāmbhoja-*
*cyutaṁ hari-kathāmṛtam*

*na*—not; *eṣā*—all this; *ati-duḥsahā*—extremely difficult to bear; *kṣut*—hunger; *mām*—unto me; *tyakta-udam*—even after giving up drinking water; *api*—also; *bādhate*—does not hinder; *pibantam*—while drinking; *tvat-mukha-ambhoja-cyutam*—emanating from your lotus mouth; *hari-kathā-amṛtam*—the nectar of topics concerning Kṛṣṇa.

## TRANSLATION

**Because of my vow on the verge of death, I have given up even drinking water, yet because I am drinking the nectar of topics about Kṛṣṇa, which is flowing from the lotus mouth of Your Lordship, my hunger and thirst, which are extremely difficult to bear, cannot hinder me.**

## PURPORT

To prepare to meet death in seven days, Mahārāja Parīkṣit gave up all food and drink. As a human being, he was certainly both hungry and thirsty, and therefore Śukadeva Gosvāmī might have wanted to stop narrating the transcendental topics of Kṛṣṇa; but despite his fast, Mahārāja Parīkṣit was not at all fatigued. "The hunger and thirst from my fast do not disturb me," he said. "Once when I felt very thirsty, I went to the *āśrama* of Śamīka Muni to drink water, but the *muni* did not supply it. I therefore wrapped a dead snake over his shoulder, and that is why I was cursed by the *brāhmaṇa* boy. Now, however, I am quite fit. I am not at all disturbed by my hunger and thirst." This indicates that although on the material platform there are disturbances from hunger and thirst, on the spiritual platform there is no such thing as fatigue.

The entire world is suffering because of spiritual thirst. Every living being is Brahman, or spirit soul, and needs spiritual food to satisfy his hunger and thirst. Unfortunately, however, the world is completely unaware of the nectar of *kṛṣṇa-kathā*. The Kṛṣṇa consciousness movement is therefore a boon to philosophers, religionists and people in general. There is certainly a charming attraction in Kṛṣṇa and *kṛṣṇa-kathā*. Therefore the Absolute Truth is called Kṛṣṇa, the most attractive.

The word *amṛta* is also an important reference to the moon, and the word *ambuja* means "lotus." The pleasing moonshine and pleasing fragrance of the lotus combined to bring pleasure to everyone hearing *kṛṣṇa-kathā* from the mouth of Śukadeva Gosvāmī. As it is said:

*matir na kṛṣṇe parataḥ svato vā*
*mitho 'bhipadyeta gṛha-vratānām*

*adānta-gobhir viśatāṁ tamisraṁ*
*punaḥ punaś carvita-carvaṇānām*

"Because of their uncontrolled senses, persons too addicted to materialistic life make progress toward hellish conditions and repeatedly chew that which has already been chewed. Their inclinations toward Kṛṣṇa are never aroused, either by the instructions of others, by their own efforts, or by a combination of both." (*Bhāg.* 7.5.30) At the present moment, all of human society is engaged in the business of chewing the chewed (*punaḥ punaś carvita-carvaṇānām*). People are prepared to undergo *mṛtyu-saṁsāra-vartmani*, taking birth in one form, dying, accepting another form and dying again. To stop this repetition of birth and death, *kṛṣṇa-kathā*, or Kṛṣṇa consciousness, is absolutely necessary. But unless one hears *kṛṣṇa-kathā* from a realized soul like Śukadeva Gosvāmī, one cannot relish the nectar of *kṛṣṇa-kathā*, which puts an end to all material fatigue, and enjoy the blissful life of transcendental existence. In relation to the Kṛṣṇa consciousness movement, we actually see that those who have tasted the nectar of *kṛṣṇa-kathā* lose all material desires, whereas those who cannot understand Kṛṣṇa or *kṛṣṇa-kathā* regard the Kṛṣṇa conscious life as "brainwashing" and "mind control." While the devotees enjoy spiritual bliss, the nondevotees are surprised that the devotees have forgotten material hankerings.

## TEXT 14

सूत उवाच
एवं निशम्य भृगुनन्दन साधुवादं
वैयासकिः स भगवानथ विष्णुरातम् ।
प्रत्यर्च्य कृष्णचरितं कलिकल्मषघ्नं
व्याहर्तुमारभत भागवतप्रधानः ॥१४॥

*sūta uvāca*
*evaṁ niśamya bhṛgu-nandana sādhu-vādaṁ*
*vaiyāsakiḥ sa bhagavān atha viṣṇu-rātam*
*pratyarcya kṛṣṇa-caritaṁ kali-kalmaṣa-ghnaṁ*
*vyāhartum ārabhata bhāgavata-pradhānaḥ*

*sūtaḥ uvāca*—Sūta Gosvāmī said; *evam*—thus; *niśamya*—hearing; *bhṛgu-nandana*—O son of the Bhṛgu dynasty, Śaunaka; *sādhu-vādam*—pious questions; *vaiyāsakiḥ*—Śukadeva Gosvāmī, the son of Vyāsadeva; *saḥ*—he; *bhagavān*—the most powerful; *atha*—thus; *viṣṇu-rātam*—unto Parīkṣit Mahārāja, who was always protected by Viṣṇu; *pratyarcya*—offering him respectful obeisances; *kṛṣṇa-caritam*—topics of Lord Kṛṣṇa; *kali-kalmaṣa-ghnam*—which diminish the troubles of this age of Kali; *vyāhartum*—to describe; *ārabhata*—began; *bhāgavata-pradhānaḥ*—Śukadeva Gosvāmī, the chief among the pure devotees.

## TRANSLATION

**Sūta Gosvāmī said: O son of Bhṛgu [Śaunaka Ṛṣi], after Śukadeva Gosvāmī, the most respectable devotee, the son of Vyāsadeva, heard the pious questions of Mahārāja Parīkṣit, he thanked the King with great respect. Then he began to discourse on topics concerning Kṛṣṇa, which are the remedy for all sufferings in this age of Kali.**

## PURPORT

In this verse the words *kṛṣṇa-caritaṁ kali-kalmaṣa-ghnam* indicate that the activities of Lord Kṛṣṇa are certainly the greatest panacea for all miseries, especially in this age of Kali. It is said that in Kali-yuga people have only short lives, and they have no culture of spiritual consciousness. If anyone is at all interested in spiritual culture, he is misled by many bogus *svāmīs* and *yogīs* who do not refer to *kṛṣṇa-kathā*. Therefore most people are unfortunate and disturbed by many calamities. Śrīla Vyāsadeva prepared *Śrīmad-Bhāgavatam* at the request of Nārada Muni in order to give relief to the suffering people of this age (*kali-kalmaṣa-ghnam*). The Kṛṣṇa consciousness movement is seriously engaged in enlightening people through the pleasing topics of *Śrīmad-Bhāgavatam*. All over the world, the message of *Śrīmad-Bhāgavatam* and *Bhagavad-gītā* is being accepted in all spheres of life, especially in advanced, educated circles.

Śrīla Śukadeva Gosvāmī is described in this verse as *bhāgavata-pradhānaḥ*, whereas Mahārāja Parīkṣit is described as *viṣṇu-rātam*. Both words bear the same meaning; that is, Mahārāja Parīkṣit was a great devotee of Kṛṣṇa, and Śukadeva Gosvāmī was also a great saintly person and a great devotee of Kṛṣṇa. Combined together to present *kṛṣṇa-kathā*, they give great relief to suffering humanity.

*anarthopaśamaṁ sākṣād*
*bhakti-yogam adhokṣaje*
*lokasyājānato vidvāṁś*
*cakre sātvata-saṁhitām*

"The material miseries of the living entity, which are superfluous to him, can be directly mitigated by the linking process of devotional service. But the mass of people do not know this, and therefore the learned Vyāsadeva compiled this Vedic literature, *Śrīmad-Bhāgavatam*, which is in relation to the Supreme Truth." (*Bhāg.* 1.7.6) People in general are unaware that the message of *Śrīmad-Bhāgavatam* can give all of human society relief from the pangs of Kali-yuga (*kali-kalmaṣa-ghnam*).

## TEXT 15

श्रीशुक उवाच
सम्यग्व्यवसिता बुद्धिस्तव राजर्षिसत्तम ।
वासुदेवकथायां ते यज्जाता नैष्ठिकी रतिः ॥१५॥

*śrī-śuka uvāca*
*samyag vyavasitā buddhis*
*tava rājarṣi-sattama*
*vāsudeva-kathāyāṁ te*
*yaj jātā naiṣṭhikī ratiḥ*

*śrī-śukaḥ uvāca*—Śrī Śukadeva Gosvāmī said; *samyak*—completely; *vyavasitā*—fixed; *buddhiḥ*—intelligence; *tava*—of Your Majesty; *rāja-ṛṣi-sattama*—O best of *rājarṣis*, saintly kings; *vāsudeva-kathāyām*—in hearing about the topics of Vāsudeva, Kṛṣṇa; *te*—your; *yat*—because; *jātā*—developed; *naiṣṭhikī*—without cessation; *ratiḥ*—attraction or ecstatic devotional service.

## TRANSLATION

**Śrīla Śukadeva Gosvāmī said: O Your Majesty, best of all saintly kings, because you are greatly attracted to topics of Vāsudeva, it is certain that your intelligence is firmly fixed in spiritual understanding, which is the only true goal for humanity. Because that attraction is unceasing, it is certainly sublime.**

## PURPORT

*Kṛṣṇa-kathā* is compulsory for the *rājarṣi,* or executive head of government. This is also mentioned in *Bhagavad-gītā* (*imaṁ rājarṣayo viduḥ*). Unfortunately, however, in this age the governmental power is gradually being captured by third-class and fourth-class men who have no spiritual understanding, and society is therefore very quickly becoming degraded. *Kṛṣṇa-kathā* must be understood by the executive heads of government, for otherwise how will people be happy and gain relief from the pangs of materialistic life? One who has fixed his mind in Kṛṣṇa consciousness should be understood to have very sharp intelligence in regard to the value of life. Mahārāja Parīkṣit was *rājarṣi-sattama,* the best of all saintly kings, and Śukadeva Gosvāmī was *muni-sattama,* the best of *munis.* Both of them were elevated because of their common interest in *kṛṣṇa-kathā.* The exalted position of the speaker and the audience will be explained very nicely in the next verse. *Kṛṣṇa-kathā* is so enlivening that Mahārāja Parīkṣit forgot everything material, even his personal comfort in relation to food and drink. This is an example of how the Kṛṣṇa consciousness movement should spread all over the world to bring both the speaker and the audience to the transcendental platform and back home, back to Godhead.

## TEXT 16

वासुदेवकथाप्रश्नः पुरुषांस्त्रीन् पुनाति हि ।
वक्तारं प्रच्छकं श्रोतॄंस्तत्पादसलिलं यथा ॥१६॥

*vāsudeva-kathā-praśnaḥ*
*puruṣāṁs trīn punāti hi*
*vaktāraṁ pracchakaṁ śrotṝṁs*
*tat-pāda-salilaṁ yathā*

*vāsudeva-kathā-praśnaḥ*—questions about the pastimes and characteristics of Vāsudeva, Kṛṣṇa; *puruṣān*—persons; *trīn*—three; *punāti*—purify; *hi*—indeed; *vaktāram*—the speaker, such as Śukadeva Gosvāmī; *pracchakam*—and an inquisitive hearer like Mahārāja Parīkṣit; *śrotṝn*—and, between them, the listeners hearing about the topics; *tat-pāda-salilam yathā*—exactly as the entire world is purified by the Ganges water emanating from the toe of Lord Viṣṇu.

## TRANSLATION

**The Ganges, emanating from the toe of Lord Viṣṇu, purifies the three worlds, the upper, middle and lower planetary systems. Similarly, when one asks questions about the pastimes and characteristics of Lord Vāsudeva, Kṛṣṇa, three varieties of men are purified: the speaker or preacher, he who inquires, and the people in general who listen.**

## PURPORT

It is said, *tasmād guruṁ prapadyeta jijñāsuḥ śreya uttamam* (*Bhāg.* 11.3.21). Those interested in understanding transcendental subject matters as the goal of life must approach the bona fide spiritual master. *Tasmād guruṁ prapadyeta.* One must surrender to such a *guru*, who can give right information about Kṛṣṇa. Herein, Mahārāja Parīkṣit has surrendered to the right personality, Śukadeva Gosvāmī, for enlightenment in *vāsudeva-kathā.* Vāsudeva is the original Personality of Godhead, who has unlimited spiritual activities. *Śrīmad-Bhāgavatam* is a record of such activities, and *Bhagavad-gītā* is the record of Vāsudeva speaking personally. Therefore, since the Kṛṣṇa consciousness movement is full of *vāsudeva-kathā*, anyone who hears, anyone who joins the movement and anyone who preaches will be purified.

## TEXT 17

भूमिर्दृप्तनृपव्याजदैत्यानीकशतायुतैः ।
आक्रान्ता भूरिभारेण ब्रह्माणं शरणं ययौ ॥१७॥

*bhūmir dṛpta-nṛpa-vyāja-*
*daityānīka-śatāyutaiḥ*

*ākrāntā bhūri-bhāreṇa*
*brahmāṇaṁ śaraṇaṁ yayau*

*bhūmiḥ*—mother earth; *dṛpta*—puffed up; *nṛpa-vyāja*—posing as kings, or the supreme power personified in the state; *daitya*—of demons; *anīka*—of military phalanxes of soldiers; *śata-ayutaiḥ*—unlimitedly, by many hundreds of thousands; *ākrāntā*—being overburdened; *bhūri-bhāreṇa*—by a burden of unnecessary fighting power; *brahmāṇam*—unto Lord Brahmā; *śaraṇam*—to take shelter; *yayau*—went.

## TRANSLATION

**Once when mother earth was overburdened by hundreds of thousands of military phalanxes of various conceited demons dressed like kings, she approached Lord Brahmā for relief.**

## PURPORT

When the world is overburdened by unnecessary military arrangements and when various demoniac kings are the executive heads of state, this burden causes the appearance of the Supreme Personality of Godhead. As the Lord says in *Bhagavad-gītā* (4.7):

*yadā yadā hi dharmasya*
*glānir bhavati bhārata*
*abhyutthānam adharmasya*
*tadātmānaṁ sṛjāmy aham*

"Whenever and wherever there is a decline in religious practice, O descendant of Bharata, and a predominant rise of irreligion—at that time I appear Myself." When the residents of this earth become atheistic and godless, they descend to the status of animals like dogs and hogs, and thus their only business is to bark among themselves. This is *dharmasya glāni*, deviation from the goal of life. Human life is meant for attaining the highest perfection of Kṛṣṇa consciousness, but when people are godless and the presidents or kings are unnecessarily puffed up with military power, their business is to fight and increase the military strength of their different states. Nowadays, therefore, it appears that every state is busy manufacturing atomic weapons to prepare for a third world war. Such preparations are certainly unnecessary; they reflect the false pride of the heads of state. The real business of a chief executive is to see to the happiness of the mass of people by training them in Kṛṣṇa consciousness in different divisions of life. *Cātur-varṇyaṁ mayā sṛṣṭaṁ guṇa-karma-vibhāgaśaḥ* (Bg. 4.13). A leader should train the people as *brāhmaṇas, kṣatriyas, vaiśyas* and *śūdras* and engage them in various occupational duties, thus helping them progress toward Kṛṣṇa consciousness. Instead, however, rogues and thieves in the guise of protectors arrange for a voting system, and in the name of democracy they come to power by hook or crook and exploit the citizens. Even long, long ago, *asuras*, persons devoid of God consciousness, became the heads of state, and now this is happening again. The various states of the world are preoccupied with arranging for military strength. Sometimes they spend sixty-five percent of the government's revenue for this purpose. But why should people's hard-earned money be spent in this way? Because of the present world situation, Kṛṣṇa has descended in the form of the Kṛṣṇa consciousness movement. This is quite natural, for without the Kṛṣṇa consciousness movement the world cannot be peaceful and happy.

## TEXT 18

गौर्भूत्वाश्रुमुखी खिन्ना क्रन्दन्ती करुणं विभोः ।
उपस्थितान्तिके तस्मै व्यसनं समवोचत ॥१८॥

*gaur bhūtvāśru-mukhī khinnā*
*krandantī karuṇaṁ vibhoḥ*
*upasthitāntike tasmai*
*vyasanaṁ samavocata*

*gauḥ*—the shape of a cow; *bhūtvā*—assuming; *aśru-mukhī*—with tears in the eyes; *khinnā*—very much distressed; *krandantī*—weeping; *karuṇam*—piteously; *vibhoḥ*—of Lord Brahmā; *upasthitā*—appeared; *antike*—in front; *tasmai*—unto him (Lord Brahmā); *vyasanam*—her distress; *samavocata*—submitted.

## TRANSLATION

**Mother earth assumed the form of a cow. Very much distressed, with tears in her eyes, she appeared before Lord Brahmā and told him about her misfortune.**

## TEXT 19

ब्रह्मा तदुपधार्याथ सह देवैस्तया सह ।
जगाम सत्रिनयनस्तीरं क्षीरपयोनिधेः ॥१९॥

*brahmā tad-upadhāryātha*
*saha devais tayā saha*
*jagāma sa-tri-nayanas*
*tīraṁ kṣīra-payo-nidheḥ*

*brahmā*—Lord Brahmā; *tat-upadhārya*—understanding everything rightly; *atha*—thereafter; *saha*—with; *devaiḥ*—the demigods; *tayā saha*—with mother earth; *jagāma*—approached; *sa-tri-nayanaḥ*—with Lord Śiva, who has three eyes; *tīram*—the shore; *kṣīra-payaḥ-nidheḥ*—of the ocean of milk.

## TRANSLATION

**Thereafter, having heard of the distress of mother earth, Lord Brahmā, with mother earth, Lord Śiva and all the other demigods, approached the shore of the ocean of milk.**

## PURPORT

After Lord Brahmā understood the precarious condition of the earth, he first visited the demigods headed by Lord Indra, who are in charge of the various affairs of this universe, and Lord Śiva, who is responsible for annihilation. Both maintenance and annihilation go on perpetually, under the order of the Supreme Personality of Godhead. As stated in *Bhagavad-gītā* (4.8), *paritrāṇāya sādhūnāṁ vināśāya ca duṣkṛtām.* Those who are obedient to the laws of God are protected by different servants and demigods, whereas those who are undesirable are vanquished by Lord Śiva. Lord Brahmā first met all the demigods, including Lord

Śiva. Then, along with mother earth, they went to the shore of the ocean of milk, where Lord Viṣṇu lies on a white island, Śvetadvīpa.

## TEXT 20

तत्र गत्वा जगन्नाथं देवदेवं वृषाकपिम् ।
पुरुषं पुरुषसूक्तेन उपतस्थे समाहितः ॥२०॥

*tatra gatvā jagannāthaṁ*
*deva-devaṁ vṛṣākapim*
*puruṣaṁ puruṣa-sūktena*
*upatasthe samāhitaḥ*

*tatra*—there (on the shore of the ocean of milk); *gatvā*—after going; *jagannātham*—unto the master of the entire universe, the Supreme Being; *deva-devam*—the Supreme God of all gods; *vṛṣākapim*—the Supreme Person, Viṣṇu, who provides for everyone and diminishes everyone's suffering; *puruṣam*—the Supreme Person; *puruṣa-sūktena*—with the Vedic *mantra* known as *Puruṣa-sūkta; upatasthe*—worshiped; *samāhitaḥ*—with full attention.

## TRANSLATION

**After reaching the shore of the ocean of milk, the demigods worshiped the Supreme Personality of Godhead, Lord Viṣṇu, the master of the whole universe, the supreme God of all gods, who provides for everyone and diminishes everyone's suffering. With great attention, they worshiped Lord Viṣṇu, who lies on the ocean of milk, by reciting the Vedic mantras known as the Puruṣa-sūkta.**

## PURPORT

The demigods, such as Lord Brahmā, Lord Śiva, King Indra, Candra and Sūrya, are all subordinate to the Supreme Personality of Godhead. Aside from the demigods, even in human society there are many influential personalities supervising various businesses or establishments. Lord Viṣṇu, however, is the God of gods (*parameśvara*). He is *parama-puruṣa*, the Supreme Being, Paramātmā. As confirmed in the

*Brahma-saṁhitā* (5.1), *īśvaraḥ paramaḥ kṛṣṇaḥ sac-cid-ānanda-vigrahaḥ:* "Kṛṣṇa, known as Govinda, is the supreme controller. He has an eternal, blissful, spiritual body." No one is equal to or greater than the Supreme Personality of Godhead, and therefore He is described here by many words: *jagannātha, deva-deva, vṛṣākapi* and *puruṣa.* The supremacy of Lord Viṣṇu is also confirmed in *Bhagavad-gītā* (10.12) in this statement by Arjuna:

*paraṁ brahma paraṁ dhāma*
*pavitraṁ paramaṁ bhavān*
*puruṣaṁ śāśvataṁ divyam*
*ādi-devam ajaṁ vibhum*

"You are the Supreme Brahman, the ultimate, the supreme abode and purifier, the Absolute Truth and the eternal divine person. You are the primal God, transcendental and original, and You are the unborn and all-pervading beauty." Kṛṣṇa is *ādi-puruṣa,* the original Personality of Godhead (*govindam ādi-puruṣaṁ tam ahaṁ bhajāmi*). Viṣṇu is a plenary expansion of Lord Kṛṣṇa, and all the *viṣṇu-tattvas* are *parameśvara, deva-deva.*

## TEXT 21

**गिरं समाधौ गगने समीरितां**
**निशम्य वेधास्त्रिदशानुवाच ह ।**
**गां पौरुषीं मे श‍ृणुतामराः पुन-**
**र्विधीयतामाशु तथैव मा चिरम् ॥२१॥**

*giraṁ samādhau gagane samīritāṁ*
*niśamya vedhās tridaśān uvāca ha*
*gāṁ pauruṣīṁ me śṛṇutāmarāḥ punar*
*vidhīyatām āśu tathaiva mā ciram*

*giram*—a vibration of words; *samādhau*—in trance; *gagane*—in the sky; *samīritām*—vibrated; *niśamya*—hearing; *vedhāḥ*—Lord Brahmā; *tridaśān*—unto the demigods; *uvāca*—said; *ha*—oh; *gām*—the order;

*pauruṣīm*—received from the Supreme Person; *me*—from me; *śṛṇuta*—just hear; *amarāḥ*—O demigods; *punaḥ*—again; *vidhīyatām*—execute; *āśu*—immediately; *tathā eva*—just so; *mā*—do not; *ciram*—delay.

## TRANSLATION

**While in trance, Lord Brahmā heard the words of Lord Viṣṇu vibrating in the sky. Thus he told the demigods: O demigods, hear from me the order of Kṣīrodakaśāyī Viṣṇu, the Supreme Person, and execute it attentively without delay.**

## PURPORT

It appears that the words of the Supreme Personality of Godhead can be heard in trance by competent persons. Modern science gives us telephones, by which one can hear sound vibrations from a distant place. Similarly, although other persons cannot hear the words of Lord Viṣṇu, Lord Brahmā is able to hear the Lord's words within himself. This is confirmed in the beginning of *Śrīmad-Bhāgavatam* (1.1.1): *tene brahma hṛdā ya ādi-kavaye. Ādi-kavi* is Lord Brahmā. In the beginning of the creation, Lord Brahmā received the instructions of Vedic knowledge from Lord Viṣṇu through the medium of the heart (*hṛdā*). The same principle is confirmed herewith. While Brahmā was in trance, he was able to hear the words of Kṣīrodakaśāyī Viṣṇu, and he carried the Lord's message to the demigods. Similarly, in the beginning, Brahmā first received the Vedic knowledge from the Supreme Personality of Godhead through the core of the heart. In both instances the same process was used in transmitting the message to Lord Brahmā. In other words, although Lord Viṣṇu was invisible even to Lord Brahmā, Lord Brahmā could hear Lord Viṣṇu's words through the heart. The Supreme Personality of Godhead is invisible even to Lord Brahmā, yet He descends on this earth and becomes visible to people in general. This is certainly an act of His causeless mercy, but fools and nondevotees think that Kṛṣṇa is an ordinary historical person. Because they think that the Lord is an ordinary person like them, they are described as *mūḍha* (*avajānanti māṁ mūḍhāḥ*). The causeless mercy of the Supreme Personality of Godhead is neglected by such demoniac persons, who cannot understand the instructions of *Bhagavad-gītā* and who therefore misinterpret them.

## TEXT 22

पुरैव पुंसावधृतो धराज्वरो
भवद्भिरंशैर्यदुषूपजन्यताम् ।
स यावदुर्व्या भरमीश्वरेश्वरः
स्वकालशक्त्या क्षपयंश्चरेद् भुवि ॥२२॥

*puraiva puṁsāvadhṛto dharā-jvaro*
*bhavadbhir aṁśair yaduṣūpajanyatām*
*sa yāvad urvyā bharam īśvareśvaraḥ*
*sva-kāla-śaktyā kṣapayaṁś cared bhuvi*

*purā*—even before this; *eva*—indeed; *puṁsā*—by the Supreme Personality of Godhead; *avadhṛtaḥ*—was certainly known; *dharā-jvaraḥ*—the distress on the earth; *bhavadbhiḥ*—by your good selves; *aṁśaiḥ*—expanding as plenary portions; *yaduṣu*—in the family of King Yadu; *upajanyatām*—take your birth and appear there; *saḥ*—He (the Supreme Personality of Godhead); *yāvat*—as long as; *urvyāḥ*—of the earth; *bharam*—the burden; *īśvara-īśvaraḥ*—the Lord of lords; *sva-kāla-śaktyā*—by His own potency the time factor; *kṣapayan*—diminishing; *caret*—should move; *bhuvi*—on the surface of the earth.

## TRANSLATION

**Lord Brahmā informed the demigods: Before we submitted our petition to the Lord, He was already aware of the distress on earth. Consequently, for as long as the Lord moves on earth to diminish its burden by His own potency in the form of time, all of you demigods should appear through plenary portions as sons and grandsons in the family of the Yadus.**

## PURPORT

As stated in the *Brahma-saṁhitā* (5.39):

*rāmādi-mūrtiṣu kalā-niyamena tiṣṭhan*
*nānāvatāram akarod bhuvaneṣu kintu*

*kṛṣṇaḥ svayaṁ samabhavat paramaḥ pumān yo*
*govindam ādi-puruṣaṁ tam ahaṁ bhajāmi*

"I worship the Supreme Personality of Godhead, Govinda, who is always situated in various incarnations such as Rāma, Nṛsiṁha and many subincarnations as well, but who is the original Personality of Godhead, known as Kṛṣṇa, and who incarnates personally also."

In this verse from *Śrīmad-Bhāgavatam* we find the words *puraiva puṁsāvadhṛto dharā-jvaraḥ*. The word *puṁsā* refers to Kṛṣṇa, who was already aware of how the whole world was suffering because of the increase of demons. Without reference to the supreme power of the Personality of Godhead, demons assert themselves to be independent kings and presidents, and thus they create a disturbance by increasing their military power. When such disturbances are very prominent, Kṛṣṇa appears. At present also, various demoniac states all over the world are increasing their military power in many ways, and the whole situation has become distressful. Therefore Kṛṣṇa has appeared by His name, in the Hare Kṛṣṇa movement, which will certainly diminish the burden of the world. Philosophers, religionists, and people in general must take to this movement very seriously, for man-made plans and devices will not help bring peace on earth. The transcendental sound Hare Kṛṣṇa is not different from the person Kṛṣṇa.

*nāma cintāmaṇiḥ kṛṣṇaś*
*caitanya-rasa-vigrahaḥ*
*pūrṇaḥ śuddho nitya-mukto*
*'bhinnatvān nāma-nāminoḥ*
(*Padma Purāṇa*)

There is no difference between the sound Hare Kṛṣṇa and Kṛṣṇa the person.

## TEXT 23

वसुदेवगृहे साक्षाद् भगवान् पुरुषः परः ।
जनिष्यते तत्प्रियार्थं सम्भवन्तु सुरस्त्रियः ॥२३॥

*vasudeva-gṛhe sākṣād*
*bhagavān puruṣaḥ paraḥ*
*janiṣyate tat-priyārthaṁ*
*sambhavantu sura-striyaḥ*

*vasudeva-gṛhe*—in the house of Vasudeva (who would be the father of Kṛṣṇa when the Lord appeared); *sākṣāt*—personally; *bhagavān*—the Supreme Personality of Godhead, who has full potency; *puruṣaḥ*—the original person; *paraḥ*—who is transcendental; *janiṣyate*—will appear; *tat-priya-artham*—and for His satisfaction; *sambhavantu*—should take birth; *sura-striyaḥ*—all the wives of the demigods.

## TRANSLATION

**The Supreme Personality of Godhead, Śrī Kṛṣṇa, who has full potency, will personally appear as the son of Vasudeva. Therefore all the wives of the demigods should also appear in order to satisfy Him.**

## PURPORT

In *Bhagavad-gītā* (4.9) the Lord says, *tyaktvā dehaṁ punar janma naiti mām eti:* after giving up the material body, the devotee of the Lord returns home, back to Godhead. This means that the devotee is first transferred to the particular universe where the Lord is at that time staying to exhibit His pastimes. There are innumerable universes, and the Lord is appearing in one of these universes at every moment. Therefore His pastimes are called *nitya-līlā,* eternal pastimes. The Lord's appearance as a child in the house of Devakī takes place continuously in one universe after another. Therefore, the devotee is first transferred to that particular universe where the pastimes of the Lord are current. As stated in *Bhagavad-gītā,* even if a devotee does not complete the course of devotional service, he enjoys the happiness of the heavenly planets, where the most pious people dwell, and then takes birth in the house of a *śuci* or *śrīmān,* a pious *brāhmaṇa* or a wealthy *vaiśya* (*śucīnāṁ śrīmatāṁ gehe yoga-bhraṣṭo 'bhijāyate*). Thus a pure devotee, even if unable to execute devotional service completely, is transferred to the upper planetary system, where pious people reside. From there, if his devotional service is complete, such a devotee is transferred to the place where the Lord's pastimes are going on. Herein it is said, *sambhavantu sura-striyaḥ. Sura-strī*, the women of the heavenly planets, were thus ordered to appear in the Yadu dynasty in Vṛndāvana to enrich the pastimes of Lord Kṛṣṇa. These *sura-strī*, when further trained to live with Kṛṣṇa, would be transferred to the original Goloka Vṛndāvana. During Lord Kṛṣṇa's pastimes within this world, the *sura-strī* were to appear in different ways in different families to give pleasure to the Lord, just so that they would be fully trained before going to the eternal Goloka Vṛndāvana. With the association of Lord Kṛṣṇa, either at Dvārakā-purī, Mathurā-purī or Vṛndāvana, they would certainly return home, back to Godhead. Among the *sura-strī*, the women of the heavenly planets, there are many devotees, such as the mother of the Upendra incarnation of Kṛṣṇa. It was such devoted women who were called for in this connection.

## TEXT 24

वासुदेवकलानन्तः सहस्रवदनः स्वराट् ।
अग्रतो भविता देवो हरेः प्रियचिकीर्षया ॥२४॥

*vāsudeva-kalānantaḥ*
*sahasra-vadanaḥ svarāṭ*
*agrato bhavitā devo*
*hareḥ priya-cikīrṣayā*

***vāsudeva-kalā anantaḥ***—the plenary expansion of Lord Kṛṣṇa known as Anantadeva or Saṅkarṣaṇa Ananta, the all-pervasive incarnation of the Supreme Lord; *sahasra-vadanaḥ*—having thousands of hoods; *svarāṭ*—fully independent; *agrataḥ*—previously; *bhavitā*—will appear; *devaḥ*—the Lord; *hareḥ*—of Lord Kṛṣṇa; *priya-cikīrṣayā*—with the desire to act for the pleasure.

## TRANSLATION

**The foremost manifestation of Kṛṣṇa is Saṅkarṣaṇa, who is known as Ananta. He is the origin of all incarnations within this**

**material world. Previous to the appearance of Lord Kṛṣṇa, this original Saṅkarṣaṇa will appear as Baladeva, just to please the Supreme Lord Kṛṣṇa in His transcendental pastimes.**

## PURPORT

Śrī Baladeva is the Supreme Personality of Godhead Himself. He is equal in supremacy to the Supreme Godhead, yet wherever Kṛṣṇa appears, Śrī Baladeva appears as His brother, sometimes elder and sometimes younger. When Kṛṣṇa appears, all His plenary expansions and other incarnations appear with Him. This is elaborately explained in *Caitanya-caritāmṛta.* This time, Baladeva would appear before Kṛṣṇa as Kṛṣṇa's elder brother.

## TEXT 25

विष्णोर्माया भगवती यया सम्मोहितं जगत् ।
आदिष्टा प्रभुणांशेन कार्यार्थे सम्भविष्यति ॥२५॥

*viṣṇor māyā bhagavatī*
*yayā sammohitaṁ jagat*
*ādiṣṭā prabhuṇāṁśena*
*kāryārthe sambhaviṣyati*

*viṣṇoḥ māyā*—the potency of the Supreme Personality of Godhead, Viṣṇu; *bhagavatī*—as good as Bhagavān and therefore known as Bhagavatī; *yayā*—by whom; *sammohitam*—captivated; *jagat*—all the worlds, both material and spiritual; *ādiṣṭā*—being ordered; *prabhuṇā*—by the master; *aṁśena*—with her different potential factors; *kārya-arthe*—for executing business; *sambhaviṣyati*—would also appear.

## TRANSLATION

**The potency of the Lord, known as viṣṇu-māyā, who is as good as the Supreme Personality of Godhead, will also appear with Lord Kṛṣṇa. This potency, acting in different capacities, captivates all the worlds, both material and spiritual. At the request of her master, she will appear with her different potencies in order to execute the work of the Lord.**

## PURPORT

*Parāsya śaktir vividhaiva śrūyate* (*Śvetāśvatara Upaniṣad* 6.8). In the *Vedas* it is said that the potencies of the Supreme Personality of Godhead are called by different names, such as *yogamāyā* and *mahāmāyā.* Ultimately, however, the Lord's potency is one, exactly as electric potency is one although it can act both to cool and to heat. The Lord's potency acts in both the spiritual and material worlds. In the spiritual world the Lord's potency works as *yogamāyā,* and in the material world the same potency works as *mahāmāyā,* exactly as electricity works in both a heater and a cooler. In the material world, this potency, working as *mahāmāyā,* acts upon the conditioned souls to deprive them more and more of devotional service. It is said, *yayā sammohito jīva ātmānaṁ tri-guṇātmakam.* In the material world the conditioned soul thinks of himself as a product of *tri-guṇa,* the three modes of material nature. This is the bodily conception of life. Because of associating with the three *guṇas* of the material potency, everyone identifies himself with his body. Someone is thinking he is a *brāhmaṇa,* someone a *kṣatriya,* and someone a *vaiśya* or *śūdra.* Actually, however, one is neither a *brāhmaṇa,* a *kṣatriya,* a *vaiśya* nor a *śūdra;* one is part and parcel of the Supreme Lord (*mamaivāṁśaḥ*), but because of being covered by the material energy, *mahāmāyā,* one identifies himself in these different ways. When the conditioned soul becomes liberated, however, he thinks himself an eternal servant of Kṛṣṇa. *Jīvera 'svarūpa' haya—kṛṣṇera 'nitya-dāsa.'* When he comes to that position, the same potency, acting as *yogamāyā,* increasingly helps him become purified and devote his energy to the service of the Lord.

In either case, whether the soul is conditioned or liberated, the Lord is supreme. As stated in *Bhagavad-gītā* (9.10), *mayādhyakṣeṇa prakṛtiḥ sūyate sa-carācaram:* it is by the order of the Supreme Personality of Godhead that the material energy, *mahāmāyā,* works upon the conditioned soul.

*prakṛteḥ kriyamāṇāni*
*guṇaiḥ karmāṇi sarvaśaḥ*
*ahaṅkāra-vimūḍhātmā*
*kartāham iti manyate*

"The bewildered spirit soul, under the influence of the three modes of material nature, thinks himself to be the doer of activities which are in actuality carried out by nature." (Bg. 3.27) Within conditioned life, no one has freedom, but because one is bewildered, being subject to the rule of *mahāmāyā*, one foolishly thinks himself independent (*ahaṅkāra-vimūḍhātmā kartāham iti manyate*). But when the conditioned soul becomes liberated by executing devotional service, he is given a greater and greater chance to relish a relationship with the Supreme Personality of Godhead in different transcendental statuses, such as *dāsya-rasa, sakhya-rasa, vātsalya-rasa* and *mādhurya-rasa.*

Thus the Lord's potency, *viṣṇu-māyā*, has two features—*āvaraṇikā* and *unmukha.* When the Lord appeared, His potency came with Him and acted in different ways. She acted as *yogamāyā* with Yaśodā, Devakī and other intimate relations of the Lord, and she acted in a different way with Kaṁsa, Śālva and other *asuras.* By the order of Lord Kṛṣṇa, His potency *yogamāyā* came with Him and exhibited different activities according to the time and circumstances. *Kāryārthe sambhaviṣyati. Yogamāyā* acted differently to execute different purposes desired by the Lord. As confirmed in *Bhagavad-gītā* (9.13), *mahātmānas tu māṁ pārtha daivīṁ prakṛtim āśritāḥ.* The *mahātmās*, who fully surrender to the lotus feet of the Lord, are directed by *yogamāyā*, whereas the *durātmās*, those who are devoid of devotional service, are directed by *mahāmāyā.*

## TEXT 26

श्रीशुक उवाच

इत्यादिश्यामरगणान् प्रजापतिपतिर्विभुः ।
आश्वास्य च महीं गीर्भिः स्वधाम परमं ययौ ॥२६॥

*śrī-śuka uvāca*
*ity ādiśyāmara-gaṇān*
*prajāpati-patir vibhuḥ*
*āśvāsya ca mahīṁ gīrbhiḥ*
*sva-dhāma paramaṁ yayau*

*śrī-śukaḥ uvāca*—Śrī Śukadeva Gosvāmī said; *iti*—thus; *ādiśya*—after informing; *amara-gaṇān*—all the demigods; *prajāpati-patiḥ*—

Lord Brahmā, the master of the Prajāpatis; *vibhuḥ*—all-powerful; *āśvāsya*—after pacifying; *ca*—also; *mahīm*—mother earth; *gīrbhiḥ*—by sweet words; *sva-dhāma*—his own planet, known as Brahmaloka; *paramam*—the best (within the universe); *yayau*—returned.

## TRANSLATION

**Śukadeva Gosvāmī continued: After thus advising the demigods and pacifying mother earth, the very powerful Lord Brahmā, who is the master of all other Prajāpatis and is therefore known as Prajāpati-pati, returned to his own abode, Brahmaloka.**

## TEXT 27

शूरसेनो यदुपतिर्मथुरामावसन् पुरीम् ।
माथुराञ्छूरसेनांश्च विषयान् बुभुजे पुरा ॥२७॥

*śūraseno yadupatir*
*mathurām āvasan purīm*
*māthurāñ chūrasenāṁś ca*
*viṣayān bubhuje purā*

*śūrasenaḥ*—King Śūrasena; *yadu-patiḥ*—the chief of the Yadu dynasty; *mathurām*—at the place known as Mathurā; *āvasan*—went to live; *purīm*—in that city; *māthurān*—at the place known as the Māthura district; *śūrasenān ca*—and the place known as Śūrasena; *viṣayān*—such kingdoms; *bubhuje*—enjoyed; *purā*—formerly.

## TRANSLATION

**Formerly, Śūrasena, the chief of the Yadu dynasty, had gone to live in the city of Mathurā. There he enjoyed the places known as Māthura and Śūrasena.**

## TEXT 28

राजधानी ततः साभूत् सर्वयादवभूभुजाम् ।
मथुरा भगवान् यत्र नित्यं संनिहितो हरिः ॥२८॥

*rājadhānī tataḥ sābhūt*
*sarva-yādava-bhūbhujām*
*mathurā bhagavān yatra*
*nityaṁ sannihito hariḥ*

*rājadhānī*—the capital; *tataḥ*—from that time; *sā*—the country and the city known as Mathurā; *abhūt*—became; *sarva-yādava-bhūbhujām*—of all the kings who appeared in the Yadu dynasty; *mathurā*—the place known as Mathurā; *bhagavān*—the Supreme Personality of Godhead; *yatra*—wherein; *nityam*—eternally; *sannihitaḥ*—intimately connected, living eternally; *hariḥ*—the Lord, the Supreme Personality of Godhead.

## TRANSLATION

**Since that time, the city of Mathurā had been the capital of all the kings of the Yadu dynasty. The city and district of Mathurā are very intimately connected with Kṛṣṇa, for Lord Kṛṣṇa lives there eternally.**

## PURPORT

It is understood that Mathurā City is the transcendental abode of Lord Kṛṣṇa; it is not an ordinary material city, for it is eternally connected with the Supreme Personality of Godhead. Vṛndāvana is within the jurisdiction of Mathurā, and it still continues to exist. Because Mathurā and Vṛndāvana are intimately connected with Kṛṣṇa eternally, it is said that Lord Kṛṣṇa never leaves Vṛndāvana (*vṛndāvanaṁ parityajya padam ekaṁ na gacchati*). At present, the place known as Vṛndāvana, in the district of Mathurā, continues its position as a transcendental place, and certainly anyone who goes there becomes transcendentally purified. Navadvīpa-dhāma is also intimately connected with Vrajabhūmi. Śrīla Narottama dāsa Ṭhākura therefore says:

*śrī gauḍa-maṇḍala-bhūmi, yebā jāne cintāmaṇi,*
*tā'ra haya vrajabhūme vāsa*

"Vrajabhūmi" refers to Mathurā-Vṛndāvana, and Gauḍa-maṇḍala-bhūmi includes Navadvīpa. These two places are nondifferent. Therefore, anyone living in Navadvīpa-dhāma, knowing Kṛṣṇa and Śrī Caitanya Mahāprabhu to be the same personality, lives in Vrajabhūmi, Mathurā-Vṛndāvana. The Lord has made it convenient for the conditioned soul to live in Mathurā, Vṛndāvana and Navadvīpa and thus be directly connected with the Supreme Personality of Godhead. Simply by living in these places, one can immediately come in contact with the Lord. There are many devotees who vow never to leave Vṛndāvana and Mathurā. This is undoubtedly a good vow, but if one leaves Vṛndāvana, Mathurā or Navadvīpa-dhāma for the service of the Lord, he is not disconnected from the Supreme Personality of Godhead. At any rate, we must understand the transcendental importance of Mathurā-Vṛndāvana and Navadvīpa-dhāma. Anyone who executes devotional service in these places certainly goes back home, back to Godhead, after giving up his body. Thus the words *mathurā bhagavān yatra nityaṁ sannihito hariḥ* are particularly important. A devotee should fully utilize this instruction to the best of his ability. Whenever the Supreme Lord personally appears, He appears in Mathurā because of His intimate connection with this place. Therefore although Mathurā and Vṛndāvana are situated on this planet earth, they are transcendental abodes of the Lord.

## TEXT 29

तस्यां तु कर्हिचिच्छौरिर्वसुदेवः कृतोद्वहः ।
देवक्या सूर्यया सार्धं प्रयाणे रथमारुहत् ॥२९॥

*tasyāṁ tu karhicic chaurir*
*vasudevaḥ kṛtodvahaḥ*
*devakyā sūryayā sārdhaṁ*
*prayāṇe ratham āruhat*

*tasyām*—in that place known as Mathurā; *tu*—indeed; *karhicit*—some time ago; *śauriḥ*—the demigod, descendant of Śūra; *vasudevaḥ*—who appeared as Vasudeva; *kṛta-udvahaḥ*—after being married; *devakyā*—Devakī; *sūryayā*—his newly married wife; *sārdham*—along with; *prayāṇe*—for returning home; *ratham*—the chariot; *āruhat*—mounted.

## TRANSLATION

**Some time ago, Vasudeva, who belonged to the demigod family [or to the Śūra dynasty], married Devakī. After the marriage, he mounted his chariot to return home with his newly married wife.**

## TEXT 30

उग्रसेनसुतः कंसः स्वसुः प्रियचिकीर्षया ।
रश्मीन् हयानां जग्राह रौक्मै रथशतैर्वृतः ॥३०॥

*ugrasena-sutaḥ kaṁsaḥ*
*svasuḥ priya-cikīrṣayā*
*raśmīn hayānāṁ jagrāha*
*raukmai ratha-śatair vṛtaḥ*

*ugrasena-sutaḥ*—the son of Ugrasena; *kaṁsaḥ*—by the name Kaṁsa; *svasuḥ*—of his own sister Devakī; *priya-cikīrṣayā*—to please her on the occasion of her marriage; *raśmīn*—the reins; *hayānām*—of the horses; *jagrāha*—took; *raukmaiḥ*—made of gold; *ratha-śataiḥ*—by hundreds of chariots; *vṛtaḥ*—surrounded.

## TRANSLATION

**Kaṁsa, the son of King Ugrasena, in order to please his sister Devakī on the occasion of her marriage, took charge of the reins of the horses and became the chariot driver. He was surrounded by hundreds of golden chariots.**

## TEXTS 31–32

चतुःशतं पारिबर्हं गजानां हेममालिनाम् ।
अश्वानामयुतं सार्धं रथानां च त्रिषट्शतम् ॥३१॥
दासीनां सुकुमारीणां द्वे शते समलङ्कृते ।
दुहित्रे देवकः प्रादाद् याने दुहितृवत्सलः ॥३२॥

*catuḥ-śataṁ pāribarhaṁ*
*gajānāṁ hema-mālinām*

*aśvānāṁ ayutaṁ sārdhaṁ*
*rathānāṁ ca tri-ṣaṭ-śatam*
*dāsīnāṁ sukumārīṇāṁ*
*dve śate samalaṅkṛte*
*duhitre devakaḥ prādād*
*yāne duhitṛ-vatsalaḥ*

*catuḥ-śatam*—four hundred; *pāribarham*—dowry; *gajānām*—of elephants; *hema-mālinām*—decorated with garlands of gold; *aśvānām*—of horses; *ayutam*—ten thousand; *sārdham*—along with; *rathānām*—of chariots; *ca*—and; *tri-ṣaṭ-śatam*—three times six hundred (eighteen hundred); *dāsīnām*—of maidservants; *su-kumārīṇām*—very young and beautiful unmarried girls; *dve*—two; *śate*—hundred; *samalaṅkṛte*—fully decorated with ornaments; *duhitre*—unto his daughter; *devakaḥ*—King Devaka; *prādāt*—gave as a gift; *yāne*—while going away; *duhitṛ-vatsalaḥ*—who was very fond of his daughter Devakī.

## TRANSLATION

**Devakī's father, King Devaka, was very much affectionate to his daughter. Therefore, while she and her husband were leaving home, he gave her a dowry of four hundred elephants nicely decorated with golden garlands. He also gave ten thousand horses, eighteen hundred chariots, and two hundred very beautiful young maidservants, fully decorated with ornaments.**

## PURPORT

The system of giving a dowry to one's daughter has existed in Vedic civilization for a very long time. Even today, following the same system, a father who has money will give his daughter an opulent dowry. A daughter would never inherit the property of her father, and therefore an affectionate father, during the marriage of his daughter, would give her as much as possible. A dowry, therefore, is never illegal according to the Vedic system. Here, of course, the gift offered as a dowry by Devaka to Devakī was not ordinary. Because Devaka was a king, he gave a dowry quite suitable to his royal position. Even an ordinary man, especially a high-class *brāhmaṇa*, *kṣatriya* or *vaiśya*, is supposed to give his daughter a liberal dowry. Immediately after the marriage, the daughter goes to her husband's house, and it is also a custom for the brother of the bride to accompany his sister and brother-in-law to exhibit affection for her. This system was followed by Kaṁsa. These are all old customs in the society of *varṇāśrama-dharma*, which is now wrongly designated as Hindu. These long-standing customs are nicely described here.

## TEXT 33

शङ्खतूर्यमृदङ्गाश्च नेदुर्दुन्दुभयः समम् ।
प्रयाणप्रक्रमे तात वरवध्वोः सुमङ्गलम् ॥३३॥

*śaṅkha-tūrya-mṛdaṅgāś ca*
*nedur dundubhayaḥ samam*
*prayāṇa-prakrame tāta*
*vara-vadhvoḥ sumaṅgalam*

*śaṅkha*—conchshells; *tūrya*—bugles; *mṛdaṅgāḥ*—drums; *ca*—also; *neduḥ*—vibrated; *dundubhayaḥ*—kettledrums; *samam*—in concert; *prayāṇa-prakrame*—at the time of departure; *tāta*—O beloved son; *vara-vadhvoḥ*—of the bridegroom and the bride; *su-maṅgalam*—for the purpose of their auspicious departure.

## TRANSLATION

**O beloved son, Mahārāja Parīkṣit, when the bride and bridegroom were ready to start, conchshells, bugles, drums and kettledrums all vibrated in concert for their auspicious departure.**

## TEXT 34

पथि प्रग्रहिणं कंसमाभाष्याहाशरीरवाक् ।
अस्यास्त्वामष्टमो गर्भो हन्ता यां वहसेऽबुध ॥३४॥

*pathi pragrahiṇaṁ kaṁsam*
*ābhāṣyāhāśarīra-vāk*

*asyās tvām aṣṭamo garbho*
*hantā yāṁ vahase 'budha*

*pathi*—on the way; *pragrahiṇam*—who was managing the reins of the horses; *kaṁsam*—unto Kaṁsa; *ābhāṣya*—addressing; *āha*—said; *a-śarīra-vāk*—a voice coming from someone whose body was invisible; *asyāḥ*—of this girl (Devakī); *tvām*—you; *aṣṭamaḥ*—the eighth; *garbhaḥ*—pregnancy; *hantā*—killer; *yām*—her whom; *vahase*—you are carrying; *abudha*—you foolish rascal.

## TRANSLATION

**While Kaṁsa, controlling the reins of the horses, was driving the chariot along the way, an unembodied voice addressed him, "You foolish rascal, the eighth child of the woman you are carrying will kill you!"**

## PURPORT

The omen spoke of *aṣṭamo garbhaḥ,* referring to the eighth pregnancy, but did not clearly say whether the child was to be a son or a daughter. Even if Kaṁsa were to see that the eighth child of Devakī was a daughter, he should have no doubt that the eighth child was to kill him. According to the *Viśva-kośa* dictionary, the word *garbha* means "embryo" and also *arbhaka,* or "child." Kaṁsa was affectionate toward his sister, and therefore he had become the chariot driver to carry her and his brother-in-law to their home. The demigods, however, did not want Kaṁsa to be affectionate toward Devakī, and therefore, from an unseen position, they encouraged Kaṁsa to offend her. Moreover, the six sons of Marīci had been cursed to take birth from the womb of Devakī, and upon being killed by Kaṁsa they would be delivered. When Devakī understood that Kaṁsa would be killed by the Supreme Personality of Godhead, who would appear from her womb, she felt great joy. The word *vahase* is also significant because it indicates that the ominous vibration condemned Kaṁsa for acting just like a beast of burden by carrying his enemy's mother.

## TEXT 35

इत्युक्तः स खलः पापो भोजानां कुलपांसनः ।
भगिनीं हन्तुमारब्धं खड्गपाणिः कचेऽग्रहीत् ॥३५॥

*ity uktaḥ sa khalaḥ pāpo*
*bhojānāṁ kula-pāṁsanaḥ*
*bhaginīṁ hantum ārabdhaṁ*
*khaḍga-pāṇiḥ kace 'grahīt*

*iti uktaḥ*—thus being addressed; *saḥ*—he (Kaṁsa); *khalaḥ*—envious; *pāpaḥ*—sinful; *bhojānām*—of the Bhoja dynasty; *kula-pāṁsanaḥ*—one who can degrade the reputation of his family; *bhaginīm*—unto his sister; *hantum ārabdham*—being inclined to kill; *khaḍga-pāṇiḥ*—taking a sword in his hand; *kace*—hair; *agrahīt*—took up.

## TRANSLATION

**Kaṁsa was a condemned personality in the Bhoja dynasty because he was envious and sinful. Therefore, upon hearing this omen from the sky, he caught hold of his sister's hair with his left hand and took up his sword with his right hand to sever her head from her body.**

## PURPORT

Kaṁsa was driving the chariot and controlling the reins with his left hand, but as soon as he heard the omen that his sister's eighth child would kill him, he gave up the reins, caught hold of his sister's hair, and with his right hand took up a sword to kill her. Before, he had been so affectionate that he was acting as his sister's chariot driver, but as soon as he heard that his self-interest or his life was at risk, he forgot all affection for her and immediately became a great enemy. This is the nature of demons. No one should trust a demon, despite any amount of affection. Aside from this, a king, a politician or a woman cannot be trusted, since they can do anything abominable for their personal interest. Cāṇakya Paṇḍita therefore says, *viśvāso naiva kartavyaḥ strīṣu rāja-kuleṣu ca.*

## TEXT 36

तं जुगुप्सितकर्माणं नृशंसं निरपत्रपम् ।
वसुदेवो महाभाग उवाच परिसान्त्वयन् ॥३६॥

*taṁ jugupsita-karmāṇaṁ*
*nṛśaṁsaṁ nirapatrapam*
*vasudevo mahā-bhāga*
*uvāca parisāntvayan*

*tam*—unto him (Kaṁsa); *jugupsita-karmāṇam*—who was ready to commit such an offensive act; *nṛśaṁsam*—very cruel; *nirapatrapam*—shameless; *vasudevaḥ*—Vasudeva; *mahā-bhāgaḥ*—the greatly fortunate father of Vāsudeva; *uvāca*—said; *parisāntvayan*—pacifying.

## TRANSLATION

**Wanting to pacify Kaṁsa, who was so cruel and envious that he was shamelessly ready to kill his sister, the great soul Vasudeva, who was to be the father of Kṛṣṇa, spoke to him in the following words.**

## PURPORT

Vasudeva, who was to be the father of Kṛṣṇa, is described here as *mahā-bhāga*, a very upright and sober personality, because although Kaṁsa was ready to kill Vasudeva's wife, Vasudeva remained sober and unagitated. In a peaceful attitude, Vasudeva began to address Kaṁsa by putting forward reasonable arguments. Vasudeva was a great personality because he knew how to pacify a cruel person and how to forgive even the bitterest enemy. One who is fortunate is never caught, even by tigers or snakes.

## TEXT 37

श्रीवसुदेव उवाच
श्लाघनीयगुणः शूरैर्भवान् भोजयशस्करः ।
स कथं भगिनीं हन्यात् स्त्रियमुद्वाहपर्वणि ॥३७॥

*śrī-vasudeva uvāca*
*ślāghanīya-guṇaḥ śūrair*
*bhavān bhoja-yaśaskaraḥ*
*sa kathaṁ bhaginīṁ hanyāt*
*striyam udvāha-parvaṇi*

*śrī-vasudevaḥ uvāca*—the great personality Vasudeva said; *ślāgha-nīya-guṇaḥ*—a person who possesses praiseworthy qualities; *śūraiḥ*—by great heroes; *bhavān*—your good self; *bhoja-yaśaḥ-karaḥ*—a brilliant star in the Bhoja dynasty; *saḥ*—one such as your good self; *katham*—how; *bhaginīm*—your sister; *hanyāt*—can kill; *striyam*—especially a woman; *udvāha-parvaṇi*—at the time of the marriage ceremony.

## TRANSLATION

**Vasudeva said: My dear brother-in-law Kaṁsa, you are the pride of your family, the Bhoja dynasty, and great heroes praise your qualities. How could such a qualified person as you kill a woman, your own sister, especially on the occasion of her marriage?**

## PURPORT

According to Vedic principles, a *brāhmaṇa*, an old man, a woman, a child or a cow cannot be killed under any circumstances. Vasudeva stressed that Devakī was not only a woman but a member of Kaṁsa's family. Because she was now married to Vasudeva, she was *para-strī*, another man's wife, and if such a woman were killed, not only would Kaṁsa be implicated in sinful activities, but his reputation as king of the Bhoja dynasty would be damaged. Thus Vasudeva tried in many ways to convince Kaṁsa in order to stop him from killing Devakī.

## TEXT 38

मृत्युर्जन्मवतां वीर देहेन सह जायते ।
अद्य वाब्दशतान्ते वा मृत्युर्वै प्राणिनां ध्रुवः ॥३८॥

*mṛtyur janmavatāṁ vīra*
*dehena saha jāyate*
*adya vābda-śatānte vā*
*mṛtyur vai prāṇināṁ dhruvaḥ*

*mṛtyuḥ*—death; *janma-vatām*—of the living entities who have taken birth; *vīra*—O great hero; *dehena saha*—along with the body; *jāyate*—is born (one who has taken birth is sure to die); *adya*—today; *vā*—

either; *abda-śata*—of hundreds of years; *ante*—at the end; *vā*—or; *mṛtyuḥ*—death; *vai*—indeed; *prāṇinām*—for every living entity; *dhruvaḥ*—is assured.

## TRANSLATION

**O great hero, one who takes birth is sure to die, for death is born with the body. One may die today or after hundreds of years, but death is sure for every living entity.**

## PURPORT

Vasudeva wanted to impress upon Kaṁsa that although Kaṁsa feared dying and therefore wanted to kill even a woman, he could not avoid death. Death is sure. Why then should Kaṁsa do something that would be detrimental to his reputation and that of his family? As confirmed in *Bhagavad-gītā* (2.27):

*jātasya hi dhruvo mṛtyur*
*dhruvaṁ janma mṛtasya ca*
*tasmād aparihārye 'rthe*
*na tvaṁ śocitum arhasi*

"For one who has taken his birth, death is certain; and for one who is dead, birth is certain. Therefore, in the unavoidable discharge of your duty, you should not lament." One should not fear death. Rather, one should prepare oneself for the next birth. One should utilize one's time in this human form to end the process of birth and death. It is not that to save oneself from death one should entangle oneself in sinful activities. This is not good.

## TEXT 39

देहे पञ्चत्वमापन्ने देही कर्मानुगोऽवशः ।
देहान्तरमनुप्राप्य प्राक्तनं त्यजते वपुः ॥३९॥

*dehe pañcatvam āpanne*
*dehī karmānugo 'vaśaḥ*

*dehāntaram anuprāpya*
*prāktanaṁ tyajate vapuḥ*

*dehe*—when the body; *pañcatvam āpanne*—turns into five elements; *dehī*—the proprietor of the body, the living being; *karma-anugaḥ*—following the reactions of his own fruitive activities; *avaśaḥ*—spontaneously, automatically; *deha-antaram*—another body (made of material elements); *anuprāpya*—receiving as a result; *prāktanam*—the former; *tyajate*—gives up; *vapuḥ*—body.

## TRANSLATION

**When the present body turns to dust and is again reduced to five elements—earth, water, fire, air and ether—the proprietor of the body, the living being, automatically receives another body of material elements according to his fruitive activities. When the next body is obtained, he gives up the present body.**

## PURPORT

This is confirmed in *Bhagavad-gītā*, which presents the beginning of spiritual understanding.

*dehino 'smin yathā dehe*
*kaumāraṁ yauvanaṁ jarā*
*tathā dehāntara-prāptir*
*dhīras tatra na muhyati*

"As the embodied soul continually passes, in this body, from boyhood to youth to old age, the soul similarly passes into another body at death. The self-realized soul is not bewildered by such a change." (Bg. 2.13) A person or an animal is not the material body; rather, the material body is the covering of the living being. *Bhagavad-gītā* compares the body to a dress and elaborately explains how one changes dresses one after another. The same Vedic knowledge is confirmed here. The living being, the soul, is constantly changing bodies one after another. Even in the present life, the body changes from childhood to boyhood, from boyhood to youth, and from youth to old age; similarly, when the body is too old to continue, the living being gives up this body and, by the laws of nature, automatically gets another body according to his fruitive activities, desires and ambitions. The laws of nature control this sequence, and therefore as long as the living entity is under the control of the external, material energy, the process of bodily change takes place automatically, according to one's fruitive activities. Vasudeva therefore wanted to impress upon Kaṁsa that if he committed this sinful act of killing a woman, in his next life he would certainly get a material body still more conditioned to the sufferings of material existence. Thus Vasudeva advised Kaṁsa not to commit sinful activities.

One who commits sinful activities because of ignorance, *tamo-guṇa*, obtains a lower body. *Kāraṇaṁ guṇa-sango 'sya sad-asad-yoni-janmasu* (Bg. 13.22). There are hundreds and thousands of different species of life. Why are there higher and lower bodies? One receives these bodies according to the contaminations of material nature. If in this life one is contaminated by the mode of ignorance and sinful activities (*duṣkṛtī*), in the next life, by the laws of nature, one will certainly get a body full of suffering. The laws of nature are not subservient to the whimsical desires of the conditioned soul. Our endeavor, therefore, should be to associate always with *sattva-guṇa* and not indulge in *rajo-guṇa* or *tamo-guṇa* (*rajas-tamo-bhāvāḥ*). Lusty desires and greed keep the living entity perpetually in ignorance and prevent him from being elevated to the platform of *sattva-guṇa* or *śuddha-sattva-guṇa*. One is advised to be situated in *śuddha-sattva-guṇa*, devotional service, for thus one is immune to the reactions of the three modes of material nature.

## TEXT 40

**व्रजंस्तिष्ठन् पदैकेन यथैवैकेन गच्छति ।**
**यथा तृणजलौकैवं देही कर्मगतिं गतः ॥४०॥**

*vrajaṁs tiṣṭhan padaikena*
*yathaivaikena gacchati*
*yathā tṛṇa-jalaukaivaṁ*
*dehī karma-gatiṁ gataḥ*

*vrajan*—a person, while traveling on the road; *tiṣṭhan*—while standing; *padā ekena*—on one foot; *yathā*—as; *eva*—indeed; *ekena*—by another foot; *gacchati*—goes; *yathā*—as; *tṛṇa-jalaukā*—a worm on a vegetable; *evam*—in this way; *dehī*—the living entity; *karma-gatim*—the reactions of fruitive activities; *gataḥ*—undergoes.

## TRANSLATION

**Just as a person traveling on the road rests one foot on the ground and then lifts the other, or as a worm on a vegetable transfers itself to one leaf and then gives up the previous one, the conditioned soul takes shelter of another body and then gives up the one he had before.**

## PURPORT

This is the process of the soul's transmigration from one body to another. At the time of death, according to his mental condition, the living being is carried by the subtle body, consisting of mind, intelligence and ego, to another gross body. When higher authorities have decided what kind of gross body the living entity will have, he is forced to enter such a body, and thus he automatically gives up his previous body. Dull-minded persons who do not have the intelligence to understand this process of transmigration take for granted that when the gross body is finished, one's life is finished forever. Such persons have no brains with which to understand the process of transmigration. At the present moment there is great opposition to the Hare Kṛṣṇa movement, which is being called a "brainwashing" movement. But actually the so-called scientists, philosophers and other leaders in the Western countries have no brains at all. The Hare Kṛṣṇa movement is trying to elevate such foolish persons by enlightening their intelligence so that they will take advantage of the human body. Unfortunately, because of gross ignorance, they regard the Hare Kṛṣṇa movement as a brainwashing movement. They do not know that without God consciousness one is forced to continue transmigrating from one body to another. Because of their devilish brains, they will next be forced to accept an abominable life and practically never be able to liberate themselves from the conditional life of material existence. How this transmigration of the soul takes place is very clearly explained in this verse.

## TEXT 41

स्वप्ने यथा पश्यति देहमीदृशं
मनोरथेनाभिनिविष्टचेतनः ।
दृष्टश्रुताभ्यां मनसानुचिन्तयन्
प्रपद्यते तत् किमपि ह्यपस्मृतिः ॥४१॥

*svapne yathā paśyati deham īdṛśaṁ*
*manorathenābhiniviṣṭa-cetanaḥ*
*dṛṣṭa-śrutābhyāṁ manasānucintayan*
*prapadyate tat kim api hy apasmṛtiḥ*

*svapne*—in a dream; *yathā*—as; *paśyati*—one sees; *deham*—the kind of body; *īdṛśam*—similarly; *manorathena*—by mental speculation; *abhiniviṣṭa*—is fully absorbed; *cetanaḥ*—he whose consciousness; *dṛṣṭa*—by whatever has been experienced by seeing with the eyes; *śrutābhyām*—and by hearing a description of something else; *manasā*—by the mind; *anucintayan*—thinking, feeling and willing; *prapadyate*—surrenders; *tat*—to that situation; *kim api*—what to speak of; *hi*—indeed; *apasmṛtiḥ*—experiencing forgetfulness of the present body.

## TRANSLATION

**Having experienced a situation by seeing or hearing about it, one contemplates and speculates about that situation, and thus one surrenders to it, not considering his present body. Similarly, by mental adjustments one dreams at night of living under different circumstances, in different bodies, and forgets his actual position. Under this same process, one gives up his present body and accepts another [tathā dehāntara-prāptiḥ].**

## PURPORT

Transmigration of the soul is very clearly explained in this verse. One sometimes forgets his present body and thinks of his childhood body, a body of the past, and of how one was playing, jumping, talking and so on. When the material body is no long workable, it becomes dust: "For dust thou art, and unto dust shalt thou return." But when the body again mixes with the five material elements—earth, water, fire, air and ether—the mind continues to work. The mind is the subtle substance in which the body is created, as we actually experience in our dreams and also when we are awake in contemplation. One must understand that the process of mental speculation develops a new type of body that does not actually exist. If one can understand the nature of the mind (*manorathena*) and its thinking, feeling and willing, one can very easily understand how from the mind different types of bodies develop.

The Kṛṣṇa consciousness movement, therefore, offers a process of transcendental activities wherein the mind is fully absorbed in affairs pertaining to Kṛṣṇa. The presence of the soul is perceived by consciousness, and one must purify his consciousness from material to spiritual, or, in other words, to Kṛṣṇa consciousness. That which is spiritual is eternal, and that which is material is temporary. Without Kṛṣṇa consciousness, one's consciousness is always absorbed in temporary things. For everyone, therefore, Kṛṣṇa recommends in *Bhagavad-gītā* (9.34), *man-manā bhava mad-bhakto mad-yājī māṁ namaskuru.* One should always be absorbed in thought of Kṛṣṇa, one should become His devotee, one should always engage in His service and worship Him as the supreme great, and one should always offer Him obeisances. In the material world one is always a servant of a greater person, and in the spiritual world our constitutional position is to serve the Supreme, the greatest, *paraṁ brahma.* This is the instruction of Śrī Caitanya Mahāprabhu. *Jīvera 'svarūpa' haya—kṛṣṇera 'nitya-dāsa'* (Cc. *Madhya* 20.108).

To act in Kṛṣṇa consciousness is the perfection of life and the highest perfection of *yoga.* As Lord Kṛṣṇa says in *Bhagavad-gītā* (6.47):

*yoginām api sarveṣāṁ*
*mad-gatenāntarātmanā*
*śraddhāvān bhajate yo māṁ*
*sa me yuktatamo mataḥ*

"Of all *yogīs,* he who always abides in Me with great faith, worshiping Me in transcendental loving service, is most intimately united with Me in *yoga* and is the highest of all."

The condition of the mind, which flickers between *saṅkalpa* and *vikalpa*, accepting something and rejecting it, is very important in transferring the soul to another material body at the time of death.

*yaṁ yaṁ vāpi smaran bhāvaṁ*
*tyajaty ante kalevaram*
*taṁ tam evaiti kaunteya*
*sadā tad-bhāva-bhāvitaḥ*

"Whatever state of being one remembers when he quits his body, that state he will attain without fail." (Bg. 8.6) Therefore one must train the mind in the system of *bhakti-yoga*, as did Mahārāja Ambarīṣa, who kept himself always in Kṛṣṇa consciousness. *Sa vai manaḥ kṛṣṇa-padāravindayoḥ.* One must fix the mind at the lotus feet of Kṛṣṇa twenty-four hours a day. If the mind is fixed upon Kṛṣṇa's lotus feet, the activities of the other senses will be engaged in Kṛṣṇa's service. *Hṛṣīkeṇa hṛṣīkeśa-sevanaṁ bhaktir ucyate:* to serve Hṛṣīkeśa, the master of the senses, with purified senses is called *bhakti.* Those who constantly engage in devotional service are situated in a transcendental state, above the material modes of nature. As Kṛṣṇa says in *Bhagavad-gītā* (14.26):

*māṁ ca yo 'vyabhicāreṇa*
*bhakti-yogena sevate*
*sa guṇān samatītyaitān*
*brahma-bhūyāya kalpate*

"One who engages in full devotional service, who does not fall down in any circumstance, at once transcends the modes of material nature and thus comes to the level of Brahman." One must learn the secret of success from the Vedic literatures, especially when the cream of Vedic knowledge is presented by *Bhagavad-gītā* as it is.

Because the mind is ultimately controlled by the Supreme Personality of Godhead, Kṛṣṇa, the word *apasmṛtiḥ* is significant. Forgetfulness of one's own identity is called *apasmṛtiḥ.* This *apasmṛtiḥ* can be controlled by the Supreme Lord, for the Lord says, *mattaḥ smṛtir jñānam apohanaṁ ca:* "From Me come remembrance, knowledge and forgetfulness." Instead of allowing one to forget one's real position, Kṛṣṇa can revive one's original identity at the time of one's death, even though the mind may be flickering. Although the mind may work imperfectly at the time of death, Kṛṣṇa gives a devotee shelter at His lotus feet. Therefore when a devotee gives up his body, the mind does not take him to another material body (*tyaktvā dehaṁ punar janma naiti mām eti*); rather, Kṛṣṇa takes the devotee to that place where He is engaged in His pastimes (*mām eti*), as we have already discussed in previous verses. One's consciousness, therefore, must always be absorbed in Kṛṣṇa, and then one's life will be successful. Otherwise the mind will carry the soul to another material body. The soul will be placed in the semen of a father and discharged into the womb of a mother. The semen and ovum create a particular type of body according to the form of the father and mother, and when the body is mature, the soul emerges in that body and begins a new life. This is the process of transmigration of the soul from one body to another (*tathā dehāntara-prāptiḥ*). Unfortunately, those who are less intelligent think that when the body disappears, everything is finished. The entire world is being misled by such fools and rascals. But as stated in *Bhagavad-gītā* (2.20), *na hanyate hanyamāne śarīre*. The soul does not die when the body is destroyed. Rather, the soul takes on another body.

## TEXT 42

यतो यतो धावति दैवचोदितं
मनो विकारात्मकमाप पञ्चसु ।
गुणेषु मायारचितेषु देह्यसौ
प्रपद्यमानः सह तेन जायते ॥४२॥

*yato yato dhāvati daiva-coditaṁ*
*mano vikārātmakam āpa pañcasu*
*guṇeṣu māyā-raciteṣu dehy asau*
*prapadyamānaḥ saha tena jāyate*

*yataḥ yataḥ*—from one place to another or from one position to another; *dhāvati*—speculates; *daiva-coditam*—impelled by accident or deliberation; *manaḥ*—the mind; *vikāra-ātmakam*—changing from one type of thinking, feeling and willing to another; *āpa*—at the end, he obtains (a mentality); *pañcasu*—at the time of death (when the material body turns totally into matter); *guṇeṣu*—(the mind, not being liberated, becomes attached) to the material qualities; *māyā-raciteṣu*—where the material energy creates a similar body; *dehī*—the spirit soul who accepts such a body; *asau*—he; *prapadyamānaḥ*—being surrendered (to such a condition); *saha*—with; *tena*—a similar body; *jāyate*—takes birth.

## TRANSLATION

**At the time of death, according to the thinking, feeling and willing of the mind, which is involved in fruitive activities, one receives a particular body. In other words, the body develops according to the activities of the mind. Changes of body are due to the flickering of the mind, for otherwise the soul could remain in its original, spiritual body.**

## PURPORT

One can very easily understand that the mind is constantly flickering, changing in the quality of its thinking, feeling and willing. This is explained by Arjuna in *Bhagavad-gītā* (6.34):

*cañcalaṁ hi manaḥ kṛṣṇa*
*pramāthi balavad dṛḍham*
*tasyāhaṁ nigrahaṁ manye*
*vāyor iva suduṣkaram*

The mind is *cañcala*, flickering, and it changes very strongly. Therefore Arjuna admitted that controlling the mind is not at all possible; this would be as difficult as controlling the wind. For example, if one were in a boat moving according to the wind on a river or the sea, and the wind were uncontrollable, the tilting boat would be very much disturbed and extremely difficult to control. It might even capsize. Therefore, in the *bhava-samudra*, the ocean of mental speculation and transmigration to different types of bodies, one must first control the mind.

By regulative practice one can control the mind, and this is the purpose of the *yoga* system (*abhyāsa-yoga-yuktena*). But there is a chance of failure with the *yoga* system, especially in this age of Kali, because the *yoga* system uses artificial means. If the mind is engaged in *bhakti-yoga*, however, by the grace of Kṛṣṇa one can very easily control it. Therefore Śrī Caitanya Mahāprabhu has recommended, *harer nāma harer nāma harer nāmaiva kevalam.* One should chant the holy name of the Lord constantly, for the holy name of the Lord is nondifferent from Hari, the Supreme Person.

By chanting the Hare Kṛṣṇa *mantra* constantly, one can fix the mind on the lotus feet of Kṛṣṇa (*sa vai manaḥ kṛṣṇa-padāravindayoḥ*) and in this way achieve the perfection of *yoga.* Otherwise, the flickering mind will hover on the platform of mental speculation for sense enjoyment, and one will have to transmigrate from one type of body to another because the mind is trained only in relation to the material elements, or, in other words, to sense gratification, which is false. *Māyā-sukhāya bharam udvahato vimūḍhān* (*Bhāg.* 7.9.43). Rascals (*vimūḍhān*), being controlled by mental speculation, make huge arrangements by which to enjoy life temporarily, but they must give up the body at the time of death, when everything is taken away by Kṛṣṇa's external energy (*mṛtyuḥ sarva-haraś cāham*). At that time, whatever one has created in this life is lost, and one must automatically accept a new body by the force of material nature. In this life one may have constructed a very tall skyscraper, but in the next life, because of one's mentality, one may have to accept a body like that of a cat, a dog, a tree or perhaps a demigod. Thus the body is offered by the laws of material nature. *Kāraṇaṁ guṇa-saṅgo 'sya sad-asad-yoni-janmasu* (Bg. 13.22). The spirit soul takes birth in higher and lower species of life only because of his association with the three qualities of material nature.

*ūrdhvaṁ gacchanti sattva-sthā*
*madhye tiṣṭhanti rājasāḥ*
*jaghanya-guṇa-vṛtti-sthā*
*adho gacchanti tāmasāḥ*

"Those situated in the mode of goodness gradually go upward to the higher planets; those in the mode of passion live on the earthly planets; and those in the mode of ignorance go down to the hellish worlds." (Bg. 14.18)

In conclusion, the Kṛṣṇa consciousness movement offers the topmost welfare activity for human society. The saner section of human society must therefore take this movement very seriously for the benefit of all humanity. To save oneself from the repetition of birth and death, one must purify his consciousness. *Sarvopādhi-vinirmuktaṁ tat-paratvena nirmalam.* One must be freed from all designations—"I am American," "I am Indian," "I am this," "I am that"—and come to the platform of understanding that Kṛṣṇa is the original master and we are His eternal servants. When the senses are purified and engaged in Kṛṣṇa's service, one achieves the highest perfection. *Hṛṣīkeṇa hṛṣīkeśa-sevanaṁ bhaktir ucyate.* The Kṛṣṇa consciousness movement is a movement of *bhakti-yoga. Vairāgya-vidyā-nija-bhakti-yoga.* By following the principles of this movement, one becomes disassociated from material mental concoctions and is established on the original platform of the eternal relationship between the living entity and the Supreme Personality of Godhead as servant and master. This, in summary, is the purpose of the Kṛṣṇa consciousness movement.

## TEXT 43

ज्योतिर्यथैवोदकपार्थिवेष्वदः
समीरवेगानुगतं विभाव्यते ।
एवं स्वमायारचितेष्वसौ पुमान्
गुणेषु रागानुगतो विमुह्यति ॥४३॥

*jyotir yathaivodaka-pārthiveṣv adaḥ*
*samīra-vegānugataṁ vibhāvyate*
*evaṁ sva-māyā-raciteṣv asau pumān*
*guṇeṣu rāgānugato vimuhyati*

*jyotiḥ*—the luminaries in the sky, such as the sun, the moon and the stars; *yathā*—as; *eva*—indeed; *udaka*—in water; *pārthiveṣu*—or in other liquids, like oil; *adaḥ*—directly; *samīra-vega-anugatam*—being forced by the movements of the wind; *vibhāvyate*—appear in different shapes; *evam*—in this way; *sva-māyā-raciteṣu*—in the situation created by one's mental concoctions; *asau*—the living entity; *pumān*—person; *guṇeṣu*—in the material world, manifested by the modes of nature; *rāga-anugataḥ*—according to his attachment; *vimuhyati*—becomes bewildered by identification.

## TRANSLATION

**When the luminaries in the sky, such as the moon, the sun and the stars, are reflected in liquids like oil or water, they appear to be of different shapes—sometimes round, sometimes long, and so on—because of the movements of the wind. Similarly, when the living entity, the soul, is absorbed in materialistic thoughts, he accepts various manifestations as his own identity because of ignorance. In other words, one is bewildered by mental concoctions because of agitation from the material modes of nature.**

## PURPORT

This verse gives a very good example by which to understand the different positions of the eternal spiritual soul in the material world and how the soul takes on different bodies (*dehāntara-prāptiḥ*). The moon is stationary and is one, but when it is reflected in water or oil, it appears to take different shapes because of the movements of the wind. Similarly, the soul is the eternal servant of Kṛṣṇa, the Supreme Personality of Godhead, but when put into the material modes of nature, it takes different bodies, sometimes as a demigod, sometimes a man, a dog, a tree and so on. By the influence of *māyā*, the illusory potency of the Supreme Personality of Godhead, the living entity thinks that he is this person, that person, American, Indian, cat, dog, tree or whatever. This is called *māyā*. When one is freed from this bewilderment and understands that the soul does not belong to any shape of this material world, one is situated on the spiritual platform (*brahma-bhūta*).

This realization is sometimes explained as *nirākāra*, or formlessness. This formlessness, however, does not mean that the soul has no form. The soul has form, but the external, agitating form he has acquired because of material contamination is false. Similarly, God is also described as *nirākāra*, which means that God has no material form but is *sac-cid-ānanda-vigraha*. The living entity is part and parcel of the supreme *sac-cid-ānanda-vigraha*, but his material forms are temporary, or illusory. Both the living entity and the Supreme Lord have original, spiritual forms (*sac-cid-ānanda-vigraha*), but the Lord, the Supreme, does not change His form. The Lord appears as He is, whereas the living entity appears because material nature forces him to accept different forms.

When the living entity receives these different forms, he identifies with them, and not with his original, spiritual form. As soon as the living entity returns to his original, spiritual form and understanding, he immediately surrenders to the supreme form, the Personality of Godhead. This is explained in *Bhagavad-gītā* (7.19). *Bahūnāṁ janmanām ante jñānavān māṁ prapadyate.* When the living entity, after many, many births in different forms, returns to his original form of Kṛṣṇa consciousness, he immediately surrenders unto the lotus feet of the supreme form, Kṛṣṇa. This is liberation. As the Lord says in *Bhagavad-gītā* (18.54):

*brahma-bhūtaḥ prasannātmā*
*na śocati na kāṅkṣati*
*samaḥ sarveṣu bhūteṣu*
*mad-bhaktiṁ labhate parām*

"One who is thus transcendentally situated at once realizes the Supreme Brahman and becomes fully joyful. He never laments nor desires to have anything; he is equally disposed to every living entity. In that state he attains pure devotional service unto Me." Surrender unto the supreme form is the result of *bhakti.* This *bhakti,* or understanding of one's own position, is the complete liberation. As long as one is under an impersonal understanding of the Absolute Truth, he is not in pure knowledge, but must still struggle for pure knowledge. *Kleśo 'dhikataras teṣām avyaktāsakta-cetasām* (Bg. 12.5). Although one may be spiritually advanced, if one is attached to the impersonal feature of the Absolute Truth one must still work very hard, as indicated by the words *kleśo 'dhikataraḥ,* which mean "greater suffering." A devotee, however, easily attains his original position as a spiritual form and understands the Supreme Personality of Godhead in His original form.

Kṛṣṇa Himself explains the forms of the living entities in the Second Chapter of *Bhagavad-gītā,* where He clearly says to Arjuna that He, Arjuna and all other living entities, who were previously in their original forms, are separate individual identities. They were individuals in the past, they are now situated in individuality, and in the future they will all continue to maintain their individual forms. The only difference is that the conditioned living entity appears in various material forms, whereas Kṛṣṇa appears in His original, spiritual form. Unfortunately, those who are not advanced in spiritual knowledge think that Kṛṣṇa is like one of them and that His form is like their material forms. *Avajānanti māṁ mūḍhā mānuṣīṁ tanum āśritam* (Bg. 9.11). Kṛṣṇa is never puffed up by material knowledge and is therefore called *acyuta*, whereas the living entities fall down and are agitated by material nature. This is the difference between the Supreme Lord and the living entities.

In this connection it is to be noted that Vasudeva, who was situated in a transcendental position, advised Kaṁsa not to commit further sinful activities. Kaṁsa, a representative of the demons, was always ready to kill Kṛṣṇa, or God, whereas Vasudeva represents a transcendentally situated person to whom Kṛṣṇa is born (Vāsudeva is the son of Vasudeva). Vasudeva wanted his brother-in-law Kaṁsa to refrain from the sinful act of killing his sister, since the result of being agitated by material nature would be that Kaṁsa would have to accept a body in which to suffer again and again. Elsewhere in *Śrīmad-Bhāgavatam* (5.5.4), Ṛṣabhadeva also says:

*na sādhu manye yata ātmano 'yam*
*asann api kleśada āsa dehaḥ*

As long as the living entity is entangled in the fruitive activities of so-called happiness and distress, he will receive a particular type of body in which to endure the three kinds of suffering due to material nature (*tri-tāpa-yantraṇā*). An intelligent person, therefore, must free himself from the influence of the three modes of material nature and revive his original, spiritual body by engaging in the service of the Supreme Person, Kṛṣṇa. As long as one is materially attached, one must accept the process of birth, death, old age and disease. One is therefore advised that an intelligent person, instead of being entangled in so-called good and bad fruitive activities, should engage his life in advancing in Kṛṣṇa consciousness so that instead of accepting another material body (*tyaktvā dehaṁ punar janma naiti*), he will return home, back to Godhead.

## TEXT 44

तस्मान्न कस्यचिद् द्रोहमाचरेत् स तथाविधः ।
आत्मनः क्षेममन्विच्छन् द्रोग्धुर्वै परतो भयम् ॥४४॥

*tasmān na kasyacid droham*
*ācaret sa tathā-vidhaḥ*
*ātmanaḥ kṣemam anvicchan*
*drogdhur vai parato bhayam*

*tasmāt*—therefore; *na*—not; *kasyacit*—of anyone; *droham*—envy; *ācaret*—one should act; *saḥ*—a person (Kaṁsa); *tathā-vidhaḥ*—who has been advised in such a way (by Vasudeva); *ātmanaḥ*—his own; *kṣemam*—welfare; *anvicchan*—if he desires; *drogdhuḥ*—of one who is envious of others; *vai*—indeed; *parataḥ*—from others; *bhayam*—there is a cause of fear.

## TRANSLATION

**Therefore, since envious, impious activities cause a body in which one suffers in the next life, why should one act impiously? Considering one's welfare, one should not envy anyone, for an envious person must always fear harm from his enemies, either in this life or in the next.**

## PURPORT

Instead of being inimical toward other living entities, one should act piously by engaging in the service of the Supreme Lord, thus avoiding a fearful situation both in this life and in the next. In this regard, the following moral instruction by the great politician Cāṇakya Paṇḍita is very meaningful:

*tyaja durjana-saṁsargaṁ*
*bhaja sādhu-samāgamam*
*kuru puṇyam aho rātraṁ*
*smara nityam anityatām*

One should give up the company of devils, demons and nondevotees and should always associate with devotees and saintly persons. One should always act piously, thinking that this life is temporary, and not be attached to temporary happiness and distress. The Kṛṣṇa consciousness movement is teaching all of human society this principle of becoming Kṛṣṇa conscious and thus solving the problems of life forever (*tyaktvā dehaṁ punar janma naiti mām eti so 'rjuna*).

## TEXT 45

एषा तवानुजा बाला कृपणा पुत्रिकोपमा ।
हन्तुं नार्हसि कल्याणीमिमां त्वं दीनवत्सलः ॥४५॥

*eṣā tavānujā bālā*
*kṛpaṇā putrikopamā*
*hantuṁ nārhasi kalyāṇīm*
*imāṁ tvaṁ dīna-vatsalaḥ*

*eṣā*—this; *tava*—your; *anujā*—younger sister; *bālā*—innocent woman; *kṛpaṇā*—completely dependent on you; *putrikā-upamā*—exactly like your own daughter; *hantum*—to kill her; *na*—not; *arhasi*—you deserve; *kalyāṇīm*—who is under your affection; *imām*—her; *tvam*—you; *dīna-vatsalaḥ*—very compassionate to the poor and innocent.

## TRANSLATION

**As your younger sister, this poor girl Devakī is like your own daughter and deserves to be affectionately maintained. You are merciful, and therefore you should not kill her. Indeed, she deserves your affection.**

## TEXT 46

श्रीशुक उवाच
एवं स सामभिर्भेदैर्बोध्यमानोऽपि दारुणः ।
न न्यवर्तत कौरव्य पुरुषादाननुव्रतः ॥४६॥

*śrī-śuka uvāca*
*evaṁ sa sāmabhir bhedair*
*bodhyamāno 'pi dāruṇaḥ*
*na nyavartata kauravya*
*puruṣādān anuvrataḥ*

*śrī-śukaḥ uvāca*—Śrī Śukadeva Gosvāmī said; *evam*—in this way; *saḥ*—he (Kaṁsa); *sāmabhiḥ*—by attempts to pacify him (Kaṁsa); *bhedaiḥ*—by moral instructions that one should not be cruel to anyone else; *bodhyamānaḥ api*—even being pacified; *dāruṇaḥ*—he who was the most fiercely cruel; *na nyavartata*—could not be stopped (from the grievous act); *kauravya*—O Mahārāja Parīkṣit; *puruṣa-adān*—the Rākṣasas, man-eaters; *anuvrataḥ*—following in their footsteps.

## TRANSLATION

**Śukadeva Gosvāmī continued: O best of the Kuru dynasty, Kaṁsa was fiercely cruel and was actually a follower of the Rākṣasas. Therefore he could be neither pacified nor terrified by the good instructions given by Vasudeva. He did not care about the results of sinful activities, either in this life or in the next.**

## TEXT 47

निर्बन्धं तस्य तं ज्ञात्वा विचिन्त्यानकदुन्दुभिः ।
प्राप्तं कालं प्रतिव्योढुमिदं तत्रान्वपद्यत ॥४७॥

*nirbandhaṁ tasya taṁ jñātvā*
*vicintyānakadundubhiḥ*
*prāptaṁ kālaṁ prativyoḍhum*
*idaṁ tatrānvapadyata*

*nirbandham*—determination to do something; *tasya*—of him (Kaṁsa); *tam*—that (determination); *jñātvā*—understanding; *vicintya*—thinking deeply; *ānakadundubhiḥ*—Vasudeva; *prāptam*—had arrived; *kālam*—imminent danger of death; *prativyoḍhum*—to stop him from such activities; *idam*—this; *tatra*—thereupon; *anvapadyata*—thought of other ways.

## TRANSLATION

**When Vasudeva saw that Kaṁsa was determined to kill his sister Devakī, he thought to himself very deeply. Considering the imminent danger of death, he thought of another plan to stop Kaṁsa.**

## PURPORT

Although Vasudeva saw the imminent danger that his wife Devakī would be killed, he was convinced of his welfare because at his birth the demigods had played drums and kettledrums. He therefore attempted another way to save Devakī.

## TEXT 48

मृत्युर्बुद्धिमतापोह्यो यावद्बुद्धिबलोदयम् ।
यद्यसौ न निवर्तेत नापराधोऽस्ति देहिनः ॥४८॥

*mṛtyur buddhimatāpohyo*
*yāvad buddhi-balodayam*
*yady asau na nivarteta*
*nāparādho 'sti dehinaḥ*

*mṛtyuḥ*—death; *buddhi-matā*—by an intelligent person; *apohyaḥ*—should be avoided; *yāvat*—as long as; *buddhi-bala-udayam*—intelligence and bodily strength are present; *yadi*—if; *asau*—that (death); *na nivarteta*—cannot be checked; *na*—not; *aparādhaḥ*—offense; *asti*—there is; *dehinaḥ*—of the person in danger of death.

## TRANSLATION

**As long as he has intelligence and bodily strength, an intelligent person must try to avoid death. This is the duty of every embodied person. But if death cannot be avoided in spite of one's endeavors, a person facing death commits no offense.**

## PURPORT

It is natural for a person facing untimely death to try his best to save himself. This is one's duty. Although death is sure, everyone should try to avoid it and not meet death without opposition because every living soul is by nature eternal. Because death is a punishment imposed in the condemned life of material existence, the Vedic culture is based on avoiding death (*tyaktvā dehaṁ punar janma naiti*). Everyone should try to avoid death and rebirth by cultivating spiritual life and should not submit to death without struggling to survive. One who is not trying to stop death is not an intelligent human being. Because Devakī was face to face with imminent death, it was Vasudeva's duty to save her, as he was trying his best to do. He therefore considered another way to approach Kaṁsa so that Devakī would be saved.

## TEXTS 49–50

प्रदाय मृत्यवे पुत्रान् मोचये कृपणामिमाम् ।
सुता मे यदि जायेरन् मृत्युर्वा न म्रियेत चेत ॥४९॥
विपर्ययो वा किं न स्याद् गतिर्धातुर्दुरत्यया ।
उपस्थितो निवर्तेत निवृत्तः पुनरापतेत ॥५०॥

*pradāya mṛtyave putrān*
*mocaye kṛpaṇām imām*
*sutā me yadi jāyeran*
*mṛtyur vā na mriyeta cet*

*viparyayo vā kiṁ na syād*
*gatir dhātur duratyayā*
*upasthito nivarteta*
*nivṛttaḥ punar āpatet*

*pradāya*—promising to deliver; *mṛtyave*—unto Kaṁsa, who is death personified for Devakī; *putrān*—my sons; *mocaye*—I am releasing her from imminent danger; *kṛpaṇām*—innocent; *imām*—Devakī; *sutāḥ*—sons; *me*—my; *yadi*—whether; *jāyeran*—should take birth; *mṛtyuḥ*—Kaṁsa; *vā*—or; *na*—not; *mriyeta*—should die; *cet*—if; *viparyayaḥ*—just the opposite; *vā*—or; *kim*—whether; *na*—not; *syāt*—it may happen; *gatiḥ*—the movement; *dhātuḥ*—of providence; *duratyayā*—very difficult to understand; *upasthitaḥ*—that which is presently obtained; *nivarteta*—may stop; *nivṛttaḥ*—Devakī's death being stopped; *punaḥ āpatet*—in the future it may happen again (but what can I do).

## TRANSLATION

**Vasudeva considered: By delivering all my sons to Kaṁsa, who is death personified, I shall save the life of Devakī. Perhaps Kaṁsa will die before my sons take birth, or, since he is already destined**

**to die at the hands of my son, one of my sons may kill him. For the time being, let me promise to hand over my sons so that Kaṁsa will give up this immediate threat, and if in due course of time Kaṁsa dies, I shall have nothing to fear.**

## PURPORT

Vasudeva wanted to save the life of Devakī by promising to deliver his sons to Kaṁsa. "In the future," he thought, "Kaṁsa may die, or I may not beget any sons. Even if a son is born and I deliver him to Kaṁsa, Kaṁsa may die at his hands, for by providence anything could happen. It is very difficult to understand how things are managed by providence." Thus Vasudeva decided that he would promise to deliver his sons to the hands of Kaṁsa in order to save Devakī from the imminent danger of death.

## TEXT 51

अग्नेर्यथा दारुवियोगयोगयो-
रदृष्टतोऽन्यन्न निमित्तमस्ति ।
एवं हि जन्तोरपि दुर्विभाव्यः
शरीरसंयोगवियोगहेतुः ॥५१॥

*agner yathā dāru-viyoga-yogayor*
*adṛṣṭato 'nyan na nimittam asti*
*evaṁ hi jantor api durvibhāvyaḥ*
*śarīra-saṁyoga-viyoga-hetuḥ*

*agneḥ*—of a fire in the forest; *yathā*—as; *dāru*—of wood; *viyoga-yogayoḥ*—of both the escaping and the capturing; *adṛṣṭataḥ*—than unseen providence; *anyat*—some other reason or accident; *na*—not; *nimittam*—a cause; *asti*—there is; *evam*—in this way; *hi*—certainly; *jantoḥ*—of the living being; *api*—indeed; *durvibhāvyaḥ*—cannot be found out; *śarīra*—of the body; *saṁyoga*—of the accepting; *viyoga*—or of the giving up; *hetuḥ*—the cause.

## TRANSLATION

**When a fire, for some unseen reason, leaps over one piece of wood and sets fire to the next, the reason is destiny. Similarly,**

**when a living being accepts one kind of body and leaves aside another, there is no other reason than unseen destiny.**

## PURPORT

When there is a fire in a village, the fire sometimes jumps over one house and burns another. Similarly, when there is a forest fire, the fire sometimes jumps over one tree and catches another. Why this happens, no one can say. One may set forth some imaginary reason why the nearest tree or house did not catch fire whereas a tree or house in a distant place did, but actually the reason is destiny. This reason also applies to the transmigration of the soul, by which a prime minister in one life may become a dog in the next. The work of unseen destiny cannot be ascertained by practical experimental knowledge, and therefore one must be satisfied by reasoning that everything is done by supreme providence.

## TEXT 52

एवं विमृश्य तं पापं यावदात्मनिदर्शनम् ।
पूजयामास वै शौरिर्बहुमानपुरःसरम् ॥५२॥

*evaṁ vimṛśya taṁ pāpaṁ*
*yāvad-ātmani-darśanam*
*pūjayām āsa vai śaurir*
*bahu-māna-puraḥsaram*

*evam*—in this way; *vimṛśya*—after contemplating; *tam*—unto Kaṁsa; *pāpam*—the most sinful; *yāvat*—as far as possible; *ātmani-darśanam*—with all the intelligence possible within himself; *pūjayām āsa*—praised; *vai*—indeed; *śauriḥ*—Vasudeva; *bahu-māna*—offering all respect; *puraḥsaram*—before him.

## TRANSLATION

**After thus considering the matter as far as his knowledge would allow, Vasudeva submitted his proposal to the sinful Kaṁsa with great respect.**

## TEXT 53

प्रसन्नवदनाम्भोजो नृशंसं निरपत्रपम् ।
मनसा दूयमानेन विहसन्निदमब्रवीत् ॥५३॥

*prasanna-vadanāmbhojo*
*nṛśaṁsaṁ nirapatrapam*
*manasā dūyamānena*
*vihasann idam abravīt*

*prasanna-vadana-ambhojaḥ*—Vasudeva, who externally presented himself as if very happy; *nṛśaṁsam*—unto the most cruel; *nirapatrapam*—shameless Kaṁsa; *manasā*—with the mind; *dūyamānena*—which was full of anxiety and sorrow; *vihasan*—smiling externally; *idaṁ abravīt*—and spoke as follows.

## TRANSLATION

**Vasudeva's mind was full of anxiety because his wife was facing danger, but in order to please the cruel, shameless and sinful Kaṁsa, he externally smiled and spoke to him as follows.**

## PURPORT

Sometimes one must act duplicitously in a dangerous position, as Vasudeva did to save his wife. The material world is complicated, and to execute one's duties, one cannot avoid adopting such diplomacy. Vasudeva did everything possible to save his wife for the sake of begetting Kṛṣṇa. This indicates that one may act duplicitously for the purpose of saving Kṛṣṇa and His interests. According to the arrangement already foretold, Kṛṣṇa was to appear through Vasudeva and Devakī to kill Kaṁsa. Vasudeva, therefore, had to do everything to save the situation. Although all the events were prearranged by Kṛṣṇa, a devotee must try his best to serve the purpose of Kṛṣṇa. Kṛṣṇa Himself is all-powerful, but it is not that a devotee should therefore sit idly and leave everything to Him. This instruction is also found in *Bhagavad-gītā*. Although Kṛṣṇa was doing everything for Arjuna, Arjuna never sat down idly as a nonviolent gentleman. Rather, he tried his best to fight the battle and be victorious.

## TEXT 54

श्रीवसुदेव उवाच
न ह्यस्यास्ते भयं सौम्य यद् वै साहाशरीरवाक् ।
पुत्रान् समर्पयिष्येऽस्या यतस्ते भयमुत्थितम् ॥५४॥

*śrī-vasudeva uvāca*
*na hy asyās te bhayaṁ saumya*
*yad vai sāhāśarīra-vāk*
*putrān samarpayiṣye 'syā*
*yatas te bhayam utthitam*

*śrī-vasudevaḥ uvāca*—Śrī Vasudeva said; *na*—not; *hi*—indeed; *asyāḥ*—from Devakī; *te*—of you; *bhayam*—fear; *saumya*—O most sober; *yat*—which; *vai*—indeed; *sā*—that omen; *āha*—dictated; *a-śarīra-vāk*—a vibration without a body; *putrān*—all my sons; *samar-payiṣye*—I shall deliver to you; *asyāḥ*—of her (Devakī); *yataḥ*—from whom; *te*—your; *bhayam*—fear; *utthitam*—has arisen.

## TRANSLATION

**Vasudeva said: O best of the sober, you have nothing to fear from your sister Devakī because of what you have heard from the unseen omen. The cause of death will be her sons. Therefore I promise that when she gives birth to the sons from whom your fear has arisen, I shall deliver them all unto your hands.**

## PURPORT

Kaṁsa feared Devakī's existence because after her eighth pregnancy she would give birth to a son who would kill him. Vasudeva, therefore, to assure his brother-in-law the utmost safety, promised to bring him all the sons. He would not wait for the eighth son, but from the very beginning would deliver to the hands of Kaṁsa all the sons to which Devakī would give birth. This was the most liberal proposition offered by Vasudeva to Kaṁsa.

## TEXT 55

श्रीशुक उवाच
स्वसुर्वधान्निववृते कंसस्तद्वाक्यसारवित् ।
वसुदेवोऽपि तं प्रीतः प्रशस्य प्राविशद् गृहम् ॥५५॥

*śrī-śuka uvāca*
*svasur vadhān nivavṛte*
*kaṁsas tad-vākya-sāra-vit*
*vasudevo 'pi taṁ prītaḥ*
*praśasya prāviśad gṛham*

*śrī-śukaḥ uvāca*—Śrī Śukadeva Gosvāmī said; *svasuḥ*—of his sister (Devakī); *vadhāt*—from the act of killing; *nivavṛte*—stopped for the time being; *kaṁsaḥ*—Kaṁsa; *tat-vākya*—the words of Vasudeva; *sāra-vit*—knowing to be perfectly correct; *vasudevaḥ*—Vasudeva; *api*—also; *tam*—to him (Kaṁsa); *prītaḥ*—being satisfied; *praśasya*—pacifying more; *prāviśat gṛham*—entered his own house.

### TRANSLATION

**Śrīla Śukadeva Gosvāmī continued: Kaṁsa agreed to the logical arguments of Vasudeva, and, having full faith in Vasudeva's words, he refrained from killing his sister. Vasudeva, being pleased with Kaṁsa, pacified him further and entered his own house.**

### PURPORT

Although Kaṁsa was a sinful demon, he believed that Vasudeva would never deviate from his word. The character of a pure devotee like Vasudeva is such that even so great a demon as Kaṁsa firmly believed in his words and was satisfied. *Yasyāsti bhaktir bhagavaty akiñcanā sarvair guṇais tatra samāsate surāḥ* (*Bhāg.* 5.18.12). All good attributes are present in a devotee, so much so that even Kaṁsa believed in Vasudeva's words without a doubt.

## TEXT 56

अथ काल उपावृत्ते देवकी सर्वदेवता ।
पुत्रान् प्रसुषुवे चाष्टौ कन्यां चैवानुवत्सरम् ॥५६॥

*atha kāla upāvṛtte*
*devakī sarva-devatā*
*putrān prasuṣuve cāṣṭau*
*kanyāṁ caivānuvatsaram*

*atha*—thereafter; *kāle*—in due course of time; *upāvṛtte*—when it was ripe; *devakī*—Devakī, the wife of Vasudeva, Kṛṣṇa's father; *sarva-devatā*—Devakī, to whom all the demigods and God Himself appeared; *putrān*—sons; *prasuṣuve*—gave birth to; *ca*—and; *aṣṭau*—eight; *kanyāṁ ca*—and one daughter named Subhadrā; *eva*—indeed; *anuvatsaram*—year after year.

## TRANSLATION

**Each year thereafter, in due course of time, Devakī, the mother of God and all the demigods, gave birth to a child. Thus she bore eight sons, one after another, and a daughter named Subhadrā.**

## PURPORT

The spiritual master is sometimes glorified as *sarva-devamayo guruḥ* (*Bhāg.* 11.7.27). By the grace of the *guru,* the spiritual master, one can understand the different kinds of *devas.* The word *deva* refers to God, the Supreme Personality of Godhead, who is the original source of all the demigods, who are also called *devas.* In *Bhagavad-gītā* (10.2) the Lord says, *aham ādir hi devānām:* "I am the source of all the *devas.*" The Supreme Lord, Viṣṇu, the Original Person, expands in different forms. *Tad aikṣata bahu syām* (*Chāndogya Upaniṣad* 6.2.3). He alone has expanded into many. *Advaitam acyutam anādim ananta-rūpam* (*Brahma-saṁhitā* 5.33). There are different grades of forms, known as *svāṁśa* and *vibhinnāṁśa.* The *svāṁśa* expansions, or *viṣṇu-tattva,* are the Supreme Personality of Godhead, whereas the *vibhinnāṁśa* are *jīva-tattva,* who are part and parcel of the Lord (*mamaivāṁśo jīva-loke jīva-bhūtaḥ sanātanaḥ*). If we accept Kṛṣṇa as the Supreme Personality of Godhead and worship Him, all the parts and expansions of the Lord are automatically worshiped. *Sarvārhaṇam acyutejyā* (*Bhāg.* 4.31.14). Kṛṣṇa is known as Acyuta (*senayor ubhayor madhye rathaṁ sthāpaya me 'cyuta*). By worshiping Acyuta, Kṛṣṇa, one automatically worships all the demigods. There is no need of separately worshiping either the *viṣṇu-tattva* or *jīva-tattva*. If one concentrates upon Kṛṣṇa, one worships everyone. Therefore, because mother Devakī gave birth to Kṛṣṇa, she is described here as *sarva-devatā*.

## TEXT 57

कीर्तिमन्तं प्रथमजं कंसायानकदुन्दुभिः ।
अर्पयामास कृच्छ्रेण सोऽनृतादतिविह्वलः ॥५७॥

*kīrtimantaṁ prathamajaṁ*
*kaṁsāyānakadundubhiḥ*
*arpayām āsa kṛcchreṇa*
*so 'nṛtād ativihvalaḥ*

*kīrtimantam*—by the name Kīrtimān; *prathama-jam*—the first-born baby; *kaṁsāya*—unto Kaṁsa; *ānakadundubhiḥ*—Vasudeva; *arpayām āsa*—delivered; *kṛcchreṇa*—with great pain; *saḥ*—he (Vasudeva); *anṛtāt*—from the breaking of the promise, or from fear of being a liar; *ati-vihvalaḥ*—was very much disturbed, being afraid.

## TRANSLATION

**Vasudeva was very much disturbed by fear of becoming a liar by breaking his promise. Thus with great pain he delivered his first-born son, named Kīrtimān, into the hands of Kaṁsa.**

## PURPORT

In the Vedic system, as soon as a child is born, especially a male child, the father calls for learned *brāhmaṇas*, and according to the description of the child's horoscope, the child is immediately given a name. This ceremony is called *nāma-karaṇa*. There are ten different *saṁskāras*, or reformatory methods, adopted in the system of *varṇāśrama-dharma*, and the name-giving ceremony is one of them. Although Vasudeva's first son was to be delivered into the hands of Kaṁsa, the *nāma-karaṇa* ceremony was performed, and thus the child was named Kīrtimān. Such names are given immediately after birth.

## TEXT 58

किं दुःसहं नु साधूनां विदुषां किमपेक्षितम् ।
किमकार्यं कदर्याणां दुस्त्यजं किं धृतात्मनाम् ॥५८॥

*kiṁ duḥsahaṁ nu sādhūnāṁ*
*viduṣāṁ kim apekṣitam*
*kim akāryaṁ kadaryāṇāṁ*
*dustyajaṁ kiṁ dhṛtātmanām*

*kim*—what is; *duḥsaham*—painful; *nu*—indeed; *sādhūnām*—for saintly persons; *viduṣām*—of learned persons; *kim apekṣitam*—what is dependence; *kim akāryam*—what is forbidden work; *kadaryāṇām*—of persons in the lowest grade; *dustyajam*—very difficult to give up; *kim*—what is; *dhṛta-ātmanām*—of persons who are self-realized.

## TRANSLATION

**What is painful for saintly persons who strictly adhere to the truth? How could there not be independence for pure devotees who know the Supreme Lord as the substance? What deeds are forbidden for persons of the lowest character? And what cannot be given up for the sake of Lord Kṛṣṇa by those who have fully surrendered at His lotus feet?**

## PURPORT

Since the eighth son of Devakī was to kill Kaṁsa, one might ask what the need was for Vasudeva to deliver the first-born child. The answer is that Vasudeva had promised Kaṁsa that he would deliver all the children born of Devakī. Kaṁsa, being an *asura*, did not believe that the eighth child would kill him; he took it for granted that he might be killed by any of the children of Devakī. Vasudeva, therefore, to save Devakī, promised to give Kaṁsa every child, whether male or female. From another point of view, Vasudeva and Devakī were very pleased when they understood that the Supreme Personality of Godhead, Kṛṣṇa, would come as their eighth son. Vasudeva, a pure devotee of the Lord, was eager to see Kṛṣṇa appear as his child from the eighth pregnancy of

Devakī. Therefore he wanted to deliver all the children quickly so that the eighth turn would come and Kṛṣṇa would appear. He begot one child every year sc that Kṛṣṇa's turn to appear would come as soon as possible.

## TEXT 59

दृष्ट्वा समत्वं तच्छौरेः सत्ये चैव व्यवस्थितिम् ।
कंसस्तुष्टमना राजन् प्रहसन्निदमब्रवीत् ॥५९॥

*dṛṣṭvā samatvaṁ tac chaureḥ*
*satye caiva vyavasthitim*
*kaṁsas tuṣṭa-manā rājan*
*prahasann idam abravīt*

*dṛṣṭvā*—by seeing; *samatvam*—being equipoised, undisturbed in distress or happiness; *tat*—that; *śaureḥ*—of Vasudeva; *satye*—in truthfulness; *ca*—indeed; *eva*—certainly; *vyavasthitim*—the firm situation; *kaṁsaḥ*—Kaṁsa; *tuṣṭa-manāḥ*—being very satisfied (with Vasudeva's behavior in delivering the first child to keep his promise); *rājan*—O Mahārāja Parīkṣit; *prahasan*—with a smiling face; *idam*—this; *abravīt*—said.

## TRANSLATION

**My dear King Parīkṣit, when Kaṁsa saw that Vasudeva, being situated in truthfulness, was completely equipoised in giving him the child, he was very happy. Therefore, with a smiling face, he spoke as follows.**

## PURPORT

The word *samatvam* is very significant in this verse. *Samatvam* refers to one who is always equipoised, unaffected by either happiness or distress. Vasudeva was so steadily equipoised that he did not seem in the least agitated when delivering his first-born child into the hands of Kaṁsa to be killed. In *Bhagavad-gītā* (2.56) it is said, *duḥkheṣv anudvigna-manāḥ sukheṣu vigata-spṛhaḥ*. In the material world, one should not be very eager to be happy, nor should one be very much disturbed by material distress. Lord Kṛṣṇa advised Arjuna:

*mātrā-sparśās tu kaunteya*
*śītoṣṇa-sukha-duḥkha-dāḥ*
*āgamāpāyino 'nityās*
*tāṁs titikṣasva bhārata*

"O son of Kuntī, the nonpermanent appearance of happiness and distress, and their disappearance in due course, are like the appearance and disappearance of winter and summer seasons. They arise from sense perception, O scion of Bharata, and one must learn to tolerate them without being disturbed." (Bg. 2.14) The self-realized soul is never disturbed by so-called distress or happiness, and this is especially true of an exalted devotee like Vasudeva, who showed this by his practical example. Vasudeva was not at all disturbed when delivering his first child to Kaṁsa to be killed.

## TEXT 60

प्रतियातु कुमारोऽयं न ह्यस्मादस्ति मे भयम् ।
अष्टमाद् युवयोर्गर्भान्मृत्युर्मे विहितः किल ॥६०॥

*pratiyātu kumāro 'yaṁ*
*na hy asmād asti me bhayam*
*aṣṭamād yuvayor garbhān*
*mṛtyur me vihitaḥ kila*

*pratiyātu*—my dear Vasudeva, take back your child and go home; *kumāraḥ*—newborn child; *ayam*—this; *na*—not; *hi*—indeed; *asmāt*—from him; *asti*—there is; *me*—my; *bhayam*—fear; *aṣṭamāt*—from the eighth; *yuvayoḥ*—of both you and your wife; *garbhāt*—from the pregnancy; *mṛtyuḥ*—death; *me*—my; *vihitaḥ*—has been ordained; *kila*—indeed.

## TRANSLATION

**O Vasudeva, you may take back your child and go home. I have no fear of your first child. It is the eighth child of you and Devakī I am concerned with because that is the child by whom I am destined to be killed.**

## TEXT 61

तथेति सुतमादाय ययावानकदुन्दुभिः ।
नाभ्यनन्दत तद्वाक्यमसतोऽविजितात्मनः ॥६१॥

*tatheti sutam ādāya*
*yayāv ānakadundubhiḥ*
*nābhyanandata tad-vākyam*
*asato 'vijitātmanaḥ*

*tathā*—very well; *iti*—thus; *sutam ādāya*—taking back his child; *yayau*—left that place; *ānakadundubhiḥ*—Vasudeva; *na abhyanandata*—did not very much value; *tat-vākyam*—the words (of Kaṁsa); *asataḥ*—who was without character; *avijita-ātmanaḥ*—and without self-control.

## TRANSLATION

**Vasudeva agreed and took his child back home, but because Kaṁsa had no character and no self-control, Vasudeva knew that he could not rely on Kaṁsa's word.**

## TEXTS 62–63

नन्दाद्या ये व्रजे गोपा याश्चामीषां च योषितः ।
वृष्णयो वसुदेवाद्या देवक्याद्या यदुस्त्रियः ॥६२॥
सर्वे वै देवताप्राया उभयोरपि भारत ।
ज्ञातयो बन्धुसुहृदो ये च कंसमनुव्रताः ॥६३॥

*nandādyā ye vraje gopā*
*yāś cāmīṣāṁ ca yoṣitaḥ*
*vṛṣṇayo vasudevādyā*
*devaky-ādyā yadu-striyaḥ*

*sarve vai devatā-prāyā*
*ubhayor api bhārata*
*jñātayo bandhu-suhṛdo*
*ye ca kaṁsam anuvratāḥ*

*nanda-ādyāḥ*—beginning from Nanda Mahārāja; *ye*—all of which persons; *vraje*—in Vṛndāvana; *gopāḥ*—the cowherd men; *yāḥ*—which; *ca*—and; *amīṣām*—of all those (inhabitants of Vṛndāvana); *ca*—as well as; *yoṣitaḥ*—the women; *vṛṣṇayaḥ*—members of the Vṛṣṇi family; *vasudeva-ādyāḥ*—headed by Vasudeva; *devakī-ādyāḥ*—headed by Devakī; *yadu-striyaḥ*—all the women of the Yadu dynasty; *sarve*—all of them; *vai*—indeed; *devatā-prāyāḥ*—were inhabitants of heaven; *ubhayoḥ*—of both Nanda Mahārāja and Vasudeva; *api*—indeed; *bhārata*—O Mahārāja Parīkṣit; *jñātayaḥ*—the relatives; *bandhu*—friends; *suhṛdaḥ*—well-wishers; *ye*—all of whom; *ca*—and; *kaṁsam anuvratāḥ*—even though apparently followers of Kaṁsa.

## TRANSLATION

**The inhabitants of Vṛndāvana, headed by Nanda Mahārāja and including his associate cowherd men and their wives, were none but denizens of the heavenly planets, O Mahārāja Parīkṣit, best of the descendants of Bharata, and so too were the descendants of the Vṛṣṇi dynasty, headed by Vasudeva, and Devakī and the other women of the dynasty of Yadu. The friends, relatives and well-wishers of both Nanda Mahārāja and Vasudeva and even those who externally appeared to be followers of Kaṁsa were all demigods.**

## PURPORT

As previously discussed, the Supreme Personality of Godhead, Viṣṇu, informed Lord Brahmā that Lord Kṛṣṇa would personally descend to mitigate the suffering on the earth. The Lord ordered all the denizens of the heavenly planets to take birth in different families of the Yadu and Vṛṣṇi dynasties and in Vṛndāvana. Now this verse informs us that all the family and friends of the Yadu dynasty, the Vṛṣṇi dynasty, Nanda Mahārāja and the *gopas* descended from the heavenly planets to see the pastimes of the Lord. As confirmed in *Bhagavad-gītā* (4.8), the Lord's pastimes consist of *paritrāṇāya sādhūnāṁ vināśāya ca duṣkṛtām*—saving the devotees and killing the demons. To demonstrate these activities, the Lord called for devotees from different parts of the universe.

There are many devotees who are elevated to the higher planetary systems.

*prāpya puṇya-kṛtāṁ lokān*
*uṣitvā śāśvatīḥ samāḥ*
*śucīnāṁ śrīmatāṁ gehe*
*yoga-bhraṣṭo 'bhijāyate*

"The unsuccessful *yogī*, after many, many years of enjoyment on the planets of the pious living entities, is born into a family of righteous people, or into a family of rich aristocracy." (Bg. 6.41) Some devotees, having failed to complete the process of devotional service, are promoted to the heavenly planets, to which the pious are elevated, and after enjoying there they may be directly promoted to the place where the Lord's pastimes are going on. When Lord Kṛṣṇa was to appear, the denizens of the heavenly planets were invited to see the pastimes of the Lord, and thus it is stated here that the members of the Yadu and Vṛṣṇi dynasties and the inhabitants of Vṛndāvana were demigods or almost as good as demigods. Even those who externally helped the activities of Kaṁsa belonged to the higher planetary systems. The imprisonment and release of Vasudeva and the killing of various demons were all manifestations of the pastimes of the Lord, and because the devotees would be pleased to see these activities personally, they were all invited to take birth as friends and relatives of these families. As confirmed in the prayers of Kuntī (*Bhāg.* 1.8.19), *naṭo nāṭya-dharo yathā.* The Lord was to play the part of a demon-killer, and a friend, son and brother to His devotees, and thus these devotees were all summoned.

## TEXT 64

**एतत् कंसाय भगवाञ्छशंसाभ्येत्य नारदः ।**
**भूमेर्भारायमाणानां दैत्यानां च वधोद्यमम् ॥६४॥**

*etat kaṁsāya bhagavāñ*
*chaśaṁsābhyetya nāradaḥ*
*bhūmer bhārāyamāṇānāṁ*
*daityānāṁ ca vadhodyamam*

*etat*—all these words about the Yadu family and Vṛṣṇi family; *kaṁsāya*—unto King Kaṁsa; *bhagavān*—the most powerful representative of the Supreme Personality of Godhead; *śaśaṁsa*—informed (Kaṁsa, who was in doubt); *abhyetya*—after approaching him; *nāradaḥ*—the great sage Nārada; *bhūmeḥ*—on the surface of the earth; *bhārāyamāṇānām*—of those who were a burden; *daityānām ca*—and of the demons; *vadha-udyamam*—the endeavor to kill.

## TRANSLATION

**Once the great saint Nārada approached Kaṁsa and informed him of how the demoniac persons who were a great burden on the earth were going to be killed. Thus Kaṁsa was placed into great fear and doubt.**

## PURPORT

It has already been discussed that mother earth implored Lord Brahmā to give her relief from the distress created by the burdensome demons and that Lord Brahmā informed her that Lord Kṛṣṇa Himself was going to appear. Kṛṣṇa says in *Bhagavad-gītā* (4.8):

*paritrāṇāya sādhūnāṁ*
*vināśāya ca duṣkṛtām*
*dharma-saṁsthāpanārthāya*
*sambhavāmi yuge yuge*

Whenever there is a burden created by the demons and whenever the innocent devotees are distressed by demoniac rulers, the Lord appears in due course of time to kill the demons with the assistance of His real representatives, who are technically called demigods. In the *Upaniṣads* it is stated that the demigods are different parts of the Supreme Personality of Godhead. As it is the duty of the parts of the body to serve the whole, it is the duty of Kṛṣṇa's devotees to serve Kṛṣṇa as He wants. Kṛṣṇa's business is to kill the demons, and therefore this should be a devotee's business also. Because the people of Kali-yuga are fallen, however, Śrī Caitanya Mahāprabhu, out of kindness for them, did not bring any weapon to kill them. Rather, by spreading Kṛṣṇa consciousness, love of Kṛṣṇa, He wanted to kill their nefarious, demoniac activities. This is the purpose of the Kṛṣṇa consciousness movement. Unless the demoniac activities on the surface of the world are diminished or vanquished, no one can be happy. The program for the conditioned soul is fully described in *Bhagavad-gītā*, and one simply has to follow these instructions to become happy. Śrī Caitanya Mahāprabhu has therefore prescribed:

*harer nāma harer nāma*
*harer nāmaiva kevalam*
*kalau nāsty eva nāsty eva*
*nāsty eva gatir anyathā*

Let people chant the Hare Kṛṣṇa *mantra* constantly. Then their demoniac tendencies will be killed, and they will become first-class devotees, happy in this life and in the next.

## TEXTS 65–66

ऋषेर्विनिर्गमे कंसो यदून् मत्वा सुरानिति ।
देवक्या गर्भसम्भूतं विष्णुं च स्ववधं प्रति ॥६५॥
देवकीं वसुदेवं च निगृह्य निगडैर्गृहे ।
जातं जातमहन् पुत्रं तयोरजनशङ्कया ॥६६॥

*ṛṣer vinirgame kaṁso*
*yadūn matvā surān iti*
*devakyā garbha-sambhūtaṁ*
*viṣṇuṁ ca sva-vadhaṁ prati*

*devakīṁ vasudevaṁ ca*
*nigṛhya nigaḍair gṛhe*
*jātaṁ jātam ahan putraṁ*
*tayor ajana-śaṅkayā*

*ṛṣeḥ*—of the great sage Nārada; *vinirgame*—on the departure (after giving information); *kaṁsaḥ*—Kaṁsa; *yadūn*—all the members of the Yadu dynasty; *matvā*—thinking of; *surān*—as demigods; *iti*—thus; *devakyāḥ*—of Devakī; *garbha-sambhūtam*—the children born from the womb; *viṣṇum*—(accepting) as Viṣṇu; *ca*—and; *sva-vadham prati*—fearing his own death from Viṣṇu; *devakīm*—Devakī; *vasudevam ca*—and her husband, Vasudeva; *nigṛhya*—arresting; *nigaḍaiḥ*—by iron shackles; *gṛhe*—confined at home; *jātam jātam*—each one who was born, one after another; *ahan*—killed; *putram*—the sons; *tayoḥ*—of Vasudeva and Devakī; *ajana-śaṅkayā*—with the doubt that they would be Viṣṇu.

## TRANSLATION

**After the departure of the great saint Nārada, Kaṁsa thought that all the members of the Yadu dynasty were demigods and that any of the children born from the womb of Devakī might be Viṣṇu. Fearing his death, Kaṁsa arrested Vasudeva and Devakī and chained them with iron shackles. Suspecting each of the children to be Viṣṇu, Kaṁsa killed them one after another because of the prophecy that Viṣṇu would kill him.**

## PURPORT

Śrīla Jīva Gosvāmī, in his notes on this verse, has mentioned how Nārada Muni gave Kaṁsa this information. This incident is described in the *Hari-vaṁśa*. Nārada Muni went to see Kaṁsa by providence, and Kaṁsa received him very well. Nārada, therefore, informed him that any one of the sons of Devakī might be Viṣṇu. Because Viṣṇu was to kill him, Kaṁsa should not spare any of Devakī's children, Nārada Muni advised. Nārada's intention was that Kaṁsa, by killing the children, would increase his sinful activities so that Kṛṣṇa would soon appear to kill him. Upon receiving the instructions of Nārada Muni, Kaṁsa killed all the children of Devakī one after another.

The word *ajana-śaṅkayā* indicates that Lord Viṣṇu never takes birth (*ajana*) and that He therefore appeared as Kṛṣṇa, taking birth just like a human being (*mānuṣīṁ tanum āśritam*). Kaṁsa attempted to kill all the babies born of Devakī and Vasudeva, although he knew that if Viṣṇu were born, He would not be killed. Actually it came to pass that when Viṣṇu appeared as Kṛṣṇa, Kaṁsa could not kill Him; rather, as foretold, it was He who killed Kaṁsa. One should know in truth how Kṛṣṇa, who takes His birth transcendentally, acts to kill the demons but is never killed. When one perfectly understands Kṛṣṇa in this way, through the medium of *śāstra*, one becomes immortal. As the Lord says in *Bhagavad-gītā* (4.9):

*janma karma ca me divyam*
*evaṁ yo vetti tattvataḥ*
*tyaktvā dehaṁ punar janma*
*naiti mām eti so 'rjuna*

"One who knows the transcendental nature of My appearance and activities does not, upon leaving the body, take his birth again in this material world, but attains My eternal abode, O Arjuna."

## TEXT 67

मातरं पितरं भ्रातॄन् सर्वांश्च सुहृदस्तथा ।
घ्नन्ति ह्यसुतृपो लुब्धा राजानः प्रायशो भुवि ॥६७॥

*mātaraṁ pitaraṁ bhrātṝn*
*sarvāṁś ca suhṛdas tathā*
*ghnanti hy asutṛpo lubdhā*
*rājānaḥ prāyaśo bhuvi*

*mātaram*—unto the mother; *pitaram*—unto the father; *bhrātṝn*—unto brothers; *sarvān ca*—and anyone else; *suhṛdaḥ*—friends; *tathā*—as well as; *ghnanti*—they kill (as it is practically seen); *hi*—indeed; *asutṛpaḥ*—those who envy the lives of others for their personal sense gratification; *lubdhāḥ*—greedy; *rājānaḥ*—such kings; *prāyaśaḥ*—almost always; *bhuvi*—on the earth.

## TRANSLATION

**Kings greedy for sense gratification on this earth almost always kill their enemies indiscriminately. To satisfy their own whims, they may kill anyone, even their mothers, fathers, brothers or friends.**

## PURPORT

We have seen in the history of India that Aurangzeb killed his brother and nephews and imprisoned his father to fulfill political ambitions.

There have been many similar instances, and Kaṁsa was the same type of king. Kaṁsa did not hesitate to kill his nephews and imprison his sister and his father. For demons to do such things is not astonishing. Nonetheless, although Kaṁsa was a demon, he was aware that Lord Viṣṇu cannot be killed, and thus he attained salvation. Even partial understanding of the activities of Lord Viṣṇu makes one eligible for salvation. Kaṁsa knew a little about Kṛṣṇa—that He could not be killed—and therefore he attained salvation although he thought of Viṣṇu, Kṛṣṇa, as an enemy. What then is to be said of one who knows Kṛṣṇa perfectly from the descriptions of *śāstras* like *Bhagavad-gītā?* It is therefore the duty of everyone to read *Bhagavad-gītā* and understand Kṛṣṇa perfectly. This will make one's life successful.

## TEXT 68

आत्मानमिह सञ्जातं जानन् प्राग् विष्णुना हतम् ।
महासुरं कालनेमिं यदुभिः स व्यरुध्यत ॥६८॥

*ātmānam iha sañjātaṁ*
*jānan prāg viṣṇunā hatam*
*mahāsuraṁ kālanemiṁ*
*yadubhiḥ sa vyarudhyata*

*ātmānam*—personally; *iha*—in this world; *sañjātam*—born again; *jānan*—understanding well; *prāk*—previously, before this birth; *viṣṇunā*—by Lord Viṣṇu; *hatam*—was killed; *mahā-asuram*—a great demon; *kālanemim*—by the name Kālanemi; *yadubhiḥ*—with the members of the Yadu dynasty; *saḥ*—he (Kaṁsa); *vyarudhyata*—acted inimically.

## TRANSLATION

**In his previous birth, Kaṁsa had been a great demon named Kālanemi and been killed by Viṣṇu. Upon learning this information from Nārada, Kaṁsa became envious of everyone connected with the Yadu dynasty.**

## PURPORT

Persons who are demons, enemies of the Supreme Personality of Godhead, are called *asuras.* As stated in *Bhagavad-gītā,* the *asuras,* because of their enmity toward the Supreme Personality of Godhead, take birth after birth in *asura* families and therefore glide down to the darkest hellish regions.

### TEXT 69

**उग्रसेनं च पितरं यदुभोजान्धकाधिपम् ।**
**स्वयं निगृह्य बुभुजे शूरसेनान् महाबलः ॥६९॥**

*ugrasenaṁ ca pitaraṁ*
*yadu-bhojāndhakādhipam*
*svayaṁ nigṛhya bubhuje*
*śūrasenān mahā-balaḥ*

*ugrasenam*—unto Ugrasena; *ca*—and; *pitaram*—who was his own father; *yadu*—of the Yadu dynasty; *bhoja*—of the Bhoja dynasty; *andhaka*—of the Andhaka dynasty; *adhipam*—the king; *svayam*—personally; *nigṛhya*—subduing; *bubhuje*—enjoyed; *śūrasenān*—all the states known as Śūrasena; *mahā-balaḥ*—the extremely powerful Kaṁsa.

### TRANSLATION

**Kaṁsa, the most powerful son of Ugrasena, even imprisoned his own father, the King of the Yadu, Bhoja and Andhaka dynasties, and personally ruled the states known as Śūrasena.**

### PURPORT

The state known as Mathurā was also included within the states known as Śūrasena.

---

## ADDITIONAL NOTES FOR THIS CHAPTER

Regarding transmigration of the soul, Śrīla Madhvācārya gives the following notes. When one is awake, whatever one sees or hears is impressed upon the mind, which later works in dreams to show one different experiences, although in dreams one appears to accept a different body. For example, when one is awake one does business and talks with customers, and similarly in dreams one meets various customers, talks about business and gives quotations. Madhvācārya says, therefore, that dreams take place according to what one sees, hears and remembers. When one reawakens, of course, one forgets the body of the dream. This forgetfulness is called *apasmṛti.* Thus we are changing bodies because we are sometimes dreaming, sometimes awake and sometimes forgetful. Forgetfulness of our previously created body is called death, and our work in the present body is called life. After death, one cannot remember the activities of one's previous body, whether imaginary or factual.

The agitated mind is compared to agitated water reflecting the sun and the moon. Actually the sun and moon reflected on the water do not exist there; nonetheless, they are reflected according to the movements of the water. Similarly, when our minds are agitated, we wander in different material atmospheres and receive different types of bodies. This is described in *Bhagavad-gītā* as *guṇa-saṅga. Kāraṇaṁ guṇa-saṅgo 'sya.* Madhvācārya says, *guṇānubaddhaḥ san.* And Śrī Caitanya Mahāprabhu says, *brahmāṇḍa bhramite kona bhāgyavān jīva* (Cc. *Madhya* 19.151). The living entity rotates up and down throughout the universe, sometimes in the upper planetary system, sometimes in the middle and lower planetary systems, sometimes as a man, sometimes a god, a dog, a tree and so on. This is all due to the agitation of the mind. The mind must therefore be steadily fixed. As it is said, *sa vai manaḥ kṛṣṇa-padāravindayoḥ.* One should fix one's mind at the lotus feet of Kṛṣṇa, and then one will become free from agitation. This is the instruction of the *Garuḍa Purāṇa,* and in the *Nāradīya Purāṇa* the same process is described. As stated in *Bhagavad-gītā, yānti deva-vratā devān.* The agitated mind goes to different planetary systems because it is attached to different kinds of demigods, but one does not go to the abode of the Supreme Personality of Godhead by worshiping the demigods, for this is not supported by any Vedic literature. Man is the architect of his own fortune. In this human life one has the facility with which to understand one's real situation, and one can decide whether to wander around the universe forever or return home, back to Godhead. This is also confirmed in *Bhagavad-gītā* (*aprāpya māṁ nivartante mṛtyu-saṁsāra-vartmani*).

There is no such thing as chance. When a tree is burning in a forest fire and although the nearest tree is spared a distant tree catches fire, this may appear to be chance. Similarly, one may seem to get different types of bodies by chance, but actually one receives these bodies because of the mind. The mind flickers between accepting and rejecting, and according to the acceptance and rejection of the mind, we receive different types of bodies, although we superficially seem to obtain these bodies by chance. Even if we accept the theory of chance, the immediate cause for the change of body is the agitation of the mind.

Notes on *aṁśa.* This chapter describes that Kṛṣṇa appeared *aṁśena*, with His parts and parcels or His partial manifestation. In this connection, Śrīdhara Svāmī says that Kṛṣṇa is one hundred percent Bhagavān (*kṛṣṇas tu bhagavān svayam*). Because of our imperfections, however, we cannot appreciate Kṛṣṇa in fullness, and therefore whatever Kṛṣṇa exhibited when present on earth was but a partial manifestation of His opulence. Again, Kṛṣṇa appeared with His plenary expansion Baladeva. Kṛṣṇa, however, is full; there is no question of His appearing partially. In the *Vaiṣṇava-toṣaṇī*, Śrīla Sanātana Gosvāmī says that to accept that Kṛṣṇa was partially manifested would contradict the statement *kṛṣṇas tu bhagavān svayam.* Śrīla Jīva Gosvāmī says that the word *aṁśena* means that Kṛṣṇa appeared with all His plenary expansions. The words *aṁśena viṣṇoḥ* do not mean that Kṛṣṇa is a partial representative of Viṣṇu. Rather, Kṛṣṇa appeared in fullness, and He manifests Himself partially in the Vaikuṇṭhalokas. In other words, Lord Viṣṇu is a partial representation of Kṛṣṇa; Kṛṣṇa is not a partial representation of Viṣṇu. In the *Caitanya-caritāmṛta, Ādi-līlā*, Chapter Four, this subject matter is explained very clearly. Śrīla Viśvanātha Cakravartī Ṭhākura also notes that no one can describe Kṛṣṇa in fullness. Whatever descriptions we find in *Śrīmad-Bhāgavatam* are partial explanations of Kṛṣṇa. In conclusion, therefore, the word *aṁśena* indicates that Lord Viṣṇu is a partial representation of Kṛṣṇa, not that Kṛṣṇa is a partial representation of Viṣṇu.

Śrīla Sanātana Gosvāmī's *Vaiṣṇava-toṣaṇī* has explained the word *dharma-śīlasya.* The exact meaning of *dharma-śīla* is "an unadulterated devotee." Real *dharma* consists of full surrender to Kṛṣṇa (*sarva-dharmān parityajya mām ekaṁ śaraṇaṁ vraja*). One who has fully surrendered to Kṛṣṇa is actually religious. One such religious person was Mahārāja Parīkṣit. Anyone who accepts the principle of surrender to the lotus feet of the Lord, giving up all other systems of religion, is actually *dharma-śīla*, perfectly religious.

The word *nivṛtta-tarṣaiḥ* refers to one who no longer has any material desires (*sarvopādhi-vinirmuktam*). One may have many material desires because of contamination in this material world, but when one is completely free from all material desires, he is called *nivṛtta-tṛṣṇa*, which indicates that he no longer has any thirst for material enjoyment. *Svāmin kṛtārtho 'smi varaṁ na yāce* (*Hari-bhakti-sudhodaya*). Materialistic persons want some material profit from executing devotional service, but this is not the purpose of service. The perfection of devotional service lies in complete surrender unto the lotus feet of Kṛṣṇa, with no material desires. One who surrenders in this way is already liberated. *Jīvan-muktaḥ sa ucyate.* One who is always busy serving Kṛṣṇa, in whatever condition he may live, is understood to be liberated even in this life. Such a person, who is a pure devotee, does not need to change his body; indeed, he does not possess a material body, for his body has already been spiritualized. An iron rod kept constantly within a fire will ultimately become fire, and whatever it touches will burn. Similarly, the pure devotee is in the fire of spiritual existence, and therefore his body is *cin-maya;* that is, it is spiritual, not material, because the pure devotee has no desire but the transcendental desire to serve the Lord. In text four the word *upagīyamānāt* is used: *nivṛtta-tarṣair upagīyamānāt.* Who will chant the glories of the Lord unless he is a devotee? Therefore the word *nivṛtta-tarṣaiḥ* indicates the devotee, and no one else. These are the remarks of *ācāryas* like Vīrarāghava Ācārya and Vijayadhvaja. To desire anything other than devotional service will diminish one's freedom from material desires, but when one is free from all such desires one is called *nivṛtta-tarṣaiḥ.*

*Vinā paśu-ghnāt.* The word *paśu* means "animal." An animal killer, *paśu-ghna*, cannot enter into Kṛṣṇa consciousness. In our Kṛṣṇa consciousness movement, therefore, animal killing is completely prohibited.

*Uttamaśloka-guṇānuvādāt.* The word *uttamaśloka* means "one who is famous as the best of those who are good." The Lord is good in all circumstances. That is His natural reputation. His goodness is unlimited, and He uses it unlimitedly. A devotee is also sometimes described as *uttamaśloka*, meaning that he is eager to glorify the Supreme Personality of Godhead or the Lord's devotees. Glorifying the Lord and glorifying the Lord's devotees are the same. Or, rather, glorifying the devotee is more important than glorifying the Lord directly. Narottama dāsa Ṭhākura explains this fact: *chāḍiyā vaiṣṇava-sevā, nistāra pāyeche kebā.* One cannot be liberated from material contamination without sincerely serving a devotee of Kṛṣṇa.

*Bhavauṣadhāt* means "from the universal remedy." Chanting the holy name and glorifying the Supreme Lord are the universal remedy for all the miseries of materialistic life. Persons who desire to be freed from this material world are called *mumukṣu.* Such persons can understand the miseries of materialistic life, and by glorifying the activities of the Lord they can be released from all these miseries. The transcendental sound vibrations concerning the Lord's name, fame, form, qualities and paraphernalia are all nondifferent from the Lord. Therefore the very sound vibration of the Lord's glorification and name are pleasing to the ears, and by understanding the absolute nature of the Lord's name, form and qualities the devotee becomes joyful. Even those who are not devotees, however, enjoy the pleasing narrations of the Lord's transcendental activities. Even ordinary persons not very much advanced in Kṛṣṇa consciousness take pleasure in describing the narrations depicted in *Śrīmad-Bhāgavatam.* When a materialistic person is purified in this way, he engages in hearing and chanting the glories of the Lord. Because glorification of the Lord's pastimes is very pleasing to the ear and heart of the devotee, it is simultaneously his subject and object.

In this world there are three kinds of men: those who are liberated, those trying to be liberated, and those entangled in sense enjoyment. Of these three, those who are already liberated chant and hear the holy name of the Lord, knowing perfectly that to glorify the Lord is the only way to keep oneself in a transcendental position. Those who are trying to be liberated, the second class, may regard the chanting and hearing of the Lord's holy name as a process of liberation, and they too will feel the transcendental pleasure of this chanting. As for *karmīs* and persons engaged in sense gratification, they also may take pleasure in hearing the pastimes of the Lord, like His fighting on the Battlefield of Kurukṣetra and His dancing in Vṛndāvana with the *gopīs.*

The word *uttamaśloka-guṇānuvāda* refers to the transcendental qualities of the Supreme Lord, such as His affection for mother Yaśodā and His friends the cowherd boys and His loving attitude toward the *gopīs.* The Lord's devotees like Mahārāja Yudhiṣṭhira are also described by the qualification *uttamaśloka-guṇānuvāda.* The word *anuvāda* refers to describing the qualities of the Supreme Lord or His devotees. When these qualities are described, other devotees are interested in hearing them. The more one is interested in hearing about these transcendental qualities, the more one transcendentally enjoys. Everyone, therefore, including the *mumukṣus*, the *vimuktas* and the *karmīs*, should chant and hear the glories of the Lord, and in this way everyone will benefit.

Although the sound vibration of the transcendental qualities of the Lord is equally beneficial to all, for those who are *muktas*, liberated, it is especially pleasing. As described in *Śrīmad-Bhāgavatam,* Eighth Canto, Third Chapter, verse twenty, because pure devotees, who no longer have any material desires, surrender fully to the lotus feet of the Lord, they always merge in the ocean of bliss by chanting and hearing the Lord's holy name. According to this verse, devotees like Nārada and other residents of Śvetadvīpa are seen always engaged in chanting the holy name of the Lord because by such chanting they are always externally and internally blissful. The *mumukṣus*, persons desiring to be liberated, do not depend on the pleasures of the senses; instead, they concentrate fully on becoming liberated by chanting the holy name of the Lord. *Karmīs* like to create something pleasing to their ears and hearts, and although they sometimes like to chant or hear the glories of the Lord, they do not do it openly. Devotees, however, always spontaneously hear, chant about and remember the activities of the Lord, and by this process they are fully satisfied, even though these may seem like topics of sense gratification. Simply by hearing the transcendental narrations of the Lord's activities, Parīkṣit Mahārāja was liberated. He was therefore *śrotramano-'bhirāma;* that is, he glorified the process of hearing. This process should be accepted by all living entities.

To distinguish persons who are bereft of these transcendental pleasures, Parīkṣit Mahārāja has used the words *virajyeta pumān.* The word *pumān* refers to any person, whether man, woman or in-between. Because of the bodily conception of life, we are subject to lamentation, but one who has no such bodily conceptions can take pleasure in transcendental hearing and chanting. Therefore a person fully absorbed in the bodily concept of life is surely killing himself by not making spiritual progress. Such a person is called *paśu-ghna.* Especially excluded from spiritual life are the animal hunters, who are not interested in hearing and chanting the holy name of the Lord. Such hunters are always unhappy, both in this life and in the next. It is therefore said that a hunter should neither die nor live because for such persons both living and dying are troublesome. Animal hunters are completely different from ordinary *karmīs*, and thus they have been excluded from the process of hearing and chanting. *Vinā paśu-ghnāt.* They cannot enter into the transcendental pleasure of chanting and hearing the holy name of the Lord.

The word *mahā-ratha* refers to a great hero who can fight alone against eleven thousand other heroes, and the word *atiratha*, as found in text five, refers to one who can fight against an unlimited number. This is mentioned in the *Mahābhārata* as follows:

*ekādaśa-sahasrāṇi*
*yodhayed yas tu dhanvinām*
*astra-śastra-pravīṇaś ca*
*mahā-ratha iti smṛtaḥ*
*amitān yodhayed yas tu*
*samprokto 'tirathas tu saḥ*

This is the description given in the *Bṛhad-vaiṣṇava-toṣaṇī* by Śrīla Sanātana Gosvāmī.

*Māyā-manuṣyasya* (10.1.17). Because of being covered by *yogamāyā* (*nāhaṁ prakāśaḥ sarvasya yogamāyā-samāvṛtaḥ*), Kṛṣṇa is sometimes called *māyā-manuṣya*, indicating that although He is the Supreme Personality of Godhead, He appears like an ordinary person. A misunderstanding arises because *yogamāyā* covers the vision of the general public. The Lord's position is actually different from that of an ordinary person, for although He appears to act like an ordinary man, He is always transcendental. The word *māyā* also indicates "mercy," and sometimes it also means "knowledge." The Lord is always full of all transcendental knowledge, and therefore although He acts like a human being, He is the Supreme Personality of Godhead, full of knowledge. In His original identity, the Lord is the controller of *māyā* (*mayādhyakṣeṇa prakṛtiḥ sūyate sa-carācaram*). Therefore the Lord may be called *māyā-manuṣya*, or the Supreme Personality of Godhead playing like an ordinary human being, although He is the controller of both the material and spiritual energies. The Lord is the Supreme Person, Puruṣottama, but because we are deluded by *yogamāyā,* He appears to be an ordinary person. Ultimately, however, *yogamāyā* induces even a nondevotee to understand the Lord as the Supreme Person, Puruṣottama. In *Bhagavad-gītā* we find two statements given by the Supreme Personality of Godhead. For the devotees, the Lord says:

*teṣāṁ satata-yuktānāṁ*
*bhajatāṁ prīti-pūrvakam*
*dadāmi buddhi-yogaṁ taṁ*
*yena mām upayānti te*

"To those who are constantly devoted and worship Me with love, I give the understanding by which they can come to Me." (Bg. 10.10) Thus for the willing devotee the Lord gives intelligence by which to understand Him and return home, back to Godhead. For others, for nondevotees, the Lord says, *mṛtyuḥ sarva-haraś cāham:* "I am all-plundering, inevitable death." A devotee like Prahlāda enjoys the activities of Lord Nṛsiṁhadeva, whereas nondevotees like Prahlāda's father, Hiraṇyakaśipu, meet death before Lord Nṛsiṁhadeva. The Lord therefore acts in two ways, by sending some onto the path of repeated birth and death and sending others back home, back to Godhead.

The word *kāla,* meaning "black," indicates the color of the Supreme Personality of Godhead, Kṛṣṇa. Lord Kṛṣṇa and Lord Rāmacandra, who both look blackish, give liberation and transcendental bliss to Their devotees. Among persons possessing material bodies, sometimes someone is able to subject death to his own will. For such a person, death is almost impossible because no one wants to die. But although Bhīṣmadeva possessed this power, Bhīṣma, by the supreme will of the Lord, died very easily in the Lord's presence. There have also been many demons who had no hope of salvation, yet Kaṁsa attained salvation by the supreme will of the Lord. Not to speak of Kaṁsa, even Pūtanā attained salvation and reached the level of the Lord's mother. Parīkṣit Mahārāja, therefore, was very eager to hear about the Lord, who has inconceivable qualities by which to give liberation to anyone. Parīkṣit Mahārāja, at the point of his death, was certainly interested in his liberation. When such a great and exalted personality as the Lord behaves like an ordinary human being although possessing inconceivable qualities, His behavior is called *māyā*. Therefore the Lord is described as *māyā-manuṣya*. This is the opinion of Śrīla Jīva Gosvāmī. *Mu* refers to *mukti*, or salvation, and *ku* refers to that which is bad or very obnoxious. Thus *muku* refers to the Supreme Personality of Godhead, who saves one from the bad condition of material existence. The Lord is called *mukunda* because He not only saves the devotee from material existence but offers him transcendental bliss in love and service.

As for Keśava, *ka* means Brahmā, and *īśa* means Lord Śiva. The Personality of Godhead captivates both Lord Brahmā and Lord Mahādeva, or Śiva, by His transcendental qualities. Thereforc He is called Keśava. This opinion is given by Sanātana Gosvāmī in his *Vaiṣṇava-toṣaṇī* commentary.

It is said that all the demigods, accompanied by Tri-nayana, Lord Śiva, went to the shore of the ocean of milk and offered their prayers through the *mantra* known as *Puruṣa-sūkta*. From this statement it is understood that the demigods cannot directly approach Lord Viṣṇu, who lies on the ocean of milk, or enter His abode. This is also clearly stated in the *Mahābhārata*, *Mokṣa-dharma*, and the next chapter of *Śrīmad-Bhāgavatam*. Kṛṣṇa, the Supreme Personality of Godhead, has His abode in Goloka (*goloka-nāmni nija-dhāmni tale ca tasya*). From Lord Kṛṣṇa come the *catur-vyūha*, the quadruple expansions Saṅkarṣaṇa, Aniruddha, Pradyumna and Vāsudeva. There are innumerable *brahmāṇḍas*, all of which emanate from the pores of Kāraṇodakaśāyī Viṣṇu, and in every *brahmāṇḍa* there is a Garbhodakaśāyī Viṣṇu, who is a partial expansion of Aniruddha. This Aniruddha is a partial expansion of Pradyumna, who is partially represented as Kṣīrodakaśāyī Viṣṇu, the Supersoul of all living entities. These Viṣṇu expansions are different from Kṛṣṇa, who resides in Goloka Vṛndāvana. When it is said that the demigods offered prayers to the Lord by chanting the *Puruṣa-sūkta*, this indicates that they pleased the Lord by enunciating prayers of *bhakti*.

The word *vṛṣākapi* refers to one who satisfies His devotee in every way and frees His devotee from all material anxieties. *Vṛṣa* refers to religious performances like sacrifices. Even without the execution of sacrifices, the Lord can still enjoy the supermost comforts of the heavenly planets. The statement that Puruṣottama, Jagannātha, would appear in the house of

Vasudeva distinguishes the Supreme Personality of Godhead from ordinary persons. The statement that He personally appeared indicates that He did not send His plenary expansion. The word *priyārtham* indicates that the Lord appeared to please Rukmiṇī and Rādhārāṇī. *Priyā* means "the most beloved."

In the commentary of Śrī Vīrarāghava Ācārya, the following extra verse is accepted after text twenty-three:

*ṛṣayo 'pi tad-ādeśāt*
*kalpyantāṁ paśu-rūpiṇaḥ*
*payo-dāna-mukhenāpi*
*viṣṇuṁ tarpayituṁ surāḥ*

"O demigods, even great sages, following the order of Viṣṇu, appeared in the forms of cows and calves to please the Supreme Personality of Godhead by delivering milk."

Rāmānujācārya sometimes accepts Baladeva as a *śaktyāveśa-avatāra*, but Śrīla Jīva Gosvāmī has explained that Baladeva is an expansion of Kṛṣṇa and that a part of Baladeva is Saṅkarṣaṇa. Although Baladeva is identical with Saṅkarṣaṇa, He is the origin of Saṅkarṣaṇa. Therefore the word *svarāṭ* has been used to indicate that Baladeva always exists in His own independence. The word *svarāṭ* also indicates that Baladeva is beyond the material conception of existence. *Māyā* cannot attract Him, but because He is fully independent, He can appear by His spiritual potency wherever He likes. *Māyā* is fully under the control of Viṣṇu. Because the material potency and *yogamāyā* mingle in the Lord's appearance, they are described as *ekānaṁśā*. Sometimes *ekānaṁśā* is interpreted to mean "without differentiation." Saṅkarṣaṇa and Śeṣa-nāga are identical. As stated by Yamunādevī, "O Rāma, O great-armed master of the world, who have extended Yourself throughout the entire universe by one plenary expansion, it is not possible to understand You fully." Therefore *ekāṁśā* refers to Śeṣa-nāga. In other words, Baladeva, merely by His partial expansion, sustains the entire universe.

The word *kāryārthe* refers to one who attracted the pregnancy of Devakī and bewildered mother Yaśodā. These pastimes are very confidential. The Supreme Personality of Godhead ordered *yogamāyā* to bewilder His associates in His pastimes and bewilder demons like Kaṁsa.

As stated previously, *yogamāyāṁ samādiśat.* To give service to the Lord, *yogamāyā* appeared along with *mahāmāyā. Mahāmāyā* refers to *yayā sammohitaṁ jagat,* "one who bewilders the entire material world." From this statement it is to be understood that *yogamāyā,* in her partial expansion, becomes *mahāmāyā* and bewilders the conditioned souls. In other words, the entire creation has two divisions—transcendental, or spiritual, and material. *Yogamāyā* manages the spiritual world, and by her partial expansion as *mahāmāyā* she manages the material world. As stated in the *Nārada-pañcarātra, mahāmāyā* is a partial expansion of *yogamāyā.* The *Nārada-pañcarātra* clearly states that the Supreme Personality has one potency, which is sometimes described as Durgā. The *Brahma-saṁhitā* says, *chāyeva yasya bhuvanāni bibharti durgā.* Durgā is not different from *yogamāyā.* When one understands Durgā properly, he is immediately liberated, for Durgā is originally the spiritual potency, *hlādinī-śakti,* by whose mercy one can understand the Supreme Personality of Godhead very easily. *Rādhā kṛṣṇa-praṇaya-vikṛtir hlādinī-śaktir asmād.* The *mahāmāyā-śakti,* however, is a covering of *yogamāyā,* and she is therefore called the covering potency. By this covering potency, the entire material world is bewildered (*yayā sammohitaṁ jagat*). In conclusion, bewildering the conditioned souls and liberating the devotees are both functions belonging to *yogamāyā.* Transferring the pregnancy of Devakī and keeping mother Yaśodā in deep sleep were both done by *yogamāyā; mahāmāyā* cannot act upon such devotees, for they are always liberated. But although it is not possible for *mahāmāyā* to control liberated souls or the Supreme Personality of Godhead, she did bewilder Kaṁsa. The action of *yogamāyā* in presenting herself before Kaṁsa was the action of *mahāmāyā,* not *yogamāyā. Yogamāyā* cannot even see or touch such polluted persons as Kaṁsa. In *Caṇḍī,* in the *Mārkaṇḍeya Purāṇa,* Eleventh Chapter, Mahāmāyā says, "During the twenty-eighth *yuga* in the period of Vaivasvata Manu, I shall take birth as the daughter of Yaśodā and be known as Vindhyācala-vāsinī."

The distinction between the two *māyās—yogamāyā* and *mahāmāyā*—is described as follows. Kṛṣṇa's *rāsa-līlā* with the *gopīs* and the *gopīs'* bewilderment in respect to their husbands, fathers-in-law and other such relatives were arrangements of *yogamāyā* in which *mahāmāyā* had no influence. The *Bhāgavatam* gives sufficient evidence of this when it clearly says, *yogamāyām upāśritaḥ.* On the other hand, there were *asuras* headed by Śālva and *kṣatriyas* like Duryodhana who were bereft of devotional service in spite of seeing Kṛṣṇa's carrier Garuḍa and the universal form, and who could not understand Kṛṣṇa to be the Supreme Personality of Godhead. This was also bewilderment, but this bewilderment was due to *mahāmāyā.* Therefore it is to be concluded that the *māyā* which drags a person from the Supreme Personality of Godhead is called *jaḍamāyā,* and the *māyā* which acts on the transcendental platform is called *yogamāyā.* When Nanda Mahārāja was taken away by Varuṇa, he saw Kṛṣṇa's opulence, but nonetheless he thought of Kṛṣṇa as his son. Such feelings of parental love in the spiritual world are acts of *yogamāyā,* not of *jaḍamāyā,* or *mahāmāyā.* This is the opinion of Śrīla Viśvanātha Cakravartī Ṭhākura.

*Śūrasenāṁś ca.* The son of Kārtavīryārjuna was Śūrasena, and the countries he ruled were also called Śūrasena. This is noted by Sanātana Gosvāmī in his *Vaiṣṇava-toṣaṇī* commentary.

In regard to Mathurā, we find this quotation:

*mathyate tu jagat sarvaṁ*
*brahma-jñānena yena vā*
*tat-sāra-bhūtaṁ yad yasyāṁ*
*mathurā sā nigadyate*

When a self-realized soul acts in his transcendental position, his situation is called Mathurā. In other words, when one acts in the process of *bhakti-yoga,* he may live anywhere, but actually he lives in Mathurā, Vṛndāvana. Devotion to Kṛṣṇa, the son of Nanda Mahārāja, is the essence of all knowledge, and wherever such knowledge is manifested is called Mathurā. Also, when one establishes *bhakti-yoga,* excluding all other methods, one's situation is called Mathurā. *Yatra nityaṁ sannihito hariḥ:* the place where Hari, the Supreme Personality of Godhead, lives eternally is called Mathurā. The word *nitya* indicates eternality. The Supreme Lord is eternal, and His abode is also eternal. *Goloka eva nivasaty akhilātma-bhūtaḥ.* Although the Lord is always stationed in His abode, Goloka Vṛndāvana, He is present everywhere in fullness. This means that when the Supreme Lord descends on the surface of the world, His original abode is not vacant, for He can remain in His original abode and simultaneously descend upon Mathurā, Vṛndāvana, Ayodhyā and other places. He does not need to descend, since He is already present there; He simply manifests Himself.

Śrīla Śukadeva Gosvāmī has addressed Mahārāja Parīkṣit as *tāta*, or "beloved son." This is due to parental love in the heart of Śukadeva Gosvāmī. Because Kṛṣṇa was soon coming as the son of Vasudeva and Devakī, out of parental affection Śukadeva Gosvāmī addressed Mahārāja Parīkṣit as *tāta*, "my dear son."

In the *Viśva-kośa* dictionary, the word *garbha* is explained: *garbho bhrūṇe arbhake kukṣāv ity ādi.* When Kaṁsa was about to kill Devakī, Vasudeva wanted to dissuade him by the diplomacy of *sāma* and *bheda. Sāma* means "pacifying." Vasudeva wanted to pacify Kaṁsa by indicating relations, gain, welfare, identity and glorification. Reference to these five concerns constitutes *sāma*, and Vasudeva's presentation of fear in two situations—in this life and the next—is called *bheda.* Thus Vasudeva used both *sāma* and *bheda* to pacify Kaṁsa. Praising Kaṁsa's qualifications was glorification, and praising him as a descendant of the *bhoja-vaṁśa* appealed to *sambandha*, relationship. Speaking of "your sister" was an appeal to identity. Speaking about killing a woman raises questions about fame and welfare, and arousing fear of the sinful act of killing one's sister during her marriage ceremony is an aspect of *bheda.* The Bhoja dynasty refers to those who were simply interested in sense gratification and were therefore not very aristocratic. Another meaning of *bhoja* is "fighting." These were indications of defamation for Kaṁsa. When Vasudeva addressed Kaṁsa as *dīna-vatsala*, this was excessive praise. Kaṁsa would accept calves as a form of revenue from his poor constituents, and therefore he was called *dīna-vatsala.* Vasudeva knew very well that he could not by force rescue Devakī from the imminent danger. Devakī was actually the daughter of Kaṁsa's uncle, and therefore she is described as *suhṛt*, meaning "relative." It is stated that Kaṁsa refrained from killing his close relation Devakī because if he had killed her, a great fight would have ensued among the other members of the family. Kaṁsa refrained from provoking this great danger of a family fight, for it would have caused many persons to lose their lives.

Formerly an *asura* named Kālanemi had six sons, named Haṁsa, Suvikrama, Krātha, Damana, Ripurmardana and Krodhahantā. They were known as the *ṣaḍ-garbhas*, or six *garbhas*, and they were all equally powerful and expert in military affairs. These *ṣaḍ-garbhas* gave up the association of Hiraṇyakaśipu, their grandfather, and underwent great austerities to satisfy Lord Brahmā, who, upon being satisfied, agreed to give them whatever benediction they might desire. When asked by Lord Brahmā to state what they wanted, the *ṣaḍ-garbhas* replied, "Dear Lord Brahmā, if you want to give us a benediction, give us the blessing that we will not be killed by any demigod, *mahā-roga*, Yakṣa, Gandharva-pati, Siddha, Cāraṇa or human being, nor by great sages who are perfect in their penances and austerities." Brahmā understood their purpose and fulfilled their desire. But when Hiraṇyakaśipu came to know of these events, he was very angry at his grandsons. "You have given up my association and have gone to worship Lord Brahmā," he said, "and therefore I no longer have any affection for you. You have tried to save yourselves from the hands of the demigods, but I curse you in this way: Your father will take birth as Kaṁsa and kill all of you because you will take birth as sons of Devakī." Because of this curse, the grandsons of Hiraṇyakaśipu had to take birth from the womb of Devakī and be killed by Kaṁsa, although he was previously their father. This description is mentioned in the *Hari-vaṁśa, Viṣṇu-parva*, Second Chapter. According to the comments of the *Vaiṣṇava-toṣaṇī*, the son of Devakī known as Kīrtimān was the third incarnation. In his first incarnation he was known as Smara and was the son of Marīci, and later he became the son of Kālanemi. This is mentioned in the histories.

An additional verse in this chapter of *Śrīmad-Bhāgavatam* is accepted by the Madhvācārya-sampradāya, represented by Vijayadhvaja Tīrtha. The verse is as follows:

*atha kaṁsam upāgamya*
*nārado brahma-nandanaḥ*
*ekāntam upasaṅgamya*
*vākyam etad uvāca ha*

*atha*—in this way; *kaṁsam*—unto Kaṁsa; *upāgamya*—after going; *nāradaḥ*—the great sage Nārada; *brahma-nandanaḥ*—who is the son of Brahmā; *ekāntam upasaṅgamya*—after going to a very solitary place;

*vākyam*—the following instruction; *etat*—this; *uvāca*—said; *ha*—in the past.

Translation: "Thereafter, Nārada, the mental son of Lord Brahmā, approached Kaṁsa and, in a very solitary place, informed him of the following news."

The great saint Nārada descended from the heavenly planets to the forest of Mathurā and sent his messenger to Kaṁsa. When the messenger approached Kaṁsa and informed him of Nārada's arrival, Kaṁsa, the leader of the *asuras*, was very happy and immediately came out of his palace to receive Nārada, who was as bright as the sun, as powerful as fire, and free from all tinges of sinful activities. Kaṁsa accepted Nārada as his guest, offered him respectful obeisances and gave him a golden seat, brilliant like the sun. Nārada was a friend of the King of heaven, and thus he told Kaṁsa, the son of Ugrasena, "My dear hero, you have satisfied me with a proper reception, and therefore I shall tell you something secret and confidential. While I was coming here from Nandakānana through the Caitraratha forest, I saw a great meeting of the demigods, who followed me to Sumeru Parvata. We traveled through many holy places, and finally we saw the holy Ganges. While Lord Brahmā was consulting the other demigods at the top of Sumeru Hill, I was also present with my stringed instrument, the *vīṇā*. I shall tell you confidentially that the meeting was held just to plan to kill the *asuras*, headed by you. You have a younger sister named Devakī, and it is a fact that her eighth son will kill you." (reference: *Hari-vaṁśa, Viṣṇu-parva* 1.2–16)

No one can blame Nāradajī for encouraging Kaṁsa to kill the sons of Devakī. The saint Nārada is always a well-wisher for human society, and he wanted the Supreme Personality of Godhead, Kṛṣṇa, to descend to this world as soon as possible so that the society of demigods would be pleased and would see Kaṁsa and his friends killed by Kṛṣṇa. Kaṁsa would also attain salvation from his nefarious activities, and this too would very much please the demigods and their followers. Śrīla Viśvanātha Cakravartī Ṭhākura remarks in this connection that Nārada Muni sometimes did things that were beneficial to the demigods and the demons simultaneously. Śrī Vīrarāghava Ācārya, in his commentary, has included the following half-verse in this regard: *asurāḥ sarva evaita lokopadrava-kāriṇaḥ*. *Asuras* are always disturbing elements for human society.

*Thus end the Bhaktivedanta purports of the Tenth Canto, First Chapter, of the* Śrīmad-Bhāgavatam, *entitled "The Advent of Lord Kṛṣṇa: Introduction."*

CHAPTER TWO

# Prayers by the Demigods for Lord Kṛṣṇa in the Womb

As described in this chapter, when the Supreme Personality of Godhead entered the womb of Devakī to kill Kaṁsa, all the demigods understood that the Lord was living within Devakī's womb, and therefore in veneration they offered Him the *Garbha-stuti* prayers.

Kaṁsa, under the protection of his father-in-law, Jarāsandha, and with the help of his demoniac friends like Pralamba, Baka, Cāṇūra, Tṛṇāvarta, Aghāsura, Muṣṭika, Bāṇa and Bhaumāsura, began oppressing the members of the Yadu dynasty. Therefore, the members of the Yadu dynasty left their homes and sought shelter in such states as Kuru, Pañcāla, Kekaya, Śālva and Vidarbha. Only some of them stayed with Kaṁsa, as nominal friends.

After Kaṁsa killed the *ṣaḍ-garbhas*, the six sons of Devakī, one after another, Anantadeva entered Devakī's womb and was transferred to the womb of Rohiṇī by the manipulation of Yogamāyā, who was following the order of the Supreme Personality of Godhead. The Lord Himself, who was soon to appear as the eighth son of Devakī, ordered Yogamāyā to take birth from the womb of Yaśodādevī. Because Kṛṣṇa and His potency, Yogamāyā, appeared simultaneously as brother and sister, the world is full of Vaiṣṇavas and *śāktas*, and there is certainly some rivalry between them. Vaiṣṇavas worship the Supreme Lord, whereas *śaktas*, according to their desires, worship Yogamāyā in forms like Durgā, Bhadrakālī and Caṇḍikā. Following the orders of the Supreme Personality of Godhead, Yogamāyā transferred Baladeva, Saṅkarṣaṇa, the seventh child of Devakī, from the womb of Devakī to the womb of Rohiṇī. Because Saṅkarṣaṇa appears in order to increase love of Kṛṣṇa, He is known as Baladeva. One may take auspicious strength from Him to become a devotee of the Lord, and therefore He is also known as Balabhadra.

After Yogamāyā transferred the seventh child of Devakī to the womb of Rohiṇī, the Supreme Personality of Godhead appeared within the heart of Vasudeva and transferred Himself into the heart of Devakī. Because the Lord was present in her heart, Devakī, as her pregnancy continued, appeared effulgent. Upon seeing this effulgence, Kaṁsa was full of anxiety, but he could not harm Devakī because of their family relationship. Thus he began indirectly thinking of Kṛṣṇa and became fully Kṛṣṇa conscious.

Meanwhile, because of the Lord's presence within the womb of Devakī, all the demigods came to offer the Lord their prayers. The Supreme Personality of Godhead, they said, is eternally the Absolute Truth. The spiritual soul is more important than the gross body, and the Supersoul, Paramātmā, is still more important than the soul. The Supreme Godhead is absolutely independent, and His incarnations are transcendental. The prayers of the demigods glorify and exalt devotees and explain the fate of persons who superficially consider themselves liberated from the conditions of material nature. A devotee is always safe. When a devotee fully surrenders at the lotus feet of the Lord, he is completely liberated from the fear of material existence. By explaining why the Supreme Personality of Godhead descends, the prayers of the demigods clearly confirm the Lord's statement in *Bhagavad-gītā* (4.7):

*yadā yadā hi dharmasya*
*glānir bhavati bhārata*
*abhyutthānam adharmasya*
*tadātmānaṁ sṛjāmy aham*

"Whenever and wherever there is a decline in religious practice, O descendant of Bharata, and a predominant rise of irreligion—at that time I descend Myself."

## TEXTS 1–2

श्रीशुक उवाच

प्रलम्बबकचाणूरतृणावर्तमहाशनैः ।
मुष्टिकारिष्टद्विविदपूतनाकेशिधेनुकैः ॥ १ ॥
अन्यैश्चासुरभूपालैर्बाणभौमादिभिर्युतः ।
यदूनां कदनं चक्रे बली मागधसंश्रयः ॥ २ ॥

*śrī-śuka uvāca*
*pralamba-baka-cāṇūra-*
*tṛṇāvarta-mahāśanaiḥ*
*muṣṭikāriṣṭa-dvivida-*
*pūtanā-keśi-dhenukaiḥ*

*anyaiś cāsura-bhūpālair*
*bāṇa-bhaumādibhir yutaḥ*
*yadūnāṁ kadanaṁ cakre*
*balī māgadha-saṁśrayaḥ*

*śrī-śukaḥ uvāca*—Śrī Śukadeva Gosvāmī said; *pralamba*—by the *asura* named Pralamba; *baka*—by the *asura* named Baka; *cāṇūra*—by the *asura* named Cāṇūra; *tṛṇāvarta*—by the *asura* named Tṛṇāvarta; *mahāśanaiḥ*—by Aghāsura; *muṣṭika*—by the *asura* named Muṣṭika; *ariṣṭa*—by the *asura* Ariṣṭa; *dvivida*—by the *asura* named Dvivida; *pūtanā*—by Pūtanā; *keśi*—by Keśī; *dhenukaiḥ*—by Dhenuka; *anyaiḥ ca*—and by many others; *asura-bhūpālaiḥ*—by demoniac kings on the surface of the globe; *bāṇa*—by King Bāṇa; *bhauma*—by Bhaumāsura; *ādibhiḥ*—and by others as well; *yutaḥ*—being assisted; *yadūnām*—of the kings of the Yadu dynasty; *kadanam*—persecution; *cakre*—regularly performed; *balī*—very powerful; *māgadha-saṁśrayaḥ*—under the protection of Jarāsandha, the King of Magadha.

## TRANSLATION

**Śukadeva Gosvāmī said: Under the protection of Magadharāja, Jarāsandha, the powerful Kaṁsa began persecuting the kings of the Yadu dynasty. In this he had the cooperation of demons like Pralamba, Baka, Cāṇūra, Tṛṇāvarta, Aghāsura, Muṣṭika, Ariṣṭa, Dvivida, Pūtanā, Keśī, Dhenuka, Bāṇāsura, Narakāsura and many other demoniac kings on the surface of the earth.**

## PURPORT

This verse supports the following statement given by the Lord in *Bhagavad-gītā* (4.7–8):

*yadā yadā hi dharmasya*
*glānir bhavati bhārata*
*abhyutthānam adharmasya*
*tadātmānaṁ sṛjāmy aham*

*paritrāṇāya sādhūnāṁ*
*vināśāya ca duṣkṛtām*
*dharma-saṁsthāpanārthāya*
*sambhavāmi yuge yuge*

"Whenever and wherever there is a decline in religious practice, O descendant of Bharata, and a predominant rise of irreligion—at that time I descend Myself. To deliver the pious and to annihilate the miscreants, as well as to reestablish the principles of religion, I advent Myself millennium after millennium."

The Lord's purpose in maintaining this material world is to give everyone a chance to go back home, back to Godhead, but kings and political leaders unfortunately try to hinder the purpose of the Lord, and therefore the Lord appears, either personally or with His plenary portions, to set things right. It is therefore said:

*garbhaṁ sañcārya rohiṇyāṁ*
*devakyā yogamāyayā*
*tasyāḥ kukṣiṁ gataḥ kṛṣṇo*
*dvitīyo vibudhaiḥ stutaḥ*

"Kṛṣṇa appeared in the womb of Devakī after transferring Baladeva to the womb of Rohiṇī by the power of Yogamāyā." *Yadubhiḥ sa vyarudhyata.* The kings of the Yadu dynasty were all devotees, but there were many powerful demons, such as Śālva, who began to persecute them. At that time, Jarāsandha, who was Kaṁsa's father-in-law, was extremely powerful, and therefore Kaṁsa took advantage of his protection and the help of the demons in persecuting the kings of the Yadu dynasty. The demons naturally appeared more powerful than the demigods, but ultimately, because of help received from the Supreme Personality of Godhead, the demons were defeated and the demigods triumphant.

## TEXT 3

ते पीडिता निविविशुः कुरुपञ्चालकेकयान् ।
शाल्वान् विदर्भान् निषधान् विदेहान् कोशलानपि ॥३॥

*te pīḍitā nivivíśuḥ*
*kuru-pañcāla-kekayān*
*śālvān vidarbhān niṣadhān*
*videhān kośalān api*

*te*—they (the kings of the Yadu dynasty); *pīḍitāḥ*—being persecuted; *nivivíśuḥ*—took shelter or entered (the kingdoms); *kuru-pañcāla*—the countries occupied by the Kurus and Pañcālas; *kekayān*—the countries of the Kekayas; *śālvān*—the countries occupied by the Śālvas; *vidarbhān*—the countries occupied by the Vidarbhas; *niṣadhān*—the countries occupied by the Niṣadhas; *videhān*—the country of Videha; *kośalān api*—as well as the countries occupied by the Kośalas.

## TRANSLATION

**Persecuted by the demoniac kings, the Yādavas left their own kingdom and entered various others, like those of the Kurus, Pañcālas, Kekayas, Śālvas, Vidarbhas, Niṣadhas, Videhas and Kośalas.**

## TEXTS 4–5

एके तमनुरुन्धाना ज्ञातयः पर्युपासते ।
हतेषु षट्सु बालेषु देवक्या औग्रसेनिना ॥ ४ ॥
सप्तमो वैष्णवं धाम यमनन्तं प्रचक्षते ।
गर्भो बभूव देवक्या हर्षशोकविवर्धनः ॥ ५ ॥

*eke tam anurundhānā*
*jñātayaḥ paryupāsate*
*hateṣu ṣaṭsu bāleṣu*
*devakyā augraseninā*

*saptamo vaiṣṇavaṁ dhāma*
*yam anantaṁ pracakṣate*
*garbho babhūva devakyā*
*harṣa-śoka-vivardhanaḥ*

*eke*—some of them; *tam*—unto Kaṁsa; *anurundhānāḥ*—exactly following his policy; *jñātayaḥ*—relatives; *paryupāsate*—began to agree with him; *hateṣu*—having been killed; *ṣaṭsu*—six; *bāleṣu*—children; *devakyāḥ*—born of Devakī; *augraseninā*—by the son of Ugrasena (Kaṁsa); *saptamaḥ*—the seventh; *vaiṣṇavam*—of Lord Viṣṇu; *dhāma*—a plenary expansion; *yam*—unto whom; *anantam*—by the name Ananta; *pracakṣate*—is celebrated; *garbhaḥ*—embryo; *babhūva*—there was; *devakyāḥ*—of Devakī; *harṣa-śoka-vivardhanaḥ*—simultaneously arousing pleasure and lamentation.

## TRANSLATION

**Some of their relatives, however, began to follow Kaṁsa's principles and act in his service. After Kaṁsa, the son of Ugrasena, killed the six sons of Devakī, a plenary portion of Kṛṣṇa entered her womb as her seventh child, arousing her pleasure and her lamentation. That plenary portion is celebrated by great sages as Ananta, who belongs to Kṛṣṇa's second quadruple expansion.**

## PURPORT

Some of the chief devotees, such as Akrūra, stayed with Kaṁsa to satisfy him. This they did for various purposes. They all expected the Supreme Personality of Godhead to appear as the eighth child as soon as Devakī's other children were killed by Kaṁsa, and they were eagerly awaiting His appearance. By remaining in Kaṁsa's association, they would be able to see the Supreme Personality of Godhead take birth and display His childhood pastimes, and Akrūra would later go to Vṛndāvana to bring Kṛṣṇa and Balarāma to Mathurā. The word *paryupāsate* is significant because it indicates that some devotees wanted to stay near Kaṁsa in order to see all these pastimes of the Lord. The six children killed by Kaṁsa had formerly been sons of Marīci, but because of having been cursed by a *brāhmaṇa*, they were obliged to take birth as grandsons of Hiraṇyakaśipu. Kaṁsa had taken birth as Kālanemi, and now he was obliged to kill his own sons. This was a mystery. As soon as the sons of Devakī were killed, they would return to their original place. The devotees wanted to see this also. Generally speaking, no one kills his own nephews, but Kaṁsa was so cruel that he did so without hesitation. Ananta, Saṅkarṣaṇa, belongs to the second *catur-vyūha,* or quadruple expansion. This is the opinion of experienced commentators.

## TEXT 6

भगवानपि विश्वात्मा विदित्वा कंसजं भयम् ।
यदूनां निजनाथानां योगमायां समादिशत् ॥ ६ ॥

*bhagavān api viśvātmā*
*viditvā kaṁsajaṁ bhayam*
*yadūnāṁ nija-nāthānāṁ*
*yogamāyāṁ samādiśat*

*bhagavān*—Śrī Kṛṣṇa, the Supreme Personality of Godhead; *api*—also; *viśvātmā*—who is the Supersoul of everyone; *viditvā*—understanding the position of the Yadus and His other devotees; *kaṁsa-jam*—because of Kaṁsa; *bhayam*—fear; *yadūnām*—of the Yadus; *nija-nāthānām*—who had accepted Him, the Supreme Lord, as their supreme shelter; *yogamāyām*—unto Yogamāyā, the spiritual potency of Kṛṣṇa; *samādiśat*—ordered as follows.

## TRANSLATION

**To protect the Yadus, His personal devotees, from Kaṁsa's attack, the Personality of Godhead, Viśvātmā, the Supreme Soul of everyone, ordered Yogamāyā as follows.**

## PURPORT

The words *bhagavān api viśvātmā viditvā kaṁsajaṁ bhayam* are commented upon by Śrīla Sanātana Gosvāmī. *Bhagavān svayam* is Kṛṣṇa (*kṛṣṇas tu bhagavān svayam*). He is Viśvātmā, the original Supersoul of everyone, because his plenary portion expands as the Supersoul. This is confirmed in *Bhagavad-gītā* (13.3): *kṣetra-jñaṁ cāpi māṁ viddhi sarva-kṣetreṣu bhārata.* Lord Kṛṣṇa is the *kṣetra-jña*, or Supersoul, of all living entities. He is the original source of all expansions of the Personality of Godhead. There are hundreds and thousands of plenary expansions of Viṣṇu, such as Saṅkarṣaṇa, Pradyumna, Aniruddha and Vāsudeva, but here in this material world, the Viśvātmā, the Supersoul for all living entities, is Kṣīrodakaśāyī Viṣṇu. As stated in *Bhagavad-gītā* (18.61), *īśvaraḥ sarva-bhūtānāṁ hṛd-deśe 'rjuna tiṣṭhati:* "The Supreme Lord is situated in the heart of all living entities, O Arjuna." Kṛṣṇa is actually Viśvātmā by His plenary expansion as *viṣṇu-tattva*, yet because of His affection for His devotees, He acts as Supersoul to give them directions (*sarvasya cāhaṁ hṛdi sanniviṣṭo mattaḥ smṛtir jñānam apohanaṁ ca*).

The affairs of the Supersoul pertain to Kṣīrodakaśāyī Viṣṇu, but Kṛṣṇa took compassion on Devakī, His devotee, because He understood her fear of Kaṁsa's persecution. A pure devotee is always fearful of material existence. No one knows what will happen next, for one may have to change his body at any moment (*tathā dehāntara-prāptiḥ*). Knowing this fact, a pure devotee acts in such a way that he will not have his life spoiled by being obliged to accept another body and undergo the tribulations of material existence. This is *bhayam*, or fear. *Bhayaṁ dvitīyābhiniveśataḥ syāt* (*Bhāg.* 11.2.37). This fear is due to material existence. Properly speaking, everyone should always be alert and fearful of material existence, but although everyone is prone to be affected by the ignorance of material existence, the Supreme Personality of Godhead, Kṛṣṇa, is always alert to the protection of His devotees. Kṛṣṇa is so kind and affectionate toward His devotees that He helps them by giving them the intelligence by which to exist in this material world without forgetting Him even for a moment. The Lord says:

*teṣām evānukampārtham*
*aham ajñānajaṁ tamaḥ*
*nāśayāmy ātma-bhāvastho*
*jñāna-dīpena bhāsvatā*

"Out of compassion for them, I, dwelling in their hearts, destroy with the shining lamp of knowledge the darkness born of ignorance." (Bg. 10.11)

The word *yoga* means "link." Any system of *yoga* is an attempt to reconnect our broken relationship with the Supreme Personality of Godhead. There are different types of *yoga*, of which *bhakti-yoga* is the best. In other *yoga* systems, one must undergo various processes before attaining perfection, but *bhakti-yoga* is direct. The Lord says in *Bhagavad-gītā* (6.47):

*yoginām api sarveṣāṁ*
*mad-gatenāntarātmanā*
*śraddhāvān bhajate yo māṁ*
*sa me yuktatamo mataḥ*

"Of all *yogīs*, he who always abides in Me with great faith, worshiping Me in transcendental loving service, is most intimately united with Me in *yoga* and is the highest of all." For the *bhakti-yogī*, a human body is guaranteed in his next existence, as stated by Lord Kṛṣṇa (*śucīnāṁ śrīmatāṁ gehe yoga-bhraṣṭo 'bhijāyate*). *Yogamāyā* is the spiritual potency of the Lord. Out of affection for His devotees, the Lord always stays in spiritual touch with them, although otherwise His *māyā* potency is so strong that she bewilders even exalted demigods like Brahmā. Therefore the Lord's potency is called *yogamāyā*. Since the Lord is Viśvātmā, He immediately ordered Yogamāyā to give protection to Devakī.

## TEXT 7

गच्छ देवि व्रजं भद्रे गोपगोभिरलङ्कृतम् ।
रोहिणी वसुदेवस्य भार्यास्ते नन्दगोकुले ।
अन्याश्च कंससंविग्ना विवरेषु वसन्ति हि ॥ ७ ॥

*gaccha devi vrajaṁ bhadre*
*gopa-gobhir alaṅkṛtam*
*rohiṇī vasudevasya*
*bhāryāste nanda-gokule*
*anyāś ca kaṁsa-saṁvignā*
*vivareṣu vasanti hi*

*gaccha*—now go; *devi*—O you who are worshipable for the whole world; *vrajam*—to the land of Vraja; *bhadre*—O you who are auspicious for all living entities; *gopa-gobhiḥ*—with cowherds and cows; *alaṅkṛtam*—decorated; *rohiṇī*—by the name Rohiṇī; *vasudevasya*—of Vasudeva, Kṛṣṇa's father; *bhāryā*—one of the wives; *āste*—is living; *nanda-gokule*—in the estate of Nanda Mahārāja known as Gokula, where hundreds and thousands of cows are maintained; *anyāḥ ca*—and other wives; *kaṁsa-saṁvignāḥ*—being afraid of Kaṁsa; *vivareṣu*—in secluded places; *vasanti*—are living; *hi*—indeed.

## TRANSLATION

**The Lord ordered Yogamāyā: O My potency, who are worshipable for the entire world and whose nature is to bestow good fortune upon all living entities, go to Vraja, where there live many cowherd men and their wives. In that very beautiful land, where many cows reside, Rohiṇī, the wife of Vasudeva, is living at the home of Nanda Mahārāja. Other wives of Vasudeva are also living there incognito because of fear of Kaṁsa. Please go there.**

## PURPORT

Nanda-gokula, the residence of King Nanda, was itself very beautiful, and when Yogamāyā was ordered to go there and encourage the devotees with fearlessness, it became even more beautiful and safe. Because Yogamāyā had the ability to create such an atmosphere, the Lord ordered her to go to Nanda-gokula.

## TEXT 8

देवक्या जठरे गर्भं शेषाख्यं धाम मामकम् ।
तत् संनिकृष्य रोहिण्या उदरे संनिवेशय ॥ ८ ॥

*devakyā jaṭhare garbhaṁ*
*śeṣākhyaṁ dhāma māmakam*
*tat sannikṛṣya rohiṇyā*
*udare sanniveśaya*

*devakyāḥ*—of Devakī; *jaṭhare*—within the womb; *garbham*—the embryo; *śeṣa-ākhyam*—known as Śeṣa, the plenary expansion of Kṛṣṇa;

*dhāma*—the plenary expansion; *māmakam*—of Me; *tat*—Him; *sannikṛṣya*—attracting; *rohiṇyāḥ*—of Rohiṇī; *udare*—within the womb; *sanniveśaya*—transfer without difficulty.

## TRANSLATION

**Within the womb of Devakī is My partial plenary expansion known as Saṅkarṣaṇa or Śeṣa. Without difficulty, transfer Him into the womb of Rohiṇī.**

## PURPORT

The first plenary expansion of Kṛṣṇa is Baladeva, also known as Śeṣa. The Śeṣa incarnation of the Supreme Personality of Godhead supports the entire universe, and the eternal mother of this incarnation is mother Rohiṇī. "Because I am going into the womb of Devakī," the Lord told Yogamāyā, "the Śeṣa incarnation has already gone there and made suitable arrangements so that I may live there. Now He should enter the womb of Rohiṇī, His eternal mother."

In this connection, one may ask how the Supreme Personality of Godhead, who is always situated transcendentally, could enter the womb of Devakī, which had previously been entered by the six *asuras*, the *ṣaḍ-garbhas*. Does this mean that the *ṣaḍ-garbhāsuras* were equal to the transcendental body of the Supreme Personality of Godhead? The following answer is given by Śrīla Viśvanātha Cakravartī Ṭhākura.

The entire creation, as well as its individual parts, is an expansion of the energy of the Supreme Personality of Godhead. Therefore, even though the Lord enters the material world, He does not do so. This is explained by the Lord Himself in *Bhagavad-gītā* (9.4–5):

*mayā tatam idaṁ sarvaṁ*
*jagad avyakta-mūrtinā*
*mat-sthāni sarva-bhūtāni*
*na cāhaṁ teṣv avasthitaḥ*

*na ca mat-sthāni bhūtāni*
*paśya me yogam aiśvaram*

*bhūta-bhṛn na ca bhūta-stho*
*mamātmā bhūta-bhāvanaḥ*

"By Me, in My unmanifested form, this entire universe is pervaded. All beings are in Me, but I am not in them. And yet everything that is created does not rest in Me. Behold My mystic opulence! Although I am the maintainer of all living entities, and although I am everywhere, My Self is the very source of creation." *Sarvaṁ khalv idaṁ brahma.* Everything is an expansion of Brahman, the Supreme Personality of Godhead, yet everything is not the Supreme Godhead, and He is not everywhere. Everything rests upon Him and yet does not rest upon Him. This can be explained only through the *acintya-bhedābheda* philosophy. Such truths cannot be understood, however, unless one is a pure devotee, for the Lord says in *Bhagavad-gītā* (18.55), *bhaktyā mām abhijānāti yāvān yaś cāsmi tattvataḥ:* "One can understand the Supreme Personality as He is only by devotional service." Even though the Lord cannot be understood by ordinary persons, this principle should be understood from the statement of the *śāstras.*

A pure devotee is always transcendentally situated because of executing nine different processes of *bhakti-yoga* (*śravaṇaṁ kīrtanaṁ viṣṇoḥ smaraṇaṁ pāda-sevenam/ arcanaṁ vandanaṁ dāsyaṁ sakhyam ātma-nivedanam*). Thus situated in devotional service, a devotee, although in the material world, is not in the material world. Yet a devotee always fears, "Because I am associated with the material world, so many contaminations affect me." Therefore he is always alert in fear, which gradually diminishes his material association.

Symbolically, mother Devakī's constant fear of Kaṁsa was purifying her. A pure devotee should always fear material association, and in this way all the *asuras* of material association will be killed, as the *ṣaḍ-garbhāsuras* were killed by Kaṁsa. It is said that from the mind, Marīci appears. In other words, Marīci is an incarnation of the mind. Marīci has six sons: Kāma, Krodha, Lobha, Moha, Mada and Mātsarya (lust, anger, greed, illusion, madness and envy). The Supreme Personality of Godhead appears in pure devotional service. This is confirmed in the *Vedas: bhaktir evainaṁ darśayati.* Only *bhakti* can bring one in contact with the Supreme Personality of Godhead. The Supreme Personality of Godhead appeared from the womb of Devakī, and therefore Devakī symbolically represents *bhakti*, and Kaṁsa symbolically represents material fear. When a pure devotee always fears material association, his real position of *bhakti* is manifested, and he naturally becomes uninterested in material enjoyment. When the six sons of Marīci are killed by such fear and one is freed from material contamination, within the womb of *bhakti* the Supreme Personality of Godhead appears. Thus the seventh pregnancy of Devakī signifies the appearance of the Supreme Personality of Godhead. After the six sons Kāma, Krodha, Lobha, Moha, Mada and Mātsarya are killed, the Śeṣa incarnation creates a suitable situation for the appearance of the Supreme Personality of Godhead. In other words, when one awakens his natural Kṛṣṇa consciousness, Lord Kṛṣṇa appears. This is the explanation given by Śrīla Viśvanātha Cakravartī Ṭhākura.

## TEXT 9

अथाहमंशभागेन देवक्याः पुत्रतां शुभे ।
प्राप्स्यामि त्वं यशोदायां नन्दपत्न्यां भविष्यसि ॥९॥

*athāham aṁśa-bhāgena*
*devakyāḥ putratāṁ śubhe*
*prāpsyāmi tvaṁ yaśodāyāṁ*
*nanda-patnyāṁ bhaviṣyasi*

*atha*—therefore; *aham*—I; *aṁśa-bhāgena*—by My plenary expansion; *devakyāḥ*—of Devakī; *putratām*—the son; *śubhe*—O all-auspicious Yogamāyā; *prāpsyāmi*—I shall become; *tvam*—you; *yaśodāyām*—in the womb of mother Yaśodā; *nanda-patnyām*—in the wife of Mahārāja Nanda; *bhaviṣyasi*—shall also appear.

## TRANSLATION

**O all-auspicious Yogamāyā, I shall then appear with My full six opulences as the son of Devakī, and you will appear as the daughter of mother Yaśodā, the queen of Mahārāja Nanda.**

## PURPORT

The word *aṁśa-bhāgena* is important in this verse. In *Bhagavad-gītā* (10.42) the Lord says:

*athavā bahunaitena*
*kim jñātena tavārjuna*
*viṣṭabhyāham idaṁ kṛtsnam*
*ekāṁśena sthito jagat*

"But what need is there, Arjuna, for all this detailed knowledge? With a single fragment of Myself I pervade and support this entire universe." Everything is situated as a part of the Supreme Lord's potency. In regard to Lord Kṛṣṇa's appearance in the womb of Devakī, Brahmā played a part also because on the bank of the milk ocean he requested the Supreme Personality of Godhead to appear. A part was also played by Baladeva, the first expansion of Godhead. Similarly, Yogamāyā, who appeared as the daughter of mother Yaśodā, also played a part. Thus *jīva-tattva, viṣṇu-tattva* and *śakti-tattva* are all integrated with the Supreme Personality of Godhead, and when Kṛṣṇa appears, He appears with all His integrated parts. As explained in previous verses, Yogamāyā was requested to attract Saṅkarṣaṇa, Baladeva, from the womb of Devakī to the womb of Rohiṇī, and this was a very heavy task for her. Yogamāyā naturally could not see how it was possible for her to attract Saṅkarṣaṇa. Therefore Kṛṣṇa addressed her as *śubhe*, auspicious, and said, "Be blessed. Take power from Me, and you will be able to do it." By the grace of the Supreme Personality of Godhead, anyone can do anything, for the Lord is present in everything, all things being His parts and parcels (*aṁśa-bhāgena*) and increasing or decreasing by His supreme will. Balarāma was only fifteen days older than Kṛṣṇa. By the blessings of Kṛṣṇa, Yogamāyā became the daughter of mother Yaśodā, but by the supreme will she was not able to enjoy the parental love of her father and mother. Kṛṣṇa, however, although not actually born from the womb of mother Yaśodā, enjoyed the parental love of mother Yaśodā and Nanda. By the blessings of Kṛṣṇa, Yogamāyā was able to achieve the reputation of being the daughter of mother Yaśodā, who also became famous by the blessings of Kṛṣṇa. Yaśodā means "one who gives fame."

## TEXT 10

अर्चिष्यन्ति मनुष्यास्त्वां सर्वकामवरेश्वरीम् ।
धूपोपहारबलिभिः सर्वकामवरप्रदाम् ॥१०॥

*arciṣyanti manuṣyās tvāṁ*
*sarva-kāma-vareśvarīm*
*dhūpopahāra-balibhiḥ*
*sarva-kāma-vara-pradām*

*arciṣyanti*—will worship; *manuṣyāḥ*—human society; *tvām*—unto you; *sarva-kāma-vara-īśvarīm*—because you are the best of the demigods who can fulfill all material desires; *dhūpa*—by incense; *upahāra*—by presentations; *balibhiḥ*—by different types of worship through sacrifice; *sarva-kāma*—of all material desires; *vara*—the blessings; *pradām*—one who can bestow.

## TRANSLATION

**By sacrifices of animals, ordinary human beings will worship you gorgeously, with various paraphernalia, because you are supreme in fulfilling the material desires of everyone.**

## PURPORT

As stated in *Bhagavad-gītā* (7.20), *kāmais tais tair hṛta-jñānāḥ prapadyante 'nya-devatāḥ:* "Those whose minds are distorted by material desires surrender unto demigods." Therefore the word *manuṣya*, meaning "human being," here refers to one who does not know the actual goal of life. Such a person wants to enjoy the material world by taking birth in a highly elevated family with the benefits of education, beauty and immense wealth, which in this material world are desirable. One who has forgotten the real aim of life may worship goddess Durgā, *māyā-śakti*, under various names, for different purposes, and in different places. As there are many holy places for the worship of Kṛṣṇa, there are also many holy places in India for the worship of Durgādevī, or Māyādevī, who took birth as the daughter of Yaśodā. After cheating Kaṁsa, Māyādevī dispersed herself to various places, especially in Vindhyācala, to accept regular worship from ordinary men. A human being should actually be interested in understanding *ātma-tattva*, the truth of *ātmā*, the spirit soul, and Paramātmā, the supreme soul. Those who are interested in *ātma-tattva* worship the Supreme Personality of Godhead (*yasmin vijñāte sarvam evaṁ vijñātaṁ bhavati*). However, as explained in the next verse of this chapter, those who cannot understand *ātma-tattva* (*apaśyatām ātma-tattvam*) worship Yogamāyā in her different features. Therefore *Śrīmad-Bhāgavatam* (2.1.2) says:

*śrotavyādīni rājendra*
*nṛṇāṁ santi sahasraśaḥ*
*apaśyatām ātma-tattvaṁ*
*gṛheṣu gṛha-medhinām*

"Those persons who are materially engrossed, being blind to the knowledge of ultimate truth, have many subject matters for hearing in human society, O Emperor." Those who are interested in remaining in this material world and are not interested in spiritual salvation have many duties, but for one who is interested in spiritual salvation, the only duty is to surrender fully unto Kṛṣṇa (*sarva-dharmān parityajya mām ekaṁ śaraṇaṁ vraja*). Such a person is not interested in material enjoyment.

## TEXTS 11–12

नामधेयानि कुर्वन्ति स्थानानि च नरा भुवि ।
दुर्गेति भद्रकालीति विजया वैष्णवीति च ॥११॥
कुमुदा चण्डिका कृष्णा माधवी कन्यकेति च ।
माया नारायणीशानी शारदेत्यम्बिकेति च ॥१२॥

*nāmadheyāni kurvanti*
*sthānāni ca narā bhuvi*
*durgeti bhadrakālīti*
*vijayā vaiṣṇavīti ca*

*kumudā caṇḍikā kṛṣṇā*
*mādhavī kanyaketi ca*
*māyā nārāyaṇīśānī*
*śāradety ambiketi ca*

*nāmadheyāni*—different names; *kurvanti*—will give; *sthānāni*—in different places; *ca*—also; *narāḥ*—persons interested in material enjoyment; *bhuvi*—on the surface of the globe; *durgā iti*—the name Durgā; *bhadrakālī iti*—the name Bhadrakālī; *vijayā*—the name Vijayā; *vaiṣṇavī iti*—the name Vaiṣṇavī; *ca*—also; *kumudā*—the name Kumudā; *caṇḍikā*—the name Caṇḍikā; *kṛṣṇā*—the name Kṛṣṇā; *mādhavī*—the name Mādhavī; *kanyakā iti*—the name Kanyakā or Kanyā-kumārī; *ca*—also; *māyā*—the name Māyā; *nārāyaṇī*—the name Nārāyaṇī; *īśānī*—the name Īśānī; *śāradā*—the name Śāradā; *iti*—thus; *ambikā*—the name Ambikā; *iti*—also; *ca*—and.

## TRANSLATION

**Lord Kṛṣṇa blessed Māyādevī by saying: In different places on the surface of the earth, people will give you different names, such as Durgā, Bhadrakālī, Vijayā, Vaiṣṇavī, Kumudā, Caṇḍikā, Kṛṣṇā, Mādhavī, Kanyakā, Māyā, Nārāyaṇī, Īśānī, Śāradā and Ambikā.**

## PURPORT

Because Kṛṣṇa and His energy appeared simultaneously, people have generally formed two groups—the *śāktas* and the Vaiṣṇavas—and sometimes there is rivalry between them. Essentially, those who are interested in material enjoyment are *śāktas*, and those interested in spiritual salvation and attaining the spiritual kingdom are Vaiṣṇavas. Because people are generally interested in material enjoyment, they are interested in worshiping Māyādevī, the energy of the Supreme Personality of Godhead. Vaiṣṇavas, however, are *śuddha-śāktas*, or pure *bhaktas*, because the Hare Kṛṣṇa *mahā-mantra* indicates worship of the Supreme Lord's energy, Harā. A Vaiṣṇava prays to the energy of the Lord for the opportunity to serve the Lord along with His spiritual energy. Thus Vaiṣṇavas all worship such Deities as Rādhā-Kṛṣṇa, Sītā-Rāma, Lakṣmī-Nārāyaṇa and Rukmiṇī-Dvārakādhīśa, whereas *durgā-śāktas* worship the material energy under different names.

The names by which Māyādevī is known in different places have been listed by Vallabhācārya as follows. In Vārāṇasī she is known as Durgā, in Avantī she is known as Bhadrakālī, in Orissa she is known as Vijayā, and in Kulahāpura she is known as Vaiṣṇavī or Mahālakṣmī. (The representatives of Mahālakṣmī and Ambikā are present in Bombay.) In the country known as Kāmarūpa she is known as Caṇḍikā, in Northern India as

Śāradā, and in Cape Comorin as Kanyakā. Thus she is distributed according to various names in various places.

Śrīla Vijayadhvaja Tīrthapāda, in his *Pada-ratnāvalī-ṭīkā*, has explained the meanings of the different representations. *Māyā* is known as Durgā because she is approached with great difficulty, as Bhadrā because she is auspicious, and as Kālī because she is deep blue. Because she is the most powerful energy, she is known as Vijayā; because she is one of the different energies of Viṣṇu, she is known as Vaiṣṇavī; and because she enjoys in this material world and gives facilities for material enjoyment, she is known as Kumudā. Because she is very severe to her enemies, the *asuras*, she is known as Caṇḍikā, and because she gives all sorts of material facilities, she is called Kṛṣṇā. In this way the material energy is differently named and situated in different places on the surface of the globe.

## TEXT 13

गर्भसंकर्षणात् तं वै प्राहुः संकर्षणं भुवि ।
रामेति लोकरमणाद् बलभद्रं बलोच्छ्रयात् ॥१३॥

*garbha-saṅkarṣaṇāt taṁ vai*
*prāhuḥ saṅkarṣaṇaṁ bhuvi*
*rāmeti loka-ramaṇād*
*balabhadraṁ balocchrayāt*

*garbha-saṅkarṣaṇāt*—because He will be taken from the womb of Devakī to that of Rohiṇī; *tam*—Him (Rohiṇī-nandana, the son of Rohiṇī); *vai*—indeed; *prāhuḥ*—people will call; *saṅkarṣaṇam*—by the name Saṅkarṣaṇa; *bhuvi*—in the world; *rāma iti*—He will also be called Rāma; *loka-ramaṇāt*—because of His special mercy in enabling people in general to become devotees; *balabhadram*—He will also be called Balabhadra; *bala-ucchrayāt*—because of extensive bodily strength.

## TRANSLATION

**The son of Rohiṇī will also be celebrated as Saṅkarṣaṇa because of being sent from the womb of Devakī to the womb of Rohiṇī. He**

**will be called Rāma because of His ability to please all the inhabitants of Gokula, and He will be known as Balabhadra because of His extensive physical strength.**

## PURPORT

These are some of the reasons why Balarāma is known as Saṅkarṣaṇa, Balarāma or sometimes Rāma. In the *mahā-mantra*—Hare Kṛṣṇa, Hare Kṛṣṇa, Kṛṣṇa Kṛṣṇa, Hare Hare/ Hare Rāma, Hare Rāma, Rāma Rāma, Hare Hare—people sometimes object when Rāma is accepted as Balarāma. But although devotees of Lord Rāma may object, they should know that there is no difference between Balarāma and Lord Rāma. Here *Śrīmad-Bhāgavatam* clearly states that Balarāma is also known as Rāma (*rāmeti*). Therefore, it is not artificial for us to speak of Lord Balarāma as Lord Rāma. Jayadeva Gosvāmī also speaks of three Rāmas: Paraśurāma, Raghupati Rāma and Balarāma. All of them are Rāmas.

## TEXT 14

सन्दिष्टैवं भगवता तथेत्योमिति तद्वचः ।
प्रतिगृह्य परिक्रम्य गां गता तत् तथाकरोत् ॥१४॥

*sandiṣṭaivaṁ bhagavatā*
*tathety om iti tad-vacaḥ*
*pratigṛhya parikramya*
*gāṁ gatā tat tathākarot*

*sandiṣṭā*—having been ordered; *evam*—thus; *bhagavatā*—by the Supreme Personality of Godhead; *tathā iti*—so be it; *oṁ*—affirmation by the mantra *oṁ; iti*—thus; *tat-vacaḥ*—His words; *pratigṛhya*—accepting the order; *parikramya*—after circumambulating Him; *gām*—to the surface of the globe; *gatā*—she immediately went; *tat*—the order, as given by the Supreme Personality of Godhead; *tathā*—just so; *akarot*—executed.

## TRANSLATION

**Thus instructed by the Supreme Personality of Godhead, Yogamāyā immediately agreed. With the Vedic mantra oṁ, she**

**confirmed that she would do what He asked. Thus having accepted the order of the Supreme Personality of Godhead, she circumambulated Him and started for the place on earth known as Nanda-gokula. There she did everything just as she had been told.**

## PURPORT

After receiving the orders of the Supreme Personality of Godhead, Yogamāyā twice confirmed her acceptance by saying, "Yes, sir, I shall do as You order," and then saying *oṁ*. Śrīla Viśvanātha Cakravartī Ṭhākura comments that *oṁ* signifies Vedic confirmation. Thus Yogamāyā very faithfully received the Lord's order as a Vedic injunction. It is a fact that whatever is spoken by the Supreme Personality of Godhead is a Vedic injunction that no one should neglect. In Vedic injunctions there are no mistakes, illusions, cheating or imperfection. Unless one understands the authority of the Vedic version, there is no purpose in quoting *śāstra*. No one should violate the Vedic injunctions. Rather, one should strictly execute the orders given in the *Vedas*. As stated in *Bhagavad-gītā* (16.24):

*tasmāc chāstraṁ pramāṇaṁ te*
*kāryākārya-vyavasthitau*
*jñātvā śāstra-vidhānoktaṁ*
*karma kartum ihārhasi*

"One should understand what is duty and what is not duty by the regulations of the scriptures. Knowing such rules and regulations, one should act so that one may gradually be elevated."

## TEXT 15

गर्भे प्रणीते देवक्या रोहिणीं योगनिद्रया ।
अहो विस्रंसितो गर्भ इति पौरा विचुक्रुशुः ॥१५॥

*garbhe praṇīte devakyā*
*rohiṇīṁ yoga-nidrayā*
*aho visraṁsito garbha*
*iti paurā vicukruśuḥ*

*garbhe*—when the embryo; *praṇīte*—was carried from the womb; *devakyāḥ*—of Devakī; *rohiṇīm*—to the womb of Rohiṇī; *yoga-nidrayā*—by the spiritual energy called Yogamāyā; *aho*—alas; *visraṁsitaḥ*—is lost; *garbhaḥ*—the embryo; *iti*—thus; *paurāḥ*—all the inhabitants of the house; *vicukruśuḥ*—lamented.

## TRANSLATION

**When the child of Devakī was attracted and transferred into the womb of Rohiṇī by Yogamāyā, Devakī seemed to have a miscarriage. Thus all the inhabitants of the palace loudly lamented, "Alas, Devakī has lost her child!"**

## PURPORT

"All the inhabitants of the palace" includes Kaṁsa. When everyone lamented, Kaṁsa joined in compassion, thinking that perhaps because of drugs or some other external means, Devakī had undergone this abortion. The real story of what happened after Yogamāyā attracted the child of Devakī into the womb of Rohiṇī in the seventh month of Rohiṇī's pregnancy is described as follows in the *Hari-vaṁśa.* At midnight, while Rohiṇī was deeply sleeping, she experienced, as if in a dream, that she had undergone a miscarriage. After some time, when she awoke, she saw that this had indeed happened, and she was in great anxiety. But Yogamāyā then informed her, "O auspicious lady, your child is now being replaced. I am attracting a child from the womb of Devakī, and therefore your child will be known as Saṅkarṣaṇa."

The word *yoga-nidrā* is significant. When one is spiritually reconnected through self-realization, one regards his material life as having been like a dream. As stated in *Bhagavad-gītā* (2.69):

*yā niśā sarva-bhūtānāṁ*
*tasyāṁ jāgarti saṁyamī*
*yasyāṁ jāgrati bhūtāni*
*sā niśā paśyato muneḥ*

"What is night for all beings is the time of awakening for the self-controlled; and the time of awakening for all beings is night for the introspective sage." The stage of self-realization is called *yoga-nidrā*. All material activities appear to be a dream when one is spiritually awakened. Thus *yoga-nidrā* may be explained to be Yogamāyā.

## TEXT 16

भगवानपि विश्वात्मा भक्तानामभयङ्करः ।
आविवेशांशभागेन मन आनकदुन्दुभेः ॥१६॥

*bhagavān api viśvātmā*
*bhaktānām abhayaṅkaraḥ*
*āviveśāṁśa-bhāgena*
*mana ānakadundubheḥ*

*bhagavān*—the Supreme Personality of Godhead; *api*—also; *viśvātmā*—the Supersoul of all living entities; *bhaktānām*—of His devotees; *abhayam-karaḥ*—always killing the causes of fear; *āviveśa*—entered; *aṁśa-bhāgena*—with all of His potential opulences (*ṣaḍ-aiśvarya-pūrṇa*); *manaḥ*—in the mind; *ānakadundubheḥ*—of Vasudeva.

## TRANSLATION

**Thus the Supreme Personality of Godhead, who is the Supersoul of all living entities and who vanquishes all the fear of His devotees, entered the mind of Vasudeva in full opulence.**

## PURPORT

The word *viśvātmā* refers to one who is situated in everyone's heart (*īśvaraḥ sarva-bhūtānāṁ hṛd-deśe 'rjuna tiṣṭhati*). Another meaning of *viśvātmā* is "the only lovable object for everyone." Because of forgetfulness of this object, people are suffering in this material world, but if one fortunately revives his old consciousness of loving Kṛṣṇa and connects with Viśvātmā, one becomes perfect. The Lord is described in the Third Canto (3.2.15) as follows: *parāvareśo mahad-aṁśa-yukto hy ajo 'pi jāto bhagavān*. Although unborn, the Lord, the master of everything, appears like a born child by entering the mind of a devotee. The Lord is already there within the mind, and consequently it is not astonishing for Him to appear as if born from a devotee's body. The word *āviveśa* signifies that the Lord appeared within the mind of Vasudeva. There was no need for a discharge of semen. That is the opinion of Śrīpāda Śrīdhara Svāmī and Śrīla Viśvanātha Cakravartī Ṭhākura. In the *Vaiṣṇava-toṣaṇī*, Śrīla Sanātana Gosvāmī says that consciousness was awakened within the mind of Vasudeva. Śrīla Vīrarāghava Ācārya also says that Vasudeva was one of the demigods and that within his mind the Supreme Personality of Godhead appeared as an awakening of consciousness.

## TEXT 17

स बिभ्रत् पौरुषं धाम भ्राजमानो यथा रविः ।
दुरासदोऽतिदुर्धर्षो भूतानां सम्बभूव ह ॥१७॥

*sa bibhrat pauruṣaṁ dhāma*
*bhrājamāno yathā raviḥ*
*durāsado 'tidurdharṣo*
*bhūtānāṁ sambabhūva ha*

*saḥ*—he (Vasudeva); *bibhrat*—carried; *pauruṣam*—pertaining to the Supreme Person; *dhāma*—the spiritual effulgence; *bhrājamānaḥ*—illuminating; *yathā*—as; *raviḥ*—the sunshine; *durāsadaḥ*—very difficult even to look at, difficult to understand by sensory perception; *ati-durdharṣaḥ*—approachable with great difficulty; *bhūtānām*—of all living entities; *sambabhūva*—so he became; *ha*—positively.

## TRANSLATION

**While carrying the form of the Supreme Personality of Godhead within the core of his heart, Vasudeva bore the Lord's transcendentally illuminating effulgence, and thus he became as bright as the sun. He was therefore very difficult to see or approach through sensory perception. Indeed, he was unapproachable and unperceivable even for such formidable men as Kaṁsa, and not only for Kaṁsa but for all living entities.**

## PURPORT

The word *dhāma* is significant. *Dhāma* refers to the place where the Supreme Personality of Godhead resides. In the beginning of *Śrīmad-Bhāgavatam* (1.1.1) it is said, *dhāmnā svena sadā nirasta-kuhakaṁ satyaṁ paraṁ dhīmahi.* In the abode of the Supreme Personality of Godhead, there is no influence of material energy (*dhāmnā svena sadā nirasta-kuhakam*). Any place where the Supreme Personality of Godhead is present by His name, form, qualities or paraphernalia immediately becomes a *dhāma.* For example, we speak of Vṛndāvana-dhāma, Dvārakā-dhāma and Mathurā-dhāma because in these places the name, fame, qualities and paraphernalia of the Supreme Godhead are always present. Similarly, if one is empowered by the Supreme Personality of Godhead to do something, the core of his heart becomes a *dhāma*, and thus he becomes so extraordinarily powerful that not only his enemies but also people in general are astonished to observe his activities. Because he is unapproachable, his enemies are simply struck with wonder, as explained here by the words *durāsado 'tidurdharṣaḥ.*

The words *pauruṣaṁ dhāma* have been explained by various *ācāryas.* Śrī Vīrarāghava Ācārya says that these words refer to the effulgence of the Supreme Personality of Godhead. Vijayadhvaja says that they signify *viṣṇu-tejas*, and Śukadeva says *bhagavat-svarūpa.* The *Vaiṣṇava-toṣaṇī* says that these words indicate the influence of the Supreme Lord's effulgence, and Viśvanātha Cakravartī Ṭhākura says that they signify the appearance of the Supreme Personality of Godhead.

## TEXT 18

ततो जगन्मङ्गलमच्युतांशं
समाहितं शूरसुतेन देवी ।
दधार सर्वात्मकमात्मभूतं
काष्ठा यथानन्दकरं मनस्तः ॥१८॥

*tato jagan-maṅgalam acyutāṁśaṁ*
*samāhitaṁ śūra-sutena devī*
*dadhāra sarvātmakam ātma-bhūtaṁ*
*kāṣṭhā yathānanda-karaṁ manastaḥ*

*tataḥ*—thereafter; *jagat-maṅgalam*—auspiciousness for all living entities in all the universes of the creation; *acyuta-aṁśam*—the Supreme Personality of Godhead, who is never bereft of the six opulences, all of which are present in all His plenary expansions; *samāhitam*—fully transferred; *śūra-sutena*—by Vasudeva, the son of Śūrasena; *devī*—Devakī-devī; *dadhāra*—carried; *sarva-ātmakam*—the Supreme Soul of everyone; *ātma-bhūtam*—the cause of all causes; *kāṣṭhā*—the east; *yathā*—just as; *ānanda-karam*—the blissful (moon); *manastaḥ*—being placed within the mind.

## TRANSLATION

**Thereafter, accompanied by plenary expansions, the fully opulent Supreme Personality of Godhead, who is all-auspicious for the entire universe, was transferred from the mind of Vasudeva to the mind of Devakī. Devakī, having thus been initiated by Vasudeva, became beautiful by carrying Lord Kṛṣṇa, the original consciousness for everyone, the cause of all causes, within the core of her heart, just as the east becomes beautiful by carrying the rising moon.**

## PURPORT

As indicated here by the word *manastaḥ*, the Supreme Personality of Godhead was transferred from the core of Vasudeva's mind or heart to the core of the heart of Devakī. We should note carefully that the Lord was transferred to Devakī not by the ordinary way for a human being, but by *dīkṣā*, initiation. Thus the importance of initiation is mentioned here. Unless one is initiated by the right person, who always carries within his heart the Supreme Personality of Godhead, one cannot acquire the power to carry the Supreme Godhead within the core of one's own heart.

The word *acyutāṁśam* is used because the Supreme Personality of Godhead is *ṣaḍ-aiśvarya-pūrṇa,* full in the opulences of wealth, strength, fame, knowledge, beauty and renunciation. The Supreme Godhead is never separated from His personal opulences. As stated in the *Brahma-saṁhitā* (5.39), *rāmādi-mūrtiṣu kalā-niyamena tiṣṭhan:* the Lord is always situated with all His plenary expansions, such as Rāma, Nṛsiṁha and Varāha. Therefore the word *acyutāṁśam* is specifically used here, signifying that the Lord is always present with His plenary expansions and opulences. There is no need to think of the Lord artificially as *yogīs* do. *Dhyānāvasthita-tad-gatena manasā paśyanti yaṁ yoginaḥ* (*Bhāg.* 12.13.1). *Yogīs* meditate upon the Supreme Person within the mind. For a devotee, however, the Lord is present, and His presence need only be awakened through initiation by a bona fide spiritual master. The Lord did not need to live within the womb of Devakī, for His presence within the core of her heart was sufficient to carry Him. One is here forbidden to think that Kṛṣṇa was begotten by Vasudeva within the womb of Devakī and that she carried the child within her womb.

When Vasudeva was sustaining the form of the Supreme Personality of Godhead within his heart, he appeared just like the glowing sun, whose shining rays are always unbearable and scorching to the common man. The form of the Lord situated in the pure, unalloyed heart of Vasudeva is not different from the original form of Kṛṣṇa. The appearance of the form of Kṛṣṇa anywhere, and specifically within the heart, is called *dhāma. Dhāma* refers not only to Kṛṣṇa's form, but to His name, His form, His quality and His paraphernalia. Everything becomes manifest simultaneously.

Thus the eternal form of the Supreme Personality of Godhead with full potencies was transferred from the mind of Vasudeva to the mind of Devakī, exactly as the setting sun's rays are transferred to the full moon rising in the east.

Kṛṣṇa, the Supreme Personality of Godhead, entered the body of Devakī from the body of Vasudeva. He was beyond the conditions of the ordinary living entity. When Kṛṣṇa is there, it is to be understood that all His plenary expansions, such as Nārāyaṇa, and incarnations like Lord Nṛsiṁha and Varāha, are with Him, and they are not subject to the conditions of material existence. In this way, Devakī became the residence of the Supreme Personality of Godhead, who is one without a second and the cause of all creation. Devakī became the residence of the Absolute Truth, but because she was within the house of Kaṁsa, she looked just like a suppressed fire, or like misused education. When fire is covered by the walls of a pot or is kept in a jug, the illuminating rays of the fire cannot be very much appreciated. Similarly, misused knowledge, which does not benefit the people in general, is not very much appreciated. So Devakī was kept within the prison walls of Kaṁsa's palace, and no one could see her transcendental beauty, which resulted from her conceiving the Supreme Personality of Godhead.

Commenting upon this verse, Śrī Vīrarāghava Ācārya writes, *vasudeva-devakī-jaṭharayor hṛdayayor bhagavataḥ sambandhaḥ*. The Supreme Lord's entrance into the womb of Devakī from the heart of Vasudeva was a heart-to-heart relationship.

## TEXT 19

सा देवकी सर्वजगन्निवास-
निवासभूता नितरां न रेजे ।
भोजेन्द्रगेहेऽग्निशिखेव रुद्धा
सरस्वती ज्ञानखले यथा सती ॥१९॥

*sā devakī sarva-jagan-nivāsa-*
*nivāsa-bhūtā nitarāṁ na reje*
*bhojendra-gehe 'gni-śikheva ruddhā*
*sarasvatī jñāna-khale yathā satī*

*sā devakī*—that Devakīdevī; *sarva-jagat-nivāsa*—of the Supreme Personality of Godhead, the sustainer of all the universes (*mat-sthāni sarva-bhūtāni*); *nivāsa-bhūtā*—the womb of Devakī has now become the residence; *nitarām*—extensively; *na*—not; *reje*—became illuminated; *bhojendra-gehe*—within the limits of the house of Kaṁsa; *agni-śikhā iva*—like the flames of a fire; *ruddhā*—covered; *sarasvatī*—knowledge; *jñāna-khale*—in a person known as *jñāna-khala*, one who possesses knowledge but cannot distribute it; *yathā*—or just as; *satī*—so being.

## TRANSLATION

**Devakī then kept within herself the Supreme Personality of Godhead, the cause of all causes, the foundation of the entire cosmos, but because she was under arrest in the house of Kaṁsa, she was like the flames of a fire covered by the walls of a pot, or like a person who has knowledge but cannot distribute it to the world for the benefit of human society.**

## PURPORT

In this verse the word *jñāna-khala* is most significant. Knowledge is meant for distribution. Although there is already much scientific knowledge, whenever scientists or philosophers awaken to a particular type of knowledge, they try to distribute it throughout the world, for otherwise the knowledge gradually dries up and no one benefits from it. India has the knowledge of *Bhagavad-gītā*, but unfortunately, for some reason or other, this sublime knowledge of the science of God was not distributed throughout the world, although it is meant for all of human society. Therefore Kṛṣṇa Himself appeared as Śrī Caitanya Mahāprabhu and ordered all Indians to take up the cause of distributing the knowledge of *Bhagavad-gītā* throughout the entire world.

*yāre dekha, tāre kaha 'kṛṣṇa'-upadeśa*
*āmāra ājñāya guru hañā tāra' ei deśa*

"Instruct everyone to follow the orders of Lord Śrī Kṛṣṇa as they are given in *Bhagavad-gītā* and *Śrīmad-Bhāgavatam.* In this way become a spiritual master and try to liberate everyone in this land." (Cc. *Madhya* 7.128) Although India has the sublime knowledge of *Bhagavad-gītā,* Indians have not done their proper duty of distributing it. Now, therefore, the Kṛṣṇa consciousness movement has been set up to distribute this knowledge as it is, without distortion. Although previously there were attempts to distribute the knowledge of *Bhagavad-gītā,* these attempts involved distortion and compromise with mundane knowledge. But now the Kṛṣṇa consciousness movement, without mundane compromises, is distributing *Bhagavad-gītā* as it is, and people are deriving the benefits of awakening to Kṛṣṇa consciousness and becoming devotees of Lord Kṛṣṇa. Therefore the proper distribution of knowledge has begun by which not only will the whole world benefit, but India's glory will be magnified in human society. Kaṁsa tried to arrest Kṛṣṇa consciousness within his house (*bhojendra-gehe*), with the result that Kaṁsa, with all his opulences, was later vanquished. Similarly, the real knowledge of *Bhagavad-gītā* was being choked by unscrupulous Indian leaders, with the result that India's culture, and knowledge of the Supreme were being lost. Now, however, because Kṛṣṇa consciousness is spreading, the proper use of *Bhagavad-gītā* is being attempted.

## TEXT 20

तां वीक्ष्य कंसः प्रभयाजितान्तरां
विरोचयन्तीं भवनं शुचिस्मिताम् ।
आहैष मे प्राणहरो हरिर्गुहां
ध्रुवं श्रितो यन्न पुरेयमीदृशी ॥२०॥

*tāṁ vīkṣya kaṁsaḥ prabhayājitāntarāṁ*
*virocayantīṁ bhavanaṁ śuci-smitām*
*āhaiṣa me prāṇa-haro harir guhāṁ*
*dhruvaṁ śrito yan na pureyam īdṛśī*

*tām*—her (Devakī); *vīkṣya*—after seeing; *kaṁsaḥ*—her brother Kaṁsa; *prabhayā*—with the enhancement of her beauty and influence; *ajita-antarām*—because of keeping Ajita, the Supreme Personality of Godhead, Viṣṇu, within herself; *virocayantīm*—illuminating; *bhavanam*—the whole atmosphere of the house; *śuci-smitām*—smiling and brilliant; *āha*—said to himself; *eṣaḥ*—this (Supreme Person); *me*—my; *prāṇa-haraḥ*—who will kill me; *hariḥ*—Lord Viṣṇu; *guhām*—within the womb of Devakī; *dhruvam*—certainly; *śritaḥ*—has taken shelter; *yat*—because; *na*—was not; *purā*—formerly; *iyam*—Devakī; *īdṛśī*—like this.

## TRANSLATION

**Because the Supreme Personality of Godhead was within her womb, Devakī illuminated the entire atmosphere in the place where she was confined. Seeing her jubilant, pure and smiling, Kaṁsa thought, "The Supreme Personality of Godhead, Viṣṇu, who is now within her, will kill me. Devakī has never before looked so brilliant and jubilant."**

## PURPORT

The Lord says in *Bhagavad-gītā* (4.7):

*yadā yadā hi dharmasya*
*glānir bhavati bhārata*

*abhyutthānam adharmasya*
*tadātmānaṁ sṛjāmy aham*

"Whenever and wherever there is a decline in religious practice, O descendant of Bharata, and a predominant rise of irreligion—at that time I descend Myself." In this age, at the present moment, there are inordinate discrepancies in the discharge of human duties. Human life is meant for God realization, but unfortunately the materialistic civilization is stressing only the senses of the body, not understanding the living force within the body. As clearly stated in *Bhagavad-gītā* (*dehino 'smin yathā dehe*), within the body is the body's proprietor, the living force, which is more important. But human society has become so fallen that instead of understanding the living force within the body, people have become busy with external things. This is a discrepancy in human duties. Therefore Kṛṣṇa has taken birth or taken shelter within the womb of the Kṛṣṇa consciousness movement. Men of Kaṁsa's class, therefore, are very much afraid and are busy trying to stop this movement, especially in the Western countries. One politician has remarked that the Kṛṣṇa consciousness movement is spreading like an epidemic and that if not checked immediately, within ten years it may capture governmental power. There is, of course, such potency in the Kṛṣṇa consciousness movement. As stated by authorities (Cc. *Ādi* 17.22), *kali-kāle nāma-rūpe kṛṣṇa-avatāra:* in this age, Kṛṣṇa has appeared in the Hare Kṛṣṇa *mahā-mantra.* The Kṛṣṇa consciousness movement is spreading like wildfire all over the world, and it will go on doing so. Men who are like Kaṁsa are very much afraid of the movement's progress and acceptance by the younger generation, but as Kṛṣṇa could not be killed by Kaṁsa, this movement cannot be checked by men of Kaṁsa's class. The movement will go on increasing more and more, provided the leaders of the movement remain firmly Kṛṣṇa conscious by following the regulative principles and the primary activities of chanting the Hare Kṛṣṇa *mantra* regularly.

## TEXT 21

किमद्य तस्मिन् करणीयमाशु मे
यदर्थतन्त्रो न विहन्ति विक्रमम् ।

स्त्रियाः स्वसुर्गुरुमत्या वधोऽयं
यशः श्रियं हन्त्यनुकालमायुः ॥२१॥

*kim adya tasmin karaṇīyam āśu me*
*yad artha-tantro na vihanti vikramam*
*striyāḥ svasur gurumatyā vadho 'yaṁ*
*yaśaḥ śriyaṁ hanty anukālam āyuḥ*

*kim*—what; *adya*—now, immediately; *tasmin*—in this situation; *karaṇīyam*—is to be done; *āśu*—without delay; *me*—my duty; *yat*—because; *artha-tantraḥ*—the Supreme Personality of Godhead, who is always determined to protect the *sādhus* and kill the *asādhus; na*—does not; *vihanti*—give up; *vikramam*—His prowess; *striyāḥ*—of a woman; *svasuḥ*—of my sister; *guru-matyāḥ*—especially when she is pregnant; *vadhaḥ ayam*—the killing; *yaśaḥ*—fame; *śriyam*—opulence; *hanti*—will vanquish; *anukālam*—forever; *āyuḥ*—and the duration of life.

## TRANSLATION

**Kaṁsa thought: What is my duty now? The Supreme Lord, who knows His purpose [paritrāṇāya sādhūnāṁ vināśāya ca duṣkṛtām], will not give up His prowess. Devakī is a woman, she is my sister, and moreover she is now pregnant. If I kill her, my reputation, opulence and duration of life will certainly be vanquished.**

## PURPORT

According to Vedic principles, a woman, a *brāhmaṇa*, an old man, a child and a cow should never be killed. It appears that Kaṁsa, although a great enemy of the Supreme Personality of Godhead, was aware of the Vedic culture and conscious of the fact that the soul transmigrates from one body to another and that one suffers in the next life according to the *karmas* of this life. Therefore he was afraid of killing Devakī, since she was a woman, she was his sister, and she was pregnant. A *kṣatriya* becomes famous by performing heroic acts. But what would be heroic about killing a woman who, while confined in his custody, was under his shelter? Therefore, he did not want to act drastically by killing Devakī. Kaṁsa's enemy was within Devakī's womb, but killing an enemy in such a nescient state would not be an exhibition of prowess. According to *kṣatriya* rules, an enemy should be fought face to face and with proper weapons. Then if the enemy is killed, the victor becomes famous. Kaṁsa very conscientiously deliberated upon these facts and therefore refrained from killing Devakī, although he was completely confident that his enemy had already appeared within her womb.

## TEXT 22

स एष जीवन् खलु सम्परेतो
वर्तेत योऽत्यन्तनृशंसितेन ।
देहे मृते तं मनुजाः शपन्ति
गन्ता तमोऽन्धं तनुमानिनो ध्रुवम् ॥२२॥

*sa eṣa jīvan khalu sampareto*
*varteta yo 'tyanta-nṛśaṁsitena*
*dehe mṛte taṁ manujāḥ śapanti*
*gantā tamo 'ndhaṁ tanu-mānino dhruvam*

*saḥ*—he; *eṣaḥ*—that jealous person; *jīvan*—while living; *khalu*—even; *samparetaḥ*—is dead; *varteta*—continues to live; *yaḥ*—anyone who; *atyanta*—very much; *nṛśaṁsitena*—by executing cruel activities; *dehe*—when the body; *mṛte*—is finished; *tam*—him; *manujāḥ*—all human beings; *śapanti*—condemn; *gantā*—he will go; *tamaḥ andham*—to hellish life; *tanu-māninaḥ*—of a person in the bodily concept of life; *dhruvam*—without a doubt.

## TRANSLATION

**A person who is very cruel is regarded as dead even while living, for while he is living or after his death, everyone condemns him. And after the death of a person in the bodily concept of life, he is undoubtedly transferred to the hell known as Andhatama.**

## PURPORT

Kaṁsa considered that if he killed his sister, while living he would be condemned by everyone, and after death he would go to the darkest region of hellish life because of his cruelty. It is said that a cruel person like a butcher is advised not to live and not to die. While living, a cruel person creates a hellish condition for his next birth, and therefore he should not live; but he is also advised not to die, because after death he must go to the darkest region of hell. Thus in either circumstance he is condemned. Kaṁsa, therefore, having good sense about the science of the soul's transmigration, deliberately refrained from killing Devakī.

In this verse the words *gantā tamo 'ndhaṁ tanu-mānino dhruvam* are very important and require extensive understanding. Śrīla Jīva Gosvāmī, in his *Vaiṣṇava-toṣaṇī-ṭīkā*, says: *tatra tanu-māninaḥ pāpina iti dehātma-buddhyaiva pāpābhiniveśo bhavati.* One who lives in the bodily concept, thinking, "I am this body," involves himself, by the very nature of this conception, in a life of sinful activities. Anyone living in such a conception is to be considered a candidate for hell.

*adānta-gobhir viśatāṁ tamisraṁ*
*punaḥ punaś carvita-carvaṇānām*
(*Bhāg.* 7.5.30)

One who is in a bodily concept of life has no control over sense gratification. Such a person can do anything sinful to eat, drink, be merry and enjoy a life of sense gratification, not knowing of the soul's transmigration from one body to another. Such a person does whatever he likes, whatever he imagines, and therefore, being subject to the laws of nature, he suffers miserably again and again in different material bodies.

*yāvat kriyās tāvad idaṁ mano vai*
*karmātmakaṁ yena śarīra-bandhaḥ*
(*Bhāg.* 5.5.5)

In the bodily concept of life, a person is *karmānubandha*, or conditioned by *karma*, and as long as the mind is absorbed in *karma*, one must accept a material body. *Śarīra-bandha*, bondage to the material body, is a source of misery (*kleśa-da*).

*na sādhu manye yata ātmano 'yam*
*asann api kleśada āsa dehaḥ*

Although the body is temporary, it always gives one trouble in many ways, but human civilization is now unfortunately based on *tanu-mānī*, the bodily concept of life, by which one thinks, "I belong to this nation," "I belong to this group," "I belong to that group," and so on. Each of us has his own ideas, and we are becoming increasingly involved, individually, socially, communally and nationally, in the complexities of *karmānubandha*, sinful activities. For the maintenance of the body, men are killing so many other bodies and becoming implicated in *karmānubandha*. Therefore Śrīla Jīva Gosvāmī says that *tanu-mānī*, those in the bodily concept of life, are *pāpī*, sinful persons. For such sinful persons, the ultimate destination is the darkest region of hellish life (*gantā tamo 'ndham*). In particular, a person who wants to maintain his body by killing animals is most sinful and cannot understand the value of spiritual life. In *Bhagavad-gītā* (16.19–20) the Lord says:

*tān ahaṁ dviṣataḥ krūrān*
*saṁsāreṣu narādhamān*
*kṣipāmy ajasram aśubhān*
*āsurīṣv eva yoniṣu*

*āsurīṁ yonim āpannā*
*mūḍhā janmani janmani*
*mām aprāpyaiva kaunteya*
*tato yānty adhamāṁ gatim*

"Those who are envious and mischievous, who are the lowest among men, are cast by Me into the ocean of material existence, into various demoniac species of life. Attaining repeated birth among the species of demoniac life, such persons can never approach Me. Gradually they sink down to the most abominable type of existence." A human being is meant to understand the value of human life, which is a boon obtained after many, many births. Therefore one must free oneself from *tanu-mānī*, the bodily concept of life, and realize the Supreme Personality of Godhead.

## TEXT 23

इति घोरतमाद् भावात् सन्निवृत्तः स्वयं प्रभुः ।
आस्ते प्रतीक्षंस्तज्जन्म हरेर्वैरानुबन्धकृत् ॥२३॥

*iti ghoratamād bhāvāt*
*sannivṛttaḥ svayaṁ prabhuḥ*
*āste pratīkṣaṁs taj-janma*
*harer vairānubandha-kṛt*

*iti*—thus (thinking in the above-mentioned way); *ghora-tamāt bhāvāt*—from the most ghastly contemplation of how to kill his sister; *sannivṛttaḥ*—refrained; *svayam*—personally deliberating; *prabhuḥ*—one who was in full knowledge (Kaṁsa); *āste*—remained; *pratīkṣan*—awaiting the moment; *tat-janma*—until the birth of Him; *hareḥ*—of the Supreme Personality of Godhead, Hari; *vaira-anubandha-kṛt*—determined to continue such enmity.

## TRANSLATION

**Śukadeva Gosvāmī said: Deliberating in this way, Kaṁsa, although determined to continue in enmity toward the Supreme Personality of Godhead, refrained from the vicious killing of his sister. He decided to wait until the Lord was born and then do what was needed.**

## TEXT 24

आसीनः संविशंस्तिष्ठन् भुञ्जानः पर्यटन् महीम् ।
चिन्तयानो हृषीकेशमपश्यत् तन्मयं जगत् ॥२४॥

*āsīnaḥ saṁviśaṁs tiṣṭhan*
*bhuñjānaḥ paryaṭan mahīm*
*cintayāno hṛṣīkeśam*
*apaśyat tanmayaṁ jagat*

*āsīnaḥ*—while sitting comfortably in his sitting room or on the throne; *saṁviśan*—or lying on his bed; *tiṣṭhan*—or staying anywhere; *bhuñjānaḥ*—while eating; *paryaṭan*—while walking or moving; *mahīm*—on the ground, going hither and thither; *cintayānaḥ*—always inimically thinking of; *hṛṣīkeśam*—the Supreme Personality of Godhead, the controller of everything; *apaśyat*—observed; *tat-mayam*—consisting of Him (Kṛṣṇa), and nothing more; *jagat*—the entire world.

## TRANSLATION

**While sitting on his throne or in his sitting room, while lying on his bed, or, indeed, while situated anywhere, and while eating, sleeping or walking, Kaṁsa saw only his enemy, the Supreme Lord, Hṛṣīkeśa. In other words, by thinking of his all-pervading enemy, Kaṁsa became unfavorably Kṛṣṇa conscious.**

## PURPORT

Śrīla Rūpa Gosvāmī has described the finest pattern of devotional service as *ānukūlyena kṛṣṇānuśīlanam,* or cultivating Kṛṣṇa consciousness favorably. Kaṁsa, of course, was also Kṛṣṇa conscious, but because he regarded Kṛṣṇa as his enemy, even though he was fully absorbed in Kṛṣṇa consciousness, his Kṛṣṇa consciousness was not favorable for his existence. Kṛṣṇa consciousness, favorably cultivated, makes one completely happy, so much so that a Kṛṣṇa conscious person does not consider *kaivalya-sukham,* or merging into the existence of Kṛṣṇa, to be a great gain. *Kaivalyaṁ narakāyate.* For a Kṛṣṇa conscious person, even merging into the existence of Kṛṣṇa, or Brahman, as impersonalists aspire to do, is uncomfortable. *Kaivalyaṁ narakāyate tridaśa-pūr ākāśa-puṣpāyate. Karmīs* hanker to be promoted to the heavenly planets, but a Kṛṣṇa conscious person considers such promotion a will-o'-the-wisp, good for nothing. *Durdāntendriya-kāla-sarpa-paṭalī protkhāta-daṁṣṭrāyate. Yogīs* try to control their senses and thus become happy, but a Kṛṣṇa conscious person neglects the methods of *yoga.* He is unconcerned with the greatest of enemies, the senses, which are compared to snakes. For a Kṛṣṇa conscious person who is cultivating Kṛṣṇa consciousness favorably, the happiness conceived by the *karmīs, jñānīs* and *yogīs* is treated as less than a fig. Kaṁsa, however, because of cultivating Kṛṣṇa consciousness in a different way—that is, inimically—was uncomfortable in all the affairs of his life; whether sitting, sleeping, walking or eating, he was always in danger. This is the difference between a devotee and a nondevotee. A nondevotee or atheist also cultivates God consciousness—by trying to avoid God in everything. For example, so-called scientists who want to create life by a combination of chemicals regard the external, material elements as supreme. Such scientists do not like the idea that life is part and parcel of the Supreme Lord. As clearly stated in *Bhagavad-gītā* (*mamaivāṁśo jīva-loke jīva-bhūtaḥ*), the living entities do not arise from a combination of material elements, such as earth, water, air and fire, but are separated portions of the Supreme Personality of Godhead. If one can understand the position of the living entity as a separated portion of the Supreme Personality of Godhead, by studying the nature of the living entity one can understand the nature of the Supreme Godhead, since the living entity is a fragmental sample of the Godhead. But because atheists are not interested in God consciousness, they try to be happy by cultivating Kṛṣṇa consciousness in various unfavorable ways.

Although Kaṁsa was always absorbed in thoughts of Hari, the Supreme Personality of Godhead, he was not happy. A devotee, however, whether sitting on a throne or beneath a tree, is always happy. Śrīla Rūpa Gosvāmī resigned from office as a government minister to sit beneath a tree, yet he was happy. *Tyaktvā tūrṇam aśeṣa-maṇḍalapati-śreṇīṁ sadā tucchavat* (*Ṣaḍ-gosvāmy-aṣṭaka* 4). He did not care for his comfortable position as minister; he was happy even beneath a tree in Vṛndāvana, favorably serving the Supreme Personality of Godhead. This is the difference between a devotee and a nondevotee. For a nondevotee, the world is full of problems, whereas for a devotee the entire world is full of happiness.

> *viśvaṁ pūrṇa-sukhāyate vidhi-mahendrādiś ca kīṭāyate*
> *yat-kāruṇya-kaṭākṣa-vaibhavavatāṁ taṁ gauram eva stumaḥ*
> (*Caitanya-candrāmṛta* 95)

This comfortable position of a devotee can be established by the mercy of Lord Caitanya Mahāprabhu. *Yasmin sthito na duḥkhena guruṇāpi vicālyate* (Bg. 6.22). Even when a devotee is superficially put into great difficulty, he is never disturbed.

## TEXT 25

ब्रह्मा भवश्च तत्रैत्य मुनिभिर्नारदादिभिः ।
देवैः सानुचरैः साकं गीर्भिर्वृषणमैडयन् ॥२५॥

*brahmā bhavaś ca tatraitya*
*munibhir nāradādibhiḥ*
*devaiḥ sānucaraiḥ sākaṁ*
*gīrbhir vṛṣaṇam aiḍayan*

*brahmā*—the supreme four-headed demigod; *bhavaḥ ca*—and Lord Śiva; *tatra*—there; *etya*—arriving; *munibhiḥ*—accompanied by great sages; *nārada-ādibhiḥ*—by Nārada and others; *devaiḥ*—and by demigods like Indra, Candra and Varuṇa; *sa-anucaraiḥ*—with their followers; *sākam*—all together; *gīrbhiḥ*—by their transcendental prayers; *vṛṣaṇam*—the Supreme Personality of Godhead, who can bestow blessings upon everyone; *aiḍayan*—pleased.

## TRANSLATION

**Lord Brahmā and Lord Śiva, accompanied by great sages like Nārada, Devala and Vyāsa and by other demigods like Indra, Candra and Varuṇa, invisibly approached the room of Devakī, where they all joined in offering their respectful obeisances and prayers to please the Supreme Personality of Godhead, who can bestow blessings upon everyone.**

## PURPORT

*Dvau bhūta-sargau loke 'smin daiva āsura eva ca* (*Padma Purāṇa*). There are two classes of men—the *daivas* and the *asuras*— and there is a great difference between them. Kaṁsa, being an *asura*, was always planning how to kill the Supreme Personality of Godhead or His mother, Devakī. Thus he was also Kṛṣṇa conscious. But devotees are Kṛṣṇa conscious favorably (*viṣṇu-bhaktaḥ smṛto daivaḥ*). Brahmā is so powerful that he is in charge of creating an entire universe, yet he personally came to receive the Supreme Personality of Godhead. Bhava, Lord Śiva, is always jubilant in chanting the holy name of the Lord. And what to speak of Nārada? *Nārada-muni, bājāya vīṇā, rādhikā-ramaṇa-nāme.* Nārada Muni is always chanting the glories of the Lord, and his engagement is to travel all over the universe and find a devotee or make someone a devotee. Even a hunter was made a devotee by the grace of Nārada. Śrīla Sanātana Gosvāmī, in his *Toṣaṇī*, says that the word *nārada-ādibhiḥ* means that Nārada and the demigods were accompanied by other saintly persons, like Sanaka and Sanātana, all of whom came to congratulate or welcome the Supreme Personality of Godhead. Even though Kaṁsa was planning to kill Devakī, he too awaited the arrival of the Supreme Personality of Godhead (*pratīkṣaṁs taj-janma*).

## TEXT 26

सत्यव्रतं सत्यपरं त्रिसत्यं
सत्यस्य योनिं निहितं च सत्ये ।
सत्यस्य सत्यमृतसत्यनेत्रं
सत्यात्मकं त्वां शरणं प्रपन्नाः ॥२६॥

*satya-vrataṁ satya-paraṁ tri-satyaṁ*
*satyasya yoniṁ nihitaṁ ca satye*
*satyasya satyam ṛta-satya-netraṁ*
*satyātmakaṁ tvāṁ śaraṇaṁ prapannāḥ*

*satya-vratam*—the Personality of Godhead, who never deviates from His vow;* *satya-param*—who is the Absolute Truth (as stated in the beginning of *Śrīmad-Bhāgavatam, satyaṁ paraṁ dhīmahi*); *tri-satyam*—He is always present as the Absolute Truth, before the creation of this cosmic manifestation, during its maintenance, and even after its annihilation; *satyasya*—of all relative truths, which are emanations from the Absolute Truth, Kṛṣṇa; *yonim*—the cause; *nihitam*—entered;† *ca*—and; *satye*—in the factors that create this material world (namely, the five elements—earth, water, fire, air and ether); *satyasya*—of all that is accepted as the truth; *satyam*—the Lord is the original truth; *ṛta-satya-netram*—He is the origin of whatever truth is pleasing (*sunetram*); *satya-ātmakam*—everything pertaining to the Lord is truth (*sac-cid-ānanda:* His body is truth, His knowledge is truth,

---

*The Lord vows: *yadā yadā hi dharmasya glānir bhavati bhārata/ abhyutthānam adharmasya tadātmānaṁ sṛjāmy aham* (Bg. 4.7). To honor this vow, the Lord appeared.

†The Lord enters everything, even the atom: *aṇḍāntara-stha-paramāṇu-cayāntara-stham* (*Brahma-saṁhitā* 5.44). Therefore He is called *antaryāmī*, the inner force.

and His pleasure is truth); *tvām*—unto You, O Lord; *śaraṇam*—offering our full surrender; *prapannāḥ*—we are completely under Your protection.

## TRANSLATION

**The demigods prayed: O Lord, You never deviate from Your vow, which is always perfect because whatever You decide is perfectly correct and cannot be stopped by anyone. Being present in the three phases of cosmic manifestation—creation, maintenance and annihilation—You are the Supreme Truth. Indeed, unless one is completely truthful, one cannot achieve Your favor, which therefore cannot be achieved by hypocrites. You are the active principle, the real truth, in all the ingredients of creation, and therefore you are known as antaryāmī, the inner force. You are equal to everyone, and Your instructions apply for everyone, for all time. You are the beginning of all truth. Therefore, offering our obeisances, we surrender unto You. Kindly give us protection.**

## PURPORT

The demigods or devotees know perfectly well that the Supreme Personality of Godhead is the true substance, whether within this material world or in the spiritual world. *Śrīmad-Bhāgavatam* begins, therefore, with the words *oṁ namo bhagavate vāsudevāya . . . satyaṁ paraṁ dhīmahi.* Vāsudeva, Kṛṣṇa, is the *paraṁ satyam*, the Supreme Truth. The Supreme Truth can be approached or understood by the supreme method, as declared by the Supreme Truth: *bhaktyā mām abhijānāti yāvān yaś cāsmi tattvataḥ* (Bg. 18.55). *Bhakti*, devotional service, is the only way to understand the Absolute Truth. For protection, therefore, the demigods surrender to the Supreme Truth, not to the relative truth. There are persons who worship various demigods, but the Supreme Truth, Kṛṣṇa, declares in *Bhagavad-gītā* (7.23), *antavat tu phalaṁ teṣāṁ tad bhavaty alpa-medhasām:* "Men of small intelligence worship the demigods, and their fruits are limited and temporary." Worship of demigods may be useful for a limited time, but the result is *antavat*, perishable. This material world is impermanent, the demigods are impermanent, and the benedictions derived from the demigods are also impermanent, whereas the living entity is eternal (*nityo nityānāṁ cetanaś cetanānām)*. Every living entity, therefore, must search for eternal happiness, not temporary happiness. The words *satyaṁ paraṁ dhīmahi* indicate that one should search for the Absolute Truth, not the relative truth.

While offering prayers to the Supreme Personality of Godhead, Nṛsiṁhadeva, Prahlāda Mahārāja said:

*bālasya neha śaraṇaṁ pitarau nṛsiṁha*
*nārtasya cāgadam udanvati majjato nauḥ*

Generally it is understood that the protectors for a child are his parents, but this is not actually the fact. The real protector is the Supreme Personality of Godhead.

*taptasya tat-pratividhir ya ihāñjaseṣṭas*
*tāvad vibho tanu-bhṛtāṁ tvad-upekṣitānām*
(*Bhāg.* 7.9.19)

If neglected by the Supreme Personality of Godhead, a child, despite the presence of his parents, will suffer, and a diseased person, despite all medical help, will die. In this material world, where there is a struggle for existence, men have invented many means for protection, but these are useless if the Supreme Personality of Godhead rejects them. Therefore the demigods purposefully say, *satyātmakaṁ tvāṁ śaraṇaṁ prapannāḥ:* "Real protection can be obtained from You, O Lord, and therefore we surrender unto You."

The Lord demands that one surrender unto Him (*sarva-dharmān parityajya mām ekaṁ śaraṇaṁ vraja)*, and He further says:

*sakṛd eva prapanno yas*
*tavāsmīti ca yācate*
*abhayaṁ sarvadā tasmai*
*dadāmy etad vrataṁ mama*

"If one surrenders unto Me sincerely, saying, 'My Lord, from this day I am fully surrendered unto You,' I always give him protection. That is My vow." (*Rāmāyaṇa, Yuddha-kāṇḍa* 18.33) The demigods offered their prayers to the Supreme Personality of Godhead because He had now appeared in the womb of His devotee Devakī to protect all the devotees harassed by Kaṁsa and his lieutenants. Thus the Lord acts as *satya-vrata.* The protection given by the Supreme Personality of Godhead cannot be compared to the protection given by the demigods. It is said that Rāvaṇa was a great devotee of Lord Śiva, but when Lord Rāmacandra went to kill him, Lord Śiva could not give him protection.

Lord Brahmā and Lord Śiva, accompanied by great sages like Nārada and followed by many other demigods, had now invisibly appeared in the house of Kaṁsa. They began to pray for the Supreme Personality of Godhead in select prayers which are very pleasing to the devotees and which award fulfillment of devotional desires. The first words they spoke acclaimed that the Lord is true to His vow. As stated in the *Bhagavad-gītā,* Kṛṣṇa descends upon this material world just to protect the pious and destroy the impious. That is His vow. The demigods could understand that the Lord had taken His residence within the womb of Devakī to fulfill this vow. They were very glad that the Lord was appearing to fulfill His mission, and they addressed Him as *satyaṁ param,* or the Supreme Absolute Truth.

Everyone is searching after the truth. That is the philosophical way of life. The demigods give information that the Supreme Absolute Truth is Kṛṣṇa. One who becomes fully Kṛṣṇa conscious can attain the Absolute Truth. Kṛṣṇa is the Absolute Truth. Relative truth is not truth in all the three phases of eternal time. Time is divided into past, present and future. Kṛṣṇa is Truth always, past, present and future. In the material world, everything is being controlled by supreme time, in the course of past, present and future. But before the creation, Kṛṣṇa was existing, and when there is creation, everything is resting in Kṛṣṇa, and when this creation is finished, Kṛṣṇa will remain. Therefore, He is Absolute Truth in all circumstances. If there is any truth within this material world, it emanates from the Supreme Truth, Kṛṣṇa. If there is any opulence within this material world, the cause of the opulence is Kṛṣṇa. If there is any reputation within this material world, the cause of the reputation is Kṛṣṇa. If there is any strength within this material world, the cause of such strength is Kṛṣṇa. If there is any wisdom and education within this material world, the cause of such wisdom and education is Kṛṣṇa. Therefore Kṛṣṇa is the source of all relative truths.

Devotees, therefore, following in the footsteps of Lord Brahmā, pray, *govindam ādi-puruṣaṁ tam ahaṁ bhajāmi,* worshiping the *ādi-puruṣa,* the supreme truth, Govinda. Everything, everywhere, is performed in terms of three principles, *jñāna-bala-kriyā*—knowledge, strength and activity. In every field, if there is not full knowledge, full strength and full activity, an endeavor is never successful. Therefore, if one wants success in everything, one must be backed by these three principles. In the *Vedas* (*Śvetāśvatara Upaniṣad* 6.8) there is this statement about the Supreme Personality of Godhead:

*na tasya kāryaṁ karaṇaṁ ca vidyate*
*na tat samaś cābhyadhikaś ca dṛśyate*
*parāsya śaktir vividhaiva śrūyate*
*svābhāvikī jñāna-bala-kriyā ca*

The Supreme Personality of Godhead does not need to do anything personally, for He has such potencies that anything He wants done will be done perfectly well through the control of material nature (*svābhāvikī jñāna-bala-kriyā ca*). Similarly, those who are engaged in the service of the Lord are not meant to struggle for existence. The devotees who are fully engaged in spreading the Kṛṣṇa consciousness movement, more than ten thousand men and women all over the world, have no steady or permanent occupation, yet we actually see that they are maintained very opulently. The Lord says in *Bhagavad-gītā* (9.22):

*ananyāś cintayanto māṁ*
*ye janāḥ paryupāsate*
*teṣāṁ nityābhiyuktānāṁ*
*yoga-kṣemaṁ vahāmy aham*

"For those who worship Me with devotion, meditating on My transcendental form, I carry to them what they lack and preserve what they have." The devotees have no anxiety over what will happen next, where they will stay or what they will eat, for everything is maintained and supplied by the Supreme Personality of Godhead, who has promised, *kaunteya pratijānīhi na me bhaktaḥ praṇaśyati:* "O son of Kuntī, declare it boldly that My devotee never perishes." (Bg. 9.31) From all angles of vision, therefore, in all circumstances, if one fully surrenders unto the Supreme Personality of Godhead, there is no question of one's struggling for existence. In this connection, the commentary by Śrīpāda Madhvācārya, who quotes from the *Tantra-bhāgavata*, is very meaningful:

*sac-chadba uttamaṁ brūyād*
*ānandantīti vai vadet*
*yetijñānaṁ samuddiṣṭaṁ*
*pūrṇānanda-dṛśis tataḥ*

. . .

*attṛtvāc ca tadā dānāt*
*satyāttya cocyate vibhuḥ*

Explaining the words *satyasya yonim*, Śrīla Viśvanātha Cakravartī Ṭhākura says that Kṛṣṇa is the *avatārī*, the origin of all incarnations. All incarnations are the Absolute Truth, yet the Supreme Personality of Godhead Kṛṣṇa is the origin of all incarnations. *Dīpārcir eva hi daśāntaram abhyupetya dīpāyate* (*Brahma-saṁhitā* 5.46). There may be many lamps, all equal in power, yet there is a first lamp, a second lamp, a third lamp and so on. Similarly, there are many incarnations, who are compared to lamps, but the first lamp, the original Personality of Godhead, is Kṛṣṇa. *Govindam ādi-puruṣaṁ tam ahaṁ bhajāmi.*

The demigods must offer worship in obedience to the Supreme Personality of Godhead, but one might argue that since the Supreme Godhead was within the womb of Devakī, He was also coming in a material body. Why then should He be worshiped? Why should one make a distinction between an ordinary living entity and the Supreme Personality of Godhead? These questions are answered in the following verses.

## TEXT 27

एकायनोऽसौ द्विफलस्त्रिमूल-
श्चतूरसः पञ्चविधः षडात्मा ।

समप्तत्वगष्टविटपो नवाक्षो
दशच्छदी द्विखगो ह्यादिवृक्षः ॥२७॥

*ekāyano 'sau dvi-phalas tri-mūlaś*
*catū-rasaḥ pañca-vidhaḥ ṣaḍ-ātmā*
*sapta-tvag aṣṭa-viṭapo navākṣo*
*daśa-cchadī dvi-khago hy ādi-vṛkṣaḥ*

*eka-ayanaḥ*—the body of an ordinary living being is fully dependent on the material elements; *asau*—that; *dvi-phalaḥ*—in this body we are subject to material happiness and distress, which result from *karma; tri-mūlaḥ*—having three roots, the three modes of nature (goodness, passion and ignorance), upon which the body is created; *catuḥ-rasaḥ*—four *rasas,* or tastes;* *pañca-vidhaḥ*—consisting of five senses for acquiring knowledge (the eyes, ears, nose, tongue and touch); *ṣaṭ-ātmā*—six circumstances (lamentation, illusion, old age, death, hunger and thirst); *sapta-tvak*—having seven coverings (skin, blood, muscle, fat, bone, marrow and semen); *aṣṭa-viṭapaḥ*—eight branches (the five gross elements—earth, water, fire, air and ether—and also the mind, intelligence and ego); *nava-akṣaḥ*—nine holes; *daśa-chadī*—ten kinds of life air, resembling the leaves of a tree; *dvi-khagaḥ*—two birds (the individual soul and the Supersoul); *hi*—indeed; *ādi-vṛkṣaḥ*—this is the original tree or construction of the material body, whether individual or universal.

## TRANSLATION

**The body [the total body and the individual body are of the same composition] may figuratively be called "the original tree." From this tree, which fully depends on the ground of material nature, come two kinds of fruit—the enjoyment of happiness and the suffering of distress. The cause of the tree, forming its three roots, is association with the three modes of material nature—goodness,**

---

*As the root of a tree extracts water (*rasa*) from the earth, the body tastes *dharma, artha, kāma* and *mokṣa*—religion, economic development, sense gratification and liberation. These are four kinds of *rasa,* or taste.

**passion and ignorance. The fruits of bodily happiness have four tastes—religiosity, economic development, sense gratification and liberation—which are experienced through five senses for acquiring knowledge in the midst of six circumstances: lamentation, illusion, old age, death, hunger and thirst. The seven layers of bark covering the tree are skin, blood, muscle, fat, bone, marrow and semen, and the eight branches of the tree are the five gross and three subtle elements—earth, water, fire, air, ether, mind, intelligence and false ego. The tree of the body has nine hollows—the eyes, the ears, the nostrils, the mouth, the rectum and the genitals—and ten leaves, the ten airs passing through the body. In this tree of the body there are two birds: one is the individual soul, and the other is the Supersoul.**

## PURPORT

This material world is composed of five principal elements—earth, water, fire, air and ether—all of which are emanations from Kṛṣṇa. Although materialistic scientists may accept these five primary elements as the cause of the material manifestation, these elements in their gross and subtle states are produced by Kṛṣṇa, whose marginal potency also produces the living entities working within this material world. The Seventh Chapter of *Bhagavad-gītā* clearly states that the entire cosmic manifestation is a combination of two of Kṛṣṇa's energies—the superior energy and the inferior energy. The living entities are the superior energy, and the inanimate material elements are His inferior energy. In the dormant stage, everything rests in Kṛṣṇa.

Material scientists cannot give such a thorough analysis of the material structure of the body. The analysis of the material scientists concerns itself only with inanimate matter, but this is inadequate because the living entity is completely separate from the material bodily structure. In *Bhagavad-gītā* (7.5) the Lord says:

*apareyam itas tv anyāṁ*
*prakṛtiṁ viddhi me parām*
*jīva-bhūtāṁ mahā-bāho*
*yayedaṁ dhāryate jagat*

"Besides this inferior nature, O mighty-armed Arjuna, there is a superior energy of Mine, which consists of all the living entities who are struggling with material nature and are sustaining the universe." Although the material elements emanate from the Supreme Personality of Godhead, Kṛṣṇa, they are separated elements and are sustained by the living elements.

As indicated by the word *dvi-khagaḥ*, the living elements within the body resemble two birds in a tree. *Kha* means "sky," and *ga* means "one who flies." Thus the word *dvi-khagaḥ* refers to birds. In the tree of the body there are two birds, or two living elements, and they are always different. In *Bhagavad-gītā* (13.3), the Lord says, *kṣetra-jñaṁ cāpi māṁ viddhi sarva-kṣetreṣu bhārata:* "O scion of Bharata, you should understand that I am also the knower in all bodies." The *kṣetra-jña*, the owner of the body, is also called the *khaga*, the living entity. Within the body there are two such *kṣetra-jñas*—the individual soul and the Supersoul. The individual soul is the owner of his individual body, but the Supersoul is present within the bodies of all living entities. Such a thorough analysis and understanding of the bodily structure cannot be obtained anywhere but in the Vedic literature.

When two birds enter a tree, one may foolishly think that the birds become one or merge with the tree, but actually they do not. Rather, each bird keeps its individual identity. Similarly, the individual soul and the Supersoul do not become one, nor do they merge with matter. The living entity lives close to matter, but this does not mean that he merges or mixes with it (*asaṅgo hy ayaṁ puruṣaḥ*), although material scientists mistakenly see the organic and inorganic, or animate and inanimate, to be mixed.

Vedic knowledge has been kept imprisoned or concealed, but every human being needs to understand it in truth. The modern civilization of ignorance is simply engaged in analyzing the body, and thus people come to the erroneous conclusion that the living force within the body is generated under certain material conditions. People have no information of the soul, but this verse gives the perfect explanation that there are two living forces (*dvi-khaga*): the individual soul and the Supersoul. The Supersoul is present in every body (*īśvaraḥ sarva-bhūtānāṁ hṛd-deśe 'rjuna tiṣṭhati*), whereas the individual soul is situated only in his own body (*dehī*) and is transmigrating from one body to another.

## TEXT 28

त्वमेक एवास्य सतः प्रसूति-
स्त्वं सन्निधानं त्वमनुग्रहश्च ।
त्वन्मायया संवृतचेतसस्त्वां
पश्यन्ति नाना न विपश्चितो ये ॥२८॥

*tvam eka evāsya sataḥ prasūtis*
*tvaṁ sannidhānaṁ tvam anugrahaś ca*
*tvan-māyayā saṁvṛta-cetasas tvāṁ*
*paśyanti nānā na vipaścito ye*

*tvam*—You (O Lord); *ekaḥ*—being one without a second, You are everything; *eva*—indeed; *asya sataḥ*—of this cosmic manifestation now visible; *prasūtiḥ*—the original source; *tvam*—Your Lordship; *sannidhānam*—the conservation of all such energy when everything is annihilated; *tvam*—Your Lordship; *anugrahaḥ ca*—and the maintainer; *tvat-māyayā*—by Your illusory, external energy; *saṁvṛta-cetasaḥ*—those whose intelligence is covered by such illusory energy; *tvām*—unto You; *paśyanti*—observe; *nānā*—many varieties; *na*—not; *vipaścitaḥ*—learned scholars or devotees; *ye*—who are.

## TRANSLATION

**The efficient cause of this material world, manifested with its many varieties as the original tree, is You, O Lord. You are also the maintainer of this material world, and after annihilation You are the one in whom everything is conserved. Those who are covered by Your external energy cannot see You behind this manifestation, but theirs is not the vision of learned devotees.**

## PURPORT

Various demigods, beginning from Lord Brahmā, Lord Śiva and even Viṣṇu, are supposed to be the creator, maintainer and annihilator of this material world, but actually they are not. The fact is that everything is the Supreme Personality of Godhead, manifested in varieties of energy. *Ekam evādvitīyaṁ brahma.* There is no second existence. Those who are truly *vipaścit,* learned, are those who have reached the platform of understanding and observing the Supreme Personality of Godhead in any condition of life. *Premāñjana-cchurita-bhakti-vilocanena santaḥ sadaiva hṛdayeṣu vilokayanti* (*Brahma-saṁhitā* 5.38). Learned devotees accept even conditions of distress as representing the presence of the Supreme Lord. When a devotee is in distress, he sees that the Lord has appeared as distress just to relieve or purify the devotee from the contamination of the material world. While one is within this material world, one is in various conditions, and therefore a devotee sees a condition of distress as but another feature of the Lord. *Tat te 'nukampāṁ susamīkṣamāṇaḥ* (*Bhāg.* 10.14.8). A devotee, therefore, regards distress as a great favor of the Lord because he understands that he is being cleansed of contamination. *Teṣām ahaṁ samuddhartā mṛtyu-saṁsāra-sāgarāt* (Bg. 12.7). The appearance of distress is a negative process intended to give the devotee relief from this material world, which is called *mṛtyu-saṁsāra,* or the constant repetition of birth and death. To save a surrendered soul from repeated birth and death, the Lord purifies him of contamination by offering him a little distress. This cannot be understood by a nondevotee, but a devotee can see this because he is *vipaścit,* or learned. A nondevotee, therefore, is perturbed in distress, but a devotee welcomes distress as another feature of the Lord. *Sarvaṁ khalv idaṁ brahma.* A devotee can actually see that there is only the Supreme Personality of Godhead and no second entity. *Ekam evādvitīyam.* There is only the Lord, who presents Himself in different energies.

Persons who are not in real knowledge think that Brahmā is the creator, Viṣṇu the maintainer and Śiva the annihilator and that the different demigods are intended to fulfill diverse purposes. Thus they create diverse purposes and worship various demigods to have these purposes fulfilled (*kāmais tais tair hṛta-jñānāḥ prapadyante 'nya-devatāḥ*). A devotee, however, knows that these various demigods are but different parts of the Supreme Personality of Godhead and that these parts need not be worshiped. As the Lord says in *Bhagavad-gītā* (9.23):

*ye 'py anya-devatā bhaktā*
*yajante śraddhayānvitāḥ*
*te 'pi mām eva kaunteya*
*yajanty avidhi-pūrvakam*

"Whatever a man may sacrifice to other gods, O son of Kuntī, is really meant for Me alone, but it is offered without true understanding." There is no need to worship the demigods, for this is *avidhi*, not in order. Simply by surrendering oneself at the lotus feet of Kṛṣṇa, one can completely discharge one's duties; there is no need to worship various deities or demigods. These various divinities are observed by the *mūḍhas*, fools, who are bewildered by the three modes of material nature (*tribhir guṇamayair bhāvair ebhiḥ sarvam idaṁ jagat*). Such fools cannot understand that the real source of everything is the Supreme Personality of Godhead (*mohitaṁ nābhijānāti mām ebhyaḥ param avyayam*). Not being disturbed by the Lord's various features, one should concentrate upon and worship the Supreme Lord (*mām ekaṁ śaraṇaṁ vraja*). This should be the guiding principle of one's life.

## TEXT 29

बिभर्षि रूपाण्यवबोध आत्मा
क्षेमाय लोकस्य चराचरस्य ।
सत्त्वोपपन्नानि सुखावहानि
सतामभद्राणि मुहुः खलानाम् ॥२९॥

*bibharṣi rūpāṇy avabodha ātmā*
*kṣemāya lokasya carācarasya*
*sattvopapannāni sukhāvahāni*
*satām abhadrāṇi muhuḥ khalānām*

*bibharṣi*—You accept; *rūpāṇi*—varieties of forms, such as Matsya, Kūrma, Varāha, Rāma and Nṛsiṁha; *avabodhaḥ ātmā*—in spite of having different incarnations, You remain the Supreme, full of knowledge; *kṣemāya*—for the benefit of everyone, and especially the devotees; *lokasya*—of all living entities; *cara-acarasya*—moving and nonmoving; *sattva-upapannāni*—all such incarnations are transcendental (*śuddha-sattva*); *sukha-avahāni*—full of transcendental bliss; *satām*—of the devotees; *abhadrāṇi*—all inauspiciousness or annihilation; *muhuḥ*—again and again; *khalānām*—of the nondevotees.

## TRANSLATION

**O Lord, You are always in full knowledge, and to bring all good fortune to all living entities, You appear in different incarnations, all of them transcendental to the material creation. When You appear in these incarnations, You are pleasing to the pious and religious devotees, but for nondevotees You are the annihilator.**

## PURPORT

This verse explains why the Supreme Personality of Godhead appears as an incarnation again and again. The incarnations of the Supreme Personality of Godhead all function differently, but their main purpose is *paritrāṇāya sādhūnāṁ vināśāya ca duṣkṛtām*—to protect the devotees and annihilate the miscreants. Yet even though the *duṣkṛtīs*, or miscreants, are annihilated, this is ultimately good for them.

## TEXT 30

त्वय्यम्बुजाक्षाखिलसत्त्वधाम्नि
समाधिनावेशितचेतसैके ।
त्वत्पादपोतेन महत्कृतेन
कुर्वन्ति गोवत्सपदं भवाब्धिम् ॥३०॥

*tvayy ambujākṣākhila-sattva-dhāmni*
*samādhināveśita-cetasaike*
*tvat-pāda-potena mahat-kṛtena*
*kurvanti govatsa-padaṁ bhavābdhim*

*tvayi*—in You; *ambhuja-akṣa*—O lotus-eyed Lord; *akhila-sattva-dhāmni*—who are the original cause of all existence, from whom everything emanates and in whom all potencies reside; *samādhinā*—by constant meditation and complete absorption (in thoughts of You, the Supreme Personality of Godhead); *āveśita*—fully absorbed, fully engaged; *cetasā*—but by such a mentality; *eke*—the one process of always thinking of Your lotus feet; *tvat-pāda-potena*—by boarding such a boat as Your lotus feet; *mahat-kṛtena*—by that action which is considered the most powerful original existence or which is executed by *mahājanas; kurvanti*—they make; *govatsa-padam*—like the hoofprint of a calf; *bhava-abdhim*—the great ocean of nescience.

## TRANSLATION

**O lotus-eyed Lord, by concentrating one's meditation on Your lotus feet, which are the reservoir of all existence, and by accepting those lotus feet as the boat by which to cross the ocean of nescience, one follows in the footsteps of mahājanas [great saints, sages and devotees]. By this simple process, one can cross the ocean of nescience as easily as one steps over the hoofprint of a calf.**

## PURPORT

The true mission in life is to cross the ocean of nescience, of repeated birth and death. Those in the darkness of ignorance, however, do not know this mission. Instead, being carried away by the waves of material nature (*prakṛteḥ kriyamāṇāni guṇaiḥ karmāṇi sarvaśaḥ*), they are undergoing the tribulations of *mṛtyu-saṁsāra-vartmani*, repeated birth and death. But persons who have achieved knowledge by the association of devotees follow the *mahājanas* (*mahat-kṛtena*). Such a person always concentrates his mind upon the lotus feet of the Lord and executes one or more of the nine varieties of devotional service (*śravaṇaṁ kīrtanaṁ viṣṇoḥ smaraṇaṁ pāda-sevanam*). Simply by this process, one can cross the insurmountable ocean of nescience.

Devotional service is powerful in any form. *Śrī-viṣṇoḥ śravaṇe parīkṣid abhavad vaiyāsakiḥ kīrtane* (*Bhakti-rasāmṛta-sindhu* 1.2.265). According to this verse, Mahārāja Parīkṣit became liberated by fully concentrating his mind on hearing the Lord's holy name, attributes and pastimes. Similarly, Śukadeva Gosvāmī simply glorified the Lord, and by speaking on the subject matters of Kṛṣṇa that constitute the entire *Śrīmad-Bhāgavatam*, he too was liberated. One may also be liberated simply by *sakhya*, friendly behavior with the Lord. Such is the power of devotional service, as we learn from the examples set by the Lord's many pure devotees.

*svayambhūr nāradaḥ śambhuḥ*
*kumāraḥ kapilo manuḥ*
*prahlādo janako bhīṣmo*
*balir vaiyāsakir vayam*
(*Bhāg.* 6.3.20)

We have to follow in the footsteps of such devotees, for by this one easy process one can cross the great ocean of nescience just as one might cross a small hole created by the hoof of a calf.

Here the Lord is described as *ambujākṣa*, or lotus-eyed. By seeing the eyes of the Lord, which are compared to lotus flowers, one becomes so satisfied that one does not want to turn his eyes to anything else. Simply by seeing the transcendental form of the Lord, a devotee is at once fully absorbed in the Lord in his heart. This absorption is called *samādhi. Dhyānāvasthita-tad-gatena manasā paśyanti yaṁ yoginaḥ* (*Bhāg.* 12.13.1). A *yogī* is fully absorbed in thoughts of the Supreme Personality of Godhead, for he has no other business than to think of the Lord always within the heart. It is also said:

*samāśritā ye pada-pallava-plavaṁ*
*mahat-padaṁ puṇya-yaśo murāreḥ*
*bhavāmbudhir vatsa-padaṁ paraṁ padaṁ*
*padaṁ padaṁ yad vipadāṁ na teṣām*

"For one who has accepted the boat of the lotus feet of the Lord, who is the shelter of the cosmic manifestation and is famous as Murāri, the enemy of the demon Mura, the ocean of the material world is like the water contained in a calf's hoofprint. His goal is *paraṁ padam*, or Vaikuṇṭha, the place where there are no material miseries, not the place where there is danger at every step." (*Bhāg.* 10.14.58) This process is recommended here by authorities like Lord Brahmā and Lord Śiva (*svayambhūr nāradaḥ śambhuḥ*), and therefore we must take to this process in order to transcend nescience. This is very easy, but we must follow in the footsteps of great personalities, and then success will be possible.

In regard to the word *mahat-kṛtena*, it is also significant that the process shown by great devotees is not only for them but also for others. If things are made easy, this affords facility for the person who has made them easy and also for others who follow the same principles. The process recommended in this verse for crossing the ocean of nescience is easy not only for the devotee but also for common persons who follow the devotee (*mahājano yena gataḥ sa panthāḥ*).

## TEXT 31

स्वयं समुत्तीर्य सुदुस्तरं द्युमन्
भवार्णवं भीममदभ्रसौहृदाः ।
भवत्पदाम्भोरुहनावमत्र ते
निधाय याताः सदनुग्रहो भवान् ॥३१॥

*svayaṁ samuttīrya sudustaraṁ dyuman*
*bhavārṇavaṁ bhīmam adabhra-sauhṛdāḥ*
*bhavat-padāmbhoruha-nāvam atra te*
*nidhāya yātāḥ sad-anugraho bhavān*

*svayam*—personally; *samuttīrya*—perfectly crossing; *su-dustaram*—which is very difficult to cross; *dyuman*—O Lord, who appear exactly like the sun, illuminating the darkness of this world of ignorance; *bhava-arṇavam*—the ocean of nescience; *bhīmam*—which is extremely fierce; *adabhra-sauhṛdāḥ*—devotees who are incessantly friendly to the fallen souls; *bhavat-pada-ambhoruha*—Your lotus feet; *nāvam*—the boat for crossing; *atra*—in this world; *te*—they (the Vaiṣṇavas); *nidhāya*—leaving behind; *yātāḥ*—on to the ultimate destination, Vaikuṇṭha; *sat-anugrahaḥ*—who are always kind and merciful to the devotees; *bhavān*—You.

## TRANSLATION

**O Lord, who resemble the shining sun, You are always ready to fulfill the desire of Your devotee, and therefore You are known as a desire tree [vāñchā-kalpataru]. When ācāryas completely take shelter under Your lotus feet in order to cross the fierce ocean of nescience, they leave behind on earth the method by which they**

**cross, and because You are very merciful to Your other devotees, You accept this method to help them.**

## PURPORT

This statement reveals how the merciful *ācāryas* and the merciful Supreme Personality of Godhead together help the serious devotee who wants to return home, back to Godhead. Śrī Caitanya Mahāprabhu, in His teachings to Rūpa Gosvāmī, said:

*brahmāṇḍa bhramite kona bhāgyavān jīva*
*guru-kṛṣṇa-prasāde pāya bhakti-latā-bīja*
(Cc. *Madhya* 19.151)

One can achieve the seed of *bhakti-latā,* devotional service, by the mercy of *guru* and Kṛṣṇa. The duty of the *guru* is to find the means, according to the time, the circumstances and the candidate, by which one can be induced to render devotional service, which Kṛṣṇa accepts from a candidate who wants to be successful in going back home, back to Godhead. After wandering throughout the universe, a fortunate person within this material world seeks shelter of such a *guru,* or *ācārya,* who trains the devotee in the suitable ways to render service according to the circumstances so that the Supreme Personality of Godhead will accept the service. This makes it easier for the candidate to reach the ultimate destination. The *ācārya's* duty, therefore, is to find the means by which devotees may render service according to references from *śāstra.* Rūpa Gosvāmī, for example, in order to help subsequent devotees, published such devotional books as *Bhakti-rasāmṛta-sindhu.* Thus it is the duty of the *ācārya* to publish books that will help future candidates take up the method of service and become eligible to return home, back to Godhead, by the mercy of the Lord. In our Kṛṣṇa consciousness movement, this same path is being prescribed and followed. Thus the devotees have been advised to refrain from four sinful activities—illicit sex, intoxication, meat-eating and gambling—and to chant sixteen rounds a day. These are bona fide instructions. Because in the Western countries constant chanting is not possible, one should not artificially imitate Haridāsa Ṭhākura, but should follow this method. Kṛṣṇa will accept a devotee who strictly follows the regulative principles and the method prescribed in the various books and literatures published by the authorities. The *ācārya* gives the suitable method for crossing the ocean of nescience by accepting the boat of the Lord's lotus feet, and if this method is strictly followed, the followers will ultimately reach the destination, by the grace of the Lord. This method is called *ācārya-sampradāya.* It is therefore said, *sampradāya-vihīnā ye mantrās te niṣphalā matāḥ* (*Padma Purāṇa*). The *ācārya-sampradāya* is strictly bona fide. Therefore one must accept the *ācārya-sampradāya;* otherwise one's endeavor will be futile. Śrīla Narottama dāsa Ṭhākura therefore sings:

*tāṅdera caraṇa sevi bhakta sane vāsa*
*janame janame haya, ei abhilāṣa*

One must worship the lotus feet of the *ācārya* and live within the society of devotees. Then one's endeavor to cross over nescience will surely be successful.

## TEXT 32

येऽन्येऽरविन्दाक्ष विमुक्तमानिन-
स्त्वय्यस्तभावादविशुद्धबुद्धयः ।
आरुह्य कृच्छ्रेण परं पदं ततः
पतन्त्यधोऽनादृतयुष्मदङ्घ्रयः ॥३२॥

*ye 'nye 'ravindākṣa vimukta-māninas*
*tvayy asta-bhāvād aviśuddha-buddhayaḥ*
*āruhya kṛcchreṇa paraṁ padaṁ tataḥ*
*patanty adho 'nādṛta-yuṣmad-aṅghrayaḥ*

*ye anye*—anyone, or all others; *aravinda-akṣa*—O lotus-eyed one; *vimukta-māninaḥ*—falsely considering themselves free from the bondage of material contamination; *tvayi*—unto You; *asta-bhāvāt*—speculating in various ways but not knowing or desiring more information of Your lotus feet; *aviśuddha-buddhayaḥ*—whose intelligence is still not purified and who do not know the goal of life; *āruhya*—even though achieving; *kṛcchreṇa*—by undergoing severe austerities, penances and hard labor; *param padam*—the highest position (according to their imagination and speculation); *tataḥ*—from that position; *patanti*—they fall; *adhaḥ*—down into material existence again; *anādṛta*—neglecting devotion to; *yuṣmat*—Your; *aṅghrayaḥ*—lotus feet.

## TRANSLATION

**[Someone may say that aside from devotees, who always seek shelter at the Lord's lotus feet, there are those who are not devotees but who have accepted different processes for attaining salvation. What happens to them? In answer to this question, Lord Brahmā and the other demigods said:] O lotus-eyed Lord, although nondevotees who accept severe austerities and penances to achieve the highest position may think themselves liberated, their intelligence is impure. They fall down from their position of imagined superiority because they have no regard for Your lotus feet.**

## PURPORT

Aside from devotees, there are many others, nondevotees, known as *karmīs, jñānīs* or *yogīs*, philanthropists, altruists, politicians, impersonalists and voidists. There are many varieties of nondevotees who have their respective ways of liberation, but simply because they do not know the shelter of the Lord's lotus feet, although they falsely think that they have been liberated and elevated to the highest position, they fall down. As clearly stated by the Lord Himself in *Bhagavad-gītā* (9.3):

*aśraddadhānāḥ puruṣā*
*dharmasyāsya parantapa*
*aprāpya māṁ nivartante*
*mṛtyu-saṁsāra-vartmani*

"Those who are not faithful on the path of devotional service cannot attain Me, O conqueror of foes, but return to birth and death in this material world." It doesn't matter whether one is a *karmī, jñānī, yogī*, philanthropist, politician or whatever; if one has no love for the lotus feet of the Lord, one falls down. That is the verdict given by Lord Brahmā in this verse.

There are persons who advocate accepting any process and who say that whatever process one accepts will lead to the same goal, but that is refuted in this verse, where such persons are referred to as *vimukta-māninaḥ*, signifying that although they think they have attained the highest perfection, in fact they have not. In the present day, big, big politicians all over the world think that by scheming they can occupy the highest political post, that of president or prime minister, but we actually see that even in this life such big prime ministers, presidents and other politicians, because of being nondevotees, fall down (*patanty adhaḥ*). To become president or prime minister is not easy; one must work very hard (*āruhya kṛcchreṇa*) to achieve the post. And even though one may reach his goal, at any moment one may be kicked down by material nature. In human society there have been many instances in which great, exalted politicians have fallen from government and become lost in historical oblivion. The cause of this is *aviśuddha-buddhayah:* their intelligence is impure. The *śāstra* says, *na te viduḥ svārtha-gatiṁ hi viṣṇum* (*Bhāg.* 7.5.31). One achieves the perfection of life by becoming a devotee of Viṣṇu, but people do not know this. Therefore, as stated in *Bhāgavad-gītā* (12.5), *kleśo 'dhikataras teṣām avyaktāsakta-cetasām.* Persons who do not ultimately accept the Supreme Personality of Godhead and take to devotional service, but who instead are attached to impersonalism and voidism, must undergo great labor to achieve their goals.

*śreyaḥ-sṛtiṁ bhaktim udasya te vibho*
*kliśyanti ye kevála-bodha-labdhaye*
(*Bhāg.* 10.14.4)

To achieve understanding, such persons work very hard and undergo severe austerities, but their hard labor and austerities themselves are their only achievement, for they do not actually achieve the real goal of life.

Dhruva Mahārāja at first wanted to achieve the greatest material kingdom and greater material possessions than his father, but when he was actually favored by the Lord, who appeared before him to give him the benediction he desired, Dhruva Mahārāja refused it, saying, *svāmin kṛtārtho 'smi varaṁ na yāce:* "Now I am fully satisfied. I do not want any material benediction." (*Hari-bhakti-sudhodaya* 7.28) This is the perfection of life. *Yaṁ labdhvā cāparaṁ lābhaṁ manyate nādhikaṁ tataḥ* (Bg. 6.22). If one achieves the shelter of the Lord's lotus feet, one is fully satisfied and does not need to ask for any material benediction.

At night, no one can see a lotus, for lotuses blossom only during the daytime. Therefore the word *aravindākṣa* is significant. One who is not captivated by the lotus eyes or transcendental form of the Supreme Lord is in darkness, exactly like one who cannot see a lotus. One who has not come to the point of seeing the lotus eyes and transcendental form of Śyāmasundara is a failure. *Premāñjana-cchurita-bhakti-vilocanena santaḥ sadaiva hṛdayeṣu vilokayanti.* Those who are attached to the Supreme Personality of Godhead in love always see the Lord's lotus eyes and lotus feet, whereas others cannot see the Lord's beauty and are therefore classified as *anādṛta-yuṣmad-aṅghrayaḥ*, or neglectful of the Lord's personal form. Those who neglect the Lord's form are surely failures on every path in life, but if one develops even a little love for the Supreme Personality of Godhead, one is liberated without difficulty (*svalpam apy asya dharmasya trāyate mahato bhayāt*). Therefore the Supreme Personality of Godhead recommends in *Bhagavad-gītā* (9.34), *man-manā bhava mad-bhakto mad-yājī māṁ namaskuru:* "Simply think of Me, become My devotee, worship Me and offer some slight homage to Me." Simply by this process, one is guaranteed to return home, back to Godhead, and thus attain the highest perfection. The Lord further affirms in *Bhagavad-gītā* (18.54–55):

*brahma-bhūtaḥ prasannātmā*
*na śocati na kāṅkṣati*
*samaḥ sarveṣu bhūteṣu*
*mad-bhaktiṁ labhate parām*

*bhaktyā mām abhijānāti*
*yāvān yaś cāsmi tattvataḥ*
*tato māṁ tattvato jñātvā*
*viśate tad-anantaram*

"One who is thus transcendentally situated at once realizes the Supreme Brahman and becomes fully joyful. He never laments nor desires to have anything; he is equally disposed to every living entity. In that state he attains pure devotional service unto Me. One can understand the Supreme Personality as He is only by devotional service. And when one is in full consciousness of the Supreme Lord by such devotion, he can enter into the kingdom of God."

## TEXT 33

तथा न ते माधव तावकाः क्वचिद्
भ्रश्यन्ति मार्गात्त्वयि बद्धसौहृदाः ।
त्वयाभिगुप्ता विचरन्ति निर्भया
विनायकानीकपमूर्धसु प्रभो ॥३३॥

*tathā na te mādhava tāvakāḥ kvacid*
*bhraśyanti mārgāt tvayi baddha-sauhṛdāḥ*
*tvayābhiguptā vicaranti nirbhayā*
*vināyakānīkapa-mūrdhasu prabho*

*tathā*—like them (the nondevotees); *na*—not; *te*—they (the devotees); *mādhava*—O Lord, husband of the goddess of fortune; *tāvakāḥ*—the followers of the devotional path, the devotees; *kvacit*—in any circumstances; *bhraśyanti*—fall down; *mārgāt*—from the path of devotional service; *tvayi*—unto You; *baddha-sauhṛdāḥ*—because of being fully attached to Your lotus feet; *tvayā*—by You; *abhiguptāḥ*—always protected from all dangers; *vicaranti*—they move; *nirbhayāḥ*—without fear; *vināyaka-anīkapa*—the enemies who maintain paraphernalia to oppose the *bhakti* cult; *mūrdhasu*—on their heads; *prabho*—O Lord.

## TRANSLATION

**O Mādhava, Supreme Personality of Godhead, Lord of the goddess of fortune, if devotees completely in love with You sometimes fall from the path of devotion, they do not fall like nondevotees, for You still protect them. Thus they fearlessly traverse the heads of their opponents and continue to progress in devotional service.**

## PURPORT

Devotees generally do not fall down, but if circumstantially they do, the Lord, because of their strong attachment to Him, gives them protection in all circumstances. Thus even if devotees fall down, they are still strong enough to traverse the heads of their enemies. We have actually seen that our Kṛṣṇa consciousness movement has many opponents, such as the "deprogrammers," who instituted a strong legal case against the devotees. We thought that this case would take a long time to settle, but because the devotees were protected by the Supreme Personality of Godhead, we unexpectedly won the case in one day. Thus a case that was expected to continue for years was settled in a day because of the protection of the Supreme Personality of Godhead, who has promised in *Bhagavad-gītā* (9.31), *kaunteya pratijānīhi na me bhaktaḥ praṇaśyati:* "O son of Kuntī, declare it boldly that My devotee never perishes." In history there are many instances of devotees like Citraketu, Indradyumna and Mahārāja Bharata who circumstantially fell down but were still protected. Mahārāja Bharata, for example, because of his attachment to a deer, thought of the deer at the time of death, and therefore in his next life he became a deer (*yaṁ yaṁ vāpi smaran bhāvaṁ tyajaty ante kalevaram*). Because of protection by the Supreme Personality of Godhead, however, the deer remembered his relationship with the Lord and next took birth in a good brahminical family and performed devotional service (*śucīnāṁ śrīmatāṁ gehe yoga-bhraṣṭo 'bhijāyate*). Similarly, Citraketu fell down and became a demon, Vṛtrāsura, but he too was protected. Thus even if one falls down from the path of *bhakti-yoga*, one is ultimately saved. If a devotee is strongly situated in devotional service, the Supreme Personality of Godhead has promised to protect him (*kaunteya pratijānīhi na me bhaktaḥ praṇaśyati*). But even if a devotee circumstantially falls down, he is protected by Mādhava.

The word Mādhava is significant. *Mā*, mother Lakṣmī, the mother of all opulences, is always with the Supreme Personality of Godhead, and if a devotee is in touch with the Supreme Personality of Godhead, all the opulences of the Lord are ready to help him.

*yatra yogeśvaraḥ kṛṣṇo*
*yatra pārtho dhanur-dharaḥ*

*tatra śrīr vijayo bhūtir*
*dhruvā nītir matir mama*
(Bg. 18.78)

Wherever there is the Supreme Personality of Godhead, Kṛṣṇa, and His devotee Arjuna, Pārtha, there is victory, opulence, extraordinary power and morality. The opulences of a devotee are not a result of *karma-kāṇḍa-vicāra*. A devotee is always protected by all of the Supreme Lord's opulences, of which no one can deprive him (*teṣāṁ nityābhiyuktānāṁ yoga-kṣemaṁ vahāmy aham*). Thus a devotee cannot be defeated by any opponents. A devotee, therefore, should not deviate knowingly from the path of devotion. The adherent devotee is assured all protection from the Supreme Personality of Godhead.

## TEXT 34

सत्त्वं विशुद्धं श्रयते भवान् स्थितौ
शरीरिणां श्रेयउपायनं वपुः ।
वेदक्रियायोगतपःसमाधिभि-
स्तवार्हणं येन जनः समीहते ॥३४॥

*sattvaṁ viśuddhaṁ śrayate bhavān sthitau*
*śarīriṇāṁ śreya-upāyanaṁ vapuḥ*
*veda-kriyā-yoga-tapaḥ-samādhibhis*
*tavārhaṇaṁ yena janaḥ samīhate*

*sattvam*—existence; *viśuddham*—transcendental, beyond the three modes of material nature; *śrayate*—accepts; *bhavān*—Your Lordship; *sthitau*—during the maintenance of this material world; *śarīriṇām*—of all living entities; *śreyaḥ*—of supreme auspiciousness; *upāyanam*—for the benefit; *vapuḥ*—a transcendental form or body; *veda-kriyā*—by ritualistic ceremonies according to the directions of the *Vedas; yoga*—by practice of devotion; *tapaḥ*—by austerities; *samādhibhiḥ*—by becoming absorbed in transcendental existence; *tava*—Your; *arhaṇam*—worship; *yena*—by such activities; *janaḥ*—human society; *samīhate*—offers (its obligation unto You).

## TRANSLATION

**O Lord, during the time of maintenance You manifest several incarnations, all with transcendental bodies, beyond the material modes of nature. When You appear in this way, You bestow all good fortune upon the living entities by teaching them to perform Vedic activities such as ritualistic ceremonies, mystic yoga, austerities, penances, and ultimately samādhi, ecstatic absorption in thoughts of You. Thus You are worshiped by the Vedic principles.**

## PURPORT

As stated in *Bhagavad-gītā* (18.3), *yajña-dāna-tapaḥ-karma na tyājyam:* the Vedic ritualistic ceremonies, charity, austerity and all such prescribed duties are never to be given up. *Yajño dānaṁ tapaś caiva pāvanāni manīṣiṇām* (18.5): even one who is very much advanced in spiritual realization must still execute the Vedic principles. Even in the lowest stage, the *karmīs* are advised to work for the sake of the Lord.

*yajñārthāt karmaṇo 'nyatra*
*loko 'yaṁ karma-bandhanaḥ*

"Work done as a sacrifice for Viṣṇu has to be performed, otherwise work binds one to this material world." (Bg. 3.9) The words *yajñārthāt karmaṇaḥ* indicate that while performing all kinds of duties, one should remember that these duties should be performed to satisfy the Supreme Lord (*sva-karmaṇā tam abhyarcya*). According to Vedic principles, there must be divisions of human society (*cātur-varṇyaṁ mayā sṛṣṭam*). There should be *brāhmaṇas, kṣatriyas, vaiśyas* and *śūdras*, and everyone should learn to worship the Supreme Personality of Godhead (*tam abhyarcya*). This is real human society, and without this system we are left with animal society.

The modern activities of human society are described in *Śrīmad-Bhāgavatam* as the activities of *go-khara*, cows and asses (*sa eva go-kharaḥ*). Everyone is acting in a bodily concept of life involving society, friendship and love for the improvement of economic and political conditions, and thus all activities are enacted in ignorance. The Supreme

Personality therefore comes to teach us how to act according to the Vedic principles. In this age of Kali, the Supreme Personality of Godhead appeared as Śrī Caitanya Mahāprabhu and preached that in this age the Vedic activities cannot be systematically performed because people are so fallen. He gave this recommendation from the *śāstras:*

*harer nāma harer nāma*
*harer nāmaiva kevalam*
*kalau nāsty eva nāsty eva*
*nāsty eva gatir anyathā*

"In this age of quarrel and hypocrisy the only means of deliverance is chanting the holy name of the Lord. There is no other way. There is no other way. There is no other way." The Kṛṣṇa consciousness movement is therefore teaching people all over the world how to chant the Hare Kṛṣṇa *mantra*, and this has proved very much effective in all places at all times. The Supreme Personality of Godhead appears in order to teach us Vedic principles intended for understanding Him (*vedaiś ca sarvair aham eva vedyaḥ*). We should always know that when Kṛṣṇa and Lord Caitanya appeared, They appeared in *śuddha-sattva* bodies. One should not mistake the body of Kṛṣṇa or Caitanya Mahāprabhu to be a material body like ours, for Kṛṣṇa and Caitanya Mahāprabhu appeared as needed for the benefit of the entire human society. Out of causeless mercy, the Lord appears in different ages in His original *śuddha-sattva* transcendental body to elevate human society to the spiritual platform upon which they can truly benefit. Unfortunately, modern politicians and other leaders stress the bodily comforts of life (*yasyātma-buddhiḥ kuṇape tri-dhātuke*) and concentrate on the activities of this ism and that ism, which they describe in different kinds of flowery language. Essentially such activities are the activities of animals (*sa eva go-kharaḥ*). We should learn how to act from *Bhagavad-gītā*, which explains everything for human understanding. Thus we can become happy even in this age of Kali.

## TEXT 35

सत्त्वं न चेद्धातरिदं निजं भवेद्
विज्ञानमज्ञानभिदापमार्जनम् ।

गुणप्रकाशैरनुमीयते भवान्
प्रकाशते यस्य च येन वा गुणः ॥३५॥

*sattvaṁ na ced dhātar idaṁ nijaṁ bhaved*
*vijñānam ajñāna-bhidāpamārjanam*
*guṇa-prakāśair anumīyate bhavān*
*prakāśate yasya ca yena vā guṇaḥ*

*sattvam*—*śuddha-sattva*, transcendental; *na*—not; *cet*—if; *dhātaḥ*—O reservoir of all energies, cause of all causes; *idam*—this; *nijam*—personal, spiritual; *bhavet*—could have been; *vijñānam*—transcendental knowledge; *ajñāna-bhidā*—which drives away the ignorance of the material modes; *apamārjanam*—completely vanquished; *guṇa-prakāśaiḥ*—by the awakening of such transcendental knowledge; *anumīyate*—becomes manifested; *bhavān*—Your Lordship; *prakāśate*—exhibit; *yasya*—whose; *ca*—and; *yena*—by which; *vā*—either; *guṇaḥ*—quality or intelligence.

## TRANSLATION

**O Lord, cause of all causes, if Your transcendental body were not beyond the modes of material nature, one could not understand the difference between matter and transcendence. Only by Your presence can one understand the transcendental nature of Your Lordship, who are the controller of material nature. Your transcendental nature is very difficult to understand unless one is influenced by the presence of Your transcendental form.**

## PURPORT

It is said, *traiguṇya-viṣayā vedā nistraiguṇyo bhavārjuna.* Unless one is situated in transcendence, one cannot understand the transcendental nature of the Lord. As stated in *Śrīmad-Bhāgavatam* (10.14.29):

*athāpi te deva padāmbuja-dvaya-*
*prasāda-leśānugṛhīta eva hi*
*jānāti tattvaṁ bhagavan-mahimno*
*na cānya eko 'pi ciraṁ vicinvan*

Only by the mercy of the Supreme Personality of Godhead can one understand Him. Those who are in the modes of material nature, although speculating for thousands of years, cannot understand Him. The Lord has innumerable forms (*rāmādi-mūrtiṣu kalā-niyamena tiṣṭhan*), and unless these forms, such as Lord Rāmacandra, Nṛsiṁhadeva, Kṛṣṇa and Balarāma, were transcendental, how could they be worshiped by devotees since time immemorial? *Bhaktyā mām abhijānāti yāvān yaś cāsmi tattvataḥ* (Bg. 18.55). Devotees who awaken their transcendental nature in the presence of the Lord and who follow the rules and regulations of devotional service can understand Lord Kṛṣṇa, Lord Rāmacandra and other incarnations, who are not of this material world but who come from the spiritual world for the benefit of people in general. If one does not take to this process, one imagines or manufactures some form of God according to material qualities and can never awaken a real understanding of the Supreme Personality of Godhead. The words *bhaktyā mām abhijānāti yāvān yaś cāsmi tattvataḥ* signify that unless one worships the Lord according to the regulative devotional principles, one cannot awaken the transcendental nature. Deity worship, even in the absence of the Supreme Personality of Godhead, awakens the transcendental nature of the devotee, who thus becomes increasingly attached to the Lord's lotus feet.

The appearance of Kṛṣṇa is the answer to all imaginative iconography of the Supreme Personality of Godhead. Everyone imagines the form of the Supreme Personality of Godhead according to his mode of material nature. In the *Brahma-saṁhitā* it is said that the Lord is the oldest person. Therefore a section of religionists imagine that God must be very old, and therefore they depict a form of the Lord like a very old man. But in the same *Brahma-saṁhitā*, that is contradicted; although He is the oldest of all living entities, He has His eternal form as a fresh youth. The exact words used in this connection in the *Śrīmad-Bhāgavatam* are *vijñānam ajñāna-bhidāpamārjanam. Vijñāna* means transcendental knowledge of the Supreme Personality; *vijñāna* is also experienced knowledge. Transcendental knowledge has to be accepted by the descending process of disciplic succession as Brahmā presents the knowledge of Kṛṣṇa in the *Brahma-saṁhitā. Brahma-saṁhitā* is *vijñāna* as realized by Brahmā's transcendental experience, and in that way he presented the form and the pastimes of Kṛṣṇa in the transcendental abode.

*Ajñāna-bhidā* means "that which can match all kinds of speculation." In ignorance, people are imagining the form of the Lord; sometimes He has no form and sometimes He has form, according to their different imaginations. But the presentation of Kṛṣṇa in the *Brahma-saṁhitā* is *vijñāna*—scientific, experienced knowledge given by Lord Brahmā and accepted by Lord Caitanya. There is no doubt about it. Śrī Kṛṣṇa's form, Śrī Kṛṣṇa's flute, Kṛṣṇa's color—everything is reality. Here it is said that this *vijñānam* is always defeating all kinds of speculative knowledge. "Therefore," the demigods prayed, "without Your appearing as Kṛṣṇa, as You are, neither *ajñāna-bhidā* (the nescience of speculative knowledge) nor *vijñānam* would be realized. *Ajñāna-bhidāpamārjanam*—by Your appearance the speculative knowledge of ignorance will be vanquished, and the real, experienced knowledge of authorities like Lord Brahmā will be established. Men influenced by the three modes of material nature imagine their own God according to the modes of material nature. In this way God is presented in various ways, but Your appearance will establish what the real form of God is."

The highest blunder committed by the impersonalist is to think that when the incarnation of God comes, He accepts a form of matter in the mode of goodness. Actually the form of Kṛṣṇa or Nārāyaṇa is transcendental to any material idea. Even the greatest impersonalist, Śaṅkarācārya, has admitted, *nārāyaṇaḥ paro 'vyaktāt:* the material creation is caused by the *avyakta,* the impersonal manifestation of matter or the nonphenomenal total reservoir of matter, and Kṛṣṇa is transcendental to that material conception. This is expressed in the *Śrīmad-Bhāgavatam* as *śuddha-sattva,* or transcendental. The Lord does not belong to the material mode of goodness, for He is above the position of material goodness. He belongs to the transcendental, eternal status of bliss and knowledge.

"Dear Lord," the demigods prayed, "when You appear in Your different incarnations, You take different names and forms according to different situations. Lord Kṛṣṇa is Your name because You are all-attractive; You are called Śyāmasundara because of Your transcendental beauty. *Śyāma* means blackish, yet they say that You are more beautiful than thousands of cupids. *Kandarpa-koṭi-kamanīya.* Although You appear in a color which is compared to that of a blackish cloud, You are the transcendental Absolute, and therefore Your beauty is many, many times more attractive than the delicate body of Cupid. Sometimes You are called Giridhārī because You lifted the hill known as Govardhana. You are sometimes called Nanda-nandana or Vāsudeva or Devakī-nandana because You appear as the son of Mahārāja Nanda or Devakī or Vasudeva. Impersonalists think that Your many names or forms are according to a particular type of work and quality because they accept You from the position of a material observer.

"Our dear Lord, the way of understanding is not to study Your absolute nature, form and activities by mental speculation. One must engage himself in devotional service; then one can understand Your absolute nature and Your transcendental form, name and quality. Actually, only a person who has a little taste for the service of Your lotus feet can understand Your transcendental nature or form and quality. Others may go on speculating for millions of years, but it is not possible for them to understand even a single part of Your actual position." In other words, the Supreme Personality of Godhead, Kṛṣṇa, cannot be understood by the nondevotees because there is a curtain of *yogamāyā* which covers Kṛṣṇa's actual features. As confirmed in the *Bhagavad-gītā* (7.25), *nāhaṁ prakāśaḥ sarvasya.* The Lord says, "I am not exposed to anyone and everyone." When Kṛṣṇa came, He was actually present on the battlefield of Kurukṣetra, and everyone saw Him. But not everyone could understand that He was the Supreme Personality of Godhead. Still, everyone who died in His presence attained complete liberation from material bondage and was transferred to the spiritual world.

Because foolish *mūḍhas* do not awaken their spiritual nature, they do not understand Kṛṣṇa or Rāma (*avajānanti māṁ mūḍhā mānuṣīṁ tanum āśritam*). Even big academic scholars, not considering the endeavors of the *ācāryas* who have recommended devotional service in many elaborate commentaries and notes, think that Kṛṣṇa is fictitious. This is due to a lack of transcendental knowledge and a failure to awaken Kṛṣṇa consciousness. One should have the common sense to ask why, if Kṛṣṇa or Rāma were fictitious, stalwart scholars like Śrīdhara Svāmī, Rūpa Gosvāmī, Sanātana Gosvāmī, Vīrarāghava, Vijayadhvaja, Vallabhācārya and many other recognized *ācāryas* would have spent so much time to write about Kṛṣṇa in notes and commentaries on *Śrīmad-Bhāgavatam.*

## TEXT 36

न नामरूपे गुणजन्मकर्मभि-
निरूपितव्ये तव तस्य साक्षिणः ।
मनोवचोभ्यामनुमेयवर्त्मनो
देव क्रियायां प्रतियन्त्यथापि हि ॥३६॥

*na nāma-rūpe guṇa-janma-karmabhir*
*nirūpitavye tava tasya sākṣiṇaḥ*
*mano-vacobhyām anumeya-vartmano*
*deva kriyāyāṁ pratiyanty athāpi hi*

*na*—not; *nāma-rūpe*—the name and form; *guṇa*—with attributes; *janma*—appearance; *karmabhiḥ*—activities or pastimes; *nirūpitavye*—are not able to be ascertained; *tava*—Your; *tasya*—of Him; *sākṣiṇaḥ*—who is the direct observer; *manaḥ*—of the mind; *vacobhyām*—words; *anumeya*—hypothesis; *vartmanaḥ*—the path; *deva*—O Lord; *kriyāyām*—in devotional activities; *pratiyanti*—they realize; *atha api*—still; *hi*—indeed (You can be realized by the devotees).

## TRANSLATION

**O Lord, Your transcendental name and form are not ascertained by those who merely speculate on the path of imagination. Your name, form and attributes can be ascertained only through devotional service.**

## PURPORT

As stated in the *Padma Purāṇa:*

*ataḥ śrī-kṛṣṇa-nāmādi*
*na bhaved grāhyam indriyaiḥ*
*sevonmukhe hi jihvādau*
*svayam eva sphuraty adaḥ*

"One cannot understand the transcendental nature of the name, form, quality and pastimes of Śrī Kṛṣṇa through one's materially contaminated senses. Only when one becomes spiritually saturated by transcendental service to the Lord are the transcendental name, form, quality and pastimes of the Lord revealed to him." Since Kṛṣṇa and His transcendental name, form and activities are all of a transcendental nature, ordinary persons or those who are only slightly advanced cannot understand them. Even big scholars who are nondevotees think that Kṛṣṇa is fictitious. Yet although so-called scholars and commentators do not believe that Kṛṣṇa was factually a historical person whose presence on the Battlefield of Kurukṣetra is recorded in the history of *Mahābhārata*, they feel compelled to write commentaries on *Bhagavad-gītā* and other historical records. *Sevonmukhe hi jihvādau svayam eva sphuraty adaḥ:* Kṛṣṇa's transcendental name, form, attributes and activities can be revealed only when one engages in His service in full consciousness. This confirms Kṛṣṇa's own words in *Bhagavad-gītā* (18.55):

*bhaktyā mām abhijānāti*
*yāvān yaś cāsmi tattvataḥ*
*tato māṁ tattvato jñātvā*
*viśate tad-anantaram*

"One can understand the Supreme Personality of Godhead as He is only by devotional service. And when one is in full consciousness of the Supreme Lord by such devotion, he can enter into the kingdom of God." Only by *sevonmukha*, by engaging oneself in the Lord's service, can one realize the name, form and qualities of the Supreme Personality of Godhead.

"O Lord," the demigods say, "the impersonalists, who are nondevotees, cannot understand that Your name is identical with Your form." Since the Lord is absolute, there is no difference between His name and His actual form. In the material world there is a difference between form and name. The mango fruit is different from the name of the mango. One cannot taste the mango fruit simply by chanting, "Mango, mango, mango." But the devotee who knows that there is no difference between the name and the form of the Lord chants Hare Kṛṣṇa, Hare Kṛṣṇa, Kṛṣṇa Kṛṣṇa, Hare Hare/ Hare Rāma, Hare Rāma, Rāma Rāma, Hare Hare, and realizes that he is always in Kṛṣṇa's company.

For persons who are not very advanced in absolute knowledge of the

Supreme, Lord Kṛṣṇa exhibits His transcendental pastimes. They can simply think of the pastimes of the Lord and get the full benefit. Since there is no difference between the transcendental name and form of the Lord, there is no difference between the transcendental pastimes and the form of the Lord. For those who are less intelligent (like women, laborers or the mercantile class), the great sage Vyāsadeva wrote *Mahābhārata.* In the *Mahābhārata,* Kṛṣṇa is present in His different activities. *Mahābhārata* is history, and simply by studying, hearing, and memorizing the transcendental activities of Kṛṣṇa, the less intelligent can also gradually rise to the standard of pure devotees.

The pure devotees, who are always absorbed in the thought of the transcendental lotus feet of Kṛṣṇa and who are always engaged in devotional service in full Kṛṣṇa consciousness, are never to be considered to be in the material world. Śrīla Rūpa Gosvāmī has explained that those who are always engaged in Kṛṣṇa consciousness by body, mind and activities are to be considered liberated even within this body. This is also confirmed in the *Bhagavad-gītā:* those who are engaged in the devotional service of the Lord have already transcended the material position.

Kṛṣṇa appears in order to give a chance to both the devotees and the nondevotees for realization of the ultimate goal of life. The devotees get the direct chance to see Him and worship Him. Those who are not on that platform get the chance to become acquainted with His activities and thus become elevated to the same position.

The *Brahma-saṁhitā* (5.38) says:

*premāñjana-cchurita-bhakti-vilocanena*
*santaḥ sadaiva hṛdayeṣu vilokayanti*
*yaṁ śyāmasundaram acintya-guṇa-svarūpaṁ*
*govindam ādi-puruṣaṁ tam ahaṁ bhajāmi*

Although Kṛṣṇa's transcendental form is presented as black, devotees who are in love with the Supreme Personality of Godhead appreciate the Lord as Śyāmasundara, having a very beautiful blackish form. The Lord's form is so beautiful that the *Brahma-saṁhitā* (5.30) also states:

*veṇuṁ kvaṇantam aravinda-dalāyatākṣaṁ*
*barhāvataṁsam asitāmbuda-sundarāṅgam*

*kandarpa-koṭi-kamanīya-viśeṣa-śobhaṁ*
*govindam ādi-puruṣaṁ tam ahaṁ bhajāmi*

"I worship Govinda, the primeval Lord, who plays on His transcendental flute. His eyes are like lotus flowers, He is decorated with peacock plumes, and His bodily color resembles the color of a fresh black cloud, although His bodily features are more beautiful than millions of Cupids." This beauty of the Supreme Lord can be seen by devotees who are in love with Him, devotees whose eyes are anointed with love of Godhead (*premāñjana-cchurita-bhakti-vilocanena*).

The Lord is also known as Giridhārī or Girivara-dhārī. Because Kṛṣṇa, for the sake of His devotees, lifted Govardhana Hill, the devotees appreciate the Lord's inconceivable strength; but nondevotees, in spite of directly perceiving the Lord's inconceivable strength and power, regard the Lord's activities as fictitious. This is the difference between a devotee and a nondevotee. Nondevotees cannot give any nomenclature for the Supreme Personality of Godhead, yet the Lord is known as Śyāmasundara and Giridhārī. Similarly, the Lord is known as Devakī-nandana and Yaśodā-nandana because He accepted the role of son for mother Devakī and mother Yaśodā, and He is known as Gopāla because He enjoyed the sport of maintaining the cows and calves. Therefore, although He has no mundane name, He is addressed by devotees as Devakī-nandana, Yaśodā-nandana, Gopāla and Śyāmasundara. These are all transcendental names that only devotees can appreciate and nondevotees cannot.

The history of Kṛṣṇa the person has been openly seen by everyone, yet only those who are in love with the Supreme Personality of Godhead can appreciate this history, whereas nondevotees, who have not developed their loving qualities, think that the activities, form and attributes of the Supreme Personality of Godhead are fictitious. Therefore this verse explains, *na nāma-rūpe guṇa-janma-karmabhir nirūpitavye tava tasya sākṣiṇaḥ.* In this connection, Śrīla Viśvanātha Cakravartī Ṭhākura has given the example that persons suffering from jaundice cannot taste the sweetness of sugar candy, although everyone knows that sugar candy is sweet. Similarly, because of the material disease, nondevotees cannot understand the transcendental name, form, attributes and activities of the Supreme Personality of Godhead, although they actually see the

Lord's activities, either through authority or through history. The *Purāṇas* are old, authentic histories, but nondevotees cannot understand them, especially *Śrīmad-Bhāgavatam*, which is the essence of Vedic knowledge. Nondevotees cannot understand even the preliminary study of transcendental knowledge, *Bhagavad-gītā*. They simply speculate and present commentaries with absurd distortions. In conclusion, unless one elevates himself to the transcendental platform by practicing *bhakti-yoga*, one cannot understand the Supreme Personality of Godhead or His name, form, attributes or activities. But if by chance, by the association of devotees, one can actually understand the Lord and His features, one immediately becomes a liberated person. As the Lord says in *Bhagavad-gītā* (4.9):

*janma karma ca me divyam*
*evaṁ yo vetti tattvataḥ*
*tyaktvā dehaṁ punar janma*
*naiti mām eti so 'rjuna*

"One who knows the transcendental nature of My appearance and activities does not, upon leaving the body, take his birth again in this material world, but attains My eternal abode, O Arjuna."

Śrīla Rūpa Gosvāmī has therefore said that by affection and love for the Supreme Personality of Godhead, devotees can express their mind to Him with their words. Others, however, cannot do this, as confirmed in *Bhagavad-gītā* (*bhaktyā mām abhijānāti yāvān yaś cāsmi tattvataḥ*).

## TEXT 37

शृण्वन् गृणन् संस्मरयंश्च चिन्तयन्
नामानि रूपाणि च मङ्गलानि ते ।
क्रियासु यस्त्वच्चरणारविन्दयो-
राविष्टचेता न भवाय कल्पते ॥३७॥

*śṛṇvan gṛṇan saṁsmarayaṁś ca cintayan*
*nāmāni rūpāṇi ca maṅgalāni te*

*kriyāsu yas tvac-caraṇāravindayor*
*āviṣṭa-cetā na bhavāya kalpate*

*śṛṇvan*—constantly hearing about the Lord (*śravaṇaṁ kīrtanaṁ viṣṇoḥ*); *gṛṇan*—chanting or reciting (the holy name of the Lord and His activities); *saṁsmarayan*—remembering (constantly thinking of the Lord's lotus feet and His form); *ca*—and; *cintayan*—contemplating (the transcendental activities of the Lord); *nāmāni*—His transcendental names; *rūpāṇi*—His transcendental forms; *ca*—also; *maṅgalāni*—which are all transcendental and therefore auspicious; *te*—of Your Lordship; *kriyāsu*—in being engaged in the devotional service; *yaḥ*—he who; *tvat-caraṇa-aravindayoḥ*—at Your lotus feet; *āviṣṭa-cetāḥ*—the devotee who is completely absorbed (in such activities); *na*—not; *bhavāya*—for the material platform; *kalpate*—is fit.

## TRANSLATION

**Even while engaged in various activities, devotees whose minds are completely absorbed at Your lotus feet, and who constantly hear, chant, contemplate and cause others to remember Your transcendental names and forms, are always on the transcendental platform, and thus they can understand the Supreme Personality of Godhead.**

## PURPORT

How *bhakti-yoga* can be practiced is explained in this verse. Śrīla Rūpa Gosvāmī has said that anyone who has dedicated his life to the service of the Lord (*īhā yasya harer dāsye*) by his activities, his mind and his words (*karmaṇā manasā girā*) may stay in any condition of life (*nikhilāsv apy avasthāsu*) and yet is no longer actually conditioned but is liberated (*jīvan-muktaḥ sa ucyate*). Even though such a devotee is in a material body, he has nothing to do with this body, for he is transcendentally situated. *Nārāyaṇa-parāḥ sarve na kutaścana bibhyati:* because a devotee is engaged in transcendental activities, he is not afraid of being materially embodied. (*Bhāg.* 6.17.28) Illustrating this liberated position, Śrī Caitanya Mahāprabhu prayed, *mama janmani janmanīśvare bhava-*

*tād bhaktir ahaitukī tvayi:* "All I want is Your causeless devotional service in My life, birth after birth." (*Śikṣāṣṭaka* 4) Even if a devotee, by the supreme will of the Lord, takes birth in this material world, he continues his devotional service. When King Bharata made a mistake and in his next life became a deer, his devotional service did not stop, although some slight chastisement was given to him because of his negligence. Nārada Muni says that even if one falls from the platform of devotional service, he is not lost, whereas nondevotees are lost entirely because they are not engaged in service. *Bhagavad-gītā* (9.14) therefore recommends that one always engage at least in chanting the Hare Kṛṣṇa *mahā-mantra:*

*satataṁ kīrtayanto māṁ*
*yatantaś ca dṛḍha-vratāḥ*
*namasyantaś ca māṁ bhaktyā*
*nitya-yuktā upāsate*

"Always chanting My glories, endeavoring with great determination, bowing down before Me, the great souls perpetually worship Me with devotion."

One should not give up the process of devotional service, which is performed in nine different ways (*śravaṇaṁ kīrtanaṁ viṣṇoḥ smaraṇaṁ pāda-sevanam,* etc.). The most important process is hearing (*śravaṇam*) from the *guru, sādhu* and *śāstra*—the spiritual master, the saintly *ācāryas* and the Vedic literature. *Sādhu-śāstra-guru-vākya, cittete kariyā aikya.* We should not hear the commentaries and explanations of nondevotees, for this is strictly forbidden by Śrīla Sanātana Gosvāmī, who quotes from the *Padma Purāṇa:*

*avaiṣṇava-mukhodgīrṇaṁ*
*pūtaṁ hari-kathāmṛtam*
*śravaṇaṁ naiva kartavyaṁ*
*sarpocchiṣṭaṁ yathā payaḥ*

We should strictly follow this injunction and never try to hear from Māyāvādīs, impersonalists, voidists, politicians or so-called scholars.

Strictly avoiding such inauspicious association, we should simply hear from pure devotees. Śrīla Rūpa Gosvāmī therefore recommends, *śrī-guru-padāśrayaḥ:* one must seek shelter at the lotus feet of a pure devotee who can be one's *guru.* Caitanya Mahāprabhu advises that a *guru* is one who strictly follows the instructions of *Bhagavad-gītā: yare dekha, tare kaha, 'kṛṣṇa'—upadeśa* (Cc. *Madhya* 7.128). A juggler, a magician or one who speaks nonsense as an academic career is not a *guru.* Rather, a *guru* is one who presents *Bhagavad-gītā,* Kṛṣṇa's instructions, as it is. *Śravaṇa* is very important; one must hear from the Vaiṣṇava *sādhu, guru* and *śāstra.*

The word *kriyāsu,* meaning "by manual labor" or "by work," is important in this verse. One should engage in practical service to the Lord. In our Kṛṣṇa consciousness movement, all our activities are concentrated upon distributing Kṛṣṇa literature. This is very important. One may approach any person and induce him to read Kṛṣṇa literature so that in the future he also may become a devotee. Such activities are recommended in this verse. *Kriyāsu yas tvac-caraṇāravindayoḥ.* Such activities will always remind the devotees of the Lord's lotus feet. By fully concentrating on distributing books for Kṛṣṇa, one is fully absorbed in Kṛṣṇa. This is *samādhi.*

## TEXT 38

दिष्टया हरेऽस्या भवतः पदो भुवो
भारोऽपनीतस्तव जन्मनेशितुः ।
दिष्टयाङ्कितां त्वत्पदकैः सुशोभनै-
र्द्रक्ष्याम गां द्यां च तवानुकम्पिताम् ॥३८॥

*diṣṭyā hare 'syā bhavataḥ pado bhuvo*
*bhāro 'panītas tava janmaneśituḥ*
*diṣṭyāṅkitāṁ tvat-padakaiḥ suśobhanair*
*drakṣyāma gāṁ dyāṁ ca tavānukampitām*

*diṣṭyā*—by fortune; *hare*—O Lord; *asyāḥ*—of this (world); *bhavataḥ*—of Your Lordship; *padaḥ*—of the place; *bhuvaḥ*—on this earth; *bhāraḥ*—the burden created by the demons; *apanītaḥ*—now removed; *tava*—of Your Lordship; *janmanā*—by appearance as an incarnation; *īśituḥ*—You, the controller of everything; *diṣṭyā*—and by fortune; *aṅkitām*—marked; *tvat-padakaiḥ*—by Your lotus feet; *su-śobhanaiḥ*—which are transcendentally decorated with the marks of conchshell, disc, lotus and club; *drakṣyāma*—we shall surely observe; *gām*—upon this earth; *dyām ca*—in heaven also; *tava anukampitām*—due to Your causeless mercy upon us.

## TRANSLATION

**O Lord, we are fortunate because the heavy burden of the demons upon this earth is immediately removed by Your appearance. Indeed, we are certainly fortunate, for we shall be able to see upon this earth and in the heavenly planets the marks of lotus, conchshell, club and disc that adorn Your lotus feet.**

## PURPORT

The soles of the Lord's lotus feet are marked with *śaṅkha-cakra-gadā-padma*—conchshell, disc, club and lotus—and also by a flag and a thunderbolt. When Kṛṣṇa walks on this earth or in the heavenly planets, these marks are visible wherever He goes. Vṛndāvana-dhāma is a transcendental place because of Kṛṣṇa's walking on this land frequently. The inhabitants of Vṛndāvana were fortunate to see these marks here and there. When Akrūra went to Vṛndāvana to take Kṛṣṇa and Balarāma away to the festival arranged by Kaṁsa, upon seeing the marks of the Lord's lotus feet on the ground of Vṛndāvana, he fell down and began to groan. These marks are visible to devotees who receive the causeless mercy of the Supreme Personality of Godhead (*tavānukampitām*). The demigods were jubilant not only because the appearance of the Supreme Lord would do away with the burdensome demons, but also because they would be able to see upon the ground the transcendental marks from the soles of the Lord's lotus feet. The *gopīs* always thought of the Lord's lotus feet when He was walking in the pasturing grounds, and, as described in the previous verse, simply by thinking of the Lord's lotus feet, the *gopīs* were fully absorbed in transcendence (*āviṣṭa-cetā na bhavāya kalpate*). Like the *gopīs*, one who is always absorbed in thought of the Lord is beyond the material platform and will not remain in this material world. It is our duty, therefore, always to hear, chant and think about the Lord's lotus feet, as actually done by Vaiṣṇavas who have decided to live in Vṛndāvana always and think of the Lord's lotus feet twenty-four hours a day.

## TEXT 39

न तेऽभवस्येश भवस्य कारणं
विना विनोदं बत तर्कयामहे ।
भवो निरोधः स्थितिरप्यविद्यया
कृता यतस्त्वय्यभयाश्रयात्मनि ॥३९॥

*na te 'bhavasyeśa bhavasya kāraṇaṁ*
*vinā vinodaṁ bata tarkayāmahe*
*bhavo nirodhaḥ sthitir apy avidyayā*
*kṛtā yatas tvayy abhayāśrayātmani*

*na*—not; *te*—of Your Lordship; *abhavasya*—of whom there is no birth, death or maintenance as for an ordinary being; *īśa*—O Supreme Lord; *bhavasya*—of Your appearance, Your birth; *kāraṇam*—the cause; *vinā*—without; *vinodam*—the pastimes (despite what is said, You are not forced to come to this world by any cause); *bata*—however; *tarkayāmahe*—we cannot argue (but must simply understand that these are Your pastimes); *bhavaḥ*—birth; *nirodhaḥ*—death; *sthitiḥ*—maintenance; *api*—also; *avidyayā*—by the external, illusory energy; *kṛtāḥ*—done; *yataḥ*—because; *tvayi*—unto You; *abhaya-āśraya*—O fearless shelter of all; *ātmani*—of the ordinary living entity.

## TRANSLATION

**O Supreme Lord, You are not an ordinary living entity appearing in this material world as a result of fruitive activities. Therefore Your appearance or birth in this world has no other cause than Your pleasure potency. Similarly, the living entities, who are part of You, have no cause for miseries like birth, death**

**and old age, except when these living entities are conducted by Your external energy.**

## PURPORT

As stated in *Bhagavad-gītā* (15.7), *mamaivaṁśo jīva-loke jīva-bhūtaḥ sanātanaḥ:* the living entities are parts and parcels of the Supreme Lord, and thus they are qualitatively one with the Lord. We can understand that when the Supreme Lord appears or disappears as an incarnation, there is no other cause than His pleasure potency. We cannot force the Supreme Personality of Godhead to appear. As He says in *Bhagavad-gītā* (4.7):

*yadā yadā hi dharmasya*
*glānir bhavati bhārata*
*abhyutthānam adharmasya*
*tadātmānaṁ sṛjāmy aham*

"Whenever and wherever there is a decline in religious practice, O descendant of Bharata, and a predominant rise of irreligion—at that time I descend Myself." When there is a need to diminish a burden created by the demons, the Supreme Godhead can do it in many ways because He has multifarious energies. There is no need for Him to come as an incarnation, since He is not forced to do anything like ordinary living entities. The living entities come to this material world in the spirit of enjoyment, but because they want to enjoy without Kṛṣṇa (*kṛṣṇa-bahirmukha haiyā bhoja-vāñchā kare*), they suffer birth, death, old age and disease under the control of the illusory energy. When the Supreme Personality of Godhead appears, however, no such causes are involved; His descent is an act of His pleasure potency. We should always remember this distinction between the Lord and the ordinary living entity and not uselessly argue that the Lord cannot come. There are philosophers who do not believe in the Lord's incarnation and who ask, "Why should the Supreme Lord come?" But the answer is, "Why should He not come? Why should He be controlled by the desire of the living entity?" The Lord is free to do whatever He likes. Therefore this verse says, *vinā vinodaṁ bata tarkayāmahe.* It is only for His pleasure that He comes although He does not need to come.

When the living entities come to this world for material enjoyment, they are entangled in *karma* and *karma-phala* by the Lord's illusory energy. But if one seeks shelter at the Lord's lotus feet, one is again situated in his original, liberated state. As stated here, *kṛtā yatas tvayy abhayāśrayātmani:* one who seeks shelter at the lotus feet of the Lord is always fearless. Because we are dependent on the Supreme Personality of Godhead, we should give up the idea that without Kṛṣṇa we can enjoy freedom in this material world. This idea is the reason we have become entangled. Now it is our duty to seek shelter again at the Lord's lotus feet. This shelter is described as *abhaya,* or fearless. Since Kṛṣṇa is not subject to birth, death, old age or disease, and since we are part and parcel of Kṛṣṇa, we also are not subject to birth, death, old age and disease, but we have become subject to these illusory problems because of our forgetfulness of Kṛṣṇa and our position as His eternal servants (*jīvera 'svarūpa' haya—kṛṣṇera 'nitya-dāsa'*). Therefore, if we practice devotional service by always thinking of the Lord, always glorifying Him and always chanting about Him, as described in text 37 (*śṛṇvan gṛṇan saṁsmarayaṁś ca cintayan*), we will be reinstated in our original, constitutional position and thus be saved. The demigods, therefore, encouraged Devakī not to fear Kaṁsa, but to think of the Supreme Personality of Godhead, who was already within her womb.

## TEXT 40

मत्स्याश्वकच्छपनृसिंहवराहहंस-
राजन्यविप्रविबुधेषु कृतावतारः ।
त्वं पासि नस्त्रिभुवनं च यथाधुनेश
भारं भुवो हर यदूत्तम वन्दनं ते ॥४०॥

*matsyāśva-kacchapa-nṛsiṁha-varāha-haṁsa-*
*rājanya-vipra-vibudheṣu kṛtāvatāraḥ*
*tvaṁ pāsi nas tri-bhuvanaṁ ca yathādhuneśa*
*bhāraṁ bhuvo hara yadūttama vandanaṁ te*

*matsya*—the fish incarnation; *aśva*—the horse incarnation; *kacchapa*—the tortoise incarnation; *nṛsiṁha*—the Narasiṁha incarnation;

*varāha*—the Varāha incarnation; *haṁsa*—the swan incarnation; *rājanya*—incarnations as Lord Rāmacandra and other *kṣatriyas; vipra*—incarnations as *brāhmaṇas* like Vāmanadeva; *vibudheṣu*—among the demigods; *kṛta-avatāraḥ*—appeared as incarnations; *tvam*—Your Lordship; *pāsi*—please save; *naḥ*—us; *tri-bhuvanam ca*—and the three worlds; *yathā*—as well as; *adhunā*—now; *īśa*—O Supreme Lord; *bhāram*—burden; *bhuvaḥ*—of the earth; *hara*—please diminish; *yadu-uttama*—O Lord Kṛṣṇa, best of the Yadus; *vandanam te*—we offer our prayers unto You.

## TRANSLATION

**O supreme controller, Your Lordship previously accepted incarnations as a fish, a horse, a tortoise, Narasiṁhadeva, a boar, a swan, Lord Rāmacandra, Paraśurāma and, among the demigods, Vāmanadeva, to protect the entire world by Your mercy. Now please protect us again by Your mercy by diminishing the disturbances in this world. O Kṛṣṇa, best of the Yadus, we respectfully offer our obeisances unto You.**

## PURPORT

In every incarnation, the Supreme Personality of Godhead has a particular mission to execute, and this was true in His appearance as the son of Devakī in the family of the Yadus. Thus all the demigods offered their prayers to the Lord, bowing down before Him, and requested the Lord to do the needful. We cannot order the Supreme Personality of Godhead to do anything for us. We can simply offer Him our obeisances, as advised in *Bhagavad-gītā* (*man-manā bhava mad-bhakto mad-yājī māṁ namaskuru*), and pray to Him for annihilation of dangers.

## TEXT 41

दिष्ट्याम्ब ते कुक्षिगतः परः पुमा-
नंशेन साक्षाद् भगवान् भवाय नः ।
माभूद् भयं भोजपतेर्मुमूर्षो-
र्गोप्ता यदूनां भविता तवात्मजः ॥४१॥

*diṣṭyāmba te kukṣi-gataḥ paraḥ pumān*
*aṁśena sākṣād bhagavān bhavāya naḥ*
*mābhūd bhayaṁ bhoja-pater mumūrṣor*
*goptā yadūnāṁ bhavitā tavātmajaḥ*

*diṣṭyā*—by fortune; *amba*—O mother; *te*—your; *kukṣi-gataḥ*—in the womb; *paraḥ*—the Supreme; *pumān*—Personality of Godhead; *aṁśena*—with all His energies, His parts and parcels; *sākṣāt*—directly; *bhagavān*—the Supreme Personality of Godhead; *bhavāya*—for the auspiciousness; *naḥ*—of all of us; *mā abhūt*—never be; *bhayam*—fearful; *bhoja-pateḥ*—from Kaṁsa, King of the Bhoja dynasty; *mumūrṣoḥ*—who has decided to be killed by the Lord; *goptā*—the protector; *yadūnām*—of the Yadu dynasty; *bhavitā*—will become; *tava ātmajaḥ*—your son.

## TRANSLATION

**O mother Devakī, by your good fortune and ours, the Supreme Personality of Godhead Himself, with all His plenary portions, such as Baladeva, is now within your womb. Therefore you need not fear Kaṁsa, who has decided to be killed by the Lord. Your eternal son, Kṛṣṇa, will be the protector of the entire Yadu dynasty.**

## PURPORT

The words *paraḥ pumān aṁśena* signify that Kṛṣṇa is the original Supreme Personality of Godhead. This is the verdict of the *śāstra* (*kṛṣṇas tu bhagavān svayam*). Thus the demigods assured Devakī, "Your son is the Supreme Personality of Godhead, and He is appearing with Baladeva, His plenary portion. He will give you all protection and kill Kaṁsa, who has decided to continue his enmity toward the Lord and thus be killed by Him."

## TEXT 42

श्रीशुक उवाच
इत्यभिष्टूय पुरुषं यद्रूपमनिदं यथा ।
ब्रह्मेशानौ पुरोधाय देवाः प्रतिययुर्दिवम् ॥४२॥

*śrī-śuka uvāca*
*ity abhiṣṭūya puruṣaṁ*
*yad-rūpam anidaṁ yathā*
*brahmeśānau purodhāya*
*devāḥ pratiyayur divam*

*śrī-śukaḥ uvāca*—Śrī Śukadeva Gosvāmī said; *iti*—in this way; *abhiṣṭūya*—offering prayers; *puruṣam*—unto the Supreme Personality; *yat-rūpam*—whose form; *anidam*—transcendental; *yathā*—as; *brahma*—Lord Brahmā; *īśānau*—and Lord Śiva; *purodhāya*—keeping them in front; *devāḥ*—all the demigods; *pratiyayuḥ*—returned; *divam*—to their heavenly homes.

## TRANSLATION

**After thus offering prayers to the Supreme Personality of Godhead, Lord Viṣṇu, the Transcendence, all the demigods, with Lord Brahmā and Lord Śiva before them, returned to their homes in the heavenly planets.**

## PURPORT

It is said:

*adyāpiha caitanya e saba līlā kare*
*yāṅ'ra bhāgye thāke, se dekhaye nirantare*
(*Caitanya-bhāgavata, Madhya* 23.513)

The incarnations of the Supreme Personality of Godhead appear continuously, like the waves of a river or an ocean. There is no limit to the Lord's incarnations, but they can be perceived only by devotees who are fortunate. The *devatās*, the demigods, fortunately understood the incarnation of the Supreme Personality of Godhead, and thus they offered their prayers. Then Lord Śiva and Lord Brahmā led the demigods in returning to their homes.

The word *kukṣi-gataḥ*, meaning "within the womb of Devakī," has been discussed by Śrī Jīva Gosvāmī in his *Krama-sandarbha* commentary. Since it was said at first that Kṛṣṇa was present within the heart of Vasudeva and was transferred to the heart of Devakī, Śrī Jīva Gosvāmī writes, how is it that Kṛṣṇa was now in the womb? He replies that there is no contradiction. From the heart the Lord can go to the womb, or from the womb He can go to the heart. Indeed, He can go or stay anywhere. As confirmed in the *Brahma-saṁhitā* (5.35), *aṇḍāntara-stha-paramāṇu-cayāntara-sthaṁ govindam ādi-puruṣaṁ tam ahaṁ bhajāmi.* The Lord can stay wherever He likes. Devakī, therefore, in accordance with the desire of her former life, now had the opportunity to seek the benediction of having the Supreme Personality of Godhead as her son, Devakī-nandana.

*Thus end the Bhaktivedanta purports of the Tenth Canto, Second Chapter, of the* Śrīmad-Bhāgavatam, *entitled "Prayers by the Demigods for Lord Kṛṣṇa in the Womb."*

CHAPTER THREE

# The Birth of Lord Kṛṣṇa

As described in this chapter, the Supreme Personality of Godhead, Kṛṣṇa, Hari in His original form, appeared as Viṣṇu so that His father and mother could understand that their son was the Supreme Personality of Godhead. Because they were afraid of Kaṁsa, when the Lord appeared as an ordinary child they took Him to Gokula, the home of Nanda Mahārāja.

Mother Devakī, being fully transcendental, *sac-cid-ānanda,* does not belong to this material world. Thus the Supreme Personality of Godhead appeared with four hands, as if born from her womb. Upon seeing the Lord in that Viṣṇu form, Vasudeva was struck with wonder, and in transcendental happiness he and Devakī mentally gave ten thousand cows in charity to the *brāhmaṇas.* Vasudeva then offered prayers to the Lord, addressing Him as the Supreme Person, Parabrahman, the Supersoul, who is beyond duality and who is internally and externally all-pervading. The Lord, the cause of all causes, is beyond material existence, although He is the creator of this material world. When He enters this world as Paramātmā, He is all-pervading (*aṇḍāntara-stha-paramāṇu-cayāntara-stham*), yet He is transcendentally situated. For the creation, maintenance and annihilation of this material world, the Lord appears as the *guṇa-avatāras*—Brahmā, Viṣṇu and Maheśvara. Thus Vasudeva offered prayers full of meaning to the Supreme Personality of Godhead. Devakī followed her husband by offering prayers describing the transcendental nature of the Lord. Fearing Kaṁsa and desiring that the Lord not be understood by atheistic and materialistic nondevotees, she prayed that the Lord withdraw His transcendental four-armed form and appear like an ordinary child with two hands.

The Lord reminded Vasudeva and Devakī of two other incarnations in which He had appeared as their son. He had appeared as Pṛśnigarbha and Vāmanadeva, and now this was the third time He was appearing as the son of Devakī to fulfill their desire. The Lord then decided to leave the residence of Vasudeva and Devakī, in the prison house of Kaṁsa, and at this very time, Yogamāyā took birth as the daughter of Yaśodā. By the arrangement of Yogamāyā, Vasudeva was able to leave the prison house and save the child from the hands of Kaṁsa. When Vasudeva brought Kṛṣṇa to the house of Nanda Mahārāja, he saw that by Yogamāyā's arrangement, Yaśodā, as well as everyone else, was deeply asleep. Thus he exchanged the babies, taking Yogamāyā from Yaśodā's lap and placing Kṛṣṇa there instead. Then Vasudeva returned to his own place, having taken Yogamāyā as his daughter. He placed Yogamāyā on Devakī's bed and prepared to be a prisoner as before. In Gokula, Yaśodā could not understand whether she had given birth to a male or female child.

## TEXTS 1–5

श्रीशुक उवाच

अथ सर्वगुणोपेतः कालः परमशोभनः ।
यर्ह्येवाजनजन्मर्क्षं शान्तर्क्षग्रहतारकम् ॥ १ ॥
दिशः प्रसेदुर्गगनं निर्मलोडुगणोदयम् ।
मही मङ्गलभूयिष्ठपुरग्रामव्रजाकरा ॥ २ ॥
नद्यः प्रसन्नसलिला ह्रदा जलरुहश्रियः ।
द्विजालिकुलसंनादस्तवका वनराजयः ॥ ३ ॥
ववौ वायुः सुखस्पर्शः पुण्यगन्धवहः शुचिः ।
अग्नयश्च द्विजातीनां शान्तास्तत्र समिन्धत ॥ ४ ॥
मनांस्यासन् प्रसन्नानि साधूनामसुरद्रुहाम् ।
जायमानेऽजने तस्मिन् नेदुर्दुन्दुभयः समम् ॥ ५ ॥

*śrī-śuka uvāca*
*atha sarva-guṇopetaḥ*
*kālaḥ parama-śobhanaḥ*
*yarhy evājana-janmarkṣaṁ*
*śāntarkṣa-graha-tārakam*

*diśaḥ prasedur gaganaṁ*
*nirmaloḍu-gaṇodayam*

*mahī maṅgala-bhūyiṣṭha-*
*pura-grāma-vrajākarā*

*nadyaḥ prasanna-salilā*
*hradā jalaruha-śriyaḥ*
*dvijāli-kula-sannāda-*
*stavakā vana-rājayaḥ*

*vavau vāyuḥ sukha-sparśaḥ*
*puṇya-gandhavahaḥ śuciḥ*
*agnayaś ca dvijātīnāṁ*
*śāntās tatra samindhata*

*manāṁsy āsan prasannāni*
*sādhūnām asura-druhām*
*jāyamāne 'jane tasmin*
*nedur dundubhayaḥ samam*

*śrī-śukaḥ uvāca*—Śrī Śukadeva Gosvāmī said; *atha*—on the occasion of the Lord's appearance; *sarva*—all around; *guṇa-upetaḥ*—endowed with material attributes or facilities; *kālaḥ*—a favorable time; *parama-śobhanaḥ*—all-auspicious and very favorable from all points of view; *yarhi*—when; *eva*—certainly; *ajana-janma-ṛkṣam*—the constellation of stars known as Rohiṇī; *śānta-ṛkṣa*—none of the constellations were fierce (all of them were peaceful); *graha-tārakam*—and the planets and stars like Aśvinī; *diśaḥ*—all directions; *praseduḥ*—appeared very auspicious and peaceful; *gaganam*—all of outer space or the sky; *nirmala-uḍu-gaṇa-udayam*—in which all the auspicious stars were visible (in the upper strata of the universe); *mahī*—the earth; *maṅgala-bhūyiṣṭha-pura-grāma-vraja-ākarāḥ*—whose many cities, towns, pasturing grounds and mines became auspicious and very neat and clean; *nadyaḥ*—the rivers; *prasanna-salilāḥ*—the waters became clear; *hradāḥ*—the lakes or large reservoirs of water; *jalaruha-śriyaḥ*—appeared very beautiful because of blooming lotuses all around; *dvija-ali-kula-sannāda-stavakāḥ*—the birds, especially the cuckoos, and swarms of bees began to chant in sweet voices, as if praying to the Supreme

Personality of Godhead; *vana-rājayaḥ*—the green trees and plants were also very pleasing to see; *vavau*—blew; *vāyuḥ*—the breeze; *sukha-sparśaḥ*—very pleasing to the touch; *puṇya-gandha-vahaḥ*—which was full of fragrance; *śuciḥ*—without pollution by dust; *agnayaḥ ca*—and the fires (at the places of sacrifice); *dvijātīnām*—of the *brāhmaṇas; śāntāḥ*—undisturbed, steady, calm and quiet; *tatra*—there; *samindhata*—blazed; *manāṁsi*—the minds of the *brāhmaṇas* (who because of Kaṁsa had always been afraid); *āsan*—became; *prasannāni*—fully satisfied and free from disturbances; *sādhūnām*—of the *brāhmaṇas*, who were all Vaiṣṇava devotees; *asura-druhām*—who had been oppressed by Kaṁsa and other demons disturbing the discharge of religious rituals; *jāyamāne*—because of the appearance or birth; *ajane*—of Lord Viṣṇu, who is always unborn; *tasmin*—in that situation; *neduḥ*—resounded; *dundubhayaḥ*—kettledrums; *samam*—simultaneously (from the upper planets).

## TRANSLATION

**Thereafter, at the auspicious time for the appearance of the Lord, the entire universe was surcharged with all the qualities of goodness, beauty and peace. The constellation Rohiṇī appeared, as did stars like Aśvinī. The sun, the moon and the other stars and planets were very peaceful. All directions appeared extremely pleasing, and the beautiful stars twinkled in the cloudless sky. Decorated with towns, villages, mines and pasturing grounds, the earth seemed all-auspicious. The rivers flowed with clear water, and the lakes and vast reservoirs, full of lilies and lotuses, were extraordinarily beautiful. In the trees and green plants, full of flowers and leaves, pleasing to the eyes, birds like cuckoos and swarms of bees began chanting with sweet voices for the sake of the demigods. A pure breeze began to blow, pleasing the sense of touch and bearing the aroma of flowers, and when the brāhmaṇas engaging in ritualistic ceremonies ignited their fires according to Vedic principles, the fires burned steadily, undisturbed by the breeze. Thus when the birthless Lord Viṣṇu, the Supreme Personality of Godhead, was about to appear, the saints and brāhmaṇas, who had always been disturbed by demons like Kaṁsa**

**and his men, felt peace within the core of their hearts, and kettledrums simultaneously vibrated from the upper planetary system.**

## PURPORT

As stated in the *Bhagavad-gītā,* the Lord says that His appearance, birth, and activities are all transcendental and that one who factually understands them is immediately eligible to be transferred to the spiritual world. The Lord's appearance or birth is not like that of an ordinary man, who is forced to accept a material body according to his past deeds. The Lord's appearance is explained in the previous chapter: He appears out of His own sweet pleasure.

When the time was mature for the appearance of the Lord, the constellations became very auspicious. The astrological influence of the constellation known as Rohiṇī was also predominant because this constellation is considered very auspicious. Rohiṇī is under the direct supervision of Brahmā, who is born of Viṣṇu, and it appears at the birth of Lord Viṣṇu, who in fact is birthless. According to the astrological conclusion, besides the proper situation of the stars, there are auspicious and inauspicious moments due to the different situations of the different planetary systems. At the time of Kṛṣṇa's birth, the planetary systems were automatically adjusted so that everything became auspicious.

At that time, in all directions, east, west, south, north, everywhere, there was an atmosphere of peace and prosperity. Auspicious stars were visible in the sky, and on the surface in all towns and villages or pasturing grounds and within the mind of everyone there were signs of good fortune. The rivers were flowing full of water, and the lakes were beautifully decorated with lotus flowers. The forests were full with beautiful birds and peacocks. All the birds within the forests began to sing with sweet voices, and the peacocks began to dance with their consorts. The wind blew very pleasantly, carrying the aroma of different flowers, and the sensation of bodily touch was very pleasing. At home, the *brāhmaṇas,* who were accustomed to offer sacrifices in the fire, found their homes very pleasant for offerings. Because of disturbances created by the demoniac kings, the sacrificial fire had been almost stopped in the houses of *brāhmaṇas,* but now they could find the opportunity to start the fire peacefully. Being forbidden to offer sacrifices, the *brāhmaṇas* were very distressed in mind, intelligence and activities. But just on the point of Kṛṣṇa's appearance, automatically their minds became full of joy because they could hear loud vibrations in the sky of transcendental sounds proclaiming the appearance of the Supreme Personality of Godhead.

On the occasion of Lord Kṛṣṇa's birth, seasonal changes took place throughout the entire universe. Kṛṣṇa was born during the month of September, yet it appeared like springtime. The atmosphere, however, was very cool, although not chilly, and the rivers and reservoirs appeared just as they would in *śarat*, the fall. Lotuses and lilies blossom during the day, but although Kṛṣṇa appeared at twelve o'clock midnight, the lilies and lotuses were in bloom, and thus the wind blowing at that time was full of fragrance. Because of Kaṁsa's disturbances, the Vedic ritualistic ceremonies had almost stopped. The *brāhmaṇas* and saintly persons could not execute the Vedic rituals with peaceful minds. But now the *brāhmaṇas* were very pleased to perform their daily ritualistic ceremonies undisturbed. The business of the *asuras* is to disturb the *suras*, the devotees and *brāhmaṇas*, but at the time of Kṛṣṇa's appearance these devotees and *brāhmaṇas* were undisturbed.

## TEXT 6

जगुः किन्नरगन्धर्वास्तुष्टुवुः सिद्धचारणाः ।
विद्याधर्यश्च ननृतुरप्सरोभिः समं मुदा ॥ ६ ॥

*jaguḥ kinnara-gandharvās*
*tuṣṭuvuḥ siddha-cāraṇāḥ*
*vidyādharyaś ca nanṛtur*
*apsarobhiḥ samaṁ mudā*

*jaguḥ*—recited auspicious songs; *kinnara-gandharvāḥ*—the Kinnaras and Gandharvas, inhabitants of various planets in the heavenly planetary system; *tuṣṭuvuḥ*—offered their respective prayers; *siddha-cāraṇāḥ*—the Siddhas and Cāraṇas, other inhabitants of the heavenly planets; *vidyādharyaḥ ca*—and the Vidyādharīs, another group of inhabitants of the heavenly planets; *nanṛtuḥ*—danced in transcendental bliss; *apsa-*

*robhiḥ*—the Apsarās, beautiful dancers in the heavenly kingdom; *samam*—along with; *mudā*—in great jubilation.

## TRANSLATION

**The Kinnaras and Gandharvas began to sing auspicious songs, the Siddhas and Cāraṇas offered auspicious prayers, and the Vidyādharīs, along with the Apsarās, began to dance in jubilation.**

## TEXTS 7–8

मुमुचुर्मुनयो देवाः सुमनांसि मुदान्विताः ।
मन्दं मन्दं जलधरा जगर्जुरनुसागरम् ॥ ७ ॥
निशीथे तमउद्भूते जायमाने जनार्दने ।
देवक्यां देवरूपिण्यां विष्णुः सर्वगुहाशयः ।
आविरासीद् यथा प्राच्यां दिशीन्दुरिव पुष्कलः ॥ ८ ॥

*mumucur munayo devāḥ*
*sumanāṁsi mudānvitāḥ*
*mandaṁ mandaṁ jaladharā*
*jagarjur añusāgaram*

*niśīthe tama-udbhūte*
*jāyamāne janārdane*
*devakyāṁ deva-rūpiṇyāṁ*
*viṣṇuḥ sarva-guhā-śayaḥ*
*āvirāsīd yathā prācyāṁ*
*diśīndur iva puṣkalaḥ*

*mumucuḥ*—showered; *munayaḥ*—all the great sages and saintly persons; *devāḥ*—and the demigods; *sumanāṁsi*—very beautiful and fragrant flowers; *mudā anvitāḥ*—being joyous in their attitude; *mandam mandam*—very mildly; *jala-dharāḥ*—the clouds; *jagarjuḥ*—vibrated; *anusāgaram*—following the vibrations of the sea waves; *niśīthe*—late at night; *tamaḥ-udbhūte*—when it was densely dark; *jāyamāne*—on the appearance of; *janārdane*—the Supreme Personality of Godhead, Viṣṇu; *devakyām*—in the womb of Devakī; *deva-rūpiṇyām*—who was in the same category as the Supreme Personality of Godhead (*ānanda-cinmaya-rasa-pratibhāvitābhiḥ*); *viṣṇuḥ*—Lord Viṣṇu, the Supreme Lord; *sarva-guhā-śayaḥ*—who is situated in the core of everyone's heart; *āvirāsīt*—appeared; *yathā*—as; *prācyām diśi*—in the east; *induḥ iva*—like the full moon; *puṣkalaḥ*—complete in every respect.

## TRANSLATION

**The demigods and great saintly persons showered flowers in a joyous mood, and clouds gathered in the sky and very mildly thundered, making sounds like those of the ocean's waves. Then the Supreme Personality of Godhead, Viṣṇu, who is situated in the core of everyone's heart, appeared from the heart of Devakī in the dense darkness of night, like the full moon rising on the eastern horizon, because Devakī was of the same category as Śrī Kṛṣṇa.**

## PURPORT

As stated in the *Brahma-saṁhitā* (5.37):

*ānanda-cinmaya-rasa-pratibhāvitābhis*
*tābhir ya eva nija-rūpatayā kalābhiḥ*
*goloka eva nivasaty akhilātma-bhūto*
*govindam ādi-puruṣaṁ tam ahaṁ bhajāmi*

This verse indicates that Kṛṣṇa and His entourage are of the same spiritual potency (*ānanda-cinmaya-rasa*). Kṛṣṇa's father, His mother, His friends the cowherd boys, and the cows are all expansions of Kṛṣṇa, as will be explained in the *brahma-vimohana-līlā*. When Brahmā took away Kṛṣṇa's associates to test the supremacy of Lord Kṛṣṇa, the Lord expanded Himself again in the forms of the many cowherd boys and calves, all of whom, as Brahmā saw, were *viṣṇu-mūrtis*. Devakī is also an expansion of Kṛṣṇa, and therefore this verse says, *devakyāṁ deva-rūpiṇyāṁ viṣṇuḥ sarva-guhā-śayaḥ*.

At the time for the Lord's appearance, the great sages and the demigods, being pleased, began to shower flowers. At the seashore, there was the sound of mild waves, and above the sea there were clouds in the sky which began to thunder very pleasingly.

When things were adjusted like this, Lord Viṣṇu, who is residing within the heart of every living entity, appeared in the darkness of night as the Supreme Personality of Godhead before Devakī, who appeared as one of the demigoddesses. The appearance of Lord Viṣṇu at that time could be compared to the rising of the full moon in the sky on the eastern horizon. The objection may be raised that since Lord Kṛṣṇa appeared on the eighth day of the waning moon, there could be no rising of the full moon. In answer to this it may be said that Lord Kṛṣṇa appeared in the dynasty which is in the hierarchy of the moon; therefore, although the moon was incomplete on that night, because of the Lord's appearance in the dynasty wherein the moon is himself the original person, the moon was in an overjoyous condition, so by the grace of Kṛṣṇa he could appear as a full moon. To welcome the Supreme Personality of Godhead, the waning moon became a full moon in jubilation.

Instead of *deva-rūpiṇyām,* some texts of *Śrīmad-Bhāgavatam* clearly say *viṣṇu-rūpiṇyām.* In either case, the meaning is that Devakī has the same spiritual form as the Lord. The Lord is *sac-cid-ānanda-vigraha,* and Devakī is also *sac-cid-ānanda-vigraha.* Therefore no one can find any fault in the way the Supreme Personality of Godhead, *sac-cid-ānanda-vigraha,* appeared from the womb of Devakī.

Those who are not in full knowledge that the appearance and disappearance of the Lord are transcendental (*janma karma ca me divyam*) are sometimes surprised that the Supreme Personality of Godhead can take birth like an ordinary child. Actually, however, the Lord's birth is never ordinary. The Supreme Personality of Godhead is already situated within the core of everyone's heart as *antaryāmī,* the Supersoul. Thus because He was present in full potency in Devakī's heart, He was also able to appear outside her body.

One of the twelve great personalities is Bhīṣmadeva (*svayambhūr nāradaḥ śambhuḥ kumāraḥ kapilo manuḥ prahlādo janako bhīṣmaḥ*). In *Śrīmad-Bhāgavatam* (1.9.42), Bhīṣma, a great authority to be followed by devotees, says that the Supreme Personality of Godhead is situated in the core of everyone's heart, just as the sun may be on everyone's head. Yet although the sun may be on the heads of millions and millions of people, this does not mean that the sun is variously situated.

Similarly, because the Supreme Personality of Godhead has inconceivable potencies, He can be within everyone's heart and yet not be situated variously. *Ekatvam anupaśyataḥ* (*Īśopaniṣad* 7). The Lord is one, but He can appear in everyone's heart by His inconceivable potency. Thus although the Lord was within the heart of Devakī, He appeared as her child. According to the *Viṣṇu Purāṇa*, therefore, as quoted in the *Vaiṣṇava-toṣaṇī*, the Lord appeared like the sun (*anugrahāsaya*). The *Brahma-saṁhitā* (5.35) confirms that the Lord is situated even within the atom (*aṇḍāntara-stha-paramāṇu-cayāntara-stham*). He is situated in Mathurā, in Vaikuṇṭha and in the core of the heart. Therefore one should clearly understand that He did not live like an ordinary child in the heart or the womb of Devakī. Nor did He appear like an ordinary human child, although He seemed to do so in order to bewilder *asuras* like Kaṁsa. The *asuras* wrongly think that Kṛṣṇa took birth like an ordinary child and passed away from this world like an ordinary man. Such asuric conceptions are rejected by persons in knowledge of the Supreme Personality of Godhead. *Ajo 'pi sann avyayātmā bhūtānām īśvaro 'pi san* (Bg. 4.6). As stated in *Bhagavad-gītā*, the Lord is *aja*, unborn, and He is the supreme controller of everything. Nonetheless, He appeared as the child of Devakī. This verse describes the inconceivable potency of the Lord, who appeared like the full moon. Understanding the special significance of the appearance of the Supreme Godhead, one should never regard Him as having taken birth like an ordinary child.

## TEXTS 9–10

तमद्भुतं बालकमम्बुजेक्षणं
चतुर्भुजं शङ्खगदाद्युदायुधम् ।
श्रीवत्सलक्ष्मं गलशोभिकौस्तुभं
पीताम्बरं सान्द्रपयोदसौभगम् ॥ ९ ॥
महार्हवैदूर्यकिरीटकुण्डल-
त्विषा परिष्वक्तसहस्रकुन्तलम् ।
उद्दामकाञ्च्यङ्गदकङ्कणादिभि-
र्विरोचमानं वसुदेव ऐक्षत ॥१०॥

*tam adbhutaṁ bālakam ambujekṣaṇaṁ*
*catur-bhujaṁ śaṅkha-gadādy-udāyudham*
*śrīvatsa-lakṣmaṁ gala-śobhi-kaustubhaṁ*
*pītāmbaraṁ sāndra-payoda-saubhagam*

*mahārha-vaidūrya-kirīṭa-kuṇḍala-*
*tviṣā pariṣvakta-sahasra-kuntalam*
*uddāma-kāñcy-aṅgada-kaṅkaṇādibhir*
*virocamānaṁ vasudeva aikṣata*

*tam*—that; *adbhutam*—wonderful; *bālakam*—child; *ambuja-īkṣaṇam*—with eyes resembling lotuses; *catuḥ-bhujam*—with four hands; *śaṅkha-gadā-ādi*—bearing a conchshell, club, disc and lotus (in those four hands); *udāyudham*—different weapons; *śrīvatsa-lakṣmam*—decorated with a particular type of hair called Śrīvatsa, which is visible only on the chest of the Supreme Personality of Godhead; *gala-śobhi-kaustubham*—on His neck was the Kaustubha gem, which is particularly available in Vaikuṇṭhaloka; *pīta-ambaram*—His garments were yellow; *sāndra-payoda-saubhagam*—very beautiful, being present with the hue of blackish clouds; *mahā-arha-vaidūrya-kirīṭa-kuṇḍala*—of His helmet and earrings, which were studded with very valuable Vaidūrya gems; *tviṣā*—by the beauty; *pariṣvakta-sahasra-kuntalam*—brilliantly illuminated by scattered, fully grown hair; *uddāma-kāñcī-aṅgada-kaṅkaṇa-ādibhiḥ*—with a brilliant belt on His waist, armbands on His arms, bracelets on His wrists, etc.; *virocamānam*—very beautifully decorated; *vasudevaḥ*—Vasudeva, the father of Kṛṣṇa; *aikṣata*—saw.

## TRANSLATION

**Vasudeva then saw the newborn child, who had very wonderful lotuslike eyes and who bore in His four hands the four weapons śaṅkha, cakra, gadā and padma. On His chest was the mark of Śrīvatsa and on His neck the brilliant Kaustubha gem. Dressed in yellow, His body blackish like a dense cloud, His scattered hair fully grown, and His helmet and earrings sparkling uncommonly with the valuable gem Vaidūrya, the child, decorated with a brilliant belt, armlets, bangles and other ornaments, appeared very wonderful.**

## PURPORT

To support the word *adbhutam*, meaning "wonderful," the decorations and opulences of the newborn child are fully described. As confirmed in the *Brahma-saṁhitā* (5.30), *barhāvataṁsam asitāmbuda-sundarāṅgam:* the hue of the Lord's beautiful form resembles the blackish color of dense clouds (*asita* means "blackish," and *ambuda* means "cloud"). It is clear from the word *catur-bhujam* that Kṛṣṇa first appeared with four hands, as Lord Viṣṇu. No ordinary child in human society has ever been born with four hands. And when is a child born with fully grown hair? The descent of the Lord, therefore, is completely distinct from the birth of an ordinary child. The Vaidūrya gem, which sometimes appears bluish, sometimes yellow and sometimes red, is available in Vaikuṇṭhaloka. The Lord's helmet and earrings were decorated with this particular gem.

## TEXT 11

स विस्मयोत्फुल्लविलोचनो हरिं
सुतं विलोक्यानकदुन्दुभिस्तदा ।
कृष्णावतारोत्सवसम्भ्रमोऽस्पृशन्
मुदा द्विजेभ्योऽयुतमाप्लुतो गवाम् ॥११॥

*sa vismayotphulla-vilocano hariṁ*
*sutaṁ vilokyānakadundubhis tadā*
*kṛṣṇāvatārotsava-sambhramo 'spṛśan*
*mudā dvijebhyo 'yutam āpluto gavām*

*saḥ*—he (Vasudeva, also known as Ānakadundubhi); *vismaya-utphulla-vilocanaḥ*—his eyes being struck with wonder at the beautiful appearance of the Supreme Personality of Godhead; *harim*—Lord Hari, the Supreme Personality of Godhead; *sutam*—as his son; *vilokya*—observing; *ānakadundubhiḥ*—Vasudeva; *tadā*—at that time; *kṛṣṇa-avatāra-utsava*—for a festival to be observed because of Kṛṣṇa's appearance; *sambhramaḥ*—wishing to welcome the Lord with great respect; *aspṛśat*—took advantage by distributing; *mudā*—with great jubilation; *dvijebhyaḥ*—to the *brāhmaṇas; ayutam*—ten thousand; *āplutaḥ*—overwhelmed, surcharged; *gavām*—cows.

## TRANSLATION

**When Vasudeva saw his extraordinary son, his eyes were struck with wonder. In transcendental jubilation, he mentally collected ten thousand cows and distributed them among the brāhmaṇas as a transcendental festival.**

## PURPORT

Śrīla Viśvanātha Cakravartī Ṭhākura has analyzed the wonder of Vasudeva upon seeing his extraordinary child. Vasudeva was shivering with wonder to see a newborn child decorated so nicely with valuable garments and gems. He could immediately understand that the Supreme Personality of Godhead had appeared, not as an ordinary child but in His original, fully decorated, four-handed form. The first wonder was that the Lord was not afraid to appear within the prison house of Kaṁsa, where Vasudeva and Devakī were interned. Second, although the Lord, the Supreme Transcendence, is all-pervading, He had appeared from the womb of Devakī. The third point of wonder, therefore, was that a child could take birth from the womb so nicely decorated. Fourth, the Supreme Personality of Godhead was Vasudeva's worshipable Deity yet had taken birth as his son. For all these reasons, Vasudeva was transcendentally jubilant, and he wanted to perform a festival, as *kṣatriyas* do to celebrate the birth of a child, but because of his imprisonment he was unable to do it externally, and therefore he performed the festival within his mind. This was just as good. If one cannot externally serve the Supreme Personality of Godhead, one can serve the Lord within one's mind, since the activities of the mind are as good as those of the other senses. This is called the nondual or absolute situation (*advaya-jñāna*). People generally perform ritualistic ceremonies for the birth of a child. Why then should Vasudeva not have performed such a ceremony when the Supreme Lord appeared as his son?

## TEXT 12

अथैनमस्तौदवधार्य पूरुषं
परं नताङ्गः कृतधीः कृताञ्जलिः ।
स्वरोचिषा भारत सूतिकागृहं
विरोचयन्तं गतभीः प्रभाववित् ॥१२॥

*athainam astaud avadhārya pūruṣaṁ*
*paraṁ natāṅgaḥ kṛta-dhīḥ kṛtāñjaliḥ*
*sva-rociṣā bhārata sūtikā-gṛhaṁ*
*virocayantaṁ gata-bhīḥ prabhāva-vit*

*atha*—thereafter; *enam*—to the child; *astaut*—offered prayers; *avadhārya*—understanding surely that the child was the Supreme Personality of Godhead; *pūruṣam*—the Supreme Person; *param*—transcendental; *nata-aṅgaḥ*—falling down; *kṛta-dhīḥ*—with concentrated attention; *kṛta-añjaliḥ*—with folded hands; *sva-rociṣā*—by the brilliance of His personal beauty; *bhārata*—O Mahārāja Parīkṣit, descendant of Mahārāja Bharata; *sūtikā-gṛham*—the place where the Lord was born; *virocayantam*—illuminating all around; *gata-bhīḥ*—all his fear disappeared; *prabhāva-vit*—he could now understand the influence (of the Supreme Personality of Godhead).

## TRANSLATION

**O Mahārāja Parīkṣit, descendant of King Bharata, Vasudeva could understand that this child was the Supreme Personality of Godhead, Nārāyaṇa. Having concluded this without a doubt, he became fearless. Bowing down with folded hands and concentrating his attention, he began to offer prayers to the child, who illuminated His birthplace by His natural influence.**

## PURPORT

Struck with such great wonder, Vasudeva now concentrated his attention on the Supreme Personality of Godhead. Understanding the influence of the Supreme Lord, he was surely fearless, since he understood that the Lord had appeared to give him protection (*gata-bhīḥ prabhāva-vit*). Understanding that the Supreme Personality of Godhead was present, he appropriately offered prayers as follows.

## TEXT 13

श्रीवसुदेव उवाच

विदितोऽसि भवान् साक्षात् पुरुषः प्रकृतेः परः।
केवलानुभवानन्दस्वरूपः सर्वबुद्धिदृक् ॥१३॥

*śrī-vasudeva uvāca*
*vidito 'si bhavān sākṣāt*
*puruṣaḥ prakṛteḥ paraḥ*
*kevalānubhavānanda-*
*svarūpaḥ sarva-buddhi-dṛk*

*śrī-vasudevaḥ uvāca*—Śrī Vasudeva prayed; *viditaḥ asi*—now I am fully conscious of You; *bhavān*—Your Lordship; *sākṣāt*—directly; *puruṣaḥ*—the Supreme Person; *prakṛteḥ*—to material nature; *paraḥ*—transcendental, beyond everything material; *kevala-anubhava-ānanda-svarūpaḥ*—Your form is *sac-cid-ānanda-vigraha,* and whoever perceives You becomes transcendentally blissful; *sarva buddhi-dṛk*—the supreme observer, the Supersoul, the intelligence of everyone.

## TRANSLATION

**Vasudeva said: My Lord, You are the Supreme Person, beyond material existence, and You are the Supersoul. Your form can be perceived by transcendental knowledge, by which You can be understood as the Supreme Personality of Godhead. I now understand Your position perfectly.**

## PURPORT

Within Vasudeva's heart, affection for his son and knowledge of the Supreme Lord's transcendental nature both awakened. In the beginning Vasudeva thought, "Such a beautiful child has been born, but now Kaṁsa will come and kill Him." But when he understood that this was not an ordinary child but the Supreme Personality of Godhead, he became fearless. Regarding his son as the Supreme Lord, wonderful in everything, he began offering prayers appropriate for the Supreme Lord. Completely free from fear of Kaṁsa's atrocities, he accepted the child simultaneously as an object of affection and as an object of worship by prayers.

## TEXT 14

स एव स्वप्रकृत्येदं सृष्ट्वाग्रे त्रिगुणात्मकम् ।
तदनु त्वं ह्यप्रविष्टः प्रविष्ट इव भाव्यसे ॥१४॥

*sa eva svaprakṛtyedaṁ*
*sṛṣṭvāgre tri-guṇātmakam*
*tad anu tvaṁ hy apraviṣṭaḥ*
*praviṣṭa iva bhāvyase*

*saḥ*—He (the Supreme Personality of Godhead); *eva*—indeed; *sva-prakṛtyā*—by Your personal energy (*mayādhyakṣeṇa prakṛtiḥ sūyate sa-carācaram*); *idam*—this material world; *sṛṣṭvā*—after creating; *agre*—in the beginning; *tri-guṇa-ātmakam*—made of three modes of energy (*sattva-rajas-tamo-guṇa*); *tat anu*—thereafter; *tvam*—Your Lordship; *hi*—indeed; *apraviṣṭaḥ*—although You did not enter; *praviṣṭaḥ iva*—You appear to have entered; *bhāvyase*—are so understood.

## TRANSLATION

**My Lord, You are the same person who in the beginning created this material world by His personal external energy. After the creation of this world of three guṇas [sattva, rajas and tamas], You appear to have entered it, although in fact You have not.**

## PURPORT

In *Bhagavad-gītā* (7.4) the Supreme Personality of Godhead clearly explains:

*bhūmir āpo 'nalo vāyuḥ*
*khaṁ mano buddhir eva ca*
*ahaṅkāra itīyaṁ me*
*bhinnā prakṛtir aṣṭadhā*

This material world of three modes of nature—*sattva-guṇa, rajo-guṇa* and *tamo-guṇa*—is a composition of earth, water, fire, air, mind, intelligence and false ego, all of which are energies coming from Kṛṣṇa, yet Kṛṣṇa, being always transcendental, is aloof from this material world. Those who are not in pure knowledge think that Kṛṣṇa is a product of matter and that His body is material like ours (*avajānanti māṁ mūḍhāḥ*). In fact, however, Kṛṣṇa is always aloof from this material world.

In the Vedic literature, we find the creation described in relationship to Mahā-Viṣṇu. As stated in the *Brahma-saṁhitā* (5.35):

*eko 'py asau racayituṁ jagad-aṇḍa-koṭiṁ*
*yac-chaktir asti jagad-aṇḍa-cayā yad-antaḥ*
*aṇḍāntara-stha-paramāṇu-cayāntara-sthaṁ*
*govindam ādi-puruṣaṁ tam ahaṁ bhajāmi*

"I worship the primeval Lord, Govinda, the original Personality of Godhead. By His partial plenary expansion as Mahā-Viṣṇu, He enters into material nature. Then He enters every universe as Garbhodakaśāyī Viṣṇu, and He enters all the elements, including every atom of matter, as Kṣīrodakaśāyī Viṣṇu. Such manifestations of cosmic creation are innumerable, both in the universes and in the individual atoms." Govinda is partially exhibited as *antaryāmī*, the Supersoul, who enters this material world (*aṇḍāntara-stha*) and who is also within the atom. The *Brahma-saṁhitā* (5.48) further says:

*yasyaika-niśvasita-kālam athāvalambya*
*jīvanti loma-vilajā jagad-aṇḍa-nāthāḥ*
*viṣṇur mahān sa iha yasya kalā-viśeṣo*
*govindam ādi-puruṣaṁ tam ahaṁ bhajāmi*

This verse describes Mahā-Viṣṇu as a plenary expansion of Kṛṣṇa. Mahā-Viṣṇu lies on the Causal Ocean, and when He exhales, millions of *brahmāṇḍas*, or universes, come from the pores of His body. Then, when Mahā-Viṣṇu inhales, all these *brahmāṇḍas* disappear. Thus the millions of *brahmāṇḍas* controlled by the Brahmās and other demigods come and go in this material world through the breathing of Mahā-Viṣṇu.

Foolish persons think that when Kṛṣṇa appears as the son of Vasudeva, He is limited like an ordinary child. But Vasudeva was aware that although the Lord had appeared as his son, the Lord had not entered Devakī's womb and then come out. Rather, the Lord was always there. The Supreme Lord is all-pervading, present within and without. *Praviṣṭa iva bhāvyase:* He only seemed to have entered the womb of Devakī and to have now appeared as Vasudeva's child. The expression of this knowledge by Vasudeva indicates that Vasudeva knew how these events took place. Vasudeva was certainly a devotee of the Lord in full knowledge, and we must learn from devotees like him. *Bhagavad-gītā* (4.34) therefore recommends:

*tad viddhi praṇipātena*
*paripraśnena sevayā*
*upadekṣyanti te jñānaṁ*
*jñāninas tattva-darśinaḥ*

"Just try to learn the truth by approaching a spiritual master. Inquire from him submissively and render service unto him. The self-realized soul can impart knowledge unto you because he has seen the truth." Vasudeva begot the Supreme Personality of Godhead, yet he was in full knowledge of how the Supreme Lord appears and disappears. He was therefore *tattva-darśī*, a seer of the truth, because he personally saw how the Supreme Absolute Truth appeared as his son. Vasudeva was not in ignorance, thinking that because the Supreme Godhead had appeared as his son, the Lord had become limited. The Lord is unlimitedly existing and all-pervading, inside and outside. Thus there is no question of His appearance or disappearance.

## TEXTS 15–17

यथेमेऽविकृता भावास्तथा ते विकृतैः सह ।
नानावीर्याः पृथग्भूता विराजं जनयन्ति हि ॥१५॥
सन्निपत्य समुत्पाद्य दृश्यन्तेऽनुगता इव ।
प्रागेव विद्यमानत्वान्न तेषामिह सम्भवः ॥१६॥
एवं भवान् बुद्ध्यनुमेयलक्षणै-
ग्राह्यैर्गुणैः सन्नपि तद्गुणाग्रहः ।
अनावृतत्वाद् बहिरन्तरं न ते
सर्वस्य सर्वात्मन आत्मवस्तुनः ॥१७॥

*yatheme 'vikṛtā bhāvās*
*tathā te vikṛtaiḥ saha*
*nānā-vīryāḥ pṛthag-bhūtā*
*virājaṁ janayanti hi*

*sannipatya samutpādya*
*dṛśyante 'nugatā iva*
*prāg eva vidyamānatvān*
*na teṣām iha sambhavaḥ*

*evaṁ bhavān buddhy-anumeya-lakṣaṇair*
*grāhyair guṇaiḥ sann api tad-guṇāgrahaḥ*
*anāvṛtatvād bahir antaraṁ na te*
*sarvasya sarvātmana ātma-vastunaḥ*

*yathā*—as; *ime*—these material creations, made of material energy; *avikṛtāḥ*—actually not disintegrated; *bhāvāḥ*—with such a conception; *tathā*—similarly; *te*—they; *vikṛtaiḥ saha*—association with these different elements coming from the total material energy; *nānā-vīryāḥ*—every element is full of different energies; *pṛthak*—separated; *bhūtāḥ*—becoming; *virājam*—the whole cosmic manifestation; *janayanti*—create; *hi*—indeed; *sannipatya*—because of association with the spiritual energy; *samutpādya*—after being created; *dṛśyante*—they appear; *anugatāḥ*—entered within it; *iva*—as if; *prāk*—from the very beginning, before the creation of this cosmic manifestation; *eva*—indeed; *vidyamānatvāt*—due to the existence of the Supreme Personality of Godhead; *na*—not; *teṣām*—of these material elements; *iha*—in this matter of creation; *sambhavaḥ*—entering would have been possible; *evam*—in this way; *bhavān*—O my Lord; *buddhi-anumeya-lakṣaṇaiḥ*—by real intelligence and by such symptoms; *grāhyaiḥ*—with the objects of the senses; *guṇaiḥ*—with the modes of material nature; *san api*—although in touch; *tat-guṇa-agrahaḥ*—are not touched by the material qualities; *anāvṛtatvāt*—because of being situated everywhere; *bahiḥ antaram*—within the external and internal; *na te*—there is no such thing for You; *sarvasya*—of everything; *sarva-ātmanaḥ*—You are the root of everything; *ātma-vastunaḥ*—everything belongs to You, but You are outside and inside of everything.

## TRANSLATION

**The mahat-tattva, the total material energy, is undivided, but because of the material modes of nature, it appears to separate into earth, water, fire, air and ether. Because of the living energy**

**[jīva-bhūta], these separated energies combine to make the cosmic manifestation visible, but in fact, before the creation of the cosmos, the total energy is already present. Therefore, the total material energy never actually enters the creation. Similarly, although You are perceived by our senses because of Your presence, You cannot be perceived by the senses, nor experienced by the mind or words [avāṅ-mānasa-gocara]. With our senses we can perceive some things, but not everything; for example, we can use our eyes to see, but not to taste. Consequently, You are beyond perception by the senses. Although in touch with the modes of material nature, You are unaffected by them. You are the prime factor in everything, the all-pervading, undivided Supersoul. For You, therefore, there is no external or internal. You never entered the womb of Devakī; rather, You existed there already.**

## PURPORT

This same understanding is explained by the Lord Himself in *Bhagavad-gītā* (9.4):

*mayā tatam idaṁ sarvaṁ*
*jagad-avyakta-mūrtinā*
*mat-sthāni sarva-bhūtāni*
*na cāhaṁ teṣv avasthitaḥ*

"By Me, in My unmanifested form, this entire universe is pervaded. All beings are in Me, but I am not in them."

The Supreme Personality of Godhead is not perceivable through the gross material senses. It is said that Lord Śrī Kṛṣṇa's name, fame, pastimes, etc., cannot be understood by material senses. Only to one who is engaged in pure devotional service under proper guidance is He revealed. As stated in *Brahma-saṁhitā* (5.38):

*premāñjana-cchurita-bhakti-vilocanena*
*santaḥ sadaiva hṛdayeṣu vilokayanti*

One can see the Supreme Personality of Godhead, Govinda, always, within oneself and outside oneself, if one has developed the transcendental loving attitude toward Him. Thus for people in general, He is not visible. In the above-mentioned verse from *Bhagavad-gītā*, therefore, it is said that although He is all-pervading, everywhere present, He is not conceivable by the material senses. But actually, although we cannot see Him, everything is resting in Him. As discussed in the Seventh Chapter of *Bhagavad-gītā*, the entire material cosmic manifestation is only a combination of His two different energies, the superior, spiritual energy and the inferior, material energy. Just as the sunshine is spread all over the universe, the energy of the Lord is spread all over the creation, and everything is resting in that energy.

Yet one should not conclude that because He is spread all over He has lost His personal existence. To refute such arguments, the Lord says, "I am everywhere, and everything is in Me, but still I am aloof." For example, a king heads a government which is but the manifestation of the king's energy; the different governmental departments are nothing but the energies of the king, and each department is resting on the king's power. But still one cannot expect the king to be present in every department personally. That is a crude example. Similarly, all the manifestations that we see, and everything that exists, both in this material world and in the spiritual world, are resting on the energy of the Supreme Personality of Godhead. The creation takes place by the diffusion of His different energies, and, as stated in the *Bhagavad-gītā*, He is everywhere present by His personal representation, the diffusion of His different energies.

One may argue that the Supreme Personality of Godhead, who creates the whole cosmic manifestation simply by His glance, cannot come within the womb of Devakī, the wife of Vasudeva. To eradicate this argument, Vasudeva said, "My dear Lord, it is not very wonderful that You appeared within the womb of Devakī, for the creation was also made in that way. You were lying in the Causal Ocean as Mahā-Viṣṇu, and by Your breathing, innumerable universes came into existence. Then You entered into each of the universes as Garbhodakaśāyī Viṣṇu. Then again You expanded Yourself as Kṣīrodakaśāyī Viṣṇu and entered into the heart of all living entities and entered even within the atoms. Therefore Your entrance into the womb of Devakī is understandable in the same way. You appear to have entered, but You are simultaneously all-pervading. We can understand Your entrance and nonentrance from material examples.

The total material energy remains intact even after being divided into sixteen elements. The material body is nothing but a combination of the five gross elements—namely earth, water, fire, air and ether. Whenever there is a material body, it appears that such elements are newly created, but actually the elements are always existing outside of the body. Similarly, although You appear as a child in the womb of Devakī, You are also existing outside. You are always in Your abode, but still You can simultaneously expand Yourself into millions of forms.

"One has to understand Your appearance with great intelligence because the material energy is also emanating from You. You are the original source of the material energy, just as the sun is the source of the sunshine. The sunshine cannot cover the sun globe, nor can the material energy—being an emanation from You—cover You. You appear to be in the three modes of material energy, but actually the three modes of material energy cannot cover You. This is understood by the highly intellectual philosophers. In other words, although You appear to be within the material energy, You are never covered by it."

We hear from the Vedic version that the Supreme Brahman exhibits His effulgence and therefore everything is illuminated. We can understand from *Brahma-saṁhitā* that the *brahmajyoti,* or the Brahman effulgence, emanates from the body of the Supreme Lord. And from the Brahman effulgence, all creation takes place. It is further stated in the *Bhagavad-gītā* that the Lord is the support of the Brahman effulgence. Originally He is the root cause of everything. But persons who are less intelligent think that when the Supreme Personality of Godhead comes within this material world, He accepts material qualities. Such conclusions are not mature, but are made by the less intelligent.

## TEXT 18

य आत्मनो दृश्यगुणेषु सन्निति
व्यवस्यते स्वव्यतिरेकतोऽबुधः ।
विनानुवादं न च तन्मनीषितं
सम्यग् यतस्त्यक्तमुपाददत् पुमान् ॥१८॥

*ya ātmano dṛśya-guṇeṣu sann iti*
*vyavasyate sva-vyatirekato 'budhaḥ*

*vinānuvādaṁ na ca tan manīṣitaṁ*
*samyag yatas tyaktam upādadat pumān*

*yaḥ*—anyone who; *ātmanaḥ*—of his own real identity, the soul; *dṛśya-guṇeṣu*—among the visible objects, beginning with the body; *san*—being situated in that position; *iti*—thus; *vyavasyate*—continues to act; *sva-vyatirekataḥ*—as if the body were independent of the soul; *abudhaḥ*—a rascal; *vinā anuvādam*—without proper analytical study; *na*—not; *ca*—also; *tat*—the body and other visible objects; *manīṣitam*—such considerations having been discussed; *samyak*—fully; *yataḥ*—because he is a fool; *tyaktam*—are rejected; *upādadat*—accepts this body as reality; *pumān*—a person.

## TRANSLATION

**One who considers his visible body, which is a product of the three modes of nature, to be independent of the soul is unaware of the basis of existence, and therefore he is a rascal. Those who are learned have rejected his conclusion because one can understand through full discussion that with no basis in soul, the visible body and senses would be insubstantial. Nonetheless, although his conclusion has been rejected, a foolish person considers it a reality.**

## PURPORT

Without the basic principle of soul, the body cannot be produced. So-called scientists have tried in many ways to produce a living body in their chemical laboratories, but no one has been able to do it because unless the spirit soul is present, a body cannot be prepared from material elements. Since scientists are now enamored of theories about the chemical composition of the body, we have challenged many scientists to make even a small egg. The chemicals in eggs can be found very easily. There is a white substance and a yellow substance, covered by a shell, and modern scientists should very easily be able to duplicate all this. But even if they were to prepare such an egg and put it in an incubator, this man-made chemical egg would not produce a chicken. The soul must be added because there is no question of a chemical combination for life. Those who think that life can exist wihout the soul have therefore been described here as *abudhaḥ*, foolish rascals.

Again, there are those who reject the body, regarding it as insubstantial. They are of the same category of fools. One can neither reject the body nor accept it as substantial. The substance is the Supreme Personality of Godhead, and both the body and the soul are energies of the Supreme Godhead, as described by the Lord Himself in *Bhagavad-gītā* (7.4–5):

*bhūmir āpo 'nalo vāyuḥ*
*khaṁ mano buddhir eva ca*
*ahaṅkāra itīyaṁ me*
*bhinnā prakṛtir aṣṭadhā*

*apareyam itas tv anyāṁ*
*prakṛtiṁ viddhi me parām*
*jīva-bhūtāṁ mahā-bāho*
*yayedaṁ dhāryate jagat*

"Earth, water, fire, air, ether, mind, intelligence and false ego—all together these eight comprise My separated material energies. But besides this inferior nature, O mighty-armed Arjuna, there is a superior energy of Mine, which consists of all living entities who are struggling with material nature and are sustaining the universe."

The body, therefore, has a relationship with the Supreme Personality of Godhead, just as the soul does. Since both of them are energies of the Lord, neither of them is false, because they come from the reality. One who does not know this secret of life is described as *abudhaḥ.* According to the Vedic injunctions, *aitadātmyam idaṁ sarvam, sarvaṁ khalv idaṁ brahma:* everything is the Supreme Brahman. Therefore, both the body and the soul are Brahman, since matter and spirit emanate from Brahman.

Not knowing the conclusions of the *Vedas,* some people accept the material nature as substance, and others accept the spirit soul as substance, but actually Brahman is the substance. Brahman is the cause of all causes. The ingredients and the immediate cause of this manifested material world are Brahman, and we cannot make the ingredients of this world independent of Brahman. Furthermore, since the ingredients and the immediate cause of this material manifestation are Brahman, both of them are truth, *satya;* there is no validity to the expression *brahma satyaṁ jagan mithyā.* The world is not false.

*Jñānīs* reject this world, and foolish persons accept this world as reality, and in this way they are both misguided. Although the body is not as important as the soul, we cannot say that it is false. Yet the body is temporary, and only foolish, materialistic persons, who do not have full knowledge of the soul, regard the temporary body as reality and engage in decorating this body. Both of these pitfalls—rejection of the body as false and acceptance of the body as all in all—can be avoided when one is fully situated in Kṛṣṇa consciousness. If we regard this world as false, we fall into the category of *asuras,* who say that this world is unreal, with no foundation and no God in control (*asatyam apratiṣṭhaṁ te jagad āhur anīśvaram*). As described in the Sixteenth Chapter of *Bhagavad-gītā,* this is the conclusion of demons.

## TEXT 19

त्वत्तोऽस्य जन्मस्थितिसंयमान् विभो
वदन्त्यनीहादगुणादविक्रियात् ।
त्वयीश्वरे ब्रह्मणि नो विरुध्यते
त्वदाश्रयत्वादुपचर्यते गुणैः ॥१९॥

*tvatto 'sya janma-sthiti-saṁyamān vibho*
*vadanty anīhād aguṇād avikriyāt*
*tvayīśvare brahmaṇi no virudhyate*
*tvad-āśrayatvād upacaryate guṇaiḥ*

*tvattaḥ*—are from Your Lordship; *asya*—of the entire cosmic manifestation; *janma*—the creation; *sthiti*—maintenance; *saṁyamān*—and annihilation; *vibho*—O my Lord; *vadanti*—the learned Vedic scholars conclude; *anīhāt*—who are free from endeavor; *aguṇāt*—who are unaffected by the modes of material nature; *avikriyāt*—who are unchanging in Your spiritual situation; *tvayi*—in You; *īśvare*—the Supreme Personality of Godhead; *brahmaṇi*—who are Parabrahman, the Supreme Brahman; *no*—not; *virudhyate*—there is a contradiction; *tvat-āśrayatvāt*—because of being controlled by You; *upacaryate*—

things are going on automatically; *guṇaiḥ*—by the operation of the material modes.

## TRANSLATION

**O my Lord, learned Vedic scholars conclude that the creation, maintenance and annihilation of the entire cosmic manifestation are performed by You, who are free from endeavor, unaffected by the modes of material nature, and changeless in Your spiritual situation. There are no contradictions in You, who are the Supreme Personality of Godhead, Parabrahman. Because the three modes of material nature—sattva, rajas and tamas—are under Your control, everything takes place automatically.**

## PURPORT

As stated in the *Vedas:*

*na tasya kāryaṁ karaṇaṁ ca vidyate*
*na tat-samaś cābhyadhikaś ca dṛśyate*
*parāsya śaktir vividhaiva śrūyate*
*svābhāvikī jñāna-bala-kriyā ca*

"The Supreme Lord has nothing to do, and no one is found to be equal to or greater than Him, for everything is done naturally and systematically by His multifarious energies." (*Śvetāśvatara Upaniṣad* 6.8) Creation, maintenance and annihilation are all conducted personally by the Supreme Personality of Godhead, and this is confirmed in *Bhagavad-gītā* (*mayādhyakṣeṇa prakṛtiḥ sūyate sa-carācaram*). Yet ultimately the Lord does not need to do anything, and therefore He is *nirvikāra*, changeless. Because everything is done under His direction, He is called *sṛṣṭi-kartā*, the master of creation. Similarly, He is the master of annihilation. When a master sits in one place while his servants work in different duties, whatever the servants are doing is ultimately an activity of the master, although he is doing nothing (*na tasya kāryaṁ karaṇaṁ ca vidyate*). The Lord's potencies are so numerous that everything is nicely done. Therefore, He is naturally still and is not directly the doer of anything in this material world.

## TEXT 20

स त्वं त्रिलोकस्थितये स्वमायया
बिभर्षि शुक्लं खलु वर्णमात्मनः ।
सर्गाय रक्तं रजसोपबृंहितं
कृष्णं च वर्णं तमसा जनात्यये ॥२०॥

*sa tvaṁ tri-loka-sthitaye sva-māyayā*
*bibharṣi śuklaṁ khalu varṇam ātmanaḥ*
*sargāya raktaṁ rajasopabṛṁhitaṁ*
*kṛṣṇaṁ ca varṇaṁ tamasā janātyaye*

*saḥ tvam*—Your Lordship, who are the same person, the Transcendence; *tri-loka-sthitaye*—to maintain the three worlds, the upper, middle and lower planetary systems; *sva-māyayā*—by Your personal energy (*ātma-māyayā*); *bibharṣi*—assume; *śuklam*—the white form of Viṣṇu in goodness; *khalu*—as well as; *varṇam*—color; *ātmanaḥ*—of the same category as You (*viṣṇu-tattva*); *sargāya*—for the creation of the entire world; *raktam*—the reddish color of *rajo-guṇa; rajasā*—with the quality of passion; *upabṛṁhitam*—being charged; *kṛṣṇam ca*—and the quality of darkness; *varṇam*—the color; *tamasā*—which is surrounded by ignorance; *jana-atyaye*—for the ultimate destruction of the entire creation.

## TRANSLATION

**My Lord, Your form is transcendental to the three material modes, yet for the maintenance of the three worlds, You assume the white color of Viṣṇu in goodness; for creation, which is surrounded by the quality of passion, You appear reddish; and at the end, when there is a need for annihilation, which is surrounded by ignorance, You appear blackish.**

## PURPORT

Vasudeva prayed to the Lord, "You are called *śuklam. Śuklam*, or 'whiteness,' is the symbolic representation of the Absolute Truth because it is unaffected by the material qualities. Lord Brahmā is called *rakta*, or red, because Brahmā represents the qualities of passion for creation. Darkness is entrusted to Lord Śiva because he annihilates the cosmos. The creation, annihilation and maintenance of this cosmic manifestation are conducted by Your potencies, yet You are always unaffected by those qualities." As confirmed in the *Vedas*, *harir hi nirguṇaḥ sākṣāt:* the Supreme Personality of Godhead is always free from all material qualities. It is also said that the qualities of passion and ignorance are nonexistent in the person of the Supreme Lord.

In this verse, the three colors mentioned—*śukla*, *rakta* and *kṛṣṇa*—are not to be understood literally, in terms of what we experience with our senses, but rather as representatives of *sattva-guṇa*, *rajo-guṇa* and *tamo-guṇa*. After all, sometimes we see that a duck is white, although it is in *tamo-guṇa*, the mode of ignorance. Illustrating the logic called *bakāndha-nyāya*, the duck is such a fool that it runs after the testicles of a bull, thinking them to be a hanging fish that can be taken when it drops. Thus the duck is always in darkness. Vyāsadeva, however, the compiler of the Vedic literature, is blackish, but this does not mean that he is in *tamo-guṇa*; rather, he is in the highest position of *sattva-guṇa*, beyond the material modes of nature. Sometimes these colors (*śukla-raktas tathā pītaḥ*) are used to designate the *brāhmaṇas*, *kṣatriyas*, *vaiśyas* and *śūdras*. Lord Kṣīrodakaśāyī Viṣṇu is celebrated as possessing a blackish color, Lord Śiva is whitish, and Lord Brahmā is reddish, but according to Śrīla Sanātana Gosvāmī in the *Vaiṣṇava-toṣaṇī-ṭīkā*, this exhibition of colors is not what is referred to here.

The real understanding of *śukla*, *rakta* and *kṛṣṇa* is as follows. The Lord is always transcendental, but for the sake of creation He assumes the color *rakta* as Lord Brahmā. Again, sometimes the Lord becomes angry. As He says in *Bhagavad-gītā* (16.19):

*tān ahaṁ dviṣataḥ krūrān*
*saṁsāreṣu narādhamān*
*kṣipāmy ajasram aśubhān*
*āsurīṣv eva yoniṣu*

"Those who are envious and mischievous, who are the lowest among men, are cast by Me into the ocean of material existence, into various demoniac species of life." To destroy the demons, the Lord becomes angry, and therefore He assumes the form of Lord Śiva. In summary, the Supreme Personality of Godhead is always beyond the material qualities, and we should not be misled into thinking otherwise simply because of sense perception. One must understand the position of the Lord through the authorities, or *mahājanas.* As stated in *Śrīmad-Bhāgavatam* (1.3.28), *ete cāṁśa-kalāḥ puṁsaḥ kṛṣṇas tu bhagavān svayam.*

## TEXT 21

त्वमस्य लोकस्य विभो रिरक्षिषु-
गृहेऽवतीर्णोऽसि ममाखिलेश्वर ।
राजन्यसंज्ञासुरकोटियूथपै-
र्निर्व्यूह्यमाना निहनिष्यसे चमूः ॥२१॥

*tvam asya lokasya vibho rirakṣiṣur*
*gṛhe 'vatīrṇo 'si mamākhileśvara*
*rājanya-saṁjñāsura-koṭi-yūthapair*
*nirvyūhyamānā nihaniṣyase camūḥ*

*tvam*—Your Lordship; *asya*—of this world; *lokasya*—especially of this *martya-loka,* the planet earth; *vibho*—O Supreme; *rirakṣiṣuḥ*—desiring protection (from the disturbance of the *asuras*); *gṛhe*—in this house; *avatīrṇaḥ asi*—have now appeared; *mama*—my; *akhila-īśvara*—although You are the proprietor of the entire creation; *rājanya-saṁjña-asura-koṭi-yūtha-paiḥ*—with millions of demons and their followers in the roles of politicians and kings; *nirvyūhyamānāḥ*—which are moving here and there all over the world; *nihaniṣyase*—will kill; *camūḥ*—the armies, paraphernalia, soldiers and retinues.

## TRANSLATION

**O my Lord, proprietor of all creation, You have now appeared in my house, desiring to protect this world. I am sure that You will kill all the armies that are moving all over the world under the leadership of politicians who are dressed as kṣatriya rulers but who are factually demons. They must be killed by You for the protection of the innocent public.**

## PURPORT

Kṛṣṇa appears in this world for two purposes, *paritrāṇāya sādhūnāṁ vināśāya ca duṣkṛtām:* to protect the innocent, religious devotees of the Lord and to annihilate all the uneducated, uncultured *asuras,* who unnecessarily bark like dogs and fight among themselves for political power. It is said, *kali-kāle nāma-rūpe kṛṣṇa avatāra.* The Hare Kṛṣṇa movement is also an incarnation of Kṛṣṇa in the form of the holy name (*nāma-rūpe*). Every one of us who is actually afraid of the asuric rulers and politicians must welcome this incarnation of Kṛṣṇa: Hare Kṛṣṇa, Hare Kṛṣṇa, Kṛṣṇa Kṛṣṇa, Hare Hare/ Hare Rāma, Hare Rāma, Rāma Rāma, Hare Hare. Then we will surely be protected from the harassment of asuric rulers. At the present moment these rulers are so powerful that by hook or by crook they capture the highest posts in government and harass countless numbers of people on the plea of national security or some emergency. Then again, one *asura* defeats another *asura,* but the public continues to suffer. Therefore the entire world is in a precarious condition, and the only hope is this Hare Kṛṣṇa movement. Lord Nṛsiṁhadeva appeared when Prahlāda was excessively harassed by his asuric father. Because of such asuric fathers—that is, the ruling politicians—it is very difficult to press forward the Hare Kṛṣṇa movement, but because Kṛṣṇa has now appeared in His holy name through this movement, we can hope that these asuric fathers will be annihilated and the kingdom of God established all over the world. The entire world is now full of many *asuras* in the guise of politicians, *gurus, sādhus, yogīs* and incarnations, and they are misleading the general public away from Kṛṣṇa consciousness, which can offer true benefit to human society.

## TEXT 22

अयं त्वसभ्यस्तव जन्म नौ गृहे
श्रुत्वाग्रजांस्ते न्यवधीत् सुरेश्वर ।
स तेऽवतारं पुरुषैः समर्पितं
श्रुत्वाधुनैवाभिसरत्युदायुधः ॥२२॥

*ayaṁ tv asabhyas tava janma nau gṛhe*
*śrutvāgrajāṁs te nyavadhīt sureśvara*

*sa te 'vatāraṁ puruṣaiḥ samarpitaṁ*
*śrutvādhunaivābhisaraty udāyudhaḥ*

*ayam*—this (rascal); *tu*—but; *asabhyaḥ*—who is not civilized at all (*asura* means "uncivilized," and *sura* means "civilized"); *tava*—of Your Lordship; *janma*—the birth; *nau*—our; *gṛhe*—into the home; *śrutvā*—after hearing; *agrajān te*—all the brothers born before You; *nyavadhīt*—killed; *sura-īśvara*—O Lord of the *suras*, the civilized persons; *saḥ*—he (that uncivilized Kaṁsa); *te*—Your; *avatāram*—appearance; *puruṣaiḥ*—by his lieutenants; *samarpitam*—being informed of; *śrutvā*—after hearing; *adhunā*—now; *eva*—indeed; *abhisarati*—will come immediately; *udāyudhaḥ*—with raised weapons.

## TRANSLATION

**O my Lord, Lord of the demigods, after hearing the prophecy that You would take birth in our home and kill him, this uncivilized Kaṁsa killed so many of Your elder brothers. As soon as he hears from his lieutenants that You have appeared, he will immediately come with weapons to kill You.**

## PURPORT

Kaṁsa has here been described as *asabhya*, meaning "uncivilized" or "most heinous," because he killed the many children of his sister. When he heard the prophecy that he would be killed by her eighth son, this uncivilized man, Kaṁsa, was immediately ready to kill his innocent sister on the occasion of her marriage. An uncivilized man can do anything for the satisfaction of his senses. He can kill children, he can kill cows, he can kill *brāhmaṇas*, he can kill old men; he has no mercy for anyone. According to the Vedic civilization, cows, women, children, old men and *brāhmaṇas* should be excused if they are at fault. But *asuras*, uncivilized men, do not care about that. At the present moment, the killing of cows and the killing of children is going on unrestrictedly, and therefore this civilization is not at all human, and those who are conducting this condemned civilization are uncivilized *asuras*.

Such uncivilized men are not in favor of the Kṛṣṇa consciousness movement. As public officers, they declare without hesitation that the chanting of the Hare Kṛṣṇa movement is a nuisance, although *Bhagavad-gītā* clearly says, *satataṁ kīrtayanto māṁ yatantaś ca dṛḍha-vratāḥ.* According to this verse, it is the duty of the *mahātmās* to chant the Hare Kṛṣṇa *mantra* and try to spread it all over the world to the best of their ability. Unfortunately, society is in such an uncivilized state that there are so-called *mahātmās* who are prepared to kill cows and children and stop the Hare Kṛṣṇa movement. Such uncivilized activities were actually demonstrated in opposition to the Hare Kṛṣṇa movement's Bombay center, Hare Kṛṣṇa Land. As Kaṁsa was not expected to kill the beautiful child of Devakī and Vasudeva, the uncivilized society, although unhappy about the advancement of the Kṛṣṇa consciousness movement, cannot be expected to stop it. Yet we must face many difficulties in many different ways. Although Kṛṣṇa cannot be killed, Vasudeva, as the father of Kṛṣṇa, was trembling because in affection he thought that Kaṁsa would immediately come and kill his son. Similarly, although the Kṛṣṇa consciousness movement and Kṛṣṇa are not different and no *asuras* can check it, we are afraid that at any moment the *asuras* can stop this movement in any part of the world.

## TEXT 23

श्रीशुक उवाच

अथैनमात्मजं वीक्ष्य महापुरुषलक्षणम् ।

देवकी तमुपाधावत् कंसाद् भीता सुविस्मिता ॥२३॥

*śrī-śuka uvāca*
*athainam ātmajaṁ vīkṣya*
*mahā-puruṣa-lakṣaṇam*
*devakī tam upādhāvat*
*kaṁsād bhītā suvismitā*

*śrī-śukaḥ uvāca*—Śrī Śukadeva Gosvāmī said; *atha*—after this offering of prayers by Vasudeva; *enam*—this Kṛṣṇa; *ātmajam*—their son; *vīkṣya*—observing; *mahā-puruṣa-lakṣaṇam*—with all the symptoms of the Supreme Personality of Godhead, Viṣṇu; *devakī*—Kṛṣṇa's mother; *tam*—unto Him (Kṛṣṇa); *upādhāvat*—offered prayers; *kaṁsāt*—of

Kaṁsa; *bhītā*—being afraid; *su-vismitā*—and also being astonished by seeing such a wonderful child.

## TRANSLATION

**Śukadeva Gosvāmī continued: Thereafter, having seen that her child had all the symptoms of the Supreme Personality of Godhead, Devakī, who was very much afraid of Kaṁsa and unusually astonished, began to offer prayers to the Lord.**

## PURPORT

The word *suvismitā*, meaning "astonished," is significant in this verse. Devakī and her husband, Vasudeva, were assured that their child was the Supreme Personality of Godhead and could not be killed by Kaṁsa, but because of affection, as they thought of Kaṁsa's previous atrocities, they were simultaneously afraid that Kṛṣṇa would be killed. This is why the word *suvismitā* has been used. Similarly, we are also astounded upon thinking of whether this movement will be killed by the *asuras* or will continue to advance without fear.

## TEXT 24

श्रीदेवक्युवाच
रूपं यत् तत् प्राहुरव्यक्तमाद्यं
ब्रह्म ज्योतिर्निर्गुणं निर्विकारम् ।
सत्तामात्रं निर्विशेषं निरीहं
स त्वं साक्षाद् विष्णुरध्यात्मदीपः ॥२४॥

*śrī-devaky uvāca*
*rūpaṁ yat tat prāhur avyaktam ādyaṁ*
*brahma jyotir nirguṇaṁ nirvikāram*
*sattā-mātraṁ nirviśeṣaṁ nirīhaṁ*
*sa tvaṁ sākṣād viṣṇur adhyātma-dīpaḥ*

*śrī-devakī uvāca*—Śrī Devakī said; *rūpam*—form or substance; *yat tat*—because You are the same substance; *prāhuḥ*—You are sometimes called; *avyaktam*—not perceivable by the material senses (*ataḥ śrī-kṛṣṇa-nāmādi na bhaved grāhyam indriyaiḥ*); *ādyam*—You are the original cause; *brahma*—You are known as Brahman; *jyotiḥ*—light; *nirguṇam*—without material qualities; *nirvikāram*—without change, the same form of Viṣṇu perpetually; *sattā-mātram*—the original substance, the cause of everything; *nirviśeṣam*—You are present everywhere as the Supersoul (within the heart of a human being and within the heart of an animal, the same substance is present); *nirīham*—without material desires; *saḥ*—that Supreme Person; *tvam*—Your Lordship; *sākṣāt*—directly; *viṣṇuḥ*—Lord Viṣṇu; *adhyātma-dīpaḥ*—the light for all transcendental knowledge (knowing You, one knows everything: *yasmin vijñāte sarvam evaṁ vijñātaṁ bhavati*).

## TRANSLATION

**Śrī Devakī said: My dear Lord, there are different Vedas, some of which describe You as unperceivable through words and the mind. Yet You are the origin of the entire cosmic manifestation. You are Brahman, the greatest of everything, full of effulgence like the sun. You have no material cause, You are free from change and deviation, and You have no material desires. Thus the Vedas say that You are the substance. Therefore, my Lord, You are directly the origin of all Vedic statements, and by understanding You, one gradually understands everything. You are different from the light of Brahman and Paramātmā, yet You are not different from them. Everything emanates from You. Indeed, You are the cause of all causes, Lord Viṣṇu, the light of all transcendental knowledge.**

## PURPORT

Viṣṇu is the origin of everything, and there is no difference between Lord Viṣṇu and Lord Kṛṣṇa because both of Them are *viṣṇu-tattva*. From the *Ṛg Veda* we understand, *oṁ tad viṣṇoḥ paramaṁ padam:* the original substance is the all-pervading Lord Viṣṇu, who is also Paramātmā and the effulgent Brahman. The living entities are also part and parcel of Viṣṇu, who has various energies (*parāsya śaktir vividhaiva śrūyate svābhāvikī jñāna-bala-kriyā ca*). Viṣṇu, or Kṛṣṇa, is therefore everything. Lord Kṛṣṇa says in the *Bhagavad-gītā* (10.8), *ahaṁ sarvasya prabhavo mattaḥ sarvaṁ pravartate:* "I am the source of all spiritual and material worlds. Everything emanates from Me." Kṛṣṇa, therefore, is the original cause of everything (*sarva-kāraṇa-kāraṇam*). When Viṣṇu expands in His all-pervading aspect, we should understand Him to be the *nirākāra-nirviśeṣa-brahmajyoti.*

Although everything emanates from Kṛṣṇa, He is ultimately a person. *Aham ādir hi devānām:* He is the origin of Brahmā, Viṣṇu and Maheśvara, and from them many other demigods are manifested. Kṛṣṇa therefore says in *Bhagavad-gītā* (14.27), *brahmaṇo hi pratiṣṭhāham:* "Brahman rests upon Me." The Lord also says:

*ye 'py anya-devatā-bhaktā*
*yajante śraddhayānvitāḥ*
*te 'pi mām eva kaunteya*
*yajanty avidhi-pūrvakam*

"Whatever a man may sacrifice to other gods, O son of Kuntī, is really meant for Me alone, but it is offered without true understanding." (Bg. 9.23) There are many persons who worship different demigods, considering all of them to be separate gods, which in fact they are not. The fact is that every demigod, and every living entity, is part and parcel of Kṛṣṇa (*mamaivāṁśo jīva-loke jīva-bhūtaḥ*). The demigods are also in the category of living entities; they are not separate gods. But men whose knowledge is immature and contaminated by the modes of material nature worship various demigods, according to their intelligence. Therefore they are rebuked in *Bhagavad-gītā* (*kāmais tais tair hṛta-jñānāḥ prapadyante 'nya-devatāḥ*). Because they are unintelligent and not very advanced and have not properly considered the truth, they take to the worship of various demigods or speculate according to various philosophies, such as the Māyāvāda philosophy.

Kṛṣṇa, Viṣṇu, is the actual origin of everything. As stated in the *Vedas, yasya bhāṣā sarvam idaṁ vibhāti.* The Absolute Truth is described later in the *Śrīmad-Bhāgavatam* (10.28.15) as *satyaṁ jñānam anantam yad brahma-jyotiḥ sānatanam.* The *brahmajyoti* is *sanātana,* eternal, yet it is dependent on Kṛṣṇa (*brahmaṇo hi pratiṣṭhāham*). The

*Brahma-saṁhitā* states that the Lord is all-pervading. *Aṇḍāntara-stha-paramāṇu-cayāntara-stham:* He is within this universe, and He is within the atom as Paramātmā. *Yasya prabhā prabhavato jagad-aṇḍa-koṭi-koṭiṣv aśeṣa-vasudhādi-vibhūti-bhinnam:* Brahman is also not independent of Him. Therefore whatever a philosopher may describe is ultimately Kṛṣṇa, or Lord Viṣṇu (*sarvaṁ khalv idaṁ brahma, paraṁ brahma paraṁ dhāma pavitraṁ paramaṁ bhavān*). According to different phases of understanding, Lord Viṣṇu is differently described, but in fact He is the origin of everything.

Because Devakī was an unalloyed devotee, she could understand that the same Lord Viṣṇu had appeared as her son. Therefore, after the prayers of Vasudeva, Devakī offered her prayers. She was very frightened because of her brother's atrocities. Devakī said, "My dear Lord, Your eternal forms, like Nārāyaṇa, Lord Rāma, Śeṣa, Varāha, Nṛsiṁha, Vāmana, Baladeva, and millions of similar incarnations emanating from Viṣṇu, are described in the Vedic literature as original. You are original because all Your forms as incarnations are outside of this material creation. Your form was existing before this cosmic manifestation was created. Your forms are eternal and all-pervading. They are self-effulgent, changeless and uncontaminated by the material qualities. Such eternal forms are evercognizant and full of bliss; they are situated in transcendental goodness and are always engaged in different pastimes. You are not limited to a particular form only; all such transcendental, eternal forms are self-sufficient. I can understand that You are the Supreme Lord Viṣṇu." We may conclude, therefore, that Lord Viṣṇu is everything, although He is also different from everything. This is the *acintya-bhedābheda-tattva* philosophy.

### TEXT 25

नष्टे लोके द्विपरार्धावसाने
महाभूतेष्वादिभूतं गतेषु ।
व्यक्तेऽव्यक्तं कालवेगेन याते
भवानेकः शिष्यतेऽशेषसंज्ञः ॥२५॥

*naṣṭe loke dvi-parārdhāvasāne*
*mahā-bhūteṣv ādi-bhūtaṁ gateṣu*

*vyakte 'vyaktaṁ kāla-vegena yāte*
*bhavān ekaḥ śiṣyate 'śeṣa-saṁjñaḥ*

*naṣṭe*—after the annihilation; *loke*—of the cosmic manifestation; *dvi-parārdha-avasāne*—after millions and millions of years (the life of Brahmā); *mahā-bhūteṣu*—when the five primary elements (earth, water, fire, air and ether); *ādi-bhūtam gateṣu*—enter within the subtle elements of sense perception; *vyakte*—when everything manifested; *avyaktam*—into the unmanifested; *kāla-vegena*—by the force of time; *yāte*—enters; *bhavān*—Your Lordship; *ekaḥ*—only one; *śiṣyate*—remains; *aśeṣa-saṁjñaḥ*—the same one with different names.

## TRANSLATION

**After millions of years, at the time of cosmic annihilation, when everything, manifested and unmanifested, is annihilated by the force of time, the five gross elements enter into the subtle conception, and the manifested categories enter into the unmanifested substance. At that time, You alone remain, and You are known as Ananta Śeṣa-nāga.**

## PURPORT

At the time of annihilation, the five gross elements—earth, water, fire, air and ether—enter into the mind, intelligence and false ego (*ahaṅkāra*), and the entire cosmic manifestation enters into the spiritual energy of the Supreme Personality of Godhead, who alone remains as the origin of everything. The Lord is therefore known as Śeṣa-nāga, as Ādi-puruṣa and by many other names.

Devakī therefore prayed, "After many millions of years, when Lord Brahmā comes to the end of his life, the annihilation of the cosmic manifestation takes place. At that time the five elements—namely earth, water, fire, air and ether—enter into the *mahat-tattva.* The *mahat-tattva* again enters, by the force of time, into the nonmanifested total material energy; the total material energy enters into the energetic *pradhāna,* and the *pradhāna* enters into You. Therefore after the annihilation of the whole cosmic manifestation, You alone remain with Your transcendental name, form, quality and paraphernalia.

"My Lord, I offer my respectful obeisances unto You because You are the director of the unmanifested total energy, and the ultimate reservoir of the material nature. My Lord, the whole cosmic manifestation is under the influence of time, beginning from the moment up to the duration of the year. All act under Your direction. You are the original director of everything and the reservoir of all potent energies."

## TEXT 26

योऽयं कालस्तस्य तेऽव्यक्तबन्धो
चेष्टामाहुश्चेष्टते येन विश्वम् ।
निमेषादिर्वत्सरान्तो महीयां-
स्तं त्वेशानं क्षेमधाम प्रपद्ये ॥२६॥

*yo 'yaṁ kālas tasya te 'vyakta-bandho*
*ceṣṭām āhuś ceṣṭate yena viśvam*
*nimeṣādir vatsarānto mahīyāṁs*
*taṁ tveśānaṁ kṣema-dhāma prapadye*

*yaḥ*—that which; *ayam*—this; *kālaḥ*—time (minutes, hours, seconds); *tasya*—of Him; *te*—of You; *avyakta-bandho*—O my Lord, You are the inaugurator of the unmanifested (the original *mahat-tattva* or *prakṛti*); *ceṣṭām*—attempt or pastimes; *āhuḥ*—it is said; *ceṣṭate*—works; *yena*—by which; *viśvam*—the entire creation; *nimeṣa-ādiḥ*—beginning with minute parts of time; *vatsara-antaḥ*—up to the limit of a year; *mahīyān*—powerful; *tam*—unto Your Lordship; *tvā īśānam*—unto You, the supreme controller; *kṣema-dhāma*—the reservoir of all auspiciousness; *prapadye*—I offer full surrender.

## TRANSLATION

**O inaugurator of the material energy, this wonderful creation works under the control of powerful time, which is divided into seconds, minutes, hours and years. This element of time, which extends for many millions of years, is but another form of Lord Viṣṇu. For Your pastimes, You act as the controller of time, but**

**You are the reservoir of all good fortune. Let me offer my full surrender unto Your Lordship.**

## PURPORT

As stated in the *Brahma-saṁhitā* (5.52):

*yac-cakṣur eṣa savitā sakala-grahāṇāṁ*
*rājā samasta-sura-mūrtir aśeṣa-tejāḥ*
*yasyājñayā bhramati saṁbhṛta-kāla-cakro*
*govindam ādi-puruṣaṁ tam ahaṁ bhajāmi*

"The sun is the king of all planetary systems and has unlimited potency in heat and light. I worship Govinda, the primeval Lord, the Supreme Personality of Godhead, under whose control even the sun, which is considered to be the eye of the Lord, rotates within the fixed orbit of eternal time." Although we see the cosmic manifestation as gigantic and wonderful, it is within the limitations of *kāla*, the time factor. This time factor is also controlled by the Supreme Personality of Godhead, as confirmed in *Bhagavad-gītā* (*mayādhyakṣeṇa prakṛtiḥ sūyate sa-carācaram*). *Prakṛti,* the cosmic manifestation, is under the control of time. Indeed, everything is under the control of time, and time is controlled by the Supreme Personality of Godhead. Therefore the Supreme Lord has no fear of the onslaughts of time. Time is estimated according to the movements of the sun (*savitā*). Every minute, every second, every day, every night, every month and every year of time can be calculated according to the sun's movements. But the sun is not independent, for it is under time's control. *Bhramati saṁbhṛta-kāla-cakraḥ:* the sun moves within the *kāla-cakra,* the orbit of time. The sun is under the control of time, and time is controlled by the Supreme Personality of Godhead. Therefore the Lord has no fear of time.

The Lord is addressed here as *avyakta-bandhu,* or the inaugurator of the movements of the entire cosmic manifestation. Sometimes the cosmic manifestation is compared to a potter's wheel. When a potter's wheel is spinning, who has set it in motion? It is the potter, of course, although sometimes we can see only the motion of the wheel and cannot see the potter himself. Therefore the Lord, who is behind the motion of the cosmos, is called *avyakta-bandhu.* Everything is within the limits of time, but time moves under the direction of the Lord, who is therefore not within time's limit.

## TEXT 27

मर्त्यो मृत्युव्यालभीतः पलायन्
लोकान् सर्वान्निर्भयं नाध्यगच्छत् ।
त्वत्पादाब्जं प्राप्य यदृच्छयाद्य
सुस्थः शेते मृत्युरस्मादपैति ॥२७॥

*martyo mṛtyu-vyāla-bhītaḥ palāyan*
*lokān sarvān nirbhayaṁ nādhyagacchat*
*tvat-pādābjaṁ prāpya yadṛcchayādya*
*susthaḥ śete mṛtyur asmād apaiti*

*martyaḥ*—the living entities who are sure to die; *mṛtyu-vyāla-bhītaḥ*—afraid of the serpent of death; *palāyan*—running (as soon as a serpent is seen, everyone runs away, fearing immediate death); *lokān*—to the different planets; *sarvān*—all; *nirbhayam*—fearlessness; *na adhyagacchat*—do not obtain; *tvat-pāda-abjam*—of Your lotus feet; *prāpya*—obtaining the shelter; *yadṛcchayā*—by chance, by the mercy of Your Lordship and Your representative, the spiritual master (*guru-kṛpā, kṛṣṇa-kṛpā*); *adya*—presently; *su-sthaḥ*—being undisturbed and mentally composed; *śete*—are sleeping; *mṛtyuḥ*—death; *asmāt*—from those persons; *apaiti*—flees.

## TRANSLATION

**No one in this material world has become free from the four principles birth, death, old age and disease, even by fleeing to various planets. But now that You have appeared, My Lord, death is fleeing in fear of You, and the living entities, having obtained shelter at Your lotus feet by Your mercy, are sleeping in full mental peace.**

## PURPORT

There are different categories of living entities, but everyone is afraid of death. The highest aim of the *karmīs* is to be promoted to the higher, heavenly planets, where the duration of life is very long. As stated in *Bhagavad-gītā* (8.17), *sahasra-yuga-paryantam ahar yad brahmaṇo viduḥ:* one day of Brahmā equals 1,000 *yugas*, and each *yuga* consists of 4,300,000 years. Similarly, Brahmā has a night of 1,000 times 4,300,000 years. In this way, we may calculate Brahmā's month and year, but even Brahmā, who lives for millions and millions of years (*dvi-parārdha-kāla*), also must die. According to Vedic *śāstra*, the inhabitants of the higher planetary systems live for 10,000 years, and just as Brahmā's day is calculated to equal 4,300,000,000 of our years, one day in the higher planetary systems equals six of our months. *Karmīs*, therefore, try for promotion to the higher planetary systems, but this cannot free them from death. In this material world, everyone from Brahmā to the insignificant ant must die. Therefore this world is called *martya-loka*. As Kṛṣṇa says in *Bhagavad-gītā* (8.16), *ābrahma-bhuvanāl lokāḥ punar āvartino 'rjuna:* as long as one is within this material world, either on Brahmaloka or on any other *loka* within this universe, one must undergo the *kāla-cakra* of one life after another (*bhūtvā bhūtvā pralīyate*). But if one returns to the Supreme Personality of Godhead (*yad gatvā na nivartante*), one need not reenter the limits of time. Therefore, devotees who have taken shelter of the lotus feet of the Supreme Lord can sleep very peacefully with this assurance from the Supreme Personality of Godhead. As confirmed in *Bhagavad-gītā* (4.9), *tyaktvā dehaṁ punar janma naiti:* after giving up the present body, a devotee who has understood Kṛṣṇa as He is need not return to this material world.

The constitutional position for the living entity is eternity (*na hanyate hanyamāne śarīre, nityaḥ śāśvato 'yam*). Every living entity is eternal. But because of having fallen into this material world, one wanders within the universe, continually changing from one body to another. Caitanya Mahāprabhu says:

*brahmāṇḍa bhramite kona bhāgyavān jīva*
*guru-kṛṣṇa prasāde pāya bhakti-latā-bīja*
(Cc. *Madhya* 19.151)

Everyone is wandering up and down within this universe, but one who is sufficiently fortunate comes in contact with Kṛṣṇa consciousness, by the mercy of the spiritual master, and takes to the path of devotional service. Then one is assured of eternal life, with no fear of death. When Kṛṣṇa appears, everyone is freed from fear of death, yet Devakī felt, "We are still afraid of Kaṁsa, although You have appeared as our son." She was more or less bewildered as to why this should be so, and she appealed to the Lord to free her and Vasudeva from this fear.

In this connection, it may be noted that the moon is one of the heavenly planets. From the Vedic literature we understand that one who goes to the moon receives a life with a duration of ten thousand years in which to enjoy the fruits of pious activities. If our so-called scientists are going to the moon, why should they come back here? We must conclude without a doubt that they have never gone to the moon. To go to the moon, one must have the qualification of pious activities. Then one may go there and live. If one has gone to the moon, why should he return to this planet, where life is of a very short duration?

## TEXT 28

स त्वं घोरादुग्रसेनात्मजान्न-
स्त्राहि त्रस्तान् भृत्यवित्रासहासि ।
रूपं चेदं पौरुषं ध्यानधिष्ण्यं
मा प्रत्यक्षं मांसदृशां कृषीष्ठाः ॥२८॥

*sa tvaṁ ghorād ugrasenātmajān nas*
*trāhi trastān bhṛtya-vitrāsa-hāsi*
*rūpaṁ cedaṁ pauruṣaṁ dhyāna-dhiṣṇyaṁ*
*mā pratyakṣaṁ māṁsa-dṛśāṁ kṛṣīṣṭhāḥ*

*saḥ*—Your Lordship; *tvam*—You; *ghorāt*—terribly fierce; *ugrasena-ātmajāt*—from the son of Ugrasena; *naḥ*—us; *trāhi*—kindly protect; *trastān*—who are very much afraid (of him); *bhṛtya-vitrāsa-hā asi*—You are naturally the destroyer of the fear of Your servants; *rūpam*—in Your Viṣṇu form; *ca*—also; *idam*—this; *pauruṣam*—as the Supreme Personality of Godhead; *dhyāna-dhiṣṇyam*—who is appreciated by meditation; *mā*—not; *pratyakṣam*—directly visible; *māṁsa-dṛśām*—to those who see with their material eyes; *kṛṣīṣṭhāḥ*—please be.

## TRANSLATION

**My Lord, because You dispell all the fear of Your devotees, I request You to save us and give us protection from the terrible fear of Kaṁsa. Your form as Viṣṇu, the Supreme Personality of Godhead, is appreciated by yogīs in meditation. Please make this form invisible to those who see with material eyes.**

## PURPORT

The word *dhyāna-dhiṣṇyam* is significant in this verse because the form of Lord Viṣṇu is meditated upon by *yogīs* (*dhyānāvasthita-tad-gatena manasā paśyanti yaṁ yoginaḥ*). Devakī requested the Lord, who had appeared as Viṣṇu, to conceal that form, for she wanted to see the Lord as an ordinary child, like a child appreciated by persons who have material eyes. Devakī wanted to see whether the Supreme Personality of Godhead had factually appeared or she was dreaming the Viṣṇu form. If Kaṁsa were to come, she thought, upon seeing the Viṣṇu form he would immediately kill the child, but if he saw a human child, he might reconsider. Devakī was afraid of Ugrasena-ātmaja; that is, she was afraid not of Ugrasena and his men, but of the son of Ugrasena. Thus she requested the Lord to dissipate that fear, since He is always ready to give protection (*abhayam*) to His devotees. "My Lord," she prayed, "I request You to save me from the cruel hands of the son of Ugrasena, Kaṁsa. I am praying to Your Lordship to please rescue me from this fearful condition because You are always ready to give protection to Your servitors." The Lord has confirmed this statement in the *Bhagavad-gītā* by assuring Arjuna, "You may declare to the world, My devotee shall never be vanquished."

While thus praying to the Lord for rescue, mother Devakī expressed her motherly affection: "I understand that this transcendental form is generally perceived in meditation by the great sages, but I am still afraid because as soon as Kaṁsa understands that You have appeared, he might harm You. So I request that for the time being You become invisible to our material eyes." In other words, she requested the Lord to assume the form of an ordinary child. "My only cause of fear from my brother Kaṁsa is due to Your appearance. My Lord Madhusūdana, Kaṁsa may know that You are already born. Therefore I request You to conceal this four-armed form of Your Lordship, which holds the four symbols of Viṣṇu—namely the conchshell, the disc, the club and the lotus flower. My dear Lord, at the end of the annihilation of the cosmic manifestation, You put the whole universe within Your abdomen; still, by Your unalloyed mercy, You have appeared in my womb. I am surprised that You imitate the activities of ordinary human beings just to please Your devotee."

Devakī was so afraid of Kaṁsa that she could not believe that Kaṁsa would be unable to kill Lord Viṣṇu, who was personally present. Out of motherly affection, therefore, she requested the Supreme Personality of Godhead to disappear. Although because of the Lord's disappearance Kaṁsa would harass her more and more, thinking that the child born of her was hidden somewhere, she did not want the transcendental child to be harassed and killed. Therefore she requested Lord Viṣṇu to disappear. Later, when harassed, she would think of Him within her mind.

## TEXT 29

जन्म ते मय्यसौ पापो मा विद्यान्मधुसूदन ।
समुद्विजे भवद्धेतोः कंसादहमधीरधीः ॥२९॥

*janma te mayy asau pāpo*
*mā vidyān madhusūdana*
*samudvije bhavad-dhetoḥ*
*kaṁsād aham adhīra-dhīḥ*

*janma*—the birth; *te*—of Your Lordship; *mayi*—in my (womb); *asau*—that Kaṁsa; *pāpaḥ*—extremely sinful; *mā vidyāt*—may be unable to understand; *madhusūdana*—O Madhusūdana; *samudvije*—I am full of anxiety; *bhavat-hetoḥ*—because of Your appearance; *kaṁsāt*—because of Kaṁsa, with whom I have had such bad experience; *aham*—I; *adhīra-dhīḥ*—have become more and more anxious.

### TRANSLATION

**O Madhusūdana, because of Your appearance, I am becoming more and more anxious in fear of Kaṁsa. Therefore, please arrange for that sinful Kaṁsa to be unable to understand that You have taken birth from my womb.**

### PURPORT

Devakī addressed the Supreme Personality of Godhead as Madhusūdana. She was aware that the Lord had killed many demons like Madhu who were hundreds and thousands of times more powerful than Kaṁsa, yet because of affection for the transcendental child, she believed that Kaṁsa could kill Him. Instead of thinking of the unlimited power of the Lord, she thought of the Lord with affection, and therefore she requested the transcendental child to disappear.

### TEXT 30

उपसंहर विश्वात्मन्नदो रूपमलौकिकम् ।
शङ्खचक्रगदापद्मश्रिया जुष्टं चतुर्भुजम् ॥३०॥

*upasaṁhara viśvātmann*
*ado rūpam alaukikam*
*śaṅkha-cakra-gadā-padma-*
*śriyā juṣṭaṁ catur-bhujam*

*upasaṁhara*—withdraw; *viśvātman*—O all-pervading Supreme Personality of Godhead; *adaḥ*—that; *rūpam*—form; *alaukikam*—which is unnatural in this world; *śaṅkha-cakra-gadā-padma*—of the conchshell, disc, club and lotus; *śriyā*—with these opulences; *juṣṭam*—decorated; *catuḥ-bhujam*—four hands.

### TRANSLATION

**O my Lord, You are the all-pervading Supreme Personality of Godhead, and Your transcendental four-armed form, holding conchshell, disc, club and lotus, is unnatural for this world. Please**

**withdraw this form [and become just like a natural human child so that I may try to hide You somewhere].**

## PURPORT

Devakī was thinking of hiding the Supreme Personality of Godhead and not handing Him over to Kaṁsa as she had all her previous children. Although Vasudeva had promised to hand over every child to Kaṁsa, this time he wanted to break his promise and hide the child somewhere. But because of the Lord's appearance in this surprising four-armed form, He would be impossible to hide.

## TEXT 31

विश्वं यदेतत् स्वतनौ निशान्ते
यथावकाशं पुरुषः परो भवान् ।
बिभर्ति सोऽयं मम गर्भगोऽभू-
दहो नृलोकस्य विडम्बनं हि तत् ॥३१॥

*viśvaṁ yad etat sva-tanau niśānte*
*yathāvakāśaṁ puruṣaḥ paro bhavān*
*bibharti so 'yaṁ mama garbhago 'bhūd*
*aho nṛ-lokasya viḍambanaṁ hi tat*

*viśvam*—the entire cosmic manifestation; *yat etat*—containing all moving and nonmoving creations; *sva-tanau*—within Your body; *niśā-ante*—at the time of devastation; *yathā-avakāśam*—shelter in Your body without difficulty; *puruṣaḥ*—the Supreme Personality of Godhead; *paraḥ*—transcendental; *bhavān*—Your Lordship; *bibharti*—keep; *saḥ*—that (Supreme Personality of Godhead); *ayam*—this form; *mama*—my; *garbha-gaḥ*—came within my womb; *abhūt*—it so happened; *aho*—alas; *nṛ-lokasya*—within this material world of living entities; *viḍambanam*—it is impossible to think of; *hi*—indeed; *tat*—that (kind of conception).

## TRANSLATION

**At the time of devastation, the entire cosmos, containing all created moving and nonmoving entities, enters Your transcendental**

**body and is held there without difficulty. But now this transcendental form has taken birth from my womb. People will not be able to believe this, and I shall become an object of ridicule.**

## PURPORT

As explained in *Caitanya-caritāmṛta*, loving service to the Personality of Godhead is of two different kinds: *aiśvarya-pūrṇa*, full of opulence, and *aiśvarya-śīthila*, without opulence. Real love of Godhead begins with *aiśvarya-śīthila*, simply on the basis of pure love.

*premāñjana-cchurita-bhakti-vilocanena*
*santaḥ sadaiva hṛdayeṣu vilokayanti*
*yaṁ śyāmasundaram acintya-guṇa-svarūpaṁ*
*govindam ādi-puruṣaṁ tam ahaṁ bhajāmi*
(*Brahma-saṁhitā* 5.38)

Pure devotees, whose eyes are anointed with the ointment of *premā*, love, want to see the Supreme Personality of Godhead as Śyāmasundara, Muralīdhara, with a flute swaying in His two hands. This is the form available to the inhabitants of Vṛndāvana, who are all in love with the Supreme Personality of Godhead as Śyāmasundara, not as Lord Viṣṇu, Nārāyaṇa, who is worshiped in Vaikuṇṭha, where the devotees admire His opulence. Although Devakī is not on the Vṛndāvana platform, she is near the Vṛndāvana platform. On the Vṛndāvana platform the mother of Kṛṣṇa is mother Yaśodā, and on the Mathurā and Dvārakā platform the mother of Kṛṣṇa is Devakī. In Mathurā and Dvārakā the love for the Lord is mixed with appreciation of His opulence, but in Vṛndāvana the opulence of the Supreme Personality of Godhead is not exhibited.

There are five stages of loving service to the Supreme Personality of Godhead—*śānta*, *dāsya*, *sakhya*, *vātsalya* and *mādhurya*. Devakī is on the platform of *vātsalya*. She wanted to deal with her eternal son, Kṛṣṇa, in that stage of love, and therefore she wanted the Supreme Personality of Godhead to withdraw His opulent form of Viṣṇu. Śrīla Viśvanātha Cakravartī Ṭhākura illuminates this fact very clearly in his explanation of this verse.

*Bhakti*, *bhagavān* and *bhakta* do not belong to the material world. This is confirmed in *Bhagavad-gītā* (14.26):

*māṁ ca yo 'vyabhicāreṇa*
*bhakti-yogena sevate*
*sa guṇān samatītyaitān*
*brahma-bhūyāya kalpate*

"One who engages in the spiritual activities of unalloyed devotional service immediately transcends the modes of material nature and is elevated to the spiritual platform." From the very beginning of one's transactions in *bhakti*, one is situated on the transcendental platform. Vasudeva and Devakī, therefore, being situated in a completely pure devotional state, are beyond this material world and are not subject to material fear. In the transcendental world, however, because of pure devotion, there is a similar conception of fear, which is due to intense love.

As stated in *Bhagavad-gītā* (*bhaktyā mām abhijānāti yāvān yaś cāsmi tattvataḥ*) and as confirmed in *Śrīmad-Bhāgavatam* (*bhaktyāham ekayā grāhyaḥ*), without *bhakti* one cannot understand the spiritual situation of the Lord. *Bhakti* may be considered in three stages, called *guṇī-bhūta*, *pradhānī-bhūta* and *kevala*, and according to these stages there are three divisions, which are called *jñāna*, *jñānamayī* and *rati*, or *premā*—that is, simple knowledge, love mixed with knowledge, and pure love. By simple knowledge, one can perceive transcendental bliss without variety. This perception is called *māna-bhūti*. When one comes to the stage of *jñānamayī*, one realizes the transcendental opulences of the Personality of Godhead. But when one reaches pure love, one realizes the transcendental form of the Lord as Lord Kṛṣṇa or Lord Rāma. This is what is wanted. Especially in the *mādhurya-rasa*, one becomes attached to the Personality of Godhead (*śrī-vigraha-niṣṭha-rūpādi*). Then loving transactions between the Lord and the devotee begin.

The special significance of Kṛṣṇa's bearing a flute in His hands in Vrajabhūmi, Vṛndāvana, is described as *mādhurī . . . virājate*. The form of the Lord with a flute in His hands is most attractive, and the one who is most sublimely attracted is Śrīmatī Rādhārāṇī, Rādhikā. She enjoys supremely blissful association with Kṛṣṇa. Sometimes people cannot understand why Rādhikā's name is not mentioned in *Śrīmad-Bhāgavatam*. Actually, however, Rādhikā can be understood from the word *ārādhana*, which indicates that She enjoys the highest loving affairs with Kṛṣṇa.

Not wanting to be ridiculed for having given birth to Viṣṇu, Devakī wanted Kṛṣṇa, with two hands, and therefore she requested the Lord to change His form.

## TEXT 32

श्रीभगवानुवाच
त्वमेव पूर्वसर्गेऽभूः पृश्निः स्वायम्भुवे सति ।
तदायं सुतपा नाम प्रजापतिरकल्मषः ॥३२॥

*śrī-bhagavān uvāca*
*tvam eva pūrva-sarge 'bhūḥ*
*pṛśniḥ svāyambhuve sati*
*tadāyaṁ sutapā nāma*
*prajāpatir akalmaṣaḥ*

*śrī-bhagavān uvāca*—the Supreme Personality of Godhead said to Devakī; *tvam*—you; *eva*—indeed; *pūrva-sarge*—in a previous millennium; *abhūḥ*—became; *pṛśniḥ*—by the name Pṛśni; *svāyambhuve*—the millennium of Svāyambhuva Manu; *sati*—O supremely chaste; *tadā*—at that time; *ayam*—Vasudeva; *sutapā*—Sutapā; *nāma*—by the name; *prajāpatiḥ*—a Prajāpati; *akalmaṣaḥ*—a spotlessly pious person.

## TRANSLATION

**The Supreme Personality of Godhead replied: My dear mother, best of the chaste, in your previous birth, in the Svāyambhuva millennium, you were known as Pṛśni, and Vasudeva, who was the most pious Prajāpati, was named Sutapā.**

## PURPORT

The Supreme Personality of Godhead made it clear that Devakī had not become His mother only now; rather, she had been His mother previously also. Kṛṣṇa is eternal, and His selection of a father and mother from among His devotees takes place eternally. Previously also, Devakī had been the Lord's mother and Vasudeva the Lord's father, and they were named Pṛśni and Sutapā. When the Supreme Personality of Godhead appears, He accepts His eternal father and mother, and they accept

Kṛṣṇa as their son. This pastime takes place eternally and is therefore called *nitya-līlā.* Thus there was no cause for surprise or ridicule. As confirmed by the Lord Himself in *Bhagavad-gītā* (4.9):

*janma karma ca me divyam*
*evaṁ yo vetti tattvataḥ*
*tyaktvā dehaṁ punar janma*
*naiti mām eti so 'rjuna*

"One who knows the transcendental nature of My appearance and activities does not, upon leaving the body, take his birth again in this material world, but attains My eternal abode, O Arjuna." One should try to understand the appearance and disappearance of the Supreme Personality of Godhead from Vedic authorities, not from imagination. One who follows his imaginations about the Supreme Personality of Godhead is condemned.

*avajānanti māṁ mūḍhā*
*mānuṣīṁ tanum āśritam*
*paraṁ bhāvam ajānanto*
*mama bhūta-maheśvaram*
(Bg. 9.11)

The Lord appears as the son of His devotee by His *paraṁ bhāvam.* The word *bhāva* refers to the stage of pure love, which has nothing to do with material transactions.

## TEXT 33

युवां वै ब्रह्मणादिष्टौ प्रजासर्गे यदा ततः ।
सन्नियम्येन्द्रियग्रामं तेपाथे परमं तपः ॥३३॥

*yuvāṁ vai brahmaṇādiṣṭau*
*prajā-sarge yadā tataḥ*
*sanniyamyendriya-grāmaṁ*
*tepāthe paramaṁ tapaḥ*

*yuvām*—both of you (Pṛśni and Sutapā); *vai*—indeed; *brahmaṇā ādiṣṭau*—ordered by Lord Brahmā (who is known as Pitāmaha, the father of the Prajāpatis); *prajā-sarge*—in the creation of progeny; *yadā*—when; *tataḥ*—thereafter; *sanniyamya*—keeping under full control; *indriya-grāmam*—the senses; *tepāthe*—underwent; *paramam*—very great; *tapaḥ*—austerity.

## TRANSLATION

**When both of you were ordered by Lord Brahmā to create progeny, you first underwent severe austerities by controlling your senses.**

## PURPORT

Here is an instruction about how to use one's senses to create progeny. According to Vedic principles, before creating progeny one must fully control the senses. This control takes place through the *garbhādhāna-saṁskāra.* In India there is great agitation for birth control in various mechanical ways, but birth cannot be mechanically controlled. As stated in *Bhagavad-gītā* (13.9), *janma-mṛtyu-jarā-vyādhi-duḥkha-doṣānu-darśanam:* birth, death, old age and disease are certainly the primary distresses of the material world. People are trying to control birth, but they are not able to control death; and if one cannot control death, one cannot control birth either. In other words, artificially controlling birth is not any more feasible than artificially controlling death.

According to Vedic civilization, procreation should not be contrary to religious principles, and then the birthrate will be controlled. As stated in *Bhagavad-gītā* (7.11), *dharmāviruddho bhūteṣu kāmo 'smi:* sex not contrary to religious principles is a representation of the Supreme Lord. People should be educated in how to give birth to good children through *saṁskāras*, beginning with the *garbhādhāna-saṁskāra;* birth should not be controlled by artificial means, for this will lead to a civilization of animals. If one follows religious principles, he automatically practices birth control because if one is spiritually educated he knows that the aftereffects of sex are various types of misery (*bahu-duḥkha-bhāja*). One who is spiritually advanced does not indulge in uncontrolled sex. Therefore, instead of being forced to refrain from sex or refrain from giving birth to many children, people should be spiritually educated, and then birth control will automatically follow.

If one is determined to make spiritual advancement, he will not beget a child unless able to make that child a devotee. As stated in *Śrīmad-Bhāgavatam* (5.5.18), *pitā na sa syāt:* one should not become a father unless one is able to protect his child from *mṛtyu*, the path of birth and death. But where is there education about this? A responsible father never begets children like cats and dogs. Instead of being encouraged to adopt artificial means of birth control, people should be educated in Kṛṣṇa consciousness because only then will they understand their responsibility to their children. If one can beget children who will be devotees and be taught to turn aside from the path of birth and death (*mṛtyu-saṁsāra-vartmani*), there is no need of birth control. Rather, one should be encouraged to beget children. Artificial means of birth control have no value. Whether one begets children or does not, a population of men who are like cats and dogs will never make human society happy. It is therefore necessary for people to be educated spiritually so that instead of begetting children like cats and dogs, they will undergo austerities to produce devotees. This will make their lives successful.

## TEXTS 34–35

वर्षवातातपहिमघर्मकालगुणाननु ।
सहमानौ श्वासरोधविनिर्धूतमनोमलौ ॥३४॥
शीर्णपर्णानिलाहारावुपशान्तेन चेतसा ।
मत्तः कामानभीप्सन्तौ मदाराधनमीहतुः ॥३५॥

*varṣa-vātātapa-hima-*
*gharma-kāla-guṇān anu*
*sahamānau śvāsa-rodha-*
*vinirdhūta-mano-malau*

*śīrṇa-parṇānilāhārāv*
*upaśāntena cetasā*
*mattaḥ kāmān abhīpsantau*
*mad-ārādhanam īhatuḥ*

*varṣa*—the rain; *vāta*—strong wind; *ātapa*—strong sunshine; *hima*—severe cold; *gharma*—heat; *kāla-guṇān anu*—according to seasonal changes; *sahamānau*—by enduring; *śvāsa-rodha*—by practicing *yoga*, controlling the breath; *vinirdhūta*—the dirty things accumulated in the mind were completely washed away; *manaḥ-malau*—the mind became clean, free from material contamination; *śīrṇa*—rejected, dry; *parṇa*—leaves from the trees; *anila*—and air; *āhārau*—eating; *upaśāntena*—peaceful; *cetasā*—with a fully controlled mind; *mattaḥ*—from Me; *kāmān abhīpsantau*—desiring to beg some benediction; *mat*—My; *ārādhanam*—worship; *īhatuḥ*—you both executed.

## TRANSLATION

**My dear father and mother, you endured rain, wind, strong sun, scorching heat and severe cold, suffering all sorts of inconvenience according to different seasons. By practicing prāṇāyāma to control the air within the body through yoga, and by eating only air and dry leaves fallen from the trees, you cleansed from your minds all dirty things. In this way, desiring a benediction from Me, you worshiped Me with peaceful minds.**

## PURPORT

Vasudeva and Devakī did not obtain the Supreme Personality of Godhead as their son very easily, nor does the Supreme Godhead accept merely anyone as His father and mother. Here we can see how Vasudeva and Devakī obtained Kṛṣṇa as their eternal son. In our own lives, we are meant to follow the principles indicated herewith for getting good children. Of course, it is not possible for everyone to get Kṛṣṇa as his son, but at least one can get very good sons and daughters for the benefit of human society. In *Bhagavad-gītā* it is said that if human beings do not follow the spiritual way of life, there will be an increase of *varṇa-saṅkara* population, population begotten like cats and dogs, and the entire world will become like hell. Not practicing Kṛṣṇa consciousness but simply encouraging artificial means to check the population will be futile; the population will increase, and it will consist of *varṇa-saṅkara*, unwanted progeny. It is better to teach people how to beget children not like hogs and dogs, but in controlled life.

Human life is meant not for becoming a hog or dog, but for *tapo divyam*, transcendental austerity. Everyone should be taught to undergo austerity, *tapasya*. Although it may not be possible to undergo *tapasya* like that of Pṛśni and Sutapā, the *śāstra* has given an opportunity for a method of *tapasya* very easy to perform—the *saṅkīrtana* movement. One cannot expect to undergo *tapasya* to get Kṛṣṇa as one's child, yet simply by chanting the Hare Kṛṣṇa *mahā-mantra* (*kīrtanād eva kṛṣṇasya*), one can become so pure that one becomes free from all the contamination of this material world (*mukta-saṅgaḥ*) and goes back home, back to Godhead (*paraṁ vrajet*). The Kṛṣṇa consciousness movement, therefore, is teaching people not to adopt artificial means of happiness, but to take the real path of happiness as prescribed in the *śāstra*—the chanting of the Hare Kṛṣṇa *mantra*—and become perfect in every aspect of material existence.

## TEXT 36

एवं वां तप्यतोस्तीव्रं तपः परमदुष्करम् ।
दिव्यवर्षसहस्राणि द्वादशेयुर्मदात्मनोः ॥३६॥

*evaṁ vāṁ tapyatos tīvraṁ*
*tapaḥ parama-duṣkaram*
*divya-varṣa-sahasrāṇi*
*dvādaśeyur mad-ātmanoḥ*

*evam*—in this way; *vām*—for both of you; *tapyatoḥ*—executing austerities; *tīvram*—very severe; *tapaḥ*—austerity; *parama-duṣkaram*—extremely difficult to execute; *divya-varṣa*—celestial years, or years counted according to the higher planetary system; *sahasrāṇi*—thousand; *dvādaśa*—twelve; *īyuḥ*—passed; *mat-ātmanoḥ*—simply engaged in consciousness of Me.

## TRANSLATION

**Thus you spent twelve thousand celestial years performing difficult activities of tapasya in consciousness of Me [Kṛṣṇa consciousness].**

## TEXTS 37–38

तदा वां परितुष्टोऽहममुना वपुषानघे ।
तपसा श्रद्धया नित्यं भक्त्या च हृदि भावितः ॥३७॥

प्रादुरासं वरदराड युवयोः कामदित्सया ।
व्रियतां वर इत्युक्ते माद‍ृशो वां वृतः सुतः ॥३८॥

*tadā vāṁ parituṣṭo 'ham*
*amunā vapuṣānaghe*
*tapasā śraddhayā nityaṁ*
*bhaktyā ca hṛdi bhāvitaḥ*

*prādurāsaṁ varada-rāḍ*
*yuvayoḥ kāma-ditsayā*
*vriyatāṁ vara ity ukte*
*mādṛśo vāṁ vṛtaḥ sutaḥ*

*tadā*—then (after the expiry of twelve thousand celestial years); *vām*—with both of you; *parituṣṭaḥ aham*—I was very much satisfied; *amunā*—by this; *vapuṣā*—in this form as Kṛṣṇa; *anaghe*—O My dear sinless mother; *tapasā*—by austerity; *śraddhayā*—by faith; *nityam*—constantly (engaged); *bhaktyā*—by devotional service; *ca*—as well as; *hṛdi*—within the core of the heart; *bhāvitaḥ*—fixed (in determination); *prādurāsam*—appeared before you (in the same way); *vara-da-rāṭ*—the best of all who can bestow benedictions; *yuvayoḥ*—of both of you; *kāma-ditsayā*—wishing to fulfill the desire; *vriyatām*—asked you to open your minds; *varaḥ*—for a benediction; *iti ukte*—when you were requested in this way; *mādṛśaḥ*—exactly like Me; *vām*—of both of you; *vṛtaḥ*—was asked; *sutaḥ*—as Your son (you wanted a son exactly like Me).

## TRANSLATION

**O sinless mother Devakī, after the expiry of twelve thousand celestial years, in which you constantly contemplated Me within the core of your heart with great faith, devotion and austerity, I was very much satisfied with you. Since I am the best of all bestowers of benediction, I appeared in this same form as Kṛṣṇa to ask you to take from Me the benediction you desired. You then expressed your desire to have a son exactly like Me.**

## PURPORT

Twelve thousand years on the celestial planets is not a very long time for those who live in the upper planetary system, although it may be very long for those who live on this planet. Sutapā was the son of Brahmā, and as we have already understood from *Bhagavad-gītā* (8.17), one day of Brahmā equals many millions of years according to our calculation (*sahasra-yuga-paryantam ahar yad brahmaṇo viduḥ*). We should be careful to understand that to get Kṛṣṇa as one's son, one must undergo such great austerities. If we want to get the Supreme Personality of Godhead to become one of us in this material world, this requires great penance, but if we want to go back to Kṛṣṇa (*tyaktvā dehaṁ punar janma naiti mām eti so 'rjuna*), we need only understand Him and love Him. Through love only, we can very easily go back home, back to Godhead. Śrī Caitanya Mahāprabhu therefore declared, *premā pum-artho mahān:* love of Godhead is the highest achievement for anyone.

As we have explained, in worship of the Lord there are three stages—*jñāna, jñānamayī* and *rati,* or love. Sutapā and his wife, Pṛśni, inaugurated their devotional activities on the basis of full knowledge. Gradually they developed love for the Supreme Personality of Godhead, and when this love was mature, the Lord appeared as Viṣṇu, although Devakī then requested Him to assume the form of Kṛṣṇa. To love the Supreme Personality of Godhead more, we want a form of the Lord like Kṛṣṇa or Rāma. We can engage in loving transactions with Kṛṣṇa especially.

In this age, we are all fallen, but the Supreme Personality of Godhead has appeared as Caitanya Mahāprabhu to bestow upon us love of Godhead directly. This was appreciated by the associates of Śrī Caitanya Mahāprabhu. Rūpa Gosvāmī said:

*namo mahā-vadānyāya*
*kṛṣṇa-prema-pradāya te*
*kṛṣṇāya kṛṣṇa-caitanya-*
*nāmne gaura-tviṣe namaḥ*

In this verse, Śrī Caitanya Mahāprabhu is described as *mahā-vadānya,* the most munificent of charitable persons, because He gives Kṛṣṇa so easily that one can attain Kṛṣṇa simply by chanting the Hare Kṛṣṇa *mahā-mantra.* We should therefore take advantage of the benediction given by Śrī Caitanya Mahāprabhu, and when by chanting the Hare Kṛṣṇa *mantra* we are cleansed of all dirty things (*ceto-darpaṇa-mārjanam*), we shall be able to understand very easily that Kṛṣṇa is the only object of love (*kīrtanād eva kṛṣṇasya mukta-saṅgaḥ paraṁ vrajet*).

Therefore, one need not undergo severe penances for many thousands of years; one need only learn how to love Kṛṣṇa and be always engaged in His service (*sevonmukhe hi jihvādau svayam eva sphuraty adaḥ*). Then one can very easily go back home, back to Godhead. Instead of bringing the Lord here for some material purpose, to have a son or whatever else, if we go back home, back to Godhead, our real relationship with the Lord is revealed, and we eternally engage in our eternal relationship. By chanting the Hare Kṛṣṇa *mantra*, we gradually develop our eternal relationship with the Supreme Person and thus attain the perfection called *svarūpa-siddhi.* We should take advantage of this benediction and go back home, back to Godhead. Śrīla Narottama dāsa Ṭhākura has therefore sung, *patita-pāvana-hetu tava avatāra:* Caitanya Mahāprabhu appeared as an incarnation to deliver all fallen souls like us and directly bestow upon us love of Godhead. We must take advantage of this great benediction of the great Personality of Godhead.

## TEXT 39

अजुष्टग्राम्यविषयावनपत्यौ च दम्पती ।
न वव्राथेऽपवर्गं मे मोहितौ देवमायया ॥३९॥

*ajuṣṭa-grāmya-viṣayāv*
*anapatyau ca dam-patī*
*na vavrāthe 'pavargaṁ me*
*mohitau deva-māyayā*

*ajuṣṭa-grāmya-viṣayau*—for sex life and to beget a child like Me; *anapatyau*—because of possessing no son; *ca*—also; *dam-patī*—both husband and wife; *na*—never; *vavrāthe*—asked for (any other benediction); *apavargam*—liberation from this world; *me*—from Me; *mohitau*—being so much attracted; *deva-māyayā*—by transcendental love for Me (desiring Me as your beloved son).

## TRANSLATION

**Being husband and wife but always sonless, you were attracted by sexual desires, for by the influence of devamāyā, transcendental**

**love, you wanted to have Me as your son. Therefore you never desired to be liberated from this material world.**

## PURPORT

Vasudeva and Devakī had been *dam-patī,* husband and wife, since the time of Sutapā and Pṛśni, and they wanted to remain husband and wife in order to have the Supreme Personality of Godhead as their son. This attachment came about by the influence of *devamāyā.* Loving Kṛṣṇa as one's son is a Vedic principle. Vasudeva and Devakī never desired anything but to have the Lord as their son, yet for this purpose they apparently wanted to live like ordinary *gṛhasthas* for sexual indulgence. Although this was a transaction of spiritual potency, their desire appears like attachment for sex in conjugal life. If one wants to return home, back to Godhead, one must give up such desires. This is possible only when one develops intense love for the Supreme Personality of Godhead. Śrī Caitanya Mahāprabhu has said:

*niṣkiñcanasya bhagavad-bhajanonmukhasya*
*pāraṁ paraṁ jigamiṣor bhava-sāgarasya*
(Cc. *Madhya* 11.8)

If one wants to go back home, back to Godhead, one must be *niṣkiñcana,* free from all material desires. Therefore, instead of desiring to have the Lord come here and become one's son, one should desire to become free from all material desires (*anyābhilāṣitā-śūnyam*) and go back home, back to Godhead. Śrī Caitanya Mahāprabhu teaches us in His *Śikṣāṣṭaka:*

*na dhanaṁ na janaṁ na sundarīṁ*
*kavitāṁ vā jagad-īśa kāmaye*
*mama janmani janmanīśvare*
*bhavatād bhaktir ahaitukī tvayi*

"O almighty Lord, I have no desire to accumulate wealth, nor do I desire beautiful women, nor do I want any number of followers. I only want Your causeless devotional service, birth after birth." One should not ask the Lord to fulfill any materially tainted desires.

## TEXT 40

गते मयि युवां लब्ध्वा वरं मत्सदृशं सुतम् ।
ग्राम्यान् भोगानभुञ्जाथां युवां प्राप्तमनोरथौ ॥४०॥

*gate mayi yuvāṁ labdhvā*
*varaṁ mat-sadṛśaṁ sutam*
*grāmyān bhogān abhuñjāthāṁ*
*yuvāṁ prāpta-manorathau*

*gate mayi*—after My departure; *yuvām*—both of you (husband and wife); *labdhvā*—after receiving; *varam*—the benediction of (having a son); *mat-sadṛśam*—exactly like Me; *sutam*—a son; *grāmyān bhogān*—engagement in sex; *abhuñjāthām*—enjoyed; *yuvām*—both of you; *prāpta*—having been achieved; *manorathau*—the desired result of your aspirations.

## TRANSLATION

**After you received that benediction and I disappeared, you engaged yourselves in sex to have a son like Me, and I fulfilled your desire.**

## PURPORT

According to the Sanskrit dictionary *Amara-kośa*, sex life is also called *grāmya-dharma*, material desire, but in spiritual life this *grāmya-dharma*, the material desire for sex, is not very much appreciated. If one has a tinge of attachment for the material enjoyments of eating, sleeping, mating and defending, one is not *niṣkiñcana*. But one really should be *niṣkiñcana*. Therefore, one should be free from the desire to beget a child like Kṛṣṇa by sexual enjoyment. This is indirectly hinted at in this verse.

## TEXT 41

अदृष्ट्वान्यतमं लोके शीलौदार्यगुणैः समम् ।
अहं सुतो वामभवं पृश्निगर्भ इति श्रुतः ॥४१॥

*adṛṣṭvānyatamaṁ loke*
*śīlaudārya-guṇaiḥ samam*
*ahaṁ suto vām abhavaṁ*
*pṛśnigarbha iti śrutaḥ*

*adṛṣṭvā*—not finding; *anyatamam*—anyone else; *loke*—in this world; *śīla-audārya-guṇaiḥ*—with the transcendental qualities of good character and magnanimity; *samam*—equal to you; *aham*—I; *sutaḥ*—the son; *vām*—of both of you; *abhavam*—became; *pṛśni-garbhaḥ*—celebrated as born of Pṛśni; *iti*—thus; *śrutaḥ*—I am known.

## TRANSLATION

**Since I found no one else as highly elevated as you in simplicity and other qualities of good character, I appeared in this world as Pṛśnigarbha, or one who is celebrated as having taken birth from Pṛśni.**

## PURPORT

In the Tretā-yuga the Lord appeared as Pṛśnigarbha. Śrīla Viśvanātha Cakravartī Ṭhākura says, *pṛśnigarbha iti so 'yaṁ tretā-yugāvatāro lakṣyate.*

## TEXT 42

तयोर्वां पुनरेवाहमदित्यामास कश्यपात् ।
उपेन्द्र इति विख्यातो वामनत्वाच्च वामनः ॥४२॥

*tayor vāṁ punar evāham*
*adityām āsa kaśyapāt*
*upendra iti vikhyāto*
*vāmanatvāc ca vāmanaḥ*

*tayoḥ*—of you two, husband and wife; *vām*—in both of you; *punaḥ eva*—even again; *aham*—I Myself; *adityām*—in the womb of Aditi; *āsa*—appeared; *kaśyapāt*—by the semen of Kaśyapa Muni; *upendraḥ*—by the name Upendra; *iti*—thus; *vikhyātaḥ*—celebrated; *vāmanatvāt ca*—and because of being a dwarf; *vāmanaḥ*—I was known as Vāmana.

## TRANSLATION

**In the next millennium, I again appeared from the two of you, who appeared as My mother, Aditi, and My father, Kaśyapa. I was known as Upendra, and because of being a dwarf, I was also known as Vāmana.**

## TEXT 43

तृतीयेऽस्मिन् भवेऽहं वै तेनैव वपुषाथ वाम् ।
जातो भूयस्तयोरेव सत्यं मे व्याहृतं सति ॥४३॥

*tṛtīye 'smin bhave 'haṁ vai*
*tenaiva vapuṣātha vām*
*jāto bhūyas tayor eva*
*satyaṁ me vyāhṛtaṁ sati*

*tṛtīye*—for the third time; *asmin bhave*—in this appearance (as Kṛṣṇa); *aham*—I Myself; *vai*—indeed; *tena*—with the same personality; *eva*—in this way; *vapuṣā*—by the form; *atha*—as; *vām*—of both of you; *jātaḥ*—born; *bhūyaḥ*—again; *tayoḥ*—of both of you; *eva*—indeed; *satyam*—take as truth; *me*—My; *vyāhṛtam*—words; *sati*—O supremely chaste.

## TRANSLATION

**O supremely chaste mother, I, the same personality, have now appeared of you both as your son for the third time. Take My words as the truth.**

## PURPORT

The Supreme Personality of Godhead chooses a mother and father from whom to take birth again and again. The Lord took birth originally from Sutapā and Pṛśni, then from Kaśyapa and Aditi, and again from the same father and mother, Vasudeva and Devakī. "In other appearances also," the Lord said, "I took the form of an ordinary child just to become your son so that we could reciprocate eternal love." Jīva Gosvāmī has explained this verse in his *Kṛṣṇa-sandarbha*, Ninety-sixth Chapter, where he notes that in text 37 the Lord says, *amunā vapuṣa*, meaning "by this same form." In other words, the Lord told Devakī, "This time I have appeared in My original form as Śrī Kṛṣṇa." Śrīla Jīva Gosvāmī says that the other forms were partial expansions of the Lord's original form, but because of the intense love developed by Pṛśni and Sutapā, the Lord appeared from Devakī and Vasudeva in His full opulence as Śrī Kṛṣṇa. In this verse the Lord confirms, "I am the same Supreme Personality of Godhead, but I appear in full opulence as Śrī Kṛṣṇa." This is the purport of the words *tenaiva vapuṣā.* When the Lord mentioned the birth of Pṛśnigarbha, He did not say *tenaiva vapuṣā,* but He assured Devakī that in the third birth the Supreme Personality of Godhead Kṛṣṇa had appeared, not His partial expansion. Pṛśnigarbha and Vāmana were partial expansions of Kṛṣṇa, but in this third birth Kṛṣṇa Himself appeared. This is the explanation given in *Śrī Kṛṣṇa-sandarbha* by Śrīla Jīva Gosvāmī.

## TEXT 44

एतद् वां दर्शितं रूपं प्राग्जन्मस्मरणाय मे ।
नान्यथा मद्भवं ज्ञानं मर्त्यलिङ्गेन जायते ॥४४॥

*etad vāṁ darśitaṁ rūpaṁ*
*prāg-janma-smaraṇāya me*
*nānyathā mad-bhavaṁ jñānaṁ*
*martya-liṅgena jāyate*

*etat*—this form of Viṣṇu; *vām*—unto both of you; *darśitam*—has been shown; *rūpam*—My form as the Supreme Personality of Godhead with four hands; *prāk-janma*—of My previous appearances; *smaraṇāya*—just to remind you; *me*—My; *na*—not; *anyathā*—otherwise; *mat-bhavam*—Viṣṇu's appearance; *jñānam*—this transcendental knowledge; *martya-liṅgena*—by taking birth like a human child; *jāyate*—does arise.

## TRANSLATION

**I have shown you this form of Viṣṇu just to remind you of My previous births. Otherwise, if I appeared like an ordinary human child, you would not believe that the Supreme Personality of Godhead, Viṣṇu, has indeed appeared.**

## PURPORT

Devakī did not need to be reminded that the Supreme Personality of Godhead, Lord Viṣṇu, had appeared as her son; she already accepted this. Nonetheless, she was anxious, thinking that if her neighbors heard that Viṣṇu had appeared as her son, none of them would believe it. Therefore she wanted Lord Viṣṇu to transform Himself into a human child. On the other hand, the Supreme Lord was also anxious, thinking that if He appeared as an ordinary child, she would not believe that Lord Viṣṇu had appeared. Such are the dealings between devotees and the Lord. The Lord deals with His devotees exactly like a human being, but this does not mean that the Lord is one of the human beings, for this is the conclusion of nondevotees (*avajānanti māṁ mūḍhā mānuṣīṁ tanum āśritam*). Devotees know the Supreme Personality of Godhead under any circumstances. This is the difference between a devotee and a nondevotee. The Lord says, *man-manā bhava mad-bhakto mad-yājī māṁ namaskuru:* "Engage your mind always in thinking of Me, become My devotee, offer obeisances and worship Me." A nondevotee cannot believe that simply by thinking of one person, one can achieve liberation from this material world and go back home, back to Godhead. But this is a fact. The Lord comes as a human being, and if one becomes attached to the Lord on the platform of loving service, one's promotion to the transcendental world is assured.

## TEXT 45

युवां मां पुत्रभावेन ब्रह्मभावेन चासकृत् ।
चिन्तयन्तौ कृतस्नेहौ यास्येथे मद्गतिं पराम् ॥४५॥

*yuvāṁ māṁ putra-bhāvena*
*brahma-bhāvena cāsakṛt*
*cintayantau kṛta-snehau*
*yāsyethe mad-gatiṁ parām*

*yuvām*—both of you (husband and wife); *mām*—unto Me; *putra-bhāvena*—as your son; *brahma-bhāvena*—knowing that I am the Supreme Personality of Godhead; *ca*—and; *asakṛt*—constantly; *cintayantau*—thinking like that; *kṛta-snehau*—dealing with love and affection; *yāsyethe*—shall both obtain; *mat-gatim*—My supreme abode; *parām*—which is transcendental, beyond this material world.

## TRANSLATION

**Both of you, husband and wife, constantly think of Me as your son, but always know that I am the Supreme Personality of Godhead. By thus thinking of Me constantly with love and affection, you will achieve the highest perfection: returning home, back to Godhead.**

## PURPORT

This instruction by the Supreme Personality of Godhead to His father and mother, who are eternally connected with Him, is especially intended for persons eager to return home, back to Godhead. One should never think of the Supreme Personality of Godhead as an ordinary human being, as nondevotees do. Kṛṣṇa, the Supreme Personality of Godhead, personally appeared and left His instructions for the benefit of all human society, but fools and rascals unfortunately think of Him as an ordinary human being and twist the instructions of *Bhagavad-gītā* for the satisfaction of their senses. Practically everyone commenting on *Bhagavad-gītā* interprets it for sense gratification. It has become especially fashionable for modern scholars and politicians to interpret *Bhagavad-gītā* as if it were something fictitious, and by their wrong interpretations they are spoiling their own careers and the careers of others. The Kṛṣṇa consciousness movement, however, is fighting against this principle of regarding Kṛṣṇa as a fictitious person and of accepting that there was no Battle of Kurukṣetra, that everything is symbolic, and that nothing in *Bhagavad-gītā* is true. In any case, if one truly wants to be successful, one can do so by reading the text of *Bhagavad-gītā* as it is. Śrī Caitanya Mahāprabhu especially stressed the instructions of *Bhagavad-gītā: yāre dekha, tāre kaha 'kṛṣṇa'-upadeśa*. If one wants to achieve the highest success in life, one must accept *Bhagavad-gītā* as spoken by the Supreme Lord. By accepting *Bhagavad-gītā* in this way, all of human society can become perfect and happy.

It is to be noted that because Vasudeva and Devakī would be separated from Kṛṣṇa when He was carried to Gokula, the residence of Nanda

Mahārāja, the Lord personally instructed them that they should always think of Him as their son and as the Supreme Personality of Godhead. That would keep them in touch with Him. After eleven years, the Lord would return to Mathurā to be their son, and therefore there was no question of separation.

## TEXT 46

श्रीशुक उवाच
इत्युक्त्वासीद्धरिस्तूष्णीं भगवानात्ममायया ।
पित्रोः सम्पश्यतोः सद्यो बभूव प्राकृतः शिशुः ॥४६॥

*śrī-śuka uvāca*
*ity uktvāsīd dharis tūṣṇīṁ*
*bhagavān ātma-māyayā*
*pitroḥ sampaśyatoḥ sadyo*
*babhūva prākṛtaḥ śiśuḥ*

*śrī-śukaḥ uvāca*—Śrī Śukadeva Gosvāmī said; *iti uktvā*—after instructing in this way; *āsīt*—remained; *hariḥ*—the Supreme Personality of Godhead; *tūṣṇīm*—silent; *bhagavān*—Lord Viṣṇu, the Supreme Personality of Godhead; *ātma-māyayā*—by acting in His own spiritual energy; *pitroḥ sampaśyatoḥ*—while His father and mother were factually seeing Him; *sadyaḥ*—immediately; *babhūva*—He became; *prākṛtaḥ*—like an ordinary human being; *śiśuḥ*—a child.

## TRANSLATION

**Śukadeva Gosvāmī said: After thus instructing His father and mother, the Supreme Personality of Godhead, Kṛṣṇa, remained silent. In their presence, by His internal energy, He then transformed Himself into a small human child. [In other words, He transformed Himself into His original form: kṛṣṇas tu bhagavān svayam.]**

## PURPORT

As stated in *Bhagavad-gītā* (4.6), *sambhavāmy ātma-māyayā:* whatever is done by the Supreme Personality of Godhead is done by His spiritual energy; nothing is forced upon Him by the material energy. This is the difference between the Lord and an ordinary living being. The *Vedas* say:

> *parāsya śaktir vividhaiva śrūyate*
> *svābhāvikī jñāna-bala-kriyā ca*
> (*Śvetāśvatara Upaniṣad* 6.8)

It is natural for the Lord to be untinged by material qualities, and because everything is perfectly present in His spiritual energy, as soon as He desires something, it is immediately done. The Lord is not a *prākṛta-śiśu*, a child of this world, but by His personal energy He appeared like one. Ordinary people may have difficulty accepting the supreme controller, God, as a human being because they forget that He can do everything by spiritual energy (*ātma-māyayā*). Nonbelievers say, "How can the supreme controller descend as an ordinary being?" This sort of thinking is materialistic. Śrīla Jīva Gosvāmī says that unless we accept the energy of the Supreme Personality of Godhead as inconceivable, beyond the conception of our words and mind, we cannot understand the Supreme Lord. Those who doubt that the Supreme Personality of Godhead can come as a human being and turn Himself into a human child are fools who think that Kṛṣṇa's body is material, that He is born and that He therefore also dies.

In *Śrīmad-Bhāgavatam*, Third Canto, Fourth Chapter, verses 28 and 29, there is a description of Kṛṣṇa's leaving His body. Mahārāja Parīkṣit inquired from Śukadeva Gosvāmī, "When all the members of the Yadu dynasty met their end, Kṛṣṇa also put an end to Himself, and the only member of the family who remained alive was Uddhava. How was this possible?" Śukadeva Gosvāmī answered that Kṛṣṇa, by His own energy, destroyed the entire family and then thought of making His own body disappear. In this connection, Śukadeva Gosvāmī described how the Lord gave up His body. But this was not the destruction of Kṛṣṇa's body; rather, it was the disappearance of the Supreme Lord by His personal energy.

Actually, the Lord does not give up His body, which is eternal, but as He can change His body from the form of Viṣṇu to that of an ordinary human child, He can change His body to any form He likes. This does not mean that He gives up His body. By spiritual energy, the Lord can appear in a body made of wood or stone. He can change His body into anything because everything is His energy (*parāsya śaktir vividhaiva śrūyate*). As clearly said in *Bhagavad-gītā* (7.4), *bhinnā prakṛtir aṣṭadhā:* the material elements are separated energies of the Supreme Lord. If He transforms Himself into the *arcā-mūrti*, the worshipable Deity, which we see as stone or wood, He is still Kṛṣṇa. Therefore the *śāstra* warns, *arcye viṣṇau śilā-dhīr guruṣu nara-matiḥ.* One who thinks that the worshipable Deity in the temple is made of wood or stone, one who sees a Vaiṣṇava *guru* as an ordinary human being, or one who materially conceives of a Vaiṣṇava as belonging to a particular caste is *nārakī*, a resident of hell. The Supreme Personality of Godhead can appear before us in many forms, as he likes, but we must know the true facts: *janma karma ca me divyam evaṁ yo vetti tattvataḥ* (Bg. 4.9). By following the instructions of *sādhu, guru* and *śāstra*—the saintly persons, the spiritual master and the authoritative scriptures—one can understand Kṛṣṇa, and then one makes his life successful by returning home, back to Godhead.

## TEXT 47

ततश्च शौरिर्भगवत्प्रचोदितः
सुतं समादाय स सूतिकागृहात् ।
यदा बहिर्गन्तुमियेष तर्ह्यजा
या योगमायाजनि नन्दजायया ॥४७॥

*tataś ca śaurir bhagavat-pracoditaḥ*
*sutaṁ samādāya sa sūtikā-gṛhāt*
*yadā bahir gantum iyeṣa tarhy ajā*
*yā yogamāyājani nanda-jāyayā*

*tataḥ*—thereafter; *ca*—indeed; *śauriḥ*—Vasudeva; *bhagavat-pracoditaḥ*—being instructed by the Supreme Personality of Godhead; *sutam*—his son; *samādāya*—carrying very carefully; *saḥ*—he; *sūtikā-gṛhāt*—from the maternity room; *yadā*—when; *bahiḥ gantum*—to go outside; *iyeṣa*—desired; *tarhi*—exactly at that time; *ajā*—the transcendental energy, who also never takes birth; *yā*—who; *yogamāyā*—is known as Yogamāyā; *ajani*—took birth; *nanda-jāyayā*—from the wife of Nanda Mahārāja.

## TRANSLATION

**Thereafter, exactly when Vasudeva, being inspired by the Supreme Personality of Godhead, was about to take the newborn child from the delivery room, Yogamāyā, the Lord's spiritual energy, took birth as the daughter of the wife of Mahārāja Nanda.**

## PURPORT

Śrīla Viśvanātha Cakravartī Ṭhākura discusses that Kṛṣṇa appeared simultaneously as the son of Devakī and as the son of Yaśodā, along with the spiritual energy Yogamāyā. As the son of Devakī, He first appeared as Viṣṇu, and because Vasudeva was not in the position of pure affection for Kṛṣṇa, Vasudeva worshiped his son as Lord Viṣṇu. Yaśodā, however, pleased her son Kṛṣṇa without understanding His Godhood. This is the difference between Kṛṣṇa as the son of Yaśodā and as the son of Devakī. This is explained by Viśvanātha Cakravartī on the authority of *Hari-vaṁśa.*

## TEXTS 48–49

तया हृतप्रत्ययसर्ववृत्तिषु
द्वाःस्थेषु पौरेष्वपि शायितेष्वथ ।
द्वारश्च सर्वाः पिहिता दुरत्यया
बृहत्कपाटायसकीलशृङ्खलैः ॥४८॥
ताः कृष्णवाहे वसुदेव आगते
स्वयं व्यवर्यन्त यथा तमो रवेः ।
ववर्ष पर्जन्य उपांशुगर्जितः
शेषोऽन्वगाद् वारि निवारयन् फणैः ॥४९॥

*tayā hṛta-pratyaya-sarva-vṛttiṣu*
*dvāḥ-stheṣu paureṣv api śāyiteṣv atha*
*dvāraś ca sarvāḥ pihitā duratyayā*
*bṛhat-kapāṭāyasa-kīla-śṛṅkhalaiḥ*

*tāḥ kṛṣṇa-vāhe vasudeva āgate*
*svayaṁ vyavaryanta yathā tamo raveḥ*

*vavarṣa parjanya upāṁśu-garjitaḥ*
*śeṣo 'nvagād vāri nivārayan phaṇaiḥ*

*tayā*—by the influence of Yogamāyā; *hṛta-pratyaya*—deprived of all sensation; *sarva-vṛttiṣu*—having all their senses; *dvāḥ-stheṣu*—all the doormen; *paureṣu api*—as well as other members of the house; *śāyiteṣu*—sleeping very deeply; *atha*—when Vasudeva tried to take his transcendental son out of the confinement; *dvāraḥ ca*—as well as the doors; *sarvāḥ*—all; *pihitāḥ*—constructed; *duratyayā*—very hard and firm; *bṛhat-kapāṭa*—and on great doors; *āyasa-kīla-śṛṅkhalaiḥ*—strongly constructed with iron pins and closed with iron chains; *tāḥ*—all of them; *kṛṣṇa-vāhe*—bearing Kṛṣṇa; *vasudeve*—when Vasudeva; *āgate*—appeared; *svayam*—automatically; *vyavaryanta*—opened wide; *yathā*—as; *tamaḥ*—darkness; *raveḥ*—on the appearance of the sun; *vavarṣa*—showered rain; *parjanyaḥ*—the clouds in the sky; *upāṁśu-garjitaḥ*—very mildly resounding and raining very slightly; *śeṣaḥ*—Ananta-nāga; *anvagāt*—followed; *vāri*—showers of rain; *nivārayan*—stopping; *phaṇaiḥ*—by spreading His hoods.

## TRANSLATION

**By the influence of Yogamāyā, all the doorkeepers fell fast asleep, their senses unable to work, and the other inhabitants of the house also fell deeply asleep. When the sun rises, the darkness automatically disappears; similarly, when Vasudeva appeared, the closed doors, which were strongly pinned with iron and locked with iron chains, opened automatically. Since the clouds in the sky were mildly thundering and showering, Ananta-nāga, an expansion of the Supreme Personality of Godhead, followed Vasudeva, beginning from the door, with hoods expanded to protect Vasudeva and the transcendental child.**

## PURPORT

Śeṣa-nāga is an expansion of the Supreme Personality of Godhead whose business is to serve the Lord with all necessary paraphernalia. When Vasudeva was carrying the child, Śeṣa-nāga came to serve the Lord and protect Him from the mild showers of rain.

## TEXT 50

मघोनि वर्षत्यसकृद् यमानुजा
गम्भीरतोयौघजवोर्मिफेनिला ।
भयानकावर्तशताकुला नदी
मार्गं ददौ सिन्धुरिव श्रियः पतेः ॥५०॥

*maghoni varṣaty asakṛd yamānujā*
*gambhīra-toyaugha-javormi-phenilā*
*bhayānakāvarta-śatākulā nadī*
*mārgaṁ dadau sindhur iva śriyaḥ pateḥ*

*maghoni varṣati*—because of Lord Indra's showering rain; *asakṛt*—constantly; *yama-anujā*—the River Yamunā, who is considered the younger sister of Yamarāja; *gambhīra-toya-ogha*—of the very deep water; *java*—by the force; *ūrmi*—by the waves; *phenilā*—full of foam; *bhayānaka*—fierce; *āvarta-śata*—by the whirling waves; *ākulā*—agitated; *nadī*—the river; *mārgam*—way; *dadau*—gave; *sindhuḥ iva*—like the ocean; *śriyaḥ pateḥ*—unto Lord Rāmacandra, the husband of the goddess Sītā.

### TRANSLATION

**Because of constant rain sent by the demigod Indra, the River Yamunā was filled with deep water, foaming about with fiercely whirling waves. But as the great Indian Ocean had formerly given way to Lord Rāmacandra by allowing Him to construct a bridge, the River Yamunā gave way to Vasudeva and allowed him to cross.**

## TEXT 51

नन्दव्रजं शौरिरुपेत्य तत्र तान्
गोपान् प्रसुप्तानुपलभ्य निद्रया ।
सुतं यशोदाशयने निधाय त-
त्सुतामुपादाय पुनर्गृहानगात् ॥५१॥

*nanda-vrajaṁ śaurir upetya tatra tān*
*gopān prasuptān upalabhya nidrayā*

*sutaṁ yaśodā-śayane nidhāya tat-*
*sutām upādāya punar gṛhān agāt*

*nanda-vrajam*—the village or the house of Nanda Mahārāja; *śauriḥ*—Vasudeva; *upetya*—reaching; *tatra*—there; *tān*—all the members; *gopān*—the cowherd men; *prasuptān*—were fast asleep; *upalabhya*—understanding that; *nidrayā*—in deep sleep; *sutam*—the son (Vasudeva's son); *yaśodā-śayane*—on the bed where mother Yaśodā was sleeping; *nidhāya*—placing; *tat-sutām*—her daughter; *upādāya*—picking up; *punaḥ*—again; *gṛhān*—to his own house; *agāt*—returned.

## TRANSLATION

**When Vasudeva reached the house of Nanda Mahārāja, he saw that all the cowherd men were fast asleep. Thus he placed his own son on the bed of Yaśodā, picked up her daughter, an expansion of Yogamāyā, and then returned to his residence, the prison house of Kaṁsa.**

## PURPORT

Vasudeva knew very well that as soon as the daughter was in the prison house of Kaṁsa, Kaṁsa would immediately kill her; but to protect his own child, he had to kill the child of his friend. Nanda Mahārāja was his friend, but out of deep affection and attachment for his own son, he knowingly did this. Śrīla Viśvanātha Cakravartī Ṭhākura says that one cannot be blamed for protecting one's own child at the sacrifice of another's. Furthermore, Vasudeva cannot be accused of callousness, since his actions were impelled by the force of Yogamāyā.

## TEXT 52

देवक्याः शयने न्यस्य वसुदेवोऽथ दारिकाम् ।
प्रतिमुच्य पदोर्लोहमास्ते पूर्ववदावृतः ॥५२॥

*devakyāḥ śayane nyasya*
*vasudevo 'tha dārikām*
*pratimucya pador loham*
*āste pūrvavad āvṛtaḥ*

*devakyāḥ*—of Devakī; *śayane*—on the bed; *nyasya*—placing; *vasudevaḥ*—Vasudeva; *atha*—thus; *dārikām*—the female child; *pratimucya*—binding himself again; *padoḥ loham*—iron shackles on the two legs; *āste*—remained; *pūrva-vat*—like before; *āvṛtaḥ*—bound.

## TRANSLATION

**Vasudeva placed the female child on the bed of Devakī, bound his legs with the iron shackles, and thus remained there as before.**

## TEXT 53

यशोदा नन्दपत्नी च जातं परमबुध्यत ।
न तल्लिङ्गं परिश्रान्ता निद्रयापगतस्मृतिः ॥५३॥

*yaśodā nanda-patnī ca*
*jātaṁ param abudhyata*
*na tal-liṅgaṁ pariśrāntā*
*nidrayāpagata-smṛtiḥ*

*yaśodā*—Yaśodā, Kṛṣṇa's mother in Gokula; *nanda-patnī*—the wife of Nanda Mahārāja; *ca*—also; *jātam*—a child was born; *param*—the Supreme Person; *abudhyata*—could understand; *na*—not; *tat-liṅgam*—whether the child was male or female; *pariśrāntā*—because of too much labor; *nidrayā*—when overwhelmed with sleep; *apagata-smṛtiḥ*—having lost consciousness.

## TRANSLATION

**Exhausted by the labor of childbirth, Yaśodā was overwhelmed with sleep and unable to understand what kind of child had been born to her.**

## PURPORT

Nanda Mahārāja and Vasudeva were intimate friends, and so were their wives, Yaśodā and Devakī. Although their names were different, they were practically nondifferent personalities. The only difference is that Devakī was able to understand that the Supreme Personality of Godhead had been born to her and had now changed into Kṛṣṇa, whereas Yaśodā was not able to understand what kind of child had been born to her. Yaśodā was such an advanced devotee that she never regarded Kṛṣṇa as the Supreme Personality of Godhead, but simply loved Him as her own child. Devakī, however, knew from the very beginning that although Kṛṣṇa was her son, He was the Supreme Personality of Godhead. In Vṛndāvana, no one regarded Kṛṣṇa as the Supreme Personality of Godhead. When something very wonderful happened because of Kṛṣṇa's activities, the inhabitants of Vṛndāvana—the cowherd men, the cowherd boys, Nanda Mahārāja, Yaśodā and the others—were surprised, but they never considered their son Kṛṣṇa the Supreme Personality of Godhead. Sometimes they suggested that some great demigod had appeared there as Kṛṣṇa. In such an exalted status of devotional service, a devotee forgets the position of Kṛṣṇa and intensely loves the Supreme Personality of Godhead without understanding His position. This is called *kevala-bhakti* and is distinct from the stages of *jñāna* and *jñānamayī bhakti.*

*Thus end the Bhaktivedanta purports of the Tenth Canto, Third Chapter, of the* Śrīmad-Bhāgavatam, *entitled "The Birth of Lord Kṛṣṇa."*

# CHAPTER FOUR

# The Atrocities of King Kaṁsa

This chapter describes how Kaṁsa, following the advice of his demoniac friends, considered the persecution of small children to be very diplomatic.

After Vasudeva bound himself with iron shackles as before, all the doors of the prison house closed by the influence of Yogamāyā, who then began crying as a newborn child. This crying awakened the doorkeepers, who immediately informed Kaṁsa that a child had been born to Devakī. Upon hearing this news, Kaṁsa appeared with great force in the maternity room, and in spite of Devakī's pleas that the child be saved, the demon forcibly snatched the child from Devakī's hands and dashed the child against a rock. Unfortunately for Kaṁsa, however, the newborn child slipped away from his hands, rose above his head and appeared as the eight-armed form of Durgā. Durgā then told Kaṁsa, "The enemy you contemplate has taken birth somewhere else. Therefore your plan to persecute all the children will prove futile."

According to the prophecy, the eighth child of Devakī would kill Kaṁsa, and therefore when Kaṁsa saw that the eighth child was a female and heard that his so-called enemy had taken birth elsewhere, he was struck with wonder. He decided to release Devakī and Vasudeva, and he admitted before them the wrongness of his atrocities. Falling at the feet of Devakī and Vasudeva, he begged their pardon and tried to convince them that because the events that had taken place were destined to happen, they should not be unhappy for his having killed so many of their children. Devakī and Vasudeva, being naturally very pious, immediately excused Kaṁsa for his atrocities, and Kaṁsa, after seeing that his sister and brother-in-law were happy, returned to his home.

After the night passed, however, Kaṁsa called for his ministers and informed them of all that had happened. The ministers, who were all demons, advised Kaṁsa that because his enemy had already taken birth somewhere else, all the children born within the past ten days in the villages within Kaṁsa's kingdom should be killed. Although the demigods always feared Kaṁsa, they should not be treated leniently; since they were enemies, Kaṁsa should try his best to uproot their existence. The demoniac ministers further advised that Kaṁsa and the demons continue their enmity toward Viṣṇu because Viṣṇu is the original person among all the demigods. The *brāhmaṇas*, the cows, the *Vedas*, austerity, truthfulness, control of the senses and mind, faithfulness and mercy are among the different parts of the body of Viṣṇu, who is the origin of all the demigods, including Lord Brahmā and Lord Śiva. Therefore, the ministers advised, the demigods, the saintly persons, the cows and the *brāhmaṇas* should be systematically persecuted. Strongly advised in this way by his friends, the demoniac ministers, Kaṁsa approved of their instructions and considered it beneficial to be envious of the *brāhmaṇas*. Following Kaṁsa's orders, therefore, the demons began committing their atrocities all over Vrajabhūmi.

## TEXT 1

श्रीशुक उवाच
बहिरन्तःपुरद्वारः सर्वाः पूर्ववदावृताः ।
ततो बालध्वनिं श्रुत्वा गृहपालाः समुत्थिताः ॥ १ ॥

*śrī-śuka uvāca*
*bahir-antaḥ-pura-dvāraḥ*
*sarvāḥ pūrvavad āvṛtāḥ*
*tato bāla-dhvaniṁ śrutvā*
*gṛha-pālāḥ samutthitāḥ*

*śrī-śukaḥ uvāca*—Śrī Śukadeva Gosvāmī said; *bahiḥ-antaḥ-pura-dvāraḥ*—the doors inside and outside the house; *sarvāḥ*—all; *pūrva-vat*—like before; *āvṛtāḥ*—closed; *tataḥ*—thereafter; *bāla-dhvanim*—the crying of the newborn child; *śrutvā*—hearing; *gṛha-pālāḥ*—all the inhabitants of the house, especially the doormen; *samutthitāḥ*—awakened.

## TRANSLATION

**Śukadeva Gosvāmī continued: My dear King Parīkṣit, the doors inside and outside the house closed as before. Thereafter, the in-**

**habitants of the house, especially the watchmen, heard the crying of the newborn child and thus awakened from their beds.**

## PURPORT

The activities of Yogamāyā are distinctly visible in this chapter, in which Devakī and Vasudeva excuse Kaṁsa for his many devious, atrocious activities and Kaṁsa becomes repentant and falls at their feet. Before the awakening of the watchmen and the others in the prison house, many other things happened. Kṛṣṇa was born and transferred to the home of Yaśodā in Gokula, the strong doors opened and again closed, and Vasudeva resumed his former condition of being shackled. The watchmen, however, could not understand all this. They awakened only when they heard the crying of the newborn child, Yogamāyā.

Śrīla Viśvanātha Cakravartī Ṭhākura has remarked that the watchmen were just like dogs. At night the dogs in the street act like watchmen. If one dog barks, many other dogs immediately follow it by barking. Although the street dogs are not appointed by anyone to act as watchmen, they think they are responsible for protecting the neighborhood, and as soon as someone unknown enters it, they all begin to bark. Both Yogamāyā and Mahāmāyā act in all material activities (*prakṛteḥ kriyamāṇāni guṇaiḥ karmāṇi sarvaśaḥ*), but although the energy of the Supreme Personality of Godhead acts under the Supreme Lord's direction (*mayādhyakṣeṇa prakṛtiḥ sūyate sa-carācaram*), doglike watchmen such as politicians and diplomats think that they are protecting their neighborhoods from the dangers of the outside world. These are the actions of *māyā.* But one who surrenders to Kṛṣṇa is relieved of the protection afforded by the dogs and doglike guardians of this material world.

## TEXT 2

ते तु तूर्णमुपव्रज्य देवक्या गर्भजन्म तत् ।
आचख्युर्भोजराजाय यदुद्विग्नः प्रतीक्षते ॥ २ ॥

*te tu tūrṇam upavrajya*
*devakyā garbha-janma tat*
*ācakhyur bhoja-rājāya*
*yad udvignaḥ pratīkṣate*

*te*—all the watchmen; *tu*—indeed; *tūrṇam*—very quickly; *upavrajya*—going before (the King); *devakyāḥ*—of Devakī; *garbha-janma*—the deliverance from the womb; *tat*—that (child); *ācakhyuḥ*—submitted; *bhoja-rājāya*—unto the King of the Bhojas, Kaṁsa; *yat*—of whom; *udvignaḥ*—with great anxiety; *pratīkṣate*—was waiting (for the child's birth).

## TRANSLATION

**Thereafter, all the watchmen very quickly approached King Kaṁsa, the ruler of the Bhoja dynasty, and submitted the news of the birth of Devakī's child. Kaṁsa, who had awaited this news very anxiously, immediately took action.**

## PURPORT

Kaṁsa was very anxiously waiting because of the prophecy that the eighth child of Devakī would kill him. This time, naturally, he was awake and waiting, and when the watchmen approached him, he immediately took action to kill the child.

## TEXT 3

स तल्पात् तूर्णमुत्थाय कालोऽयमिति विह्वलः ।
सूतीगृहमगात् तूर्णं प्रस्खलन् मुक्तमूर्धजः ॥ ३ ॥

*sa talpāt tūrṇam utthāya*
*kālo 'yam iti vihvalaḥ*
*sūtī-gṛham agāt tūrṇaṁ*
*praskhalan mukta-mūrdhajaḥ*

*saḥ*—he (King Kaṁsa); *talpāt*—from the bed; *tūrṇam*—very quickly; *utthāya*—getting up; *kālaḥ ayam*—here is my death, the supreme time; *iti*—in this way; *vihvalaḥ*—overwhelmed; *sūti-gṛham*—to the maternity home; *agāt*—went; *tūrṇam*—without delay; *praskhalan*—scattering; *mukta*—had become opened; *mūrdha-jaḥ*—the hair on the head.

## TRANSLATION

**Kaṁsa immediately got up from bed, thinking, "Here is Kāla, the supreme time factor, which has taken birth to kill me!" Thus**

**overwhelmed, Kaṁsa, his hair scattered on his head, at once approached the place where the child had been born.**

## PURPORT

The word *kālaḥ* is significant. Although the child was born to kill Kaṁsa, Kaṁsa thought that this was the proper time to kill the child so that he himself would be saved. *Kāla* is actually another name of the Supreme Personality of Godhead when He appears only for the purpose of killing. When Arjuna inquired from Kṛṣṇa in His universal form, "Who are You?" the Lord presented Himself as *kāla*, death personified to kill. By nature's law, when there is an unwanted increase in population, *kāla* appears, and by some arrangement of the Supreme Personality of Godhead, people are killed wholesale in different ways, by war, pestilence, famine and so on. At that time, even atheistic political leaders go to a church, mosque or temple for protection by God or gods and submissively say, "God willing." Before that, they pay no attention to God, not caring to know God or His will, but when *kāla* appears, they say, "God willing." Death is but another feature of the supreme *kāla*, the Supreme Personality of Godhead. At the time of death, the atheist must submit to this supreme *kāla*, and then the Supreme Personality of Godhead takes away all his possessions (*mṛtyuḥ sarva-haraś cāham*) and forces him to accept another body (*tathā dehāntara-prāptiḥ*). This the atheists do not know, and if they do know, they neglect it so that they may go on with their normal life. The Kṛṣṇa consciousness movement is trying to teach them that although for a few years one may act as a great protector or great watchman, with the appearance of *kāla*, death, one must take another body by the laws of nature. Not knowing this, they unnecessarily waste their time in their occupation as watchdogs and do not try to get the mercy of the Supreme Personality of Godhead. As it is clearly said, *aprāpya māṁ nivartante mṛtyu-saṁsāra-vartmani:* without Kṛṣṇa consciousness, one is condemned to continue wandering in birth and death, not knowing what will happen in one's next birth.

## TEXT 4

तमाह भ्रातरं देवी कृपणा करुणं सती ।
स्नुषेयं तव कल्याण स्त्रियं मा हन्तुमर्हसि ॥ ४ ॥

*tam āha bhrātaraṁ devī*
*kṛpaṇā karuṇaṁ satī*
*snuṣeyaṁ tava kalyāṇa*
*striyaṁ mā hantum arhasi*

*tam*—unto Kaṁsa; *āha*—said; *bhrātaram*—her brother; *devī*—mother Devakī; *kṛpaṇā*—helplessly; *karuṇam*—piteously; *satī*—the chaste lady; *snuṣā iyam tava*—this child will be your daughter-in-law, the wife of your future son; *kalyāṇa*—O all-auspicious one; *striyam*—a woman; *mā*—not; *hantum*—to kill; *arhasi*—you deserve.

## TRANSLATION

**Devakī helplessly, piteously appealed to Kaṁsa: My dear brother, all good fortune unto you. Don't kill this girl. She will be your daughter-in-law. Indeed, it is unworthy of you to kill a woman.**

## PURPORT

Kaṁsa had previously excused Devakī because he thought that a woman should not be killed, especially when pregnant. But now, by the influence of *māyā*, he was prepared to kill a woman—not only a woman, but a small, helpless newborn child. Devakī wanted to save her brother from this terrible, sinful act. Therefore she told him, "Don't be so atrocious as to kill a female child. Let there be all good fortune for you." Demons can do anything for their personal benefit, not considering what is pious or vicious. But Devakī, on the contrary, although safe because she had already given birth to her own son, Kṛṣṇa, was anxious to save the daughter of someone else. This was natural for her.

## TEXT 5

बहवो हिंसिता भ्रातः शिशवः पावकोपमाः ।
त्वया दैवनिसृष्टेन पुत्रिकैका प्रदीयताम् ॥ ५ ॥

*bahavo hiṁsitā bhrātaḥ*
*śiśavaḥ pāvakopamāḥ*
*tvayā daiva-nisṛṣṭena*
*putrikaikā pradīyatām*

*bahavaḥ*—many; *hiṁsitāḥ*—killed out of envy; *bhrātaḥ*—my dear brother; *śiśavaḥ*—small children; *pāvaka-upamāḥ*—all of them equal to fire in brightness and beauty; *tvayā*—by you; *daiva-nisṛṣṭena*—as spoken by destiny; *putrikā*—daughter; *ekā*—one; *pradīyatām*—give me as your gift.

## TRANSLATION

**My dear brother, by the influence of destiny you have already killed many babies, each of them as bright and beautiful as fire. But kindly spare this daughter. Give her to me as your gift.**

## PURPORT

Here we see that Devakī first focused Kaṁsa's attention on his atrocious activities, his killing of her many sons. Then she wanted to compromise with him by saying that whatever he had done was not his fault, but was ordained by destiny. Then she appealed to him to give her the daughter as a gift. Devakī was the daughter of a *kṣatriya* and knew how to play the political game. In politics there are different methods of achieving success: first repression (*dama*), then compromise (*sāma*), and then asking for a gift (*dāna*). Devakī first adopted the policy of repression by directly attacking Kaṁsa for having cruelly, atrociously killed her babies. Then she compromised by saying that this was not his fault, and then she begged for a gift. As we learn from the history of the *Mahābhārata*, or "Greater India," the wives and daughters of the ruling class, the *kṣatriyas*, knew the political game, but we never find that a woman was given the post of chief executive. This is in accordance with the injunctions of *Manu-saṁhitā*, but unfortunately *Manu-saṁhitā* is now being insulted, and the Āryans, the members of Vedic society, cannot do anything. Such is the nature of Kali-yuga.

Nothing happens unless ordained by destiny.

*tasyaiva hetoḥ prayateta kovido*
*na labhyate yad bhramatām upary adhaḥ*
*tal labhyate duḥkhavad anyataḥ sukhaṁ*
*kālena sarvatra gabhīra-raṁhasā*
(*Bhāg.* 1.5.18)

Devakī knew very well that because the killing of her many children had been ordained by destiny, Kaṁsa was not to be blamed. There was no need to give good instructions to Kaṁsa. *Upadeśo hi murkhāṇāṁ prakopāya na śāntaye* (Cāṇakya Paṇḍita). If a foolish person is given good instructions, he becomes more and more angry. Moreover, a cruel person is more dangerous than a snake. A snake and a cruel person are both cruel, but a cruel person is more dangerous because although a snake can be charmed by *mantras* or subdued by herbs, a cruel person cannot be subdued by any means. Such was the nature of Kaṁsa.

## TEXT 6

नन्वहं ते ह्यवरजा दीना हतसुता प्रभो ।
दातुमर्हसि मन्दाया अङ्गेमां चरमां प्रजाम् ॥ ६ ॥

*nanv ahaṁ te hy avarajā*
*dīnā hata-sutā prabho*
*dātum arhasi mandāyā*
*aṅgemāṁ caramāṁ prajām*

*nanu*—however; *aham*—I am; *te*—your; *hi*—indeed; *avarajā*—younger sister; *dīnā*—very poor; *hata-sutā*—deprived of all children; *prabho*—O my lord; *dātum arhasi*—you deserve to give (some gift); *mandāyāḥ*—to me, who am so poor; *aṅga*—my dear brother; *imām*—this; *caramām*—last; *prajām*—child.

## TRANSLATION

**My lord, my brother, I am very poor, being bereft of all my children, but still I am your younger sister, and therefore it would be worthy of you to give me this last child as a gift.**

## TEXT 7

श्रीशुक उवाच
उपगुह्यात्मजामेवं रुदत्या दीनदीनवत् ।
याचितस्तां विनिर्भर्त्स्य हस्तादाचिच्छिदे खलः ॥७॥

*śrī-śuka uvāca*
*upaguhyātmajām evaṁ*
*rudatyā dīna-dīnavat*
*yācitas tāṁ vinirbhartsya*
*hastād ācicchide khalaḥ*

*śrī-śukaḥ uvāca*—Śrī Śukadeva Gosvāmī said; *upaguhya*—embracing; *ātmajām*—her daughter; *evam*—in this way; *rudatyā*—by Devakī, who was crying; *dīna-dīna-vat*—very piteously, like a poor woman; *yācitaḥ*—being begged; *tām*—her (Devakī); *vinirbhartsya*—chastising; *hastāt*—from her hands; *ācicchide*—separated the child by force; *khalaḥ*—Kaṁsa, the most cruel.

## TRANSLATION

**Śukadeva Gosvāmī continued: Piteously embracing her daughter and crying, Devakī begged Kaṁsa for the child, but he was so cruel that he chastised her and forcibly snatched the child from her hands.**

## PURPORT

Although Devakī was crying like a very poor woman, actually she was not poor, and therefore the word used here is *dīnavat.* She had already given birth to Kṛṣṇa. Therefore, who could have been richer than she? Even the demigods had come to offer prayers to Devakī, but she played the part of a poor, piteously afflicted woman because she wanted to save the daughter of Yaśodā.

## TEXT 8

तां गृहीत्वा चरणयोर्जातमात्रां स्वसुः सुताम् ।
अपोथयच्छिलापृष्ठे स्वार्थोन्मूलितसौहृदः ॥ ८ ॥

*tāṁ gṛhītvā caraṇayor*
*jāta-mātrāṁ svasuḥ sutām*
*apothayac chilā-pṛṣṭhe*
*svārthonmūlita-sauhṛdaḥ*

*tām*—the child; *gṛhītvā*—taking by force; *caraṇayoḥ*—by the two legs; *jāta-mātrām*—the newborn child; *svasuḥ*—of his sister; *sutām*—the daughter; *apothayat*—smashed; *śilā-pṛṣṭhe*—on the surface of a stone; *sva-artha-unmūlita*—uprooted because of intense selfishness; *sauhṛdaḥ*—all friendship or family relationships.

## TRANSLATION

**Having uprooted all relationships with his sister because of intense selfishness, Kaṁsa, who was sitting on his knees, grasped the newborn child by the legs and tried to dash her against the surface of a stone.**

## TEXT 9

सा तद्धस्तात् समुत्पत्य सद्यो देव्यम्बरं गता ।
अदृश्यतानुजा विष्णोः सायुधाष्टमहाभुजा ॥ ९ ॥

*sā tad-dhastāt samutpatya*
*sadyo devy ambaraṁ gatā*
*adṛśyatānujā viṣṇoḥ*
*sāyudhāṣṭa-mahābhujā*

*sā*—that female child; *tat-hastāt*—from the hand of Kaṁsa; *samutpatya*—slipped upward; *sadyaḥ*—immediately; *devī*—the form of a demigoddess; *ambaram*—into the sky; *gatā*—went; *adṛśyata*—was seen; *anujā*—the younger sister; *viṣṇoḥ*—of the Supreme Personality of Godhead; *sa-āyudhā*—with weapons; *aṣṭa*—eight; *mahā-bhujā*—with mighty arms.

## TRANSLATION

**The child, Yogamāyā-devī, the younger sister of Lord Viṣṇu, slipped upward from Kaṁsa's hands and appeared in the sky as Devī, the goddess Durgā, with eight arms, completely equipped with weapons.**

## PURPORT

Kaṁsa tried to dash the child downward against a piece of stone, but since she was Yogamāyā, the younger sister of Lord Viṣṇu, she slipped upward and assumed the form of the goddess Durgā. The word *anujā*, meaning "the younger sister," is significant. When Viṣṇu, or Kṛṣṇa, took birth from Devakī, He must have simultaneously taken birth from Yaśodā also. Otherwise how could Yogamāyā have been *anujā*, the Lord's younger sister?

## TEXTS 10–11

दिव्यस्रगम्बरालेपरत्नाभरणभूषिता ।
धनुःशूलेषुचर्मासिशङ्खचक्रगदाधरा ॥१०॥
सिद्धचारणगन्धर्वैरप्सरःकिन्नरोरगैः ।
उपाहृतोरुबलिभिः स्तूयमानेदमब्रवीत् ॥११॥

*divya-srag-ambarālepa-*
*ratnābharaṇa-bhūṣitā*
*dhanuḥ-śūleṣu-carmāsi-*
*śaṅkha-cakra-gadā-dharā*

*siddha-cāraṇa-gandharvair*
*apsaraḥ-kinnaroragaiḥ*
*upāhṛtoru-balibhiḥ*
*stūyamānedam abravīt*

*divya-srak-ambara-ālepa*—she then assumed the form of a demigoddess, completely decorated with sandalwood pulp, flower garlands and a nice dress; *ratna-ābharaṇa-bhūṣitā*—decorated with ornaments of valuable jewels; *dhanuḥ-śūla-iṣu-carma-asi*—with bow, trident, arrows, shield and sword; *śaṅkha-cakra-gadā-dharā*—and holding the weapons of Viṣṇu (conchshell, disc and club); *siddha-cāraṇa-gandharvaiḥ*—by the Siddhas, Cāraṇas and Gandharvas; *apsaraḥ-kinnara-uragaiḥ*—and by the Apsarās, Kinnaras and Uragas; *upāhṛta-uru-balibhiḥ*—who brought all kinds of presentations to her; *stūyamānā*—being praised; *idam*—these words; *abravīt*—she said.

## TRANSLATION

**The goddess Durgā was decorated with flower garlands, smeared with sandalwood pulp and dressed with excellent garments and ornaments made of valuable jewels. Holding in her hands a bow, a**

**trident, arrows, a shield, a sword, a conchshell, a disc and a club, and being praised by celestial beings like Apsarās, Kinnaras, Uragas, Siddhas, Cāraṇas and Gandharvas, who worshiped her with all kinds of presentations, she spoke as follows.**

## TEXT 12

किं मया हतया मन्द जातः खलु तवान्तकृत् ।
यत्र क्व वा पूर्वशत्रुर्मा हिंसीः कृपणान् वृथा ॥१२॥

*kiṁ mayā hatayā manda*
*jātaḥ khalu tavānta-kṛt*
*yatra kva vā pūrva-śatrur*
*mā hiṁsīḥ kṛpaṇān vṛthā*

*kim*—what is the use; *mayā*—me; *hatayā*—in killing; *manda*—O you fool; *jātaḥ*—has already been born; *khalu*—indeed; *tava anta-kṛt*—who will kill you; *yatra kva vā*—somewhere else; *pūrva-śatruḥ*—your former enemy; *mā*—do not; *hiṁsīḥ*—kill; *kṛpaṇān*—other poor children; *vṛthā*—unnecessarily.

## TRANSLATION

**O Kaṁsa, you fool, what will be the use of killing me? The Supreme Personality of Godhead, who has been your enemy from the very beginning and who will certainly kill you, has already taken His birth somewhere else. Therefore, do not unnecessarily kill other children.**

## TEXT 13

इति प्रभाष्य तं देवी माया भगवती भुवि ।
बहुनामनिकेतेषु बहुनामा बभूव ह ॥१३॥

*iti prabhāṣya taṁ devī*
*māyā bhagavatī bhuvi*
*bahu-nāma-niketeṣu*
*bahu-nāmā babhūva ha*

*iti*—in this way; *prabhāṣya*—addressing; *tam*—Kaṁsa; *devī*—the goddess Durgā; *māyā*—Yogamāyā; *bhagavatī*—possessing immense power, like that of the Supreme Personality of Godhead; *bhuvi*—on the surface of the earth; *bahu-nāma*—of different names; *niketeṣu*—in different places; *bahu-nāmā*—different names; *babhūva*—became; *ha*—indeed.

## TRANSLATION

**After speaking to Kaṁsa in this way, the goddess Durgā, Yogamāyā, appeared in different places, such as Vārāṇasī, and became celebrated by different names, such as Annapūrṇā, Durgā, Kālī and Bhadrā.**

## PURPORT

The goddess Durgā is celebrated in Calcutta as Kālī, in Bombay as Mumbādevī, in Vārāṇasī as Annapūrṇā, in Cuttack as Bhadrakālī and in Ahmedabad as Bhadrā. Thus in different places she is known by different names. Her devotees are known as *śāktas*, or worshipers of the energy of the Supreme Personality of Godhead, whereas worshipers of the Supreme Personality of Godhead Himself are called Vaiṣṇavas. Vaiṣṇavas are destined to return home, back to Godhead, in the spiritual world, whereas the *śāktas* are destined to live within this material world to enjoy different types of material happiness. In the material world, the living entity must accept different types of bodies. *Bhrāmayan sarva-bhūtāni yantrārūḍhāni māyayā* (Bg. 18.61). According to the living entity's desire, Yogamāyā, or Māyā, the goddess Durgā, gives him a particular type of body, which is mentioned as *yantra*, a machine. But the living entities who are promoted to the spiritual world do not return to the prison house of a material body (*tyaktvā dehaṁ punar janma naiti mām eti so 'rjuna*). The words *janma na eti* indicate that these living entities remain in their original, spiritual bodies to enjoy the company of the Supreme Personality of Godhead in the transcendental abodes Vaikuṇṭha and Vṛndāvana.

## TEXT 14

तयाभिहितमाकर्ण्य कंसः परमविस्मितः ।
देवकीं वसुदेवं च विमुच्य प्रश्रितोऽब्रवीत् ॥१४॥

*tayābhihitam ākarṇya*
*kaṁsaḥ parama-vismitaḥ*
*devakīṁ vasudevaṁ ca*
*vimucya praśrito 'bravīt*

*tayā*—by the goddess Durgā; *abhihitam*—the words spoken; *ākarṇya*—by hearing; *kaṁsaḥ*—Kaṁsa; *parama-vismitaḥ*—was struck with wonder; *devakīm*—unto Devakī; *vasudevam ca*—and Vasudeva; *vimucya*—releasing immediately; *praśritaḥ*—with great humility; *abravīt*—spoke as follows.

## TRANSLATION

**After hearing the words of the goddess Durgā, Kaṁsa was struck with wonder. Thus he approached his sister Devakī and brother-in-law Vasudeva, released them immediately from their shackles, and very humbly spoke as follows.**

## PURPORT

Kaṁsa was astonished because the goddess Durgā had become the daughter of Devakī. Since Devakī was a human being, how could the goddess Durgā become her daughter? This was one cause of his astonishment. Also, how is it that the eighth child of Devakī was a female? This also astonished him. *Asuras* are generally devotees of mother Durgā, Śakti, or of demigods, especially Lord Śiva. The appearance of Durgā in her original eight-armed feature, holding various weapons, immediately changed Kaṁsa's mind about Devakī's being an ordinary human. Devakī must have had some transcendental qualities; otherwise why would the goddess Durgā have taken birth from her womb? Under the circumstances, Kaṁsa, struck with wonder, wanted to compensate for his atrocities against his sister Devakī.

## TEXT 15

अहो भगिन्यहो भाम मया वां बत पाप्मना ।
पुरुषाद इवापत्यं बहवो हिंसिताः सुताः ॥१५॥

*aho bhaginy aho bhāma*
*mayā vāṁ bata pāpmanā*
*puruṣāda ivāpatyaṁ*
*bahavo hiṁsitāḥ sutāḥ*

*aho*—alas; *bhagini*—my dear sister; *aho*—alas; *bhāma*—my dear brother-in-law; *mayā*—by me; *vām*—of you; *bata*—indeed; *pāpmanā*—because of sinful activities; *puruṣa-adaḥ*—a Rākṣasa, man-eater; *iva*—like; *apatyam*—child; *bahavaḥ*—many; *hiṁsitāḥ*—have been killed; *sutāḥ*—sons.

## TRANSLATION

**Alas, my sister! Alas, my brother-in-law! I am indeed so sinful that exactly like a man-eater [Rākṣasa] who eats his own child, I have killed so many sons born of you.**

## PURPORT

Rākṣasas are understood to be accustomed to eating their own sons, as snakes and many other animals sometimes do. At the present moment in Kali-yuga, Rākṣasa fathers and mothers are killing their own children in the womb, and some are even eating the fetus with great relish. Thus the so-called civilization is gradually advancing by producing Rākṣasas.

## TEXT 16

स त्वहं त्यक्तकारुण्यस्त्यक्तज्ञातिसुहृत् खलः ।
काँल्लोकान् वै गमिष्यामि ब्रह्महेव मृतः श्वसन् ॥१६॥

*sa tv ahaṁ tyakta-kāruṇyas*
*tyakta-jñāti-suhṛt khalaḥ*
*kān lokān vai gamiṣyāmi*
*brahma-heva mṛtaḥ śvasan*

*saḥ*—that person (Kaṁsa); *tu*—indeed; *aham*—I; *tyakta-kāruṇyaḥ*—devoid of all mercy; *tyakta-jñāti-suhṛt*—my relatives and friends have been rejected by me; *khalaḥ*—cruel; *kān lokān*—which planets;

*vai*—indeed; *gamiṣyāmi*—shall go; *brahma-hā iva*—like the killer of a *brāhmaṇa; mṛtaḥ śvasan*—either after death or while breathing.

## TRANSLATION

**Being merciless and cruel, I have forsaken all my relatives and friends. Therefore, like a person who has killed a brāhmaṇa, I do not know to which planet I shall go, either after death or while breathing.**

## TEXT 17

दैवमप्यनृतं वक्ति न मर्त्या एव केवलम् ।
यद्विश्रम्भादहं पापः स्वसुर्निहतवाञ्छिशून् ॥१७॥

*daivam apy anṛtaṁ vakti*
*na martyā eva kevalam*
*yad-viśrambhād ahaṁ pāpaḥ*
*svasur nihatavāñ chiśūn*

*daivam*—providence; *api*—also; *anṛtam*—lies; *vakti*—say; *na*—not; *martyāḥ*—human beings; *eva*—certainly; *kevalam*—only; *yat-viśrambhāt*—because of believing that prophecy; *aham*—I; *pāpaḥ*—the most sinful; *svasuḥ*—of my sister; *nihatavān*—killed; *śiśūn*—so many children.

## TRANSLATION

**Alas, not only human beings but sometimes even providence lies. And I am so sinful that I believed the omen of providence and killed so many of my sister's children.**

## TEXT 18

मा शोचतं महाभागावात्मजान् स्वकृतंभुजः ।
जान्तवो न सदैकत्र दैवाधीनास्तदासते ॥१८॥

*mā śocataṁ mahā-bhāgāv*
*ātmajān sva-kṛtaṁ bhujaḥ*

*jāntavo na sadaikatra*
*daivādhīnās tadāsate*

*mā śocatam*—kindly do not be aggrieved (for what happened in the past); *mahā-bhāgau*—O you who are learned and fortunate in spiritual knowledge; *ātmajān*—for your sons; *sva-kṛtam*—only because of their own acts; *bhujaḥ*—who are suffering; *jāntavaḥ*—all living entities; *na*—not; *sadā*—always; *ekatra*—in one place; *daiva-adhīnāḥ*—who are under the control of providence; *tadā*—hence; *āsate*—live.

## TRANSLATION

**O great souls, your children have suffered their own misfortune. Therefore, please do not lament for them. All living entities are under the control of the Supreme, and they cannot always live together.**

## PURPORT

Kaṁsa addressed his sister and brother-in-law as *mahā-bhāgau* because although he killed their ordinary children, the goddess Durgā took birth from them. Because Devakī bore Durgādevī in her womb, Kaṁsa praised both Devakī and her husband. *Asuras* are very devoted to the goddess Durgā, Kālī and so forth. Kaṁsa, therefore, truly astonished, appreciated the exalted position of his sister and brother-in-law. Durgā is certainly not under the laws of nature, because she herself is the controller of the laws of nature. Ordinary living beings, however, are controlled by these laws (*prakṛteḥ kriyamāṇāni guṇaiḥ karmāṇi sarvaśaḥ*). Consequently, none of us are allowed to live together for any long period. By speaking in this way, Kaṁsa tried to pacify his sister and brother-in-law.

## TEXT 19

भुवि भौमानि भूतानि यथा यान्त्यपयान्ति च ।
नायमात्मा तथैतेषु विपर्येति यथैव भूः ॥१९॥

*bhuvi bhaumāni bhūtāni*
*yathā yānty apayānti ca*

*nāyam ātmā tathaiteṣu*
*viparyeti yathaiva bhūḥ*

*bhuvi*—on the surface of the world; *bhaumāni*—all material products from earth, such as pots; *bhūtāni*—which are produced; *yathā*—as; *yānti*—appear (in form); *apayānti*—disappear (broken or mixed with the earth); *ca*—and; *na*—not; *ayam ātmā*—the soul or spiritual identity; *tathā*—similarly; *eteṣu*—among all these (products of material elements); *viparyeti*—is changed or broken; *yathā*—as; *eva*—certainly; *bhūḥ*—the earth.

## TRANSLATION

**In this world, we can see that pots, dolls and other products of the earth appear, break and then disappear, mixing with the earth. Similarly, the bodies of all conditioned living entities are annihilated, but the living entities, like the earth itself, are unchanging and never annihilated [na hanyate hanyamāne śarīre].**

## PURPORT

Although Kaṁsa is described as a demon, he had good knowledge of the affairs of *ātma-tattva*, the truth of the self. Five thousand years ago, there were kings like Kaṁsa, who is described as an *asura*, but he was better than modern politicians and diplomats, who have no knowledge about *ātma-tattva*. As stated in the *Vedas*, *asaṅgo hy ayaṁ puruṣaḥ:* the spirit soul has no connection with the changes of the material body. The body undergoes six changes—birth, growth, sustenance, by-products, dwindling and then annihilation—but the soul undergoes no such changes. Even after the annihilation of a particular bodily form, the original source of the bodily elements does not change. The living entity enjoys the material body, which appears and disappears, but the five elements earth, water, fire, air and ether remain the same. The example given here is that pots and dolls are produced from the earth, and when broken or destroyed they mingle with their original ingredients. In any case, the source of supply remains the same.

As already discussed, the body is made according to the desires of the soul. The soul desires, and thus the body is formed. Kṛṣṇa therefore says in *Bhagavad-gītā* (18.61):

*īśvaraḥ sarva-bhūtānāṁ*
*hṛd-deśe 'rjuna tiṣṭhati*
*bhrāmayan sarva-bhūtāni*
*yantrārūḍhāni māyayā*

"The Supreme Lord is situated in everyone's heart, O Arjuna, and is directing the wanderings of all living entities, who are seated as on a machine, made of the material energy." Neither the Supersoul, Paramātmā, nor the individual soul changes its original, spiritual identity. The *ātmā* does not undergo birth, death or changes like the body. Therefore a Vedic aphorism says, *asaṅgo hy ayaṁ puruṣaḥ:* although the soul is conditioned within this material world, he has no connections with the changes of the material body.

## TEXT 20

यथानेवंविदो भेदो यत आत्मविपर्ययः ।
देहयोगवियोगौ च संसृतिर्न निवर्तते ॥२०॥

*yathānevaṁ-vido bhedo*
*yata ātma-viparyayaḥ*
*deha-yoga-viyogau ca*
*saṁsṛtir na nivartate*

*yathā*—as; *an-evam-vidaḥ*—of a person who has no knowledge (about *ātma-tattva* and the steadiness of the *ātmā* in his own identity, despite the changes of the body); *bhedaḥ*—the idea of difference between body and self; *yataḥ*—because of which; *ātma-viparyayaḥ*—the foolish understanding that one is the body; *deha-yoga-viyogau ca*—and this causes connections and separations among different bodies; *saṁsṛtiḥ*—the continuation of conditioned life; *na*—not; *nivartate*—does stop.

## TRANSLATION

**One who does not understand the constitutional position of the body and the soul [ātmā] becomes too attached to the bodily concept of life. Consequently, because of attachment to the body and its by-products, he feels affected by union with and separation**

**from his family, society and nation. As long as this continues, one continues his material life. [Otherwise, one is liberated.]**

## PURPORT

As confirmed in *Śrīmad-Bhāgavatam* (1.2.6):

*sa vai puṁsāṁ paro dharmo*
*yato bhaktir adhokṣaje*
*ahaituky apratihatā*
*yayātmā suprasīdati*

The word *dharma* means "engagement." One who is engaged in the service of the Lord (*yato bhaktir adhokṣaje*), without impediment and without cessation, is understood to be situated in his original, spiritual status. When one is promoted to this status, one is always happy in transcendental bliss. Otherwise, as long as one is in the bodily concept of life, one must suffer material conditions. *Janma-mṛtyu-jarā-vyādhi-duḥkha-doṣānudarśanam.* The body is subject to its own principles of birth, death, old age and disease, but one who is situated in spiritual life (*yato bhaktir adhokṣaje*) has no birth, no death, no old age and no disease. One may argue that we may see a person who is spiritually engaged twenty-four hours a day but is still suffering from disease. In fact, however, he is neither suffering nor diseased; otherwise he could not be engaged twenty-four hours a day in spiritual activities. The example may be given in this connection that sometimes dirty foam or garbage is seen floating on the water of the Ganges. This is called *nīra-dharma*, a function of the water. But one who goes to the Ganges does not mind the foam and dirty things floating in the water. With his hand, he pushes away such nasty things, bathes in the Ganges and gains the beneficial results. Therefore, one who is situated in the spiritual status of life is unaffected by foam and garbage—or any superficial dirty things. This is confirmed by Śrīla Rūpa Gosvāmī:

*īhā yasya harer dāsye*
*karmaṇā manasā girā*
*nikhilāsv apy avasthāsu*
*jīvan-muktaḥ sa ucyate*

"A person acting in the service of Kṛṣṇa with his body, mind and words is a liberated person, even within the material world." (*Bhakti-rasāmṛta-sindhu* 1.2.187) Therefore, one is forbidden to regard the *guru* as an ordinary human being (*guruṣu nara-matir . . . nārakī saḥ*). The spiritual master, or *ācārya*, is always situated in the spiritual status of life. Birth, death, old age and disease do not affect him. According to the *Hari-bhakti-vilāsa*, therefore, after the disappearance of an *ācārya*, his body is never burnt to ashes, for it is a spiritual body. The spiritual body is always unaffected by material conditions.

## TEXT 21

तस्माद् भद्रे स्वतनयान् मया व्यापादितानपि ।
मानुशोच यतः सर्वः स्वकृतं विन्दतेऽवशः ॥२१॥

*tasmād bhadre sva-tanayān*
*mayā vyāpāditān api*
*mānuśoca yataḥ sarvaḥ*
*sva-kṛtaṁ vindate 'vaśaḥ*

*tasmāt*—therefore; *bhadre*—my dear sister (all auspiciousness unto you); *sva-tanayān*—for your own sons; *mayā*—by me; *vyāpāditān*—unfortunately killed; *api*—although; *mā anuśoca*—do not be aggrieved; *yataḥ*—because; *sarvaḥ*—everyone; *sva-kṛtam*—the fruitive results of one's own deeds; *vindate*—suffers or enjoys; *avaśaḥ*—under the control of providence.

## TRANSLATION

**My dear sister Devakī, all good fortune unto you. Everyone suffers and enjoys the results of his own work under the control of providence. Therefore, although your sons have unfortunately been killed by me, please do not lament for them.**

## PURPORT

As stated in the *Brahma-saṁhitā* (5.54):

*yas tv indra-gopam athavendram aho sva-karma-*
*bandhānurūpa-phala-bhājanam ātanoti*

*karmāṇi nirdahati kintu ca bhakti-bhājāṁ*
*govindam ādi-puruṣaṁ tam ahaṁ bhajāmi*

Everyone, beginning from the small insect known as *indra-gopa* up to Indra, the King of the heavenly planets, is obliged to undergo the results of his fruitive activities. We may superficially see that one is suffering or enjoying because of some external causes, but the real cause is one's own fruitive activities. Even when someone kills someone else, it is to be understood that the person who was killed met the fruitive results of his own work and that the man who killed him acted as the agent of material nature. Thus Kaṁsa begged Devakī's pardon by analyzing the matter deeply. He was not the cause of the death of Devakī's sons. Rather, this was their own destiny. Under the circumstances, Devakī should excuse Kaṁsa and forget his past deeds without lamentation. Kaṁsa admitted his own fault, but whatever he had done was under the control of providence. Kaṁsa might have been the immediate cause for the death of Devakī's sons, but the remote cause was their past deeds. This was an actual fact.

## TEXT 22

यावद्धतोऽस्मि हन्तास्मीत्यात्मानं मन्यतेऽस्वदृक् ।
तावत्तदभिमान्यज्ञो बाध्यबाधकतामियात् ॥२२॥

*yāvad dhato 'smi hantāsmi-*
*ty ātmānaṁ manyate 'sva-dṛk*
*tāvat tad-abhimāny ajño*
*bādhya-bādhakatām iyāt*

*yāvat*—as long as; *hataḥ asmi*—I am now being killed (by others); *hantā asmi*—I am the killer (of others); *iti*—thus; *ātmānam*—own self; *manyate*—he considers; *a-sva-dṛk*—one who has not seen himself (because of the darkness of the bodily conception of life); *tāvat*—for that long; *tat-abhimānī*—regarding himself as the killed or the killer; *ajñaḥ*—a foolish person; *bādhya-bādhakatām*—the worldly transaction of being obliged to execute some responsibility; *iyāt*—continues.

## TRANSLATION

**In the bodily conception of life, one remains in darkness, without self-realization, thinking, "I am being killed" or "I have killed my enemies." As long as a foolish person thus considers the self to be the killer or the killed, he continues to be responsible for material obligations, and consequently he suffers the reactions of happiness and distress.**

## PURPORT

By the grace of the Lord, Kaṁsa felt sincere regret for having unnecessarily persecuted such Vaiṣṇavas as Devakī and Vasudeva, and thus he came to the transcendental stage of knowledge. "Because I am situated on the platform of knowledge," Kaṁsa said, "understanding that I am not at all the killer of your sons, I have no responsibility for their death. As long as I thought that I would be killed by your son, I was in ignorance, but now I am free from this ignorance, which was due to a bodily conception of life." As stated in *Bhagavad-gītā* (18.17):

*yasya nāhaṅkṛto bhāvo*
*buddhir yasya na lipyate*
*hatvāpi sa imāl lokān*
*na hanti na nibadhyate*

"One who is not motivated by false ego, whose intelligence is not entangled, though he kills men in this world, is not the slayer. Nor is he bound by his actions." According to this axiomatic truth, Kaṁsa pleaded that he was not responsible for having killed the sons of Devakī and Vasudeva. "Please try to excuse me for such false, external activities," he said, "and be pacified with this same knowledge."

## TEXT 23

क्षमध्वं मम दौरात्म्यं साधवो दीनवत्सलाः ।
इत्युक्त्वाश्रुमुखः पादौ श्यालः स्वस्रोरथाग्रहीत् ॥२३॥

*kṣamadhvaṁ mama daurātmyaṁ*
*sādhavo dīna-vatsalāḥ*

*ity uktvāśru-mukhaḥ pādau*
*śyālaḥ svasror athāgrahīt*

*kṣamadhvam*—kindly excuse; *mama*—my; *daurātmyam*—atrocious activities; *sādhavaḥ*—both of you are great saintly persons; *dīna-vatsalāḥ*—and are very kind to poor, cripple-minded persons; *iti uktvā*—saying this; *aśru-mukhaḥ*—his face full of tears; *pādau*—the feet; *śyālaḥ*—his brother-in-law Kaṁsa; *svasroḥ*—of his sister and brother-in-law; *atha*—thus; *agrahīt*—captured.

## TRANSLATION

**Kaṁsa begged, "My dear sister and brother-in-law, please be merciful to such a poor-hearted person as me, since both of you are saintly persons. Please excuse my atrocities." Having said this, Kaṁsa fell at the feet of Vasudeva and Devakī, his eyes full of tears of regret.**

## PURPORT

Although Kaṁsa had spoken very nicely on the subject of real knowledge, his past deeds were abominable and atrocious, and therefore he further begged forgiveness from his sister and brother-in-law by falling at their feet and admitting that he was a most sinful person.

## TEXT 24

मोचयामास निगडाद् विश्रब्धः कन्यकागिरा ।
देवकीं वसुदेवं च दर्शयन्नात्मसौहृदम् ॥२४॥

*mocayām āsa nigaḍād*
*viśrabdhaḥ kanyakā-girā*
*devakīṁ vasudevaṁ ca*
*darśayann ātma-sauhṛdam*

*mocayām āsa*—Kaṁsa released them; *nigaḍāt*—from their iron shackles; *viśrabdhaḥ*—with full confidence; *kanyakā-girā*—in the words of the goddess Durgā; *devakīm*—toward his sister Devakī;

*vasudevam ca*—and his brother-in-law Vasudeva; *darśayan*—fully exhibiting; *ātma-sauhṛdam*—his family relationship.

## TRANSLATION

**Fully believing in the words of the goddess Durgā, Kaṁsa exhibited his familial affection for Devakī and Vasudeva by immediately releasing them from their iron shackles.**

## TEXT 25

भ्रातुः समनुतप्तस्य क्षान्तरोषा च देवकी ।
व्यसृजद् वसुदेवश्च प्रहस्य तमुवाच ह ॥२५॥

*bhrātuḥ samanutaptasya*
*kṣānta-roṣā ca devakī*
*vyasṛjad vasudevaś ca*
*prahasya tam uvāca ha*

*bhrātuḥ*—toward her brother Kaṁsa; *samanutaptasya*—because of his being regretful; *kṣānta-roṣā*—was relieved of anger; *ca*—also; *devakī*—Kṛṣṇa's mother, Devakī; *vyasṛjat*—gave up; *vasudevaḥ ca*—Vasudeva also; *prahasya*—smiling; *tam*—unto Kaṁsa; *uvāca*—said; *ha*—in the past.

## TRANSLATION

**When Devakī saw her brother actually repentant while explaining ordained events, she was relieved of all anger. Similarly, Vasudeva was also free from anger. Smiling, he spoke to Kaṁsa as follows.**

## PURPORT

Devakī and Vasudeva, both highly elevated personalities, accepted the truth presented by Kaṁsa that everything is ordained by providence. According to the prophecy, Kaṁsa would be killed by the eighth child of Devakī. Therefore, Vasudeva and Devakī saw that behind all these incidents was a great plan devised by the Supreme Personality of Godhead.

Because the Lord had already taken birth, just like a human child, and was in the safe custody of Yaśodā, everything was happening according to plan, and there was no need to continue their ill feeling toward Kaṁsa. Thus they accepted Kaṁsa's words.

## TEXT 26

एवमेतन्महाभाग यथा वदसि देहिनाम् ।
अज्ञानप्रभवाहंधीः स्वपरेति भिदा यतः ॥२६॥

*evam etan mahā-bhāga*
*yathā vadasi dehinām*
*ajñāna-prabhavāhaṁ-dhīḥ*
*sva-pareti bhidā yataḥ*

*evam*—yes, this is right; *etat*—what you have said; *mahā-bhāga*—O great personality; *yathā*—as; *vadasi*—you are speaking; *dehinām*—about living entities (accepting material bodies); *ajñāna-prabhavā*—by the influence of ignorance; *aham-dhīḥ*—this is my interest (false ego); *sva-parā iti*—this is another's interest; *bhidā*—differentiation; *yataḥ*—because of such a conception of life.

## TRANSLATION

**O great personality Kaṁsa, only by the influence of ignorance does one accept the material body and bodily ego. What you have said about this philosophy is correct. Persons in the bodily concept of life, lacking self-realization, differentiate in terms of "This is mine" and "This belongs to another."**

## PURPORT

Everything is done automatically by the laws of nature, which work under the direction of the Supreme Personality of Godhead. There is no question of doing anything independently, for one who has put himself in this material atmosphere is fully under the control of nature's laws. Our main business, therefore, should be to get out of this conditioned life and again become situated in spiritual existence. Only due to ignorance does a person think, "I am a demigod," "I am a human being," "I am a dog," "I am a cat," or, when the ignorance is still further advanced, "I am God." Unless one is fully self-realized, one's life of ignorance will continue.

## TEXT 27

शोकहर्षभयद्वेषलोभमोहमदान्विताः ।
मिथो घ्नन्तं न पश्यन्ति भावैर्भावं पृथग्दृशः ॥२७॥

*śoka-harṣa-bhaya-dveṣa-*
*lobha-moha-madānvitāḥ*
*mitho ghnantaṁ na paśyanti*
*bhāvair bhāvaṁ pṛthag-dṛśaḥ*

*śoka*—lamentation; *harṣa*—jubilation; *bhaya*—fear; *dveṣa*—envy; *lobha*—greed; *moha*—illusion: *mada*—madness; *anvitāḥ*—endowed with; *mithaḥ*—one another; *ghnantam*—engaged in killing; *na paśyanti*—do not see; *bhāvaiḥ*—because of such differentiation; *bhāvam*—the situation in relation to the Supreme Lord; *pṛthak-dṛśaḥ*—persons who see everything as separate from the control of the Lord.

## TRANSLATION

**Persons with the vision of differentiation are imbued with the material qualities lamentation, jubilation, fear, envy, greed, illusion and madness. They are influenced by the immediate cause, which they are busy counteracting, because they have no knowledge of the remote, supreme cause, the Personality of Godhead.**

## PURPORT

Kṛṣṇa is the cause of all causes (*sarva-kāraṇa-kāraṇam*), but one who has no connection with Kṛṣṇa is disturbed by immediate causes and cannot restrain his vision of separation or differences. When an expert physician treats a patient, he tries to find the original cause of the disease and is not diverted by the symptoms of that original cause. Similarly, a devotee is never disturbed by reverses in life. *Tat te 'nukampāṁ susamīkṣamāṇaḥ* (*Bhāg.* 10.14.8). A devotee understands that when he is in distress, this is due to his own past misdeeds, which are now accruing reactions, although by the grace of the Supreme Personality of Godhead these are only very slight. *Karmāṇi nirdahati kintu ca bhakti-bhājām* (*Brahma-saṁhitā* 5.54). When a devotee under the protection of the Supreme Personality of Godhead is to suffer because of faults in his past deeds, he passes through only a little misery by the grace of the Lord. Although the disease of a devotee is due to mistakes committed sometime in the past, he agrees to suffer and tolerate such miseries, and he depends fully on the Supreme Personality of Godhead. Thus he is never affected by material conditions of lamentation, jubilation, fear and so on. A devotee never sees anything to be unconnected with the Supreme Personality of Godhead. Śrīla Madhvācārya, quoting from the *Bhaviṣya Purāṇa*, says:

*bhagavad-darśanād yasya*
*virodhād darśanaṁ pṛthak*
*pṛthag-dṛṣṭiḥ sa vijñeyo*
*na tu sad-bheda-darśanaḥ*

## TEXT 28

श्रीशुक उवाच
कंस एवं प्रसन्नाभ्यां विशुद्धं प्रतिभाषितः ।
देवकीवसुदेवाभ्यामनुज्ञातोऽविशद् गृहम् ॥२८॥

*śrī-śuka uvāca*
*kaṁsa evaṁ prasannābhyāṁ*
*viśuddhaṁ pratibhāṣitaḥ*
*devakī-vasudevābhyām*
*anujñāto 'viśad gṛham*

*śrī-śukaḥ uvāca*—Śrī Śukadeva Gosvāmī said; *kaṁsaḥ*—King Kaṁsa; *evam*—thus; *prasannābhyām*—who were very much appeased; *viśud-dham*—in purity; *pratibhāṣitaḥ*—being answered; *devakī-vasudevā-bhyām*—by Devakī and Vasudeva; *anujñātaḥ*—taking permission; *aviśat*—entered; *gṛham*—his own palace.

## TRANSLATION

**Śukadeva Gosvāmī continued: Thus having been addressed in purity by Devakī and Vasudeva, who were very much appeased, Kaṁsa felt pleased, and with their permission he entered his home.**

## TEXT 29

तस्यां रात्र्यां व्यतीतायां कंस आहूय मन्त्रिणः ।
तेभ्य आचष्ट तत् सर्वं यदुक्तं योगनिद्रया ॥२९॥

*tasyāṁ rātryāṁ vyatītāyāṁ*
*kaṁsa āhūya mantriṇaḥ*
*tebhya ācaṣṭa tat sarvaṁ*
*yad uktaṁ yoga-nidrayā*

*tasyām*—that; *rātryām*—night; *vyatītāyām*—having passed; *kaṁsaḥ*—King Kaṁsa; *āhūya*—calling for; *mantriṇaḥ*—all the ministers; *tebhyaḥ*—them; *ācaṣṭa*—informed; *tat*—that; *sarvam*—all; *yat uktam*—which was spoken (that Kaṁsa's murderer was already somewhere else); *yoga-nidrayā*—by Yogamāyā, the goddess Durgā.

## TRANSLATION

**After that night passed, Kaṁsa summoned his ministers and informed them of all that had been spoken by Yogamāyā [who had revealed that He who was to slay Kaṁsa had already been born somewhere else].**

## PURPORT

The Vedic scripture *Caṇḍī* describes *māyā*, the energy of the Supreme Lord, as *nidrā: durgā devī sarva-bhūteṣu nidrā-rūpeṇa samāsthitaḥ.* The energy of Yogamāyā and Mahāmāyā keeps the living entities sleeping in this material world in the great darkness of ignorance. Yogamāyā, the goddess Durgā, kept Kaṁsa in darkness about Kṛṣṇa's birth and misled him to believe that his enemy Kṛṣṇa had been born elsewhere. Kṛṣṇa was born the son of Devakī, but according to the Lord's original plan, as prophesied to Brahmā, He went to Vṛndāvana to give pleasure to mother Yaśodā and Nanda Mahārāja and other intimate friends and devotees for eleven years. Then He would return to kill Kaṁsa. Because Kaṁsa did not know this, he believed Yogamāyā's statement that Kṛṣṇa was born elsewhere, not of Devakī.

## TEXT 30

आकर्ण्य भर्तुर्गदितं तमूचुर्देवशत्रवः ।
देवान् प्रति कृतामर्षा दैतेया नातिकोविदाः ॥३०॥

*ākarṇya bhartur gaditaṁ*
*tam ūcur deva-śatravaḥ*
*devān prati kṛtāmarṣā*
*daiteyā nāti-kovidāḥ*

*ākarṇya*—after hearing; *bhartuḥ*—of their master; *gaditam*—the words or statement; *tam ūcuḥ*—replied to him; *deva-śatravaḥ*—all the *asuras*, who were enemies of the demigods; *devān*—the demigods; *prati*—toward; *kṛta-amarṣāḥ*—who were envious; *daiteyāḥ*—the *asuras; na*—not; *ati-kovidāḥ*—who were very expert in executing transactions.

## TRANSLATION

**After hearing their master's statement, the envious asuras, who were enemies of the demigods and were not very expert in their dealings, advised Kaṁsa as follows.**

## PURPORT

There are two different types of men—the *asuras* and the *suras.*

*dvau bhūta-sargau loke 'smin*
*daiva āsura eva ca*
*viṣṇu-bhakta smṛto daiva*
*āsuras tad-viparyayaḥ*
(*Padma Purāṇa*)

Those who are devotees of Lord Viṣṇu, Kṛṣṇa, are *suras*, or *devas*, whereas those who are opposed to the devotees are called *asuras*. Devotees are expert in all transactions (*yasyāsti bhaktir bhagavaty akiñcanā sarvair guṇais tatra samāsate surāḥ*). Therefore they are called *kovida*, which means "expert." *Asuras*, however, although superficially showing expertise in passionate activities, are actually all fools. They are neither sober nor expert. Whatever they do is imperfect. *Moghāśā mogha-karmāṇaḥ*. According to this description of the *asuras* given in *Bhagavad-gītā* (9.12), whatever they do will ultimately be baffled. It was such persons who advised Kaṁsa because they were his chief friends and ministers.

## TEXT 31

एवं चेत्तर्हि भोजेन्द्र पुरग्रामव्रजादिषु ।
अनिर्दशान् निर्दशांश्च हनिष्यामोऽद्य वै शिशून् ॥३१॥

*evaṁ cet tarhi bhojendra*
*pura-grāma-vrajādiṣu*
*anirdaśān nirdaśāṁś ca*
*haniṣyāmo 'dya vai śiśūn*

*evam*—thus; *cet*—if it is so; *tarhi*—then; *bhoja-indra*—O King of Bhoja; *pura-grāma-vraja-ādiṣu*—in all the towns, villages and pasturing grounds; *anirdaśān*—those who are less than ten days old; *nirdaśān ca*—and those who are just over ten days old; *haniṣyāmaḥ*—we shall kill; *adya*—beginning from today; *vai*—indeed; *śiśūn*—all such children.

## TRANSLATION

**If this is so, O King of the Bhoja dynasty, beginning today we shall kill all the children born in all the villages, towns and pasturing grounds within the past ten days or slightly more.**

## TEXT 32

किमुद्यमैः करिष्यन्ति देवाः समरभीरवः ।
नित्यमुद्विग्नमनसो ज्याघोषैर्धनुषस्तव ॥३२॥

*kim udyamaiḥ kariṣyanti*
*devāḥ samara-bhīravaḥ*
*nityam udvigna-manaso*
*jyā-ghoṣair dhanuṣas tava*

*kim*—what; *udyamaiḥ*—by their endeavors; *kariṣyanti*—will do; *devāḥ*—all the demigods; *samara-bhīravaḥ*—who are afraid of fighting; *nityam*—always; *udvigna-manasaḥ*—with agitated minds; *jyā-ghoṣaiḥ*—by the sound of the string; *dhanuṣaḥ*—of the bow; *tava*—your.

### TRANSLATION

**The demigods always fear the sound of your bowstring. They are constantly in anxiety, afraid of fighting. Therefore, what can they do by their endeavors to harm you?**

### TEXT 33

अस्यतस्ते शरव्रातैर्हन्यमानाः समन्ततः ।
जिजीविषव उत्सृज्य पलायनपरा ययुः ॥३३॥

*asyatas te śara-vrātair*
*hanyamānāḥ samantataḥ*
*jijīviṣava utsṛjya*
*palāyana-parā yayuḥ*

*asyataḥ*—pierced by your discharged arrows; *te*—your; *śara-vrātaiḥ*—by the multitude of arrows; *hanyamānāḥ*—being killed; *samantataḥ*—here and there; *jijīviṣavaḥ*—aspiring to live; *utsṛjya*—giving up the battlefield; *palāyana-parāḥ*—intent on escaping; *yayuḥ*—they fled (the fighting).

### TRANSLATION

**While being pierced by your arrows, which you discharged on all sides, some of them, who were injured by the multitude of arrows but who desired to live, fled the battlefield, intent on escaping.**

## TEXT 34

केचित् प्राञ्जलयो दीना न्यस्तशस्त्रा दिवौकसः ।
मुक्तकच्छशिखाः केचिद् भीताः स्म इति वादिनः ॥३४॥

*kecit prāñjalayo dīnā*
*nyasta-śastrā divaukasaḥ*
*mukta-kaccha-śikhāḥ kecid*
*bhītāḥ sma iti vādinaḥ*

*kecit*—some of them; *prāñjalayaḥ*—folded their hands just to please you; *dīnāḥ*—very poor; *nyasta-śastrāḥ*—being bereft of all weapons; *divaukasaḥ*—the demigods; *mukta-kaccha-śikhāḥ*—their garments and hair loosened and scattered; *kecit*—some of them; *bhītāḥ*—we are very much afraid; *sma*—so became; *iti vādinaḥ*—they spoke thus.

## TRANSLATION

**Defeated and bereft of all weapons, some of the demigods gave up fighting and praised you with folded hands, and some of them, appearing before you with loosened garments and hair, said, "O lord, we are very much afraid of you."**

## TEXT 35

न त्वं विस्मृतशस्त्रास्त्रान् विरथान् भयसंवृतान् ।
हंस्यन्यासक्तविमुखान् भग्नचापानयुध्यतः ॥३५॥

*na tvaṁ vismṛta-śastrāstrān*
*virathān bhaya-saṁvṛtān*
*haṁsy anyāsakta-vimukhān*
*bhagna-cāpān ayudhyataḥ*

*na*—not; *tvam*—Your Majesty; *vismṛta-śastra-astrān*—those who have forgotten how to use weapons; *virathān*—without chariots; *bhaya-saṁvṛtān*—bewildered by fear; *haṁsi*—does kill; *anya-āsakta-vimukhān*—persons attached not to fighting but to some other subject matter;

*bhagna-cāpān*—their bows broken; *ayudhyataḥ*—and thus not fighting.

## TRANSLATION

**When the demigods are bereft of their chariots, when they forget how to use weapons, when they are fearful or attached to something other than fighting, or when their bows are broken and they have thus lost the ability to fight, Your Majesty does not kill them.**

## PURPORT

There are principles that govern even fighting. If an enemy has no chariot, is unmindful of the fighting art because of fear, or is unwilling to fight, he is not to be killed. Kaṁsa's ministers reminded Kaṁsa that despite his power, he was cognizant of the principles of fighting, and therefore he had excused the demigods because of their incapability. "But the present emergency," the ministers said, "is not intended for such mercy or military etiquette. Now you should prepare to fight under any circumstances." Thus they advised Kaṁsa to give up the traditional etiquette in fighting and chastise the enemy at any cost.

## TEXT 36

किं क्षेमशूरैर्विबुधैरसंयुगविकत्थनैः ।
रहोजुषा किं हरिणा शम्भुना वा वनौकसा ।
किमिन्द्रेणाल्पवीर्येण ब्रह्मणा वा तपस्यता ॥३६॥

*kiṁ kṣema-śūrair vibudhair*
*asaṁyuga-vikatthanaiḥ*
*raho-juṣā kiṁ hariṇā*
*śambhunā vā vanaukasā*
*kim indreṇālpa-vīryeṇa*
*brahmaṇā vā tapasyatā*

*kim*—what is there to fear; *kṣema*—in a place where there is a scarcity of the ability to fight; *śūraiḥ*—by the demigods; *vibudhaiḥ*—by such powerful persons; *asaṁyuga-vikatthanaiḥ*—by boasting and talking uselessly, away from the fighting; *rahaḥ-juṣā*—who is living in a solitary place within the core of the heart; *kim hariṇā*—what is the fear from Lord Viṣṇu; *śambhunā*—(and what is the fear) from Lord Śiva; *vā*—either; *vana-okasā*—who is living in the forest; *kim indreṇa*—what is the fear from Indra; *alpa-vīryeṇa*—he is not at all powerful (having no power to fight with you); *brahmaṇā*—and what is the fear from Brahmā; *vā*—either; *tapasyatā*—who is always engaged in meditation.

## TRANSLATION

**The demigods boast uselessly while away from the battlefield. Only where there is no fighting can they show their prowess. Therefore, from such demigods we have nothing to fear. As for Lord Viṣṇu, He is in seclusion in the core of the hearts of the yogis. As for Lord Śiva, he has gone to the forest. And as for Lord Brahmā, he is always engaged in austerities and meditation. The other demigods, headed by Indra, are devoid of prowess. Therefore you have nothing to fear.**

## PURPORT

Kaṁsa's ministers told Kaṁsa that all the exalted demigods had fled in fear of him. One had gone to the forest, one to the core of the heart, and one to engage in *tapasya*. "Thus you can be free from all fear of the demigods," they said. "Just prepare to fight."

## TEXT 37

तथापि देवाः सापत्न्यान्नोपेक्ष्या इति मन्महे ।
ततस्तन्मूलखनने नियुङ्क्ष्वास्माननुव्रतान् ॥३७॥

*tathāpi devāḥ sāpatnyān*
*nopekṣyā iti manmahe*
*tatas tan-mūla-khanane*
*niyuṅkṣvāsmān anuvratān*

*tathā api*—still; *devāḥ*—the demigods; *sāpatnyāt*—due to enmity; *na upekṣyāḥ*—should not be neglected; *iti manmahe*—this is our opinion; *tataḥ*—therefore; *tat-mūla-khanane*—to uproot them completely;

*niyuṅkṣva*—engage; *asmān*—us; *anuvratān*—who are ready to follow you.

### TRANSLATION

**Nonetheless, because of their enmity, our opinion is that the demigods should not be neglected. Therefore, to uproot them completely, engage us in fighting with them, for we are ready to follow you.**

### PURPORT

According to moral instructions, one should not neglect to extinguish fire completely, treat diseases completely, and clear debts completely. Otherwise they will increase and later be difficult to stop. Therefore the minsters advised Kaṁsa to uproot his enemies completely.

## TEXT 38

यथामयोऽङ्गे समुपेक्षितो नृभि-
र्न शक्यते रूढपदश्चिकित्सितुम् ।
यथेन्द्रियग्राम उपेक्षितस्तथा
रिपुर्महान् बद्धबलो न चाल्यते ॥३८॥

*yathāmayo 'ṅge samupekṣito nṛbhir*
*na śakyate rūḍha-padaś cikitsitum*
*yathendriya-grāma upekṣitas tathā*
*ripur mahān baddha-balo na cālyate*

*yathā*—as; *āmayaḥ*—a disease; *aṅge*—in the body; *samupekṣitaḥ*—being neglected; *nṛbhiḥ*—by men; *na*—not; *śakyate*—is able; *rūḍha-padaḥ*—when it is acute; *cikitsitum*—to be treated; *yathā*—and as; *indriya-grāmaḥ*—the senses; *upekṣitaḥ*—not controlled in the beginning; *tathā*—similarly; *ripuḥ mahān*—a great enemy; *baddha-balaḥ*—if he becomes strong; *na*—not; *cālyate*—can be controlled.

### TRANSLATION

**As a disease, if initially neglected, becomes acute and impossible to cure, or as the senses, if not controlled at first, are impossible to**

**control later, an enemy, if neglected in the beginning, later becomes insurmountable.**

## TEXT 39

मूलं हि विष्णुर्देवानां यत्र धर्मः सनातनः ।
तस्य च ब्रह्म गोविप्रास्तपो यज्ञाः सदक्षिणाः ॥३९॥

*mūlaṁ hi viṣṇur devānāṁ*
*yatra dharmaḥ sanātanaḥ*
*tasya ca brahma-go-viprās*
*tapo yajñāḥ sa-dakṣiṇāḥ*

*mūlam*—the foundation; *hi*—indeed; *viṣṇuḥ*—is Lord Viṣṇu; *devānām*—of the demigods; *yatra*—wherein; *dharmaḥ*—religious principles; *sanātanaḥ*—traditional or eternal; *tasya*—of this (foundation); *ca*—also; *brahma*—brahminical civilization; *go*—cow protection; *viprāḥ—brāhmaṇas; tapaḥ*—austerity; *yajñāḥ*—performing sacrifices; *sa-dakṣiṇāḥ*—with proper remuneration.

## TRANSLATION

**The foundation of all the demigods is Lord Viṣṇu, who lives and is worshiped wherever there are religious principles, traditional culture, the Vedas, cows, brāhmaṇas, austerities, and sacrifices with proper remuneration.**

## PURPORT

Here is a description of *sanātana-dharma,* eternal religious principles, which must include brahminical culture, *brāhmaṇas,* sacrifices and religion. These principles establish the kingdom of Viṣṇu. Without the kingdom of Viṣṇu, the kingdom of God, no one can be happy. *Na te viduḥ svārtha-gatiṁ hi viṣṇum:* in this demoniac civilization, people unfortunately do not understand that the self-interest of human society lies in Viṣṇu. *Durāśayā ye bahir-artha-māninaḥ:* thus they are involved in a hopeless hope. People want to be happy without God consciousness, or Kṛṣṇa consciousness, because they are led by blind leaders who lead human society to chaos. The asuric adherents of Kaṁsa wanted to disrupt the traditional condition of human happiness and thus defeat the *devatās*, the devotees and demigods. Unless the devotees and demigods predominate, the *asuras* will increase, and human society will be in a chaotic condition.

## TEXT 40

तस्मात् सर्वात्मना राजन् ब्राह्मणान् ब्रह्मवादिनः।
तपस्विनो यज्ञशीलान् गाश्च हन्मो हविर्दुघाः ॥४०॥

*tasmāt sarvātmanā rājan*
*brāhmaṇān brahma-vādinaḥ*
*tapasvino yajña-śīlān*
*gāś ca hanmo havir-dughāḥ*

*tasmāt*—therefore; *sarva-ātmanā*—in every respect; *rājan*—O King; *brāhmaṇān*—the *brāhmaṇas; brahma-vādinaḥ*—who maintain the brahminical culture, centered around Viṣṇu; *tapasvinaḥ*—persons who are engaged in austerities; *yajña-śīlān*—persons engaged in offering sacrifices; *gāḥ ca*—cows and persons engaged in protecting cows; *hanmaḥ*—we shall kill; *haviḥ-dughāḥ*—because they supply milk, from which clarified butter is obtained for the offering of sacrifice.

## TRANSLATION

**O King, we, who are your adherents in all respects, shall therefore kill the Vedic brāhmaṇas, the persons engaged in offering sacrifices and austerities, and the cows that supply milk, from which clarified butter is obtained for the ingredients of sacrifice.**

## TEXT 41

विप्रा गावश्च वेदाश्च तपः सत्यं दमः शमः ।
श्रद्धा दया तितिक्षा च क्रतवश्च हरेस्तनूः ॥४१॥

*viprā gāvaś ca vedāś ca*
*tapaḥ satyaṁ damaḥ śamaḥ*

*śraddhā dayā titikṣā ca*
*kratavaś ca hares tanūḥ*

*viprāḥ*—the *brāhmaṇas; gāvaḥ ca*—and the cows; *vedāḥ ca*—and the Vedic knowledge; *tapaḥ*—austerity; *satyam*—truthfulness; *damaḥ*—control of the senses; *śamaḥ*—control of the mind; *śraddhā*—faith; *dayā*—mercy; *titikṣā*—tolerance; *ca*—also; *kratavaḥ ca*—as well as sacrifices; *hareḥ tanūḥ*—are the different parts of the body of Lord Viṣṇu.

## TRANSLATION

**The brāhmaṇas, the cows, Vedic knowledge, austerity, truthfulness, control of the mind and senses, faith, mercy, tolerance and sacrifice are the different parts of the body of Lord Viṣṇu, and they are the paraphernalia for a godly civilization.**

## PURPORT

When we offer our obeisances to the Personality of Godhead, we say:

*namo brahmaṇya-devāya*
*go-brāhmaṇa-hitāya ca*
*jagad-dhitāya kṛṣṇāya*
*govindāya namo namaḥ*

When Kṛṣṇa comes to establish real perfection in the social order, He personally gives protection to the cows and the *brāhmaṇas* (*go-brāhmaṇa-hitāya ca*). This is His first interest because without protection of the *brāhmaṇas* and the cows, there can be no human civilization and no question of happy, peaceful life. *Asuras*, therefore, are always interested in killing the *brāhmaṇas* and cows. Especially in this age, Kali-yuga, cows are being killed all over the world, and as soon as there is a movement to establish brahminical civilization, people in general rebel. Thus they regard the Kṛṣṇa consciousness movement as a form of "brainwashing." How can such envious persons be happy in their godless civilization? The Supreme Personality of Godhead punishes them by keeping them in darkness, birth after birth, and pushing them lower and lower into wretched conditions of hellish life. The Kṛṣṇa consciousness movement has started a brahminical civilization, but especially when it is introduced in the Western countries, the *asuras* try to impede it in many ways. Nonetheless, we must push forward this movement tolerantly for the benefit of human society.

## TEXT 42

स हि सर्वसुराध्यक्षो ह्यसुरद्विड् गुहाशयः ।
तन्मूला देवताः सर्वाः सेश्वराः सचतुर्मुखाः ।
अयं वै तद्वधोपायो यदृषीणां विहिंसनम् ॥४२॥

*sa hi sarva-surādhyakṣo*
*hy asura-dviḍ guhā-śayaḥ*
*tan-mūlā devatāḥ sarvāḥ*
*seśvarāḥ sa-catur-mukhāḥ*
*ayaṁ vai tad-vadhopāyo*
*yad ṛṣīṇāṁ vihiṁsanam*

*saḥ*—He (Lord Viṣṇu); *hi*—indeed; *sarva-sura-adhyakṣaḥ*—the leader of all the demigods; *hi*—indeed; *asura-dviṭ*—the enemy of the *asuras; guhā-śayaḥ*—He is the Supersoul within the core of everyone's heart; *tat-mūlāḥ*—taking shelter at His lotus feet; *devatāḥ*—the demigods exist; *sarvāḥ*—all of them; *sa-īśvarāḥ*—including Lord Śiva; *sa-catuḥ-mukhāḥ*—as well as Lord Brahmā, who has four faces; *ayam*—this is; *vai*—indeed; *tat-vadha-upāyaḥ*—the only means of killing Him (Viṣṇu); *yat*—which; *ṛṣīṇām*—of great sages, saintly persons, or Vaiṣṇavas; *vihiṁsanam*—suppression with all kinds of persecution.

## TRANSLATION

**Lord Viṣṇu, the Supersoul within the core of everyone's heart, is the ultimate enemy of the asuras and is therefore known as asura-dviṭ. He is the leader of all the demigods because all the demigods, including Lord Śiva and Lord Brahmā, exist under His protection. The great saintly persons, sages and Vaiṣṇavas also depend upon Him. To persecute the Vaiṣṇavas, therefore, is the only way to kill Viṣṇu.**

## PURPORT

The demigods and the Vaiṣṇavas especially are part and parcel of the Supreme Lord, Viṣṇu, because they are always obedient to His orders (*oṁ tad viṣṇoḥ paramaṁ padaṁ sadā paśyanti sūrayaḥ*). The demoniac followers of Kaṁsa thought that if the Vaiṣṇavas, saintly persons and sages were persecuted, the original body of Viṣṇu would naturally be destroyed. Thus they decided to suppress Vaiṣṇavism. The *asuras* perpetually struggle to persecute the Vaiṣṇavas because they do not want Vaiṣṇavism to spread. Vaiṣṇavas preach only devotional service, not encouraging *karmīs, jñānīs* and *yogīs*, because if one must liberate oneself from material, conditional life, one must ultimately become a Vaiṣṇava. Our Kṛṣṇa consciousness movement is directed with this understanding, and therefore the *asuras* always try to suppress it.

## TEXT 43

श्रीशुक उवाच
एवं दुर्मन्त्रिभिः कंसः सह सम्मन्त्र्य दुर्मतिः ।
ब्रह्महिंसां हितं मेने कालपाशावृतोऽसुरः ॥४३॥

*śrī-śuka uvāca*
*evaṁ durmantribhiḥ kaṁsaḥ*
*saha sammantrya durmatiḥ*
*brahma-hiṁsāṁ hitaṁ mene*
*kāla-pāśāvṛto 'suraḥ*

*śrī-śukaḥ uvāca*—Śrī Śukadeva Gosvāmī said; *evam*—in this way; *durmantribhiḥ*—his bad ministers; *kaṁsaḥ*—King Kaṁsa; *saha*—along with; *sammantrya*—after considering very elaborately; *durmatiḥ*—without good intelligence; *brahma-hiṁsām*—persecution of the *brāhmaṇas; hitam*—as the best way; *mene*—accepted; *kāla-pāśa-āvṛtaḥ*—being bound by the rules and regulations of Yamarāja; *asuraḥ*—because he was a demon.

## TRANSLATION

**Śukadeva Gosvāmī continued: Thus, having considered the instructions of his bad ministers, Kaṁsa, who was bound by the laws**

**of Yamarāja and devoid of good intelligence because he was a demon, decided to persecute the saintly persons, the brāhmaṇas, as the only way to achieve his own good fortune.**

## PURPORT

Śrīla Locana dāsa Ṭhākura has sung, *āpana karama, bhuñjāye śamana, kahaye locana dāsa.* Instead of taking good instructions from the sages and the *śāstras,* godless nondevotees act whimsically, according to their own plans. Actually, however, no one has his own plans because everyone is bound by the laws of nature and must act according to his tendency in material, conditional life. Therefore one must change one's own decision and follow the decision of Kṛṣṇa and Kṛṣṇa's devotees. Then one is rescued from punishment by Yamarāja. Kaṁsa was not uneducated. It appears from his talks with Vasudeva and Devakī that he knew all about the laws of nature. But because of his association with bad ministers, he could not make a clear decision about his welfare. Therefore the *Caitanya-caritāmṛta* (*Madhya* 22.54) says:

*'sādhu-saṅga,' 'sādhu-saṅga'—sarva-śāstre kaya*
*lava-mātra sādhu-saṅge sarva-siddhi haya*

If one desires his real welfare, he must associate with devotees and saintly persons and in this way rectify the material condition of his life.

## TEXT 44

सन्दिश्य साधुलोकस्य कदने कदनप्रियान् ।
कामरूपधरान् दिक्षु दानवान् गृहमाविशत् ॥४४॥

*sandiśya sādhu-lokasya*
*kadane kadana-priyān*
*kāma-rūpa-dharān dikṣu*
*dānavān gṛham āviśat*

*sandiśya*—after giving permission; *sādhu-lokasya*—of the saintly persons; *kadane*—in persecution; *kadana-priyān*—to the demons, who were very expert at persecuting others; *kāma-rūpa-dharān*—who could assume any form, according to their own desire; *dikṣu*—in all directions; *dānavān*—to the demons; *gṛham āviśat*—Kaṁsa entered his own palace.

## TRANSLATION

**These demons, the followers of Kaṁsa, were expert at persecuting others, especially the Vaiṣṇavas, and could assume any form they desired. After giving these demons permission to go everywhere and persecute the saintly persons, Kaṁsa entered his palace.**

## TEXT 45

ते वै रजःप्रकृतयस्तमसा मूढचेतसः ।
सतां विद्वेषमाचेरुरारादागतमृत्यवः ॥४५॥

*te vai rajaḥ-prakṛtayas*
*tamasā mūḍha-cetasaḥ*
*satāṁ vidveṣam ācerur*
*ārād āgata-mṛtyavaḥ*

*te*—all the asuric ministers; *vai*—indeed; *rajaḥ-prakṛtayaḥ*—surcharged with the mode of passion; *tamasā*—overwhelmed by the mode of ignorance; *mūḍha-cetasaḥ*—foolish persons; *satām*—of saintly persons; *vidveṣam*—persecution; *āceruḥ*—executed; *ārāt āgata-mṛtyavaḥ*—impending death having already overtaken them.

## TRANSLATION

**Surcharged with passion and ignorance and not knowing what was good or bad for them, the asuras, for whom impending death was waiting, began the persecution of the saintly persons.**

## PURPORT

As stated in *Bhagavad-gītā* (2.13):

*dehino 'smin yathā dehe*
*kaumāraṁ yauvanaṁ jarā*

*tathā dehāntara-prāptir*
*dhīras tatra na muhyati*

"As the embodied soul continually passes, in this body, from boyhood to youth to old age, the soul similarly passes into another body at death. The self-realized soul is not bewildered by such a change." Irresponsible persons, surcharged with passion and ignorance, foolishly do things that are not to be done (*nūnaṁ pramattaḥ kurute vikarma*). But one should know the results of irresponsible actions, as explained in the next verse.

## TEXT 46

आयुः श्रियं यशो धर्मं लोकानाशिष एव च ।
हन्ति श्रेयांसि सर्वाणि पुंसो महदतिक्रमः ॥४६॥

*āyuḥ śriyaṁ yaśo dharmaṁ*
*lokān āśiṣa eva ca*
*hanti śreyāṁsi sarvāṇi*
*puṁso mahad-atikramaḥ*

*āyuḥ*—the duration of life; *śriyam*—beauty; *yaśaḥ*—fame; *dharmam*—religion; *lokān*—elevation to higher planets; *āśiṣaḥ*—blessings; *eva*—indeed; *ca*—also; *hanti*—destroys; *śreyāṁsi*—benedictions; *sarvāṇi*—all; *puṁsaḥ*—of a person; *mahat-atikramaḥ*—trespassing against great personalities.

## TRANSLATION

**My dear King, when a man persecutes great souls, all his benedictions of longevity, beauty, fame, religion, blessings and promotion to higher planets will be destroyed.**

*Thus end the Bhaktivedanta purports of the Tenth Canto, Fourth Chapter, of the* Śrīmad-Bhāgavatam, *entitled "The Atrocities of King Kaṁsa."*

CHAPTER FIVE

# The Meeting of Nanda Mahārāja and Vasudeva

As described in this chapter, Nanda Mahārāja very gorgeously performed the birth ceremony for his newborn child. Then he went to Kaṁsa to pay taxes due and met his intimate friend Vasudeva.

There was great jubilation all over Vṛndāvana due to Kṛṣṇa's birth. Everyone was overwhelmed with joy. Therefore the King of Vraja, Mahārāja Nanda, wanted to perform the birth ceremony for his child, and this he did. During this great festival, Nanda Mahārāja gave in charity to all present whatever they desired. After the festival, Nanda Mahārāja put the cowherd men in charge of protecting Gokula, and then he went to Mathurā to pay official taxes to Kaṁsa. In Mathurā, Nanda Mahārāja met Vasudeva. Nanda Mahārāja and Vasudeva were brothers, and Vasudeva praised Nanda Mahārāja's good fortune because he knew that Kṛṣṇa had accepted Nanda Mahārāja as His father. When Vasudeva inquired from Nanda Mahārāja about the welfare of the child, Nanda Mahārāja informed him all about Vṛndāvana, and Vasudeva was very much satisfied by this, although he expressed his grief because Devakī's many children had been killed by Kaṁsa. Nanda Mahārāja consoled Vasudeva by saying that everything happens according to destiny and that one who knows this is not aggrieved. Expecting many disturbances in Gokula, Vasudeva then advised Nanda Mahārāja not to wait in Mathurā, but to return to Vṛndāvana as soon as possible. Thus Nanda Mahārāja took leave of Vasudeva and returned to Vṛndāvana with the other cowherd men on their bullock carts.

## TEXTS 1–2

श्रीशुक उवाच

नन्दस्त्वात्मज उत्पन्ने जाताह्लादो महामनाः ।
आहूय विप्रान् वेदज्ञान् स्नातः शुचिरलङ्कृतः ॥ १ ॥

वाचयित्वा स्वस्त्ययनं जातकर्मात्मजस्य वै ।
कारयामास विधिवत् पितृदेवार्चनं तथा ॥ २ ॥

*śrī-śuka uvāca*
*nandas tv ātmaja utpanne*
*jātāhlādo mahā-manāḥ*
*āhūya viprān veda-jñān*
*snātaḥ śucir alaṅkṛtaḥ*

*vācayitvā svastyayanaṁ*
*jāta-karmātmajasya vai*
*kārayām āsa vidhivat*
*pitṛ-devārcanaṁ tathā*

*śrī-śukaḥ uvāca*—Śrī Śukadeva Gosvāmī said; *nandaḥ*—Mahārāja Nanda; *tu*—indeed; *ātmaje*—his son; *utpanne*—having been born; *jāta*—overwhelmed; *āhlādaḥ*—in great jubilation; *mahā-manāḥ*—who was great minded; *āhūya*—invited; *viprān*—the *brāhmaṇas; veda-jñān*—who were fully conversant in Vedic knowledge; *snātaḥ*—taking a full bath; *śuciḥ*—purifying himself; *alaṅkṛtaḥ*—being dressed very nicely with ornaments and fresh garments; *vācayitvā*—after causing to be recited; *svasti-ayanam*—Vedic *mantras* (by the *brāhmaṇas*); *jāta-karma*—the festival for the birth of the child; *ātmajasya*—of his own son; *vai*—indeed; *kārayām āsa*—caused to be performed; *vidhi-vat*—according to the Vedic regulations; *pitṛ-deva-arcanam*—the worship of the forefathers and the demigods; *tathā*—as well as.

## TRANSLATION

**Śukadeva Gosvāmī said: Nanda Mahārāja was naturally very magnanimous, and when Lord Śrī Kṛṣṇa appeared as his son, he was overwhelmed by jubilation. Therefore, after bathing and purifying himself and dressing himself properly, he invited brāhmaṇas who knew how to recite Vedic mantras. After having these qualified brāhmaṇas recite auspicious Vedic hymns, he arranged to have the Vedic birth ceremony celebrated for his newborn child according to the rules and regulations, and he also arranged for worship of the demigods and forefathers.**

## PURPORT

Śrīla Viśvanātha Cakravartī Ṭhākura has discussed the significance of the words *nandas tu.* The word *tu,* he says, is not used to fulfill the sentence, because without *tu* the sentence is complete. Therefore the word *tu* is used for a different purpose. Although Kṛṣṇa appeared as the son of Devakī, Devakī and Vasudeva did not enjoy the *jāta-karma,* the festival of the birth ceremony. Instead, this ceremony was enjoyed by Nanda Mahārāja, as stated here (*nandas tv ātmaja utpanne jātāhlādo mahāmanāḥ*). When Nanda Mahārāja met Vasudeva, Vasudeva could not disclose, "Your son Kṛṣṇa is actually my son. You are His father in a different way, spiritually." Because of fear of Kaṁsa, Vasudeva could not observe the festival for Kṛṣṇa's birth. Nanda Mahārāja, however, took full advantage of this opportunity.

The *jāta-karma* ceremony can take place when the umbilical cord, connecting the child and the placenta, is cut. However, since Kṛṣṇa was brought by Vasudeva to the house of Nanda Mahārāja, where was the chance for this to happen? In this regard, Viśvanātha Cakravartī Ṭhākura desires to prove with evidence from many *śāstras* that Kṛṣṇa actually took birth as the son of Yaśodā before the birth of Yogamāyā, who is therefore described as the Lord's younger sister. Even though there may be doubts about the cutting of the umbilical cord, and even though it is possible that this was not done, when the Supreme Personality of Godhead appears, such events are regarded as factual. Kṛṣṇa appeared as Varāhadeva from the nostril of Brahmā, and therefore Brahmā is described as the father of Varāhadeva. Also significant are the words *kārayām āsa vidhivat.* Being overwhelmed with jubilation over the birth of his son, Nanda Mahārāja did not see whether the cord was cut or not. Thus he performed the ceremony very gorgeously. According to the opinion of some authorities, Kṛṣṇa was actually born as the son of Yaśodā. In any case, without regard for material understandings, we can accept that Nanda Mahārāja's celebration for the ceremony of Kṛṣṇa's birth was proper. This ceremony is therefore well known everywhere as Nandotsava.

## TEXT 3

धेनूनां नियुते प्रादाद् विप्रेभ्यः समलङ्कृते ।
तिलाद्रीन् सप्त रत्नौघशातकौम्भाम्बरावृतान् ॥ ३ ॥

*dhenūnāṁ niyute prādād*
*viprebhyaḥ samalaṅkṛte*
*tilādrīn sapta ratnaugha-*
*śātakaumbhāmbarāvṛtān*

*dhenūnām*—of milk-giving cows; *niyute*—two million; *prādāt*—gave in charity; *viprebhyaḥ*—unto the *brāhmaṇas; samalaṅkṛte*—completely decorated; *tila-adrīn*—hills of grain; *sapta*—seven; *ratna-ogha-śāta-kaumbha-ambara-āvṛtān*—covered with jewels and cloth embroidered with gold.

## TRANSLATION

**Nanda Mahārāja gave two million cows, completely decorated with cloth and jewels, in charity to the brāhmaṇas. He also gave them seven hills of grain, covered with jewels and with cloth decorated with golden embroidery.**

## TEXT 4

कालेन स्नानशौचाभ्यां संस्कारैस्तपसेज्यया ।
शुध्यन्ति दानैःसन्तुष्ट्या द्रव्याण्यात्मात्मविद्यया ॥ ४ ॥

*kālena snāna-śaucābhyāṁ*
*saṁskārais tapasejyayā*
*śudhyanti dānaiḥ santuṣṭyā*
*dravyāṇy ātmātma-vidyayā*

*kālena*—by due course of time (the land and other material things become purified); *snāna-śaucābhyām*—by bathing (the body becomes purified) and by cleansing (unclean things become purified); *saṁskāraiḥ*—by purificatory processes (birth becomes purified); *tapasā*—by austerity (the senses become purified); *ijyayā*—by worship (the *brāhmaṇas* become purified); *śudhyanti*—become purified; *dānaiḥ*—by charity (wealth becomes purified); *santuṣṭyā*—by satisfaction (the mind becomes purified); *dravyāṇi*—all material possessions, such as cows, land and gold; *ātmā*—the soul (becomes purified); *ātma-vidyayā*—by self-realization.

## TRANSLATION

**O King, by the passing of time, land and other material possessions are purified; by bathing, the body is purified; and by being cleansed, unclean things are purified. By purificatory ceremonies, birth is purified; by austerity, the senses are purified; and by worship and charity offered to the brāhmaṇas, material possessions are purified. By satisfaction, the mind is purified; and by self-realization, or Kṛṣṇa consciousness, the soul is purified.**

## PURPORT

These are śāstric injunctions concerning how one can purify everything according to Vedic civilization. Unless purified, anything we use will infect us with contamination. In India five thousand years ago, even in the villages such as that of Nanda Mahārāja, people knew how to purify things, and thus they enjoyed even material life without contamination.

## TEXT 5

सौमङ्गल्यगिरो विप्राः सूतमागधवन्दिनः ।
गायकाश्च जगुर्नेदुर्भेर्यो दुन्दुभयो मुहुः ॥ ५ ॥

*saumaṅgalya-giro viprāḥ*
*sūta-māgadha-vandinaḥ*
*gāyakāś ca jagur nedur*
*bheryo dundubhayo muhuḥ*

*saumaṅgalya-giraḥ*—whose chanting of *mantras* and hymns purified the environment by their vibration; *viprāḥ*—the *brāhmaṇas; sūta*—experts in reciting all the histories; *māgadha*—experts in reciting the histories of special royal families; *vandinaḥ*—general professional reciters; *gāyakāḥ*—singers; *ca*—as well as; *jaguḥ*—chanted; *neduḥ*—vibrated; *bheryaḥ*—a kind of musical instrument; *dundubhayaḥ*—a kind of musical instrument; *muhuḥ*—constantly.

## TRANSLATION

**The brāhmaṇas recited auspicious Vedic hymns, which purified the environment by their vibration. The experts in reciting old**

**histories like the Purāṇas, the experts in reciting the histories of royal families, and general reciters all chanted, while singers sang and many kinds of musical instruments, like bherīs and dundubhis, played in accompaniment.**

## TEXT 6

व्रजः सम्मृष्टसंसिक्तद्वाराजिरगृहान्तरः ।
चित्रध्वजपताकास्रक्चैलपल्लवतोरणैः ॥ ६ ॥

*vrajaḥ sammṛṣṭa-saṁsikta-*
*dvārājira-gṛhāntaraḥ*
*citra-dhvaja-patākā-srak-*
*caila-pallava-toraṇaiḥ*

*vrajaḥ*—the land occupied by Nanda Mahārāja; *sammṛṣṭa*—very nicely cleaned; *saṁsikta*—very nicely washed; *dvāra*—all the doors or entrances; *ajira*—courtyards; *gṛha-antaraḥ*—everything within the house; *citra*—variegated; *dhvaja*—of festoons; *patākā*—of flags; *srak*—of flower garlands; *caila*—of pieces of cloth; *pallava*—of the leaves of mango trees; *toraṇaiḥ*—(decorated) by gates in different places.

## TRANSLATION

**Vrajapura, the residence of Nanda Mahārāja, was fully decorated with varieties of festoons and flags, and in different places, gates were made with varieties of flower garlands, pieces of cloth, and mango leaves. The courtyards, the gates near the roads, and everything within the rooms of the houses were perfectly swept and washed with water.**

## TEXT 7

गावो वृषा वत्सतरा हरिद्रातैलरूषिताः ।
विचित्रधातुबर्हस्रग्वस्त्रकाञ्चनमालिनः ॥ ७ ॥

*gāvo vṛṣā vatsatarā*
*haridrā-taila-rūṣitāḥ*

*vicitra-dhātu-barhasrag-*
*vastra-kāñcana-mālinaḥ*

*gāvaḥ*—the cows; *vṛṣāḥ*—the bulls; *vatsatarāḥ*—the calves; *hari-drā*—with a mixture of turmeric; *taila*—and oil; *rūṣitāḥ*—their entire bodies smeared; *vicitra*—decorated varieties of; *dhātu*—colored minerals; *barha-srak*—peacock-feather garlands; *vastra*—cloths; *kāñ-cana*—golden ornaments; *mālinaḥ*—being decorated with garlands.

## TRANSLATION

**The cows, the bulls and the calves were thoroughly smeared with a mixture of turmeric and oil, mixed with varieties of minerals. Their heads were bedecked with peacock feathers, and they were garlanded and covered with cloth and golden ornaments.**

## PURPORT

The Supreme Personality of Godhead has instructed in *Bhagavad-gītā* (18.44), *kṛṣi-go-rakṣya-vāṇijyaṁ vaiśya-karma-svabhāvajam:* "Farming, cow protection and trade are the qualities of work for the *vaiśyas.*" Nanda Mahārāja belonged to the *vaiśya* community, the agriculturalist community. How to protect the cows and how rich this community was are explained in these verses. We can hardly imagine that cows, bulls and calves could be cared for so nicely and decorated so well with cloths and valuable golden ornaments. How happy they were. As described elsewhere in the *Bhāgavatam,* during Mahārāja Yudhiṣṭhira's time the cows were so happy that they used to muddy the pasturing ground with milk. This is Indian civilization. Yet in the same place, India, Bhāratavarṣa, how much people are suffering by giving up the Vedic way of life and not understanding the teachings of *Bhagavad-gītā.*

## TEXT 8

महार्हवस्त्राभरणकञ्चुकोष्णीषभूषिताः ।
गोपाः समाययू राजन् नानोपायनपाणयः ॥ ८ ॥

*mahārha-vastrābharaṇa-*
*kañcukoṣṇīṣa-bhūṣitāḥ*
*gopāḥ samāyayū rājan*
*nānopāyana-pāṇayaḥ*

*mahā-arha*—extremely valuable; *vastra-ābharaṇa*—with garments and ornaments; *kañcuka*—by a particular type of garment used in Vṛndāvana; *uṣṇīṣa*—with turbans; *bhūṣitāḥ*—being nicely dressed; *gopāḥ*—all the cowherd men; *samāyayuḥ*—came there; *rājan*—O King (Mahārāja Parīkṣit); *nānā*—various; *upāyana*—presentations; *pāṇayaḥ*—holding in their hands.

## TRANSLATION

**O King Parīkṣit, the cowherd men dressed very opulently with valuable ornaments and garments such as coats and turbans. Decorated in this way and carrying various presentations in their hands, they approached the house of Nanda Mahārāja.**

## PURPORT

When we consider the past condition of the agriculturalist in the village, we can see how opulent he was, simply because of agricultural produce and protection of cows. At the present, however, agriculture having been neglected and cow protection given up, the agriculturalist is suffering pitiably and is dressed in a niggardly torn cloth. This is the distinction between the India of history and the India of the present day. By the atrocious activities of *ugra-karma*, how we are killing the opportunity of human civilization!

## TEXT 9

गोप्यश्चाकर्ण्य मुदिता यशोदायाः सुतोद्भवम् ।
आत्मानं भूषयाञ्चक्रुर्वस्त्राकल्पाञ्जनादिभिः ॥ ९ ॥

*gopyaś cākarṇya muditā*
*yaśodāyāḥ sutodbhavam*
*ātmānaṁ bhūṣayāṁ cakrur*
*vastrākalpāñjanādibhiḥ*

*gopyaḥ*—the feminine community, the wives of the cowherd men; *ca*—also; *ākarnya*—after hearing; *muditāḥ*—became very glad; *yaśodāyāḥ*—of mother Yaśodā; *suta-udbhavam*—the birth of a male child; *ātmānam*—personally; *bhūṣayām cakruḥ*—dressed very nicely to attend the festival; *vastra-ākalpa-añjana-ādibhiḥ*—with proper dress, ornaments, black ointment, and so on.

## TRANSLATION

**The gopī wives of the cowherd men were very pleased to hear that mother Yaśodā had given birth to a son, and they began to decorate themselves very nicely with proper dresses, ornaments, black ointment for the eyes, and so on.**

## TEXT 10

नवकुङ्कुमकिञ्जल्कमुखपङ्कजभूतयः ।
बलिभिस्त्वरितं जग्मुः पृथुश्रोण्यश्चलत्कुचाः ॥१०॥

*nava-kuṅkuma-kiñjalka-*
*mukha-paṅkaja-bhūtayaḥ*
*balibhis tvaritaṁ jagmuḥ*
*pṛthu-śroṇyaś calat-kucāḥ*

*nava-kuṅkuma-kiñjalka*—with saffron and newly grown *kuṅkuma* flower; *mukha-paṅkaja-bhūtayaḥ*—exhibiting an extraordinary beauty in their lotuslike faces; *balibhiḥ*—with presentations in their hands; *tvaritam*—very quickly; *jagmuḥ*—went (to the house of mother Yaśodā); *pṛthu-śroṇyaḥ*—bearing full hips, fulfilling womanly beauty; *calat-kucāḥ*—their developed breasts were moving.

## TRANSLATION

**Their lotuslike faces extraordinarily beautiful, being decorated with saffron and newly grown kuṅkuma, the wives of the cowherd men hurried to the house of mother Yaśodā with presentations in their hands. Because of natural beauty, the wives had full hips and full breasts, which moved as they hurried along.**

## PURPORT

The cowherd men and women in the villages lived a very natural life, and the women developed a natural feminine beauty, with full hips and breasts. Because women in modern civilization do not live naturally, their hips and breasts do not develop this natural fullness. Because of artificial living, women have lost their natural beauty, although they claim to be independent and advanced in material civilization. This description of the village women gives a clear example of the contrast between natural life and the artificial life of a condemned society, such as that of the Western countries, where topless, bottomless beauty may be easily purchased in clubs and shops and for public advertisements. The word *balibhiḥ* indicates that the women were carrying gold coins, jeweled necklaces, nice cloths, newly grown grass, sandalwood pulp, flower garlands and similar offerings on plates made of gold. Such offerings are called *bali.* The words *tvaritaṁ jagmuḥ* indicate how happy the village women were to understand that mother Yaśodā had given birth to a wonderful child known as Kṛṣṇa.

## TEXT 11

गोप्यः सुमृष्टमणिकुण्डलनिष्ककण्ठ्य-
श्चित्राम्बराः पथि शिखाच्युतमाल्यवर्षाः ।
नन्दालयं सवलया व्रजतीर्विरेजु-
र्व्यालोलकुण्डलपयोधरहारशोभाः ॥११॥

*gopyaḥ sumṛṣṭa-maṇi-kuṇḍala-niṣka-kaṇṭhyaś*
*citrāmbarāḥ pathi śikhā-cyuta-mālya-varṣāḥ*
*nandālayaṁ sa-valayā vrajatīr virejur*
*vyālola-kuṇḍala-payodhara-hāra-śobhāḥ*

*gopyaḥ*—the *gopīs; su-mṛṣṭa*—very dazzling; *maṇi*—made of jewels; *kuṇḍala*—wearing earrings; *niṣka-kaṇṭhyaḥ*—and having little keys and lockets hanging from their necks; *citra-ambarāḥ*—dressed with varieties of colored embroidery; *pathi*—on their way to Yaśodāmayī's house; *śikhā-cyuta*—fell from their hair; *mālya-varṣāḥ*—a shower of flower garlands; *nanda-ālayam*—to the house of Mahārāja Nanda; *sa-valayāḥ*—with bangles on their hands; *vrajatīḥ*—while going (in that costume); *virejuḥ*—they looked very, very beautiful; *vyālola*—moving; *kuṇḍala*—with earrings; *payodhara*—with breasts; *hāra*—with flower garlands; *śobhāḥ*—who appeared so beautiful.

## TRANSLATION

**In the ears of the gopīs were brilliantly polished jeweled earrings, and from their necks hung metal lockets. Their hands were decorated with bangles, their dresses were of varied colors, and from their hair, flowers fell onto the street like showers. Thus while going to the house of Mahārāja Nanda, the gopīs, their earrings, breasts and garlands moving, were brilliantly beautiful.**

## PURPORT

The description of the *gopīs*, who were going to the house of Mahārāja Nanda to welcome Kṛṣṇa, is especially significant. The *gopīs* were not ordinary women, but expansions of Kṛṣṇa's pleasure potency, as described in the *Brahma-saṁhitā:*

*ānanda-cinmaya-rasa-pratibhāvitābhis*
*tābhir ya eva nija-rūpatayā kalābhiḥ*
*goloka eva nivasaty akhilātma-bhūto*
*govindam ādi-puruṣaṁ tam ahaṁ bhajāmi*
(5.37)

*cintāmaṇi-prakara-sadmasu kalpa-vṛkṣa-*
*lakṣāvṛteṣu surabhīr abhipālayantam*
*lakṣmī-sahasra-śata-sambhrama-sevyamānaṁ*
*govindum ādi-puruṣaṁ tam ahaṁ bhajāmi*
(5.29)

Kṛṣṇa is always worshiped by the *gopīs* wherever He goes. Therefore Kṛṣṇa is so vividly described in *Śrīmad-Bhāgavatam.* Śrī Caitanya Mahāprabhu has also described Kṛṣṇa in this way: *ramyā kācid upāsanā vrajavadhū-vargeṇa yā kalpitā.* All these *gopīs* were going to offer Kṛṣṇa their presentations because the *gopīs* are eternal associates of the Lord. Now the *gopīs* were more jubilant because of the news of Kṛṣṇa's appearance in Vṛndāvana.

## TEXT 12

ता आशिषः प्रयुञ्जानाश्चिरं पाहीति बालके ।
हरिद्राचूर्णतैलाद्भिः सिञ्चन्त्योऽजनमुज्जगुः ॥१२॥

*tā āśiṣaḥ prayuñjānāś*
*ciraṁ pāhīti bālake*
*haridrā-cūrṇa-tailādbhiḥ*
*siñcantyo 'janam ujjaguḥ*

*tāḥ*—all the women, the wives and daughters of the cowherd men; *āśiṣaḥ*—blessings; *prayuñjānāḥ*—offering; *ciram*—for a long time; *pāhi*—may You become the King of Vraja and maintain all its inhabitants; *iti*—thus; *bālake*—unto the newborn child; *haridrā-cūrṇa*—powder of turmeric; *taila-adbhiḥ*—mixed with oil; *siñcantyaḥ*—sprinkling; *ajanam*—the Supreme Personality of Godhead, who is unborn; *ujjaguḥ*—offered prayers.

## TRANSLATION

**Offering blessings to the newborn child, Kṛṣṇa, the wives and daughters of the cowherd men said, "May You become the King of Vraja and long maintain all its inhabitants." They sprinkled a mixture of turmeric powder, oil and water upon the birthless Supreme Lord and offered their prayers.**

## TEXT 13

अवाद्यन्त विचित्राणि वादित्राणि महोत्सवे ।
कृष्णे विश्वेश्वरेऽनन्ते नन्दस्य व्रजमागते ॥१३॥

*avādyanta vicitrāṇi*
*vāditrāṇi mahotsave*

*kṛṣṇe viśveśvare 'nante*
*nandasya vrajam āgate*

*avādyanta*—vibrated in celebration of Vasudeva's son; *vicitrāṇi*—various; *vāditrāṇi*—musical instruments; *mahā-utsave*—in the great festival; *kṛṣṇe*—when Lord Kṛṣṇa; *viśva-īśvare*—the master of the entire cosmic manifestation; *anante*—unlimitedly; *nandasya*—of Mahārāja Nanda; *vrajam*—at the pasturing place; *āgate*—had so arrived.

## TRANSLATION

**Now that the all-pervading, unlimited Lord Kṛṣṇa, the master of the cosmic manifestation, had arrived within the estate of Mahārāja Nanda, various types of musical instruments resounded to celebrate the great festival.**

## PURPORT

The Lord says in *Bhagavad-gītā* (4.7):

*yadā yadā hi dharmasya*
*glānir bhavati bhārata*
*abhyutthānam adharmasya*
*tadātmānaṁ sṛjāmy aham*

"Whenever and wherever there is a decline in religious practice, O descendant of Bharata, and a predominant rise of irreligion—at that time I descend Myself." Whenever Kṛṣṇa comes, once in a day of Brahmā, He comes to the house of Nanda Mahārāja in Vṛndāvana. Kṛṣṇa is the master of all creation (*sarva-loka-maheśvaram*). Therefore, not only in the neighborhood of Nanda Mahārāja's estate, but all over the universe—and in all the other universes—musical sounds celebrated the auspicious arrival of the Lord.

## TEXT 14

गोपाः परस्परं हृष्टा दधिक्षीरघृताम्बुभिः ।
आसिञ्चन्तो विलिम्पन्तो नवनीतैश्च चिक्षिपुः ॥१४॥

*gopāḥ parasparaṁ hṛṣṭā*
*dadhi-kṣīra-ghṛtāmbubhiḥ*
*āsiñcanto vilimpanto*
*navanītaiś ca cikṣipuḥ*

*gopāḥ*—the cowherd men; *parasparam*—on one another; *hṛṣṭāḥ*—being so pleased; *dadhi*—with curd; *kṣīra*—with condensed milk; *ghṛta-ambubhiḥ*—with water mixed with butter; *āsiñcantaḥ*—sprinkling; *vilimpantaḥ*—smearing; *navanītaiḥ ca*—and with butter; *cikṣipuḥ*—they threw on one another.

## TRANSLATION

**In gladness, the cowherd men enjoyed the great festival by splashing one another's bodies with a mixture of curd, condensed milk, butter and water. They threw butter on one another and smeared it on one another's bodies.**

## PURPORT

From this statement we can understand that five thousand years ago not only was there enough milk, butter and curd to eat, drink and cook with, but when there was a festival it would be thrown about without restriction. There was no limit to how extensively milk, butter, curd and other such products were used in human society. Everyone had an ample stock of milk, and by using it in many varied milk preparations, people would keep good health in natural ways and thus enjoy life in Kṛṣṇa consciousness.

## TEXTS 15–16

नन्दो महामनास्तेभ्यो वासोऽलङ्कारगोधनम् ।
सूतमागधवन्दिभ्यो येऽन्ये विद्योपजीविनः ॥१५॥
तैस्तैः कामैरदीनात्मा यथोचितमपूजयत् ।
विष्णोराराधनार्थाय स्वपुत्रस्योदयाय च ॥१६॥

*nando mahā-manās tebhyo*
*vāso 'laṅkāra-go-dhanam*

*sūta-māgadha-vandibhyo*
*ye 'nye vidyopajīvinaḥ*

*tais taiḥ kāmair adīnātmā*
*yathocitam apūjayat*
*viṣṇor ārādhanārthāya*
*sva-putrasyodayāya ca*

*nandaḥ*—Mahārāja Nanda; *mahā-manāḥ*—who among the cowherd men was the greatest of all upright persons; *tebhyaḥ*—unto the cowherd men; *vāsaḥ*—clothing; *alaṅkāra*—ornaments; *go-dhanam*—and cows; *sūta-māgadha-vandibhyaḥ*—unto the *sūtas* (the professional reciters of the old histories), the *māgadhas* (the professional reciters of the histories of royal dynasties) and the *vandīs* (general singers of prayers); *ye anye*—as well as others; *vidyā-upajīvinaḥ*—who were continuing their livelihood on the basis of educational qualifications; *taiḥ taiḥ*—with whatever; *kāmaiḥ*—improvements of desire; *adīna-ātmā*—Mahārāja Nanda, who was so magnanimous; *yathā-ucitam*—as was suitable; *apūjayat*—worshiped them or satisfied them; *viṣṇoḥ ārādhana-arthāya*—for the purpose of satisfying Lord Viṣṇu; *sva-putrasya*—of his own child; *udayāya*—for the improvement in all respects; *ca*—and.

## TRANSLATION

**The great-minded Mahārāja Nanda gave clothing, ornaments and cows in charity to the cowherd men in order to please Lord Viṣṇu, and thus he improved the condition of his own son in all respects. He distributed charity to the sūtas, the māgadhas, the vandīs, and men of all other professions, according to their educational qualifications, and satisfied everyone's desires.**

## PURPORT

Although it has become fashionable to speak of *daridra-nārāyaṇa*, the words *viṣṇor ārādhanārthāya* do not mean that all the people satisfied by Nanda Mahārāja in this great ceremony were Viṣṇus. They were not *daridra*, nor were they Nārāyaṇa. Rather, they were devotees of Nārāyaṇa, and by their educational qualifications they would satisfy

Nārāyaṇa. Therefore, satisfying them was an indirect way of satisfying Lord Viṣṇu. *Mad-bhakta-pūjābhyadhikā* (*Bhāg.* 11.19.21). The Lord says, "Worshiping My devotees is better than worshiping Me directly." The *varṇāśrama* system is entirely meant for *viṣṇu-ārādhana*, worship of Lord Viṣṇu. *Varṇāśramācāravatā puruṣeṇa paraḥ pumān/ viṣṇur ārādhyate* (*Viṣṇu Purāṇa* 3.8.9). The ultimate goal of life is to please Lord Viṣṇu, the Supreme Lord. The uncivilized man or materialistic person, however, does not know this aim of life. *Na te viduḥ svārtha-gatiṁ hi viṣṇum* (*Bhāg.* 7.5.31). One's real self-interest lies in satisfying Lord Viṣṇu. Not satisfying Lord Viṣṇu but instead attempting to become happy through material adjustments (*bahir-artha-māninaḥ*) is the wrong way for happiness. Because Viṣṇu is the root of everything, if Viṣṇu is pleased, everyone is pleased; in particular, one's children and family members become happy in all respects. Nanda Mahārāja wanted to see his newborn child happy. That was his purpose. Therefore he wanted to satisfy Lord Viṣṇu, and to satisfy Lord Viṣṇu it was necessary to satisfy His devotees, such as the learned *brāhmaṇas*, *māgadhas* and *sūtas*. Thus, in a roundabout way, ultimately it was Lord Viṣṇu who was to be satisfied.

## TEXT 17

रोहिणी च महाभागा नन्दगोपाभिनन्दिता ।
व्यचरद् दिव्यवासस्रक्कण्ठाभरणभूषिता ॥१७॥

*rohiṇī ca mahā-bhāgā*
*nanda-gopābhinanditā*
*vyacarad divya-vāsa-srak-*
*kaṇṭhābharaṇa-bhūṣitā*

*rohiṇī*—Rohiṇī, the mother of Baladeva; *ca*—also; *mahā-bhāgā*—the most fortunate mother of Baladeva (greatly fortunate because of having the opportunity to raise Kṛṣṇa and Balarāma together); *nanda-gopā-abhinanditā*—being honored by Mahārāja Nanda and mother Yaśodā; *vyacarat*—was busy wandering here and there; *divya*—beautiful; *vāsa*—with a dress; *srak*—with a garland; *kaṇṭha-ābharaṇa*—and with an ornament covering the neck; *bhūṣitā*—decorated.

## TRANSLATION

**The most fortunate Rohiṇī, the mother of Baladeva, was honored by Nanda Mahārāja and Yaśodā, and thus she also dressed gorgeously and decorated herself with a necklace, a garland and other ornaments. She was busy wandering here and there to receive the women who were guests at the festival.**

## PURPORT

Rohiṇī, another wife of Vasudeva's, was also kept under the care of Nanda Mahārāja with her son Baladeva. Because her husband was imprisoned by Kaṁsa, she was not very happy, but on the occasion of Kṛṣṇa-janmāṣṭamī, Nandotsava, when Nanda Mahārāja gave dresses and ornaments to others, he also gave gorgeous garments and ornaments to Rohiṇī so that she could take part in the festival. Thus she also was busy receiving the women who were guests. Because of her good fortune in being able to raise Kṛṣṇa and Balarāma together, she is described as *mahā-bhāgā*, greatly fortunate.

## TEXT 18

तत आरभ्य नन्दस्य व्रजः सर्वसमृद्धिमान् ।
हरेर्निवासात्मगुणै रमाक्रीडमभून्नृप ॥१८॥

*tata ārabhya nandasya*
*vrajaḥ sarva-samṛddhimān*
*harer nivāsātma-guṇai*
*ramākrīḍam abhūn nṛpa*

*tataḥ ārabhya*—beginning from that time; *nandasya*—of Mahārāja Nanda; *vrajaḥ*—Vrajabhūmi, the land for protecting and breeding cows; *sarva-samṛddhimān*—became opulent with all kinds of riches; *hareḥ nivāsa*—of the residence of the Supreme Personality of Godhead; *ātma-guṇaiḥ*—by the transcendental qualities; *ramā-ākrīḍam*—the place of pastimes for the goddess of fortune; *abhūt*—became; *nṛpa*—O King (Mahārāja Parīkṣit).

## TRANSLATION

**O Mahārāja Parīkṣit, the home of Nanda Mahārāja is eternally the abode of the Supreme Personality of Godhead and His transcendental qualities and is therefore always naturally endowed with the opulence of all wealth. Yet beginning from Lord Kṛṣṇa's appearance there, it became the place for the pastimes of the goddess of fortune.**

## PURPORT

As stated in the *Brahma-saṁhitā* (5.29), *lakṣmī-sahasra-śata-sambhrama-sevyamānaṁ govindam ādi-puruṣaṁ tam ahaṁ bhajāmi.* The abode of Kṛṣṇa is always served by hundreds and thousands of goddesses of fortune. Wherever Kṛṣṇa goes, the goddess of fortune naturally resides with Him. The chief of the goddesses of fortune is Śrīmatī Rādhārāṇī. Therefore, Kṛṣṇa's appearance in the land of Vraja indicated that the chief goddess of fortune, Rādhārāṇī, would also appear there very soon. Nanda Mahārāja's abode was already opulent, and since Kṛṣṇa had appeared, it would be opulent in all respects.

## TEXT 19

गोपान् गोकुलरक्षायां निरूप्य मथुरां गतः ।
नन्दः कंसस्य वार्षिक्यं करं दातुं कुरूद्वह ॥१९॥

*gopān gokula-rakṣāyāṁ*
*nirūpya mathurāṁ gataḥ*
*nandaḥ kaṁsasya vārṣikyaṁ*
*karaṁ dātuṁ kurūdvaha*

*gopān*—the cowherd men; *gokula-rakṣāyām*—in giving protection to the state of Gokula; *nirūpya*—after appointing; *mathurām*—to Mathurā; *gataḥ*—went; *nandaḥ*—Nanda Mahārāja; *kaṁsasya*—of Kaṁsa; *vārṣikyam*—yearly taxes; *karam*—the share of profit; *dātum*—to pay; *kuru-udvaha*—O Mahārāja Parīkṣit, best protector of the Kuru dynasty.

## TRANSLATION

**Śukadeva Gosvāmī continued: Thereafter, my dear King Parīkṣit, O best protector of the Kuru dynasty, Nanda Mahārāja ap-**

**pointed the local cowherd men to protect Gokula and then went to Mathurā to pay the yearly taxes to King Kaṁsa.**

## PURPORT

Because the killing of babies was going on and had already become known, Nanda Mahārāja was very much afraid for his newborn child. Thus he appointed the local cowherd men to protect his home and child. He wanted to go immediately to Mathurā to pay the taxes due and also to offer some presentation for the sake of his newborn son. For the protection of the child, he had worshiped various demigods and forefathers and given charity to everyone's satisfaction. Similarly, Nanda Mahārāja wanted not only to pay Kaṁsa the yearly taxes but also to offer some presentation so that Kaṁsa too would be satisfied. His only concern was how to protect his transcendental child, Kṛṣṇa.

## TEXT 20

वसुदेव उपश्रुत्य भ्रातरं नन्दमागतम् ।
ज्ञात्वा दत्तकरं राज्ञे ययौ तदवमोचनम् ॥२०॥

*vasudeva upaśrutya*
*bhrātaraṁ nandam āgatam*
*jñātvā datta-karaṁ rājñe*
*yayau tad-avamocanam*

*vasudevaḥ*—Vasudeva; *upaśrutya*—when he heard; *bhrātaram*—that his dear friend and brother; *nandam*—Nanda Mahārāja; *āgatam*—had come to Mathurā; *jñātvā*—when he learned; *datta-karam*—and had already paid the taxes; *rājñe*—unto the King; *yayau*—he went; *tat-avamocanam*—to the residential quarters of Nanda Mahārāja.

## TRANSLATION

**When Vasudeva heard that Nanda Mahārāja, his very dear friend and brother, had come to Mathurā and already paid the taxes to Kaṁsa, he went to Nanda Mahārāja's residence.**

## PURPORT

Vasudeva and Nanda Mahārāja were so intimately connected that they lived like brothers. Furthermore, it is learned from the notes of Śrīpāda Madhvācārya that Vasudeva and Nanda Mahārāja were stepbrothers. Vasudeva's father, Śūrasena, married a *vaiśya* girl, and from her Nanda Mahārāja was born. Later, Nanda Mahārāja himself married a *vaiśya* girl, Yaśodā. Therefore his family is celebrated as a *vaiśya* family, and Kṛṣṇa, identifying Himself as their son, took charge of *vaiśya* activities (*kṛṣi-go-rakṣya-vāṇijyam*). Balarāma represents plowing the land for agriculture and therefore always carries in His hand a plow, whereas Kṛṣṇa tends cows and therefore carries a flute in His hand. Thus the two brothers represent *kṛṣi-rakṣya* and *go-rakṣya.*

## TEXT 21

तं दृष्ट्वा सहसोत्थाय देहः प्राणमिवागतम् ।
प्रीतः प्रियतमं दोर्भ्यां सस्वजे प्रेमविह्वलः ॥२१॥

*taṁ dṛṣṭvā sahasotthāya*
*dehaḥ prāṇam ivāgatam*
*prītaḥ priyatamaṁ dorbhyāṁ*
*sasvaje prema-vihvalaḥ*

*tam*—him (Vasudeva); *dṛṣṭvā*—seeing; *sahasā*—suddenly; *utthāya*—getting up; *dehaḥ*—the same body; *prāṇam*—life; *iva*—as if; *āgatam*—had returned; *prītaḥ*—so pleased; *priya-tamam*—his dear friend and brother; *dorbhyām*—by his two arms; *sasvaje*—embraced; *prema-vihvalaḥ*—overwhelmed with love and affection.

## TRANSLATION

**When Nanda Mahārāja heard that Vasudeva had come, he was overwhelmed with love and affection, being as pleased as if his body had regained its life. Seeing Vasudeva suddenly present, he got up and embraced him with both arms.**

## PURPORT

Nanda Mahārāja was older than Vasudeva. Therefore Nanda Mahārāja embraced him, and Vasudeva offered him *namaskāra.*

## TEXT 22

पूजितः सुखमासीनः पृष्ट्वानामयमादृतः ।
प्रसक्तधीः स्वात्मजयोरिदमाह विशाम्पते ॥२२॥

*pūjitaḥ sukham āsīnaḥ*
*pṛṣṭvānāmayam ādṛtaḥ*
*prasakta-dhīḥ svātmajayor*
*idam āha viśāmpate*

*pūjitaḥ*—Vasudeva having been so dearly welcomed; *sukham āsīnaḥ*—having been given a place to sit comfortably; *pṛṣṭvā*—asking; *anāmayam*—all-auspicious inquiries; *ādṛtaḥ*—being honored and respectfully received; *prasakta-dhīḥ*—because of his being very much attached; *sva-ātmajayoḥ*—to his own two sons, Kṛṣṇa and Balarāma; *idam*—the following; *āha*—inquired; *viśām-pate*—O Mahārāja Parīkṣit.

## TRANSLATION

**O Mahārāja Parīkṣit, having thus been received and welcomed by Nanda Mahārāja with honor, Vasudeva sat down very peacefully and inquired about his own two sons because of intense love for them.**

## TEXT 23

दिष्ट्या भ्रातः प्रवयस इदानीमप्रजस्य ते ।
प्रजाशाया निवृत्तस्य प्रजा यत् समपद्यत ॥२३॥

*diṣṭyā bhrātaḥ pravayasa*
*idānīm aprajasya te*
*prajāśāyā nivṛttasya*
*prajā yat samapadyata*

*diṣṭyā*—it is by great fortune; *bhrātaḥ*—O my dear brother; *pravayasaḥ*—of you whose age is now quite advanced; *idānīm*—at the present moment; *aprajasya*—of one who did not have a son before; *te*—of you; *prajā-āśāyāḥ nivṛttasya*—of one who was almost hopeless of getting a son at this age; *prajā*—a son; *yat*—whatever; *samapadyata*—has been gotten by chance.

## TRANSLATION

**My dear brother Nanda Mahārāja, at an advanced age you had no son at all and were hopeless of having one. Therefore, that you now have a son is a sign of great fortune.**

## PURPORT

At an advanced age one generally cannot beget a male child. If by chance one does beget a child at this age, the child is generally female. Thus Vasudeva indirectly asked Nanda Mahārāja whether he had actually begotten a male child or a female child. Vasudeva knew that Yaśodā had given birth to a female child, whom he had stolen and replaced with a male child. This was a great mystery, and Vasudeva wanted to determine whether this mystery was already known to Nanda Mahārāja. On inquiring, however, he was confident that the mystery of Kṛṣṇa's birth and His being placed in the care of Yaśodā was still hidden. There was no danger, since Kaṁsa at least could not learn what had already happened.

## TEXT 24

दिष्ट्या संसारचक्रेऽस्मिन् वर्तमानः पुनर्भवः ।
उपलब्धो भवानद्य दुर्लभं प्रियदर्शनम् ॥२४॥

*diṣṭyā saṁsāra-cakre 'smin*
*vartamānaḥ punar-bhavaḥ*
*upalabdho bhavān adya*
*durlabhaṁ priya-darśanam*

*diṣṭyā*—it is also by great fortune; *saṁsāra-cakre asmin*—in this world of birth and death; *vartamānaḥ*—although I was existing; *punaḥ-bhavaḥ*—my meeting with you is just like another birth; *upalabdhaḥ*—being obtained by me; *bhavān*—you; *adya*—today; *durlabham*—although it was never to happen; *priya-darśanam*—to see you again, my very dear friend and brother.

## TRANSLATION

**It is also by good fortune that I am seeing you. Having obtained this opportunity, I feel as if I have taken birth again. Even though**

**one is present in this world, to meet with intimate friends and dear relatives in this material world is extremely difficult.**

## PURPORT

Vasudeva had been imprisoned by Kaṁsa, and therefore, although present in Mathurā, he was unable to see Nanda Mahārāja for many years. Therefore when they met again, Vasudeva considered this meeting to be another birth.

## TEXT 25

नैकत्र प्रियसंवासः सुहृदां चित्रकर्मणाम् ।
ओघेन व्यूह्यमानानां प्लवानां स्रोतसो यथा ॥२५॥

*naikatra priya-saṁvāsaḥ*
*suhṛdāṁ citra-karmaṇām*
*oghena vyūhyamānānāṁ*
*plavānāṁ srotaso yathā*

*na*—not; *ekatra*—in one place; *priya-saṁvāsaḥ*—living together with dear friends and relatives; *suhṛdām*—of friends; *citra-karmaṇām*—of all of us who have had varieties of reactions to our past *karma; oghena*—by the force; *vyūhyamānānām*—carried away; *plavānām*—of sticks and other objects floating in the water; *srotasaḥ*—of the waves; *yathā*—as.

## TRANSLATION

**Many planks and sticks, unable to stay together, are carried away by the force of a river's waves. Similarly, although we are intimately related with friends and family members, we are unable to stay together because of our varied past deeds and the waves of time.**

## PURPORT

Vasudeva was lamenting because he and Nanda Mahārāja could not live together. Yet how could they live together? Vasudeva warns that all of us, even if intimately related, are carried away by the waves of time according to the results of past *karma.*

## TEXT 26

कच्चित् पशव्यं निरुजं भूर्यम्बुतृणवीरुधम् ।
बृहद्वनं तदधुना यत्रास्से त्वं सुहृद्वृतः ॥२६॥

*kaccit paśavyaṁ nirujaṁ*
*bhūry-ambu-tṛṇa-vīrudham*
*bṛhad vanaṁ tad adhunā*
*yatrāsse tvaṁ suhṛd-vṛtaḥ*

*kaccit*—whether; *paśavyam*—protection of the cows; *nirujam*—without difficulties or disease; *bhūri*—sufficient; *ambu*—water; *tṛṇa*—grass; *vīrudham*—plants; *bṛhat vanam*—the great forest; *tat*—all these arrangements are there; *adhunā*—now; *yatra*—where; *āsse*—are living; *tvam*—you; *suhṛt-vṛtaḥ*—surrounded by friends.

## TRANSLATION

**My dear friend Nanda Mahārāja, in the place where you are living with your friends, is the forest favorable for the animals, the cows? I hope there is no disease or inconvenience. The place must be full of water, grass and other plants.**

## PURPORT

For human happiness, one must care for the animals, especially the cows. Vasudeva therefore inquired whether there was a good arrangement for the animals where Nanda Mahārāja lived. For the proper pursuit of human happiness, there must be arrangements for the protection of cows. This means that there must be forests and adequate pasturing grounds full of grass and water. If the animals are happy, there will be an ample supply of milk, from which human beings will benefit by deriving many milk products with which to live happily. As enjoined in *Bhagavad-gītā* (18.44), *kṛṣi-go-rakṣya-vāṇijyaṁ vaiśya-karma-svabhāvajam.* Without giving proper facilities to the animals, how can human society be happy? That people are raising cattle to send to the slaughterhouse is a great sin. By this demoniac enterprise, people are ruining their chance for a truly human life. Because they are not giving any importance to the instructions of Kṛṣṇa, the advancement of their so-called civilization resembles the crazy efforts of men in a lunatic asylum.

## TEXT 27

भ्रातर्मम सुतः कच्चिन्मात्रा सह भवद्व्रजे ।
तातं भवन्तं मन्वानो भवद्भ्यामुपलालितः ॥२७॥

*bhrātar mama sutaḥ kaccin*
*mātrā saha bhavad-vraje*
*tātaṁ bhavantaṁ manvāno*
*bhavadbhyām upalālitaḥ*

*bhrātaḥ*—my dear brother; *mama*—my; *sutaḥ*—son (Baladeva, born of Rohiṇī); *kaccit*—whether; *mātrā saha*—with His mother, Rohiṇī; *bhavat-vraje*—in your house; *tātam*—as father; *bhavantam*—unto you; *manvānaḥ*—thinking; *bhavadbhyām*—by you and your wife, Yaśodā; *upalālitaḥ*—properly being raised.

## TRANSLATION

**My son Baladeva, being raised by you and your wife, Yaśodādevī, considers you His father and mother. Is he living very peacefully in your home with His real mother, Rohiṇī?**

## TEXT 28

पुंसस्त्रिवर्गो विहितः सुहृदो ह्यनुभावितः ।
न तेषु क्लिश्यमानेषु त्रिवर्गोऽर्थाय कल्पते ॥२८॥

*puṁsas tri-vargo vihitaḥ*
*suhṛdo hy anubhāvitaḥ*
*na teṣu kliśyamāneṣu*
*tri-vargo 'rthāya kalpate*

*puṁsaḥ*—of a person; *tri-vargaḥ*—the three aims of life (religion, economic development and sense gratification); *vihitaḥ*—enjoined according to Vedic ritualistic ceremonies; *suhṛdaḥ*—toward relatives and friends; *hi*—indeed; *anubhāvitaḥ*—when they are properly in line; *na*—not; *teṣu*—in them; *kliśyamāneṣu*—if they are actually in any difficulty; *tri-vargaḥ*—these three aims of life; *arthāya*—for any purpose; *kalpate*—does become so.

## TRANSLATION

**When one's friends and relatives are properly situated, one's religion, economic development and sense gratification, as described in the Vedic literatures, are beneficial. Otherwise, if one's friends and relatives are in distress, these three cannot offer any happiness.**

## PURPORT

Vasudeva regretfully informed Nanda Mahārāja that although he had his wife and children, he could not properly discharge his duty of maintaining them and was therefore unhappy.

## TEXT 29

श्रीनन्द उवाच
अहो ते देवकीपुत्राः कंसेन बहवो हताः ।
एकावशिष्टावरजा कन्या सापि दिवं गता ॥२९॥

*śrī-nanda uvāca*
*aho te devakī-putrāḥ*
*kaṁsena bahavo hatāḥ*
*ekāvaśiṣṭāvarajā*
*kanyā sāpi divaṁ gatā*

*śrī-nandaḥ uvāca*—Nanda Mahārāja said; *aho*—alas; *te*—your; *devakī-putrāḥ*—all the sons of your wife Devakī; *kaṁsena*—by King Kaṁsa; *bahavaḥ*—many; *hatāḥ*—have been killed; *ekā*—one; *avaśiṣṭā*—remaining child; *avarajā*—the youngest of all; *kanyā*—a daughter also; *sā api*—she also; *divam gatā*—gone to the heavenly planets.

## TRANSLATION

**Nanda Mahārāja said: Alas, King Kaṁsa killed so many of your children, born of Devakī. And your one daughter, the youngest child of all, entered the heavenly planets.**

## PURPORT

When Vasudeva understood from Nanda Mahārāja that the mystery of Kṛṣṇa's birth and His having been exchanged with Yaśodā's daughter was yet undisclosed, he was happy that things were going on nicely. By saying that Vasudeva's daughter, his youngest child, had gone to the heavenly planets, Nanda Mahārāja indicated that he did not know that this daughter was born of Yaśodā and that Vasudeva had exchanged her with Kṛṣṇa. Thus the doubts of Vasudeva were dispelled.

## TEXT 30

नूनं ह्यदृष्टनिष्ठोऽयमदृष्टपरमो जनः ।
अदृष्टमात्मनस्तत्त्वं यो वेद न स मुह्यति ॥३०॥

*nūnaṁ hy adṛṣṭa-niṣṭho 'yam*
*adṛṣṭa-paramo janaḥ*
*adṛṣṭam ātmanas tattvaṁ*
*yo veda na sa muhyati*

*nūnam*—certainly; *hi*—indeed; *adṛṣṭa*—unseen; *niṣṭhaḥ ayam*—something ends there; *adṛṣṭa*—the unseen destiny; *paramaḥ*—ultimate; *janaḥ*—every living entity within this material world; *adṛṣṭam*—that destiny; *ātmanaḥ*—of oneself; *tattvam*—ultimate truth; *yaḥ*—anyone who; *veda*—knows; *na*—not; *saḥ*—he; *muhyati*—becomes bewildered.

## TRANSLATION

**Every man is certainly controlled by destiny, which determines the results of one's fruitive activities. In other words, one has a son or daughter because of unseen destiny, and when the son or**

**daughter is no longer present, this also is due to unseen destiny. Destiny is the ultimate controller of everyone. One who knows this is never bewildered.**

## PURPORT

Nanda Mahārāja consoled his younger brother Vasudeva by saying that destiny is ultimately responsible for everything. Vasudeva should not be unhappy that his many children had been killed by Kaṁsa or that the last child, the daughter, had gone to the heavenly planets.

## TEXT 31

श्रीवसुदेव उवाच
करो वै वार्षिको दत्तो राज्ञे दृष्टा वयं च वः ।
नेह स्थेयं बहुतिथं सन्त्युत्पाताश्च गोकुले ॥३१॥

*śrī-vasudeva uvāca*
*karo vai vārṣiko datto*
*rājñe dṛṣṭā vayaṁ ca vaḥ*
*neha stheyaṁ bahu-tithaṁ*
*santy utpātāś ca gokule*

*śrī-vasudevaḥ uvāca*—Śrī Vasudeva replied; *karaḥ*—the taxes; *vai*—indeed; *vārṣikaḥ*—yearly; *dattaḥ*—have already been paid by you; *rājñe*—to the King; *dṛṣṭāḥ*—have been seen; *vayam ca*—both of us; *vaḥ*—of you; *na*—not; *iha*—in this place; *stheyam*—should be staying; *bahu-titham*—for many days; *santi*—may be; *utpātāḥ ca*—many disturbances; *gokule*—in your home, Gokula.

## TRANSLATION

**Vasudeva said to Nanda Mahārāja: Now, my dear brother, since you have paid the annual taxes to Kaṁsa and have also seen me, do not stay in this place for many days. It is better to return to Gokula, since I know that there may be some disturbances there.**

## TEXT 32

श्रीशुक उवाच

इति नन्दादयो गोपाः प्रोक्तास्ते शौरिणा ययुः ।
अनोभिरनडुद्युक्तैस्तमनुज्ञाप्य गोकुलम् ॥३२॥

*śrī-śuka uvāca*
*iti nandādayo gopāḥ*
*proktās te śauriṇā yayuḥ*
*anobhir anaḍud-yuktais*
*tam anujñāpya gokulam*

*śrī-śukaḥ uvāca*—Śrī Śukadeva Gosvāmī said; *iti*—thus; *nanda-ādayaḥ*—Nanda Mahārāja and his companions; *gopāḥ*—the cowherd men; *proktāḥ*—being advised; *te*—they; *śauriṇā*—by Vasudeva; *yayuḥ*—started from that place; *anobhiḥ*—by the bullock carts; *anaḍut-yuktaiḥ*—yoked with oxen; *tam anujñāpya*—taking permission from Vasudeva; *gokulam*—for Gokula.

## TRANSLATION

**Śukadeva Gosvāmī said: After Vasudeva advised Nanda Mahārāja in this way, Nanda Mahārāja and his associates, the cowherd men, took permission from Vasudeva, yoked their bulls to the bullock carts, and started riding for Gokula.**

*Thus end the Bhaktivedanta purports to the Tenth Canto, Fifth Chapter, of the* Śrīmad-Bhāgavatam, *entitled "The Meeting of Nanda Mahārāja and Vasudeva."*

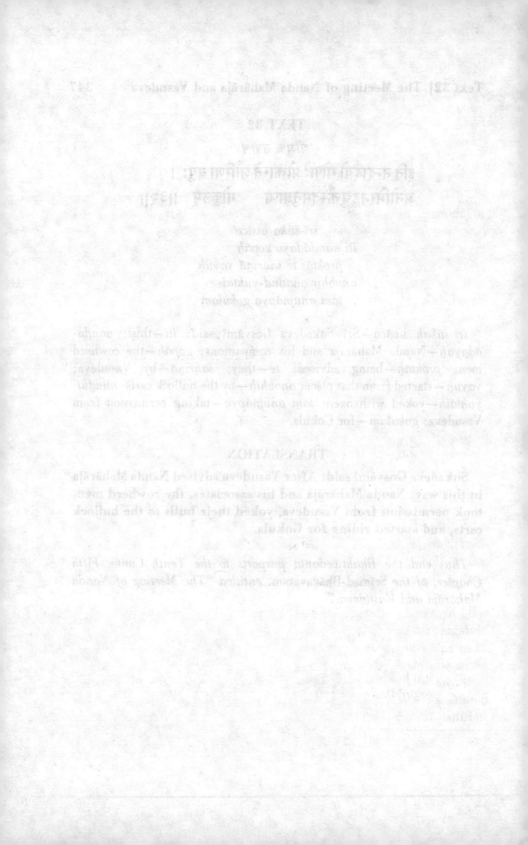

## CHAPTER SIX

# The Killing of the Demon Pūtanā

A summary of the Sixth Chapter is as follows: when Nanda Mahārāja, following the instructions of Vasudeva, was returning home, he saw a great demoniac woman lying on the road, and then he heard about her death.

While Nanda Mahārāja, the King of Vraja, was thinking about Vasudeva's words concerning disturbances in Gokula, he was a little afraid and sought shelter at the lotus feet of Śrī Hari. Meanwhile, Kaṁsa sent to the village of Gokula a Rākṣasī named Pūtanā, who was wandering here and there killing small babies. Of course, wherever there is no Kṛṣṇa consciousness, there is the danger of such Rākṣasīs, but since the Supreme Personality of Godhead Himself was in Gokula, Pūtanā could accept nothing there but her own death.

One day, Pūtanā arrived from outer space in Gokula, the home of Nanda Mahārāja, and by displaying her mystic power, she assumed the disguise of a very beautiful woman. Taking courage, she immediately entered Kṛṣṇa's bedroom without anyone's permission; by the grace of Kṛṣṇa, no one forbade her to enter the house or the room, because that was Kṛṣṇa's desire. The baby Kṛṣṇa, who resembled a fire covered by ashes, looked upon Pūtanā and thought that He would have to kill this demon, the beautiful woman. Enchanted by the influence of *yogamāyā* and the Personality of Godhead, Pūtanā took Kṛṣṇa upon her lap, and neither Rohiṇī nor Yaśodā objected. The demon Pūtanā offered her breast for Kṛṣṇa to suck, but her breast was smeared with poison. The child Kṛṣṇa, therefore, squeezed Pūtanā's breast so severely that in unbearable pain she had to assume her original body and fell to the ground. Then Kṛṣṇa began playing on her breast just like a small child. When Kṛṣṇa was playing, the *gopīs* were pacified and took the child away to their own laps. After this incident, the *gopīs* took precautions because of the attack of the Rākṣasī. Mother Yaśodā gave the child her breast to suck and then laid Him in bed.

Meanwhile, Nanda and his associates the cowherd men returned from Mathurā, and when they saw the great dead body of Pūtanā, they were struck with wonder. Everyone was astonished that Vasudeva had foretold this mishap, and they praised Vasudeva for his power of foresight. The inhabitants of Vraja cut the gigantic body of Pūtanā into pieces, but because Kṛṣṇa had sucked her breast, she had been freed from all sins, and therefore when the cowherd men burned the pieces of her body in a fire, the smoke filled the air with a very pleasing fragrance. Ultimately, although Pūtanā had desired to kill Kṛṣṇa, she attained the Lord's abode. From this incident we gain the instruction that if one is attached to Kṛṣṇa somehow or other, even as an enemy, one ultimately attains success. What then is to be said of devotees who are naturally attached to Kṛṣṇa in love? When the inhabitants of Vraja heard about the killing of Pūtanā and the welfare of the child, they were very much satisfied. Nanda Mahārāja took the baby Kṛṣṇa on his lap and was filled with satisfaction.

## TEXT 1

श्रीशुक उवाच
नन्दः पथि वचः शौरेर्न मृषेति विचिन्तयन् ।
हरिं जगाम शरणमुत्पातागमशङ्कितः ॥ १ ॥

*śrī-śuka uvāca*
*nandaḥ pathi vacaḥ śaurer*
*na mṛṣeti vicintayan*
*hariṁ jagāma śaraṇam*
*utpātāgama-śaṅkitaḥ*

*śrī-śukaḥ uvāca*—Śrī Śukadeva Gosvāmī said; *nandaḥ*—Nanda Mahārāja; *pathi*—on his way back home; *vacaḥ*—the words; *śaureḥ*—of Vasudeva; *na*—not; *mṛṣā*—without purpose or cause; *iti*—thus; *vicintayan*—while thinking about inauspiciousness for his little son, Kṛṣṇa; *harim*—unto the Supreme Lord, the controller; *jagāma*—took; *śaraṇam*—shelter; *utpāta*—of disturbances; *āgama*—with the expectation; *śaṅkitaḥ*—thus being afraid.

## TRANSLATION

**Śukadeva Gosvāmī continued: My dear King, while Nanda Mahārāja was on the way home, he considered that what Vasudeva had said could not be false or useless. There must have been some danger of disturbances in Gokula. As Nanda Mahārāja thought about the danger for his beautiful son, Kṛṣṇa, he was afraid, and he took shelter at the lotus feet of the supreme controller.**

## PURPORT

Whenever there is danger, the pure devotee thinks of the protection and shelter of the Supreme Personality of Godhead. This is also advised in *Bhagavad-gītā* (9.33): *anityam asukhaṁ lokam imaṁ prāpya bhajasva mām.* In this material world there is danger at every step (*padaṁ padaṁ yad vipadām*). Therefore a devotee has no other course than to take shelter of the Lord at every step.

## TEXT 2

कंसेन प्रहिता घोरा पूतना बालघातिनी ।
शिशूंश्चचार निघ्नन्ती पुरग्रामव्रजादिषु ॥ २ ॥

*kaṁsena prahitā ghorā*
*pūtanā bāla-ghātinī*
*śiśūṁś cacāra nighnantī*
*pura-grāma-vrajādiṣu*

*kaṁsena*—by King Kaṁsa; *prahitā*—engaged previously; *ghorā*—very fierce; *pūtanā*—by the name Pūtanā; *bāla-ghātinī*—a Rākṣasī who killed; *śiśūn*—small babies; *cacāra*—wandered; *nighnantī*—killing; *pura-grāma-vraja-ādiṣu*—in towns, cities and villages here and there.

## TRANSLATION

**While Nanda Mahārāja was returning to Gokula, the same fierce Pūtanā whom Kaṁsa had previously engaged to kill babies was wandering about in the towns, cities and villages, doing her nefarious duty.**

## TEXT 3

न यत्र श्रवणादीनि रक्षोघ्नानि स्वकर्मसु ।
कुर्वन्ति सात्वतां भर्तुर्यातुधान्यश्च तत्र हि ॥ ३ ॥

*na yatra śravaṇādīni*
*rakṣo-ghnāni sva-karmasu*
*kurvanti sātvatāṁ bhartur*
*yātudhānyaś ca tatra hi*

*na*—not; *yatra*—wherever; *śravaṇa-ādīni*—the activities of *bhakti-yoga*, beginning with hearing and chanting; *rakṣaḥ-ghnāni*—the sound vibration to kill all danger and bad elements; *sva-karmasu*—if one is engaged in his own occupational duty; *kurvanti*—such things are done; *sātvatām bhartuḥ*—of the protector of the devotees; *yātudhānyaḥ*—disturbing elements, bad elements; *ca*—also; *tatra hi*—there must be.

## TRANSLATION

**My dear King, wherever people in any position perform their occupational duties of devotional service by chanting and hearing [śravaṇaṁ kīrtanaṁ viṣṇoḥ], there cannot be any danger from bad elements. Therefore there was no need for anxiety about Gokula while the Supreme Personality of Godhead was personally present.**

## PURPORT

Śukadeva Gosvāmī spoke this verse to mitigate the anxiety of Mahārāja Parīkṣit. Mahārāja Parīkṣit was a devotee of Kṛṣṇa, and therefore when he understood that Pūtanā was causing disturbances in Gokula, he was somewhat perturbed. Śukadeva Gosvāmī therefore assured him that there was no danger in Gokula. Śrīla Bhaktivinoda Ṭhākura has sung: *nāmāśraya kari' yatane tumi, thākaha āpana kāje.* Everyone is thus advised to seek shelter in the chanting of the Hare Kṛṣṇa *mahā-mantra* and remain engaged in his own occupational duty. There is no loss in this, and the gain is tremendous. Even from a material point of view, everyone should take to chanting the Hare Kṛṣṇa *mantra* to be saved from all kinds of danger. This world is full of danger (*padaṁ padaṁ yad vipadām*). Therefore we should be encouraged to chant the

Hare Kṛṣṇa *mahā-mantra* so that in our family, society, neighborhood and nation, everything will be smooth and free from danger.

## TEXT 4

सा खेचर्येकदोत्पत्य पूतना नन्दगोकुलम् ।
योषित्वा माययात्मानं प्राविशत् कामचारिणी ॥४॥

*sā khe-cary ekadotpatya*
*pūtanā nanda-gokulam*
*yoṣitvā māyayātmānaṁ*
*prāviśat kāma-cāriṇī*

*sā*—that (Pūtanā); *khe-carī*—who traveled in outer space; *ekadā*—once upon a time; *utpatya*—was flying; *pūtanā*—the demon Pūtanā; *nanda-gokulam*—at the place of Nanda Mahārāja, Gokula; *yoṣitvā*—converting into a very beautiful woman; *māyayā*—by mystic power; *ātmānam*—herself; *prāviśat*—entered; *kāma-cāriṇī*—one who could move according to her own desire.

## TRANSLATION

**Once upon a time, Pūtanā Rākṣasi, who could move according to her desire and was wandering in outer space, converted herself by mystic power into a very beautiful woman and thus entered Gokula, the abode of Nanda Mahārāja.**

## PURPORT

Rākṣasīs learn mystic powers by which they can travel in outer space without machines. In some parts of India there are still such mystical witches, who can sit on a stick and use it to fly from one place to another in a very short time. This art was known to Pūtanā. Assuming the feature of a very beautiful woman, she entered Nanda Mahārāja's abode, Gokula.

## TEXTS 5–6

तां केशबन्धव्यतिषक्तमल्लिकां
बृहन्नितम्बस्तनकृच्छ्रमध्यमाम् ।

सुवाससं कल्पितकर्णभूषण-
त्विषोल्लसत्कुन्तलमण्डिताननाम् ॥ ५ ॥
वल्गुस्मितापाङ्गविसर्गवीक्षितै-
र्मनो हरन्तीं वनितां व्रजौकसाम् ।
अमंसताम्भोजकरेण रूपिणीं
गोप्यः श्रियं द्रष्टुमिवागतां पतिम् ॥ ६ ॥

*tāṁ keśa-bandha-vyatiṣakta-mallikāṁ*
*bṛhan-nitamba-stana-kṛcchra-madhyamām*
*suvāsasaṁ kalpita-karṇa-bhūṣaṇa-*
*tviṣollasat-kuntala-maṇḍitānanām*

*valgu-smitāpāṅga-visarga-vīkṣitair*
*mano harantīṁ vanitāṁ vrajaukasām*
*amaṁsatāmbhoja-kareṇa rūpiṇīṁ*
*gopyaḥ śriyaṁ draṣṭum ivāgatāṁ patim*

*tām*—her; *keśa-bandha-vyatiṣakta-mallikām*—whose arrangement of hair was decorated with a garland of *mallikā* flowers; *bṛhat*—very, very big; *nitamba-stana*—by her hips and firm breasts; *kṛcchra-madhyamām*—whose slim waist was overburdened; *su-vāsasam*—nicely painted or very attractively dressed; *kalpita-karṇa-bhūṣaṇa*—of the earrings arranged on her ears; *tviṣā*—by the brilliance; *ullasat*—very attractive; *kuntala-maṇḍita-ānanām*—whose beautiful face was surrounded by black hair; *valgu-smita-apāṅga-visarga-vīkṣitaiḥ*—by her casting her smiling glance on everyone very attractively; *manaḥ harantīm*—everyone's attention was attracted (by her); *vanitām*—an especially attractive woman; *vraja-okasām*—of the inhabitants of Gokula; *amaṁsata*—thought; *ambhoja*—holding a lotus flower; *kareṇa*—with her hand; *rūpiṇīm*—very beautiful; *gopyaḥ*—the *gopī* inhabitants of Gokula; *śriyam*—the goddess of fortune; *draṣṭum*—to see; *iva*—as if; *āgatām*—had come; *patim*—her husband.

## TRANSLATION

**Her hips were full, her breasts were large and firm, seeming to overburden her slim waist, and she was dressed very nicely. Her**

**hair, adorned with a garland of mallikā flowers, was scattered about her beautiful face. Her earrings were brilliant, and as she smiled very attractively, glancing upon everyone, her beauty drew the attention of all the inhabitants of Vraja, especially the men. When the gopīs saw her, they thought that the beautiful goddess of fortune, holding a lotus flower in her hand, had come to see her husband, Kṛṣṇa.**

## TEXT 7

बालग्रहस्तत्र विचिन्वती शिशून्
यदृच्छया नन्दगृहेऽसदन्तकम् ।
बालं प्रतिच्छन्ननिजोरुतेजसं
ददर्श तल्पेऽग्निमिवाहितं भसि ॥ ७ ॥

*bāla-grahas tatra vicinvatī śiśūn*
*yadṛcchayā nanda-gṛhe 'sad-antakam*
*bālaṁ praticchanna-nijoru-tejasaṁ*
*dadarśa talpe 'gnim ivāhitaṁ bhasi*

*bāla-grahaḥ*—the witch, whose business was to kill small babies; *tatra*—standing there; *vicinvatī*—thinking of, searching for; *śiśūn*—children; *yadṛcchayā*—independently; *nanda-gṛhe*—in the house of Nanda Mahārāja; *asat-antakam*—who could kill all demons; *bālam*—the child; *praticchanna*—covered; *nija-uru-tejasam*—whose unlimited power; *dadarśa*—she saw; *talpe*—(lying) on the bed; *agnim*—fire; *iva*—just like; *āhitam*—covered; *bhasi*—within ashes.

## TRANSLATION

**While searching for small children, Pūtanā, whose business was to kill them, entered the house of Nanda Mahārāja unobstructed, having been sent by the superior potency of the Lord. Without asking anyone's permission, she entered Nanda Mahārāja's room, where she saw the child sleeping in bed, His unlimited power covered like a powerful fire covered by ashes. She could understand that this child was not ordinary, but was meant to kill all demons.**

## PURPORT

Demons are always busy creating disturbances and killing. But the child lying on the bed in the house of Nanda Mahārāja was meant to kill many demons.

## TEXT 8

विबुध्य तां बालकमारिकाग्रहं
चराचरात्मा स निमीलितेक्षणः ।
अनन्तमारोपयदङ्कमन्तकं
यथोरगं सुप्तमबुद्धिरज्जुधीः ॥ ८ ॥

*vibudhya tāṁ bālaka-mārikā-grahaṁ*
*carācarātmā sa nimīlitekṣaṇaḥ*
*anantam āropayad aṅkam antakaṁ*
*yathoragaṁ suptam abuddhi-rajju-dhīḥ*

*vibudhya*—understanding; *tām*—her (Pūtanā); *bālaka-mārikā-graham*—a witch very expert in killing small babies; *cara-acara-ātmā*—Kṛṣṇa, the all-pervading Supersoul; *saḥ*—He; *nimīlita-īkṣaṇaḥ*—closed His eyes; *anantam*—the Unlimited; *āropayat*—she placed; *aṅkam*—on her lap; *antakam*—for her own annihilation; *yathā*—as; *uragam*—a snake; *suptam*—while sleeping; *abuddhi*—a person who has no intelligence; *rajju-dhīḥ*—one who thinks a snake to be a rope.

## TRANSLATION

**Lord Śrī Kṛṣṇa, the all-pervading Supersoul, lying on the bed, understood that Pūtanā, a witch who was expert in killing small children, had come to kill Him. Therefore, as if afraid of her, Kṛṣṇa closed His eyes. Thus Pūtanā took upon her lap Him who was to be her own annihilation, just as an unintelligent person places a sleeping snake on his lap, thinking the snake to be a rope.**

## PURPORT

In this verse there are two perplexities. When Kṛṣṇa saw that Pūtanā had come to kill Him, He thought that since this woman was present with motherly affection, although artificial, He had to offer her a benediction. Therefore He looked at her with a little perplexity and then closed His eyes again. Pūtanā Rākṣasī also was perplexed. She was not intelligent enough to understand that she was taking a sleeping snake on her lap; she thought the snake to be an ordinary rope. The two words *antakam* and *anantam* are contradictory. Because of not being intelligent, Pūtanā thought that she could kill her *antakam,* the source of her annihilation; but because He is *ananta,* unlimited, no one can kill Him.

## TEXT 9

तां तीक्ष्णचित्तामतिवामचेष्टितां
वीक्ष्यान्तरा कोषपरिच्छदासिवत् ।
वरस्त्रियं तत्प्रभया च धर्षिते
निरीक्ष्यमाणे जननी ह्यतिष्ठताम् ॥ ९ ॥

*tāṁ tīkṣṇa-cittām ativāma-ceṣṭitāṁ*
*vīkṣyāntarā koṣa-paricchadāsivat*
*vara-striyaṁ tat-prabhayā ca dharṣite*
*nirīkṣyamāṇe jananī hy atiṣṭhatām*

*tām*—that (Pūtanā Rākṣasī); *tīkṣṇa-cittām*—having a very fierce heart for killing the child; *ati-vāma-ceṣṭitām*—although she was trying to treat the child better than a mother; *vīkṣya antarā*—seeing her within the room; *koṣa-paricchada-asi-vat*—like a sharp sword within a soft sheath; *vara-striyam*—the very beautiful woman; *tat-prabhayā*—by her influence; *ca*—also; *dharṣite*—being overwhelmed; *nirīkṣyamāṇe*—were seeing; *jananī*—the two mothers; *hi*—indeed; *atiṣṭhatām*—they remained silent, without prohibiting.

## TRANSLATION

**Pūtanā Rākṣasī's heart was fierce and cruel, but she looked like a very affectionate mother. Thus she resembled a sharp sword in a soft sheath. Although seeing her within the room, Yaśodā and Rohiṇī, overwhelmed by her beauty, did not stop her, but remained silent because she treated the child like a mother.**

## PURPORT

Although Pūtanā was an outsider and although she personified fierce death because the determination within her heart was to kill the child, when she directly came and placed the child on her lap to offer the child her breast to suck, the mothers were so captivated by her beauty that they did not prohibit her. Sometimes a beautiful woman is dangerous because everyone, being captivated by external beauty (*māyā-mohita*), is unable to understand what is in her mind. Those who are captivated by the beauty of the external energy are called *māyā-mohita. Mohitaṁ nābhijānāti mām ebhyaḥ param avyayam* (Bg. 7.13). *Na te viduḥ svārtha-gatiṁ hi viṣṇuṁ durāśayā ye bahir-artha-māninaḥ* (*Bhāg*. 7.5.31). Here, of course, the two mothers Rohiṇī and Yaśodā were not *māyā-mohita*, deluded by the external energy, but to develop the pastimes of the Lord, they were captivated by *yogamāyā*. Such *māyā-moha* is the action of *yogamāyā*.

## TEXT 10

तस्मिन् स्तनं दुर्जरवीर्यमुल्वणं
घोराङ्कमादाय शिशोर्ददावथ ।
गाढं कराभ्यां भगवान् प्रपीड्य तत्-
प्राणैः समं रोषसमन्वितोऽपिबत् ॥१०॥

*tasmin stanaṁ durjara-vīryam ulbaṇaṁ*
*ghorāṅkam ādāya śiśor dadāv atha*
*gāḍhaṁ karābhyāṁ bhagavān prapīḍya tat-*
*prāṇaiḥ samaṁ roṣa-samanvito 'pibat*

*tasmin*—in that very spot; *stanam*—the breast; *durjara-vīryam*—a very powerful weapon mixed with poison; *ulbaṇam*—which was fierce; *ghorā*—the most ferocious Pūtanā; *aṅkam*—on her lap; *ādāya*—placing; *śiśoḥ*—in the mouth of the child; *dadau*—pushed; *atha*—thereupon; *gāḍham*—very hard; *karābhyām*—with both hands; *bhagavān*—the Supreme Personality of Godhead; *prapīḍya*—giving her great pain; *tat-prāṇaiḥ*—her life; *samam*—along with; *roṣa-samanvitaḥ*—being very angry at her; *apibat*—sucked the breast.

## TRANSLATION

**On that very spot, the fiercely dangerous Rākṣasī took Kṛṣṇa on her lap and pushed her breast into His mouth. The nipple of her breast was smeared with a dangerous, immediately effective poison, but the Supreme Personality of Godhead, Kṛṣṇa, becoming very angry at her, took hold of her breast, squeezed it very hard with both hands, and sucked out both the poison and her life.**

## PURPORT

Lord Kṛṣṇa was not angry at Pūtanā for His own sake. Rather, He was angry because the Rākṣasī had killed so many small children in Vrajabhūmi. Therefore He decided that she should be punished by having to forfeit her life.

## TEXT 11

सा मुञ्च मुञ्चालमिति प्रभाषिणी
निष्पीड्यमानाखिलजीवमर्मणि ।
विवृत्य नेत्रे चरणौ भुजौ मुहुः
प्रस्विन्नगात्रा क्षिपती रुरोद ह ॥११॥

*sā muñca muñcālam iti prabhāṣiṇī*
*niṣpīḍyamānākhila-jīva-marmaṇi*
*vivṛtya netre caraṇau bhujau muhuḥ*
*prasvinna-gātrā kṣipatī ruroda ha*

*sā*—she (Pūtanā Rākṣasī); *muñca*—give up; *muñca*—give up; *alam*—suck my breast no longer; *iti*—thus; *prabhāṣiṇī*—crying; *niṣpīḍyamānā*—being pressed severely; *akhila-jīva-marmaṇi*—in every center of her vitality; *vivṛtya*—opening wide; *netre*—her two eyes; *caraṇau*—two legs; *bhujau*—two hands; *muhuḥ*—again and again; *prasvinna-gātrā*—with her body perspiring; *kṣipatī*—throwing; *ruroda*—cried severely; *ha*—indeed.

## TRANSLATION

**Unbearably pressed in every vital point, the demon Pūtanā began to cry, "Please leave me, leave me! Suck my breast no**

**longer!" Perspiring, her eyes wide open and her arms and legs flailing, she cried very loudly again and again.**

## PURPORT

The Rākṣasī was severely punished by Kṛṣṇa. She threw her arms and legs about, and Kṛṣṇa also began to kick her with His legs to punish her properly for her mischievous activities.

## TEXT 12

तस्याः स्वनेनातिगभीररंहसा
साद्रिर्मही द्यौश्च चचाल सग्रहा ।
रसा दिशश्च प्रतिनेदिरे जनाः
पेतुः क्षितौ वज्रनिपातशङ्कया ॥१२॥

*tasyāḥ svanenātigabhīra-raṁhasā*
*sādrir mahī dyauś ca cacāla sa-grahā*
*rasā diśaś ca pratinedire janāḥ*
*petuḥ kṣitau vajra-nipāta-śaṅkayā*

*tasyāḥ*—of the great Rākṣasī Pūtanā; *svanena*—by the vibration of the sound; *ati*—very; *gabhīra*—deep; *raṁhasā*—forceful; *sa-adriḥ*—with the mountains; *mahī*—the surface of the world; *dyauḥ ca*—and outer space; *cacāla*—trembled; *sa-grahā*—with the stars; *rasā*—below the planet earth; *diśaḥ ca*—and all directions; *pratinedire*—vibrated; *janāḥ*—people in general; *petuḥ*—fell down; *kṣitau*—on the surface of the world; *vajra-nipāta-śaṅkayā*—by suspecting that thunderbolts were falling.

## TRANSLATION

**As Pūtanā screamed loudly and forcefully, the earth with its mountains, and outer space with its planets, trembled. The lower planets and all directions vibrated, and people fell down, fearing that thunderbolts were falling upon them.**

## PURPORT

Śrīla Viśvanātha Cakravartī Ṭhākura remarks that in this verse the word *rasā* refers to the planetary systems below the earth, such as Rasātala, Atala, Vitala, Sutala and Talātala.

## TEXT 13

निशाचरीत्थं व्यथितस्तना व्यसु-
व्यादाय केशांश्चरणौ भुजावपि ।
प्रसार्य गोष्ठे निजरूपमास्थिता
वज्राहतो वृत्र इवापतन्नृप ॥१३॥

*niśā-carīttham vyathita-stanā vyasur*
*vyādāya keśāṁś caraṇau bhujāv api*
*prasārya goṣṭhe nija-rūpam āsthitā*
*vajrāhato vṛtra ivāpatan nṛpa*

*niśā-carī*—the Rākṣasī; *ittham*—in this way; *vyathita-stanā*—being severely aggrieved because of pressure on her breast; *vyasuḥ*—lost her life; *vyādāya*—opening her mouth wide; *keśān*—bunch of hairs; *caraṇau*—her two legs; *bhujau*—her two hands; *api*—also; *prasārya*—expanding; *goṣṭhe*—in the pasturing ground; *nija-rūpam āsthitā*—remained in her original demoniac form; *vajra-āhataḥ*—killed by the thunderbolt of Indra; *vṛtraḥ*—Vṛtrāsura; *iva*—as if; *apatat*—fell down; *nṛpa*—O King.

## TRANSLATION

**In this way the demon Pūtanā, very much aggrieved because her breast was being attacked by Kṛṣṇa, lost her life. O King Parīkṣit, opening her mouth wide and spreading her arms, legs and hair, she fell down in the pasturing ground in her original form as a Rākṣasī, as Vṛtrāsura had fallen when killed by the thunderbolt of Indra.**

## PURPORT

Pūtanā was a great Rākṣasī who knew the art of covering her original form by mystic power, but when she was killed her mystic power could not hide her, and she appeared in her original form.

## TEXT 14

पतमानोऽपि तद्देहस्त्रिगव्यूत्यन्तरद्रुमान् ।
चूर्णयामास राजेन्द्र महदासीत्तदद्भुतम् ॥१४॥

*patamāno 'pi tad-dehas*
*tri-gavyūty-antara-drumān*
*cūrṇayām āsa rājendra*
*mahad āsīt tad adbhutam*

*patamānaḥ api*—even while falling down; *tat-dehaḥ*—her gigantic body; *tri-gavyūti-antara*—within a limit of twelve miles; *drumān*—all kinds of trees; *cūrṇayām āsa*—smashed; *rājendra*—O King Parīkṣit; *mahat āsīt*—was quite gigantic; *tat*—that body; *adbhutam*—and very, very wonderful.

## TRANSLATION

**O King Parīkṣit, when the gigantic body of Pūtanā fell to the ground, it smashed all the trees within a limit of twelve miles. Appearing in a gigantic body, she was certainly extraordinary.**

## PURPORT

Because of the grievous hurt imposed upon her by Kṛṣṇa's sucking her breast, Pūtanā, while dying, not only left the room but abandoned the village and fell down in the pasturing ground in her gigantic body.

## TEXTS 15–17

ईषामात्रोग्रदंष्ट्रास्यं गिरिकन्दरनासिकम् ।
गण्डशैलस्तनं रौद्रं प्रकीर्णारुणमूर्धजम् ॥१५॥
अन्धकूपगभीराक्षं पुलिनारोहभीषणम् ।
बद्धसेतुभुजोर्वङ्घ्रि शून्यतोयह्रदोदरम् ॥१६॥
सन्तत्रसुः स्म तद् वीक्ष्य गोपा गोप्यः कलेवरम् ।
पूर्वं तु तन्निःस्वनितभिन्नहृत्कर्णमस्तकाः ॥१७॥

*īṣā-mātrogra-daṁṣṭrāsyaṁ*
*giri-kandara-nāsikam*
*gaṇḍa-śaila-stanaṁ raudraṁ*
*prakīrṇāruṇa-mūrdhajam*

*andha-kūpa-gabhīrākṣaṁ*
*pulināroha-bhīṣaṇam*
*baddha-setu-bhujorv-aṅghri*
*śūnya-toya-hradodaram*

*santatrasuḥ sma tad vīkṣya*
*gopā gopyaḥ kalevaram*
*pūrvaṁ tu tan-niḥsvanita-*
*bhinna-hṛt-karṇa-mastakāḥ*

*īṣā-mātra*—like the front of a plow; *ugra*—fierce; *daṁṣṭra*—the teeth; *āsyam*—having a mouth in which; *giri-kandara*—like mountain caves; *nāsikam*—the nostrils of whom; *gaṇḍa-śaila*—like big slabs of stone; *stanam*—the breasts of whom; *raudram*—very fierce; *prakīrṇa*—scattered; *aruṇa-mūrdha-jam*—whose hair was the color of copper; *andha-kūpa*—like blind wells; *gabhīra*—deep; *akṣam*—eye sockets; *pulina-āroha-bhīṣaṇam*—whose thighs were fearful like the banks of a river; *baddha-setu-bhuja-uru-aṅghri*—whose arms, thighs and feet were strongly built bridges; *śūnya-toya-hrada-udaram*—whose abdomen was like a lake without water; *santatrasuḥ sma*—became frightened; *tat*—that; *vīkṣya*—seeing; *gopāḥ*—the cowherd men; *gopyaḥ*—and the cowherd women; *kalevaram*—such a gigantic body; *pūrvam tu*—before that; *tat-niḥsvanita*—because of her loud vibration; *bhinna*—were shocked; *hṛt*—whose hearts; *karṇa*—ears; *mastakāḥ*—and heads.

## TRANSLATION

**The Rākṣasī's mouth was full of teeth, each resembling the front of a plow, her nostrils were deep like mountain caves, and her breasts resembled big slabs of stone fallen from a hill. Her scattered hair was the color of copper. The sockets of her eyes**

**appeared like deep blind wells, her fearful thighs resembled the banks of a river, her arms, legs and feet seemed like big bridges, and her abdomen appeared like a dried-up lake. The hearts, ears and heads of the cowherd men and women were already shocked by the Rākṣasī's screaming, and when they saw the fierce wonder of her body, they were even more frightened.**

## TEXT 18

बालं च तस्या उरसि क्रीडन्तमकुतोभयम् ।
गोप्यस्तूर्णं समभ्येत्य जगृहुर्जातसम्भ्रमाः ॥१८॥

*bālaṁ ca tasyā urasi*
*krīḍantam akutobhayam*
*gopyas tūrṇaṁ samabhyetya*
*jagṛhur jāta-sambhramāḥ*

*bālam ca*—the child also; *tasyāḥ*—of that (Rākṣasī Pūtanā); *urasi*—on the upper portion of the breast; *krīḍantam*—engaged in playing; *akutobhayam*—without fear; *gopyaḥ*—all the cowherd women; *tūrṇam*—immediately; *samabhyetya*—coming near; *jagṛhuḥ*—picked up; *jāta-sambhramāḥ*—with the same affection and respect they always maintained.

## TRANSLATION

**Without fear, the child Kṛṣṇa was playing on the upper portion of Pūtanā Rākṣasī's breast, and when the gopīs saw the child's wonderful activities, they immediately came forward with great jubilation and picked Him up.**

## PURPORT

Here is the Supreme Personality of Godhead—Kṛṣṇa. Although the Rākṣasī Pūtanā could increase or decrease her bodily size by her mystic abilities and thus gain proportionate power, the Supreme Personality of Godhead is equally powerful in any transcendental form. Kṛṣṇa is the real Personality of Godhead because whether as a child or as a grown-up young man, He is the same person. He does not need to become powerful by meditation or any other external endeavor. Therefore when the greatly powerful Pūtanā expanded her body, Kṛṣṇa remained the same small child and fearlessly played on the upper portion of her breast. *Ṣaḍ-aiśvarya-pūrṇa.* Bhagavān, the Supreme Personality of Godhead, is always full in all potencies, regardless of whether He is present in this form or that. His potencies are always full. *Parāsya śaktir vividhaiva śrūyate.* He can display all potencies under any circumstances.

## TEXT 19

यशोदारोहिणीभ्यां ताः समं बालस्य सर्वतः ।
रक्षां विदधिरे सम्यग्गोपुच्छभ्रमणादिभिः ॥१९॥

*yaśodā-rohiṇībhyāṁ tāḥ*
*samaṁ bālasya sarvataḥ*
*rakṣāṁ vidadhire samyag*
*go-puccha-bhramaṇādibhiḥ*

*yaśodā-rohiṇībhyām*—with mother Yaśodā and mother Rohiṇī, who principally took charge of the child; *tāḥ*—the other *gopīs; samam*—equally as important as Yaśodā and Rohiṇī; *bālasya*—of the child; *sarvataḥ*—from all dangers; *rakṣām*—protection; *vidadhire*—executed; *samyak*—completely; *go-puccha-bhramaṇa-ādibhiḥ*—by waving around the switch of a cow.

## TRANSLATION

**Thereafter, mother Yaśodā and Rohiṇī, along with the other elderly gopīs, waved about the switch of a cow to give full protection to the child Śrī Kṛṣṇa.**

## PURPORT

When Kṛṣṇa was saved from such a great danger, mother Yaśodā and Rohiṇī were principally concerned, and the other elderly *gopīs*, who were almost equally concerned, followed the activities of mother Yaśodā and Rohiṇī. Here we find that in household affairs, ladies could take charge of protecting a child simply by taking help from the cow. As described here, they knew how to wave about the switch of a cow so as to protect the child from all types of danger. There are so many facilities afforded by cow protection, but people have forgotten these arts. The importance of protecting cows is therefore stressed by Kṛṣṇa in *Bhagavad-gītā* (*kṛṣi-go-rakṣya-vāṇijyaṁ vaiśya-karma svabhāvajam*). Even now in the Indian villages surrounding Vṛndāvana, the villagers live happily simply by giving protection to the cow. They keep cow dung very carefully and dry it to use as fuel. They keep a sufficient stock of grains, and because of giving protection to the cows, they have sufficient milk and milk products to solve all economic problems. Simply by giving protection to the cow, the villagers live so peacefully. Even the urine and stool of cows have medicinal value.

### TEXT 20

गोमूत्रेण स्नापयित्वा पुनर्गोरजसार्भकम् ।
रक्षां चक्रुश्च शकृता द्वादशाङ्गेषु नामभिः ॥२०॥

*go-mūtreṇa snāpayitvā*
*punar go-rajasārbhakam*
*rakṣāṁ cakruś ca śakṛtā*
*dvādaśāṅgeṣu nāmabhiḥ*

*go-mūtreṇa*—with the urine of the cows; *snāpayitvā*—after thoroughly washing; *punaḥ*—again; *go-rajasā*—with the dust floating because of the movements of the cows; *arbhakam*—unto the child; *rakṣām*—protection; *cakruḥ*—executed; *ca*—also; *śakṛtā*—with the cow dung; *dvādaśa-aṅgeṣu*—in twelve places (*dvādaśa-tilaka*); *nāmabhiḥ*—by imprinting the holy names of the Lord.

### TRANSLATION

**The child was thoroughly washed with cow urine and then smeared with the dust raised by the movements of the cows. Then different names of the Lord were applied with cow dung on twelve different parts of His body, beginning with the forehead, as done in applying tilaka. In this way, the child was given protection.**

## TEXT 21

गोप्यः संस्पृष्टसलिला अङ्गेषु करयोः पृथक् ।
न्यस्यात्मन्यथ बालस्य बीजन्यासमकुर्वत ॥२१॥

*gopyaḥ saṁspṛṣṭa-salilā*
*aṅgeṣu karayoḥ pṛthak*
*nyasyātmany atha bālasya*
*bīja-nyāsam akurvata*

*gopyaḥ*—the *gopīs; saṁspṛṣṭa-salilāḥ*—touching a cup of water and drinking; *aṅgeṣu*—on their bodies; *karayoḥ*—on their two hands; *pṛthak*—separately; *nyasya*—after placing the letters of the *mantra; ātmani*—on their own; *atha*—then; *bālasya*—of the child; *bīja-nyāsam*—the process of *mantra-nyāsa; akurvata*—executed.

## TRANSLATION

**The gopīs first executed the process of ācamana, drinking a sip of water from the right hand. They purified their bodies and hands with the nyāsa-mantra and then applied the same mantra upon the body of the child.**

## PURPORT

*Nyāsa-mantra* includes *ācamana,* or first drinking a sip of water kept in the right hand. There are different *viṣṇu-mantras* to purify the body. The *gopīs,* and in fact any householders, knew the process for being purified by chanting Vedic hymns. The *gopīs* executed this process first to purify themselves and then to purify the child Kṛṣṇa. One executes the process of *aṅga-nyāsa* and *kara-nyāsa* simply by drinking a little sip of water and chanting the *mantra.* The *mantra* is preceded with the first letter of the name, followed by *anusvāra* and the word *namaḥ: aṁ namo 'jas tavāṅghrī avyāt, maṁ mano maṇimāṁs tava jānunī avyāt,* and so on. By losing Indian culture, Indian householders have forgotten how to execute the *aṅga-nyāsa* and are simply busy in sense gratification, without any advanced knowledge of human civilization.

## TEXTS 22–23

अव्यादजोऽङ्घ्रि मणिमांस्तव जान्वथोरू
यज्ञोऽच्युतः कटितटं जठरं हयास्यः ।
हृत् केशवस्त्वदुर ईश इनस्तु कण्ठं
विष्णुर्भुजं मुखमुरुक्रम ईश्वरः कम् ॥२२॥

चक्र्यग्रतः सहगदो हरिरस्तु पश्चात्
त्वत्पार्श्वयोर्धनुरसी मधुहाजनश्च ।
कोणेषु शङ्ख उरुगाय उपर्युपेन्द्र-
स्तार्क्ष्यः क्षितौ हलधरः पुरुषः समन्तात् ॥२३॥

*avyād ajo 'ṅghri maṇimāṁs tava jānv athorū*
*yajño 'cyutaḥ kaṭi-taṭaṁ jaṭharaṁ hayāsyaḥ*
*hṛt keśavas tvad-ura īśa inas tu kaṇṭhaṁ*
*viṣṇur bhujaṁ mukham urukrama īśvaraḥ kam*

*cakry agrataḥ saha-gado harir astu paścāt*
*tvat-pārśvayor dhanur-asī madhu-hājanaś ca*
*koṇeṣu śaṅkha urugāya upary upendras*
*tārkṣyaḥ kṣitau haladharaḥ puruṣaḥ samantāt*

*avyāt*—may protect; *ajaḥ*—Lord Aja; *aṅghri*—legs; *maṇimān*—Lord Maṇimān; *tava*—Your; *jānu*—knees; *atha*—thereafter; *urū*—thighs; *yajñaḥ*—Lord Yajña; *acyutaḥ*—Lord Acyuta; *kaṭi-taṭam*—the upper part of the waist; *jaṭharam*—abdomen; *hayāsyaḥ*—Lord Hayagrīva; *hṛt*—the heart; *keśavaḥ*—Lord Keśava; *tvat*—Your; *uraḥ*—chest; *īśaḥ*—the supreme controller, Lord Īśa; *inaḥ*—Sūrya, the sun-god; *tu*—but; *kaṇṭham*—neck; *viṣṇuḥ*—Lord Viṣṇu; *bhujam*—arms; *mukham*—the mouth; *urukramaḥ*—Lord Urukrama; *īśvaraḥ*—Lord Īśvara; *kam*—head; *cakrī*—the carrier of the disc; *agrataḥ*—in front; *saha-gadaḥ*—the carrier of the club; *hariḥ*—Lord Hari; *astu*—may He remain; *paścāt*—on the back; *tvat-pārśvayoḥ*—on both sides; *dhanuḥ-asī*—the carrier of the bow and the sword; *madhu-hā*—the killer of the demon Madhu; *ajanaḥ*—Lord Viṣṇu; *ca*—and; *koṇeṣu*—in the corners;

*śaṅkhaḥ*—the carrier of the conchshell; *urugāyaḥ*—who is well worshiped; *upari*—above; *upendraḥ*—Lord Upendra; *tārkṣyaḥ*—Garuḍa; *kṣitau*—on the surface; *haladharaḥ*—Lord Haladhara; *puruṣaḥ*—the Supreme Person; *samantāt*—on all sides.

## TRANSLATION

**[Śukadeva Gosvāmī informed Mahārāja Parīkṣit that the gopīs, following the proper system, protected Kṛṣṇa, their child, with this mantra.] May Aja protect Your legs, may Maṇimān protect Your knees, Yajña Your thighs, Acyuta the upper part of Your waist, and Hayagrīva Your abdomen. May Keśava protect Your heart, Īśa Your chest, the sun-god Your neck, Viṣṇu Your arms, Urukrama Your face, and Īśvara Your head. May Cakrī protect You from the front; may Śrī Hari, Gadādharī, the carrier of the club, protect You from the back; and may the carrier of the bow, who is known as the enemy of Madhu, and Lord Ajana, the carrier of the sword, protect Your two sides. May Lord Urugāya, the carrier of the conchshell, protect You from all corners; may Upendra protect You from above; may Garuḍa protect You on the ground; and may Lord Haladhara, the Supreme Person, protect You on all sides.**

## PURPORT

Even in the houses of the cultivators, who were not very advanced in the modern ways of civilization, the ladies used to know how to chant *mantras* to give protection to children with the help of cow dung and cow urine. This was a simple and practical way to give the greatest protection from the greatest dangers. People should know how to do this, for this is a part of Vedic civilization.

## TEXT 24

इन्द्रियाणि हृषीकेशः प्राणान् नारायणोऽवतु ।
श्वेतद्वीपपतिश्चित्तं मनो योगेश्वरोऽवतु ॥२४॥

*indriyāṇi hṛṣīkeśaḥ*
*prāṇān nārāyaṇo 'vatu*

*śvetadvīpa-patiś cittaṁ*
*mano yogeśvaro 'vatu*

*indriyāṇi*—all the senses; *hṛṣīkeśaḥ*—Lord Hṛṣīkeśa, the proprietor of all the senses; *prāṇān*—all kinds of life air; *nārāyaṇaḥ*—Lord Nārāyaṇa; *avatu*—may He give protection; *śvetadvīpa-patiḥ*—the master of Śvetadvīpa, Viṣṇu; *cittam*—the core of the heart; *manaḥ*—the mind; *yogeśvaraḥ*—Lord Yogeśvara; *avatu*—may He give protection.

## TRANSLATION

**May Hṛṣīkeśa protect Your senses, and Nārāyaṇa Your life air. May the master of Śvetadvīpa protect the core of Your heart, and may Lord Yogeśvara protect Your mind.**

## TEXTS 25–26

पृश्निगर्भस्तु ते बुद्धिमात्मानं भगवान् परः ।
क्रीडन्तं पातु गोविन्दः शयानं पातु माधवः ॥२५॥
व्रजन्तमव्याद् वैकुण्ठ आसीनं त्वां श्रियः पतिः।
भुञ्जानं यज्ञभुक् पातु सर्वग्रहभयङ्करः ॥२६॥

*pṛśnigarbhas tu te buddhim*
*ātmānaṁ bhagavān paraḥ*
*krīḍantaṁ pātu govindaḥ*
*śayānaṁ pātu mādhavaḥ*

*vrajantam avyād vaikuṇṭha*
*āsīnaṁ tvāṁ śriyaḥ patiḥ*
*bhuñjānaṁ yajñabhuk pātu*
*sarva-graha-bhayaṅkaraḥ*

*pṛśnigarbhaḥ*—Lord Pṛśnigarbha; *tu*—indeed; *te*—Your; *buddhim*—intelligence; *ātmānam*—Your soul; *bhagavān*—the Supreme Personality of Godhead; *paraḥ*—transcendental; *krīḍantam*—while playing; *pātu*—may He protect; *govindaḥ*—Lord Govinda; *śayānam*—while sleeping; *pātu*—may He protect; *mādhavaḥ*—Lord Mādhava;

*vrajantam*—while walking; *avyāt*—may He protect; *vaikuṇṭhaḥ*—Lord Vaikuṇṭha; *āsīnam*—while sitting down; *tvām*—unto You; *śriyaḥ patiḥ*—Nārāyaṇa, the husband of the goddess of fortune (may protect); *bhuñjānam*—while enjoying life; *yajñabhuk*—Yajñabhuk; *pātu*—may He protect; *sarva-graha-bhayam-karaḥ*—who is fearful to all evil planets.

## TRANSLATION

**May Lord Pṛśnigarbha protect Your intelligence, and the Supreme Personality of Godhead Your soul. While You are playing, may Govinda protect You, and while You are sleeping may Mādhava protect You. May Lord Vaikuṇṭha protect You while You are walking, and may Lord Nārāyaṇa, the husband of the goddess of fortune, protect You while You are sitting. Similarly, may Lord Yajñabhuk, the fearful enemy of all evil planets, always protect You while You enjoy life.**

## TEXTS 27–29

डाकिन्यो यातुधान्यश्च कुष्माण्डा येऽर्भकग्रहाः ।
भूतप्रेतपिशाचाश्च यक्षरक्षोविनायकाः ॥२७॥
कोटरा रेवती ज्येष्ठा पूतना मातृकादयः ।
उन्मादा ये ह्यपस्मारा देहप्राणेन्द्रियद्रुहः ॥२८॥
स्वप्नदृष्टा महोत्पाता वृद्धा बालग्रहाश्च ये ।
सर्वे नश्यन्तु ते विष्णोर्नामग्रहणभीरवः ॥२९॥

*ḍākinyo yātudhānyaś ca*
*kuṣmāṇḍā ye 'rbhaka-grahāḥ*
*bhūta-preta-piśācāś ca*
*yakṣa-rakṣo-vināyakāḥ*

*koṭarā revatī jyeṣṭhā*
*pūtanā mātṛkādayaḥ*
*unmādā ye hy apasmārā*
*deha-prāṇendriya-druhaḥ*

*svapna-dṛṣṭā mahotpātā*
*vṛddhā bāla-grahāś ca ye*
*sarve naśyantu te viṣṇor*
*nāma-grahaṇa-bhīravaḥ*

*ḍākinyaḥ yātudhānyaḥ ca kuṣmāṇḍāḥ*—witches and devils, enemies of children; *ye*—those who are; *arbhaka-grahāḥ*—like evil stars for children; *bhūta*—evil spirits; *preta*—evil hobgoblins; *piśācāḥ*—similar bad spirits; *ca*—also; *yakṣa*—the living entities known as Yakṣas; *rakṣaḥ*—those known as Rākṣasas; *vināyakāḥ*—those by the name Vināyaka; *koṭarā*—by the name Koṭarā; *revatī*—by the name Revatī; *jyeṣṭhā*—by the name Jyeṣṭhā; *pūtanā*—by the name Pūtanā; *mātṛkā-ādayaḥ*—and evil women like Mātṛkā; *unmādāḥ*—those who cause madness; *ye*—which others; *hi*—indeed; *apasmārāḥ*—causing loss of memory; *deha-prāṇa-indriya*—to the body, life air and senses; *druhaḥ*—give trouble; *svapna-dṛṣṭāḥ*—the evil spirits that cause bad dreams; *mahā-utpātāḥ*—those causing great disturbances; *vṛddhāḥ*—the most experienced; *bāla-grahāḥ ca*—and those attacking children; *ye*—who; *sarve*—all of them; *naśyantu*—let be vanquished; *te*—those; *viṣṇoḥ*—of Lord Viṣṇu; *nāma-grahaṇa*—by the chanting of the name; *bhīravaḥ*—become afraid.

## TRANSLATION

**The evil witches known as Ḍākinīs, Yātudhānīs and Kuṣmāṇḍas are the greatest enemies of children, and the evil spirits like Bhūtas, Pretas, Piśācas, Yakṣas, Rākṣasas and Vināyakas, as well as witches like Koṭarā, Revatī, Jyeṣṭhā, Pūtanā and Mātṛkā, are always ready to give trouble to the body, the life air and the senses, causing loss of memory, madness and bad dreams. Like the most experienced evil stars, they all create great disturbances, especially for children, but one can vanquish them simply by uttering Lord Viṣṇu's name, for when Lord Viṣṇu's name resounds, all of them become afraid and go away.**

## PURPORT

As stated in the *Brahma-saṁhitā* (5.33):

*advaitam acyutam anādim ananta-rūpam*
*ādyaṁ purāṇa-puruṣaṁ nava-yauvanaṁ ca*

*vedeṣu durlabham adurlabham ātma-bhaktau*
*govindam ādi-puruṣaṁ tam ahaṁ bhajāmi*

"I worship the Supreme Personality of Godhead, Govinda, who is the original person—nondual, infallible, and without beginning. Although He expands into unlimited forms, He is still the original, and although He is the oldest person, He always appears as a fresh youth. Such eternal, blissful and all-knowing forms of the Lord cannot be understood by the academic wisdom of the *Vedas*, but they are always manifest to pure, unalloyed devotees."

While decorating the body with *tilaka*, we give protection to the body by chanting twelve names of Viṣṇu. Although Govinda, or Lord Viṣṇu, is one, He has different names and forms with which to act differently. But if one cannot remember all the names at one time, one may simply chant, "Lord Viṣṇu, Lord Viṣṇu, Lord Viṣṇu," and always think of Lord Viṣṇu. *Viṣṇor ārādhanaṁ param:* this is the highest form of worship. If one remembers Viṣṇu always, even though one is disturbed by many bad elements, one can be protected without a doubt. The *Āyurveda-śāstra* recommends, *auṣadhi cintayet viṣṇum:* even while taking medicine, one should remember Viṣṇu, because the medicine is not all and all and Lord Viṣṇu is the real protector. The material world is full of danger (*padaṁ padaṁ yad vipadām*). Therefore one must become a Vaiṣṇava and think of Viṣṇu constantly. This is made easier by the chanting of the Hare Kṛṣṇa *mahā-mantra.* Therefore Śrī Caitanya Mahāprabhu has recommended, *kīrtanīyaḥ sadā hariḥ, paraṁ vijayate śrī-kṛṣṇa-saṅkīrtanam,* and *kīrtanād eva kṛṣṇasya mukta-saṅgaḥ paraṁ vrajet.*

## TEXT 30

श्रीशुक उवाच

इति प्रणयबद्धाभिर्गोपीभिः कृतरक्षणम् ।
पाययित्वा स्तनं माता संन्यवेशयदात्मजम् ॥३०॥

*śrī-śuka uvāca*
*iti praṇaya-baddhābhir*
*gopībhiḥ kṛta-rakṣaṇam*
*pāyayitvā stanaṁ mātā*
*sannyaveśayad ātmajam*

*śrī-śukaḥ uvāca*—Śrī Śukadeva Gosvāmī said; *iti*—in this way; *praṇaya-baddhābhiḥ*—who were bound with maternal affection; *gopībhiḥ*—by the elderly *gopīs*, headed by mother Yaśodā; *kṛta-rakṣaṇam*—all measures were taken to protect the child; *pāyayitvā*—and after that, feeding the child; *stanam*—the nipple; *mātā*—mother Yaśodā; *sannyaveśayat*—made to lie down on the bed; *ātmajam*—her son.

## TRANSLATION

**Śrīla Śukadeva Gosvāmī continued: All the gopīs, headed by mother Yaśodā, were bound by maternal affection. After they thus chanted mantras to protect the child, mother Yaśodā gave the child the nipple of her breast to suck and then got Him to lie down on His bed.**

## PURPORT

When a baby drinks milk from the breast of his mother, this is a good sign of health. So the elderly *gopīs* were not satisfied with chanting *mantras* to give protection to Kṛṣṇa; they also tested whether their child's health was in order. When the child sucked the breast, this confirmed that He was healthy, and when the *gopīs* were fully satisfied, they had the child lie down on His bed.

## TEXT 31

तावन्नन्दादयो गोपा मथुराया व्रजं गताः ।
विलोक्य पूतनादेहं बभूवुरतिविस्मिताः ॥३१॥

*tāvan nandādayo gopā*
*mathurāyā vrajaṁ gatāḥ*
*vilokya pūtanā-dehaṁ*
*babhūvur ativismitāḥ*

*tāvat*—in the meantime; *nanda-ādayaḥ*—headed by Nanda Mahārāja; *gopāḥ*—all the cowherd men; *mathurāyāḥ*—from Mathurā; *vrajam*—to Vṛndāvana; *gatāḥ*—came back; *vilokya*—when they saw; *pūtanā-deham*—the gigantic body of Pūtanā lying dead; *babhūvuḥ*—became; *ati*—very much; *vismitāḥ*—struck with wonder.

## TRANSLATION

**Meanwhile, all the cowherd men, headed by Nanda Mahārāja, returned from Mathurā, and when they saw on the way the gigantic body of Pūtanā lying dead, they were struck with great wonder.**

## PURPORT

Nanda Mahārāja's wonder may be understood in various ways. First of all, the cowherd men had never before seen such a gigantic body in Vṛndāvana, and therefore they were struck with wonder. Then they began to consider where such a body had come from, whether it had dropped from the sky, or whether, by some mistake or by the power of some mystic *yoginī*, they had come to some place other than Vṛndāvana. They could not actually guess what had happened, and therefore they were struck with wonder.

## TEXT 32

नूनं बतर्षिः संजातो योगेशो वा समास सः ।
स एव दृष्टो ह्युत्पातो यदाहानकदुन्दुभिः ॥३२॥

*nūnaṁ batarṣiḥ sañjāto*
*yogeśo vā samāsa saḥ*
*sa eva dṛṣṭo hy utpāto*
*yad āhānakadundubhiḥ*

*nūnam*—certainly; *bata*—O my friends; *ṛṣiḥ*—a great saintly person; *sañjātaḥ*—has become; *yoga-īśaḥ*—a master of mystic power; *vā*—or; *samāsa*—has become; *saḥ*—he (Vasudeva); *saḥ*—that; *eva*—indeed; *dṛṣṭaḥ*—has been seen (by us); *hi*—because; *utpātaḥ*—kind of disturbance; *yat*—that which; *āha*—predicted; *ānakadundubhiḥ*—Ānakadundubhi (another name of Vasudeva).

## TRANSLATION

**Nanda Mahārāja and the other gopas exclaimed: My dear friends, you must know that Ānakadundubhi, Vasudeva, has become a great saint or a master of mystic power. Otherwise how could he have foreseen this calamity and predicted it to us?**

## PURPORT

This verse illustrates the difference between *kṣatriyas* and innocent *vaiśyas.* By studying the political situation, Vasudeva could see what would happen, whereas Nanda Mahārāja, the king of the agriculturalists, could only guess that Vasudeva was a great saintly person and had developed mystic powers. Vasudeva actually had all mystic powers under his control; otherwise he could not have become the father of Kṛṣṇa. But in fact he foresaw the calamities in Vraja by studying Kaṁsa's political activities and thus warned Nanda Mahārāja to take precautions, although Nanda Mahārāja thought that Vasudeva had predicted this incident through wonderful mystic powers. By mystic powers gained through the practice of *haṭha-yoga,* one can study and understand the future.

## TEXT 33

कलेवरं परशुभिश्छित्त्वा तत्ते व्रजौकसः ।
दूरे क्षिप्त्वावयवशो न्यदहन् काष्ठवेष्टितम् ॥३३॥

*kalevaraṁ paraśubhiś*
*chittvā tat te vrajaukasaḥ*
*dūre kṣiptvāvayavaśo*
*nyadahan kāṣṭha-veṣṭitam*

*kalevaram*—the gigantic body of Pūtanā; *paraśubhiḥ*—with the aid of axes; *chittvā*—after cutting to pieces; *tat*—that (body); *te*—all of those; *vraja-okasaḥ*—inhabitants of Vraja; *dūre*—far, far away; *kṣiptvā*—after throwing; *avayavaśaḥ*—different parts of the body, piece by piece; *nyadahan*—burned to ashes; *kāṣṭha-veṣṭitam*—covered by wood.

## TRANSLATION

**The inhabitants of Vraja cut the gigantic body of Pūtanā into pieces with the help of axes. Then they threw the pieces far away, covered them with wood and burned them to ashes.**

## PURPORT

It is the practice that after a snake has been killed, its body is cut into various pieces for fear that it may come to life again simply by interacting with air. Merely killing a serpent is not sufficient; after it is killed, it must be cut to pieces and burned, and then the danger will be over. Pūtanā resembled a great serpent, and therefore the cowherd men took the same precautions by burning her body to ashes.

## TEXT 34

दह्यमानस्य देहस्य धूमश्चागुरुसौरभः ।
उत्थितः कृष्णनिर्भुक्तसपद्याहतपाप्मनः ॥३४॥

*dahyamānasya dehasya*
*dhūmaś cāguru-saurabhaḥ*
*utthitaḥ kṛṣṇa-nirbhukta-*
*sapady āhata-pāpmanaḥ*

*dahyamānasya*—while being burnt to ashes; *dehasya*—of the body of Pūtanā; *dhūmaḥ*—the smoke; *ca*—and; *aguru-saurabhaḥ*—turned into saintly scented smoke of the *aguru* herb; *utthitaḥ*—emanating from her body; *kṛṣṇa-nirbhukta*—because of Kṛṣṇa's having sucked her breast; *sapadi*—immediately; *āhata-pāpmanaḥ*—her material body became spiritualized or relieved of all material conditions.

## TRANSLATION

**Because of Kṛṣṇa's having sucked the breast of the Rākṣasī Pūtanā, when Kṛṣṇa killed her she was immediately freed of all material contamination. Her sinful reactions automatically vanished, and therefore when her gigantic body was being burnt, the smoke emanating from her body was fragrant like aguru incense.**

## PURPORT

Such are the effects of Kṛṣṇa consciousness. If one somehow or other becomes Kṛṣṇa conscious by applying his senses in the service of the Lord, one is immediately freed from material contamination. *Śṛṇvatāṁ sva-kathāḥ kṛṣṇaḥ puṇya-śravaṇa-kīrtanaḥ* (*Bhāg.* 1.2.17). Hearing about the activities of Kṛṣṇa is the beginning of purified life. *Puṇya-śravaṇa-kīrtanaḥ:* simply by hearing and chanting, one becomes purified. Therefore, in discharging devotional service, *śravaṇa-kīrtana* (hearing and chanting) is most important. Then, with purified senses, one begins to render service to the Lord (*hṛṣīkeṇa hṛṣīkeśa-sevanam*). *Bhaktir ucyate:* this is called *bhakti.* When Pūtanā was somehow or other, directly or indirectly, induced to render some service to the Lord by feeding Him with her breast, she was immediately purified, so much so that when her nasty material body was burnt to ashes, it gave off the fragrance of *aguru*, the most agreeably scented herb.

### TEXTS 35–36

पूतना लोकबालघ्नी राक्षसी रुधिराशना ।
जिघांसयापि हरये स्तनं दत्त्वाप सद्गतिम् ॥३५॥
किं पुनः श्रद्धया भक्त्या कृष्णाय परमात्मने ।
यच्छन् प्रियतमं किं नु रक्तास्तन्मातरो यथा ॥३६॥

*pūtanā loka-bāla-ghnī*
*rākṣasī rudhirāśanā*
*jighāṁsayāpi haraye*
*stanaṁ dattvāpa sad-gatim*

*kiṁ punaḥ śraddhayā bhaktyā*
*kṛṣṇāya paramātmane*
*yacchan priyatamaṁ kiṁ nu*
*raktās tan-mātaro yathā*

*pūtanā*—Pūtanā, the professional Rākṣasī; *loka-bāla-ghnī*—who used to kill human children; *rākṣasī*—the she-demon; *rudhira-aśanā*—simply hankering for blood; *jighāṁsayā*—with the desire to kill Kṛṣṇa (being envious of Kṛṣṇa and having been instructed by Kaṁsa); *api*—still; *haraye*—unto the Supreme Personality of Godhead; *stanam*—her breast; *dattvā*—after offering; *āpa*—obtained; *sat-gatim*—the most elevated position of spiritual existence; *kim*—what to speak of; *punaḥ*—again; *śraddhayā*—with faith; *bhaktyā*—by devotion; *kṛṣṇāya*—unto Lord Kṛṣṇa; *paramātmane*—who is the Supreme Person; *yacchan*—offering; *priya-tamam*—the dearmost; *kim*—something; *nu*—indeed;

*raktāḥ*—those who have an affinity; *tat-mātaraḥ*—Kṛṣṇa's affectionate mothers (offering the beloved child their breasts); *yathā*—exactly like.

## TRANSLATION

**Pūtanā was always hankering for the blood of human children, and with that desire she came to kill Kṛṣṇa; but because she offered her breast to the Lord, she attained the greatest achievement. What then is to be said of those who had natural devotion and affection for Kṛṣṇa as mothers and who offered Him their breasts to suck or offered something very dear, as a mother offers something to a child?**

## PURPORT

Pūtanā had no affection for Kṛṣṇa; rather, she was envious and wanted to kill Him. Nonetheless, because with or without knowledge she offered her breast, she attained the highest achievement in life. But the offerings of devotees attracted to Kṛṣṇa in parental love are always sincere. A mother likes to offer something to her child with affection and love; there is no question of envy. So here we can make a comparative study. If Pūtanā could attain such an exalted position in spiritual life by neglectfully, enviously making an offering to Kṛṣṇa, what is to be said of mother Yaśodā and the other *gopīs*, who served Kṛṣṇa with such great affection and love, offering everything for Kṛṣṇa's satisfaction? The *gopīs* automatically achieved the highest perfection. Therefore Śrī Caitanya Mahāprabhu recommended the affection of the *gopīs*, either in maternal affection or in conjugal love, as the highest perfection in life (*ramyā kācid upāsanā vrajavadhū-vargeṇa yā kalpitā*).

## TEXTS 37–38

पद्भ्यां भक्तहृदिस्थाभ्यां वन्द्याभ्यां लोकवन्दितैः ।
अङ्गं यस्याः समाक्रम्य भगवानपिबत् स्तनम् ॥३७॥
यातुधान्यपि सा स्वर्गमवाप जननीगतिम् ।
कृष्णभुक्तस्तनक्षीराः किमु गावोऽनुमातरः ॥३८॥

*padbhyāṁ bhakta-hṛdi-sthābhyāṁ*
*vandyābhyāṁ loka-vanditaiḥ*
*aṅgaṁ yasyāḥ samākramya*
*bhagavān api tat-stanam*

*yātudhāny api sā svargam*
*avāpa jananī-gatim*
*kṛṣṇa-bhukta-stana-kṣīrāḥ*
*kim u gāvo 'numātaraḥ*

*padbhyām*—by the two lotus feet; *bhakta-hṛdi-sthābhyām*—which are always thought of by pure devotees, in whose heart the Lord is therefore situated constantly; *vandyābhyām*—which are always to be praised; *loka-vanditaiḥ*—by Lord Brahmā and Lord Śiva, who are praised by all the inhabitants of the three worlds; *aṅgam*—the body; *yasyāḥ*—of whom (Pūtanā); *samākramya*—embracing; *bhagavān*—the Supreme Personality of Godhead; *api*—also; *tat-stanam*—that breast; *yātudhānī api*—although she was a witch (whose only business was to kill small children and who had tried to kill Kṛṣṇa also); *sā*—she; *svargam*—the transcendental abode; *avāpa*—achieved; *jananī-gatim*—the position of a mother; *kṛṣṇa-bhukta-stana-kṣīrāḥ*—therefore, because their breasts were sucked by Kṛṣṇa, who drank the milk flowing from their bodies; *kim u*—what to speak of; *gāvaḥ*—the cows; *anumātaraḥ*—exactly like mothers (who allowed their nipples to be sucked by Kṛṣṇa).

## TRANSLATION

**The Supreme Personality of Godhead, Kṛṣṇa, is always situated within the core of the heart of the pure devotee, and He is always offered prayers by such worshipable personalities as Lord Brahmā and Lord Śiva. Because Kṛṣṇa embraced Pūtanā's body with great pleasure and sucked her breast, although she was a great witch, she attained the position of a mother in the transcendental world and thus achieved the highest perfection. What then is to be said of the cows whose nipples Kṛṣṇa sucked with great pleasure and who offered their milk very jubilantly with affection exactly like that of a mother?**

## PURPORT

These verses explain how devotional service rendered to the Supreme Personality of Godhead, whether directly or indirectly, knowingly or unknowingly, becomes successful. Pūtanā was neither a devotee nor a nondevotee; she was actually a demoniac witch instructed by Kaṁsa to kill Kṛṣṇa. Nonetheless, in the beginning she assumed the form of a very beautiful woman and approached Kṛṣṇa exactly like an affectionate mother, so that mother Yaśodā and Rohiṇī did not doubt her sincerity. The Lord took all this into consideration, and thus she was automatically promoted to a position like that of mother Yaśodā. As explained by Viśvanātha Cakravartī Ṭhākura, there are various roles one may play in such a position. Pūtanā was immediately promoted to Vaikuṇṭhaloka, which is also sometimes described as Svarga. The Svarga mentioned in this verse is not the material heavenly planet, but the transcendental world. In Vaikuṇṭhaloka, Pūtanā attained the position of a nurse (*dhātry-ucitām*), as described by Uddhava. Pūtanā was elevated to the position of a nurse and maidservant in Goloka Vṛndāvana to assist mother Yaśodā.

## TEXTS 39–40

पयांसि यासामपिबत् पुत्रस्नेहस्नुतान्यलम् ।
भगवान् देवकीपुत्रः कैवल्याद्यखिलप्रदः ॥३९॥
तासामविरतं कृष्णे कुर्वतीनां सुतेक्षणम् ।
न पुनः कल्पते राजन् संसारोऽज्ञानसम्भवः ॥४०॥

*payāṁsi yāsām apibat*
*putra-sneha-snutāny alam*
*bhagavān devakī-putraḥ*
*kaivalyādy-akhila-pradaḥ*

*tāsām aviratam kṛṣṇe*
*kurvatīnāṁ suteksaṇam*
*na punaḥ kalpate rājan*
*saṁsāro 'jñāna-sambhavaḥ*

*payāṁsi*—milk (coming from the body); *yāsām*—of all of whom; *apibat*—Lord Kṛṣṇa drank; *putra-sneha-snutāni*—that milk coming from the bodies of the *gopīs*, not artificially but because of maternal affection; *alam*—sufficiently; *bhagavān*—the Supreme Personality of Godhead; *devakī-putraḥ*—who appeared as the son of Devakī; *kaivalya-ādi*—like liberation or merging into the Brahman effulgence; *akhila-pradaḥ*—the bestower of all similar blessings; *tāsām*—of all of them (of all the *gopīs*); *aviratam*—constantly; *kṛṣṇe*—unto Lord Kṛṣṇa; *kurvatīnām*—making; *suta-īkṣaṇam*—as a mother looks upon her child; *na*—never; *punaḥ*—again; *kalpate*—can be imagined; *rājan*—O King Parīkṣit; *saṁsāraḥ*—the material bondage of birth and death; *ajñāna-sambhavaḥ*—which is to be accepted by foolish persons ignorantly trying to become happy.

## TRANSLATION

**The Supreme Personality of Godhead, Kṛṣṇa, is the bestower of many benedictions, including liberation [kaivalya], or oneness with the Brahman effulgence. For that Personality of Godhead, the gopīs always felt maternal love, and Kṛṣṇa sucked their breasts with full satisfaction. Therefore, because of their relationship as mother and son, although the gopīs were engaged in various family activities, one should never think that they returned to this material world after leaving their bodies.**

## PURPORT

The advantage of Kṛṣṇa consciousness is described herein. Kṛṣṇa consciousness gradually develops on the transcendental platform. One may think of Kṛṣṇa as the supreme personality, one may think of Kṛṣṇa as the supreme master, one may think of Kṛṣṇa as the supreme friend, one may think of Kṛṣṇa as the supreme son, or one may think of Kṛṣṇa as the supreme conjugal lover. If one is connected with Kṛṣṇa in any of these transcendental relationships, the course of one's material life is understood to have already ended. As confirmed in *Bhagavad-gītā* (4.9), *tyaktvā dehaṁ punar janma naiti mām eti:* for such devotees, going back home, back to Godhead, is guaranteed. *Na punaḥ kalpate rājan saṁsāro 'jñāna-sambhavaḥ.* This verse also guarantees that devotees who constantly think of Kṛṣṇa in a particular relationship will never return to this material world. In this material world of *saṁsāra*, there are the same relationships. One thinks, "Here is my son," "Here is my wife," "Here is my lover," or "Here is my friend." But these relationships are temporary illusions. *Ajñāna-sambhavaḥ:* such a consciousness awakens in ignorance. But when the same relationships awaken in Kṛṣṇa consciousness, one's spiritual life is revived, and one is guaranteed to return home, back to Godhead. Even though the *gopīs* who were friends of Rohiṇī and mother Yaśodā and who allowed their breasts to be sucked by Kṛṣṇa were not directly Kṛṣṇa's mothers, they all had the same chance as Rohiṇī and Yaśodā to go back to Godhead and act as Kṛṣṇa's mothers-in-law, servants and so on. The word *saṁsāra* refers to attachment for one's body, home, husband or wife, and children, but although the *gopīs* and all the other inhabitants of Vṛndāvana had the same affection and attachment for husband and home, their central affection was for Kṛṣṇa in some transcendental relationship, and therefore they were guaranteed to be promoted to Goloka Vṛndāvana in the next life, to live with Kṛṣṇa eternally in spiritual happiness. The easiest way to attain spiritual elevation, to be liberated from this material world, and to go back home, back to Godhead, is recommended by Bhaktivinoda Ṭhākura: *kṛṣṇera saṁsāra kara chāḍi' anācāra.* One should give up all sinful activities and remain in the family of Kṛṣṇa. Then one's liberation is guaranteed.

## TEXT 41

कटधूमस्य सौरभ्यमवघ्राय व्रजौकसः ।
किमिदं कुत एवेति वदन्तो व्रजमाययुः ॥४१॥

*kaṭa-dhūmasya saurabhyam*
*avaghrāya vrajaukasaḥ*
*kim idaṁ kuta eveti*
*vadanto vrajam āyayuḥ*

*kaṭa-dhūmasya*—of the smoke emanating from the fire burning the different parts of Pūtanā's body; *saurabhyam*—the fragrance; *avaghrāya*—when they smelled through their nostrils; *vraja-okasaḥ*—the inhabitants of Vrajabhūmi in distant places; *kim idam*—what is this fragrance; *kutaḥ*—where does it come from; *eva*—indeed; *iti*—in this way; *vadantaḥ*—speaking; *vrajam*—the place of Nanda Mahārāja, Vrajabhūmi; *āyayuḥ*—reached.

## TRANSLATION

**Upon smelling the fragrance of the smoke emanating from Pūtanā's burning body, many inhabitants of Vrajabhūmi in distant places were astonished. "Where is this fragrance coming from?" they asked. Thus they went to the spot where Pūtanā's body was being burnt.**

## PURPORT

The aroma of the smoke emanating from a burning fire is not always very favorable. Therefore upon smelling such a wonderful fragrance, the inhabitants of Vraja were astonished.

## TEXT 42

ते तत्र वर्णितं गोपैः पूतनागमनादिकम् ।
श्रुत्वा तन्निधनं स्वस्ति शिशोश्चासन् सुविस्मिताः ॥४२॥

*te tatra varṇitaṁ gopaiḥ*
*pūtanāgamanādikam*
*śrutvā tan-nidhanaṁ svasti*
*śiśoś cāsan suvismitāḥ*

*te*—all those persons who arrived; *tatra*—there (in the vicinity of Nanda Mahārāja's estate); *varṇitam*—described; *gopaiḥ*—by the cowherd men; *pūtanā-āgamana-ādikam*—everything about how Pūtanā the witch had come there and played havoc; *śrutvā*—after hearing; *tat-nidhanam*—and about how Pūtanā had died; *svasti*—all auspiciousness; *śiśoḥ*—for the baby; *ca*—and; *āsan*—offered; *su-vismitāḥ*—being struck with great wonder because of what had happened.

## TRANSLATION

**When the inhabitants of Vraja who had come from distant places heard the whole story of how Pūtanā had come and then been**

**killed by Kṛṣṇa, they were certainly astonished, and they offered their blessings to the child for His wonderful deed of killing Pūtanā. Nanda Mahārāja, of course, was very much obliged to Vasudeva, who had foreseen the incident, and simply thanked him, thinking how wonderful Vasudeva was.**

## TEXT 43

नन्दः स्वपुत्रमादाय प्रेत्यागतमुदारधीः ।
मूर्ध्न्युपाघ्राय परमां मुदं लेभे कुरूद्वह ॥४३॥

*nandaḥ sva-putram ādāya*
*pretyāgatam udāra-dhīḥ*
*mūrdhny upāghrāya paramām*
*mudaṁ lebhe kurūdvaha*

*nandaḥ*—Mahārāja Nanda; *sva-putram ādāya*—taking his son Kṛṣṇa on his lap; *pretya-āgatam*—as if Kṛṣṇa had returned from death (no one could even imagine that from such danger a child could be saved); *udāra-dhīḥ*—because he was always liberal and simple; *mūrdhni*—on the head of Kṛṣṇa; *upāghrāya*—formally smelling; *paramām*—highest; *mudam*—peace; *lebhe*—achieved; *kuru-udvaha*—O Mahārāja Parīkṣit.

## TRANSLATION

**O Mahārāja Parīkṣit, best of the Kurus, Nanda Mahārāja was very liberal and simple. He immediately took his son Kṛṣṇa on his lap as if Kṛṣṇa had returned from death, and by formally smelling his son's head, Nanda Mahārāja undoubtedly enjoyed transcendental bliss.**

## PURPORT

Nanda Mahārāja could not understand how the inhabitants of his house had allowed Pūtanā to enter the house, nor could he imagine the gravity of the situation. He did not understand that Kṛṣṇa had wanted to kill Pūtanā and that His pastimes were performed by *yogamāyā.* Nanda Mahārāja simply thought that someone had entered his house and created havoc. This was Nanda Mahārāja's simplicity.

## TEXT 44

य एतत् पूतनामोक्षं कृष्णस्यार्भकमद्भुतम् ।
शृणुयाच्छ्रद्धया मर्त्यो गोविन्दे लभते रतिम् ॥४४॥

*ya etat pūtanā-mokṣaṁ*
*kṛṣṇasyārbhakam adbhutam*
*śṛṇuyāc chraddhayā martyo*
*govinde labhate ratim*

*yaḥ*—anyone who; *etat*—this; *pūtanā-mokṣam*—salvation of Pūtanā; *kṛṣṇasya*—of Kṛṣṇa; *ārbhakam*—the childhood pastimes; *adbhutam*—wonderful; *śṛṇuyāt*—should hear; *śraddhayā*—with faith and devotion; *martyaḥ*—any person within this material world; *govinde*—for the Supreme Person, Govinda, Ādi-puruṣa; *labhate*—gains; *ratim*—attachment.

## TRANSLATION

**Any person who hears with faith and devotion about how Kṛṣṇa, the Supreme Personality of Godhead, killed Pūtanā, and who thus invests his hearing in such childhood pastimes of Kṛṣṇa, certainly attains attachment for Govinda, the supreme, original person.**

## PURPORT

The incident in which the great witch attempted to kill the child but was killed herself is certainly wonderful. Therefore this verse uses the word *adbhutam*, meaning "specifically wonderful." Kṛṣṇa has left us many wonderful narrations about Him. Simply by reading these narrations, as they are described in *Kṛṣṇa, the Supreme Personality of Godhead*, one gains salvation from this material world and gradually develops attachment to and devotion for Govinda, Ādi-puruṣa.

*Thus end the Bhaktivedanta purports of the Tenth Canto, Sixth Chapter, of the* Śrīmad-Bhāgavatam, *entitled "The Killing of the Demon Pūtanā."*

# CHAPTER SEVEN

# The Killing of the Demon Tṛṇāvarta

In this chapter, Śrī Kṛṣṇa's pastimes of breaking the cart (*śakaṭa-bhañjana*), killing the *asura* known as Tṛṇāvarta, and demonstrating the entire universe within His mouth are especially described.

When Śukadeva Gosvāmī saw that Mahārāja Parīkṣit was eagerly waiting to hear about Lord Kṛṣṇa's pastimes as a child, he was very much pleased, and he continued to speak. When Śrī Kṛṣṇa was only three months old and was just trying to turn backside up, before He even attempted to crawl, mother Yaśodā wanted to observe a ritualistic ceremony with her friends for the good fortune of the child. Such a ritualistic ceremony is generally performed with ladies who also have small children. When mother Yaśodā saw that Kṛṣṇa was falling asleep, because of other engagements she put the child underneath a household cart, called *śakaṭa*, and while the child was sleeping, she engaged herself in other business pertaining to the auspicious ritualistic ceremony. Underneath the cart was a cradle, and mother Yaśodā placed the child in that cradle. The child was sleeping, but suddenly He awakened and, as usual for a child, began to kick His small legs. This kicking shook the cart, which collapsed with a great sound, breaking completely and spilling all its contents. Children who were playing nearby immediately informed mother Yaśodā that the cart had broken, and therefore she hastily arrived there in great anxiety with the other *gopīs*. Mother Yaśodā immediately took the child on her lap and allowed Him to suck her breast. Then various types of Vedic ritualistic ceremonies were performed with the help of the *brāhmaṇas*. Not knowing the real identity of the child, the *brāhmaṇas* showered the child with blessings.

Another day, when mother Yaśodā was sitting with her child on her lap, she suddenly observed that he had assumed the weight of the entire universe. She was so astonished that she had to put the child down, and in the meantime Tṛṇāvarta, one of the servants of Kaṁsa, appeared there as a whirlwind and took the child away. The whole tract of land known as Gokula became surcharged with dust, no one could see where the child had been taken, and all the *gopīs* were overwhelmed because He had been taken away in the dust storm. But up in the sky, the *asura*, being overburdened by the child, could not carry the child far away, although he also could not drop the child because the child had caught him so tightly that it was difficult for him to separate the child from his body. Thus Tṛṇāvarta himself fell down from a very great height, the child grasping him tightly by the shoulder, and immediately died. The demon having fallen, the *gopīs* picked the child up and delivered Him to the lap of mother Yaśodā. Thus mother Yaśodā was struck with wonder, but because of *yogamāyā's* influence, no one could understand who Kṛṣṇa was and what had actually happened. Rather, everyone began to praise fortune for the child's having been saved from such a calamity. Nanda Mahārāja, of course, was thinking of the wonderful foretelling of Vasudeva and began to praise him as a great *yogī*. Later, when the child was on the lap of mother Yaśodā, the child yawned, and mother Yaśodā could see within His mouth the entire universal manifestation.

## TEXTS 1–2

श्रीराजोवाच

येन येनावतारेण भगवान् हरिरीश्वरः ।
करोति कर्णरम्याणि मनोज्ञानि च नः प्रभो ॥ १ ॥
यच्छृण्वतोऽपैत्यरतिर्वितृष्णा
सत्त्वं च शुद्धयत्यचिरेण पुंसः ।
भक्तिर्हरौ तत्पुरुषे च सख्यं
तदेव हारं वद मन्यसे चेत् ॥ २ ॥

*śrī-rājovāca*
*yena yenāvatāreṇa*
*bhagavān harir īśvaraḥ*
*karoti karṇa-ramyāṇi*
*mano-jñāni ca naḥ prabho*

*yac-chṛṇvato 'paity aratir vitṛṣṇā*
*sattvaṁ ca śuddhyaty acireṇa puṁsaḥ*

*bhaktir harau tat-puruṣe ca sakhyaṁ*
*tad eva hāraṁ vada manyase cet*

*śrī-rājā uvāca*—the King inquired (from Śukadeva Gosvāmī); *yena yena avatāreṇa*—the pastimes exhibited by different varieties of incarnations; *bhagavān*—the Supreme Personality of Godhead; *hariḥ*—the Lord; *īśvaraḥ*—the controller; *karoti*—presents; *karṇa-ramyāṇi*—were all very pleasing to the ear; *manaḥ-jñāni*—very attractive to the mind; *ca*—also; *naḥ*—of us; *prabho*—my lord, Śukadeva Gosvāmī; *yat-śṛṇvataḥ*—of anyone who simply hears these narrations; *apaiti*—vanishes; *aratiḥ*—unattractiveness; *vitṛṣṇā*—dirty things within the mind that make us uninterested in Kṛṣṇa consciousness; *sattvam ca*—the existential position in the core of the heart; *śuddhyati*—becomes purified; *acireṇa*—very soon; *puṁsaḥ*—of any person; *bhaktiḥ harau*—devotional attachment and service to the Lord; *tat-puruṣe*—with Vaiṣṇavas; *ca*—also; *sakhyam*—attraction to association; *tat eva*—that only; *hāram*—the activities of the Lord, which should be heard and kept on the neck as a garland; *vada*—kindly speak; *manyase*—you think it fit; *cet*—if.

## TRANSLATION

**King Parīkṣit said: My lord, Śukadeva Gosvāmī, all the various activities exhibited by the incarnations of the Supreme Personality of Godhead are certainly pleasing to the ear and to the mind. Simply by one's hearing of these activities, the dirty things in one's mind immediately vanish. Generally we are reluctant to hear about the activities of the Lord, but Kṛṣṇa's childhood activities are so attractive that they are automatically pleasing to the mind and ear. Thus one's attachment for hearing about material things, which is the root cause of material existence, vanishes, and one gradually develops devotional service to the Supreme Lord, attachment for Him, and friendship with devotees who give us the contribution of Kṛṣṇa consciousness. If you think it fit, kindly speak about those activities of the Lord.**

## PURPORT

As stated in the *Prema-vivarta:*

*kṛṣṇa-bahirmukha haiyā bhoga-vāñchā kare*
*nikaṭa-stha māyā tāre jāpaṭiyā dhare*

Our material existence is *māyā,* or illusion, in which we desire different varieties of material enjoyment and therefore change to different varieties of bodies (*bhrāmayan sarva-bhūtāni yantrārūḍhāni māyayā*). *Asann api kleśada āsa dehaḥ:* as long as we have these temporary bodies, they give us many varieties of tribulation—*ādhyātmika, ādhibhautika* and *ādhidaivika.* This is the root cause of all suffering, but this root cause of suffering can be removed by revival of our Kṛṣṇa consciousness. All the Vedic literatures presented by Vyāsadeva and other great sages are therefore intended to revive our Kṛṣṇa consciousness, which begins to revive with *śravaṇa-kīrtanam. Śṛṇvatāṁ sva-kathāḥ kṛṣṇaḥ* (*Bhāg.* 1.2.17). *Śrīmad-Bhāgavatam* and other Vedic literatures exist simply to give us a chance to hear about Kṛṣṇa. Kṛṣṇa has different *avatāras,* or incarnations, all of which are wonderful and which arouse one's inquisitiveness, but generally such *avatāras* as Matsya, Kūrma and Varāha are not as attractive as Kṛṣṇa. First of all, however, we have no attraction for hearing about Kṛṣṇa, and this is the root cause of our suffering.

But Parīkṣit Mahārāja specifically mentions that the wonderful activities of baby Kṛṣṇa, which amazed mother Yaśodā and the other inhabitants of Vraja, are especially attractive. From the very beginning of His childhood, Kṛṣṇa killed Pūtanā, Tṛṇāvarta and Śakaṭāsura and showed the entire universe within His mouth. Thus the pastimes of Kṛṣṇa, one after another, kept mother Yaśodā and all the inhabitants of Vraja in great astonishment. The process to revive one's Kṛṣṇa consciousness is *ādau śraddhā tataḥ sādhu-saṅgaḥ* (*Bhakti-rasāmṛta-sindhu* 1.4.15). The pastimes of Kṛṣṇa can be properly received from devotees. If one has developed a little bit of Kṛṣṇa consciousness by hearing from Vaiṣṇavas about the activities of Kṛṣṇa, one becomes attached to Vaiṣṇavas who are interested only in Kṛṣṇa consciousness. Therefore Parīkṣit Mahārāja recommends that one hear about Kṛṣṇa's childhood activities, which are more attractive than the activities of other incarnations, such as Matsya, Kūrma and Varāha. Wanting to hear more and more from Śukadeva Gosvāmī, Mahārāja Parīkṣit requested him to continue describing Kṛṣṇa's childhood activities, which are especially easy to hear and which create more and more inquisitiveness.

## TEXT 3

अथान्यदपि कृष्णस्य तोकाचरितमद्भुतम् ।
मानुषं लोकमासाद्य तज्जातिमनुरुन्धतः ॥ ३ ॥

*athānyad api kṛṣṇasya*
*tokācaritam adbhutam*
*mānuṣaṁ lokam āsādya*
*taj-jātim anurundhataḥ*

*atha*—also; *anyat api*—other pastimes also; *kṛṣṇasya*—of child Kṛṣṇa; *toka-ācaritam adbhutam*—they are also wonderful childhood pastimes; *mānuṣam*—as if playing as a human child; *lokam āsādya*—appearing on this planet earth in human society; *tat-jātim*—exactly like a human child; *anurundhataḥ*—who was imitating.

## TRANSLATION

**Please describe other pastimes of Kṛṣṇa, the Supreme Personality, who appeared on this planet earth, imitating a human child and performing wonderful activities like killing Pūtanā.**

## PURPORT

Mahārāja Parīkṣit requested Śukadeva Gosvāmī to narrate other childhood pastimes exhibited by Kṛṣṇa while playing as a human child. The Supreme Personality of Godhead incarnates at different times in different planets and universes, and according to the nature of those places, He exhibits His unlimited potency. That a child sitting on the lap of his mother was able to kill the gigantic Pūtanā is extremely wonderful for the inhabitants of this planet, but on other planets the inhabitants are more advanced, and therefore the pastimes the Lord performs there are still more wonderful. Kṛṣṇa's appearance on this planet like a human being makes us more fortunate than the demigods in the higher planets, and therefore Mahārāja Parīkṣit was very much interested in hearing about Him.

### TEXT 4

श्रीशुक उवाच
कदाचिदौत्थानिककौतुकाप्लवे
जन्मर्क्षयोगे समवेतयोषिताम् ।
वादित्रगीतद्विजमन्त्रवाचकै-
श्चकार सूनोरभिषेचनं सती ॥ ४ ॥

*śrī-śuka uvāca*
*kadācid autthānika-kautukāplave*
*janmarkṣa-yoge samaveta-yoṣitām*
*vāditra-gīta-dvija-mantra-vācakaiś*
*cakāra sūnor abhiṣecanaṁ satī*

*śrī-śukaḥ uvāca*—Śrī Śukadeva Gosvāmī continued to speak (at the request of Mahārāja Parīkṣit); *kadācit*—at that time (when Kṛṣṇa was three months old); *autthānika-kautuka-āplave*—when Kṛṣṇa was three or four months old and His body was developing, He attempted to turn around, and this pleasing occasion was observed with a festival and bathing ceremony; *janma-ṛkṣa-yoge*—at that time, there was also a conjunction of the moon with the auspicious constellation Rohiṇī; *samaveta-yoṣitām*—(the ceremony was observed) among the assembled women, a ceremony of mothers; *vāditra-gīta*—different varieties of music and singing; *dvija-mantra-vācakaiḥ*—with chanting of Vedic hymns by qualified *brāhmaṇas; cakāra*—executed; *sūnoḥ*—of her son; *abhiṣecanam*—the bathing ceremony; *satī*—mother Yaśodā.

### TRANSLATION

**Śukadeva Gosvāmī said: When mother Yaśodā's baby was slanting His body to attempt to rise and turn around, this attempt was observed by a Vedic ceremony. In such a ceremony, called utthāna, which is performed when a child is due to leave the house for the first time, the child is properly bathed. Just after Kṛṣṇa turned three months old, mother Yaśodā celebrated this ceremony with**

**other women of the neighborhood. On that day, there was a conjunction of the moon with the constellation Rohiṇī. As the brāhmaṇas joined by chanting Vedic hymns and professional musicians also took part, this great ceremony was observed by mother Yaśodā.**

## PURPORT

There is no question of overpopulation or of children's being a burden for their parents in a Vedic society. Such a society is so well organized and people are so advanced in spiritual consciousness that childbirth is never regarded as a burden or a botheration. The more a child grows, the more his parents become jubilant, and the child's attempts to turn over are also a source of jubilation. Even before the child is born, when the mother is pregnant, many recommended ritualistic ceremonies are performed. For example, when the child has been within the womb for three months and for seven months, there is a ceremony the mother observes by eating with neighboring children. This ceremony is called *svāda-bhakṣaṇa.* Similarly, before the birth of the child there is the *garbhādhāna* ceremony. In Vedic civilization, childbirth or pregnancy is never regarded as a burden; rather, it is a cause for jubilation. In contrast, people in modern civilization do not like pregnancy or childbirth, and when there is a child, they sometimes kill it. We can just consider how human society has fallen since the inauguration of Kali-yuga. Although people still claim to be civilized, at the present moment there is actually no human civilization, but only an assembly of two-legged animals.

## TEXT 5

नन्दस्य पत्नी कृतमज्जनादिकं
विप्रैः कृतस्वस्त्ययनं सुपूजितैः ।
अन्नाद्यवासःस्रगभीष्टधेनुभिः
संजातनिद्राक्षमशीशयच्छनैः ॥५॥

*nandasya patnī kṛta-majjanādikaṁ*
*vipraiḥ kṛta-svastyayanaṁ supūjitaiḥ*
*annādya-vāsaḥ-srag-abhīṣṭa-dhenubhiḥ*
*sañjāta-nidrākṣam aśīśayac chanaiḥ*

*nandasya*—of Mahārāja Nanda; *patnī*—the wife (mother Yaśodā); *kṛta-majjana-ādikam*—after she and the other members of the house had bathed and the child had been bathed also; *vipraiḥ*—by the *brāhmaṇas; kṛta-svastyayanam*—engaging them in chanting auspicious Vedic hymns; *su-pūjitaiḥ*—who were all received and worshiped with proper respect; *anna-ādya*—by offering them sufficient grains and other eatables; *vāsaḥ*—garments; *srak-abhīṣṭa-dhenubhiḥ*—by offering flower garlands and very desirable cows; *sañjāta-nidrā*—had become sleepy; *akṣam*—whose eyes; *aśīśayat*—laid the child down; *śanaiḥ*—for the time being.

## TRANSLATION

**After completing the bathing ceremony for the child, mother Yaśodā received the brāhmaṇas by worshiping them with proper respect and giving them ample food grains and other eatables, clothing, desirable cows, and garlands. The brāhmaṇas properly chanted Vedic hymns to observe the auspicious ceremony, and when they finished and mother Yaśodā saw that the child felt sleepy, she lay down on the bed with the child until He was peacefully asleep.**

## PURPORT

An affectionate mother takes great care of her child and is always anxious to see that the child is not disturbed even for a moment. As long as the child wants to remain with the mother, the mother stays with the child, and the child feels very comfortable. Mother Yaśodā saw that her child felt sleepy, and to give Him all facilities for sleep, she lay down with the child, and when He was peaceful, she got up to attend to her other household affairs.

## TEXT 6

औत्थानिकौत्सुक्यमना मनस्विनी
समागतान् पूजयती व्रजौकसः ।
नैवाशृणोद्द् वै रुदितं सुतस्य सा
रुदन् स्तनार्थी चरणावुदक्षिपत् ॥ ६ ॥

*autthānikautsukya-manā manasvinī*
*samāgatān pūjayatī vrajaukasaḥ*
*naivāśṛṇod vai ruditaṁ sutasya sā*
*rudan stanārthī caraṇāv udakṣipat*

*autthānika-autsukya-manāḥ*—mother Yaśodā was very busy celebrating the *utthāna* ceremony of her child; *manasvinī*—very liberal in distributing food, clothing, ornaments and cows, according to necessity; *samāgatān*—to the assembled guests; *pūjayatī*—just to satisfy them; *vraja-okasaḥ*—to the inhabitants of Vraja; *na*—not; *eva*—certainly; *aśṛṇot*—did hear; *vai*—indeed; *ruditam*—the crying; *sutasya*—of her child; *sā*—mother Yaśodā; *rudan*—crying; *stana-arthī*—Kṛṣṇa, who was hankering to drink His mother's milk by sucking her breast; *caraṇau udakṣipat*—out of anger, threw His two legs hither and thither.

## TRANSLATION

**The liberal mother Yaśodā, absorbed in celebrating the utthāna ceremony, was busy receiving guests, worshiping them with all respect and offering them clothing, cows, garlands and grains. Thus she could not hear the child crying for His mother. At that time, the child Kṛṣṇa, demanding to drink the milk of His mother's breast, angrily threw His legs upward.**

## PURPORT

Kṛṣṇa had been placed underneath a household handcart, but this handcart was actually another form of the Śakaṭāsura, a demon who had come there to kill the child. Now, on the plea of demanding to suck His mother's breast, Kṛṣṇa took this opportunity to kill the demon. Thus He kicked Śakaṭāsura just to expose him. Although Kṛṣṇa's mother was engaged in receiving guests, Lord Kṛṣṇa wanted to draw her attention by killing the Śakaṭāsura, and therefore he kicked that cart-shaped demon. Such are the pastimes of Kṛṣṇa. Kṛṣṇa wanted to draw the attention of His mother, but while doing so He created a great havoc not understandable by ordinary persons. These narrations are wonderfully enjoyable, and those who are fortunate are struck with wonder upon hearing of these extraordinary activities of the Lord. Although the less intelligent regard them as mythological because a dull brain cannot understand them, they are real facts. These narrations are actually so enjoyable and enlightening that Mahārāja Parīkṣit and Śukadeva Gosvāmī took pleasure in them, and other liberated persons, following in their footsteps, become fully jubilant by hearing about the wonderful activities of the Lord.

## TEXT 7

अधःशयानस्य शिशोरनोऽल्पक-
प्रवालमृद्वङ्घ्रिहतं व्यवर्तत ।
विध्वस्तनानारसकुप्यभाजनं
व्यत्यस्तचक्राक्षविभिन्नकूबरम् ॥ ७ ॥

*adhaḥ-śayānasya śiśor ano 'lpaka-*
*pravāla-mṛdv-aṅghri-hataṁ vyavartata*
*vidhvasta-nānā-rasa-kupya-bhājanaṁ*
*vyatyasta-cakrākṣa-vibhinna-kūbaram*

*adhaḥ-śayānasya*—who was put underneath the handcart; *śiśoḥ*—of the child; *anaḥ*—the cart; *alpaka*—not very much grown; *pravāla*—just like a new leaf; *mṛdu-aṅghri-hatam*—struck by His beautiful, delicate legs; *vyavartata*—turned over and fell down; *vidhvasta*—scattered; *nānā-rasa-kupya-bhājanam*—utensils made of various metals; *vyatyasta*—dislocated; *cakra-akṣa*—the two wheels and the axle; *vibhinna*—broken; *kūbaram*—the pole of the handcart.

## TRANSLATION

**Lord Śrī Kṛṣṇa was lying down underneath the handcart in one corner of the courtyard, and although His little legs were as soft as leaves, when He struck the cart with His legs, it turned over violently and collapsed. The wheels separated from the axle, the hubs and spokes fell apart, and the pole of the handcart broke. On the cart there were many little utensils made of various metals, and all of them scattered hither and thither.**

## PURPORT

Śrīla Viśvanātha Cakravartī Ṭhākura has commented on this verse as follows. When Lord Kṛṣṇa was of a very tender age, His hands and legs resembled soft new leaves, yet simply by touching the handcart with His legs, He made the cart fall to pieces. It was quite possible for Him to act in this way and yet not exert Himself very much. The Lord in His Vāmana *avatāra* had to extend His foot to the greatest height to penetrate the covering of the universe, and when the Lord killed the gigantic demon Hiraṇyakaśipu, He had to assume the special bodily feature of Nṛsiṁhadeva. But in His Kṛṣṇa *avatāra*, the Lord did not need to exert such energy. Therefore, *kṛṣṇas tu bhagavān svayam:* Kṛṣṇa is the Supreme Personality of Godhead Himself. In other incarnations, the Lord had to exert some energy according to the time and circumstances, but in this form He exhibited unlimited potency. Thus the handcart collapsed, its joints broken, and all the metal pots and utensils scattered.

The *Vaiṣṇava-toṣaṇī* remarks that although the handcart was higher than the child, the child could easily touch the wheel of the cart, and this was sufficient to send the demon down to the earth. The Lord simultaneously pushed the demon to the earth and superficially broke the handcart.

## TEXT 8

दृष्ट्वा यशोदाप्रमुखा व्रजस्त्रिय
औत्थानिके कर्मणि याः समागताः ।
नन्दादयश्चाद्भुतदर्शनाकुलाः
कथं स्वयं वै शकटं विपर्यगात् ॥ ८ ॥

*dṛṣṭvā yaśodā-pramukhā vraja-striya*
*autthānike karmaṇi yāḥ samāgatāḥ*
*nandādayaś cādbhuta-darśanākulāḥ*
*kathaṁ svayaṁ vai śakaṭaṁ viparyagāt*

*dṛṣṭvā*—after seeing; *yaśodā-pramukhāḥ*—headed by mother Yaśodā; *vraja-striyaḥ*—all the ladies of Vraja; *autthānike karmaṇi*—in the celebration of the *utthāna* ceremony; *yāḥ*—those who; *samāgatāḥ*—

assembled there; *nanda-ādayaḥ ca*—and the men, headed by Nanda Mahārāja; *adbhuta-darśana*—by seeing the wonderful calamity (that the heavily loaded cart had broken upon the small baby, who still lay there unhurt); *ākulāḥ*—and thus they were very much perturbed as to how it had happened; *katham*—how; *svayam*—by itself; *vai*—indeed; *śakaṭam*—the handcart; *viparyagāt*—became so heavily damaged, dismantled.

## TRANSLATION

**When mother Yaśodā and the other ladies who had assembled for the utthāna festival, and all the men, headed by Nanda Mahārāja, saw the wonderful situation, they began to wonder how the handcart had collapsed by itself. They began to wander here and there, trying to find the cause, but were unable to do so.**

## TEXT 9

ऊचुरव्यवसितमतीन् गोपान् गोपीश्च बालकाः ।
रुदतानेन पादेन क्षिप्तमेतन्न संशयः ॥ ९ ॥

*ūcur avyavasita-matīn*
*gopān gopīś ca bālakāḥ*
*rudatānena pādena*
*kṣiptam etan na saṁśayaḥ*

*ūcuḥ*—said; *avyavasita-matīn*—who had lost all intelligence in the present situation; *gopān*—to the cowherd men; *gopīḥ ca*—and to the ladies; *bālakāḥ*—the children; *rudatā anena*—as soon as the child cried; *pādena*—with one leg; *kṣiptam etat*—this cart was dashed apart and immediately fell dismantled; *na saṁśayaḥ*—there is no doubt about it.

## TRANSLATION

**The assembled cowherd men and ladies began to contemplate how this thing had happened. "Is it the work of some demon or evil planet?" they asked. At that time, the small children present asserted that the cart had been kicked apart by the baby Kṛṣṇa. As**

**soon as the crying baby had kicked the cart's wheel, the cart had collapsed. There was no doubt about it.**

## PURPORT

We have heard of people's being haunted by ghosts. Having no gross material body, a ghost seeks shelter of a gross body to stay in and haunt. The Śakaṭāsura was a ghost who had taken shelter of the handcart and was looking for the opportunity to do mischief to Kṛṣṇa. When Kṛṣṇa kicked the cart with His small and very delicate legs, the ghost was immediately pushed down to the earth and his shelter dismantled, as already described. This was possible for Kṛṣṇa because He has full potency, as confirmed in the *Brahma-saṁhitā* (5.32):

*aṅgāni yasya sakalendriya-vṛttimanti*
*paśyanti pānti kalayanti ciraṁ jaganti*
*ānanda-cinmaya-sad-ujjvala-vigrahasya*
*govindam ādi-puruṣaṁ tam ahaṁ bhajāmi*

Kṛṣṇa's body is *sac-cid-ānanda-vigraha,* or *ānanda-cinmaya-rasa-vigraha.* That is, any of the parts of His *ānanda-cinmaya* body can act for any other part. Such are the inconceivable potencies of the Supreme Personality of Godhead. The Supreme Lord does not need to acquire these potencies; He already has them. Thus Kṛṣṇa kicked His little legs, and His whole purpose was fulfilled. Also, when the handcart broke, an ordinary child could have been injured in many ways, but because Kṛṣṇa is the Supreme Personality of Godhead, He enjoyed the dismantling of the cart, and nothing injured Him. Everything done by Him is *ānanda-cinmaya-rasa,* full transcendental bliss. Thus Kṛṣṇa factually enjoyed.

The nearby children saw that actually Kṛṣṇa had kicked the wheel of the cart and this was how the accident happened. By the arrangement of *yogamāyā,* all the *gopīs* and *gopas* thought that the accident had taken place because of some bad planet or some ghost, but in fact everything was done by Kṛṣṇa and enjoyed by Him. Those who enjoy the activities of Kṛṣṇa are also on the platform of *ānanda-cinmaya-rasa;* they are liberated from the material platform. When one develops the practice of hearing *kṛṣṇa-kathā,* he is certainly transcendental to material existence, as confirmed in *Bhagavad-gītā* (*sa guṇān samatītyaitān brahma-bhūyāya kalpate*). Unless one is on the spiritual platform, one cannot enjoy the transcendental activities of Kṛṣṇa; or in other words, whoever engages in hearing the transcendental activities of Kṛṣṇa is not on the material platform, but on the transcendental, spiritual platform.

## TEXT 10

न ते श्रद्दधिरे गोपा बालभाषितमित्युत ।
अप्रमेयं बलं तस्य बालकस्य न ते विदुः ॥१०॥

*na te śraddadhire gopā*
*bāla-bhāṣitam ity uta*
*aprameyaṁ balaṁ tasya*
*bālakasya na te viduḥ*

*na*—not; *te*—the cowherd men and ladies; *śraddadhire*—put their faith (in such statements); *gopāḥ*—the cowherd men and women; *bāla-bhāṣitam*—childish talk from the assembled children; *iti uta*—thus spoken; *aprameyam*—unlimited, inconceivable; *balam*—the power; *tasya bālakasya*—of the small baby Kṛṣṇa; *na*—not; *te*—the *gopīs* and *gopas*; *viduḥ*—were aware of.

## TRANSLATION

**The assembled gopīs and gopas, unaware that Kṛṣṇa is always unlimited, could not believe that baby Kṛṣṇa had such inconceivable power. They could not believe the statements of the children, and therefore they neglected these statements as being childish talk.**

## TEXT 11

रुदन्तं सुतमादाय यशोदा ग्रहशङ्किता ।
कृतस्वस्त्ययनं विप्रैः सूक्तैः स्तनमपाययत् ॥११॥

*rudantaṁ sutam ādāya*
*yaśodā graha-śaṅkitā*
*kṛta-svastyayanaṁ vipraiḥ*
*sūktaiḥ stanam apāyayat*

*rudantam*—crying; *sutam*—son; *ādāya*—picking up; *yaśodā*—mother Yaśodā; *graha-śaṅkitā*—fearing some bad planet; *kṛta-svastyayanam*—immediately performed a ritualistic ceremony for good fortune; *vipraiḥ*—by calling all the *brāhmaṇas; sūktaiḥ*—by Vedic hymns; *stanam*—her breast; *apāyayat*—made the child suck.

## TRANSLATION

**Thinking that some bad planet had attacked Kṛṣṇa, mother Yaśodā picked up the crying child and allowed Him to suck her breast. Then she called for experienced brāhmaṇas to chant Vedic hymns and perform an auspicious ritualistic ceremony.**

## PURPORT

Whenever there is some danger or some inauspicious occurrence, it is the custom of Vedic civilization to have qualified *brāhmaṇas* immediately chant Vedic hymns to counteract it. Mother Yaśodā did this properly and allowed the baby to suck her breast.

## TEXT 12

पूर्ववत् स्थापितं गोपैर्बलिभिः सपरिच्छदम् ।
विप्रा हुत्वार्चयाञ्चक्रुर्दध्यक्षतकुशाम्बुभिः ॥१२॥

*pūrvavat sthāpitaṁ gopair*
*balibhiḥ sa-paricchadam*
*viprā hutvārcayāṁ cakrur*
*dadhy-akṣata-kuśāmbubhiḥ*

*pūrva-vat*—as the handcart had been situated before; *sthāpitam*—again assembled with the pots situated properly; *gopaiḥ*—by the cowherd men; *balibhiḥ*—all of whom were very strong and stout and who could therefore assemble the parts without difficulty; *sa-paricchadam*—with all the paraphernalia kept on it; *viprāḥ*—the *brāhmaṇas; hutvā*—after performing a fire ceremony; *arcayām cakruḥ*—performed ritualistic ceremonies; *dadhi*—with curd; *akṣata*—grains of rice; *kuśa*—and *kuśa* grass; *ambubhiḥ*—with water.

## TRANSLATION

**After the strong, stout cowherd men assembled the pots and paraphernalia on the handcart and set it up as before, the brāhmaṇas performed a ritualistic ceremony with a fire sacrifice to appease the bad planet, and then, with rice grains, kuśa, water and curd, they worshiped the Supreme Lord.**

## PURPORT

The handcart was loaded with heavy utensils and other paraphernalia. To set the cart back in its original position required much strength, but this was easily done by the cowherd men. Then, according to the system of the *gopa-jāti*, various Vedic ceremonies were performed to appease the calamitous situation.

## TEXTS 13–15

येऽसूयानृतदम्भेर्षाहिंसामानविवर्जिताः ।
न तेषां सत्यशीलानामाशिषो विफलाः कृताः ॥१३॥
इति बालकमादाय सामर्ग्यजुरुपाकृतैः ।
जलैः पवित्रौषधिभिरभिषिच्य द्विजोत्तमैः ॥१४॥
वाचयित्वा स्वस्त्ययनं नन्दगोपः समाहितः ।
हुत्वा चाग्निं द्विजातिभ्यः प्रादादन्नं महागुणम् ॥१५॥

*ye 'sūyānṛta-dambherṣā-*
*hiṁsā-māna-vivarjitāḥ*
*na teṣāṁ satya-śīlānām*
*āśiṣo viphalāḥ kṛtāḥ*

*iti bālakam ādāya*
*sāmarg-yajur-upākṛtaiḥ*
*jalaiḥ pavitrauṣadhibhir*
*abhiṣicya dvijottamaiḥ*

*vāciyitvā svastyayanaṁ*
*nanda-gopaḥ samāhitaḥ*

*hutvā cāgniṁ dvijātibhyaḥ*
*prādād annaṁ mahā-guṇam*

*ye*—those *brāhmaṇas* who; *asūya*—envy; *anṛta*—untruthfulness; *dambha*—false pride; *īrṣā*—grudges; *hiṁsā*—being disturbed by the opulence of others; *māna*—false prestige; *vivarjitāḥ*—completely devoid of; *na*—not; *teṣām*—of such *brāhmaṇas; satya-śīlānām*—who are endowed with perfect brahminical qualifications (*satya, śama, dama,* etc.); *āśiṣaḥ*—the blessings; *viphalāḥ*—useless; *kṛtāḥ*—have become; *iti*—considering all these things; *bālakam*—the child; *ādāya*—taking care of; *sāma*—according to the *Sāma Veda; ṛk*—according to the *Ṛg Veda; yajuḥ*—and according to the *Yajur Veda; upākṛtaiḥ*—purified by such means; *jalaiḥ*—with water; *pavitra-auṣadhibhiḥ*—mixed with pure herbs; *abhiṣicya*—after bathing (the child); *dvija-uttamaiḥ*—with ceremonies performed by first-class *brāhmaṇas* with the above qualifications; *vācayitvā*—requested to be chanted; *svasti-ayanam*—auspicious hymns; *nanda-gopaḥ*—Mahārāja Nanda, the head of the cowherd men; *samāhitaḥ*—liberal and good; *hutvā*—after offering oblations; *ca*—also; *agnim*—unto the sacred fire; *dvijātibhyaḥ*—unto those first-class *brāhmaṇas; prādāt*—gave in charity; *annam*—food grains; *mahā-guṇam*—excellent.

## TRANSLATION

**When brāhmaṇas are free from envy, untruthfulness, unnecessary pride, grudges, disturbance by the opulence of others, and false prestige, their blessings never go in vain. Considering this, Nanda Mahārāja soberly took Kṛṣṇa on his lap and invited such truthful brāhmaṇas to perform a ritualistic ceremony according to the holy hymns of the Sāma Veda, Ṛg Veda and Yajur Veda. Then, while the hymns were being chanted, he bathed the child with water mixed with pure herbs, and after performing a fire ceremony, he sumptuously fed all the brāhmaṇas with first-class grains and other food.**

## PURPORT

Nanda Mahārāja was very confident about the qualifications of the *brāhmaṇas* and their blessings. He was fully confident that simply if the good *brāhmaṇas* showered their blessings, the child Kṛṣṇa would be happy. The blessings of qualified *brāhmaṇas* can bring happiness not only to Kṛṣṇa, the Supreme Personality of Godhead, but to everyone. Because Kṛṣṇa is self-sufficient, He does not require anyone's blessings, yet Nanda Mahārāja thought that Kṛṣṇa required the blessings of the *brāhmaṇas*. What then is to be said of others? In human society, therefore, there must be an ideal class of men, *brāhmaṇas*, who can bestow blessings upon others, namely, upon the *kṣatriyas, vaiśyas* and *śūdras*, so that everyone will be happy. Kṛṣṇa therefore says in *Bhagavad-gītā* (4.13) that human society must have four social orders (*cātur-varṇyaṁ mayā sṛṣṭaṁ guṇa-karma-vibhāgaśaḥ*); it is not that everyone should become a *śūdra* or a *vaiśya* and human society will prosper. As enunciated in *Bhagavad-gītā*, there must be a class of *brāhmaṇas* with qualities like *satya* (truthfulness), *śama* (peacefulness), *dama* (self-control) and *titikṣā* (tolerance).

Here also, in the *Bhāgavatam*, Nanda Mahārāja invites qualified *brāhmaṇas*. There may be caste *brāhmaṇas*, and we have all respect for them, but their birth in *brāhmaṇa* families does not mean that they are qualified to bestow blessings upon the other members of human society. This is the verdict of the *śāstras*. In Kali-yuga, caste *brāhmaṇas* are accepted as *brāhmaṇas*. *Vipratve sūtram eva hi* (*Bhāg*. 12.2.3): in Kali-yuga, simply by putting on a thread worth two paise, one becomes a *brāhmaṇa*. Such *brāhmaṇas* were not called for by Nanda Mahārāja. As stated by Nārada Muni (*Bhāg*. 7.11.35), *yasya yal lakṣaṇaṁ proktam*. The symptoms of a *brāhmaṇa* are stated in *śāstra*, and one must be qualified with these symptoms.

The blessings of *brāhmaṇas* who are not envious, disturbed or puffed up with pride and false prestige and who are fully qualified with truthfulness will be useful. Therefore a class of men must be trained as *brāhmaṇas* from the very beginning. *Brahmacārī guru-kule vasan dānto guror hitam* (*Bhāg*. 7.12.1). The word *dāntaḥ* is very important. *Dāntaḥ* refers to one who is not envious, disturbing or puffed up with false prestige. With the Kṛṣṇa consciousness movement, we are trying to introduce such *brāhmaṇas* in society. *Brāhmaṇas* must ultimately be Vaiṣṇavas, and if one is a Vaiṣṇava, he has already acquired the qualifications of a *brāhmaṇa*. *Brahma-bhūtaḥ prasannātmā* (Bg. 18.54). The word *brahma-bhūta* refers to becoming a *brāhmaṇa*, or understanding what is Brahman (*brahma jānātīti brāhmaṇaḥ*). One who is *brahma-bhūta* is always happy (*prasannātmā*). *Na śocati na kāṅkṣati:* he is never disturbed about material necessities. *Samaḥ sarveṣu bhūteṣu:* he is ready to bestow blessings upon everyone equally. *Mad-bhaktiṁ labhate parām:* then he becomes a Vaiṣṇava. In this age, Śrīla Bhaktisiddhānta Sarasvatī Ṭhākura introduced the sacred thread ceremony for his Vaiṣṇava disciples, with the idea that people should understand that when one becomes a Vaiṣṇava he has already acquired the qualifications of a *brāhmaṇa.* Therefore in the International Society for Krishna Consciousness, those who are twice initiated so as to become *brāhmaṇas* must bear in mind their great responsibility to be truthful, control the mind and senses, be tolerant, and so on. Then their life will be successful. It was such *brāhmaṇas* that Nanda Mahārāja invited to chant the Vedic hymns, not ordinary *brāhmaṇas.* Verse thirteen distinctly mentions *hiṁsā-māna.* The word *māna* refers to false prestige or false pride. Those who were falsely proud, thinking that they were *brāhmaṇas* because they were born in *brāhmaṇa* families, were never invited by Nanda Mahārāja on such occasions.

Verse fourteen mentions *pavitrauṣadhi.* In any ritualistic ceremony, many herbs and leaves were required. These were known as *pavitra-patra.* Sometimes there were *nimba* leaves, sometimes bael leaves, mango leaves, *aśvattha* leaves or *āmalakī* leaves. Similarly, there were *pañca-gavya, pañca-śasya* and *pañca-ratna.* Although Nanda Mahārāja belonged to the *vaiśya* community, everything was known to him.

The most important word in these verses is *mahā-guṇam,* indicating that the *brāhmaṇas* were offered very palatable food of exalted quality. Such palatable dishes were generally prepared with two things, namely food grains and milk products. *Bhagavad-gītā* (18.44) therefore enjoins that human society must give protection to the cows and encourage agriculture (*kṛṣi-go-rakṣya-vāṇijyaṁ vaiśya-karma svabhāvajam*). Simply by expert cooking, hundreds and thousands of palatable dishes can be prepared from agricultural produce and milk products. This is indicated here by the words *annaṁ mahā-guṇam.* Still today in India, from these two things, namely food grains and milk, hundreds and thousands of varieties of food are prepared, and then they are offered to the Supreme Personality of Godhead. (*Catur-vidha-śrī-bhagavat-prasāda. Patraṁ puṣpaṁ phalaṁ toyaṁ yo me bhaktyā prayacchati.*) Then the *prasāda* is distributed. Even today in Jagannātha-kṣetra and other big temples, very palatable dishes are offered to the Deity, and *prasāda* is distributed profusely. Cooked by first-class *brāhmaṇas* with expert knowledge and then distributed to the public, this *prasāda* is also a blessing from the *brāhmaṇas* or Vaiṣṇavas. There are four kinds of *prasāda* (*catur-vidha*). Salty, sweet, sour and pungent tastes are made with different types of spices, and the food is prepared in four divisions, called *carvya, cūṣya, lehya* and *pehya—prasāda* that is chewed, *prasāda* that is licked, *prasāda* tasted with the tongue, and *prasāda* that is drunk. Thus there are many varieties of *prasāda*, prepared very nicely with grains and ghee, offered to the Deity and distributed to the *brāhmaṇas* and Vaiṣṇavas and then to the general public. This is the way of human society. Killing the cows and spoiling the land will not solve the problem of food. This is not civilization. Uncivilized men living in the jungle and being unqualified to produce food by agriculture and cow protection may eat animals, but a perfect human society advanced in knowledge must learn how to produce first-class food simply by agriculture and protection of cows.

## TEXT 16

गावः सर्वगुणोपेता वासःस्रग्रुक्ममालिनीः ।
आत्मजाभ्युदयार्थाय प्रादात्ते चान्वयुञ्जत ॥१६॥

*gāvaḥ sarva-guṇopetā*
*vāsaḥ-srag-rukma-mālinīḥ*
*ātmajābhyudayārthāya*
*prādāt te cānvayuñjata*

*gāvaḥ*—cows; *sarva-guṇa-upetāḥ*—being fully qualified by giving sufficient milk, etc.; *vāsaḥ*—well dressed; *srak*—with flower garlands; *rukma-mālinīḥ*—and with garlands of gold; *ātmaja-abhyudaya-arthāya*—for the purpose of his son's affluence; *prādāt*—gave in charity; *te*—those *brāhmaṇas; ca*—also; *anvayuñjata*—accepted them.

## TRANSLATION

**Nanda Mahārāja, for the sake of the affluence of his own son Kṛṣṇa, gave the brāhmaṇas cows fully decorated with garments,**

**flower garlands and gold necklaces. These cows, fully qualified to give ample milk, were given to the brāhmaṇas in charity, and the brāhmaṇas accepted them and bestowed blessings upon the whole family, and especially upon Kṛṣṇa.**

## PURPORT

Nanda Mahārāja first fed the *brāhmaṇas* sumptuously and then gave them in charity first-class cows fully decorated with golden necklaces, garments and flower garlands.

## TEXT 17

विप्रा मन्त्रविदो युक्तास्तैर्याः प्रोक्तास्तथाशिषः ।
ता निष्फला भविष्यन्ति न कदाचिदपि स्फुटम् ॥१७॥

*viprā mantra-vido yuktās*
*tair yāḥ proktās tathāśiṣaḥ*
*tā niṣphalā bhaviṣyanti*
*na kadācid api sphuṭam*

*viprāḥ*—the *brāhmaṇas; mantra-vidaḥ*—completely expert in chanting the Vedic hymns; *yuktāḥ*—perfect mystic *yogīs; taiḥ*—by them; *yāḥ*—whatsoever; *proktāḥ*—was spoken; *tathā*—becomes just so; *āśiṣaḥ*—all blessings; *tāḥ*—such words; *niṣphalāḥ*—useless, without fruit; *bhaviṣyanti na*—never will become; *kadācit*—at any time; *api*—indeed; *sphuṭam*—always factual, as it is.

## TRANSLATION

**The brāhmaṇas, who were completely expert in chanting the Vedic hymns, were all yogīs fully equipped with mystic powers. Whatever blessings they spoke were certainly never fruitless.**

## PURPORT

*Brāhmaṇas* fully equipped with the brahminical qualifications are always *yogīs* fully powerful in mystic *yoga*. Their words never fail. In every transaction with other members of society, *brāhmaṇas* are certainly dependable. In this age, however, one must take into account that the *brāhmaṇas* are uncertain in their qualifications. Because there are no yajñic *brāhmaṇas,* all *yajñas* are forbidden. The only *yajña* recommended in this age is *saṅkīrtana-yajña. Yajñaiḥ saṅkīrtana-prāyair yajanti hi sumedhasaḥ* (*Bhāg.* 11.5.32). *Yajña* is meant to satisfy Viṣṇu (*yajñārthāt karmaṇo 'nyatra loko 'yaṁ karma-bandhanaḥ*). Because in this age there are no qualified *brāhmaṇas,* people should perform *yajña* by chanting the Hare Kṛṣṇa *mantra* (*yajñaiḥ saṅkīrtana-prāyair yajanti hi sumedhasaḥ*). Life is meant for *yajña,* and *yajña* is performed by the chanting of Hare Kṛṣṇa, Hare Kṛṣṇa, Kṛṣṇa Kṛṣṇa, Hare Hare/ Hare Rāma, Hare Rāma, Rāma Rāma, Hare Hare.

## TEXT 18

एकदारोहमारूढं लालयन्ती सुतं सती ।
गरिमाणं शिशोर्वोढुं न सेहे गिरिकूटवत् ॥१८॥

*ekadāroham ārūḍhaṁ*
*lālayantī sutaṁ satī*
*garimāṇaṁ śiśor voḍhuṁ*
*na sehe giri-kūṭavat*

*ekadā*—one time (estimated to have been when Kṛṣṇa was one year old); *āroham*—on His mother's lap; *ārūḍham*—who was sitting; *lālayantī*—was patting; *sutam*—her son; *satī*—mother Yaśodā; *garimāṇam*—because of an increase in heaviness; *śiśoḥ*—of the child; *voḍhum*—to bear Him; *na*—not; *sehe*—was able; *giri-kūṭa-vat*—appearing like the weight of a mountain peak.

## TRANSLATION

**One day, a year after Kṛṣṇa's appearance, mother Yaśodā was patting her son on her lap. But suddenly she felt the child to be heavier than a mountain peak, and she could no longer bear His weight.**

## PURPORT

*Lālayantī.* Sometimes a mother lifts her child, and when the child falls in her hands, the child laughs, and the mother also enjoys pleasure. Yaśodā used to do this, but this time Kṛṣṇa became very heavy, and she could not bear His weight. Under the circumstances, it is to be understood that Kṛṣṇa was aware of the coming of Tṛṇāvartāsura, who would take Him far away from His mother. Kṛṣṇa knew that when Tṛṇāvarta came and took Him away from His mother's lap, mother Yaśodā would be greatly bereaved. He did not want His mother to suffer any difficulty from the demon. Therefore, because He is the source of everything (*janmādy asya yataḥ*), He assumed the heaviness of the entire universe. The child was on the lap of Yaśodā, who was therefore in possession of everything in the world, but when the child assumed such heaviness, she had to put Him down in order to give Tṛṇāvartāsura an opportunity to take Him away and play with Him for some time before the child returned to the lap of His mother.

## TEXT 19

भूमौ निधाय तं गोपी विस्मिता भारपीडिता ।
महापुरुषमादध्यौ जगतामास कर्मसु ॥१९॥

*bhūmau nidhāya taṁ gopī*
*vismitā bhāra-pīḍitā*
*mahā-puruṣam ādadhyau*
*jagatām āsa karmasu*

*bhūmau*—on the ground; *nidhāya*—placing; *tam*—the child; *gopī*—mother Yaśodā; *vismitā*—being astonished; *bhāra-pīḍitā*—being aggrieved by the weight of the child; *mahā-puruṣam*—Lord Viṣṇu, Nārāyaṇa; *ādadhyau*—took shelter of; *jagatām*—as if the weight of the whole world; *āsa*—engaged herself; *karmasu*—in other household affairs.

## TRANSLATION

**Feeling the child to be as heavy as the entire universe and therefore being anxious, thinking that perhaps the child was being attacked by some other ghost or demon, the astonished mother Yaśodā put the child down on the ground and began to think of Nārāyaṇa. Foreseeing disturbances, she called for the brāhmaṇas to counteract this heaviness, and then she engaged in her other household affairs. She had no alternative than to remember the lotus feet of Nārāyaṇa, for she could not understand that Kṛṣṇa was the original source of everything.**

## PURPORT

Mother Yaśodā did not understand that Kṛṣṇa is the heaviest of all heavy things and that Kṛṣṇa rests within everything (*mat-sthāni sarva-bhūtāni*). As confirmed in *Bhagavad-gītā* (9.4), *mayā tatam idaṁ sarvaṁ jagad avyakta-mūrtinā:* Kṛṣṇa is everywhere in His impersonal form, and everything rests upon Him. Nonetheless, *na cāhaṁ teṣv avasthitaḥ:* Kṛṣṇa is not everywhere. Mother Yaśodā was unable to understand this philosophy because she was dealing with Kṛṣṇa as His real mother by the arrangement of *yogamāyā.* Not understanding the importance of Kṛṣṇa, she could only seek shelter of Nārāyaṇa for Kṛṣṇa's safety and call the *brāhmaṇas* to counteract the situation.

## TEXT 20

दैत्यो नाम्ना तृणावर्तः कंसभृत्यः प्रणोदितः ।
चक्रवातस्वरूपेण जहारासीनमर्भकम् ॥२०॥

*daityo nāmnā tṛṇāvartaḥ*
*kaṁsa-bhṛtyaḥ praṇoditaḥ*
*cakravāta-svarūpeṇa*
*jahārāsīnam arbhakam*

*daityaḥ*—another demon; *nāmnā*—by the name; *tṛṇāvartaḥ*—Tṛṇāvartāsura; *kaṁsa-bhṛtyaḥ*—a servant of Kaṁsa; *praṇoditaḥ*—having been induced by him; *cakravāta-svarūpeṇa*—in the form of a whirlwind; *jahāra*—swept away; *āsīnam*—the sitting; *arbhakam*—child.

## TRANSLATION

**While the child was sitting on the ground, a demon named Tṛṇāvarta, who was a servant of Kaṁsa's, came there as a whirlwind, at Kaṁsa's instigation, and very easily carried the child away into the air.**

## PURPORT

Kṛṣṇa's heaviness was unbearable for the child's mother, but when Tṛṇāvartāsura came, he immediately carried the child away. This was another demonstration of Kṛṣṇa's inconceivable energy. When the Tṛṇāvarta demon came, Kṛṣṇa became lighter than the grass so that the demon could carry Him away. This was *ānanda-cinmaya-rasa*, Kṛṣṇa's blissful, transcendental pleasure.

## TEXT 21

गोकुलं सर्वमावृण्वन् मुष्णंश्चक्षूंषि रेणुभिः ।
ईरयन् सुमहाघोरशब्देन प्रदिशो दिशः ॥२१॥

*gokulaṁ sarvam āvṛṇvan*
*muṣṇaṁś cakṣūṁṣi reṇubhiḥ*
*īrayan sumahā-ghora-*
*śabdena pradiśo diśaḥ*

*gokulam*—the whole tract of land known as Gokula; *sarvam*—everywhere; *āvṛṇvan*—covering; *muṣṇan*—taking away; *cakṣūṁṣi*—the power of vision; *reṇubhiḥ*—by particles of dust; *īrayan*—was vibrating; *su-mahā-ghora*—very fierce and heavy; *śabdena*—with a sound; *pradiśaḥ diśaḥ*—entered everywhere, in all directions.

## TRANSLATION

**Covering the whole land of Gokula with particles of dust, that demon, acting as a strong whirlwind, covered everyone's vision and began vibrating everywhere with a greatly fearful sound.**

## PURPORT

Tṛṇāvartāsura assumed the form of a whirlwind and covered with a dust storm the whole tract of land known as Gokula, so that no one could see even the nearest thing.

## TEXT 22

मुहूर्तमभवद् गोष्ठं रजसा तमसावृतम् ।
सुतं यशोदा नापश्यत्तस्मिन् न्यस्तवती यतः ॥२२॥

*muhūrtam abhavad goṣṭhaṁ*
*rajasā tamasāvṛtam*
*sutaṁ yaśodā nāpaśyat*
*tasmin nyastavatī yataḥ*

*muhūrtam*—for a moment; *abhavat*—there was; *goṣṭham*—throughout the whole pasturing ground; *rajasā*—by big particles of dust; *tamasā āvṛtam*—covered with darkness; *sutam*—her son; *yaśodā*—mother Yaśodā; *na apaśyat*—could not find; *tasmin*—in that very spot; *nyastavatī*—she had placed Him; *yataḥ*—where.

## TRANSLATION

**For a moment, the whole pasturing ground was overcast with dense darkness from the dust storm, and mother Yaśodā was unable to find her son where she had placed Him.**

## TEXT 23

नापश्यत् कश्चनात्मानं परं चापि विमोहितः ।
तृणावर्तनिसृष्टाभिः शर्कराभिरुपद्रुतः ॥२३॥

*nāpaśyat kaścanātmānaṁ*
*paraṁ cāpi vimohitaḥ*
*tṛṇāvarta-nisṛṣṭābhiḥ*
*śarkarābhir upadrutaḥ*

*na*—not; *apaśyat*—saw; *kaścana*—anyone; *ātmānam*—himself; *param ca api*—or another; *vimohitaḥ*—being illusioned; *tṛṇāvarta-nisṛṣṭābhiḥ*—thrown by Tṛṇāvartāsura; *śarkarābhiḥ*—by the sands; *upadrutaḥ*—and thus being disturbed.

## TRANSLATION

**Because of the bits of sand thrown about by Tṛṇāvarta, people could not see themselves or anyone else, and thus they were illusioned and disturbed.**

## TEXT 24

इति खरपवनचक्रपांशुवर्षे
सुतपदवीमबलाविलक्ष्य माता ।
अतिकरुणमनुस्मरन्त्यशोचद्
भुवि पतिता मृतवत्सका यथा गौः ॥२४॥

*iti khara-pavana-cakra-pāṁśu-varṣe*
*suta-padavīm abalāvilakṣya mātā*
*atikaruṇam anusmaranty aśocad*
*bhuvi patitā mṛta-vatsakā yathā gauḥ*

*iti*—thus; *khara*—very strong; *pavana-cakra*—by a whirlwind; *pāṁśu-varṣe*—when there were showers of dust and small dust particles; *suta-padavīm*—the place of her son; *abalā*—the innocent woman; *avilakṣya*—not seeing; *mātā*—because of being His mother; *ati-karuṇam*—very pitifully; *anusmarantī*—she was thinking of her son; *aśocat*—lamented extraordinarily; *bhuvi*—on the ground; *patitā*—fell down; *mṛta-vatsakā*—who has lost her calf; *yathā*—like; *gauḥ*—a cow.

## TRANSLATION

**Because of the dust storm stirred up by the strong whirlwind, mother Yaśodā could find no trace of her son, nor could she understand why. Thus she fell down on the ground like a cow who has lost her calf and began to lament very pitifully.**

## TEXT 25

रुदितमनुनिशम्य तत्र गोप्यो
भृशमनुतप्तधियोऽश्रुपूर्णमुख्यः ।
रुरुदुरनुपलभ्य नन्दसूनुं
पवन उपारतपांशुवर्षवेगे ॥२५॥

*ruditam anuniśamya tatra gopyo*
*bhṛśam anutapta-dhiyo 'śru-pūrṇa-mukhyaḥ*

*rurudur anupalabhya nanda-sūnuṁ*
*pavana upārata-pāṁśu-varṣa-vege*

*ruditam*—mother Yaśodā, crying pitifully; *anuniśamya*—after hearing; *tatra*—there; *gopyaḥ*—the other ladies, the *gopīs; bhṛśam*—highly; *anutapta*—lamenting sympathetically after mother Yaśodā; *dhiyaḥ*—with such feelings; *aśru-pūrṇa-mukhyaḥ*—and the other *gopīs*, their faces full of tears; *ruruduḥ*—they were crying; *anupalabhya*—without finding; *nanda-sūnum*—the son of Nanda Mahārāja, Kṛṣṇa; *pavane*—when the whirlwind; *upārata*—had ceased; *pāṁśu-varṣa-vege*—its force of showering dust.

## TRANSLATION

**When the force of the dust storm and the winds subsided, Yaśodā's friends, the other gopīs, approached mother Yaśodā, hearing her pitiful crying. Not seeing Kṛṣṇa present, they too felt very much aggrieved and joined mother Yaśodā in crying, their eyes full of tears.**

## PURPORT

This attachment of the *gopīs* to Kṛṣṇa is wonderful and transcendental. The center of all the activities of the *gopīs* was Kṛṣṇa. When Kṛṣṇa was there they were happy, and when Kṛṣṇa was not there, they were unhappy. Thus when mother Yaśodā was lamenting Kṛṣṇa's absence, the other ladies also began to cry.

## TEXT 26

तृणावर्तः शान्तरयो वात्यारूपधरो हरन् ।
कृष्णं नभोगतो गन्तुं नाशक्नोद् भूरिभारभृत् ॥२६॥

*tṛṇāvartaḥ śānta-rayo*
*vātyā-rūpa-dharo haran*
*kṛṣṇaṁ nabho-gato gantuṁ*
*nāśaknod bhūri-bhāra-bhṛt*

*tṛṇāvartaḥ*—the demon Tṛṇāvarta; *śānta-rayaḥ*—the force of the blast reduced; *vātyā-rūpa-dharaḥ*—who had assumed the form of a forceful whirlwind; *haran*—and had thus taken away; *kṛṣṇam*—Kṛṣṇa, the Supreme Personality of Godhead; *nabhaḥ-gataḥ*—went up to the top of the sky; *gantum*—to go further; *na aśaknot*—was not able; *bhūri-bhāra-bhṛt*—because Kṛṣṇa then became more powerful and heavy than the demon.

## TRANSLATION

**Having assumed the form of a forceful whirlwind, the demon Tṛṇāvarta took Kṛṣṇa very high in the sky, but when Kṛṣṇa became heavier than the demon, the demon had to stop his force and could go no further.**

## PURPORT

Here is a competition in yogic power between Kṛṣṇa and Tṛṇāvartāsura. By practicing mystic *yoga, asuras* generally attain some perfection in the eight *siddhis*, or perfections, namely *aṇimā, laghimā, mahimā, prāpti, prākāmya, īśitva, vaśitva* and *kāmāvasāyitā.* But although a demon may acquire such powers to a very limited extent, he cannot compete with the mystic power of Kṛṣṇa, for Kṛṣṇa is Yogeśvara, the source of all mystic power (*yatra yogeśvaro hariḥ*). No one can compete with Kṛṣṇa. Sometimes, of course, having acquired a fragmental portion of Kṛṣṇa's mystic power, *asuras* demonstrate their power to the foolish public and assert themselves to be God, not knowing that God is the supreme Yogeśvara. Here also we see that Tṛṇāvarta assumed the *mahimā-siddhi* and took Kṛṣṇa away as if Kṛṣṇa were an ordinary child. But Kṛṣṇa also became a mystic *mahimā-siddha.* When mother Yaśodā was carrying Him, He became so heavy that His mother, who was usually accustomed to carrying Him, could not bear Him and had to place Him down on the ground. Thus Tṛṇāvarta had been able to take Kṛṣṇa away in the presence of mother Yaśodā. But when Kṛṣṇa, high in the sky, assumed the *mahimā-siddhi,* the demon, unable to go further, was obliged to stop his force and come down according to Kṛṣṇa's desire. One should not, therefore, compete with Kṛṣṇa's mystic power.

Devotees automatically have all mystic power, but they do not like to compete with Kṛṣṇa. Instead, they fully surrender to Kṛṣṇa, and their yogic power is demonstrated by Kṛṣṇa's mercy. Devotees can show mystic *yoga* so powerful that a demon could not even dream of it, but they never try to demonstrate it for their personal sense gratification.

Whatever they do is for the service of the Lord, and therefore they are always in a position superior to that of the demons. There are many *karmīs*, *yogīs* and *jñānīs* who artificially try to compete with Kṛṣṇa, and thus ordinary, foolish people who do not care to hear *Śrīmad-Bhāgavatam* from authorities consider some rascal *yogī* to be Bhagavān, the Supreme Personality of Godhead. At the present moment there are many so-called *bābās* who present themselves as incarnations of God by showing some insignificant mystic wonder, and foolish people regard them as God because of lacking knowledge of Kṛṣṇa.

## TEXT 27

तमश्मानं मन्यमान आत्मनो गुरुमत्तया ।
गले गृहीत उत्स्रष्टुं नाशक्नोदद्भुतार्भकम् ॥२७॥

*tam aśmānaṁ manyamāna*
*ātmano guru-mattayā*
*gale gṛhīta utsraṣṭuṁ*
*nāśaknod adbhutārbhakam*

*tam*—Kṛṣṇa; *aśmānam*—very heavy stone like a lump of iron; *manyamānaḥ*—thinking like that; *ātmanaḥ guru-mattayā*—because of being heavier than he could personally perceive; *gale*—his neck; *gṛhīte*—being embraced or encircled by His arms; *utsraṣṭum*—to give up; *na aśaknot*—was not able; *adbhuta-arbhakam*—this wonderful child who was different from an ordinary child.

## TRANSLATION

**Because of Kṛṣṇa's weight, Tṛṇāvarta considered Him to be like a great mountain or a hunk of iron. But because Kṛṣṇa had caught the demon's neck, the demon was unable to throw Him off. He therefore thought of the child as wonderful, since he could neither bear the child nor cast aside the burden.**

## PURPORT

Tṛṇāvarta intended to take Kṛṣṇa up in the sky and kill Him, but Kṛṣṇa enjoyed the pastime of riding on Tṛṇāvarta's body and traveling for a while in the sky. Thus Tṛṇāvarta's attempt to kill Kṛṣṇa failed, while Kṛṣṇa, *ānanda-cinmaya-rasa-vigraha,* enjoyed this pastime. Now, since Tṛṇāvarta was falling because of Kṛṣṇa's heaviness, he wanted to save himself by throwing Kṛṣṇa off from his neck, but was unable to do so because Kṛṣṇa held him very tightly. Consequently, this would be the last time for Tṛṇāvarta's yogic power. Now he was going to die by the arrangement of Kṛṣṇa.

## TEXT 28

गलग्रहणनिश्चेष्टो दैत्यो निर्गतलोचनः ।
अव्यक्तरावो न्यपतत् सहबालो व्यसुर्व्रजे ॥२८॥

*gala-grahaṇa-niścesṭo*
*daityo nirgata-locanaḥ*
*avyakta-rāvo nyapatat*
*saha-bālo vyasur vraje*

*gala-grahaṇa-niśceṣṭaḥ*—because of Kṛṣṇa's grasping the neck of the demon Tṛṇāvarta, the demon choked and could not do anything; *daityaḥ*—the demon; *nirgata-locanaḥ*—his eyes popped out because of pressure; *avyakta-rāvaḥ*—because of choking, he could not even make a sound; *nyapatat*—fell down; *saha-bālaḥ*—with the child; *vyasuḥ vraje*—lifeless on the ground of Vraja.

## TRANSLATION

**With Kṛṣṇa grasping him by the throat, Tṛṇāvarta choked, unable to make even a sound or even to move his hands and legs. His eyes popping out, the demon lost his life and fell, along with the little boy, down to the ground of Vraja.**

## TEXT 29

तमन्तरिक्षात् पतितं शिलायां
विशीर्णसर्वावयवं करालम् ।
पुरं यथा रुद्रशरेण विद्धं
स्त्रियो रुदत्यो ददृशुः समेताः ॥२९॥

*tam antarikṣāt patitaṁ śilāyāṁ*
*viśīrṇa-sarvāvayavaṁ karālam*
*puraṁ yathā rudra-śareṇa viddhaṁ*
*striyo rudatyo dadṛśuḥ sametāḥ*

*tam*—unto the demon Tṛṇāvarta; *antarikṣāt*—from outer space; *patitam*—fallen; *śilāyām*—on a slab of stone; *viśīrṇa*—scattered, separated; *sarva-avayavam*—all the parts of his body; *karālam*—very fierce hands and legs; *puram*—the place of Tripurāsura; *yathā*—as; *rudra-śareṇa*—by the arrow of Lord Śiva; *viddham*—pierced; *striyaḥ*—all the women, the *gopīs; rudatyaḥ*—although crying because Kṛṣṇa was separated from them; *dadṛśuḥ*—they saw in front of them; *sametāḥ*—all together.

## TRANSLATION

**While the gopīs who had gathered were crying for Kṛṣṇa, the demon fell from the sky onto a big slab of stone, his limbs dislocated, as if he had been pierced by the arrow of Lord Śiva like Tripurāsura.**

## PURPORT

In transcendental life, as soon as devotees of the Lord merge in lamentation, they immediately experience the Lord's transcendental activities and merge in transcendental bliss. Actually such devotees are always in transcendental bliss, and such apparent calamities provide a further impetus for that bliss.

## TEXT 30

प्रादाय मात्रे प्रतिहृत्य विस्मिताः
कृष्णं च तस्योरसि लम्बमानम् ।
तं स्वस्तिमन्तं पुरुषादनीतं
विहायसा मृत्युमुखात् प्रमुक्तम् ।
गोप्यश्च गोपाः किल नन्दमुख्या
लब्ध्वा पुनः प्रापुरतीव मोदम् ॥३०॥

*prādāya mātre pratihṛtya vismitāḥ*
*kṛṣṇaṁ ca tasyorasi lambamānam*
*taṁ svastimantaṁ puruṣāda-nītaṁ*
*vihāyasā mṛtyu-mukhāt pramuktam*
*gopyaś ca gopāḥ kila nanda-mukhyā*
*labdhvā punaḥ prāpur atīva modam*

*prādāya*—after picking up; *mātre*—unto His mother (Yaśodā); *pratihṛtya*—delivered; *vismitāḥ*—all surprised; *kṛṣṇam ca*—and Kṛṣṇa; *tasya*—of the demon; *urasi*—on the chest; *lambamānam*—situated; *tam*—Kṛṣṇa; *svastimantam*—endowed with all auspiciousness; *puruṣa-ada-nītam*—who was taken by the man-eating demon; *vihāyasā*—into the sky; *mṛtyu-mukhāt*—from the mouth of death; *pramuktam*—now liberated; *gopyaḥ*—the *gopīs; ca*—and; *gopāḥ*—the cowherd men; *kila*—indeed; *nanda-mukhyāḥ*—headed by Nanda Mahārāja; *labdhvā*—after getting; *punaḥ*—again (their son); *prāpuḥ*—enjoyed; *atīva*—very much; *modam*—bliss.

## TRANSLATION

**The gopīs immediately picked Kṛṣṇa up from the chest of the demon and delivered Him, free from all inauspiciousness, to mother Yaśodā. Because the child, although taken into the sky by the demon, was unhurt and now free from all danger and misfortune, the gopīs and cowherd men, headed by Nanda Mahārāja, were extremely happy.**

## PURPORT

The demon fell flat from the sky, and Kṛṣṇa was playing on his chest very happily, uninjured and free from misfortune. Not at all disturbed because of being taken high in the sky by the demon, Kṛṣṇa was playing and enjoying. This is *ānanda-cinmaya-rasa-vigraha.* In any condition, Kṛṣṇa is *sac-cid-ānanda-vigraha.* He has no unhappiness. Others might have thought that He was in difficulty, but because the demon's chest was sufficiently broad to play on, the baby was happy in all respects. It was most astonishing that although the demon went so high in the sky, the child did not fall down. Therefore, the child had been saved virtually from the mouth of death. Now that He was saved, all the inhabitants of Vṛndāvana were happy.

### TEXT 31

अहो बतात्यद्भुतमेष रक्षसा
बालो निवृत्तिं गमितोऽभ्यगात् पुनः ।
हिंस्रः स्वपापेन विहिंसितः खलः
साधुः समत्वेन भयाद् विमुच्यते ॥३१॥

*aho batāty-adbhutam eṣa rakṣasā*
*bālo nivṛttiṁ gamito 'bhyagāt punaḥ*
*hiṁsraḥ sva-pāpena vihiṁsitaḥ khalaḥ*
*sādhuḥ samatvena bhayād vimucyate*

*aho*—alas; *bata*—indeed; *ati*—very much; *adbhutam*—this incident is wonderfully astonishing; *eṣaḥ*—this (child); *rakṣasā*—by the man-eating demon; *bālaḥ*—the innocent child Kṛṣṇa; *nivṛttim*—taken away just to be killed and eaten; *gamitaḥ*—went away; *abhyagāt punaḥ*—but He has come back again unhurt; *hiṁsraḥ*—one who is envious; *sva-pāpena*—because of his own sinful activities; *vihiṁsitaḥ*—now (that demon) has been killed; *khalaḥ*—because he was envious and polluted; *sādhuḥ*—any person who is innocent and free from sinful life; *samatvena*—being equal to everyone; *bhayāt*—from all kinds of fear; *vimucyate*—becomes relieved.

### TRANSLATION

**It is most astonishing that although this innocent child was taken away by the Rākṣasa to be eaten, He has returned without having been killed or even injured. Because this demon was envious, cruel and sinful, he has been killed for his own sinful activities. This is the law of nature. An innocent devotee is always protected by the Supreme Personality of Godhead, and a sinful person is always vanquished for his sinful life.**

### PURPORT

Kṛṣṇa conscious life means innocent devotional life, and a *sādhu* is one who is fully devoted to Kṛṣṇa. As confirmed by Kṛṣṇa in *Bhagavad-gītā*

(9.30), *bhajate māṁ ananya-bhāk sādhur eva sa mantavyaḥ:* anyone fully attached to Kṛṣṇa is a *sādhu.* Nanda Mahārāja and the *gopīs* and other cowherd men could not understand that Kṛṣṇa was the Supreme Personality of Godhead playing as a human child and that His life was not in danger under any circumstances. Rather, because of their intense parental love for Kṛṣṇa, they thought that Kṛṣṇa was an innocent child and had been saved by the Supreme Lord.

In the material world, because of intense lust and desire for enjoyment, one becomes implicated in sinful life more and more (*kāma eṣa krodha eṣa rajo-guṇa-samudbhavaḥ*). Therefore the quality of fear is one of the aspects of material life (*āhāra-nidrā-bhaya-maithunaṁ ca*). But if one becomes Kṛṣṇa conscious, the process of devotional service, *śravaṇaṁ kīrtanam,* diminishes one's polluted life of material existence, and one is purified and protected by the Supreme Personality of Godhead. *Śṛṇvatāṁ sva-kathāḥ kṛṣṇaḥ puṇya-śravaṇa-kīrtanaḥ.* In devotional life, one has faith in this process. Such faith is one of the six kinds of surrender. *Rakṣiṣyatīti viśvāsaḥ* (*Hari-bhakti-vilāsa* 11.676). One of the processes of surrender is that one should simply depend on Kṛṣṇa, convinced that He will give one all protection. That Kṛṣṇa will protect His devotee is a fact, and Nanda Mahārāja and the other inhabitants of Vṛndāvana accepted this very simply, although they did not know that the Supreme Lord Himself was present before them. There have been many instances in which a devotee like Prahlāda Mahārāja or Dhruva Mahārāja has been put in difficulty even by his father but has been saved under all circumstances. Therefore our only business is to become Kṛṣṇa conscious and depend fully on Kṛṣṇa for all protection.

## TEXT 32

किं नस्तपश्चीर्णमधोक्षजार्चनं
पूर्तेष्टदत्तमुत भूतसौहृदम् ।
यत्संपरेतः पुनरेव बालको
दिष्ट्या स्वबन्धून् प्रणयन्नुपस्थितः ॥३२॥

*kiṁ nas tapaś cīrṇam adhokṣajārcanaṁ*
*pūrteṣṭa-dattam uta bhūta-sauhṛdam*

*yat samparetaḥ punar eva bālako*
*diṣṭyā sva-bandhūn praṇayann upasthitaḥ*

*kim*—what kind of; *naḥ*—by us; *tapaḥ*—austerity; *cīrṇam*—has been done for a very long time; *adhokṣaja*—of the Supreme Personality of Godhead; *arcanam*—worshiping; *pūrta*—constructing public roads, etc.; *iṣṭa*—activities for public benefit; *dattam*—giving charity; *uta*—or else; *bhūta-sauhṛdam*—because of love for the general public; *yat*—by the result of which; *samparetaḥ*—even though the child was practically lost in death; *punaḥ eva*—even again because of pious activities; *bālakaḥ*—the child; *diṣṭyā*—by fortune; *sva-bandhūn*—all His relatives; *praṇayan*—to please; *upasthitaḥ*—is present here.

## TRANSLATION

**Nanda Mahārāja and the others said: We must previously have performed austerities for a very long time, worshiped the Supreme Personality of Godhead, performed pious activities for public life, constructing public roads and wells, and also given charity, as a result of which this boy, although faced with death, has returned to give happiness to His relatives.**

## PURPORT

Nanda Mahārāja confirmed that by pious activities one can become a *sādhu* so that one will be happy at home and one's children will be protected. In *śāstra* there are many injunctions for *karmīs* and *jñānīs*, especially for *karmīs*, by which they can become pious and happy even in material life. According to Vedic civilization, one should perform activities for the benefit of the public, such as constructing public roads, planting trees on both sides of the road so that people can walk in the shade, and constructing public wells so that everyone can take water without difficulty. One should perform austerity to control one's desires, and one must simultaneously worship the Supreme Personality of Godhead. Thus one becomes pious, and as a result one is happy even in material conditions of life.

## TEXT 33

दृष्ट्वाद्भुतानि बहुशो नन्दगोपो बृहद्वने ।
वसुदेववचो भूयो मानयामास विस्मितः ॥३३॥

*dṛṣṭvādbhutāni bahuśo*
*nanda-gopo bṛhadvane*
*vasudeva-vaco bhūyo*
*mānayām āsa vismitaḥ*

*dṛṣṭvā*—after seeing; *adbhutāni*—the very wonderful and astonishing incidents; *bahuśaḥ*—many times; *nanda-gopaḥ*—Nanda Mahārāja, the head of the cowherd men; *bṛhadvane*—in Bṛhadvana; *vasudeva-vacaḥ*—the words spoken by Vasudeva when Nanda Mahārāja was in Mathurā; *bhūyaḥ*—again and again; *mānayām āsa*—accepted how true they were; *vismitaḥ*—in great astonishment.

## TRANSLATION

**Having seen all these incidents in Bṛhadvana, Nanda Mahārāja became more and more astonished, and he remembered the words spoken to him by Vasudeva in Mathurā.**

## TEXT 34

एकदार्भकमादाय स्वाङ्कमारोप्य भामिनी ।
प्रस्नुतं पाययामास स्तनं स्नेहपरिप्लुता ॥३४॥

*ekadārbhakam ādāya*
*svāṅkam āropya bhāminī*
*prasnutaṁ pāyayām āsa*
*stanaṁ sneha-pariplutā*

*ekadā*—once upon a time; *arbhakam*—the child; *ādāya*—taking; *sva-aṅkam*—on her own lap; *āropya*—and placing Him; *bhāminī*—mother Yaśodā; *prasnutam*—breast milk oozing out; *pāyayām āsa*—fed the child; *stanam*—her breast; *sneha-pariplutā*—with great affection and love.

## TRANSLATION

**One day mother Yaśodā, having taken Kṛṣṇa up and placed Him on her lap, was feeding Him milk from her breast with maternal affection. The milk was flowing from her breast, and the child was drinking it.**

## TEXTS 35–36

पीतप्रायस्य जननी सुतस्य रुचिरस्मितम् ।
मुखं लालयती राजञ्जृम्भतो ददृशे इदम् ॥३५॥
खं रोदसी ज्योतिरनीकमाशाः
सूर्येन्दुवह्निश्वसनाम्बुधींश्च ।
द्वीपान् नगांस्तद्दुहितॄर्वनानि
भूतानि यानि स्थिरजङ्गमानि ॥३६॥

*pīta-prāyasya jananī*
*sutasya rucira-smitam*
*mukhaṁ lālayatī rājañ*
*jṛmbhato dadṛśe idam*

*khaṁ rodasī jyotir-anīkam āśāḥ*
*sūryendu-vahni-śvasanāmbudhīṁś ca*
*dvīpān nagāṁs tad-duhitṝr vanāni*
*bhūtāni yāni sthira-jaṅgamāni*

*pīta-prāyasya*—of child Kṛṣṇa, who was being offered breast milk and was almost satisfied; *jananī*—mother Yaśodā; *sutasya*—of her son; *rucira-smitam*—seeing the child fully satisfied and smiling; *mukham*—the face; *lālayatī*—patting and softly rubbing with her hand; *rājan*—O King; *jṛmbhataḥ*—while the child was yawning; *dadṛśe*—she saw; *idam*—the following; *kham*—the sky; *rodasī*—both the higher planetary system and the earth; *jyotiḥ-anīkam*—the luminaries; *āśāḥ*—the directions; *sūrya*—the sun; *indu*—the moon; *vahni*—fire; *śvasana*—the air; *ambudhīn*—the seas; *ca*—and; *dvīpān*—the islands; *nagān*—the mountains; *tat-duhitṝḥ*—the daughters of the mountains (the rivers); *vanāni*—forests; *bhūtāni*—all kinds of living entities; *yāni*—which are; *sthira-jaṅgamāni*—nonmoving and moving.

## TRANSLATION

**O King Parīkṣit, when the child Kṛṣṇa was almost finished drinking His mother's milk and mother Yaśodā was touching Him and looking at His beautiful, brilliantly smiling face, the baby yawned, and mother Yaśodā saw in His mouth the whole sky, the higher planetary system and the earth, the luminaries in all directions, the sun, the moon, fire, air, the seas, islands, mountains, rivers, forests, and all kinds of living entities, moving and nonmoving.**

## PURPORT

By the arrangement of *yogamāyā,* Kṛṣṇa's pastimes with mother Yaśodā were all regarded as ordinary. So here was an opportunity for Kṛṣṇa to show His mother that the whole universe is situated within Him. In His small form, Kṛṣṇa was kind enough to show His mother the *virāṭ-rūpa*, the universal form, so that she could enjoy seeing what kind of child she had on her lap. The rivers have been mentioned here as the daughters of the mountains (*nagāṁs tad-duhitṝḥ*). It is the flowing of the rivers that makes big forests possible. There are living entities everywhere, some of them moving and some of them not moving. No place is vacant. This is a special feature of God's creation.

## TEXT 37

सा वीक्ष्य विश्वं सहसा राजन् सञ्जातवेपथुः ।
सम्मील्य मृगशावाक्षी नेत्रे आसीत् सुविस्मिता ॥३७॥

*sā vīkṣya viśvaṁ sahasā*
*rājan sañjāta-vepathuḥ*
*sammīlya mṛgaśāvākṣī*
*netre āsīt suvismitā*

*sā*—mother Yaśodā; *vīkṣya*—by seeing; *viśvam*—the whole universe; *sahasā*—suddenly within the mouth of her son; *rājan*—O King

(Mahārāja Parīkṣit); *sañjāta-vepathuḥ*—whose heart was beating; *sammīlya*—opening; *mṛgaśāva-akṣī*—like the eyes of a deer cub; *netre*—her two eyes; *āsīt*—became; *su-vismitā*—astonished.

## TRANSLATION

**When mother Yaśodā saw the whole universe within the mouth of her child, her heart began to throb, and in astonishment she wanted to close her restless eyes.**

## PURPORT

Because of her pure maternal love, mother Yaśodā thought that this wonderful child playing so many tricks must have had some disease. She did not appreciate the wonders shown by her child; rather, she wanted to close her eyes. She was expecting another danger, and therefore her eyes became restless like those of a deer cub. This was all the arrangement of *yogamāyā*. The relationship between mother Yaśodā and Kṛṣṇa is one of pure maternal love. In that love, mother Yaśodā did not very much appreciate the display of the Supreme Personality of Godhead's opulences.

At the beginning of this chapter, two extra verses sometimes appear:

*evaṁ bahūni karmāṇi*
*gopānāṁ śaṁ sa-yoṣitām*
*nandasya gehe vavṛdhe*
*kurvan viṣṇu-janārdanaḥ*

"In this way, to chastise and kill the demons, the child Kṛṣṇa demonstrated many activities in the house of Nanda Mahārāja, and the inhabitants of Vraja enjoyed these incidents."

*evaṁ sa vavṛdhe viṣṇur*
*nanda-gehe janārdanaḥ*
*kurvann aniśam ānandaṁ*
*gopālānāṁ sa-yoṣitām*

"To increase the transcendental pleasure of the *gopas* and the *gopīs*, Kṛṣṇa, the killer of all demons, was thus raised by His father and mother, Nanda and Yaśodā."

Śrīpāda Vijayadhvaja Tīrtha also adds another verse after the third verse in this chapter:

*vistareṇeha kāruṇyāt*
*sarva-pāpa-praṇāśanam*
*vaktum arhasi dharma-jña*
*dayālus tvam iti prabho*

"Parīkṣit Mahārāja then requested Śukadeva Gosvāmī to continue speaking such narrations about the pastimes of Kṛṣṇa, so that the King could enjoy from them transcendental bliss."

*Thus end the Bhaktivedanta purports of the Tenth Canto, Seventh Chapter, of the* Śrīmad-Bhāgavatam, *entitled "The Killing of the Demon Tṛṇāvarta."*

# CHAPTER EIGHT

# Lord Kṛṣṇa Shows the Universal Form Within His Mouth

The summary of the Eighth Chapter is as follows. This chapter describes the ceremony of giving a name to Kṛṣṇa. It also describes His crawling, His playing with the cows, and His eating earth and again showing the universal form to His mother.

One day, Vasudeva sent for Gargamuni, the family priest of the *yadu-vaṁśa,* and thus Gargamuni went to the house of Nanda Mahārāja, who received him very well and requested him to give names to Kṛṣṇa and Balarāma. Gargamuni, of course, reminded Nanda Mahārāja that Kaṁsa was looking for the son of Devakī and said that if he performed the ceremony very gorgeously, the ceremony would come to the notice of Kaṁsa, who would then suspect that Kṛṣṇa was the son of Devakī. Nanda Mahārāja therefore requested Gargamuni to perform this ceremony without anyone's knowledge, and Gargamuni did so. Because Balarāma, the son of Rohiṇī, increases the transcendental bliss of others, His name is Rāma, and because of His extraordinary strength, He is called Baladeva. He attracts the Yadus to follow His instructions, and therefore His name is Saṅkarṣaṇa. Kṛṣṇa, the son of Yaśodā, previously appeared in many other colors, such as white, red and yellow, and He had now assumed the color black. Because He was sometimes the son of Vasudeva, His name is Vāsudeva. According to His various activities and qualities, He has many other names. After thus informing Nanda Mahārāja and completing the name-giving ceremony, Gargamuni advised Nanda Mahārāja to protect his son very carefully and then departed.

Śukadeva Gosvāmī next described how the two children crawled, walked on Their small legs, played with the cows and calves, stole butter and other milk products and broke the butter pots. In this way, he described many naughty activities of Kṛṣṇa and Balarāma. The most wonderful of these occurred when Kṛṣṇa's playmates complained to mother Yaśodā that Kṛṣṇa was eating earth. Mother Yaśodā wanted to open

Kṛṣṇa's mouth to see the evidence so that she could chastise Him. Sometimes she assumed the position of a chastising mother, and at the next moment she was overwhelmed with maternal love. After describing all this to Mahārāja Parīkṣit, Śukadeva Gosvāmī, at Mahārāja Parīkṣit's request, praised the fortune of mother Yaśodā and Nanda. Nanda and Yaśodā were formerly Droṇa and Dharā, and by the order of Brahmā they came to this earth and had the Supreme Personality of Godhead as their son.

## TEXT 1

श्रीशुक उवाच

गर्गः पुरोहितो राजन् यदूनां सुमहातपाः ।
व्रजं जगाम नन्दस्य वसुदेवप्रचोदितः ॥ १ ॥

*śrī-śuka uvāca*
*gargaḥ purohito rājan*
*yadūnāṁ sumahā-tapāḥ*
*vrajaṁ jagāma nandasya*
*vasudeva-pracoditaḥ*

*śrī-śukaḥ uvāca*—Śrī Śukadeva Gosvāmī said; *gargaḥ*—Gargamuni; *purohitaḥ*—the priest; *rājan*—O King Parīkṣit; *yadūnām*—of the Yadu dynasty; *su-mahā-tapāḥ*—highly elevated in austerity and penance; *vrajam*—to the village known as Vrajabhūmi; *jagāma*—went; *nandasya*—of Mahārāja Nanda; *vasudeva-pracoditaḥ*—being inspired by Vasudeva.

## TRANSLATION

**Śukadeva Gosvāmī said: O Mahārāja Parīkṣit, the priest of the Yadu dynasty, namely Gargamuni, who was highly elevated in austerity and penance, was then inspired by Vasudeva to go see Nanda Mahārāja at his home.**

## TEXT 2

तं दृष्ट्वा परमप्रीतः प्रत्युत्थाय कृताञ्जलिः ।
आनर्चाधोक्षजधिया प्रणिपातपुरःसरम् ॥ २ ॥

*taṁ dṛṣṭvā parama-prītaḥ*
*pratyutthāya kṛtāñjaliḥ*
*ānarcādhokṣaja-dhiyā*
*praṇipāta-puraḥsaram*

*tam*—him (Gargamuni); *dṛṣṭvā*—after seeing; *parama-prītaḥ*—Nanda Mahārāja was very much pleased; *pratyutthāya*—standing up to receive him; *kṛta-añjaliḥ*—with folded hands; *ānarca*—worshiped; *adhokṣaja-dhiyā*—although Gargamuni was visible to the senses, Nanda Mahārāja maintained a very high respect for him; *praṇipāta-puraḥsaram*—Nanda Mahārāja fell down before him and offered obeisances.

## TRANSLATION

**When Nanda Mahārāja saw Gargamuni present at his home, Nanda was so pleased that he stood up to receive him with folded hands. Although seeing Gargamuni with his eyes, Nanda Mahārāja could appreciate that Gargamuni was adhokṣaja; that is, he was not an ordinary person seen by material senses.**

## TEXT 3

सूपविष्टं कृतातिथ्यं गिरा सूनृतया मुनिम् ।
नन्दयित्वाब्रवीद् ब्रह्मन् पूर्णस्य करवाम किम् ॥ ३ ॥

*sūpaviṣṭaṁ kṛtātithyaṁ*
*girā sūnṛtayā munim*
*nandayitvābravīd brahman*
*pūrṇasya karavāma kim*

*su-upaviṣṭam*—when Gargamuni was seated very comfortably; *kṛta-ātithyam*—and he had been properly received as a guest; *girā*—by words; *sūnṛtayā*—very sweet; *munim*—Gargamuni; *nandayitvā*—pleasing him in this way; *abravīt*—said; *brahman*—O *brāhmaṇa; pūrṇasya*—of one who is full in everything; *karavāma kim*—what can I do for you (kindly order me).

## TRANSLATION

**When Gargamuni had been properly received as a guest and was very comfortably seated, Nanda Mahārāja submitted with gentle and submissive words: Dear sir, because you are a devotee, you are full in everything. Yet my duty is to serve you. Kindly order me. What can I do for you?**

## TEXT 4

महद्विचलनं नृणां गृहिणां दीनचेतसाम् ।
निःश्रेयसाय भगवन् कल्पते नान्यथा क्वचित् ॥ ४ ॥

*mahad-vicalanaṁ nṛṇāṁ*
*gṛhiṇāṁ dīna-cetasām*
*niḥśreyasāya bhagavan*
*kalpate nānyathā kvacit*

*mahat-vicalanam*—the movement of great personalities; *nṛṇām*—in the houses of ordinary persons; *gṛhiṇām*—especially householders; *dīna-cetasām*—who are very simple-minded, being engaged in family maintenance and nothing more; *niḥśreyasāya*—a great personality has no reason to go to the *gṛhastha* but to benefit him; *bhagavan*—O most powerful devotee; *kalpate*—is to be taken that way; *na anyathā*—not for any other purpose; *kvacit*—at any time.

## TRANSLATION

**O my lord, O great devotee, persons like you move from one place to another not for their own interests but for the sake of poor-hearted gṛhasthas [householders]. Otherwise they have no interest in going from one place to another.**

## PURPORT

As factually stated by Nanda Mahārāja, Gargamuni, being a devotee, had no needs. Similarly, when Kṛṣṇa comes He has no needs, for He is *pūrṇa, ātmārāma*. Nonetheless, He descends to this material world to protect the devotees and vanquish miscreants (*paritrāṇāya sādhūnām vināśāya ca duṣkṛtām*). This is the mission of the Supreme Personality of Godhead, and devotees also have the same mission. One who executes this mission of *para-upakāra*, performing welfare activities for people in general, is recognized by Kṛṣṇa, the Supreme Personality of Godhead, as being very, very dear to Him (*na ca tasmān manuṣyeṣu kaścin me priya-kṛttamaḥ*). Similarly, Caitanya Mahāprabhu has advised this *para-upakāra*, and He has especially advised the inhabitants of India:

*bhārata-bhūmite haila manuṣya-janma yāra*
*janma sārthaka kari' kara para-upakāra*

"One who has taken his birth as a human being in the land of India [Bhāratavarṣa] should make his life successful and work for the benefit of all other people." (Cc. *Ādi.* 9.41) On the whole, the duty of a pure Vaiṣṇava devotee is to act for the welfare of others.

Nanda Mahārāja could understand that Gargamuni had come for this purpose and that his own duty now was to act according to Gargamuni's advice. Thus he said, "Please tell me what is my duty." This should be the attitude of everyone, especially the householder. The *varṇāśrama* society is organized into eight divisions: *brāhmaṇa, kṣatriya, vaiśya, śūdra, brahmacarya, gṛhastha, vānaprastha* and *sannyāsa.* Nanda Mahārāja represented himself as *gṛhiṇām*, a householder. A *brahmacārī* factually has no needs, but *gṛhī*, householders, are engaged in sense gratification. As stated in *Bhagavad-gītā* (2.44), *bhogaiśvarya-prasaktānāṁ tayāpahṛta-cetasām.* Everyone has come to this material world for sense gratification, and the position of those who are too attached to sense gratification and who therefore accept the *gṛhastha-āśrama* is very precarious. Since everyone in this material world is searching for sense gratification, *gṛhasthas* are required to be trained as *mahat*, great *mahātmās.* Therefore Nanda Mahārāja specifically used the word *mahad-vicalanam.* Gargamuni had no interest to serve by going to Nanda Mahārāja, but Nanda Mahārāja, as a *gṛhastha*, was always perfectly ready to receive instructions from a *mahātmā* to gain the real benefit in life. Thus he was ready to execute Gargamuni's order.

## TEXT 5

ज्योतिषामयनं साक्षाद् यत्तज्ज्ञानमतीन्द्रियम् ।
प्रणीतं भवता येन पुमान् वेद परावरम् ॥ ५ ॥

*jyotiṣām ayanaṁ sākṣād*
*yat taj jñānam atīndriyam*
*praṇītaṁ bhavatā yena*
*pumān veda parāvaram*

*jyotiṣām*—knowledge of astrology (along with other aspects of culture in human society, and specifically in civilized society, there must be knowledge of astrology); *ayanam*—the movements of the stars and planets in relationship to human society; *sākṣāt*—directly; *yat tat jñānam*—such knowledge; *ati-indriyam*—which an ordinary person cannot understand because it is beyond his vision; *praṇītam bhavatā*—you have prepared a perfect book of knowledge; *yena*—by which; *pumān*—any person; *veda*—can understand; *para-avaram*—the cause and effect of destiny.

## TRANSLATION

**O great saintly person, you have compiled the astrological knowledge by which one can understand past and present unseen things. By the strength of this knowledge, any human being can understand what he has done in his past life and how it affects his present life. This is known to you.**

## PURPORT

The word "destiny" is now defined. Unintelligent persons who do not understand the meaning of life are just like animals. Animals do not know the past, present and future of life, nor are they able to understand it. But a human being can understand this, if he is sober. Therefore, as stated in *Bhagavad-gītā* (2.13), *dhīras tatra na muhyati:* a sober person is not bewildered. The simple truth is that although life is eternal, in this material world one changes from one body to another. Foolish people, especially in this age, do not understand this simple truth. Kṛṣṇa says:

*dehino 'smin yathā dehe*
*kaumāraṁ yauvanaṁ jarā*
*tathā dehāntara-prāptir*
*dhīras tatra na muhyati*

"As the embodied soul continually passes, in this body, from boyhood to youth to old age, the soul similarly passes into another body at death. The self-realized soul is not bewildered by such a change." (Bg. 2.13) Kṛṣṇa, the greatest authority, says that the body will change. And as soon as the body changes, one's whole program of work changes also. Today I am a human being or a great personality, but with a little deviation from nature's law, I shall have to accept a different type of body. Today I am a human being, but tomorrow I may become a dog, and then whatever activities I have performed in this life will be a failure. This simple truth is now rarely understood, but one who is a *dhīra* can understand this. Those in this material world for material enjoyment should know that because their present position will cease to exist, they must be careful in how they act. This is also stated by Ṛṣabhadeva. *Na sādhu manye yata ātmano 'yam asann api kleśada āsa dehaḥ* (*Bhāg.* 5.5.4). Although this body is temporary, as long as we have to live in this body we must suffer. Whether one has a short life or a long life, one must suffer the threefold miseries of material life. Therefore any gentleman, *dhīra*, must be interested in *jyotiṣa*, astrology.

Nanda Mahārāja was trying to take advantage of the opportunity afforded by Gargamuni's presence, for Gargamuni was a great authority in this knowledge of astrology, by which one can see the unseen events of past, present and future. It is the duty of a father to understand the astrological position of his children and do what is needed for their happiness. Now, taking advantage of the opportunity afforded by the presence of Gargamuni, Nanda Mahārāja suggested that Gargamuni prepare a horoscope for Nanda's two sons, Kṛṣṇa and Balarāma.

## TEXT 6

त्वं हि ब्रह्मविदां श्रेष्ठः संस्कारान् कर्तुमर्हसि ।
बालयोरनयोर्नॄणां जन्मना ब्राह्मणो गुरुः ॥ ६ ॥

*tvaṁ hi brahma-vidāṁ śreṣṭhaḥ*
*saṁskārān kartum arhasi*
*bālayor anayor nṝṇāṁ*
*janmanā brāhmaṇo guruḥ*

*tvam*—Your Holiness; *hi*—indeed; *brahma-vidām*—of all *brāhmaṇas*, or persons who understand what is Brahman (*brahma jānātīti brāhmaṇaḥ*); *śreṣṭhaḥ*—you are the best; *saṁskārān*—ceremonies performed for reformation (because by these reformatory activities one takes one's second birth: *saṁskārād bhaved dvijaḥ*); *kartum arhasi*—because you have kindly come here, kindly execute; *bālayoḥ*—of these two sons (Kṛṣṇa and Balarāma); *anayoḥ*—of both of Them; *nṛṇām*—not only of Them, but of all human society; *janmanā*—as soon as he takes birth; *brāhmaṇaḥ*—immediately the *brāhmaṇa* becomes; *guruḥ*—the guide.*

## TRANSLATION

**My lord, you are the best of the brāhmaṇas, especially because you are fully aware of the jyotiḥ-śāstra, the astrological science. Therefore you are naturally the spiritual master of every human being. This being so, since you have kindly come to my house, kindly execute the reformatory activities for my two sons.**

## PURPORT

The Supreme Personality of Godhead, Kṛṣṇa, says in *Bhagavad-gītā* (4.13), *cātur-varṇyaṁ mayā sṛṣṭaṁ guṇa-karma-vibhāgaśaḥ:* the four *varṇas*—*brāhmaṇa, kṣatriya, vaiśya* and *śūdra*—must be present in society. The *brāhmaṇas* are required for the guidance of the whole society. If there is no such institution as *varṇāśrama-dharma* and if human society has no such guide as the *brāhmaṇa*, human society will be hellish. In Kali-yuga, especially at the present moment, there is no such thing as a real *brāhmaṇa*, and therefore society is in a chaotic condition. Formerly there were qualified *brāhmaṇas*, but at present, although there are certainly persons who think themselves *brāhmaṇas*, they actually have no ability to guide society. The Kṛṣṇa consciousness movement is therefore very much eager to reintroduce the *varṇāśrama* system into human society so that those who are bewildered or less intelligent will be able to take guidance from qualified *brāhmaṇas*.

*Brāhmaṇa* means Vaiṣṇava. After one becomes a *brāhmaṇa*, the next stage of development in human society is to become a Vaiṣṇava. People

---

*The *śāstras* enjoin, *tad-vijñānārthaṁ sa gurum evābhigacchet* (*Muṇḍaka Upaniṣad* 1.2.12). It is the duty of everyone to approach a *brāhmaṇa* as the *guru*.

in general must be guided to the destination or goal of life, and therefore they must understand Viṣṇu, the Supreme Personality of Godhead. The whole system of Vedic knowledge is based on this principle, but people have lost the clue (*na te viduḥ svārtha-gatiṁ hi viṣṇum*), and they are simply pursuing sense gratification, with the risk of gliding down to a lower grade of life (*mṛtyu-saṁsāra-vartmani*). It doesn't matter whether one is born a *brāhmaṇa* or not. No one is born a *brāhmaṇa;* everyone is born a *śūdra.* But by the guidance of a *brāhmaṇa* and by *saṁskāra,* one can become *dvija,* twice-born, and then gradually become a *brāhmaṇa.* Brahmanism is not a system meant to create a monopoly for a particular class of men. Everyone should be educated so as to become a *brāhmaṇa.* At least there must be an opportunity to allow everyone to attain the destination of life. Regardless of whether one is born in a *brāhmaṇa* family, a *kṣatriya* family or a *śūdra* family, one may be guided by a proper *brāhmaṇa* and be promoted to the highest platform of being a Vaiṣṇava. Thus the Kṛṣṇa consciousness movement affords an opportunity to develop the right destiny for human society. Nanda Mahārāja took advantage of the opportunity of Gargamuni's presence by requesting him to perform the necessary reformatory activities for his sons to guide Them toward the destination of life.

## TEXT 7

श्रीगर्ग उवाच

यदूनामहमाचार्यः ख्यातश्च भुवि सर्वदा ।
सुतं मया संस्कृतं ते मन्यते देवकीसुतम् ॥ ७ ॥

*śrī-garga uvāca*
*yadūnām aham ācāryaḥ*
*khyātaś ca bhuvi sarvadā*
*sutaṁ mayā saṁskṛtaṁ te*
*manyate devakī-sutam*

*śrī-gargaḥ uvāca*—Gargamuni said; *yadūnām*—of the Yadu dynasty; *aham*—I am; *ācāryaḥ*—the priestly guide, or *purohita; khyātaḥ ca*—this is already known; *bhuvi*—everywhere; *sarvadā*—always; *sutam*—the son; *mayā*—by me; *saṁskṛtam*—having undergone the purificatory process; *te*—of you; *manyate*—would be considered; *devakī-sutam*—the son of Devakī.

## TRANSLATION

**Gargamuni said: My dear Nanda Mahārāja, I am the priestly guide of the Yadu dynasty. This is known everywhere. Therefore, if I perform the purificatory process for your sons, Kaṁsa will consider Them the sons of Devakī.**

## PURPORT

Gargamuni indirectly disclosed that Kṛṣṇa was the son of Devakī, not of Yaśodā. Since Kaṁsa was already searching for Kṛṣṇa, if the purificatory process were undertaken by Gargamuni, Kaṁsa might be informed, and that would create a catastrophe. It may be argued that although Gargamuni was the priest of the Yadu dynasty, Nanda Mahārāja also belonged to that dynasty. Nanda Mahārāja, however, was not acting as a *kṣatriya*. Therefore Gargamuni said, "If I act as your priest, this will confirm that Kṛṣṇa is the son of Devakī."

## TEXTS 8–9

कंसः पापमतिः सख्यं तव चानकदुन्दुभेः ।
देवक्या अष्टमो गर्भो न स्त्री भवितुमर्हति ॥८॥
इति सञ्चिन्तयञ्छ्रुत्वा देवक्या दारिकावचः ।
अपि हन्ता गताशङ्कस्तर्हि तन्नोऽनयो भवेत् ॥९॥

*kaṁsaḥ pāpa-matiḥ sakhyaṁ*
*tava cānakadundubheḥ*
*devakyā aṣṭamo garbho*
*na strī bhavitum arhati*

*iti sañcintayañ chrutvā*
*devakyā dārikā-vacaḥ*
*api hantā gatāśaṅkas*
*tarhi tan no 'nayo bhavet*

*kaṁsaḥ*—King Kaṁsa; *pāpa-matiḥ*—very, very sinful, having a polluted mind; *sakhyam*—friendship; *tava*—your; *ca*—also; *ānaka-dundubheḥ*—of Vasudeva; *devakyāḥ*—of Devakī; *aṣṭamaḥ garbhaḥ*—the eighth pregnancy; *na*—not; *strī*—a woman; *bhavitum arhati*—is possible to be; *iti*—in this way; *sañcintayan*—considering; *śrutvā*—and hearing (this news); *devakyāḥ*—of Devakī; *dārikā-vacaḥ*—the message from the daughter; *api*—although there was; *hantā gata-āśaṅkaḥ*—there is a possibility that Kaṁsa would take steps to kill this child; *tarhi*—therefore; *tat*—that incident; *naḥ*—for us; *anayaḥ bhavet*—may not be very good.

## TRANSLATION

**Kaṁsa is both a great diplomat and a very sinful man. Therefore, having heard from Yogamāyā, the daughter of Devakī, that the child who will kill him has already been born somewhere else, having heard that the eighth pregnancy of Devakī could not bring forth a female child, and having understood your friendship with Vasudeva, Kaṁsa, upon hearing that the purificatory process has been performed by me, the priest of the Yadu dynasty, may certainly consider all these points and suspect that Kṛṣṇa is the son of Devakī and Vasudeva. Then he might take steps to kill Kṛṣṇa. That would be a catastrophe.**

## PURPORT

Kaṁsa knew very well that Yogamāyā was, after all, the maidservant of Kṛṣṇa and Viṣṇu and that although Yogamāyā had appeared as the daughter of Devakī, she might have been forbidden to disclose this fact. Actually this was what had happened. Gargamuni argued very soberly that his taking part in performing the reformatory process for Kṛṣṇa would give rise to many doubts, so that Kaṁsa might take very severe steps to kill the child. Kaṁsa had already sent many demons to attempt to kill this child, but none of them had survived. If Gargamuni were to perform the purificatory process, Kaṁsa's suspicions would be fully confirmed, and he would take very severe steps. Gargamuni gave this warning to Nanda Mahārāja.

### TEXT 10

श्रीनन्द उवाच
अलक्षितोऽस्मिन् रहसि मामकैरपि गोव्रजे ।
कुरु द्विजातिसंस्कारं स्वस्तिवाचनपूर्वकम् ॥१०॥

*śrī-nanda uvāca*
*alakṣito 'smin rahasi*
*māmakair api go-vraje*
*kuru dvijāti-saṁskāraṁ*
*svasti-vācana-pūrvakam*

*śrī-nandaḥ uvāca*—Nanda Mahārāja said (to Gargamuni); *alakṣitaḥ*—without Kaṁsa's knowledge; *asmin*—in this cow shed; *rahasi*—in a very solitary place; *māmakaiḥ*—even by my relatives; *api*—a still more secluded place; *go-vraje*—in the cow shed; *kuru*—just execute; *dvijāti-saṁskāram*—the purificatory process of second birth (*saṁskārād bhaved dvijaḥ*); *svasti-vācana-pūrvakam*—by chanting the Vedic hymns to perform the purificatory process.

### TRANSLATION

**Nanda Mahārāja said: My dear great sage, if you think that your performing this process of purification will make Kaṁsa suspicious, then secretly chant the Vedic hymns and perform the purifying process of second birth here in the cow shed of my house, without the knowledge of anyone else, even my relatives, for this process of purification is essential.**

### PURPORT

Nanda Mahārāja did not like the idea of avoiding the purificatory process. Despite the many obstacles, he wanted to take advantage of Gargamuni's presence and do what was needed. The purificatory process is essential specifically for *brāhmaṇas, kṣatriyas* and *vaiśyas.* Therefore, since Nanda Mahārāja presented himself as a *vaiśya,* this process of purification was essential. Formerly, such institutional activities were compulsory. *Cātur-varṇyaṁ mayā sṛṣṭaṁ guṇa-karma-vibhāgaśaḥ*

(Bg. 4.13). Without these activities of purification, the society would be considered a society of animals. To take advantage of Gargamuni's presence, Nanda Mahārāja wanted to perform the *nāma-karaṇa* ceremonies, even secretly, without any gorgeous arrangements. Therefore, the opportunity for purification should be regarded as the essential duty of human society. In Kali-yuga, however, people have forgotten the essence. *Mandāḥ sumanda-matayo manda-bhāgyā hy upadrutāḥ* (*Bhāg.* 1.1.10). In this age, people are all bad and unfortunate, and they do not accept Vedic instructions to make their life successful. Nanda Mahārāja, however, did not want to neglect anything. To keep intact a happy society advanced in spiritual knowledge, he took full advantage of Gargamuni's presence to do what was necessary. How degraded society has become within five thousand years. *Mandāḥ sumanda-matayo manda-bhāgyāḥ.* The human life is obtained after many, many millions of births, and it is intended for purification. Previously, a father was eager to give all kinds of help to elevate his children, but at present, because of being misguided, people are prepared even to kill to avoid the responsibility of raising children.

## TEXT 11

श्रीशुक उवाच
एवं सम्प्रार्थितो विप्रः स्वचिकीर्षितमेव तत् ।
चकार नामकरणं गूढो रहसि बालयोः ॥११॥

*śrī-śuka uvāca*
*evaṁ samprārthito vipraḥ*
*sva-cikīrṣitam eva tat*
*cakāra nāma-karaṇaṁ*
*gūḍho rahasi bālayoḥ*

*śrī-śukaḥ uvāca*—Śrī Śukadeva Gosvāmī said; *evam*—in this way; *samprārthitaḥ*—being eagerly requested; *vipraḥ*—the *brāhmaṇa* Gargamuni; *sva-cikīrṣitam eva*—which he already desired to do and for which he had gone there; *tat*—that; *cakāra*—performed; *nāma-karaṇam*—the name-giving ceremony; *gūḍhaḥ*—confidentially; *rahasi*—in a secluded place; *bālayoḥ*—of the two boys (Kṛṣṇa and Balarāma).

## TRANSLATION

**Śukadeva Gosvāmī continued: Having thus been especially requested by Nanda Mahārāja to do that which he already desired to do, Gargamuni performed the name-giving ceremony for Kṛṣṇa and Balarāma in a solitary place.**

## TEXT 12

श्रीगर्ग उवाच
अयं हि रोहिणीपुत्रो रमयन् सुहृदो गुणैः ।
आख्यास्यते राम इति बलाधिक्याद् बलं विदुः ।
यदूनामपृथग्भावात् सङ्कर्षणमुशन्त्यपि ॥१२॥

*śrī-garga uvāca*
*ayaṁ hi rohiṇī-putro*
*ramayan suhṛdo guṇaiḥ*
*ākhyāsyate rāma iti*
*balādhikyād balaṁ viduḥ*
*yadūnām apṛthag-bhāvāt*
*saṅkarṣaṇam uśanty api*

*śrī-gargaḥ uvāca*—Gargamuni said; *ayam*—this; *hi*—indeed; *rohiṇī-putraḥ*—the son of Rohiṇī; *ramayan*—pleasing; *suhṛdaḥ*—all His friends and relatives; *guṇaiḥ*—by transcendental qualities; *ākhyāsyate*—will be called; *rāmaḥ*—by the name Rāma, the supreme enjoyer; *iti*—in this way; *bala-ādhikyāt*—because of extraordinary strength; *balam viduḥ*—will be known as Balarāma; *yadūnām*—of the Yadu dynasty; *apṛthak-bhāvāt*—because of not being separated from you; *saṅkarṣaṇam*—by the name Saṅkarṣaṇa, or uniting two families; *uśanti*—attracts; *api*—also.

## TRANSLATION

**Gargamuni said: This child, the son of Rohiṇī, will give all happiness to His relatives and friends by His transcendental qualities. Therefore He will be known as Rāma. And because He will manifest extraordinary bodily strength, He will also be known as**

**Bala. Moreover, because He unites two families—Vasudeva's family and the family of Nanda Mahārāja—He will be known as Saṅkarṣaṇa.**

## PURPORT

Baladeva was actually the son of Devakī, but He was transferred from Devakī's womb to that of Rohiṇī. This fact was not disclosed. According to a statement in the *Hari-vaṁśa:*

*pratyuvāca tato rāmaḥ*
*sarvāṁs tān abhitaḥ sthitān*
*yādaveṣv api sarveṣu*
*bhavanto mama vallabhāḥ*

Gargamuni did disclose to Nanda Mahārāja that Balarāma would be known as Saṅkarṣaṇa because of uniting two families—the *yadu-vaṁśa* and the *vaṁśa* of Nanda Mahārāja—one of which was known as *kṣatriya* and the other as *vaiśya.* Both families had the same original forefather, the only difference being that Nanda Mahārāja was born of a *vaiśya* wife whereas Vasudeva was born of a *kṣatriya* wife. Later, Nanda Mahārāja married a *vaiśya* wife, and Vasudeva married a *kṣatriya* wife. So although the families of Nanda Mahārāja and Vasudeva both came from the same father, they were divided as *kṣatriya* and *vaiśya.* Now Baladeva united them, and therefore He was known as Saṅkarṣaṇa.

## TEXT 13

आसन् वर्णास्त्रयो ह्यस्य गृह्णतोऽनुयुगं तनूः ।
शुक्लो रक्तस्तथा पीत इदानीं कृष्णतां गतः ॥१३॥

*āsan varṇās trayo hy asya*
*gṛhṇato 'nuyugaṁ tanūḥ*
*śuklo raktas tathā pīta*
*idānīṁ kṛṣṇatāṁ gataḥ*

*āsan*—were assumed; *varṇāḥ trayaḥ*—three colors; *hi*—indeed; *asya*—of your son Kṛṣṇa; *gṛhṇataḥ*—accepting; *anuyugam tanūḥ*—

transcendental bodies according to the different *yugas; śuklaḥ*—sometimes white; *raktaḥ*—sometimes red; *tathā*—as well as; *pītaḥ*—sometimes yellow; *idānīm kṛṣṇatām gataḥ*—at the present moment He has assumed a blackish color.

## TRANSLATION

**Your son Kṛṣṇa appears as an incarnation in every millennium. In the past, He assumed three different colors—white, red and yellow—and now He has appeared in a blackish color. [In another Dvāpara-yuga, He appeared (as Lord Rāmacandra) in the color of śuka, a parrot. All such incarnations have now assembled in Kṛṣṇa.]**

## PURPORT

Partially explaining the position of Lord Kṛṣṇa and partially covering the facts, Gargamuni indicated, "Your son is a great personality, and He can change the color of His body in different ages." The word *gṛhṇataḥ* indicates that Kṛṣṇa is free to make His choice. In other words, He is the Supreme Personality of Godhead and may therefore do whatever He desires. In Vedic literature the different colors assumed by the Personality of Godhead in different millenniums are stated, and therefore when Gargamuni said, "Your son has assumed these colors," he indirectly said, "He is the Supreme Personality of Godhead." Because of Kaṁsa's atrocities, Gargamuni tried to avoid disclosing this fact, but he indirectly informed Nanda Mahārāja that Kṛṣṇa, his son, was the Supreme Personality of Godhead.

It may be noted that Śrīla Jīva Gosvāmī, in his book *Krama-sandarbha*, has enunciated the purport of this verse. In every millennium, Kṛṣṇa appears in a different form, either as white, red or yellow, but this time He personally appeared in His original, blackish form and, as predicted by Gargamuni, exhibited the power of Nārāyaṇa. Because in this form the Supreme Personality of Godhead exhibits Himself fully, His name is Śrī Kṛṣṇa, the all-attractive.

Factually, Kṛṣṇa is the source of all *avatāras*, and therefore all the different features of the different *avatāras* are present in Kṛṣṇa. When Kṛṣṇa incarnates, all the features of other incarnations are already present within Him. Other incarnations are partial representations of Kṛṣṇa, who is the full-fledged incarnation of the Supreme Being. It is to be understood that the Supreme Being, whether appearing as *śukla*, *rakta* or *pīta* (white, red or yellow), is the same person. When He appears in different incarnations, He appears in different colors, just like the sunshine, which contains seven colors. Sometimes the colors of sunshine are represented separately; otherwise the sunshine is observed mainly as bright light. The different *avatāras*, such as the *manvantara-avatāras*, *līlā-avatāras* and *daśa-avatāras*, are all included in the *kṛṣṇa-avatāra*. When Kṛṣṇa appears, all the *avatāras* appear with Him. As described in *Śrīmad-Bhāgavatam* (1.3.26):

*avatārā hy asaṅkhyeyā*
*hareḥ sattva-nidher dvijāḥ*
*yathāvidāsinaḥ kulyāḥ*
*sarasaḥ syuḥ sahasraśaḥ*

The *avatāras* incessantly appear, like incessantly flowing water. No one can count how many waves there are in flowing water, and similarly there is no limitation of the *avatāras*. And Kṛṣṇa is the full representation of all *avatāras* because He is the source of all *avatāras*. Kṛṣṇa is *aṁśī*, whereas others are *aṁśa*, part of Kṛṣṇa. All living entities, including us, are *aṁśas* (*mamaivāṁśo jīva-loke jīva-bhūtaḥ sanātanaḥ*). These *aṁśas* are of different magnitude. Human beings (who are minute *aṁśas*) and the demigods, *viṣṇu-tattva* and all other living beings are all part of the Supreme. *Nityo nityānāṁ cetanaś cetanānām* (*Kaṭha Upaniṣad* 2.2.13). Kṛṣṇa is the full representation of all living entities, and when Kṛṣṇa is present, all *avatāras* are included in Him.

The Eleventh Canto of *Śrīmad-Bhāgavatam* describes the incarnations for each *yuga* in chronological order. The *Bhāgavatam* says, *kṛte śuklaś catur-bāhuḥ, tretāyāṁ rakta-varṇo 'sau, dvāpare bhagavān śyāmaḥ* and *kṛṣṇa-varṇaṁ tviṣākṛṣṇam.* We actually see that in Kali-yuga, Bhagavān has appeared in *pīta-varṇa*, or a yellow color, as Gaurasundara, although the *Bhāgavatam* speaks of *kṛṣṇa-varṇam.* To adjust all these statements, one should understand that although in some *yugas* some of the colors are prominent, in every *yuga*, whenever Kṛṣṇa appears, all the colors are present. *Kṛṣṇa-varṇaṁ tviṣākṛṣṇam:* although Caitanya Mahāprabhu appears without *kṛṣṇa*, or a blackish color, He is understood to be Kṛṣṇa Himself. *Idānīṁ kṛṣṇatāṁ gataḥ.* The same original Kṛṣṇa who appears in different *varṇas* has now appeared. The word *āsan* indicates that He is always present. Whenever the Supreme Personality of Godhead appears in His full feature, He is understood to be *kṛṣṇa-varṇam*, although He appears in different colors. Prahlāda Mahārāja states that Caitanya Mahāprabhu is *channa;* that is, although He is Kṛṣṇa, He is covered by a yellow color. Thus the Gauḍīya Vaiṣṇavas accept the conclusion that although Caitanya Mahāprabhu appeared in *pīta* color, He is Kṛṣṇa.

*kṛṣṇa-varṇaṁ tviṣākṛṣṇaṁ*
*sāṅgopāṅgāstra-pārṣadam*
*yajñaiḥ saṅkīrtana-prāyair*
*yajanti hi sumedhasaḥ*
(*Bhāg.* 11.5.32)

## TEXT 14

प्रागयं वसुदेवस्य क्वचिज्जातस्तवात्मजः ।
वासुदेव इति श्रीमानभिज्ञाः सम्प्रचक्षते ॥१४॥

*prāg ayaṁ vasudevasya*
*kvacij jātas tavātmajaḥ*
*vāsudeva iti śrīmān*
*abhijñāḥ sampracakṣate*

*prāk*—before; *ayam*—this child; *vasudevasya*—of Vasudeva; *kvacit*—sometimes; *jātaḥ*—was born; *tava*—your; *ātmajaḥ*—Kṛṣṇa, who has taken birth as your child; *vāsudevaḥ*—therefore He may be given the name Vāsudeva; *iti*—thus; *śrīmān*—very beautiful; *abhijñāḥ*—those who are learned; *sampracakṣate*—also say that Kṛṣṇa is Vāsudeva.

## TRANSLATION

**For many reasons, this beautiful son of yours sometimes appeared previously as the son of Vasudeva. Therefore, those who are learned sometimes call this child Vāsudeva.**

## PURPORT

Gargamuni indirectly disclosed, "This child was originally born as the son of Vasudeva, although He is acting as your child. Generally He is your child, but sometimes He is the son of Vasudeva."

## TEXT 15

**बहूनि सन्ति नामानि रूपाणि च सुतस्य ते ।**
**गुणकर्मानुरूपाणि तान्यहं वेद नो जनाः ॥१५॥**

*bahūni santi nāmāni*
*rūpāṇi ca sutasya te*
*guṇa-karmānurūpāṇi*
*tāny ahaṁ veda no janāḥ*

*bahūni*—various; *santi*—there are; *nāmāni*—names; *rūpāṇi*—forms; *ca*—also; *sutasya*—of the son; *te*—your; *guṇa-karma-anu-rūpāṇi*—according to His attributes and activities; *tāni*—them; *aham*—I; *veda*—know; *no janāḥ*—not ordinary persons.

## TRANSLATION

**For this son of yours there are many forms and names according to His transcendental qualities and activities. These are known to me, but people in general do not understand them.**

## PURPORT

*Bahūni:* the Lord has many names. *Advaitam acyutam anādim ananta-rūpam ādyaṁ purāṇa-puruṣaṁ nava-yauvanaṁ ca.* As stated in the *Brahma-saṁhitā* (5.33), the Lord is one, but He has many forms and many names. It was not that because Gargamuni gave the child the name Kṛṣṇa, that was His only name. He has other names, such as Bhakta-vatsala, Giridhārī, Govinda and Gopāla. If we analyze the *nirukti*, or semantic derivation, of the word "Kṛṣṇa," we find that *na* signifies that He stops the repetition of birth and death, and *kṛṣ* means *sattārtha*, or "existence." (Kṛṣṇa is the whole of existence.) Also, *kṛṣ* means "attraction," and *na* means *ānanda*, or "bliss." Kṛṣṇa is known as Mukunda because He wants to give everyone spiritual, eternal, blissful life. Unfortunately, because of the living entity's little independence, the living entity wants to "deprogram" the program of Kṛṣṇa. This is the material disease. Nonetheless, because Kṛṣṇa wants to give transcendental bliss to the living entities, He appears in various forms. Therefore He is called Kṛṣṇa. Because Gargamuni was an astrologer, he knew what others did not know. Yet Kṛṣṇa has so many names that even Gargamuni did not know them all. It is to be concluded that Kṛṣṇa, according to His transcendental activities, has many names and many forms.

## TEXT 16

एष वः श्रेय आधास्यद् गोपगोकुलनन्दनः ।
अनेन सर्वदुर्गाणि यूयमञ्जस्तरिष्यथ ॥१६॥

*eṣa vaḥ śreya ādhāsyad*
*gopa-gokula-nandanaḥ*
*anena sarva-durgāṇi*
*yūyam añjas tariṣyatha*

*eṣaḥ*—this child; *vaḥ*—for all of you people; *śreyaḥ*—the most auspicious; *ādhāsyat*—will act all-auspiciously; *gopa-gokula-nandanaḥ*—just like a cowherd boy, born in a family of cowherd men as the son of the estate of Gokula; *anena*—by Him; *sarva-durgāṇi*—all kinds of miserable conditions; *yūyam*—all of you; *añjaḥ*—easily; *tariṣyatha*—will overcome.

## TRANSLATION

**To increase the transcendental bliss of the cowherd men of Gokula, this child will always act auspiciously for you. And by His grace only, you will surpass all difficulties.**

## PURPORT

For the cowherd men and the cows, Kṛṣṇa is the supreme friend. Therefore He is worshiped by the prayer *namo brahmaṇya-devāya go-brāhmaṇa-hitāya ca.* His pastimes in Gokula, His *dhāma*, are always favorable to the *brāhmaṇas* and the cows. His first business is to give all comfort to the cows and the *brāhmaṇas.* In fact, comfort for the *brāhmaṇas* is secondary, and comfort for the cows is His first concern. Because of His presence, all people would overcome all difficulties and always be situated in transcendental bliss.

## TEXT 17

पुरानेन व्रजपते साधवो दस्युपीडिताः ।
अराजके रक्ष्यमाणा जिग्युर्दस्यून् समेधिताः ॥१७॥

*purānena vraja-pate*
*sādhavo dasyu-pīḍitāḥ*
*arājake rakṣyamāṇā*
*jigyur dasyūn samedhitāḥ*

*purā*—formerly; *anena*—by Kṛṣṇa; *vraja-pate*—O King of Vraja; *sādhavaḥ*—those who were honest; *dasyu-pīḍitāḥ*—being disturbed by rogues and thieves; *arājake*—when there was an irregular government; *rakṣyamāṇāḥ*—were protected; *jigyuḥ*—conquered; *dasyūn*—the rogues and thieves; *samedhitāḥ*—flourished.

## TRANSLATION

**O Nanda Mahārāja, as recorded in history, when there was an irregular, incapable government, Indra having been dethroned, and people were being harassed and disturbed by thieves, this child appeared in order to protect the people and enable them to flourish, and He curbed the rogues and thieves.**

## PURPORT

Indra is the king of the universe. Demons, thieves and rogues always disturb Indra (*indrāri-vyākulaṁ lokam*), but when *indrāris*, the enemies of Indra, become prominent, Kṛṣṇa appears. *Kṛṣṇas tu bhagavān svayaṁ/ indrāri-vyākulaṁ lokaṁ mṛḍayanti yuge yuge* (*Bhāg*. 1.3.28).

## TEXT 18

य एतस्मिन् महाभागाः प्रीतिं कुर्वन्ति मानवाः।
नारयोऽभिभवन्त्येतान् विष्णुपक्षानिवासुराः॥१८॥

*ya etasmin mahā-bhāgāḥ*
*prītiṁ kurvanti mānavāḥ*
*nārayo 'bhibhavanty etān*
*viṣṇu-pakṣān ivāsurāḥ*

*ye*—those persons who; *etasmin*—unto this child; *mahā-bhāgāḥ*—very fortunate; *prītim*—affection; *kurvanti*—execute; *mānavāḥ*—such persons; *na*—not; *arayaḥ*—the enemies; *abhibhavanti*—do overcome; *etān*—those who are attached to Kṛṣṇa; *viṣṇu-pakṣān*—the demigods, who always have Lord Viṣṇu on their side; *iva*—like; *asurāḥ*—the demons.

## TRANSLATION

**Demons [asuras] cannot harm the demigods, who always have Lord Viṣṇu on their side. Similarly, any person or group attached to Kṛṣṇa is extremely fortunate. Because such persons are very much affectionate toward Kṛṣṇa, they cannot be defeated by demons like the associates of Kaṁsa [or by the internal enemies, the senses].**

## TEXT 19

तस्मान्नन्दात्मजोऽयं ते नारायणसमो गुणैः ।
श्रिया कीर्त्यानुभावेन गोपायस्व समाहितः ॥१९॥

*tasmān nandātmajo 'yaṁ te*
*nārāyaṇa-samo guṇaiḥ*
*śriyā kīrtyānubhāvena*
*gopāyasva samāhitaḥ*

*tasmāt*—therefore; *nanda*—O Nanda Mahārāja; *ātmajaḥ*—your son; *ayam*—this; *te*—of you; *nārāyaṇa-samaḥ*—is as good as Nārāyaṇa (Nārāyaṇa Himself showing transcendental qualities); *guṇaiḥ*—by qualities; *śriyā*—by opulence; *kīrtyā*—especially by His name and fame; *anubhāvena*—and by His influence; *gopāyasva*—just raise this child; *samāhitaḥ*—with great attention and precaution.

## TRANSLATION

**In conclusion, therefore, O Nanda Mahārāja, this child of yours is as good as Nārāyaṇa. In His transcendental qualities, opulence,**

**name, fame and influence, He is exactly like Nārāyaṇa. You should all raise this child very carefully and cautiously.**

## PURPORT

In this verse, the word *nārāyaṇa-samaḥ* is significant. Nārāyaṇa has no equal. He is *asamaurdhva:* no one is equal to Him, and no one is greater than He is. As stated in *śāstra:*

*yas tu nārāyaṇaṁ devaṁ*
*brahma-rudrādi-daivataiḥ*
*samatvenaiva vīkṣeta*
*sa pāṣaṇḍī bhaved dhruvam*

One who equates Nārāyaṇa even with great exalted demigods like Lord Śiva or Lord Brahmā is a *pāṣaṇḍī,* an agnostic. No one can equal Nārāyaṇa. Nonetheless, Gargamuni used the word *sama,* meaning "equal," because he wanted to treat Kṛṣṇa as the Supreme Personality of Godhead who had become Nanda Mahārāja's son. Gargamuni wanted to impress upon the mind of Nanda Mahārāja, "Your worshipable Deity, Nārāyaṇa, is so pleased with you that He has sent you a son almost equal to Him in qualifications. Therefore you may designate your son with a similar name, such as Mukunda or Madhusūdana. But you must always remember that whenever you want to do something very good, there will be many hindrances. Therefore you should raise and protect this child with great care. If you can protect this child very cautiously, as Nārāyaṇa always protects you, the child will be as good as Nārāyaṇa." Gargamuni also indicated that although the child was exaltedly qualified like Nārāyaṇa, He would enjoy more than Nārāyaṇa as *rāsa-vihārī,* the central enjoyer of the *rāsa* dance. As stated in the *Brahma-saṁhitā, lakṣmī-sahasra-śata-sambhrama-sevyamānam:* He would be served by many *gopīs,* who would all be as good as the goddess of fortune.

## TEXT 20

श्रीशुक उवाच

इत्यात्मानं समादिश्य गर्गे च स्वगृहं गते ।
नन्दः प्रमुदितो मेने आत्मानं पूर्णमाशिषाम् ॥२०॥

*śrī-śuka uvāca*
*ity ātmānaṁ samādiśya*
*garge ca sva-gṛhaṁ gate*
*nandaḥ pramudito mene*
*ātmānaṁ pūrṇam āśiṣām*

*śrī-śukaḥ uvāca*—Śrī Śukadeva Gosvāmī said; *iti*—thus; *ātmānam*—about the Absolute Truth, the Supreme Soul; *samādiśya*—after fully instructing; *garge*—when Gargamuni; *ca*—also; *sva-gṛham*—to his own abode; *gate*—had departed; *nandaḥ*—Mahārāja Nanda; *pramuditaḥ*—became extremely pleased; *mene*—considered; *ātmānam*—his own self; *pūrṇam āśiṣām*—full of all good fortune.

## TRANSLATION

**Śrīla Śukadeva Gosvāmī continued: After Gargamuni, having instructed Nanda Mahārāja about Kṛṣṇa, departed for his own home, Nanda Mahārāja was very pleased and considered himself full of all good fortune.**

## PURPORT

Kṛṣṇa is the Supersoul, and Nanda Mahārāja is the individual soul. By the instructions of Gargamuni, both of them were blessed. Nanda Mahārāja was thinking of Kṛṣṇa's safety from the hands of demons like Pūtanā and Śakaṭāsura, and because he possessed such a son, he thought of himself as most fortunate.

## TEXT 21

कालेन व्रजताल्पेन गोकुले रामकेशवौ ।
जानुभ्यां सह पाणिभ्यां रिङ्गमाणौ विजह्रतुः ॥२१॥

*kālena vrajatālpena*
*gokule rāma-keśavau*
*jānubhyāṁ saha pāṇibhyāṁ*
*riṅgamāṇau vijahratuḥ*

*kālena*—of time; *vrajatā*—passing; *alpena*—a very small duration; *gokule*—in Gokula, Vraja-dhāma; *rāma-keśavau*—both Balarāma and

Kṛṣṇa; *jānubhyām*—by the strength of Their knees; *saha pāṇibhyām*—resting on Their hands; *riṅgamāṇau*—crawling; *vijahratuḥ*—enjoyed childhood play.

## TRANSLATION

**After a short time passed, both brothers, Rāma and Kṛṣṇa, began to crawl on the ground of Vraja with the strength of Their hands and knees and thus enjoy Their childhood play.**

## PURPORT

One *brāhmaṇa* devotee says:

*śrutim apare smṛtim itare bhāratam anye bhajantu bhava-bhītāḥ*
*aham iha nandaṁ vande yasyālinde paraṁ brahma*

"Let others, fearing material existence, worship the *Vedas*, the Vedic supplementary *Purāṇas* and the *Mahābhārata*, but I shall worship Nanda Mahārāja, in whose courtyard the Supreme Brahman is crawling." For a highly exalted devotee, *kaivalya*, merging into the existence of the Supreme, appears no better than hell (*narakāyate*). But here one can simply think of the crawling of Kṛṣṇa and Balarāma in the courtyard of Nanda Mahārāja and always merge in transcendental happiness. As long as one is absorbed in thoughts of *kṛṣṇa-līlā*, especially Kṛṣṇa's childhood pastimes, as Parīkṣit Mahārāja desired to be, one is always merged in actual *kaivalya*. Therefore Vyāsadeva compiled *Śrīmad-Bhāgavatam. Lokasyājānato vidvāṁś cakre sātvata-saṁhitām* (*Bhāg.* 1.7.6). Vyāsadeva compiled *Śrīmad-Bhāgavatam*, under the instruction of Nārada, so that anyone can take advantage of this literature, think of Kṛṣṇa's pastimes and always be liberated.

*śrutim apare smṛtim itare bhāratam anye bhajantu bhava-bhītāḥ*
*aham iha nandaṁ vande yasyālinde paraṁ brahma*

## TEXT 22

तावङ्घ्रियुग्ममनुकृष्य सरीसृपन्तौ
घोषप्रघोषरुचिरं व्रजकर्दमेषु ।

तन्नादहृष्टमनसावनुसृत्य लोकं
मुग्धप्रभीतवदुपेयतुरन्ति मात्रोः ॥२२॥

*tāv aṅghri-yugmam anukṛṣya sarīsṛpantau*
*ghoṣa-praghoṣa-ruciraṁ vraja-kardameṣu*
*tan-nāda-hṛṣṭa-manasāv anusṛtya lokaṁ*
*mugdha-prabhītavad upeyatur anti mātroḥ*

*tau*—Kṛṣṇa and Balarāma; *aṅghri-yugmam anukṛṣya*—dragging Their legs; *sarīsṛpantau*—crawling like snakes; *ghoṣa-praghoṣa-ruciram*—producing a sound with Their ankle bells that was very, very sweet to hear; *vraja-kardameṣu*—in the mud created by cow dung and cow urine on the earth of Vrajabhūmi; *tat-nāda*—by the sound of those ankle bells; *hṛṣṭa-manasau*—being very much pleased; *anusṛtya*—following; *lokam*—other persons; *mugdha*—thus being enchanted; *prabhīta-vat*—then again being afraid of them; *upeyatuḥ*—immediately returned; *anti mātroḥ*—toward Their mothers.

## TRANSLATION

**When Kṛṣṇa and Balarāma, with the strength of Their legs, crawled in the muddy places created in Vraja by cow dung and cow urine, Their crawling resembled the crawling of serpents, and the sound of Their ankle bells was very charming. Very much pleased by the sound of other people's ankle bells, They used to follow these people as if going to Their mothers, but when They saw that these were other people, They became afraid and returned to Their real mothers, Yaśodā and Rohiṇī.**

## PURPORT

When Kṛṣṇa and Balarāma were crawling about Vrajabhūmi, They were enchanted by the sound of ankle bells. Thus They sometimes followed other people, who would enjoy the crawling of Kṛṣṇa and Balarāma and exclaim, "Oh, see how Kṛṣṇa and Balarāma are crawling!" Upon hearing this, Kṛṣṇa and Balarāma could understand that these were not Their mothers They were following, and They would return to Their actual mothers. Thus the crawling of Kṛṣṇa and Balarāma was enjoyed by the people of the neighborhood, as well as by mother Yaśodā and Rohiṇī and the two children Themselves.

## TEXT 23

तन्मातरौ निजसुतौ घृणया स्नुवन्त्यौ
पङ्काङ्गरागरुचिरावुपगृह्य दोर्भ्याम् ।
दत्त्वा स्तनं प्रपिबतोः स मुखं निरीक्ष्य
मुग्धस्मिताल्पदशनं ययतुः प्रमोदम् ॥२३॥

*tan-mātarau nija-sutau ghṛṇayā snuvantyau*
*paṅkāṅga-rāga-rucirāv upagṛhya dorbhyām*
*dattvā stanaṁ prapibatoḥ sma mukhaṁ nirīkṣya*
*mugdha-smitālpa-daśanaṁ yayatuḥ pramodam*

*tat-mātarau*—Their mothers (Rohiṇī and Yaśodā); *nija-sutau*—their own respective sons; *ghṛṇayā*—with great affection; *snuvantyau*—allowed to suck the flowing milk from Their breasts very happily; *paṅka-aṅga-rāga-rucirau*—whose beautiful transcendental bodies were covered with muddy cow dung and urine; *upagṛhya*—taking care of; *dorbhyām*—by their arms; *dattvā*—delivering Them; *stanam*—the breast; *prapibatoḥ*—when the babies were sucking; *sma*—indeed; *mukham*—the mouth; *nirīkṣya*—and seeing; *mugdha-smita-alpa-daśanam*—smiling with little teeth coming out of Their mouths (they were more and more attracted); *yayatuḥ*—and enjoyed; *pramodam*—transcendental bliss.

## TRANSLATION

**Dressed with muddy earth mixed with cow dung and cow urine, the babies looked very beautiful, and when They went to Their mothers, both Yaśodā and Rohiṇī picked Them up with great affection, embraced Them and allowed Them to suck the milk flowing from their breasts. While sucking the breast, the babies smiled, and Their small teeth were visible. Their mothers, upon seeing those beautiful teeth, enjoyed great transcendental bliss.**

## PURPORT

As the mothers cared for their respective babies, by the arrangement of *yogamāyā* the babies thought, "Here is My mother," and the mothers thought, "Here is my son." Because of affection, milk naturally flowed from the mothers' breasts, and the babies drank it. When the mothers saw small teeth coming in, they would count them and be happy, and when the babies saw Their mothers allowing Them to drink their breast milk, the babies also felt transcendental pleasure. As this transcendental affection continued between Rohiṇī and Balarāma and Yaśodā and Kṛṣṇa, they all enjoyed transcendental bliss.

## TEXT 24

यर्ह्यङ्गनादर्शनीयकुमारलीला-
वन्तर्व्रजे तदबलाः प्रगृहीतपुच्छैः ।
वत्सैरितस्तत उभावनुकृष्यमाणौ
प्रेक्षन्त्य उज्झितगृहा जहृषुर्हसन्त्यः ॥२४॥

*yarhy aṅganā-darśanīya-kumāra-līlāv*
*antar-vraje tad abalāḥ pragṛhīta-pucchaiḥ*
*vatsair itas tata ubhāv anukṛṣyamāṇau*
*prekṣantya ujjhita-gṛhā jahṛṣur hasantyaḥ*

*yarhi*—when; *aṅganā-darśanīya*—visible only to the ladies within the house; *kumāra-līlau*—the pastimes Śrī Kṛṣṇa and Balarāma exhibited as children; *antaḥ-vraje*—within the inside of Vraja, in the house of Nanda Mahārāja; *tat*—at that time; *abalāḥ*—all the ladies; *pragṛhīta-pucchaiḥ*—the ends of their tails having been caught by Kṛṣṇa and Balarāma; *vatsaiḥ*—by the calves; *itaḥ tataḥ*—here and there; *ubhau*—both Kṛṣṇa and Balarāma; *anukṛṣyamāṇau*—being dragged; *prekṣantyaḥ*—seeing such things; *ujjhita*—given up; *gṛhāḥ*—their household affairs; *jahṛṣuḥ*—enjoyed very much; *hasantyah*—while laughing.

## TRANSLATION

**Within the house of Nanda Mahārāja, the cowherd ladies would enjoy seeing the pastimes of the babies Rāma and Kṛṣṇa. The**

**babies would catch the ends of the calves' tails, and the calves would drag Them here and there. When the ladies saw these pastimes, they certainly stopped their household activities and laughed and enjoyed the incidents.**

## PURPORT

While crawling in curiosity, Kṛṣṇa and Balarāma would sometimes catch the ends of the tails of calves. The calves, feeling that someone had caught them, would begin to flee here and there, and the babies would hold on very tightly, being afraid of how the calves were moving. The calves, seeing that the babies were holding them tightly, would also become afraid. Then the ladies would come to rescue the babies and gladly laugh. This was their enjoyment.

## TEXT 25

शृङ्ग्यग्निदंष्ट्र्यसिजलद्विजकण्टकेभ्यः
क्रीडापरावतिचलौ स्वसुतौ निषेद्धुम् ।
गृह्याणि कर्तुमपि यत्र न तज्जनन्यौ
शेकात आपतुरलं मनसोऽनवस्थाम् ॥२५॥

*śṛṅgy-agni-daṁṣṭry-asi-jala-dvija-kaṇṭakebhyaḥ*
*krīḍā-parāv aticalau sva-sutau niṣeddhum*
*gṛhyāṇi kartum api yatra na taj-jananyau*
*śekāta āpatur alaṁ manaso 'navasthām*

*śṛṅgī*—with the cows; *agni*—fire; *daṁṣṭrī*—monkeys and dogs; *asi*—swords; *jala*—water; *dvija*—birds; *kaṇṭakebhyaḥ*—and thorns; *krīḍā-parau ati-calau*—the babies, being too restless, engaged in play; *sva-sutau*—their own two sons; *niṣeddhum*—just to stop Them; *gṛhyāṇi*—household duties; *kartum api*—by executing; *yatra*—when; *na*—not; *tat-jananyau*—Their mothers (Rohiṇī and Yaśodā); *śekāte*—able; *āpatuḥ*—obtained; *alam*—indeed; *manasaḥ*—of the mind; *ana-vasthām*—equilibrium.

## TRANSLATION

**When mother Yaśodā and Rohiṇī were unable to protect the babies from calamities threatened by horned cows, by fire, by animals with claws and teeth such as monkeys, dogs and cats, and by thorns, swords and other weapons on the ground, they were always in anxiety, and their household engagements were disturbed. At that time, they were fully equipoised in the transcendental ecstasy known as the distress of material affection, for this was aroused within their minds.**

## PURPORT

All these pastimes of Kṛṣṇa, and the great enjoyment exhibited by the mothers, are transcendental; nothing about them is material. They are described in the *Brahma-saṁhitā* as *ānanda-cinmaya-rasa.* In the spiritual world there is anxiety, there is crying, and there are other feelings similar to those of the material world, but because the reality of these feelings is in the transcendental world, of which this world is only an imitation, mother Yaśodā and Rohiṇī enjoyed them transcendentally.

## TEXT 26

कालेनाल्पेन राजर्षे रामः कृष्णश्च गोकुले ।
अघृष्टजानुभिः पद्भिर्विचक्रमतुरञ्जसा ॥२६॥

*kālenālpena rājarṣe*
*rāmaḥ kṛṣṇaś ca gokule*
*aghṛṣṭa-jānubhiḥ padbhir*
*vicakramatur añjasā*

*kālena alpena*—within a very short time; *rājarṣe*—O King (Mahārāja Parīkṣit); *rāmaḥ kṛṣṇaḥ ca*—both Rāma and Kṛṣṇa; *gokule*—in the village of Gokula; *aghṛṣṭa-jānubhiḥ*—without the help of crawling on Their knees; *padbhiḥ*—by Their legs alone; *vicakramatuḥ*—began to walk; *añjasā*—very easily.

## TRANSLATION

**O King Parīkṣit, within a very short time both Rāma and Kṛṣṇa began to walk very easily in Gokula on Their legs, by Their own strength, without the need to crawl.**

## PURPORT

Instead of crawling with Their knees, the babies could now stand up by holding on to something and walk little by little, without difficulty, by the strength of Their legs.

## TEXT 27

ततस्तु भगवान् कृष्णो वयस्यैर्व्रजबालकैः ।
सहरामो व्रजस्त्रीणां चिक्रीडे जनयन् मुदम् ॥२७॥

*tatas tu bhagavān kṛṣṇo*
*vayasyair vraja-bālakaiḥ*
*saha-rāmo vraja-strīṇāṁ*
*cikrīḍe janayan mudam*

*tataḥ*—thereafter; *tu*—but; *bhagavān*—the Supreme Personality of Godhead; *kṛṣṇaḥ*—Lord Kṛṣṇa; *vayasyaiḥ*—with Their playmates; *vraja-bālakaiḥ*—with other small children in Vraja; *saha-rāmaḥ*—along with Balarāma; *vraja-strīṇām*—of all the ladies of Vraja; *cikrīḍe*—played very happily; *janayan*—awakening; *mudam*—transcendental bliss.

## TRANSLATION

**Thereafter, Lord Kṛṣṇa, along with Balarāma, began to play with the other children of the cowherd men, thus awakening the transcendental bliss of the cowherd women.**

## PURPORT

The word *saha-rāmaḥ*, meaning "along with Balarāma," is significant in this verse. In such transcendental pastimes, Kṛṣṇa is the chief hero, and Balarāma provides additional help.

## TEXT 28

कृष्णस्य गोप्यो रुचिरं वीक्ष्य कौमारचापलम् ।
शृण्वंत्याः किल तन्मातुरिति होचुः समागताः॥२८॥

*kṛṣṇasya gopyo ruciraṁ*
*vīkṣya kaumāra-cāpalam*
*śṛṇvantyāḥ kila tan-mātur*
*iti hocuḥ samāgatāḥ*

*kṛṣṇasya*—of Kṛṣṇa; *gopyaḥ*—all the *gopīs; ruciram*—very attractive; *vīkṣya*—observing; *kaumāra-cāpalam*—the restlessness of the childish pastimes; *śṛṇvantyāḥ*—just to hear them again and again; *kila*—indeed; *tat-mātuḥ*—in the presence of His mother; *iti*—thus; *ha*—indeed; *ūcuḥ*—said; *samāgatāḥ*—assembled there.

## TRANSLATION

**Observing the very attractive childish restlessness of Kṛṣṇa, all the gopīs in the neighborhood, to hear about Kṛṣṇa's activities again and again, would approach mother Yaśodā and speak to her as follows.**

## PURPORT

Kṛṣṇa's activities are always very attractive to devotees. Therefore the neighbors, who were friends of mother Yaśodā, informed mother Yaśodā of whatever they saw Kṛṣṇa doing in the neighborhood. Mother Yaśodā, just to hear about the activities of her son, stopped her household duties and enjoyed the information given by the neighborhood friends.

## TEXT 29

वत्सान् मुञ्चन् क्वचिदसमये क्रोशसंजातहासः
स्तेयं स्वाद्वत्त्यथ दधिपयः कल्पितैः स्तेययोगैः ।
मर्कान् भोक्ष्यन् विभजति स चेन्नात्ति भाण्डं भिन्नत्ति
द्रव्यालाभे सगृहकुपितो यात्युपक्रोश्य तोकान्॥२९॥

*vatsān muñcan kvacid asamaye krośa-sañjāta-hāsaḥ*
*steyaṁ svādv atty atha dadhi-payaḥ kalpitaiḥ steya-yogaiḥ*

*markān bhokṣyan vibhajati sa cen nātti bhāṇḍaṁ bhinnatti*
*dravyālābhe sagṛha-kupito yāty upakrośya tokān*

*vatsān*—the calves; *muñcan*—releasing; *kvacit*—sometimes; *asamaye*—at odd times; *krośa-sañjāta-hāsaḥ*—after this, when the head of the house is angry, Kṛṣṇa begins to smile; *steyam*—obtained by stealing; *svādu*—very tasteful; *atti*—eats; *atha*—thus; *dadhi-payaḥ*—pot of curd and milk; *kalpitaiḥ*—devised; *steya-yogaiḥ*—by some sort of stealing process; *markān*—to the monkeys; *bhokṣyan*—giving to eat; *vibhajati*—divides their portion; *saḥ*—the monkey; *cet*—if; *na*—not; *atti*—eats; *bhāṇḍam*—the pot; *bhinnatti*—He breaks; *dravya-alābhe*—when eatables are unavailable or He cannot find such pots; *sa-gṛha-kupitaḥ*—He becomes angry at the residents of the house; *yāti*—He goes away; *upakrośya*—irritating and pinching; *tokān*—the small children.

## TRANSLATION

**"Our dear friend Yaśodā, your son sometimes comes to our houses before the milking of the cows and releases the calves, and when the master of the house becomes angry, your son merely smiles. Sometimes He devises some process by which He steals palatable curd, butter and milk, which He then eats and drinks. When the monkeys assemble, He divides it with them, and when the monkeys have their bellies so full that they won't take more, He breaks the pots. Sometimes, if He gets no opportunity to steal butter or milk from a house, He will be angry at the householders, and for His revenge He will agitate the small children by pinching them. Then, when the children begin crying, Kṛṣṇa will go away.**

## PURPORT

The narration of Kṛṣṇa's naughty childhood activities would be presented to mother Yaśodā in the form of complaints. Sometimes Kṛṣṇa would enter the house of a neighbor, and if He found no one there, He would release the calves before the time for the cows to be milked. The calves are actually supposed to be released when their mothers are milked, but Kṛṣṇa would release them before that time, and naturally the calves would drink all the milk from their mothers. When the cowherd men saw this, they would chase Kṛṣṇa and try to catch Him, saying,

"Here is Kṛṣṇa doing mischief," but He would flee and enter another house, where He would again devise some means to steal butter and curd. Then the cowherd men would again try to capture Him, saying, "Here is the butter thief. Better capture Him!" And they would be angry. But Kṛṣṇa would simply smile, and they would forget everything. Sometimes, in their presence, He would begin eating the curd and butter. There was no need for Kṛṣṇa to eat butter, since His belly was always full, but He would try to eat it, or else He would break the pots and distribute the contents to the monkeys. In this way, Kṛṣṇa was always engaged in mischief-making. If in any house He could not find any butter or curd to steal, He would go into a room and agitate the small children sleeping there by pinching them, and when they cried He would go away.

## TEXT 30

हस्ताग्राह्ये रचयति विधिं पीठकोलूखलाद्यै-
श्छिद्रं ह्यन्तर्निहितवयुनः शिक्यभाण्डेषु तद्वित् ।
ध्वान्तागारे धृतमणिगणं स्वाङ्गमर्थप्रदीपं
काले गोप्यो यर्हि गृहकृत्येषु सुव्यग्रचित्ताः ॥३०॥

*hastāgrāhye racayati vidhiṁ pīṭhakolūkhalādyaiś*
*chidraṁ hy antar-nihita-vayunaḥ śikya-bhāṇḍeṣu tad-vit*
*dhvāntāgāre dhṛta-maṇi-gaṇaṁ svāṅgam artha-pradīpaṁ*
*kāle gopyo yarhi gṛha-kṛtyeṣu suvyagra-cittāḥ*

*hasta-agrāhye*—when the destination is out of the reach of His hands; *racayati*—He arranges to make; *vidhim*—a means; *pīṭhaka*—by wooden planks piled together; *ulūkhala-ādyaiḥ*—and by overturning the stone mortar for grinding spices; *chidram*—a hole; *hi*—indeed; *antaḥ-nihita*—about the contents of the pot; *vayunaḥ*—with such knowledge; *śikya*—hanging by a swing; *bhāṇḍeṣu*—in the pots; *tat-vit*—expert in that knowledge, or in full knowledge; *dhvānta-āgāre*—in a very dark room; *dhṛta-maṇi-gaṇam*—because of being decorated with valuable jewels; *sva-aṅgam*—His own body; *artha-pradīpam*—is the light required for seeing in darkness; *kāle*—after that, in due course of time;

*gopyaḥ*—the elderly *gopīs; yarhi*—as soon as; *gṛha-kṛtyeṣu*—in discharging household affairs; *su-vyagra-cittāḥ*—are busily engaged.

## TRANSLATION

**"When the milk and curd are kept high on a swing hanging from the ceiling and Kṛṣṇa and Balarāma cannot reach it, They arrange to reach it by piling up various planks and turning upside down the mortar for grinding spices. Being quite aware of the contents of a pot, They pick holes in it. While the elderly gopīs go about their household affairs, Kṛṣṇa and Balarāma sometimes go into a dark room, brightening the place with the valuable jewels and ornaments on Their bodies and taking advantage of this light by stealing.**

## PURPORT

Formerly, in every household, yogurt and butter were kept for use in emergencies. But Kṛṣṇa and Balarāma would pile up planks so that They could reach the pots and would then pick holes in the pots with Their hands so that the contents would leak out and They could drink it. This was another means for stealing butter and milk. When the butter and milk were kept in a dark room, Kṛṣṇa and Balarāma would go there and make the place bright with the valuable jewels on Their bodies. On the whole, Kṛṣṇa and Balarāma engaged in stealing butter and milk from the neighborhood houses in many ways.

## TEXT 31

एवं धार्ष्ट्यान्युशति कुरुते मेहनादीनि वास्तौ
स्तेयोपायैर्विरचितकृतिः सुप्रतीको यथास्ते ।
इत्थं स्त्रीभिः सभयनयनश्रीमुखालोकिनीभि-
र्व्याख्यातार्था प्रहसितमुखी न ह्युपालब्धुमैच्छत् ॥३१॥

*evaṁ dhārṣṭyāny uśati kurute mehanādīni vāstau*
*steyopāyair viracita-kṛtiḥ supratīko yathāste*
*itthaṁ strībhiḥ sa-bhaya-nayana-śrī-mukhālokinībhir*
*vyākhyātārthā prahasita-mukhī na hy upālabdhum aicchat*

*evam*—in this way; *dhārṣṭyāni*—naughty activities; *uśati*—in a neat and clean place; *kurute*—sometimes does; *mehana-ādīni*—passing stool and urine; *vāstau*—in our houses; *steya-upāyaiḥ*—and by inventing different devices to steal butter and milk; *viracita-kṛtiḥ*—is very expert; *su-pratīkaḥ*—is now sitting down here like a very good, well-behaved child; *yathā āste*—while staying here; *ittham*—all these topics of conversation; *strībhiḥ*—by the *gopīs; sa-bhaya-nayana*—just now sitting there with fearful eyes; *śrī-mukha*—such a beautiful face; *ālokinībhiḥ*—by the *gopīs*, who were enjoying the pleasure of seeing; *vyākhyāta-arthā*—and while complaining against Him before mother Yaśodā; *prahasita-mukhī*—they were smiling and enjoying; *na*—not; *hi*—indeed; *upālabdhum*—to chastise and threaten (rather, she enjoyed how Kṛṣṇa was sitting there as a very good boy); *aicchat*—she desired.

## TRANSLATION

**"When Kṛṣṇa is caught in His naughty activities, the master of the house will say to Him, 'Oh, You are a thief,' and artificially express anger at Kṛṣṇa. Kṛṣṇa will then reply, 'I am not a thief. You are a thief.' Sometimes, being angry, Kṛṣṇa passes urine and stool in a neat, clean place in our houses. But now, our dear friend Yaśodā, this expert thief is sitting before you like a very good boy." Sometimes all the gopīs would look at Kṛṣṇa sitting there, His eyes fearful so that His mother would not chastise Him, and when they saw Kṛṣṇa's beautiful face, instead of chastising Him they would simply look upon His face and enjoy transcendental bliss. Mother Yaśodā would mildly smile at all this fun, and she would not want to chastise her blessed transcendental child.**

## PURPORT

Kṛṣṇa's business in the neighborhood was not only to steal but sometimes to pass stool and urine in a neat, clean house. When caught by the master of the house, Kṛṣṇa would chastise him, saying, "You are a thief." Aside from being a thief in His childhood affairs, Kṛṣṇa acted as an expert thief when He was young by attracting young girls and enjoying them in the *rāsa* dance. This is Kṛṣṇa's business. He is also violent, as the killer of many demons. Although mundane people like nonviolence and other such brilliant qualities, God, the Absolute Truth, being always the same, is good in any activities, even so-called immoral activities like stealing, killing and violence. Kṛṣṇa is always pure, and He is always the Supreme Absolute Truth. Kṛṣṇa may do anything supposedly abominable in material life, yet still He is attractive. Therefore His name is Kṛṣṇa, meaning "all-attractive." This is the platform on which transcendental loving affairs and service are exchanged. Because of the features of Kṛṣṇa's face, the mothers were so attracted that they could not chastise Him. Instead of chastising Him, they smiled and enjoyed hearing of Kṛṣṇa's activities. Thus the *gopīs* remained satisfied, and Kṛṣṇa enjoyed their happiness. Therefore another name of Kṛṣṇa is Gopī-jana-vallabha because He invented such activities to please the *gopīs.*

## TEXT 32

**एकदा क्रीडमानास्ते रामाद्या गोपदारकाः ।**
**कृष्णो मृदं भक्षितवानिति मात्रे न्यवेदयन् ॥३२॥**

*ekadā krīḍamānās te*
*rāmādyā gopa-dārakāḥ*
*kṛṣṇo mṛdaṁ bhakṣitavān*
*iti mātre nyavedayan*

*ekadā*—once upon a time; *krīḍamānāḥ*—now Kṛṣṇa, being still more grown up, was playing with other children of the same age; *te*—they; *rāma-ādyāḥ*—Balarāma and others; *gopa-dārakāḥ*—other boys born in the same neighborhood of the cowherd men; *kṛṣṇaḥ mṛdam bhakṣitavān*—O Mother, Kṛṣṇa has eaten earth (a complaint was lodged); *iti*—thus; *mātre*—unto mother Yaśodā; *nyavedayan*—they submitted.

## TRANSLATION

**One day while Kṛṣṇa was playing with His small playmates, including Balarāma and other sons of the gopas, all His friends came together and lodged a complaint to mother Yaśodā. "Mother," they submitted, "Kṛṣṇa has eaten earth."**

## PURPORT

Here is another of Kṛṣṇa's transcendental activities invented to please the *gopīs*. First a complaint was lodged with mother Yaśodā about Kṛṣṇa's stealing, but mother Yaśodā did not chastise Him. Now, in an attempt to awaken mother Yaśodā's anger so that she would chastise Kṛṣṇa, another complaint was invented—that Kṛṣṇa had eaten earth.

## TEXT 33

सा गृहीत्वा करे कृष्णमुपालभ्य हितैषिणी ।
यशोदा भयसम्भ्रान्तप्रेक्षणाक्षमभाषत ॥३३॥

*sā gṛhītvā kare kṛṣṇam*
*upālabhya hitaiṣiṇī*
*yaśodā bhaya-sambhrānta-*
*prekṣaṇākṣam abhāṣata*

*sā*—mother Yaśodā; *gṛhītvā*—taking; *kare*—within the hands (being anxious about what Kṛṣṇa might have eaten); *kṛṣṇam*—Kṛṣṇa; *upālabhya*—wanted to chastise Him; *hita-eṣiṇī*—because she was anxious for the welfare of Kṛṣṇa, she became very much agitated, thinking, "How is it that Kṛṣṇa has eaten earth?"; *yaśodā*—mother Yaśodā; *bhaya-sambhrānta-prekṣaṇa-akṣam*—began to look very carefully within Kṛṣṇa's mouth in fear, to see if Kṛṣṇa had eaten something dangerous; *abhāṣata*—began to address Kṛṣṇa.

## TRANSLATION

**Upon hearing this from Kṛṣṇa's playmates, mother Yaśodā, who was always full of anxiety over Kṛṣṇa's welfare, picked Kṛṣṇa up with her hands to look into His mouth and chastise Him. Her eyes fearful, she spoke to her son as follows.**

## TEXT 34

कस्मान्मृदमदान्तात्मन् भवान् भक्षितवान् रहः ।
वदन्ति तावका ह्येते कुमारास्तेऽग्रजोऽप्ययम् ॥३४॥

*kasmān mṛdam adāntātman*
*bhavān bhakṣitavān rahaḥ*
*vadanti tāvakā hy ete*
*kumārās te 'grajo 'py ayam*

*kasmāt*—why; *mṛdam*—dirt; *adānta-ātman*—You restless boy; *bhavān*—You; *bhakṣitavān*—have eaten; *rahaḥ*—in a solitary place; *vadanti*—are lodging this complaint; *tāvakāḥ*—Your friends and playmates; *hi*—indeed; *ete*—all of them; *kumārāḥ*—boys; *te*—Your; *agrajaḥ*—older brother; *api*—also (confirms); *ayam*—this.

## TRANSLATION

**Dear Kṛṣṇa, why are You so restless that You have eaten dirt in a solitary place? This complaint has been lodged against You by all Your playmates, including Your elder brother, Balarāma. How is this?**

## PURPORT

Mother Yaśodā was agitated by Kṛṣṇa's restless misbehavior. Her house was full of sweetmeats. Why then should the restless boy eat dirt in a solitary place? Kṛṣṇa replied, "My dear mother, they have plotted together and lodged a complaint against Me so that you will punish Me. My elder brother, Balarāma, has joined them. Actually, I have not done this. Take My words as true. Do not be angry and chastise Me."

## TEXT 35

नाहं भक्षितवानम्ब सर्वे मिथ्याभिशंसिनः ।
यदि सत्यगिरस्तर्हि समक्षं पश्य मे मुखम् ॥३५॥

*nāhaṁ bhakṣitavān amba*
*sarve mithyābhiśaṁsinaḥ*
*yadi satya-giras tarhi*
*samakṣaṁ paśya me mukham*

*na*—not; *aham*—I; *bhakṣitavān*—have eaten dirt; *amba*—My dear mother; *sarve*—all of them; *mithya-abhiśaṁsinaḥ*—all liars, simply complaining against Me so that you may chastise Me; *yadi*—if it is actually a fact; *satya-giraḥ*—that they have spoken the truth; *tarhi*—then; *samakṣam*—directly; *paśya*—see; *me*—My; *mukham*—mouth.

## TRANSLATION

**Lord Śrī Kṛṣṇa replied: My dear mother, I have never eaten dirt. All My friends complaining against Me are liars. If you think they are being truthful, you can directly look into My mouth and examine it.**

## PURPORT

Kṛṣṇa presented Himself as an innocent child to increase the transcendental ecstasy of maternal affection. As described in the *śāstra, tāḍana-bhayān mithyoktir vātsalya-rasa-poṣikā.* This means that sometimes a small child speaks lies. For example, he may have stolen something or eaten something and yet deny that he has done so. We ordinarily see this in the material world, but in relation to Kṛṣṇa it is different; such activities are meant to endow the devotee with transcendental ecstasy. The Supreme Personality of Godhead was playing as a liar and accusing all the other devotees of being liars. As stated in *Śrīmad-Bhāgavatam* (10.12.11), *kṛta-puṇya-puñjāḥ:* a devotee may attain such an ecstatic position after many, many births of devotional service. Persons who have amassed the results of a vast amount of pious activities can attain the stage of associating with Kṛṣṇa and playing with Him like ordinary playmates. One should not consider these transactions of transcendental service to be untruthful accusations. One should never accuse such devotees of being ordinary boys speaking lies, for they attained this stage of associating with Kṛṣṇa by great austerities (*tapasā brahmacaryeṇa śamena ca damena ca*).

## TEXT 36

यद्येवं तर्हि व्यादेहीत्युक्तः स भगवान् हरिः ।
व्यादत्ताव्याहतैश्वर्यः क्रीडामनुजबालकः ॥३६॥

*yady evaṁ tarhi vyādehī-*
*ty uktaḥ sa bhagavān hariḥ*
*vyādattāvyāhataiśvaryaḥ*
*krīḍā-manuja-bālakaḥ*

*yadi*—if; *evam*—it is so; *tarhi*—then; *vyādehi*—open Your mouth wide (I want to see); *iti uktaḥ*—in this way ordered by mother Yaśodā; *saḥ*—He; *bhagavān*—the Supreme Personality of Godhead; *hariḥ*—the Supreme Lord; *vyādatta*—opened His mouth; *avyāhata-aiśvaryaḥ*—without minimizing any potencies of absolute opulence (*aiśvaryasya samagrasya*); *krīḍā*—pastimes; *manuja-bālakaḥ*—exactly like the child of a human being.

## TRANSLATION

**Mother Yaśodā challenged Kṛṣṇa, "If You have not eaten earth, then open Your mouth wide." When challenged by His mother in this way, Kṛṣṇa, the son of Nanda Mahārāja and Yaśodā, to exhibit pastimes like a human child, opened His mouth. Although the Supreme Personality of Godhead, Kṛṣṇa, who is full of all opulences, did not disturb His mother's parental affection, His opulence was automatically displayed, for Kṛṣṇa's opulence is never lost at any stage, but is manifest at the proper time.**

## PURPORT

Without disturbing the ecstasy of His mother's affection, Kṛṣṇa opened His mouth and displayed His own natural opulences. When a person is given varieties of food, there may be a hundred and one varieties, but if one likes ordinary *śāka*, spinach, he prefers to eat that. Similarly, although Kṛṣṇa was full of opulences, now, by the order of mother Yaśodā, He opened wide His mouth like a human child and did not neglect the transcendental humor of maternal affection.

## TEXTS 37–39

सा तत्र ददृशे विश्वं जगत् स्थास्नु च खं दिशः ।
साद्रिद्वीपाब्धिभूगोलं सवाय्वग्नीन्दुतारकम् ॥३७॥

ज्योतिश्चक्रं जलं तेजो नभस्वान् वियदेव च।
वैकारिकाणीन्द्रियाणि मनो मात्रा गुणास्त्रयः॥३८॥
एतद् विचित्रं सह जीवकाल-
स्वभावकर्माशयलिङ्गभेदम् ।
सूनोस्तनौ वीक्ष्य विदारितास्ये
व्रजं सहात्मानमवाप शङ्काम् ॥३९॥

*sā tatra dadṛśe viśvaṁ*
*jagat sthāsnu ca khaṁ diśaḥ*
*sādri-dvīpābdhi-bhūgolaṁ*
*sa-vāyv-agnīndu-tārakam*

*jyotiś-cakraṁ jalaṁ tejo*
*nabhasvān viyad eva ca*
*vaikārikāṇīndriyāṇi*
*mano mātrā guṇās trayaḥ*

*etad vicitraṁ saha-jīva-kāla-*
*svabhāva-karmāśaya-liṅga-bhedam*
*sūnos tanau vīkṣya vidāritāsye*
*vrajaṁ sahātmānam avāpa śaṅkām*

*sā*—mother Yaśodā; *tatra*—within the wide-open mouth of Kṛṣṇa; *dadṛśe*—saw; *viśvam*—the whole universe; *jagat*—moving entities; *sthāsnu*—maintenance of nonmoving entities; *ca*—and; *kham*—the sky; *diśaḥ*—the directions; *sa-adri*—with the mountains; *dvīpa*—islands; *abdhi*—and oceans; *bhū-golam*—the surface of the earth; *sa-vāyu*—with the blowing wind; *agni*—fire; *indu*—the moon; *tārakam*—stars; *jyotiḥ-cakram*—the planetary systems; *jalam*—water; *tejaḥ*—light; *nabhasvān*—outer space; *viyat*—the sky; *eva*—also; *ca*—and; *vaikārikāṇi*—creation by transformation of *ahaṅkāra; indriyāṇi*—the senses; *manaḥ*—mind; *mātrāḥ*—sense perception; *guṇāḥ trayaḥ*—the three material qualities (*sattva, rajas* and *tamas*); *etat*—all these; *vicitram*—varieties; *saha*—along with; *jīva-kāla*—the duration of life of all living entities; *svabhāva*—natural instinct; *karma-āśaya*—resultant action and desire for material enjoyment; *liṅga-bhedam*—varieties of bodies according to desire; *sūnoḥ tanau*—in the body of her son; *vīkṣya*—seeing; *vidārita-āsye*—within the wide-open mouth; *vrajam*—Vṛndāvana-dhāma, Nanda Mahārāja's place; *saha-ātmānam*—along with herself; *avāpa*—was struck; *śaṅkām*—with all doubts and wonder.

## TRANSLATION

**When Kṛṣṇa opened His mouth wide by the order of mother Yaśodā, she saw within His mouth all moving and nonmoving entities, outer space, and all directions, along with mountains, islands, oceans, the surface of the earth, the blowing wind, fire, the moon and the stars. She saw the planetary systems, water, light, air, sky, and creation by transformation of ahaṅkāra. She also saw the senses, the mind, sense perception, and the three qualities goodness, passion and ignorance. She saw the time allotted for the living entities, she saw natural instinct and the reactions of karma, and she saw desires and different varieties of bodies, moving and nonmoving. Seeing all these aspects of the cosmic manifestation, along with herself and Vṛndāvana-dhāma, she became doubtful and fearful of her son's nature.**

## PURPORT

All the cosmic manifestations that exist on the gross and subtle elements, as well as the means of their agitation, the three *guṇas*, the living entity, creation, maintenance, annihilation and everything going on in the external energy of the Lord—all this comes from the Supreme Personality of Godhead, Govinda. Everything is within the control of the Supreme Personality of Godhead. This is also confirmed in *Bhagavad-gītā* (9.10). *Mayādhyakṣeṇa prakṛtiḥ sūyate sa-carācaram:* everything in the material nature (*prakṛti*) works under His control. Because all these manifestations come from Govinda, they could all be visible within the mouth of Govinda. Quite astonishingly, mother Yaśodā was afraid because of intense maternal affection. She could not believe that within the mouth of her son such things could appear. Yet she saw them, and therefore she was struck with fear and wonder.

## TEXT 40

किं स्वप्न एतदुत देवमाया
किं वा मदीयो बत बुद्धिमोहः ।
अथो अमुष्यैव ममार्भकस्य
यः कश्चनौत्पत्तिक आत्मयोगः ॥४०॥

*kiṁ svapna etad uta devamāyā*
*kiṁ vā madīyo bata buddhi-mohaḥ*
*atho amuṣyaiva mamārbhakasya*
*yaḥ kaścanautpattika ātma-yogaḥ*

*kim*—whether; *svapnaḥ*—a dream; *etat*—all this; *uta*—or otherwise; *deva-māyā*—an illusory manifestation by the external energy; *kim vā*—or else; *madīyaḥ*—my personal; *bata*—indeed; *buddhi-mohaḥ*—illusion of intelligence; *atho*—otherwise; *amuṣya*—of such; *eva*—indeed; *mama arbhakasya*—of my child; *yaḥ*—which; *kaścana*—some; *autpattikaḥ*—natural; *ātma-yogaḥ*—personal mystic power.

## TRANSLATION

**[Mother Yaśodā began to argue within herself:] Is this a dream, or is it an illusory creation by the external energy? Has this been manifested by my own intelligence, or is it some mystic power of my child?**

## PURPORT

When mother Yaśodā saw this wonderful manifestation within the mouth of her child, she began to argue within herself about whether it was a dream. Then she considered, "I am not dreaming, because my eyes are open. I am actually seeing what is happening. I am not sleeping, nor am I dreaming. Then maybe this is an illusion created by *devamāyā*. But that is also not possible. What business would the demigods have showing such things to me? I am an insignificant woman with no connection with the demigods. Why should they take the trouble to put me into *devamāyā*? That also is not possible." Then mother Yaśodā considered whether the vision might be due to bewilderment: "I am fit in health; I am not diseased. Why should there be any bewilderment? It is not possible that my brain is deranged, since I am ordinarily quite fit to think. Then this vision must be due to some mystic power of my son, as predicted by Gargamuni." Thus she finally concluded that the vision was due to her son's activities, and nothing else.

## TEXT 41

अथो यथावन्न वितर्कगोचरं
चेतोमनःकर्मवचोभिरञ्जसा ।
यदाश्रयं येन यतः प्रतीयते
सुदुर्विभाव्यं प्रणतास्मि तत्पदम् ॥४१॥

*atho yathāvan na vitarka-gocaraṁ*
*ceto-manaḥ-karma-vacobhir añjasā*
*yad-āśrayaṁ yena yataḥ pratīyate*
*sudurvibhāvyaṁ praṇatāsmi tat-padam*

*atho*—therefore she decided to surrender unto the Supreme Lord; *yathā-vat*—as perfectly as one can perceive; *na*—not; *vitarka-gocaram*—beyond all arguments, reason and sense perception; *cetaḥ*—by consciousness; *manaḥ*—by mind; *karma*—by activities; *vacobhiḥ*—or by words; *añjasā*—taking all of them together, we cannot understand them; *yat-āśrayam*—under whose control; *yena*—by whom; *yataḥ*—from whom; *pratīyate*—can be conceived only that from Him everything emanates; *su-durvibhāvyam*—beyond our sense perception or consciousness; *praṇatā asmi*—let me surrender; *tat-padam*—at His lotus feet.

## TRANSLATION

**Therefore let me surrender unto the Supreme Personality of Godhead and offer my obeisances unto Him, who is beyond the conception of human speculation, the mind, activities, words and arguments, who is the original cause of this cosmic manifestation, by whom the entire cosmos is maintained, and by whom we can conceive of its existence. Let me simply offer my obeisances, for**

**He is beyond my contemplation, speculation and meditation. He is beyond all of my material activities.**

## PURPORT

One simply has to realize the greatness of the Supreme Personality of Godhead. One should not try to understand Him by any material means, subtle or gross. Mother Yaśodā, being a simple woman, could not find out the real cause of the vision; therefore, out of maternal affection, she simply offered obeisances unto the Supreme Lord to protect her child. She could do nothing but offer obeisances to the Lord. It is said, *acintyāḥ khalu ye bhāvā na tāṁs tarkeṇa yojayet* (*Mahābhārata, Bhīṣma Parva* 5.22). One should not try to understand the supreme cause by argument or reasoning. When we are beset by some problem for which we can find no reason, there is no alternative than to surrender to the Supreme Lord and offer Him our respectful obeisances. Then our position will be secure. This was the means adopted in this instance also by mother Yaśodā. Whatever happens, the original cause is the Supreme Personality of Godhead (*sarva-kāraṇa-kāraṇam*). When the immediate cause cannot be ascertained, let us simply offer our obeisances at the lotus feet of the Lord. Mother Yaśodā concluded that the wonderful things she saw within the mouth of her child were due to Him, although she could not clearly ascertain the cause. Therefore when a devotee cannot ascertain the cause of suffering, he concludes:

*tat te 'nukampāṁ susamīkṣamāṇo*
*bhuñjāna evātma-kṛtaṁ vipākam*
*hṛd-vāg-vapurbhir vidadhan namas te*
*jīveta yo mukti-pade sa dāya-bhāk*
(*Bhāg.* 10.14.8)

The devotee accepts that it is due to his own past misdeeds that the Supreme Personality of Godhead has caused him some small amount of suffering. Thus he offers obeisances to the Lord again and again. Such a devotee is called *mukti-pade sa dāya-bhāk*; that is, he is guaranteed his liberation from this material world. As stated in *Bhagavad-gītā* (2.14):

*mātrā-sparśās tu kaunteya*
*śītoṣṇa-sukha-duḥkha-dāḥ*
*āgamāpāyino nityās*
*tāṁs titikṣasva bhārata*

We should know that material suffering due to the material body will come and go. Therefore we must tolerate the suffering and proceed with discharging our duty as ordained by our spiritual master.

## TEXT 42

अहं ममासौ पतिरेष मे सुतो
व्रजेश्वरस्याखिलवित्तपा सती ।
गोप्यश्च गोपाः सहगोधनाश्च मे
यन्माययेत्थं कुमतिः स मे गतिः ॥४२॥

*ahaṁ mamāsau patir eṣa me suto*
*vrajeśvarasyākhila-vittapā satī*
*gopyaś ca gopāḥ saha-godhanāś ca me*
*yan-māyayetthaṁ kumatiḥ sa me gatiḥ*

*aham*—my existence ("I am something"); *mama*—my; *asau*—Nanda Mahārāja; *patiḥ*—husband; *eṣaḥ*—this (Kṛṣṇa); *me sutaḥ*—is my son; *vraja-īśvarasya*—of my husband, Nanda Mahārāja; *akhila-vitta-pā*—I am the possessor of unlimited opulence and wealth; *satī*—because I am his wife; *gopyaḥ ca*—and all the damsels of the cowherd men; *gopāḥ*—all the cowherd men (are my subordinates); *saha-godhanāḥ ca*—with the cows and calves; *me*—my; *yat-māyayā*—all such things addressed by me are, after all, given by the mercy of the Supreme; *ittham*—thus; *kumatiḥ*—I am wrongly thinking they are my possessions; *saḥ me gatiḥ*—He is therefore my only shelter (I am simply instrumental).

## TRANSLATION

**It is by the influence of the Supreme Lord's māyā that I am wrongly thinking that Nanda Mahārāja is my husband, that Kṛṣṇa**

**is my son, and that because I am the queen of Nanda Mahārāja, all the wealth of cows and calves are my possessions and all the cowherd men and their wives are my subjects. Actually, I also am eternally subordinate to the Supreme Lord. He is my ultimate shelter.**

## PURPORT

Following in the footsteps of mother Yaśodā, everyone should follow this mentality of renunciation. Whatever wealth, opulence or whatever else we may possess belongs not to us but to the Supreme Personality of Godhead, who is the ultimate shelter of everyone and the ultimate owner of everything. As stated by the Lord Himself in *Bhagavad-gītā* (5.29):

*bhoktāraṁ yajña-tapasāṁ*
*sarva-loka-maheśvaram*
*suhṛdaṁ sarva-bhūtānāṁ*
*jñātvā māṁ śāntim ṛcchati*

"The sages, knowing Me as the ultimate purpose of all sacrifices and austerities, the Supreme Lord of all planets and demigods and the benefactor and well-wisher of all living entities, attain peace from the pangs of material miseries."

We should not be proud of our possessions. As expressed by mother Yaśodā herein, "I am not the owner of possessions, the opulent wife of Nanda Mahārāja. The estate, the possessions, the cows and calves and the subjects like the *gopīs* and cowherd men are all given to me." One should give up thinking of "my possessions, my son and my husband" (*janasya moho 'yam ahaṁ mameti*). Nothing belongs to anyone but the Supreme Lord. Only because of illusion do we wrongly think, "I am existing" or "Everything belongs to me." Thus mother Yaśodā completely surrendered unto the Supreme Lord. For the moment, she was rather disappointed, thinking, "My endeavors to protect my son by charity and other auspicious activities are useless. The Supreme Lord has given me many things, but unless He takes charge of everything, there is no assurance of protection. I must therefore ultimately seek shelter of the Supreme Personality of Godhead." As stated by Prahlāda Mahārāja (*Bhāg.* 7.9.19), *bālasya neha śaraṇaṁ pitarau nṛsiṁha:* a father and mother cannot ultimately take care of their children. *Ato gṛha-kṣetra-sutāpta-vittair janasya moho 'yam ahaṁ mameti* (*Bhāg.* 5.5.8). One's land, home, wealth and all of one's possessions belong to the Supreme Personality of Godhead, although we wrongly think, "I am this" and "These things are mine."

## TEXT 43

इत्थं विदिततत्त्वायां गोपिकायां स ईश्वरः ।
वैष्णवीं व्यतनोन्मायां पुत्रस्नेहमयीं विभुः ॥४३॥

*itthaṁ vidita-tattvāyāṁ*
*gopikāyāṁ sa īśvaraḥ*
*vaiṣṇavīṁ vyatanon māyāṁ*
*putra-snehamayīṁ vibhuḥ*

*ittham*—in this way; *vidita-tattvāyām*—when she understood the truth of everything philosophically; *gopikāyām*—unto mother Yaśodā; *saḥ*—the Supreme Lord; *īśvaraḥ*—the supreme controller; *vaiṣṇavīm*—*viṣṇumāyā*, or *yogamāyā; vyatanot*—expanded; *māyām*—*yogamāyā; putra-sneha-mayīm*—very much attached because of maternal affection for her son; *vibhuḥ*—the Supreme Lord.

## TRANSLATION

**Mother Yaśodā, by the grace of the Lord, could understand the real truth. But then again, the supreme master, by the influence of the internal potency, yogamāyā, inspired her to become absorbed in intense maternal affection for her son.**

## PURPORT

Although mother Yaśodā understood the whole philosophy of life, at the next moment she was overwhelmed by affection for her son by the influence of *yogamāyā.* Unless she took care of her son Kṛṣṇa, she thought, how could He be protected? She could not think otherwise, and thus she forgot all her philosophical speculations. This forgetfulness is described by Śrīla Viśvanātha Cakravartī Ṭhākura as being inspired by the influence of *yogamāyā* (*mohana-sādharmyān māyām*). Materialistic persons are captivated by *mahāmāyā,* whereas devotees, by the arrangement of the spiritual energy, are captivated by *yogamāyā.*

## TEXT 44

सद्योनष्टस्मृतिर्गोपी सारोप्यारोहमात्मजम् ।
प्रवृद्धस्नेहकलिलहृदयासीद् यथा पुरा ॥४४॥

*sadyo naṣṭa-smṛtir gopī*
*sāropyāroham ātmajam*
*pravṛddha-sneha-kalila-*
*hṛdayāsīd yathā purā*

*sadyaḥ*—after all these philosophical speculations, mother Yaśodā fully surrendered to the Supreme Personality of Godhead; *naṣṭa-smṛtiḥ*—having gotten rid of the memory of seeing the universal form within Kṛṣṇa's mouth; *gopī*—mother Yaśodā; *sā*—she; *āropya*—seating; *āroham*—on the lap; *ātmajam*—her son; *pravṛddha*—increased; *sneha*—by affection; *kalila*—affected; *hṛdayā*—the core of her heart; *āsīt*—became situated; *yathā purā*—as she was formerly.

## TRANSLATION

**Immediately forgetting yogamāyā's illusion that Kṛṣṇa had shown the universal form within His mouth, mother Yaśodā took her son on her lap as before, feeling increased affection in her heart for her transcendental child.**

## PURPORT

Mother Yaśodā regarded the vision of the universal form within Kṛṣṇa's mouth as an arrangement of *yogamāyā,* like a dream. As one forgets everything after a dream, mother Yaśodā immediately forgot the entire incident. As her natural feeling of affection increased, she decided to herself, "Now let this incident be forgotten. I do not mind. Here is my son. Let me kiss Him."

## TEXT 45

त्रय्या चोपनिषद्भिश्च सांख्ययोगैश्च सात्वतैः ।
उपगीयमानमाहात्म्यं हरिं सामन्यतात्मजम् ॥४५॥

*trayyā copaniṣadbhiś ca*
*sāṅkhya-yogaiś ca sātvataiḥ*
*upagīyamāna-māhātmyaṁ*
*hariṁ sāmanyatātmajam*

*trayyā*—by studying the three *Vedas* (*Sāma*, *Yajur* and *Atharva*); *ca*—also; *upaniṣadbhiḥ ca*—and by studying the Vedic knowledge of the *Upaniṣads; sāṅkhya-yogaiḥ*—by reading the literature of *sāṅkhya-yoga; ca*—and; *sātvataiḥ*—by the great sages and devotees, or by reading *Vaiṣṇava-tantra, Pancarātras; upagīyamāna-māhātmyam*—whose glories are worshiped (by all these Vedic literatures); *harim*—unto the Supreme Personality of Godhead; *sā*—she; *amanyata*—considered (ordinary); *ātmajam*—as her own son.

## TRANSLATION

**The glories of the Supreme Personality of Godhead are studied through the three Vedas, the Upaniṣads, the literature of sāṅkhya-yoga, and other Vaiṣṇava literature, yet mother Yaśodā considered that Supreme Person her ordinary child.**

## PURPORT

As stated in *Bhagavad-gītā* (15.15) by the Supreme Personality of Godhead, Kṛṣṇa, the purpose of studying the *Vedas* is to understand Him (*vedaiś ca sarvair aham eva vedyaḥ*). Śrī Caitanya Mahāprabhu explained to Sanātana Gosvāmī that there are three purposes in the *Vedas.* One is to understand our relationship with Kṛṣṇa (*sambandha*), another is to act according to that relationship (*abhidheya*), and the third is to reach the ultimate goal (*prayojana*). The word *prayojana* means "necessities," and the ultimate necessity is explained by Śrī Caitanya Mahāprabhu. *Premā pum-artho mahān:* the greatest necessity for a human being is the achievement of love for the Supreme Personality of

Godhead. Here we see that mother Yaśodā is on the highest stage of necessity, for she is completely absorbed in love for Kṛṣṇa.

In the beginning, the Vedic purpose is pursued in three ways (*trayī*)—by *karma-kāṇḍa, jñāna-kāṇḍa* and *upāsanā-kāṇḍa.* When one reaches the complete, perfect stage of *upāsanā-kāṇḍa,* one comes to worship Nārāyaṇa, or Lord Viṣṇu. When Pārvatī asked Lord Mahādeva, Lord Śiva, what is the best method of *upāsanā,* or worship, Lord Śiva answered, *ārādhanānāṁ sarveṣāṁ viṣṇor ārādhanaṁ param. Viṣṇū-pāsanā,* or *viṣṇv-ārādhana,* worship of Lord Viṣṇu, is the highest stage of perfection, as realized by Devakī. But here mother Yaśodā performs no *upāsanā,* for she has developed transcendental ecstatic love for Kṛṣṇa. Therefore her position is better than that of Devakī. In order to show this, Śrīla Vyāsadeva enunciates this verse, *trayyā copaniṣadbhiḥ* etc.

When a human being enters into the study of the *Vedas* to obtain *vidyā,* knowledge, he begins to take part in human civilization. Then he advances further to study the *Upaniṣads* and gain *brahma-jñāna,* impersonal realization of the Absolute Truth, and then he advances still further, to *sāṅkhya-yoga,* in order to understand the supreme controller, who is indicated in *Bhagavad-gītā* (*paraṁ brahma paraṁ dhāma pavitraṁ paramaṁ bhavān/ puruṣaṁ śāśvatam*). When one understands that *puruṣa,* the supreme controller, to be Paramātmā, one is engaged in the method of *yoga* (*dhyānāvasthita-tad-gatena manasā paśyanti yaṁ yoginaḥ*). But mother Yaśodā has surpassed all these stages. She has come to the platform of loving Kṛṣṇa as her beloved child, and therefore she is accepted to be on the highest stage of spiritual realization. The Absolute Truth is realized in three features (*brahmeti paramātmeti bhagavān iti śabdyate*), but she is in such ecstasy that she does not care to understand what is Brahman, what is Paramātmā or what is Bhagavān. Bhagavān has personally descended to become her beloved child. Therefore there is no comparison to mother Yaśodā's good fortune, as declared by Śrī Caitanya Mahāprabhu (*ramyā kācid upāsanā vrajavadhū-vargeṇa yā kalpitā*). The Absolute Truth, the Supreme Personality of Godhead, may be realized in different stages. As the Lord says in *Bhagavad-gītā* (4.11):

*ye yathā māṁ prapadyante*
*tāṁs tathaiva bhajāmy aham*

*mama vartmānuvartante*
*manuṣyāḥ pārtha sarvaśaḥ*

"As men surrender unto Me, I reward them accordingly. Everyone follows My path in all respects, O son of Pṛthā." One may be a *karmī,* a *jñānī,* a *yogī* and then a *bhakta* or *prema-bhakta.* But the ultimate stage of realization is *prema-bhakti,* as actually demonstrated by mother Yaśodā.

## TEXT 46

श्रीराजोवाच
नन्दः किमकरोद् ब्रह्मन् श्रेय एवं महोदयम् ।
यशोदा च महाभागा पपौ यस्याः स्तनं हरिः ॥४६॥

*śrī-rājovāca*
*nandaḥ kim akarod brahman*
*śreya evaṁ mahodayam*
*yaśodā ca mahā-bhāgā*
*papau yasyāḥ stanaṁ hariḥ*

*śrī-rājā uvāca*—Mahārāja Parīkṣit further inquired (from Śukadeva Gosvāmī); *nandaḥ*—Mahārāja Nanda; *kim*—what; *akarot*—performed; *brahman*—O learned *brāhmaṇa; śreyaḥ*—auspicious activities, like performing penances and austerities; *evam*—as exhibited by him; *mahā-udayam*—from which they achieved the greatest perfection; *yaśodā*—mother Yaśodā; *ca*—also; *mahā-bhāgā*—most fortunate; *papau*—drank; *yasyāḥ*—of whom; *stanam*—the breast milk; *hariḥ*—the Supreme Personality of Godhead.

## TRANSLATION

**Having heard of the great fortune of mother Yaśodā, Parīkṣit Mahārāja inquired from Śukadeva Gosvāmī: O learned brāhmaṇa, mother Yaśodā's breast milk was sucked by the Supreme Personality of Godhead. What past auspicious activities did she and Nanda Mahārāja perform to achieve such perfection in ecstatic love?**

## PURPORT

As stated in *Bhagavad-gītā* (7.16), *catur-vidhā bhajante māṁ janāḥ sukṛtino 'rjuna.* Without *sukṛti,* or pious activities, no one can come to the shelter of the Supreme Personality of Godhead. The Lord is approached by four kinds of pious men (*ārto jijñāsur arthārthī jñānī ca*), but here we see that Nanda Mahārāja and Yaśodā surpassed all of them. Therefore Parīkṣit Mahārāja naturally inquired, "What kind of pious activities did they perform in their past lives by which they achieved such a stage of perfection?" Of course, Nanda Mahārāja and Yaśodā are accepted as the father and mother of Kṛṣṇa, yet mother Yaśodā was more fortunate than Nanda Mahārāja, Kṛṣṇa's father, because Nanda Mahārāja was sometimes separated from Kṛṣṇa whereas Yaśodā, Kṛṣṇa's mother, was not separated from Kṛṣṇa at any moment. From Kṛṣṇa's babyhood to His childhood and from His childhood to His youth, mother Yaśodā was always in association with Kṛṣṇa. Even when Kṛṣṇa was grown up, He would go to Vṛndāvana and sit on the lap of mother Yaśodā. Therefore there is no comparison to the fortune of mother Yaśodā, and Parīkṣit Mahārāja naturally inquired, *yaśodā ca mahā-bhāgā.*

## TEXT 47

पितरौ नान्वविन्देतां कृष्णोदारार्भकेहितम् ।
गायन्त्यद्यापि कवयो यल्लोकशमलापहम् ॥४७॥

*pitarau nānvavindetāṁ*
*kṛṣṇodārārbhakehitam*
*gāyanty adyāpi kavayo*
*yal loka-śamalāpaham*

*pitarau*—the actual father and mother of Kṛṣṇa; *na*—not; *anvavindetām*—enjoyed; *kṛṣṇa*—of Kṛṣṇa; *udāra*—magnanimous; *arbhaka-īhitam*—the childhood pastimes He performed; *gāyanti*—are glorifying; *adya api*—even today; *kavayaḥ*—great, great sages and saintly persons; *yat*—which is; *loka-śamala-apaham*—by hearing of which the contamination of the whole material world is vanquished.

## TRANSLATION

**Although Kṛṣṇa was so pleased with Vasudeva and Devakī that He descended as their son, they could not enjoy Kṛṣṇa's magnanimous childhood pastimes, which are so great that simply chanting about them vanquishes the contamination of the material world. Nanda Mahārāja and Yaśodā, however, enjoyed these pastimes fully, and therefore their position is always better than that of Vasudeva and Devakī.**

## PURPORT

Kṛṣṇa actually took birth from the womb of Devakī, but just after His birth He was transferred to the home of mother Yaśodā. Devakī could not even have Kṛṣṇa suck her breast. Therefore Parīkṣit Mahārāja was astonished. How had mother Yaśodā and Nanda Mahārāja become so fortunate that they enjoyed the complete childhood pastimes of Kṛṣṇa, which are still glorified by saintly persons? What had they done in the past by which they were elevated to such an exalted position?

## TEXT 48

श्रीशुक उवाच

द्रोणो वसूनां प्रवरो धरया भार्यया सह ।
करिष्यमाण आदेशान् ब्रह्मणस्तमुवाच ह ॥४८॥

*śrī-śuka uvāca*
*droṇo vasūnāṁ pravaro*
*dharayā bhāryayā saha*
*kariṣyamāṇa ādeśān*
*brahmaṇas tam uvāca ha*

*śrī-śukaḥ uvāca*—Śrī Śukadeva Gosvāmī said; *droṇaḥ*—by the name Droṇa; *vasūnām*—of the eight Vasus (a type of demigod); *pravaraḥ*—who was the best; *dharayā*—with Dharā; *bhāryayā*—His wife; *saha*—with; *kariṣyamāṇaḥ*—just to execute; *ādeśān*—the orders; *brahmaṇaḥ*—of Lord Brahmā; *tam*—unto him; *uvāca*—said; *ha*—in the past.

## TRANSLATION

**Śukadeva Gosvāmī said: To follow the orders of Lord Brahmā, Droṇa, the best of the Vasus, along with his wife, Dharā, spoke to Lord Brahmā in this way.**

## PURPORT

As stated in the *Brahma-saṁhitā* (5.37):

*ānanda-cinmaya-rasa-pratibhāvitābhis*
*tābhir ya eva nija-rūpatayā kalābhiḥ*
*goloka eva nivasaty akhilātma-bhūto*
*govindam ādi-puruṣaṁ tam ahaṁ bhajāmi*

When Kṛṣṇa descends anywhere, He is accompanied by His own associates. These associates are not ordinary living beings. Kṛṣṇa's pastimes are eternal, and when He descends, He comes with His associates. Therefore Nanda and mother Yaśodā are the eternal father and mother of Kṛṣṇa. This means that whenever Kṛṣṇa descends, Nanda and Yaśodā, as well as Vasudeva and Devakī, also descend as the Lord's father and mother. Their personalities are expansions of Kṛṣṇa's personal body; they are not ordinary living beings. Mahārāja Parīkṣit knew this, but he was curious to know from Śukadeva Gosvāmī whether it is possible for an ordinary human being to come to this stage by *sādhana-siddhi.* There are two kinds of perfection—*nitya-siddhi* and *sādhana-siddhi.* A *nitya-siddha* is one who is eternally Kṛṣṇa's associate, an expansion of Kṛṣṇa's personal body, whereas a *sādhana-siddha* is an ordinary human being who, by executing pious activities and following regulative principles of devotional service, also comes to that stage. Thus the purpose of Mahārāja Parīkṣit's inquiry was to determine whether an ordinary human being can attain the position of mother Yaśodā and Nanda Mahārāja. Śukadeva Gosvāmī answered this question as follows.

## TEXT 49

जातयोर्नौ महादेवे भुवि विश्वेश्वरे हरौ ।
भक्तिः स्यात् परमा लोके ययाञ्जो दुर्गतिं तरेत् ॥४९॥

*jātayor nau mahādeve*
*bhuvi viśveśvare harau*
*bhaktiḥ syāt paramā loke*
*yayāñjo durgatiṁ taret*

*jātayoḥ*—after we two have taken birth; *nau*—both husband and wife, Droṇa and Dharā; *mahādeve*—in the Supreme Person, the Supreme Personality of Godhead; *bhuvi*—on the earth; *viśva-īśvare*—in the master of all the planetary systems; *harau*—in the Supreme Lord; *bhaktiḥ*—devotional service; *syāt*—will be spread; *paramā*—the ultimate goal of life; *loke*—in the world; *yayā*—by which; *añjaḥ*—very easily; *durgatim*—miserable life; *taret*—one can avoid and be delivered.

## TRANSLATION

**Droṇa and Dharā said: Please permit us to be born on the planet earth so that after our appearance, the Supreme Lord, the Personality of Godhead, the supreme controller and master of all planets, will also appear and spread devotional service, the ultimate goal of life, so that those born in this material world may very easily be delivered from the miserable condition of materialistic life by accepting this devotional service.**

## PURPORT

This statement by Droṇa clearly indicates that Droṇa and Dharā are the eternal father and mother of Kṛṣṇa. Whenever there is a necessity of Kṛṣṇa's appearance, Droṇa and Dharā appear first, and then Kṛṣṇa appears. Kṛṣṇa says in *Bhagavad-gītā* that His birth is not ordinary (*janma karma ca me divyam*).

*ajo 'pi sann avyayātmā*
*bhūtānām īśvaro 'pi san*
*prakṛtiṁ svām adhiṣṭhāya*
*sambhavāmy ātma-māyayā*

"Although I am unborn and My transcendental body never deteriorates, and although I am the Lord of all sentient beings, I still appear in every millennium in My original transcendental form." (Bg. 4.6) Before Kṛṣṇa's appearance, Droṇa and Dharā appear in order to become His father and mother. It is they who appear as Nanda Mahārāja and his wife, Yaśodā. In other words, it is not possible for a *sādhana-siddha* living being to become the father or mother of Kṛṣṇa, for Kṛṣṇa's father and mother are already designated. But by following the principles exhibited by Nanda Mahārāja and Yaśodā and their associates, the inhabitants of Vṛndāvana, ordinary living beings may attain such affection as exhibited by Nanda and Yaśodā.

When Droṇa and Dharā were requested to beget children, they chose to come to this world to have the Supreme Personality of Godhead as their son, Kṛṣṇa. Kṛṣṇa's appearance means *paritrāṇāya sādhūnāṁ vināśāya ca duṣkṛtām*—the devotees are protected, and the miscreants are vanquished. Whenever Kṛṣṇa comes, He distributes the highest goal of life, devotional service. He appears as Caitanya Mahāprabhu for the same purpose because unless one comes to devotional service, one cannot be delivered from the miseries of the material world (*duḥkhālayam aśāśvatam*), where the living beings struggle for existence. The Lord says in *Bhagavad-gītā* (15.7):

*mamaivāṁśo jīva-loke*
*jīva-bhūtaḥ sanātanaḥ*
*manaḥ ṣaṣṭhānīndriyāṇi*
*prakṛti-sthāni karṣati*

"The living entities in this conditioned world are My eternal, fragmental parts. Because of conditioned life, they are struggling very hard with the six senses, which include the mind." The living entities are struggling to become happy, but unless they take to the *bhakti* cult, their happiness is not possible. Kṛṣṇa clearly says:

*aśraddadhānāḥ puruṣā*
*dharmasyāsya parantapa*
*aprāpya māṁ nivartante*
*mṛtyu-saṁsāra-vartmani*

"Those who are not faithful on the path of devotional service cannot attain Me, O conqueror of foes, but return to birth and death in this material world." (Bg. 9.3)

Foolish persons do not know how risky life is here if one does not follow the instructions of Kṛṣṇa. The Kṛṣṇa consciousness movement, therefore, has been started so that by practicing Kṛṣṇa consciousness one can avoid the risky life of this material existence. There is no question of accepting or not accepting Kṛṣṇa consciousness. It is not optional; it is compulsory. If we do not take to Kṛṣṇa consciousness, our life is very risky. Everything is explained in *Bhagavad-gītā.* Therefore, to learn how to become free from the miserable condition of material existence, *Bhagavad-gītā As It Is* is the preliminary study. Then, if one understands *Bhagavad-gītā,* one can proceed to *Śrīmad-Bhāgavatam,* and if one advances further, one may study *Caitanya-caritāmṛta.* We are therefore presenting these invaluable books to the whole world so that people may study them and be happy, being delivered from miserable conditional life.

## TEXT 50

अस्त्वित्युक्तः स भगवान् व्रजे द्रोणो महायशाः ।
जज्ञे नन्द इति ख्यातो यशोदा सा धराभवत् ॥५०॥

*astv ity uktaḥ sa bhagavān*
*vraje droṇo mahā-yaśāḥ*
*jajñe nanda iti khyāto*
*yaśodā sā dharābhavat*

*astu*—when Brahmā agreed, "Yes, it is all right"; *iti uktaḥ*—thus being ordered by him; *saḥ*—he (Droṇa); *bhagavān*—eternally the father of Kṛṣṇa (Bhagavān's father is also Bhagavān); *vraje*—in Vrajabhūmi, Vṛndāvana; *droṇaḥ*—Droṇa, the most powerful Vasu; *mahā-yaśāḥ*—the very famous transcendentalist; *jajñe*—appeared; *nandaḥ*—as Nanda Mahārāja; *iti*—thus; *khyātaḥ*—is celebrated; *yaśodā*—as mother Yaśodā; *sā*—she; *dharā*—the same Dharā; *abhavat*—appeared.

## TRANSLATION

**When Brahmā said, "Yes, let it be so," the most fortune Droṇa, who was equal to Bhagavān, appeared in Vrajapura, Vṛndāvana, as**

**the most famous Nanda Mahārāja, and his wife, Dharā, appeared as mother Yaśodā.**

## PURPORT

Because whenever Kṛṣṇa appears on this earth He superficially needs a father and mother, Droṇa and Dharā, His eternal father and mother, appeared on earth before Kṛṣṇa as Nanda Mahārāja and Yaśodā. In contrast to Sutapā and Pṛśnigarbha, they did not undergo severe penances and austerities to become the father and mother of Kṛṣṇa. This is the difference between *nitya-siddha* and *sādhana-siddha.*

## TEXT 51

ततो भक्तिर्भगवति पुत्रीभूते जनार्दने ।
दम्पत्योर्नितरामासीद् गोपगोपीषु भारत ॥५१॥

*tato bhaktir bhagavati*
*putrī-bhūte janārdane*
*dampatyor nitarām āsīd*
*gopa-gopīṣu bhārata*

*tataḥ*—thereafter; *bhaktiḥ bhagavati*—the cult of *bhakti,* devotional service unto the Supreme Personality of Godhead; *putrī-bhūte*—in the Lord, who had appeared as the son of mother Yaśodā; *janārdane*—in Lord Kṛṣṇa; *dam-patyoḥ*—of both husband and wife; *nitarām*—continuously; *āsīt*—there was; *gopa-gopīṣu*—all the inhabitants of Vṛndāvana, the *gopas* and the *gopīs,* associating with Nanda Mahārāja and Yaśodā and following in their footsteps; *bhārata*—O Mahārāja Parīkṣit.

## TRANSLATION

**Thereafter, O Mahārāja Parīkṣit, best of the Bhāratas, when the Supreme Personality of Godhead became the son of Nanda Mahārāja and Yaśodā, they maintained continuous, unswerving devotional love in parental affection. And in their association, all the other inhabitants of Vṛndāvana, the gopas and gopīs, developed the culture of kṛṣṇa-bhakti.**

## PURPORT

Although when the Supreme Personality of Godhead stole the butter, curd and milk of the neighboring *gopas* and *gopīs* this teasing superficially seemed troublesome, in fact it was an exchange of affection in the ecstasy of devotional service. The more the *gopas* and *gopīs* exchanged feelings with the Lord, the more their devotional service increased. Sometimes we may superficially see that a devotee is in difficulty because of being engaged in devotional service, but the fact is different. When a devotee suffers for Kṛṣṇa, that suffering is transcendental enjoyment. Unless one becomes a devotee, this cannot be understood. When Kṛṣṇa exhibited His childhood pastimes, not only did Nanda Mahārāja and Yaśodā increase their devotional affection, but those in their association also increased in devotional service. In other words, persons who follow the activities of Vṛndāvana will also develop devotional service in the highest perfection.

## TEXT 52

कृष्णो ब्रह्मण आदेशं सत्यं कर्तुं व्रजे विभुः ।
सहरामो वसंश्चक्रे तेषां प्रीतिं स्वलीलया ॥५२॥

*kṛṣṇo brahmaṇa ādeśaṁ*
*satyaṁ kartuṁ vraje vibhuḥ*
*saha-rāmo vasaṁś cakre*
*teṣāṁ prītiṁ sva-līlayā*

*kṛṣṇaḥ*—the Supreme Personality, Kṛṣṇa; *brahmaṇaḥ*—of Lord Brahmā; *ādeśam*—the order; *satyam*—truthful; *kartum*—to make; *vraje*—in Vrajabhūmi, Vṛndāvana; *vibhuḥ*—the supreme powerful; *saha-rāmaḥ*—along with Balarāma; *vasan*—residing; *cakre*—increased; *teṣām*—of all the inhabitants of Vṛndāvana; *prītim*—the pleasure; *sva-līlayā*—by His transcendental pastimes.

## TRANSLATION

**Thus the Supreme Personality, Kṛṣṇa, along with Balarāma, lived in Vrajabhūmi, Vṛndāvana, just to substantiate the benediction of Brahmā. By exhibiting different pastimes in His childhood,**

**He increased the transcendental pleasure of Nanda and the other inhabitants of Vṛndāvana.**

*Thus end the Bhaktivedanta purports of the Tenth Canto, Eighth Chapter, of the* Śrīmad-Bhāgavatam, *entitled, "Lord Kṛṣṇa Shows the Universal Form Within His Mouth."*

## CHAPTER NINE

# Mother Yaśodā Binds Lord Kṛṣṇa

While mother Yaśodā was allowing Kṛṣṇa to drink her breast milk, she was forced to stop because she saw the milk pan boiling over on the oven. The maidservants being engaged in other business, she stopped allowing Kṛṣṇa to drink from her breast and immediately attended to the overflowing milk pan. Kṛṣṇa became very angry because of His mother's behavior and devised a means of breaking the pots of yogurt. Because He created this disturbance, mother Yaśodā decided to bind Him. These incidents are described in this chapter.

One day, the maidservants being engaged in other work, mother Yaśodā was churning the yogurt into butter herself, and in the meantime Kṛṣṇa came and requested her to allow Him to suck her breast milk. Of course, mother Yaśodā immediately allowed Him to do so, but then she saw that the hot milk on the oven was boiling over, and therefore she immediately stopped allowing Kṛṣṇa to drink the milk of her breast and went to stop the milk on the oven from overflowing. Kṛṣṇa, however, having been interrupted in His business of sucking the breast, was very angry. He took a piece of stone, broke the churning pot and entered a room, where He began to eat the freshly churned butter. When mother Yaśodā, after attending to the overflowing milk, returned and saw the pot broken, she could understand that this was the work of Kṛṣṇa, and therefore she went to search for Him. When she entered the room, she saw Kṛṣṇa standing on the *ulūkhala*, a large mortar for grinding spices. Having turned the mortar upside down, He was stealing butter hanging from a swing and was distributing the butter to the monkeys. As soon as Kṛṣṇa saw that His mother had come, He immediately began to run away, and mother Yaśodā began to follow Him. After going some distance, mother Yaśodā was able to catch Kṛṣṇa, who because of His offense was crying. Mother Yaśodā, of course, threatened to punish Kṛṣṇa if He acted that way again, and she decided to bind Him with rope. Unfortunately, when the time came to knot the rope, the rope with which she wanted to bind Him was short by a distance equal to the width of two fingers. When she made the rope longer by adding another rope, she again saw that it was short by two fingers. Again and again she tried, and again and again she found the rope too short by two fingers. Thus she became very tired, and Kṛṣṇa, seeing His affectionate mother so tired, allowed Himself to be bound. Now, being compassionate, He did not show her His unlimited potency. After mother Yaśodā bound Kṛṣṇa and became engaged in other household affairs, Kṛṣṇa observed two *yamala-arjuna* trees, which were actually Nalakūvara and Maṇigrīva, two sons of Kuvera who had been condemned by Nārada Muni to become trees. Kṛṣṇa, by His mercy, now began to proceed toward the trees to fulfill the desire of Nārada Muni.

## TEXTS 1–2

श्रीशुक उवाच

एकदा गृहदासीषु यशोदा नन्दगेहिनी ।
कर्मान्तरनियुक्तासु निर्ममन्थ स्वयं दधि ॥ १ ॥
यानि यानीह गीतानि तद्बालचरितानि च ।
दधिनिर्मन्थने काले स्मरन्ती तान्यगायत ॥ २ ॥

*śrī-śuka uvāca*
*ekadā gṛha-dāsīṣu*
*yaśodā nanda-gehinī*
*karmāntara-niyuktāsu*
*nirmamantha svayaṁ dadhi*

*yāni yānīha gītāni*
*tad-bāla-caritāni ca*
*dadhi-nirmanthane kāle*
*smarantī tāny agāyata*

*śrī-śukaḥ uvāca*—Śrī Śukadeva Gosvāmī said; *ekadā*—one day; *gṛha-dāsīṣu*—when all the maidservants of the household were otherwise engaged; *yaśodā*—mother Yaśodā; *nanda-gehinī*—the queen of Nanda Mahārāja; *karma-antara*—in other household affairs; *niyuktāsu*—being engaged; *nirmamantha*—churned; *svayam*—personally; *dadhi*—the yogurt; *yāni*—all such; *yāni*—such; *iha*—in this connection; *gītāni*—

songs; *tat-bāla-caritāni*—in which the activities of her own child were enacted; *ca*—and; *dadhi-nirmanthane*—while churning the yogurt; *kāle*—at that time; *smarantī*—remembering; *tāni*—all of them (in the form of songs); *agāyata*—chanted.

## TRANSLATION

**Śrī Śukadeva Gosvāmī continued: One day when mother Yaśodā saw that all the maidservants were engaged in other household affairs, she personally began to churn the yogurt. While churning, she remembered the childish activities of Kṛṣṇa, and in her own way she composed songs and enjoyed singing to herself about all those activities.**

## PURPORT

Śrīla Viśvanātha Cakravartī Ṭhākura, quoting from the *Vaiṣṇava-toṣaṇī* of Śrīla Sanātana Gosvāmī, says that the incident of Kṛṣṇa's breaking the pot of yogurt and being bound by mother Yaśodā took place on the Dipavali Day, or Dīpa-mālikā. Even today in India, this festival is generally celebrated very gorgeously in the month of Kārtika by fireworks and lights, especially in Bombay. It is to be understood that among all the cows of Nanda Mahārāja, several of mother Yaśodā's cows ate only grasses so flavorful that the grasses would automatically flavor the milk. Mother Yaśodā wanted to collect the milk from these cows, make it into yogurt and churn it into butter personally, since she thought that this child Kṛṣṇa was going to the houses of neighborhood *gopas* and *gopīs* to steal butter because He did not like the milk and yogurt ordinarily prepared.

While churning the butter, mother Yaśodā was singing about the childhood activities of Kṛṣṇa. It was formerly a custom that if one wanted to remember something constantly, he would transform it into poetry or have this done by a professional poet. It appears that mother Yaśodā did not want to forget Kṛṣṇa's activities at any time. Therefore she poeticized all of Kṛṣṇa's childhood activities, such as the killing of Pūtanā, Aghāsura, Śakaṭāsura and Tṛṇāvarta, and while churning the butter, she sang about these activities in poetical form. This should be the practice of persons eager to remain Kṛṣṇa conscious twenty-four hours a day. This incident shows how Kṛṣṇa conscious mother Yaśodā was. To stay in Kṛṣṇa consciousness, we should follow such persons.

## TEXT 3

क्षौमं वासः पृथुकटितटे बिभ्रती सूत्रनद्धं
पुत्रस्नेहस्नुतकुचयुगं जातकम्पं च सुभ्रूः ।
रज्ज्वाकर्षश्रमभुजचलत्कङ्कणौ कुण्डले च
स्विन्नं वक्त्रं कबरविगलन्मालती निर्ममन्थ ॥ ३ ॥

*kṣaumaṁ vāsaḥ pṛthu-kaṭi-taṭe bibhratī sūtra-naddhaṁ*
*putra-sneha-snuta-kuca-yugaṁ jāta-kampaṁ ca subhrūḥ*
*rajjv-ākarṣa-śrama-bhuja-calat-kaṅkaṇau kuṇḍale ca*
*svinnaṁ vaktraṁ kabara-vigalan-mālatī nirmamantha*

*kṣaumam*—saffron and yellow mixed; *vāsaḥ*—mother Yaśodā was wearing such a sari; *pṛthu-kaṭi-taṭe*—surrounding her large hips; *bibhratī*—shaking; *sūtra-naddham*—bound with a belt; *putra-sneha-snuta*—because of intense love for her child, became wet with milk; *kuca-yugam*—the nipples of her breasts; *jāta-kampam ca*—as they were very nicely moving and quivering; *su-bhrūḥ*—who had very beautiful eyebrows; *rajju-ākarṣa*—by pulling on the rope of the churning rod; *śrama*—because of the labor; *bhuja*—on whose hands; *calat-kaṅkaṇau*—the two bangles were moving; *kuṇḍale*—the two earrings; *ca*—also; *svinnam*—her hair was black like a cloud, so perspiration was dropping like rain; *vaktram*—throughout her face; *kabara-vigalat-mālatī*—and *mālatī* flowers were dropping from her hair; *nir-mamantha*—thus mother Yaśodā was churning the butter.

## TRANSLATION

**Dressed in a saffron-yellow sari, with a belt tied about her full hips, mother Yaśodā pulled on the churning rope, laboring considerably, her bangles and earrings moving and vibrating and her whole body shaking. Because of her intense love for her child, her breasts were wet with milk. Her face, with its very beautiful**

**eyebrows, was wet with perspiration, and mālatī flowers were falling from her hair.**

## PURPORT

Anyone who desires to be Kṛṣṇa conscious in motherly affection or parental affection should contemplate the bodily features of mother Yaśodā. It is not that one should desire to become like Yaśodā, for this is Māyāvāda. Either in parental affection or conjugal love, friendship or servitorship—in any way—we must follow in the footsteps of the inhabitants of Vṛndāvana, not try to become like them. Therefore this description is provided here. Advanced devotees must cherish this description, always thinking of mother Yaśodā's features—how she was dressed, how she was working and perspiring, how beautifully the flowers were arranged in her hair, and so on. One should take advantage of the full description provided here by thinking of mother Yaśodā in maternal affection for Kṛṣṇa.

## TEXT 4

तां स्तन्यकाम आसाद्य मथ्नन्तीं जननीं हरिः ।
गृहीत्वा दधिमन्थानं न्यषेधत् प्रीतिमावहन् ॥ ४ ॥

*tāṁ stanya-kāma āsādya*
*mathnantīṁ jananīṁ hariḥ*
*gṛhītvā dadhi-manthānaṁ*
*nyaṣedhat prītim āvahan*

*tām*—unto mother Yaśodā; *stanya-kāmaḥ*—Kṛṣṇa, who was desiring to drink her breast milk; *āsādya*—appearing before her; *mathnantīm*—while she was churning butter; *jananīm*—to the mother; *hariḥ*—Kṛṣṇa; *gṛhītvā*—catching; *dadhi-manthānam*—the churning rod; *nyaṣedhat*—forbade; *prītim āvahan*—creating a situation of love and affection.

## TRANSLATION

**While mother Yaśodā was churning butter, Lord Kṛṣṇa, desiring to drink the milk of her breast, appeared before her, and in order**

**to increase her transcendental pleasure, He caught hold of the churning rod and began to prevent her from churning.**

## PURPORT

Kṛṣṇa was sleeping within the room, and as soon as He got up, He became hungry and went to His mother. Wanting to stop her from churning and drink the milk of her breasts, He stopped her from moving the churning rod.

## TEXT 5

तमङ्कमारूढमपाययत् स्तनं
स्नेहस्नुतं सस्मितमीक्षती मुखम् ।
अतृप्तमुत्सृज्य जवेन सा यया-
वुत्सिच्यमाने पयसि त्वधिश्रिते ॥ ५ ॥

*tam aṅkam ārūḍham apāyayat stanaṁ*
*sneha-snutaṁ sa-smitam īkṣatī mukham*
*atṛptam utsṛjya javena sā yayāv*
*utsicyamāne payasi tv adhiśrite*

*tam*—unto Kṛṣṇa; *aṅkam ārūḍham*—very affectionately allowing Him to sit down on her lap; *apāyayat*—allowed to drink; *stanam*—her breast; *sneha-snutam*—which was flowing with milk because of intense affection; *sa-smitam īkṣatī mukham*—mother Yaśodā was smiling and observing the smiling face of Kṛṣṇa; *atṛptam*—Kṛṣṇa, who was still not fully satisfied by drinking the milk; *utsṛjya*—putting Him aside; *javena*—very hastily; *sā*—mother Yaśodā; *yayau*—left that place; *utsicyamāne payasi*—because of seeing that the milk was overflowing; *tu*—but; *adhiśrite*—in the milk pan on the oven.

## TRANSLATION

**Mother Yaśodā then embraced Kṛṣṇa, allowed Him to sit down on her lap, and began to look upon the face of the Lord with great love and affection. Because of her intense affection, milk was flowing from her breast. But when she saw that the milk pan on the**

**oven was boiling over, she immediately left her son to take care of the overflowing milk, although the child was not yet fully satisfied with drinking the milk of His mother's breast.**

## PURPORT

Everything in the household affairs of mother Yaśodā was meant for Kṛṣṇa. Although Kṛṣṇa was drinking the breast milk of mother Yaśodā, when she saw that the milk pan in the kitchen was overflowing, she had to take care of it immediately, and thus she left her son, who then became very angry, not having been fully satisfied with drinking the milk of her breast. Sometimes one must take care of more than one item of important business for the same purpose. Therefore mother Yaśodā was not unjust when she left her son to take care of the overflowing milk. On the platform of love and affection, it is the duty of the devotee to do one thing first and other things later. The proper intuition by which to do this is given by Kṛṣṇa.

*teṣāṁ satata-yuktānāṁ*
*bhajatāṁ prīti-pūrvakam*
*dadāmi buddhi-yogaṁ taṁ*
*yena mām upayānti te*
(Bg. 10.10)

In Kṛṣṇa consciousness, everything is dynamic. Kṛṣṇa guides the devotee in what to do first and what to do next on the platform of absolute truth.

## TEXT 6

सञ्जातकोपः स्फुरितारुणाधरं
संदश्य दद्भिर्दधिमन्थभाजनम् ।
भित्त्वा मृषाश्रुर्दृषदश्मना रहो
जघास हैयङ्गवमन्तरं गतः ॥ ६ ॥

*sañjāta-kopaḥ sphuritāruṇādharaṁ*
*sandaśya dadbhir dadhi-mantha-bhājanam*
*bhittvā mṛṣāśrur dṛṣad-aśmanā raho*
*jaghāsa haiyaṅgavam antaraṁ gataḥ*

*sañjāta-kopaḥ*—in this way, Kṛṣṇa being very angry; *sphurita-aruṇa-adharam*—swollen reddish lips; *sandaśya*—capturing; *dadbhiḥ*—by His teeth; *dadhi-mantha-bhājanam*—the pot in which yogurt was being churned; *bhittvā*—breaking; *mṛṣā-aśruḥ*—with false tears in the eyes; *dṛṣat-aśmanā*—with a piece of stone; *rahaḥ*—in a solitary place; *jaghāsa*—began to eat; *haiyaṅgavam*—the freshly churned butter; *antaram*—within the room; *gataḥ*—having gone.

## TRANSLATION

**Being very angry and biting His reddish lips with His teeth, Kṛṣṇa, with false tears in His eyes, broke the container of yogurt with a piece of stone. Then He entered a room and began to eat the freshly churned butter in a solitary place.**

## PURPORT

It is natural that when a child becomes angry he can begin crying with false tears in his eyes. So Kṛṣṇa did this, and biting His reddish lips with His teeth, He broke the pot with a stone, entered a room and began to eat the freshly churned butter.

## TEXT 7

उत्तार्य गोपी सुश्रृतं पयः पुनः
प्रविश्य संदृश्य च दध्यमत्रकम् ।
भग्नं विलोक्य स्वसुतस्य कर्म त-
ज्जहास तं चापि न तत्र पश्यती ॥ ७ ॥

*uttārya gopī suśṛtaṁ payaḥ punaḥ*
*praviśya sandṛśya ca dadhy-amatrakam*
*bhagnaṁ vilokya sva-sutasya karma taj*
*jahāsa taṁ cāpi na tatra paśyatī*

*uttārya*—putting down from the oven; *gopī*—mother Yaśodā; *su-śṛtam*—very hot; *payaḥ*—the milk; *punaḥ*—again; *praviśya*—entered the churning spot; *sandṛśya*—by observing; *ca*—also; *dadhi-amatrakam*—the container of yogurt; *bhagnam*—broken; *vilokya*—

seeing this; *sva-sutasya*—of her own child; *karma*—work; *tat*—that; *jahāsa*—smiled; *tam ca*—Kṛṣṇa also; *api*—at the same time; *na*—not; *tatra*—there; *paśyatī*—finding.

## TRANSLATION

**Mother Yaśodā, after taking down the hot milk from the oven, returned to the churning spot, and when she saw that the container of yogurt was broken and that Kṛṣṇa was not present, she concluded that the breaking of the pot was the work of Kṛṣṇa.**

## PURPORT

Seeing the pot broken and Kṛṣṇa not present, Yaśodā definitely concluded that the breaking of the pot was the work of Kṛṣṇa. There was no doubt about it.

## TEXT 8

उलूखलाङ्घ्रेरुपरि व्यवस्थितं
मर्काय कामं ददतं शिचि स्थितम् ।
हैयङ्गवं चौर्यविशङ्कितेक्षणं
निरीक्ष्य पश्चात् सुतमागमच्छनैः ॥ ८ ॥

*ulūkhalāṅghrer upari vyavasthitaṁ*
*markāya kāmaṁ dadataṁ śici sthitam*
*haiyaṅgavaṁ caurya-viśaṅkitekṣaṇaṁ*
*nirīkṣya paścāt sutam āgamac chanaiḥ*

*ulūkhala-aṅghreḥ*—of the mortar in which spices were ground and which was being kept upside down; *upari*—on top; *vyavasthitam*—Kṛṣṇa was sitting; *markāya*—unto a monkey; *kāmam*—according to His satisfaction; *dadatam*—delivering shares; *śici sthitam*—situated in the butter pot hanging on the swing; *haiyaṅgavam*—butter and other milk preparations; *caurya-viśaṅkita*—because of stealing, were anxiously looking hither and thither; *īkṣaṇam*—whose eyes; *nirīkṣya*—by seeing these activities; *paścāt*—from behind; *sutam*—her son; *āgamat*—she reached; *śanaiḥ*—very slowly, cautiously.

## TRANSLATION

**Kṛṣṇa, at that time, was sitting on an upside-down wooden mortar for grinding spices and was distributing milk preparations such as yogurt and butter to the monkeys as He liked. Because of having stolen, He was looking all around with great anxiety, suspecting that He might be chastised by His mother. Mother Yaśodā, upon seeing Him, very cautiously approached Him from behind.**

## PURPORT

Mother Yaśodā was able to trace Kṛṣṇa by following His butter-smeared footprints. She saw that Kṛṣṇa was stealing butter, and thus she smiled. Meanwhile, the crows also entered the room and came out in fear. Thus mother Yaśodā found Kṛṣṇa stealing butter and very anxiously looking here and there.

## TEXT 9

तामात्तयष्टिं प्रसमीक्ष्य सत्वर-
स्ततोऽवरुह्यापससार भीतवत् ।
गोप्यन्वधावन्न यमाप योगिनां
क्षमं प्रवेष्टुं तपसेरितं मनः ॥ ९ ॥

*tām ātta-yaṣṭiṁ prasamīkṣya satvaras*
*tato 'varuhyāpasasāra bhītavat*
*gopy anvadhāvan na yam āpa yogināṁ*
*kṣamaṁ praveṣṭuṁ tapaseritaṁ manaḥ*

*tām*—unto mother Yaśodā; *ātta-yaṣṭim*—carrying in her hand a stick; *prasamīkṣya*—Kṛṣṇa, seeing her in that attitude; *satvaraḥ*—very quickly; *tataḥ*—from there; *avaruhya*—getting down; *apasasāra*—began to flee; *bhīta-vat*—as if very much afraid; *gopī*—mother Yaśodā; *anvadhāvat*—began to follow Him; *na*—not; *yam*—unto whom; *āpa*—failed to reach; *yoginām*—of great *yogīs*, mystics; *kṣamam*—who could reach Him; *praveṣṭum*—trying to enter into the Brahman effulgence or Paramātmā; *tapasā*—with great austerities and penances; *īritam*—trying for that purpose; *manaḥ*—by meditation.

## TRANSLATION

**When Lord Śrī Kṛṣṇa saw His mother, stick in hand, He very quickly got down from the top of the mortar and began to flee as if very much afraid. Although yogīs try to capture Him as Paramātmā by meditation, desiring to enter into the effulgence of the Lord with great austerities and penances, they fail to reach Him. But mother Yaśodā, thinking that same Personality of Godhead, Kṛṣṇa, to be her son, began following Kṛṣṇa to catch Him.**

## PURPORT

*Yogīs*, mystics, want to catch Kṛṣṇa as Paramātmā, and with great austerities and penances they try to approach Him, yet they cannot. Here we see, however, that Kṛṣṇa is going to be caught by Yaśodā and is running away in fear. This illustrates the difference between the *bhakta* and the *yogī*. *Yogīs* cannot reach Kṛṣṇa, but for pure devotees like mother Yaśodā, Kṛṣṇa is already caught. Kṛṣṇa was even afraid of mother Yaśodā's stick. This was mentioned by Queen Kuntī in her prayers: *bhaya-bhāvanayā sthitasya* (*Bhāg*. 1.8.31). Kṛṣṇa is afraid of mother Yaśodā, and *yogīs* are afraid of Kṛṣṇa. *Yogīs* try to reach Kṛṣṇa by *jñāna-yoga* and other *yogas*, but fail. Yet although mother Yaśodā was a woman, Kṛṣṇa was afraid of her, as clearly described in this verse.

## TEXT 10

अन्वञ्चमाना जननी बृहच्चल-
च्छ्रोणीभराक्रान्तगतिः सुमध्यमा ।
जवेन विस्रंसितकेशबन्धन-
च्युतप्रसूनानुगतिः परामृशत् ॥१०॥

*anvañcamānā jananī bṛhac-calac-*
*chroṇī-bharākrānta-gatiḥ sumadhyamā*
*javena visraṁsita-keśa-bandhana-*
*cyuta-prasūnānugatiḥ parāmṛśat*

*anvañcamānā*—following Kṛṣṇa very swiftly; *jananī*—mother Yaśodā; *bṛhat-calat-śroṇī-bhara-ākrānta-gatiḥ*—being overburdened by the weight of her large breasts, she became tired and had to reduce her speed; *su-madhyamā*—because of her thin waist; *javena*—because of going very fast; *visraṁsita-keśa-bandhana*—from her arrangement of hair, which had become loosened; *cyuta-prasūna-anugatiḥ*—she was followed by the flowers falling after her; *parāmṛśat*—finally captured Kṛṣṇa without fail.

## TRANSLATION

**While following Kṛṣṇa, mother Yaśodā, her thin waist overburdened by her heavy breasts, naturally had to reduce her speed. Because of following Kṛṣṇa very swiftly, her hair became loose, and the flowers in her hair were falling after her. Yet she did not fail to capture her son Kṛṣṇa.**

## PURPORT

*Yogīs* cannot capture Kṛṣṇa by severe penances and austerities, but mother Yaśodā, despite all obstacles, was finally able to catch Kṛṣṇa without difficulty. This is the difference between a *yogī* and a *bhakta. Yogīs* cannot enter even the effulgence of Kṛṣṇa. *Yasya prabhā prabhavato jagad-aṇḍa-koṭi-koṭiṣu* (*Brahma-saṁhitā* 5.40). In that effulgence there are millions of universes, but *yogīs* and *jñānīs* cannot enter that effulgence even after many, many years of austerities, whereas *bhaktas* can capture Kṛṣṇa simply by love and affection. This is the example shown here by mother Yaśodā. Kṛṣṇa therefore confirms that if one wants to capture Him, one must undertake devotional service.

*bhaktyā mām abhijānāti*
*yāvān yaś cāsmi tattvataḥ*
*tato māṁ tattvato jñātvā*
*viśate tad-anantaram*
(Bg. 18.55)

*Bhaktas* enter even the planet of Kṛṣṇa very easily, but the less intelligent *yogīs* and *jñānīs*, by their meditation, remain running after Kṛṣṇa. Even if they enter Kṛṣṇa's effulgence, they fall down.

## TEXT 11

कृतागसं तं प्ररुदन्तमक्षिणी
कषन्तमञ्जन्मषिणी स्वपाणिना ।
उद्वीक्षमाणं भयविह्वलेक्षणं
हस्ते गृहीत्वा भिषयन्त्यवागुरत् ॥११॥

*kṛtāgasaṁ taṁ prarudantam akṣiṇī*
*kaṣantam añjan-maṣiṇī sva-pāṇinā*
*udvīkṣamāṇaṁ bhaya-vihvalekṣaṇaṁ*
*haste gṛhītvā bhiṣayanty avāgurat*

*kṛta-āgasam*—who was an offender; *tam*—unto Kṛṣṇa; *prarudantam*—with a crying attitude; *akṣiṇī*—His two eyes; *kaṣantam*—rubbing; *añjat-maṣiṇī*—from whose eyes the blackish ointment was distributed all over His face with tears; *sva-pāṇinā*—with His own hand; *udvīkṣamāṇam*—who was seen in that attitude by mother Yaśodā; *bhaya-vihvala-īkṣaṇam*—whose eyes appeared distressed because of such fear of His mother; *haste*—by the hand; *gṛhītvā*—catching; *bhiṣayantī*—mother Yaśodā was threatening Him; *avāgurat*—and thus she very mildly chastised Him.

## TRANSLATION

**When caught by mother Yaśodā, Kṛṣṇa became more and more afraid and admitted to being an offender. As she looked upon Him, she saw that He was crying, His tears mixing with the black ointment around His eyes, and as He rubbed His eyes with His hands, He smeared the ointment all over His face. Mother Yaśodā, catching her beautiful son by the hand, mildly began to chastise Him.**

## PURPORT

From these dealings between mother Yaśodā and Kṛṣṇa, we can understand the exalted position of a pure devotee in loving service to the Lord. *Yogīs*, *jñānīs*, *karmīs* and Vedāntists cannot even approach Kṛṣṇa; they must remain very, very far away from Him and try to enter His bodily effulgence, although this also they are unable to do. Great demigods like Lord Brahmā and Lord Śiva always worship the Lord by meditation and by service. Even the most powerful Yamarāja fears Kṛṣṇa. Therefore, as we find in the history of Ajāmila, Yamarāja instructed his followers not even to approach the devotees, what to speak of capturing them. In other words, Yamarāja also fears Kṛṣṇa and Kṛṣṇa's devotees. Yet this Kṛṣṇa became so dependent on mother Yaśodā that when she simply showed Kṛṣṇa the stick in her hand, Kṛṣṇa admitted to being an offender and began to cry like an ordinary child. Mother Yaśodā, of course, did not want to chastise her beloved child very much, and therefore she immediately threw her stick away and simply rebuked Kṛṣṇa, saying, "Now I shall bind You so that You cannot commit any further offensive activities. Nor for the time being can You play with Your playmates." This shows the position of a pure devotee, in contrast with others, like *jñānīs*, *yogīs* and the followers of Vedic ritualistic ceremonies, in regarding the transcendental nature of the Absolute Truth.

## TEXT 12

त्यक्त्वा यष्टिं सुतं भीतं विज्ञायार्भकवत्सला ।
इयेष किल तं बद्धुं दाम्नातद्वीर्यकोविदा ॥१२॥

*tyaktvā yaṣṭiṁ sutaṁ bhītaṁ*
*vijñāyārbhaka-vatsalā*
*iyeṣa kila taṁ baddhuṁ*
*dāmnātad-vīrya-kovidā*

*tyaktvā*—throwing away; *yaṣṭim*—the stick in her hand; *sutam*—her son; *bhītam*—considering her son's great fear; *vijñāya*—understanding; *arbhaka-vatsalā*—the most affectionate mother of Kṛṣṇa; *iyeṣa*—desired; *kila*—indeed; *tam*—Kṛṣṇa; *baddhum*—to bind; *dāmnā*—with a rope; *a-tat-vīrya-kovidā*—without knowledge of the supremely powerful Personality of Godhead (because of intense love for Kṛṣṇa).

## TRANSLATION

**Mother Yaśodā was always overwhelmed by intense love for Kṛṣṇa, not knowing who Kṛṣṇa was or how powerful He was. Be-**

**cause of maternal affection for Kṛṣṇa, she never even cared to know who He was. Therefore, when she saw that her son had become excessively afraid, she threw the stick away and desired to bind Him so that He would not commit any further naughty activities.**

## PURPORT

Mother Yaśodā wanted to bind Kṛṣṇa not in order to chastise Him but because she thought that the child was so restless that He might leave the house in fear. That would be another disturbance. Therefore, because of full affection, to stop Kṛṣṇa from leaving the house, she wanted to bind Him with rope. Mother Yaśodā wanted to impress upon Kṛṣṇa that since He was afraid merely to see her stick, He should not perform such disturbing activities as breaking the container of yogurt and butter and distributing its contents to the monkeys. Mother Yaśodā did not care to understand who Kṛṣṇa was and how His power spreads everywhere. This is an example of pure love for Kṛṣṇa.

## TEXTS 13–14

न चान्तर्न बहिर्यस्य न पूर्वं नापि चापरम् ।
पूर्वापरं बहिश्चान्तर्जगतो यो जगच्च यः ॥१३॥
तं मत्वात्मजमव्यक्तं मर्त्यलिङ्गमधोक्षजम् ।
गोपिकोलूखले दाम्ना बबन्ध प्राकृतं यथा ॥१४॥

*na cāntar na bahir yasya*
*na pūrvaṁ nāpi cāparam*
*pūrvāparaṁ bahiś cāntar*
*jagato yo jagac ca yaḥ*

*taṁ matvātmajam avyaktam*
*martya-liṅgam adhokṣajam*
*gopikolūkhale dāmnā*
*babandha prākṛtaṁ yathā*

*na*—not; *ca*—also; *antaḥ*—interior; *na*—nor; *bahiḥ*—exterior; *yasya*—whose; *na*—neither; *pūrvam*—beginning; *na*—nor; *api*—

indeed; *ca*—also; *aparam*—end; *pūrva-aparam*—the beginning and the end; *bahiḥ ca antaḥ*—the external and the internal; *jagataḥ*—of the whole cosmic manifestation; *yaḥ*—one who is; *jagat ca yaḥ*—and who is everything in creation in total; *tam*—Him; *matvā*—considering; *ātma-jam*—her own son; *avyaktam*—the unmanifested; *martya-liṅgam*—appearing as a human being; *adhokṣajam*—beyond sense perception; *gopikā*—mother Yaśodā; *ulūkhale*—to the grinding mortar; *dāmnā*—by a rope; *babandha*—bound; *prākṛtam yathā*—as done to a common human child.

## TRANSLATION

**The Supreme Personality of Godhead has no beginning and no end, no exterior and no interior, no front and no rear. In other words, He is all-pervading. Because He is not under the influence of the element of time, for Him there is no difference between past, present and future; He exists in His own transcendental form at all times. Being absolute, beyond relativity, He is free from distinctions between cause and effect, although He is the cause and effect of everything. That unmanifested person, who is beyond the perception of the senses, had now appeared as a human child, and mother Yaśodā, considering Him her own ordinary child, bound Him to the wooden mortar with a rope.**

## PURPORT

In *Bhagavad-gītā* (10.12), Kṛṣṇa is described as the Supreme Brahman (*paraṁ brahma paraṁ dhāma*). The word *brahma* means "the greatest." Kṛṣṇa is greater than the greatest, being unlimited and all-pervading. How can it be possible for the all-pervading to be measured or bound? Then again, Kṛṣṇa is the time factor. Therefore, He is all-pervading not only in space but also in time. We have measurements of time, but although we are limited by past, present and future, for Kṛṣṇa these do not exist. Every individual person can be measured, but Kṛṣṇa has already shown that although He also is an individual, the entire cosmic manifestation is within His mouth. All these points considered, Kṛṣṇa cannot be measured. How then did Yaśodā want to measure Him and bind Him? We must conclude that this took place simply on the platform of pure transcendental love. This was the only cause.

*advaitam acyutam anādim ananta-rūpam*
*ādyaṁ purāṇa-puruṣaṁ nava-yauvanaṁ ca*
*vedeṣu durlabham adurlabham ātma-bhaktau*
*govindam ādi-puruṣaṁ tam ahaṁ bhajāmi*
(*Brahma-saṁhitā* 5.33)

Everything is one because Kṛṣṇa is the supreme cause of everything. Kṛṣṇa cannot be measured or calculated by Vedic knowledge (*vedeṣu durlabham*). He is available only to devotees (*adurlabham ātma-bhaktau*). Devotees can handle Him because they act on the basis of loving service (*bhaktyā mām abhijānāti yāvān yaś cāsmi tattvataḥ*). Thus mother Yaśodā wanted to bind Him.

## TEXT 15

तद् दाम बध्यमानस्य स्वार्भकस्य कृतागसः ।
द्व्यङ्गुलोनमभूत्तेन सन्दधेऽन्यच्च गोपिका ॥१५॥

*tad dāma badhyamānasya*
*svārbhakasya kṛtāgasaḥ*
*dvy-aṅgulonam abhūt tena*
*sandadhe 'nyac ca gopikā*

*tat dāma*—that binding rope; *badhyamānasya*—who was being bound by mother Yaśodā; *sva-arbhakasya*—of her own son; *kṛta-āgasaḥ*—who was an offender; *dvi-aṅgula*—by a measurement of two fingers; *ūnam*—short; *abhūt*—became; *tena*—with that rope; *sandadhe*—joined; *anyat ca*—another rope; *gopikā*—mother Yaśodā.

## TRANSLATION

**When mother Yaśodā was trying to bind the offending child, she saw that the binding rope was short by a distance the width of two fingers. Thus she brought another rope to join to it.**

## PURPORT

Here is the first chapter in Kṛṣṇa's exhibition of unlimited potency to mother Yaśodā when she tried to bind Him: the rope was too short. The

Lord had already shown His unlimited potency by killing Pūtanā, Śakaṭāsura and Tṛṇāvarta. Now Kṛṣṇa exhibited another *vibhūti*, or display of potency, to mother Yaśodā. "Unless I agree," Kṛṣṇa desired to show, "you cannot bind Me." Thus although mother Yaśodā, in her attempt to bind Kṛṣṇa, added one rope after another, ultimately she was a failure. When Kṛṣṇa agreed, however, she was successful. In other words, one must be in transcendental love with Kṛṣṇa, but that does not mean that one can control Kṛṣṇa. When Kṛṣṇa is satisfied with one's devotional service, He does everything Himself. *Sevonmukhe hi jihvādau svayam eva sphuraty adaḥ.* He reveals more and more to the devotee as the devotee advances in service. *Jihvādau:* this service begins with the tongue, with chanting and with taking the *prasāda* of Kṛṣṇa.

*ataḥ śrī-kṛṣṇa-nāmādi*
*na bhaved grāhyam indriyaiḥ*
*sevonmukhe hi jihvādau*
*svayam eva sphuraty adaḥ*
(*Bhakti-rasāmṛta-sindhu* 1.2.234)

## TEXT 16

यदासीत्तदपि न्यूनं तेनान्यदपि सन्दधे ।
तदपि द्व्यङ्गुलं न्यूनं यद् यदादत्त बन्धनम् ॥१६॥

*yadāsīt tad api nyūnaṁ*
*tenānyad api sandadhe*
*tad api dvy-aṅgulaṁ nyūnaṁ*
*yad yad ādatta bandhanam*

*yadā*—when; *āsīt*—became; *tat api*—even the new rope that had been joined; *nyūnam*—still short; *tena*—then, with the second rope; *anyat api*—another rope also; *sandadhe*—she joined; *tat api*—that also; *dvi-aṅgulam*—by a measurement of two fingers; *nyūnam*—remained short; *yat yat ādatta*—in this way, one after another, whatever ropes she joined; *bandhanam*—for binding Kṛṣṇa.

## TRANSLATION

**This new rope also was short by a measurement of two fingers, and when another rope was joined to it, it was still two fingers too short. As many ropes as she joined, all of them failed; their shortness could not be overcome.**

## TEXT 17

एवं स्वगेहदामानि यशोदा सन्दधत्यपि ।
गोपीनां सुस्मयन्तीनां स्मयन्ती विस्मिताभवत् ॥१७॥

*evaṁ sva-geha-dāmāni*
*yaśodā sandadhaty api*
*gopīnāṁ susmayantīnāṁ*
*smayantī vismitābhavat*

*evam*—in this manner; *sva-geha-dāmāni*—all the ropes available in the household; *yaśodā*—mother Yaśodā; *sandadhati api*—although she was joining one after another; *gopīnām*—when all the other elderly *gopī* friends of mother Yaśodā; *su-smayantīnām*—were all taking pleasure in this funny affair; *smayantī*—mother Yaśodā was also smiling; *vismitā abhavat*—all of them were struck with wonder.

## TRANSLATION

**Thus mother Yaśodā joined whatever ropes were available in the household, but still she failed in her attempt to bind Kṛṣṇa. Mother Yaśodā's friends, the elderly gopīs in the neighborhood, were smiling and enjoying the fun. Similarly, mother Yaśodā, although laboring in that way, was also smiling. All of them were struck with wonder.**

## PURPORT

Actually this incident was wonderful because Kṛṣṇa was only a child with small hands. To bind Him should have required only a rope not more than two feet long. All the ropes in the house combined together might have been hundreds of feet long, but still He was impossible to bind, for all the ropes together were still too short. Naturally mother Yaśodā and her *gopī* friends thought, "How is this possible?" Seeing this funny affair, all of them were smiling. The first rope was short by a measurement the width of two fingers, and after the second rope was added, it was still two fingers too short. If the shortness of all the ropes were added together, it must have amounted to the width of hundreds of fingers. Certainly this was astonishing. This was another exhibition of Kṛṣṇa's inconceivable potency to His mother and His mother's friends.

## TEXT 18

स्वमातुः स्विन्नगात्राया विस्रस्तकबरस्रजः ।
दृष्ट्वा परिश्रमं कृष्णः कृपयासीत् स्वबन्धने ॥१८॥

*sva-mātuḥ svinna-gātrāyā*
*visrasta-kabara-srajaḥ*
*dṛṣṭvā pariśramaṁ kṛṣṇaḥ*
*kṛpayāsīt sva-bandhane*

*sva-mātuḥ*—of His own mother (Kṛṣṇa's mother, Yaśodādevī); *svinna-gātrāyāḥ*—when Kṛṣṇa saw His mother perspiring all over because of unnecessary labor; *visrasta*—were falling down; *kabara*—from her hair; *srajaḥ*—of whom the flowers; *dṛṣṭvā*—by seeing the condition of His mother; *pariśramam*—He could understand that she was now overworked and feeling fatigued; *kṛṣṇaḥ*—the Supreme Personality of Godhead; *kṛpayā*—by His causeless mercy upon His devotee and mother; *āsīt*—agreed; *sva-bandhane*—in binding Him.

## TRANSLATION

**Because of mother Yaśodā's hard labor, her whole body became covered with perspiration, and the flowers and comb were falling from her hair. When child Kṛṣṇa saw His mother thus fatigued, He became merciful to her and agreed to be bound.**

## PURPORT

When mother Yaśodā and the other ladies finally saw that Kṛṣṇa, although decorated with many bangles and other jeweled ornaments, could not be bound with all the ropes available in the house, they decided that Kṛṣṇa was so fortunate that He could not be bound by any material condition. Thus they gave up the idea of binding Him. But in competition between Kṛṣṇa and His devotee, Kṛṣṇa sometimes agrees to be defeated. Thus Kṛṣṇa's internal energy, *yogamāyā*, was brought to work, and Kṛṣṇa agreed to be bound by mother Yaśodā.

## TEXT 19

एवं संदर्शिता ह्यङ्ग हरिणा भृत्यवश्यता ।
स्ववशेनापि कृष्णेन यस्येदं सेश्वरं वशे ॥१९॥

*evaṁ sandarśitā hy aṅga*
*hariṇā bhṛtya-vaśyatā*
*sva-vaśenāpi kṛṣṇena*
*yasyedaṁ seśvaraṁ vaśe*

*evam*—in this manner; *sandarśitā*—was exhibited; *hi*—indeed; *aṅga*—O Mahārāja Parīkṣit; *hariṇā*—by the Supreme Personality of Godhead; *bhṛtya-vaśyatā*—His transcendental quality of becoming subordinate to His servitor or devotee; *sva-vaśena*—who is within the control only of His own self; *api*—indeed; *kṛṣṇena*—by Kṛṣṇa; *yasya*—of whom; *idam*—the whole universe; *sa-īśvaram*—with the powerful demigods like Lord Śiva and Lord Brahmā; *vaśe*—under the control.

## TRANSLATION

**O Mahārāja Parīkṣit, this entire universe, with its great, exalted demigods like Lord Śiva, Lord Brahmā and Lord Indra, is under the control of the Supreme Personality of Godhead. Yet the Supreme Lord has one transcendental attribute: He comes under the control of His devotees. This was now exhibited by Kṛṣṇa in this pastime.**

## PURPORT

This pastime of Kṛṣṇa's is very difficult to understand, but devotees can understand it. It is therefore said, *darśayaṁs tad-vidāṁ loka ātmano bhakta-vaśyatām* (*Bhāg.* 10.11.9): the Lord displays the transcendental attribute of coming under the control of His devotees. As stated in the *Brahma-saṁhitā* (5.35):

*eko 'py asau racayituṁ jagad-aṇḍa-koṭiṁ*
*yac-chaktir asti jagad-aṇḍa-cayā yad antaḥ*
*aṇḍāntara-stha-paramāṇu-cayāntara-sthaṁ*
*govindam ādi-puruṣaṁ tam ahaṁ bhajāmi*

By His one plenary portion as Paramātmā, the Lord controls innumerable universes, with all their demigods; yet He agrees to be controlled by a devotee. In the *Upaniṣads* it is said that the Supreme Personality of Godhead can run with more speed than the mind, but here we see that although Kṛṣṇa wanted to avoid being arrested by His mother, He was finally defeated, and mother Yaśodā captured Him. *Lakṣmī-sahasra-śata-sambhrama-sevyamānam:* Kṛṣṇa is served by hundreds and thousands of goddesses of fortune. Nonetheless, He steals butter like one who is poverty-stricken. Yamarāja, the controller of all living entities, fears the order of Kṛṣṇa, yet Kṛṣṇa is afraid of His mother's stick. These contradictions cannot be understood by one who is not a devotee, but a devotee can understand how powerful is unalloyed devotional service to Kṛṣṇa; it is so powerful that Kṛṣṇa can be controlled by an unalloyed devotee. This *bhṛtya-vaśyatā* does not mean that He is under the control of the servant; rather, He is under the control of the servant's pure love. In *Bhagavad-gītā* (1.21) it is said that Kṛṣṇa became the chariot driver of Arjuna. Arjuna ordered Him, *senayor ubhayor madhye rathaṁ sthāpaya me 'cyuta:* "My dear Kṛṣṇa, You have agreed to be my charioteer and to execute my orders. Place my chariot between the two armies of soldiers." Kṛṣṇa immediately executed this order, and therefore one may argue that Kṛṣṇa also is not independent. But this is one's *ajñāna*, ignorance. Kṛṣṇa is always fully independent; when He becomes subordinate to His devotees, this is a display of *ānanda-cinmaya-rasa*, the humor of transcendental qualities that increases His transcendental pleasure. Everyone worships Kṛṣṇa as the Supreme Personality of Godhead, and therefore He sometimes desires to be controlled by someone else. Such a controller can be no one else but a pure devotee.

## TEXT 20

**नेमं विरिञ्चो न भवो न श्रीरप्यङ्गसंश्रया ।**
**प्रसादं लेभिरे गोपी यत्तत्प्राप विमुक्तिदात् ॥२०॥**

*nemaṁ viriñco na bhavo*
*na śrīr apy aṅga-saṁśrayā*
*prasādaṁ lebhire gopī*
*yat tat prāpa vimuktidāt*

*na*—not; *imam*—this exalted position; *viriñcaḥ*—Lord Brahmā; *na*—nor; *bhavaḥ*—Lord Śiva; *na*—nor; *śrīḥ*—the goddess of fortune; *api*—indeed; *aṅga-saṁśrayā*—although she is always the better half of the Supreme Personality of Godhead; *prasādam*—mercy; *lebhire*—obtained; *gopī*—mother Yaśodā; *yat tat*—as that which; *prāpa*—obtained; *vimukti-dāt*—from Kṛṣṇa, who gives deliverance from this material world.

## TRANSLATION

**Neither Lord Brahmā, nor Lord Śiva, nor even the goddess of fortune, who is always the better half of the Supreme Lord, can obtain from the Supreme Personality of Godhead, the deliverer from this material world, such mercy as received by mother Yaśodā.**

## PURPORT

This is a comparative study between mother Yaśodā and other devotees of the Lord. As stated in *Caitanya-caritāmṛta* (*Ādi* 5.142), *ekale īśvara kṛṣṇa, āra saba bhṛtya:* the only supreme master is Kṛṣṇa, and all others are His servants. Kṛṣṇa has the transcendental quality of *bhṛtya-vaśyatā*, becoming subordinate to His *bhṛtya*, or servant. Now, although everyone is *bhṛtya* and although Kṛṣṇa has the quality of becoming subordinate to His *bhṛtya*, the position of mother Yaśodā is the greatest. Lord Brahmā is *bhṛtya*, a servant of Kṛṣṇa, and he is *ādi-kavi*, the original creator of this universe (*tene brahma hṛdā ya ādi-kavaye*). Nonetheless, even he could not obtain such mercy as mother Yaśodā. As for Lord Śiva, he is the topmost Vaiṣṇava (*vaiṣṇavānāṁ yathā śambhuḥ*). What to speak of Lord

Brahmā and Lord Śiva, the goddess of fortune, Lakṣmī, is the Lord's constant companion in service, since she always associates with His body. But even she could not get such mercy. Therefore Mahārāja Parīkṣit was surprised, thinking, "What did mother Yaśodā and Nanda Mahārāja do in their previous lives by which they got such a great opportunity, the opportunity to be the affectionate father and mother of Kṛṣṇa?"

In this verse there are three negative pronouncements—*na, na, na.* When anything is uttered three times—"do it, do it, do it"—one should understand that this is meant to indicate great stress on a fact. In this verse, we find *na lebhire, na lebhire, na lebhire.* Yet mother Yaśodā is in the supermost exalted position, and thus Kṛṣṇa has become completely subordinate to her.

The word *vimuktidāt* is also significant. There are different types of liberation, such as *sāyujya, sālokya, sārūpya, sārṣṭi* and *sāmīpya,* but *vimukti* means "special *mukti.*" When after liberation one is situated on the platform of *prema-bhakti,* one is said to have achieved *vimukti,* "special *mukti.*" Therefore the word *na* is mentioned. That exalted platform of *premā* is described by Śrī Caitanya Mahāprabhu as *premā pum-artho mahān,* and mother Yaśodā naturally acts in such an exalted position in loving affairs. She is therefore a *nitya-siddha* devotee, an expansion of Kṛṣṇa's *hlādinī* potency, His potency to enjoy transcendental bliss through expansions who are special devotees (*ānanda-cinmaya-rasa-pratibhāvitābhiḥ*). Such devotees are not *sādhana-siddha.*

## TEXT 21

नायं सुखापो भगवान् देहिनां गोपिकासुतः ।
ज्ञानिनां चात्मभूतानां यथा भक्तिमतामिह ॥२१॥

*nāyaṁ sukhāpo bhagavān*
*dehināṁ gopikā-sutaḥ*
*jñānināṁ cātma-bhūtānāṁ*
*yathā bhaktimatām iha*

*na*—not; *ayam*—this; *sukha-āpaḥ*—very easily obtainable, or an object of happiness; *bhagavān*—the Supreme Personality of Godhead; *dehinām*—of persons in the bodily concept of life, especially the *karmīs;*

*gopikā-sutaḥ*—Kṛṣṇa, the son of mother Yaśodā (Kṛṣṇa as the son of Vasudeva is called Vāsudeva, and as the son of mother Yaśodā He is known as Kṛṣṇa); *jñāninām ca*—and of the *jñānīs,* who try to be free from material contamination; *ātma-bhūtānām*—of self-sufficient *yogīs; yathā*—as; *bhakti-matām*—of the devotees; *iha*—in this world.

## TRANSLATION

**The Supreme Personality of Godhead, Kṛṣṇa, the son of mother Yaśodā, is accessible to devotees engaged in spontaneous loving service, but He is not as easily accessible to mental speculators, to those striving for self-realization by severe austerities and penances, or to those who consider the body the same as the self.**

## PURPORT

Kṛṣṇa, the Supreme Personality of Godhead as the son of mother Yaśodā, is very easily available to devotees, but not to *tapasvīs, yogīs, jñānīs* and others who have a bodily concept of life. Although they may sometimes be called *śānta-bhaktas,* real *bhakti* begins with *dāsya-rasa.* Kṛṣṇa says in *Bhagavad-gītā* (4.11):

*ye yathā māṁ prapadyante*
*tāṁs tathaiva bhajāmy aham*
*mama vartmānuvartante*
*manuṣyāḥ pārtha sarvaśaḥ*

"As living entities surrender unto Me, I reward them accordingly. Everyone follows My path in all respects, O son of Pṛthā." Everyone is seeking Kṛṣṇa, for He is the Supersoul of all individual souls. Everyone loves his body and wants to protect it because he is within the body as the soul, and everyone loves the soul because the soul is part and parcel of the Supersoul. Therefore, everyone is actually seeking to achieve happiness by reviving his relationship with the Supersoul. As the Lord says in *Bhagavad-gītā* (15.15), *vedaiś ca sarvair aham eva vedyaḥ:* "By all the *Vedas,* it is I who am to be known." Therefore, the *karmīs, jñānīs, yogīs* and saintly persons are all seeking Kṛṣṇa. But by following in the footsteps of devotees who are in a direct relationship with Kṛṣṇa, especially the inhabitants of Vṛndāvana, one can reach the supreme position of associating with Kṛṣṇa. As it is said, *vṛndāvanaṁ parityajya padam ekaṁ na gacchati:* Kṛṣṇa does not leave Vṛndāvana even for a moment. The *vṛndāvana-vāsīs*—mother Yaśodā, Kṛṣṇa's friends and Kṛṣṇa's conjugal lovers, the younger *gopīs* with whom He dances—have very intimate relationships with Kṛṣṇa, and if one follows in the footsteps of these devotees, Kṛṣṇa is available. Although the *nitya-siddha* expansions of Kṛṣṇa always remain with Kṛṣṇa, if those engaged in *sādhana-siddhi* follow in the footsteps of Kṛṣṇa's *nitya-siddha* associates, such *sādhana-siddhas* also can easily attain Kṛṣṇa without difficulty. But there are those who are attached to bodily concepts of life. Lord Brahmā and Lord Śiva, for example, have very prestigious positions, and thus they have the sense of being very exalted *īśvaras.* In other words, because Lord Brahmā and Lord Śiva are *guṇa-avatāras* and have exalted positions, they have some small sense of being like Kṛṣṇa. But the pure devotees who inhabit Vṛndāvana do not possess any bodily conception. They are fully dedicated to the service of the Lord in sublime affection, *premā.* Śrī Caitanya Mahāprabhu has therefore recommended, *premā pum-artho mahān:* the highest perfection of life is *premā,* pure love in relationship with Kṛṣṇa. And mother Yaśodā appears to be the topmost of devotees who have attained this perfection.

## TEXT 22

कृष्णस्तु गृहकृत्येषु व्यग्रायां मातरि प्रभुः ।
अद्राक्षीदर्जुनौ पूर्वं गुह्यकौ धनदात्मजौ ॥२२॥

*kṛṣṇas tu gṛha-kṛtyeṣu*
*vyagrāyāṁ mātari prabhuḥ*
*adrākṣīd arjunau pūrvaṁ*
*guhyakau dhanadātmajau*

*kṛṣṇaḥ tu*—in the meantime; *gṛha-kṛtyeṣu*—in engagement in household affairs; *vyagrāyām*—very busy; *mātari*—when His mother; *prabhuḥ*—the Lord; *adrākṣīt*—observed; *arjunau*—the twin *arjuna* trees; *pūrvam*—before Him; *guhyakau*—which in a former millennium had been demigods; *dhanada-ātmajau*—the sons of Kuvera, the treasurer of the demigods.

## TRANSLATION

**While mother Yaśodā was very busy with household affairs, the Supreme Lord, Kṛṣṇa, observed twin trees known as yamala-arjuna, which in a former millennium had been the demigod sons of Kuvera.**

## TEXT 23

पुरा नारदशापेन वृक्षतां प्रापितौ मदात् ।
नलकूवरमणिग्रीवाविति ख्यातौ श्रियान्वितौ ॥२३॥

*purā nārada-śāpena*
*vṛkṣatāṁ prāpitau madāt*
*nalakūvara-maṇigrīvāv*
*iti khyātau śriyānvitau*

*purā*—formerly; *nārada-śāpena*—being cursed by Nārada Muni; *vṛkṣatām*—the forms of trees; *prāpitau*—obtained; *madāt*—because of madness; *nalakūvara*—one of them was Nalakūvara; *maṇigrīvau*—the other was Maṇigrīva; *iti*—thus; *khyātau*—well known; *śriyā anvitau*—very opulent.

## TRANSLATION

**In their former birth, these two sons, known as Nalakūvara and Maṇigrīva, were extremely opulent and fortunate. But because of pride and false prestige, they did not care about anyone, and thus Nārada Muni cursed them to become trees.**

*Thus end the Bhaktivedanta purports of the Tenth Canto, Ninth Chapter, of the* Śrīmad-Bhāgavatam, *entitled "Mother Yaśodā Binds Lord Kṛṣṇa."*

## CHAPTER TEN

# Deliverance of the Yamala-arjuna Trees

This chapter describes how Kṛṣṇa broke the twin *arjuna* trees, from which Nalakūvara and Maṇigrīva, the sons of Kuvera, then came out.

Nalakūvara and Maṇigrīva were great devotees of Lord Śiva, but because of material opulence they became so extravagant and senseless that one day they were enjoying with naked girls in a lake and shamelessly walking here and there. Suddenly Nārada Muni passed by, but they were so maddened by their wealth and false prestige that even though they saw Nārada Muni present, they remained naked and were not even ashamed. In other words, because of opulence and false prestige, they lost their sense of common decency. Of course, it is the nature of the material qualities that when one becomes very much opulent in terms of wealth and a prestigious position, one loses one's sense of etiquette and does not care about anyone, even a sage like Nārada Muni. For such bewildered persons (*ahaṅkāra-vimūḍhātmā*), who especially deride devotees, the proper punishment is to be again stricken with poverty. The Vedic rules and regulations prescribe how to control the false sense of prestige by the practice of *yama, niyama* and so on (*tapasā brahmacaryeṇa śamena ca damena ca*). A poor man can be convinced very easily that the prestige of an opulent position in this material world is temporary, but a rich man cannot. Therefore Nārada Muni set an example by cursing these two persons, Nalakūvara and Maṇigrīva, to become dull and unconscious like trees. This was a fit punishment. But because Kṛṣṇa is always merciful, even though they were punished they were fortunate enough to see the Supreme Personality of Godhead face to face. Therefore the punishment given by Vaiṣṇavas is not at all punishment; rather, it is another kind of mercy. By the curse of the *devarṣi*, Nalakūvara and Maṇigrīva became twin *arjuna* trees and remained in the courtyard of mother Yaśodā and Nanda Mahārāja, waiting for the opportunity to see Kṛṣṇa directly. Lord Kṛṣṇa, by the desire of His devotee, uprooted these *yamala-arjuna* trees, and when Nalakūvara and Maṇigrīva were thus delivered by Kṛṣṇa after one hundred years of the *devas*, their old consciousness revived, and they offered Kṛṣṇa prayers suitable to be offered by demigods. Having thus gotten the opportunity to see Kṛṣṇa face to face, they understood how merciful Nārada Muni was, and therefore they expressed their indebtedness to him and thanked him. Then, after circumambulating the Supreme Personality of Godhead, Kṛṣṇa, they departed for their respective abodes.

## TEXT 1

श्रीराजोवाच
कथ्यतां भगवन्नेतत्तयोः शापस्य कारणम् ।
यत्तद् विगर्हितं कर्म येन वा देवर्षेस्तमः ॥ १ ॥

*śrī-rājovāca*
*kathyatāṁ bhagavann etat*
*tayoḥ śāpasya kāraṇam*
*yat tad vigarhitaṁ karma*
*yena vā devarṣes tamaḥ*

*śrī-rājā uvāca*—the King further inquired; *kathyatām*—please describe; *bhagavan*—O supremely powerful one; *etat*—this; *tayoḥ*—of both of them; *śāpasya*—of cursing; *kāraṇam*—the cause; *yat*—which; *tat*—that; *vigarhitam*—abominable; *karma*—act; *yena*—by which; *vā*—either; *devarṣeḥ tamaḥ*—the great sage Nārada became so angry.

## TRANSLATION

**King Parīkṣit inquired from Śukadeva Gosvāmī: O great and powerful saint, what was the cause of Nalakūvara's and Maṇigrīva's having been cursed by Nārada Muni? What did they do that was so abominable that even Nārada, the great sage, became angry at them? Kindly describe this to me.**

## TEXTS 2–3

श्रीशुक उवाच
रुद्रस्यानुचरौ भूत्वा सुदृप्तौ धनदात्मजौ ।
कैलासोपवने रम्ये मन्दाकिन्यां मदोत्कटौ ॥ २ ॥

वारुणीं मदिरां पीत्वा मदाघूर्णितलोचनौ ।
स्त्रीजनैरनुगायद्भिश्चेरतुः पुष्पिते वने ॥ ३ ॥

*śrī-śuka uvāca*
*rudrasyānucarau bhūtvā*
*sudṛptau dhanadātmajau*
*kailāsopavane ramye*
*mandākinyāṁ madotkaṭau*

*vāruṇīṁ madirāṁ pītvā*
*madāghūrṇita-locanau*
*strī-janair anugāyadbhiś*
*ceratuḥ puṣpite vane*

*śrī-śukaḥ uvāca*—Śrī Śukadeva Gosvāmī replied; *rudrasya*—of Lord Śiva; *anucarau*—two great devotees or associates; *bhūtvā*—being elevated to that post; *su-dṛptau*—being proud of that position and their beautiful bodily features; *dhanada-ātmajau*—the two sons of Kuvera, treasurer of the demigods; *kailāsa-upavane*—in a small garden attached to Kailāsa Parvata, the residence of Lord Śiva; *ramye*—in a very beautiful place; *mandākinyām*—on the River Mandākinī; *mada-utkaṭau*—terribly proud and mad; *vāruṇīm*—a kind of liquor named Vāruṇī; *madirām*—intoxication; *pītvā*—drinking; *mada-āghūrṇita-locanau*—their eyes rolling with intoxication; *strī-janaiḥ*—with women; *anugāyadbhiḥ*—vibrating songs sung by them; *ceratuḥ*—wandered; *puṣpite vane*—in a nice flower garden.

## TRANSLATION

**Śukadeva Gosvāmī said: O King Parīkṣit, because the two sons of Kuvera had been elevated to the association of Lord Śiva, of which they were very much proud, they were allowed to wander in a garden attached to Kailāsa Hill, on the bank of the Mandākinī River. Taking advantage of this, they used to drink a kind of liquor called Vāruṇī. Accompanied by women singing after them, they would wander in that garden of flowers, their eyes always rolling in intoxication.**

## PURPORT

This verse mentions some of the material advantages afforded to persons associated with or devoted to Lord Śiva. Apart from Lord Śiva, if one is a devotee of any other demigod, one receives some material advantages. Foolish people, therefore, become devotees of demigods. This has been pointed out and criticized by Lord Kṛṣṇa in *Bhagavad-gītā* (7.20): *kāmais tais tair hṛta-jñānāḥ prapadyante 'nya-devatāḥ.* Those who are not devotees of Kṛṣṇa have a taste for women, wine and so forth, and therefore they have been described as *hṛta-jñāna,* bereft of sense. The Kṛṣṇa consciousness movement can very easily point out such foolish persons, for they have been indicated in *Bhagavad-gītā* (7.15), where Lord Kṛṣṇa says:

*na māṁ duṣkṛtino mūḍhāḥ*
*prapadyante narādhamāḥ*
*māyayāpahṛta-jñānā*
*āsuraṁ bhāvam āśritāḥ*

"Those miscreants who are grossly foolish, lowest among mankind, whose knowledge is stolen by illusion, and who partake of the atheistic nature of demons, do not surrender unto Me." Anyone who is not a devotee of Kṛṣṇa and does not surrender to Kṛṣṇa must be considered *narādhama,* the lowest of men, and *duṣkṛtī,* one who always commits sinful activities. Thus there is no difficulty in finding out who is a third-class or fourth-class man, for one's position can be understood simply by this crucial test: is he or is he not a devotee of Kṛṣṇa?

Why are devotees of the demigods greater in number than the Vaiṣṇavas? The answer is given herein. Vaiṣṇavas are not interested in such fourth-class pleasures as wine and women, nor does Kṛṣṇa allow them such facilities.

## TEXT 4

अन्तः प्रविश्य गङ्गायामम्भोजवनराजिनि ।
चिक्रीडतुर्युवतिभिर्गजाविव करेणुभिः ॥ ४ ॥

*antaḥ praviśya gaṅgāyām*
*ambhoja-vana-rājini*

*cikrīḍatur yuvatibhir*
*gajāv iva kareṇubhiḥ*

*antaḥ*—within; *praviśya*—entering; *gaṅgāyām*—the Ganges, known as Mandākinī; *ambhoja*—of lotus flowers; *vana-rājini*—where there was a congested forest; *cikrīḍatuḥ*—the two of them used to enjoy; *yuvatibhiḥ*—in the company of young girls; *gajau*—two elephants; *iva*—just like; *kareṇubhiḥ*—with female elephants.

## TRANSLATION

**Within the waters of the Mandākinī Ganges, which were crowded with gardens of lotus flowers, the two sons of Kuvera would enjoy young girls, just like two male elephants enjoying in the water with female elephants.**

## PURPORT

People generally go to the Ganges to be purified of the effects of sinful life, but here is an example of how foolish persons enter the Ganges to become involved in sinful life. It is not that everyone becomes purified by entering the Ganges. Everything, spiritual and material, depends on one's mental condition.

## TEXT 5

यदृच्छया च देवर्षिर्भगवांस्तत्र कौरव ।
अपश्यन्नारदो देवौ क्षीबाणौ समबुध्यत ॥ ५ ॥

*yadṛcchayā ca devarṣir*
*bhagavāṁs tatra kaurava*
*apaśyan nārado devau*
*kṣībāṇau samabudhyata*

*yadṛcchayā*—by chance, while wandering all over the universe; *ca*—and; *deva-ṛṣiḥ*—the supreme saintly person among the demigods; *bhagavān*—the most powerful; *tatra*—there (where the two sons of Kuvera were enjoying life); *kaurava*—O Mahārāja Parīkṣit; *apaśyat*—when he saw; *nāradaḥ*—the great saint; *devau*—the two boys of the demigods; *kṣībāṇau*—with eyes maddened by intoxication; *samabudhyata*—he could understand (their position).

## TRANSLATION

**O Mahārāja Parīkṣit, by some auspicious opportunity for the two boys, the great saint Devarṣi Nārada once appeared there by chance. Seeing them intoxicated, with rolling eyes, he could understand their situation.**

## PURPORT

It is said:

*'sādhu-saṅga,' 'sādhu-saṅga'—sarva-śāstre kaya*
*lava-mātra sādhu-saṅge sarva-siddhi haya*
(Cc. *Madhya* 22.54)

Wherever Nārada Muni goes, any moment at which he appears is understood to be extremely auspicious. It is also said:

*brahmāṇḍa bhramite kona bhāgyavān jīva*
*guru-kṛṣṇa-prasāde pāya bhakti-latā-bīja*

"According to their *karma*, all living entities are wandering throughout the entire universe. Some of them are being elevated to the upper planetary systems, and some are going down into the lower planetary systems. Out of many millions of wandering living entities, one who is very fortunate gets an opportunity to associate with a bona fide spiritual master by the grace of Kṛṣṇa. By the mercy of both Kṛṣṇa and the spiritual master, such a person receives the seed of the creeper of devotional service." (Cc. *Madhya* 19.151) Nārada appeared in the garden to give the two sons of Kuvera the seed of devotional service, even though they were intoxicated. Saintly persons know how to bestow mercy upon the fallen souls.

## TEXT 6

**तं दृष्ट्वा व्रीडिता देव्यो विवस्त्राः शापशङ्किताः ।**
**वासांसि पर्यधुः शीघ्रं विवस्त्रौ नैव गुह्यकौ ॥ ६ ॥**

*taṁ dṛṣṭvā vrīḍitā devyo*
*vivastrāḥ śāpa-śaṅkitāḥ*
*vāsāṁsi paryadhuḥ śīghraṁ*
*vivastrau naiva guhyakau*

*tam*—Nārada Muni; *dṛṣṭvā*—seeing; *vrīḍitāḥ*—being ashamed; *devyaḥ*—the young girls of the demigods; *vivastrāḥ*—although they were naked; *śāpa-śaṅkitāḥ*—being afraid of being cursed; *vāsāṁsi*—garments; *paryadhuḥ*—covered the body; *śīghram*—very swiftly; *vivastrau*—who were also naked; *na*—not; *eva*—indeed; *guhyakau*—the two sons of Kuvera.

## TRANSLATION

**Upon seeing Nārada, the naked young girls of the demigods were very much ashamed. Afraid of being cursed, they covered their bodies with their garments. But the two sons of Kuvera did not do so; instead, not caring about Nārada, they remained naked.**

## TEXT 7

तौ दृष्ट्वा मदिरामत्तौ श्रीमदान्धौ सुरात्मजौ ।
तयोरनुग्रहार्थाय शापं दास्यन्निदं जगौ ॥ ७ ॥

*tau dṛṣṭvā madirā-mattau*
*śrī-madāndhau surātmajau*
*tayor anugrahārthāya*
*śāpaṁ dāsyann idaṁ jagau*

*tau*—the two boys of the demigods; *dṛṣṭvā*—seeing; *madirā-mattau*—very intoxicated because of drinking liquor; *śrī-mada-andhau*—being blind with false prestige and opulence; *sura-ātmajau*—the two sons of the demigods; *tayoḥ*—unto them; *anugraha-arthāya*—for the purpose of giving special mercy; *śāpam*—a curse; *dāsyan*—desiring to offer them; *idam*—this; *jagau*—uttered.

## TRANSLATION

**Seeing the two sons of the demigods naked and intoxicated by opulence and false prestige, Devarṣi Nārada, in order to show them**

**special mercy, desired to give them a special curse. Thus he spoke as follows.**

## PURPORT

Although in the beginning Nārada Muni appeared very angry and cursed them, at the end the two demigods Nalakūvara and Maṇigrīva were able to see the Supreme Personality of Godhead, Kṛṣṇa, face to face. Thus the curse was ultimately auspicious and brilliant. One has to judge what kind of curse Nārada placed upon them. Śrīla Viśvanātha Cakravartī Ṭhākura gives herein a good example. When a father finds his child deeply asleep but the child has to take some medicine to cure some disease, the father pinches the child so that the child will get up and take the medicine. In a similar way, Nārada Muni cursed Nalakūvara and Maṇigrīva in order to cure their disease of material blindness.

## TEXT 8

श्रीनारद उवाच

न ह्यन्यो जुषतो जोष्यान् बुद्धिभ्रंशो रजोगुणः ।
श्रीमदादाभिजात्यादिर्यत्र स्त्री द्यूतमासवः ॥ ८ ॥

*śrī-nārada uvāca*
*na hy anyo juṣato joṣyān*
*buddhi-bhraṁśo rajo-guṇaḥ*
*śrī-madād ābhijātyādir*
*yatra strī dyūtam āsavaḥ*

*śrī-nāradaḥ uvāca*—Nārada Muni said; *na*—there is not; *hi*—indeed; *anyaḥ*—another material enjoyment; *juṣataḥ*—of one who is enjoying; *joṣyān*—things very attractive in the material world (different varieties of eating, sleeping, mating and defense); *buddhi-bhraṁśaḥ*—such enjoyments attract the intelligence; *rajaḥ-guṇaḥ*—being controlled by the mode of passion; *śrī-madāt*—than riches; *ābhijātya-ādiḥ*—among the four material principles (attractive personal bodily features, birth in an aristocratic family, being very learned, and being very rich); *yatra*—wherein; *strī*—women; *dyūtam*—gambling; *āsavaḥ*—wine (wine, women and gambling are very prominent).

## TRANSLATION

**Nārada Muni said: Among all the attractions of material enjoyment, the attraction of riches bewilders one's intelligence more than having beautiful bodily features, taking birth in an aristocratic family, and being learned. When one is uneducated but falsely puffed up by wealth, the result is that one engages his wealth in enjoying wine, women and gambling.**

## PURPORT

Among the three modes of material nature—goodness, passion and ignorance—people are certainly conducted by the lower qualities, namely passion and ignorance, and especially by passion. Conducted by the mode of passion, one becomes more and more involved in material existence. Therefore human life is meant for subduing the modes of passion and ignorance and advancing in the mode of goodness.

*tadā rajas-tamo-bhāvāḥ*
*kāma-lobhādayaś ca ye*
*ceta etair anāviddhaṁ*
*sthitaṁ sattve prasīdati*
(*Bhāg.* 1.2.19)

This is culture: one must subdue the modes of passion and ignorance. In the mode of passion, when one is falsely proud of wealth, one engages his wealth only for three things, namely wine, women and gambling. We can actually see, especially in this age, that those who have unnecessary riches simply try to enjoy these three things. In Western civilization, these three things are very prominent because of an unnecessary increase of wealth. Nārada Muni considered all this in the case of Maṇigrīva and Nalakūvara because he found in them so much pride in the wealth of their father, Kuvera.

## TEXT 9

हन्यन्ते पशवो यत्र निर्दयैरजितात्मभिः ।
मन्यमानैरिमं देहमजरामृत्यु नश्वरम् ॥ ९ ॥

*hanyante paśavo yatra*
*nirdayair ajitātmabhiḥ*
*manyamānair imaṁ deham*
*ajarāmṛtyu naśvaram*

*hanyante*—are killed in many ways (especially by slaughterhouses); *paśavaḥ*—four-legged animals (horses, sheep, cows, hogs, etc.); *yatra*—wherein; *nirdayaiḥ*—by those merciless persons who are conducted by the mode of passion; *ajita-ātmabhiḥ*—rascals who are unable to control the senses; *manyamānaiḥ*—are thinking; *imam*—this; *deham*—body; *ajara*—will never become old or diseased; *amṛtyu*—death will never come; *naśvaram*—although the body is destined to be annihilated.

## TRANSLATION

**Unable to control their senses, rascals who are falsely proud of their riches or their birth in aristocratic families are so cruel that to maintain their perishable bodies, which they think will never grow old or die, they kill poor animals without mercy. Sometimes they kill animals merely to enjoy an excursion.**

## PURPORT

When the modes of passion and ignorance increase in human society, giving rise to unnecessary economic development, the result is that people become involved with wine, women and gambling. Then, being mad, they maintain big slaughterhouses or occasionally go on pleasure excursions to kill animals. Forgetting that however one may try to maintain the body, the body is subject to birth, death, old age and disease, such foolish rascals engage in sinful activities, one after another. Being *duṣkṛtīs*, they completely forget the existence of the supreme controller, who is sitting within the core of everyone's heart (*īśvaraḥ sarva-bhūtānāṁ hṛd-deśe 'rjuna tiṣṭhati*). That supreme controller is observing every bit of one's activity, and He rewards or punishes everyone by giving one a suitable body made by material nature (*bhrāmayan sarva-bhūtāni yantrārūḍhāni māyayā*). In this way, sinful persons automatically receive punishment in different types of bodies. The root cause of this punishment is that when one unnecessarily accumulates wealth, one becomes more and more degraded, not knowing that his wealth will be finished with his next birth.

*na sādhu manye yata ātmano 'yam*
*asann api kleśada āsa dehaḥ*
(*Bhāg.* 5.5.4)

Animal killing is prohibited. Every living being, of course, has to eat something (*jīvo jīvasya jīvanam*). But one should be taught what kind of food one should take. Therefore the *Īśopaniṣad* instructs, *tena tyaktena bhuñjīthāḥ:* one should eat whatever is allotted for human beings. Kṛṣṇa says in *Bhagavad-gītā* (9.26):

*patraṁ puṣpaṁ phalaṁ toyaṁ*
*yo me bhaktyā prayacchati*
*tad ahaṁ bhakty-upahṛtam*
*aśnāmi prayatātmanaḥ*

"If one offers Me with love and devotion a leaf, a flower, fruit or water, I will accept it." A devotee, therefore, does not eat anything that would require slaughterhouses for poor animals. Rather, devotees take *prasāda* of Kṛṣṇa (*tena tyaktena bhuñjīthāḥ*). Kṛṣṇa recommends that one give Him *patraṁ puṣpaṁ phalaṁ toyam*—a leaf, a flower, fruit or water. Animal food is never recommended for human beings; instead, a human being is recommended to take *prasāda*, remnants of food left by Kṛṣṇa. *Yajña-śiṣṭāśinaḥ santo mucyante sarva-kilbiṣaiḥ* (Bg. 3.13). If one practices eating *prasāda*, even if there is some little sinful activity involved, one becomes free from the results of sinful acts.

## TEXT 10

देवसंज्ञितमप्यन्ते कृमिविड्भस्मसंज्ञितम् ।
भूतध्रुक् तत्कृते स्वार्थं किं वेद निरयो यतः ॥१०॥

*deva-saṁjñitam apy ante*
*kṛmi-viḍ-bhasma-saṁjñitam*

*bhūta-dhruk tat-kṛte svārthaṁ*
*kiṁ veda nirayo yataḥ*

*deva-saṁjñitam*—the body now known as a very exalted person, like president, minister or even demigod; *api*—even if the body is so exalted; *ante*—after death; *kṛmi*—turns into worms; *viṭ*—or into stool; *bhasma-saṁjñitam*—or into ashes; *bhūta-dhruk*—a person who does not accept the śāstric injunctions and is unnecessarily envious of other living entities; *tat-kṛte*—by acting in that way; *sva-artham*—self-interest; *kim*—who is there; *veda*—who knows; *nirayaḥ yataḥ*—because from such sinful activities one must suffer hellish conditions.

## TRANSLATION

**While living one may be proud of one's body, thinking oneself a very big man, minister, president or even demigod, but whatever one may be, after death this body will turn either into worms, into stool or into ashes. If one kills poor animals to satisfy the temporary whims of this body, one does not know that he will suffer in his next birth, for such a sinful miscreant must go to hell and suffer the results of his actions.**

## PURPORT

In this verse the three words *kṛmi-viḍ-bhasma* are significant. After death, the body may become *kṛmi,* which means "worms," for if the body is disposed of without cremation, it may be eaten by worms; or else it may be eaten by animals like hogs and vultures and be turned into stool. Those who are more civilized burn the dead body, and thus it becomes ashes (*bhasma-saṁjñitam*). Yet although the body will be turned into worms, stool or ashes, foolish persons, just to maintain it, commit many sinful activities. This is certainly regrettable. The human form of body is actually meant for *jīvasya tattva-jijñāsā,* enlightenment in knowledge of spiritual values. Therefore, one must seek shelter of a bona fide spiritual master. *Tasmād guruṁ prapadyeta:* one must approach a *guru.* Who is a *guru*? *Śābde pare ca niṣṇātam* (*Bhāg.* 11.3.21): a *guru* is one who has full transcendental knowledge. Unless one approaches a spiritual master, one remains in ignorance. *Ācāryavān puruṣo veda*

(*Chāndogya Upaniṣad* 6.14.2): one has full knowledge about life when one is *ācāryavān*, controlled by the *ācārya*. But when one is conducted by *rajo-guṇa* and *tamo-guṇa*, one does not care about anything; instead, one acts like an ordinary foolish animal, risking his life (*mṛtyu-saṁsāra-vartmani*) and therefore continuing to go through suffering after suffering. *Na te viduḥ svārtha-gatiṁ hi viṣṇum* (*Bhāg.* 7.5.31). Such a foolish person does not know how to elevate himself in this body. Instead, he indulges in sinful activities and goes deeper and deeper into hellish life.

## TEXT 11

देहः किमन्नदातुः स्वं निषेक्तुर्मातुरेव च ।
मातुः पितुर्वा बलिनः क्रेतुरग्नेः शुनोऽपि वा ॥११॥

*dehaḥ kim anna-dātuḥ svaṁ*
*niṣektur mātur eva ca*
*mātuḥ pitur vā balinaḥ*
*kretur agneḥ śuno 'pi vā*

*dehaḥ*—this body; *kim anna-dātuḥ*—does it belong to the employer who gives me the money to maintain it; *svam*—or does it belong to me personally; *niṣektuḥ*—(or does it belong) to the person who discharged the semen; *mātuḥ eva*—(or does it belong) to the mother who maintained this body within her womb; *ca*—and; *mātuḥ pituḥ vā*—or (does it belong) to the father of the mother (because sometimes the father of the mother takes a grandson as an adopted son); *balinaḥ*—(or does it belong) to the person who takes this body away by force; *kretuḥ*—or to the person who purchases the body as a slave; *agneḥ*—or to the fire (because ultimately the body is burned); *śunaḥ*—or to the dogs and vultures that ultimately eat it; *api*—even; *vā*—or.

## TRANSLATION

**While alive, does this body belong to its employer, to the self, to the father, the mother, or the mother's father? Does it belong to the person who takes it away by force, to the slave master who purchases it, or to the sons who burn it in the fire? Or, if the body is not burned, does it belong to the dogs that eat it? Among the**

**many possible claimants, who is the rightful claimant? Not to ascertain this but instead to maintain the body by sinful activities is not good.**

## TEXT 12

एवं साधारणं देहमव्यक्तप्रभवाप्ययम् ।
को विद्वानात्मसात् कृत्वा हन्ति जन्तूनृतेऽसतः ॥१२॥

*evaṁ sādhāraṇaṁ deham*
*avyakta-prabhavāpyayam*
*ko vidvān ātmasāt kṛtvā*
*hanti jantūn ṛte 'sataḥ*

*evam*—in this way; *sādhāraṇam*—common property; *deham*—the body; *avyakta*—from unmanifested nature; *prabhava*—manifested in that way; *apyayam*—and again merged with the unmanifested ("for dust thou art, and unto dust shalt thou return"); *kaḥ*—who is that person; *vidvān*—one who is actually in knowledge; *ātmasāt kṛtvā*—claiming as his own; *hanti*—kills; *jantūn*—poor animals; *ṛte*—except; *asataḥ*—rascals who have no knowledge, no clear understanding.

## TRANSLATION

**This body, after all, is produced by the unmanifested nature and again annihilated and merged in the natural elements. Therefore, it is the common property of everyone. Under the circumstances, who but a rascal claims this property as his own and while maintaining it commits such sinful activities as killing animals just to satisfy his whims? Unless one is a rascal, one cannot commit such sinful activities.**

## PURPORT

Atheists do not believe in the existence of the soul. Nonetheless, unless one is very cruel, why should one kill animals unnecessarily? The body is a manifestation of a combination of matter. In the beginning it was nothing, but by a combination of matter it has come into existence. Then again, when the combination is dismantled, the body will no longer exist.

In the beginning it was nothing, and in the end it will be nothing. Why then should one commit sinful activities when it is manifested? It is not possible for anyone to do this unless he is rascal number one.

## TEXT 13

असतः श्रीमदान्धस्य दारिद्र्यं परमञ्जनम् ।
आत्मौपम्येन भूतानि दरिद्रः परमीक्षते ॥१३॥

*asataḥ śrī-madāndhasya*
*dāridryaṁ param añjanam*
*ātmaupamyena bhūtāni*
*daridraḥ param īkṣate*

*asataḥ*—of such a foolish rascal; *śrī-mada-andhasya*—who is blinded by temporarily possessing riches and opulence; *dāridryam*—poverty; *param añjanam*—the best ointment for the eyes, by which to see things as they are; *ātma-aupamyena*—with comparison to himself; *bhūtāni*—living beings; *daridraḥ*—a poverty-stricken man; *param*—perfectly; *īkṣate*—can see things as they are.

## TRANSLATION

**Atheistic fools and rascals who are very much proud of wealth fail to see things as they are. Therefore, returning them to poverty is the proper ointment for their eyes so they may see things as they are. At least a poverty-stricken man can realize how painful poverty is, and therefore he will not want others to be in a painful condition like his own.**

## PURPORT

Even today, if a man who was formerly poverty-stricken gets money, he is inclined to utilize his money to perform many philanthropic activities, like opening schools for uneducated men and hospitals for the diseased. In this connection there is an instructive story called *punar mūṣiko bhava*, "Again Become a Mouse." A mouse was very much harassed by a cat, and therefore the mouse approached a saintly person to request to become a cat. When the mouse became a cat, he was harassed by a dog, and then when he became a dog, he was harassed by a tiger. But when he became a tiger, he stared at the saintly person, and when the saintly person asked him, "What do you want?" the tiger said, "I want to eat you." Then the saintly person cursed him, saying, "May you again become a mouse." A similar thing is going on all over the universe. One is going up and down, sometimes becoming a mouse, sometimes a tiger, and so on. Śrī Caitanya Mahāprabhu said:

*brahmāṇḍa bhramite kona bhāgyavān jīva*
*guru-kṛṣṇa-prasāde pāya bhakti-latā-bīja*
(Cc. *Madhya* 19.151)

The living entities are promoted and degraded by the laws of nature, but if one is very, very fortunate, by association with saintly persons he gets the seed of devotional service, and his life becomes successful. Nārada Muni wanted to bring Nalakūvara and Maṇigrīva to the platform of devotional service through poverty, and thus he cursed them. Such is the mercy of a Vaiṣṇava. Unless one is brought to the Vaiṣṇava platform, one cannot be a good man. *Harāv abhaktasya kuto mahad-guṇāḥ* (*Bhāg*. 5.18.12). An *avaiṣṇava* never becomes a good man, however severely he is punished.

## TEXT 14

यथा कण्टकविद्धाङ्गो जन्तोर्नेच्छति तां व्यथाम् ।
जीवसाम्यं गतो लिङ्गैर्न तथाविद्धकण्टकः ॥१४॥

*yathā kaṇṭaka-viddhāṅgo*
*jantor necchati tāṁ vyathām*
*jīva-sāmyaṁ gato liṅgair*
*na tathāviddha-kaṇṭakaḥ*

*yathā*—just as; *kaṇṭaka-viddha-aṅgaḥ*—a person whose body has been pinpricked; *jantoḥ*—of such an animal; *na*—not; *icchati*—desires; *tām*—a particular; *vyathām*—pain; *jīva-sāmyam gataḥ*—when he understands that the position is the same for everyone; *liṅgaiḥ*—by possessing a particular type of body; *na*—not; *tathā*—so; *aviddha-kaṇṭakaḥ*—a person who has not been pinpricked.

## TRANSLATION

**By seeing their faces, one whose body has been pricked by pins can understand the pain of others who are pinpricked. Realizing that this pain is the same for everyone, he does not want others to suffer in this way. But one who has never been pricked by pins cannot understand this pain.**

## PURPORT

There is a saying, "The happiness of wealth is enjoyable by a person who has tasted the distress of poverty." There is also another common saying, *vandhyā ki bujhibe prasava-vedanā:* "A woman who has not given birth to a child cannot understand the pain of childbirth." Unless one comes to the platform of actual experience, one cannot realize what is pain and what is happiness in this material world. The laws of nature act accordingly. If one has killed an animal, one must himself be killed by that same animal. This is called *māṁsa. Mām* means "me," and *sa* means "he." As I am eating an animal, that animal will have the opportunity to eat me. In every state, therefore, it is ordinarily the custom that if a person commits murder he is hanged.

## TEXT 15

दरिद्रो निरहंस्तम्भो मुक्तः सर्वमदैरिह ।
कृच्छ्रं यदृच्छयाप्नोति तद्धि तस्य परं तपः ॥१५॥

*daridro nirahaṁ-stambho*
*muktaḥ sarva-madair iha*
*kṛcchraṁ yadṛcchayāpnoti*
*tad dhi tasya paraṁ tapaḥ*

*daridraḥ*—a poverty-stricken person; *nir-aham-stambhaḥ*—is automatically freed from all false prestige; *muktaḥ*—liberated; *sarva*—all;

*madaiḥ*—from false ego; *iha*—in this world; *kṛcchram*—with great difficulty; *yadṛcchayā āpnoti*—what he gains by chance from providence; *tat*—that; *hi*—indeed; *tasya*—his; *param*—perfect; *tapaḥ*—austerity.

## TRANSLATION

**A poverty-stricken man must automatically undergo austerities and penances because he does not have the wealth to possess anything. Thus his false prestige is vanquished. Always in need of food, shelter and clothing, he must be satisfied with what is obtained by the mercy of providence. Undergoing such compulsory austerities is good for him because this purifies him and completely frees him from false ego.**

## PURPORT

A saintly person voluntarily accepts a state of poverty just to become free from material false prestige. Many great kings left their princely standard of living and went to the forest to practice austerity according to Vedic culture, just to become purified. But if one who cannot voluntarily accept such austerity is put into a situation of poverty, he automatically must practice austerity. Austerity is good for everyone because it frees one from material conditions. Therefore, if one is very much proud of his material position, putting him into poverty is the best way to rectify his foolishness. *Dāridrya-doṣo guṇa-rāśi-nāśi:* when a person is poverty-stricken, naturally his false pride in aristocracy, wealth, education and beauty is smashed. Thus corrected, he is in the right position for liberation.

## TEXT 16

नित्यं क्षुत्क्षामदेहस्य दरिद्रस्यान्नकाङ्क्षिणः ।
इन्द्रियाण्यनुशुष्यन्ति हिंसापि विनिवर्तते ॥१६॥

*nityaṁ kṣut-kṣāma-dehasya*
*daridrasyānna-kāṅkṣiṇaḥ*
*indriyāṇy anuśuṣyanti*
*hiṁsāpi vinivartate*

*nityam*—always; *kṣut*—with hunger; *kṣāma*—weak, without necessary strength; *dehasya*—of the body of a poor man; *daridrasya*—poverty-stricken; *anna-kāṅkṣiṇaḥ*—always desiring to get sufficient food; *indriyāṇi*—the senses, which are compared to snakes; *anuśuṣyanti*—gradually become weaker and weaker, with less potency; *hiṁsā api*—the tendency to be envious of others; *vinivartate*—reduces.

## TRANSLATION

**Always hungry, longing for sufficient food, a poverty-stricken man gradually becomes weaker and weaker. Having no extra potency, his senses are automatically pacified. A poverty-stricken man, therefore, is unable to perform harmful, envious activities. In other words, such a man automatically gains the results of the austerities and penances adopted voluntarily by saintly persons.**

## PURPORT

According to the opinion of experienced medical practitioners, diabetes is a result of voracious eating, and tuberculosis is a disease of undereating. We should desire neither to be diabetic nor to be tubercular. *Yāvad artha-prayojanam.* We should eat frugally and keep the body fit for advancing in Kṛṣṇa consciousness. As recommended elsewhere in *Śrīmad-Bhāgavatam* (1.2.10):

*kāmasya nendriya-prītir*
*lābho jīveta yāvatā*
*jīvasya tattva-jijñāsā*
*nārtho yaś ceha karmabhiḥ*

The real business of human life is to keep oneself fit for advancement in spiritual realization. Human life is not meant for making the senses unnecessarily strong so that one suffers from disease and one increases in an envious, fighting spirit. In this age of Kali, however, human civilization is so misled that people are unnecessarily increasing in economic development, and as a result they are opening more and more slaughterhouses, liquor shops and brothels. In this way, the whole civilization is being spoiled.

## TEXT 17

दरिद्रस्यैव युज्यन्ते साधवः समदर्शिनः ।
सद्भिः क्षिणोति तं तर्षं तत आराद् विशुद्ध्यति ॥१७॥

*daridrasyaiva yujyante*
*sādhavaḥ sama-darśinaḥ*
*sadbhiḥ kṣiṇoti taṁ tarṣaṁ*
*tata ārād viśuddhyati*

*daridrasya*—of a person who is poverty-stricken; *eva*—indeed; *yujyante*—may easily associate; *sādhavaḥ*—saintly persons; *sama-darśinaḥ*—although *sādhus* are equal to everyone, to the poor and the rich, the poor man can take advantage of their association; *sadbhiḥ*—by the association of such saintly persons; *kṣiṇoti*—reduces; *tam*—the original cause of material suffering; *tarṣam*—the desire for material enjoyment; *tataḥ*—thereafter; *ārāt*—very soon; *viśuddhyati*—his material contamination is cleansed off.

## TRANSLATION

**Saintly persons may freely associate with those who are poverty-stricken, but not with those who are rich. A poverty-stricken man, by association with saintly persons, very soon becomes uninterested in material desires, and the dirty things within the core of his heart are cleansed away.**

## PURPORT

It is said, *mahad-vicalanaṁ nṛṇāṁ gṛhiṇāṁ dīna-cetasām* (*Bhāg.* 10.8.4). The only business of a saintly person or *sannyāsī,* a person in the renounced order, is to preach Kṛṣṇa consciousness. *Sādhus,* saintly persons, want to preach to both the poor and the rich, but the poor take more advantage of the *sādhus'* preaching than the rich do. A poor man receives *sādhus* very quickly, offers them obeisances, and tries to take advantage of their presence, whereas a rich man keeps a big greyhound dog at his door so that no one can enter his house. He posts a sign saying "Beware of Dog" and avoids the association of saintly persons, whereas a poor man keeps his door open for them and thus benefits by their association more than a rich man does. Because Nārada Muni, in his previous life, was the poverty-stricken son of a maidservant, he got the association of saintly persons and later became the exalted Nārada Muni. This was his actual experience. Therefore, he is now comparing the position of a poor man with that of a rich man.

*satāṁ prasaṅgān mama vīrya-saṁvido*
*bhavanti hṛt-karṇa-rasāyanāḥ kathāḥ*
*taj-joṣaṇād āśv apavarga-vartmani*
*śraddhā ratir bhaktir anukramiṣyati*
(*Bhāg.* 3.25.25)

If one gets the advantage of association with saintly persons, by their instructions one becomes more and more purified of material desires.

*kṛṣṇa-bahirmukha haiyā bhoga-vāñchā kare*
*nikaṭa-stha māyā tāre jāpaṭiyā dhare*
(*Prema-vivarta*)

Material life means that one forgets Kṛṣṇa and that one increases in one's desires for sense gratification. But if one receives the advantage of instructions from saintly persons and forgets the importance of material desires, one is automatically purified. *Ceto-darpaṇa-mārjanaṁ bhava-mahādāvāgni-nirvāpaṇam* (*Śikṣāṣṭaka* 1). Unless the core of a materialistic person's heart is purified, he cannot get rid of the pangs of *bhava-mahādāvāgni*, the blazing fire of material existence.

## TEXT 18

साधूनां समचित्तानां मुकुन्दचरणैषिणाम् ।
उपेक्ष्यैः किं धनस्तम्भैरसद्भिरसदाश्रयैः ॥१८॥

*sādhūnāṁ sama-cittānāṁ*
*mukunda-caraṇaiṣiṇām*
*upekṣyaiḥ kiṁ dhana-stambhair*
*asadbhir asad-āśrayaiḥ*

*sādhūnām*—of saintly persons; *sama-cittānām*—of those who are equal to everyone; *mukunda-caraṇa-eṣiṇām*—whose only business is to serve Mukunda, the Supreme Personality of Godhead, and who always aspire for that service; *upekṣyaiḥ*—neglecting the association; *kim*—what; *dhana-stambhaiḥ*—rich and proud; *asadbhiḥ*—with the association of undesirable persons; *asat-āśrayaiḥ*—taking shelter of those who are *asat*, or nondevotees.

## TRANSLATION

**Saintly persons [sādhus] think of Kṛṣṇa twenty-four hours a day. They have no other interest. Why should people neglect the association of such exalted spiritual personalities and try to associate with materialists, taking shelter of nondevotees, most of whom are proud and rich?**

## PURPORT

A *sādhu* is one who is engaged in devotional service to the Lord without deviation (*bhajate mām ananya-bhāk*).

*titikṣavaḥ kāruṇikāḥ*
*suhṛdaḥ sarva-dehinām*
*ajāta-śatravaḥ śāntāḥ*
*sādhavaḥ sādhu-bhūṣaṇāḥ*

"The symptoms of a *sādhu* are that he is tolerant, merciful and friendly to all living entities. He has no enemies, he is peaceful, he abides by the scriptures, and all his characteristics are sublime." (*Bhāg.* 3.25.21) A *sādhu* is *suhṛdaḥ sarva-dehinām*, the friend of everyone. Why then should the rich, instead of associating with *sādhus*, waste their valuable time in association with other rich men who are averse to spiritual life? Both the poor man and the rich man can take advantage of the Kṛṣṇa consciousness movement, and here it is advised that everyone do so. There is no profit in avoiding the association of the members of the Kṛṣṇa consciousness movement. Narottama dāsa Ṭhākura has said:

*sat-saṅga chāḍi' kainu asate vilāsa*
*te-kāraṇe lāgila ye karma-bandha-phāṅsa*

If we give up the association of *sādhus*, saintly persons engaged in Kṛṣṇa consciousness, and associate with persons seeking sense gratification and accumulating wealth for this purpose, our life is spoiled. The word *asat* refers to an *avaiṣṇava*, one who is not a devotee of Kṛṣṇa, and *sat* refers to a Vaiṣṇava, Kṛṣṇa's devotee. One should always seek the association of Vaiṣṇavas and not spoil one's life by mixing with *avaiṣṇavas*. In *Bhagavad-gītā* (7.15), the distinction between Vaiṣṇava and *avaiṣṇava* is enunciated:

*na māṁ duṣkṛtino mūḍhāḥ*
*prapadyante narādhamāḥ*
*māyayāpahṛta-jñānā*
*āsuraṁ bhāvam āśritāḥ*

Anyone who is not surrendered to Kṛṣṇa is a most sinful person (*duṣkṛtī*), a rascal (*mūḍha*), and the lowest of men (*narādhama*). Therefore one should not avoid the association of Vaiṣṇavas, which is now available all over the world in the form of the Kṛṣṇa consciousness movement.

## TEXT 19

तदहं मत्तयोर्माध्व्या वारुण्या श्रीमदान्धयोः ।
तमोमदं हरिष्यामि स्त्रैणयोरजितात्मनोः ॥१९॥

*tad ahaṁ mattayor mādhvyā*
*vāruṇyā śrī-madāndhayoḥ*
*tamo-madaṁ hariṣyāmi*
*straiṇayor ajitātmanoḥ*

*tat*—therefore; *aham*—I; *mattayoḥ*—of these two drunken persons; *mādhvyā*—by drinking liquor; *vāruṇyā*—named Vāruṇī; *śrī-mada-andhayoḥ*—who are blinded by celestial opulence; *tamaḥ-madam*—this false prestige due to the mode of ignorance; *hariṣyāmi*—I shall take away; *straiṇayoḥ*—because they have become so attached to women; *ajita-ātmanoḥ*—being unable to control the senses.

## TRANSLATION

**Therefore, since these two persons, drunk with the liquor named Vāruṇī, or Mādhvi, and unable to control their senses, have**

**been blinded by the pride of celestial opulence and have become attached to women, I shall relieve them of their false prestige.**

## PURPORT

When a *sādhu* chastises or punishes someone, he does not do so for revenge. Mahārāja Parīkṣit had inquired why Nārada Muni was subject to such a spirit of revenge (*tamaḥ*). But this was not *tamaḥ*, for Nārada Muni, in full knowledge of what was for the good of the two brothers, wisely thought of how to cure them. Vaiṣṇavas are good physicians. They know how to protect a person from material disease. Thus they are never in *tamo-guṇa. Sa guṇān samatītyaitān brahma-bhūyāya kalpate* (Bg. 14.26). Vaiṣṇavas are always situated on the transcendental platform, the Brahman platform. They cannot be subject to mistakes or the influence of the modes of material nature. Whatever they do, after full consideration, is meant just to lead everyone back home, back to Godhead.

## TEXTS 20–22

यदिमौ लोकपालस्य पुत्रौ भूत्वा तमःप्लुतौ ।
न विवाससमात्मानं विजानीतः सुदुर्मदौ ॥२०॥
अतोऽर्हतः स्थावरतां स्यातां नैवं यथा पुनः ।
स्मृतिः स्यान्मत्प्रसादेन तत्रापि मदनुग्रहात् ॥२१॥
वासुदेवस्य सान्निध्यं लब्ध्वा दिव्यशरच्छते ।
वृत्ते स्वर्लोकतां भूयो लब्धभक्ती भविष्यतः ॥२२॥

*yad imau loka-pālasya*
*putrau bhūtvā tamaḥ-plutau*
*na vivāsasam ātmānaṁ*
*vijānītaḥ sudurmadau*

*ato 'rhataḥ sthāvaratāṁ*
*syātāṁ naivaṁ yathā punaḥ*
*smṛtiḥ syān mat-prasādena*
*tatrāpi mad-anugrahāt*

*vāsudevasya sānnidhyaṁ*
*labdhvā divya-śarac-chate*
*vṛtte svarlokatāṁ bhūyo*
*labdha-bhaktī bhaviṣyataḥ*

*yat*—because; *imau*—these two young demigods; *loka-pālasya*—of the great demigod Kuvera; *putrau*—born as sons; *bhūtvā*—being so (they should not have become like that); *tamaḥ-plutau*—so absorbed in the mode of darkness; *na*—not; *vivāsasam*—without any dress, completely naked; *ātmānam*—their personal bodies; *vijānītaḥ*—could understand that they were naked; *su-durmadau*—because they were very much fallen due to false pride; *ataḥ*—therefore; *arhataḥ*—they deserve; *sthāvaratām*—immobility like that of a tree; *syātām*—they may become; *na*—not; *evam*—in this way; *yathā*—as; *punaḥ*—again; *smṛtiḥ*—remembrance; *syāt*—may continue; *mat-prasādena*—by my mercy; *tatra api*—over and above that; *mat-anugrahāt*—by my special favor; *vāsudevasya*—of the Supreme Personality of Godhead; *sānnidhyam*—the personal association, face to face; *labdhvā*—obtaining; *divya-śarat-śate vṛtte*—after the expiry of one hundred years by the measurement of the demigods; *svarlokatām*—the desire to live in the celestial world; *bhūyaḥ*—again; *labdha-bhaktī*—having revived their natural condition of devotional service; *bhaviṣyataḥ*—will become.

## TRANSLATION

**These two young men, Nalakūvara and Maṇigrīva, are by fortune the sons of the great demigod Kuvera, but because of false prestige and madness after drinking liquor, they are so fallen that they are naked but cannot understand that they are. Therefore, because they are living like trees (for trees are naked but are not conscious), these two young men should receive the bodies of trees. This will be proper punishment. Nonetheless, after they become trees and until they are released, by my mercy they will have remembrance of their past sinful activities. Moreover, by my special favor, after the expiry of one hundred years by the measurement of the demigods, they will be able to see the Supreme Personality of Godhead, Vāsudeva, face to face, and thus revive their real position as devotees.**

## PURPORT

A tree has no consciousness: when cut, it feels no pain. But Nārada Muni wanted the consciousness of Nalakūvara and Maṇigrīva to continue, so that even after being released from the life of trees, they would not forget the circumstances under which they had been punished. Therefore, to bestow upon them special favor, Nārada Muni arranged things in such a way that after being released, they would be able to see Kṛṣṇa in Vṛndāvana and thus revive their dormant *bhakti.*

Each day of the demigods in the upper planetary system equals six months of our measurement. Although the demigods in the upper planetary system are attached to material enjoyment, they are all devotees, and therefore they are called demigods. There are two kinds of persons, namely the *devas* and the *asuras. Asuras* forget their relationship with Kṛṣṇa (*āsuraṁ bhāvam āśritāḥ*), whereas the *devas* do not forget.

*dvau bhūta-sargau loke 'smin*
*daiva āsura eva ca*
*viṣṇu-bhaktaḥ smṛto daiva*
*āsuras tad-viparyayaḥ*
(*Padma Purāṇa*)

The distinction between a pure devotee and a *karma-miśra* devotee is this: a pure devotee does not desire anything for material enjoyment, whereas a mixed devotee becomes a devotee to become a first-class enjoyer of this material world. One who is in direct touch with the Supreme Personality of Godhead in devotional service remains pure, uncontaminated by material desires (*anyābhilāṣitā-śūnyaṁ jñāna-karmādy-anāvṛtam*).

By *karma-miśra-bhakti* one is elevated to the celestial kingdom, by *jñāna-miśra-bhakti* one is able to merge in the Brahman effulgence, and by *yoga-miśra-bhakti* one is able to realize the omnipotency of the Supreme Personality of Godhead. But pure *bhakti* does not depend on *karma, jñāna* or *yoga,* for it simply consists of loving affairs. The liberation of the *bhakta,* therefore, which is called not just *mukti* but *vimukti,* surpasses the five other kinds of liberation—*sāyujya, sārūpya, sālokya, sārṣṭi* and *sāmīpya.* A pure devotee always engages in pure service (*ānukūlyena kṛṣṇānuśīlanaṁ bhaktir uttamā*). Taking birth in the upper planetary system as a demigod is a chance to become a further purified devotee and go back home, back to Godhead. Nārada Muni indirectly gave Maṇigrīva and Nalakūvara the greatest opportunity by his so-called curse.

## TEXT 23

श्रीशुक उवाच
एवमुक्त्वा स देवर्षिर्गतो नारायणाश्रमम् ।
नलकूवरमणिग्रीवावासतुर्यमलार्जुनौ ॥२३॥

*śrī-śuka uvāca*
*evam uktvā sa devarṣir*
*gato nārāyaṇāśramam*
*nalakūvara-maṇigrīvāv*
*āsatur yamalārjunau*

*śrī-śukaḥ uvāca*—Śrī Śukadeva Gosvāmī continued to speak; *evam uktvā*—thus uttering; *saḥ*—he; *devarṣiḥ*—the greatest saintly person, Nārada; *gataḥ*—left that place; *nārāyaṇa-āśramam*—for his own *āśrama*, known as Nārāyaṇa-āśrama; *nalakūvara*—Nalakūvara; *maṇi-grīvau*—and Maṇigrīva; *āsatuḥ*—remained there to become; *yamala-arjunau*—twin *arjuna* trees.

## TRANSLATION

**Śukadeva Gosvāmī continued: Having thus spoken, the great saint Devarṣi Nārada returned to his āśrama, known as Nārāyaṇa-āśrama, and Nalakūvara and Maṇigrīva became twin arjuna trees.**

## PURPORT

*Arjuna* trees are still found in many forests, and their skin is used by cardiologists to prepare medicine for heart trouble. This means that even though they are trees, they are disturbed when skinned for medical science.

## TEXT 24

ऋषेर्भागवतमुख्यस्य सत्यं कर्तुं वचो हरिः ।
जगाम शनकैस्तत्र यत्रास्तां यमलार्जुनौ ॥२४॥

*ṛṣer bhāgavata-mukhyasya*
*satyaṁ kartuṁ vaco hariḥ*
*jagāma śanakais tatra*
*yatrāstāṁ yamalārjunau*

*ṛṣeḥ*—of the great sage and saintly person Nārada; *bhāgavata-mukhyasya*—of the topmost of all devotees; *satyam*—truthful; *kartum*—to prove; *vacaḥ*—his words; *hariḥ*—the Supreme Personality of Godhead, Kṛṣṇa; *jagāma*—went there; *śanakaiḥ*—very slowly; *tatra*—there; *yatra*—to the spot where; *āstām*—there were; *yamala-arjunau*—the twin *arjuna* trees.

## TRANSLATION

**The Supreme Personality of Godhead, Śrī Kṛṣṇa, to fulfill the truthfulness of the words of the greatest devotee, Nārada, slowly went to that spot where the twin arjuna trees were standing.**

## TEXT 25

देवर्षिर्मे प्रियतमो यदिमौ धनदात्मजौ ।
तत्तथा साधयिष्यामि यद् गीतं तन्महात्मना ॥२५॥

*devarṣir me priyatamo*
*yad imau dhanadātmajau*
*tat tathā sādhayiṣyāmi*
*yad gītaṁ tan mahātmanā*

*devarṣiḥ*—the great saint Devarṣi Nārada; *me*—My; *priya-tamaḥ*—most beloved devotee; *yat*—although; *imau*—these two persons (Nalakūvara and Maṇigrīva); *dhanada-ātmajau*—born of a rich father and being nondevotees; *tat*—the words of Devarṣi; *tathā*—just so; *sādhayiṣyāmi*—I shall execute (because he wanted Me to come face to face with the *yamala-arjuna*, I shall do so); *yat gītam*—as already stated; *tat*—that; *mahātmanā*—by Nārada Muni.

## TRANSLATION

**"Although these two young men are the sons of the very rich Kuvera and I have nothing to do with them, Devarṣi Nārada is My very dear and affectionate devotee, and therefore because he wanted Me to come face to face with them, I must do so for their deliverance."**

## PURPORT

Nalakūvara and Maṇigrīva actually had nothing to do with devotional service or seeing the Supreme Personality of Godhead face to face, for this is not an ordinary opportunity. It is not that because one is very rich or learned or was born in an aristocratic family one will be able to see the Supreme Personality of Godhead face to face. This is impossible. But in this case, because Nārada Muni desired that Nalakūvara and Maṇigrīva see Vāsudeva face to face, the Supreme Personality of Godhead wanted to fulfill the words of His very dear devotee Nārada Muni. If one seeks the favor of a devotee instead of directly asking favors from the Supreme Personality of Godhead, one is very easily successful. Śrīla Bhaktivinoda Ṭhākura has therefore recommended: *vaiṣṇava ṭhākura tomāra kukkura bhuliyā jānaha more, kṛṣṇa se tomāra kṛṣṇa dite pāra.* One should desire to become like a dog in strictly following a devotee. Kṛṣṇa is in the hand of a devotee. *Adurlabham ātma-bhaktau.* Thus without the favor of a devotee, one cannot directly approach Kṛṣṇa, what to speak of engaging in His service. Narottama dāsa Ṭhākura therefore sings, *chāḍiyā vaiṣṇava-sevā nistāra pāyeche kebā:* unless one becomes a servant of a pure devotee, one cannot be delivered from the material condition of life. In our Gauḍīya Vaiṣṇava society, following in the footsteps of Rūpa Gosvāmī, our first business is to seek shelter of a bona fide spiritual master (*ādau gurv-āśrayaḥ*).

## TEXT 26

इत्यन्तरेणार्जुनयोः कृष्णस्तु यमयोर्ययौ ।
आत्मनिर्वेशमात्रेण तिर्यग्गतमुलूखलम् ॥२६॥

*ity antareṇārjunayoḥ*
*kṛṣṇas tu yamayor yayau*
*ātma-niveśa-mātreṇa*
*tiryag-gatam ulūkhalam*

*iti*—thus deciding; *antareṇa*—between; *arjunayoḥ*—the two *arjuna* trees; *kṛṣṇaḥ tu*—Lord Kṛṣṇa; *yamayoḥ yayau*—entered between the two trees; *ātma-niveśa-mātreṇa*—as soon as He entered (between the two trees); *tiryak*—crossways; *gatam*—so became; *ulūkhalam*—the big mortar for grinding spices.

## TRANSLATION

**Having thus spoken, Kṛṣṇa soon entered between the two arjuna trees, and thus the big mortar to which He was bound turned crosswise and stuck between them.**

## TEXT 27

बालेन निष्कर्षयतान्वगुलूखलं तद्
दामोदरेण तरसोत्कलिताङ्घ्रिबन्धौ ।
निष्पेततुः परमविक्रमितातिवेप-
स्कन्धप्रवालविटपौ कृतचण्डशब्दौ ॥२७॥

*bālena niṣkarṣayatānvag ulūkhalaṁ tad*
*dāmodareṇa tarasotkalitāṅghri-bandhau*
*niṣpetatuḥ parama-vikramitātivepa-*
*skandha-pravāla-viṭapau kṛta-caṇḍa-śabdau*

*bālena*—by the boy Kṛṣṇa; *niṣkarṣayatā*—who was dragging; *anvak*—following the dragging of Kṛṣṇa; *ulūkhalam*—the wooden mortar; *tat*—that; *dāma-udareṇa*—by Kṛṣṇa, who was tied by the belly; *tarasā*—with great force; *utkalita*—uprooted; *aṅghri-bandhau*—the roots of the two trees; *niṣpetatuḥ*—fell down; *parama-vikramita*—by the supreme power; *ati-vepa*—trembling severely; *skandha*—trunk; *pravāla*—bunches of leaves; *viṭapau*—those two trees, along with their branches; *kṛta*—having made; *caṇḍa-śabdau*—a fierce sound.

## TRANSLATION

**By dragging behind Him with great force the wooden mortar tied to His belly, the boy Kṛṣṇa uprooted the two trees. By the great strength of the Supreme Person, the two trees, with their trunks, leaves and branches, trembled severely and fell to the ground with a great crash.**

## PURPORT

This is the pastime of Kṛṣṇa known as *dāmodara-līlā*. Therefore another of Kṛṣṇa's names is Dāmodara. As stated in the *Hari-vaṁśa:*

*sa ca tenaiva nāmnā tu*
*kṛṣṇo vai dāma-bandhanāt*
*goṣṭhe dāmodara iti*
*gopībhiḥ parigīyate*

## TEXT 28

तत्र श्रिया परमया ककुभः स्फुरन्तौ
सिद्धावुपेत्य कुजयोरिव जातवेदाः ।
कृष्णं प्रणम्य शिरसाखिललोकनाथं
बद्धाञ्जली विरजसाविदमूचतुः स्म ॥२८॥

*tatra śriyā paramayā kakubhaḥ sphurantau*
*siddhāv upetya kujayor iva jāta-vedāḥ*
*kṛṣṇaṁ praṇamya śirasākhila-loka-nāthaṁ*
*baddhāñjalī virajasāv idam ūcatuḥ sma*

*tatra*—there, on the very spot where the two *arjunas* fell; *śriyā*—with beautification; *paramayā*—superexcellent; *kakubhaḥ*—all directions; *sphurantau*—illuminating by effulgence; *siddhau*—two perfect persons; *upetya*—then coming out; *kujayoḥ*—from between the two trees; *iva*—like; *jāta-vedāḥ*—fire personified; *kṛṣṇam*—unto Lord Kṛṣṇa; *praṇamya*—offering obeisances; *śirasā*—with the head; *akhila-loka-nātham*—to the Supreme Person, the controller of everything;

*baddha-añjalī*—with folded hands; *virajasau*—fully cleansed of the mode of ignorance; *idam*—the following words; *ūcatuḥ sma*—uttered.

## TRANSLATION

**Thereafter, in that very place where the two arjuna trees had fallen, two great, perfect personalities, who appeared like fire personified, came out of the two trees. The effulgence of their beauty illuminating all directions, with bowed heads they offered obeisances to Kṛṣṇa, and with hands folded they spoke the following words.**

## TEXT 29

कृष्ण कृष्ण महायोगिंस्त्वमाद्यः पुरुषः परः ।
व्यक्ताव्यक्तमिदं विश्वं रूपं ते ब्राह्मणा विदुः ॥२९॥

*kṛṣṇa kṛṣṇa mahā-yogiṁs*
*tvam ādyaḥ puruṣaḥ paraḥ*
*vyaktāvyaktam idaṁ viśvaṁ*
*rūpaṁ te brāhmaṇā viduḥ*

*kṛṣṇa kṛṣṇa*—O Lord Kṛṣṇa, O Lord Kṛṣṇa; *mahā-yogin*—O master of mysticism; *tvam*—You, the exalted personality; *ādyaḥ*—the root cause of everything; *puruṣaḥ*—the Supreme Person; *paraḥ*—beyond this material creation; *vyakta-avyaktam*—this material cosmic manifestation, consisting of cause and effect, or gross and subtle forms; *idam*—this; *viśvam*—whole world; *rūpam*—form; *te*—Your; *brāhmaṇāḥ*—learned *brāhmaṇas; viduḥ*—know.

## TRANSLATION

**O Lord Kṛṣṇa, Lord Kṛṣṇa, Your opulent mysticism is inconceivable. You are the supreme, original person, the cause of all causes, immediate and remote, and You are beyond this material creation. Learned brāhmaṇas know [on the basis of the Vedic statement sarvaṁ khalv idaṁ brahma] that You are everything and that this cosmic manifestation, in its gross and subtle aspects, is Your form.**

## PURPORT

The two demigods Nalakūvara and Maṇigrīva, because of their continuing memory, could understand the supremacy of Kṛṣṇa by the grace of Nārada. Now they admitted, "That we should be delivered by the blessings of Nārada Muni was all Your plan. Therefore You are the supreme mystic. Everything—past, present and future—is known to You. Your plan was made so nicely that although we stayed here as twin *arjuna* trees, You have appeared as a small boy to deliver us. This was all Your inconceivable arrangement. Because You are the Supreme Person, You can do everything."

## TEXTS 30–31

त्वमेकः सर्वभूतानां देहास्वात्मेन्द्रियेश्वरः ।
त्वमेव कालो भगवान् विष्णुरव्यय ईश्वरः ॥३०॥
त्वं महान् प्रकृतिः सूक्ष्मा रजःसत्त्वतमोमयी ।
त्वमेव पुरुषोऽध्यक्षः सर्वक्षेत्रविकारवित् ॥३१॥

*tvam ekaḥ sarva-bhūtānāṁ*
*dehāsv-ātmendriyeśvaraḥ*
*tvam eva kālo bhagavān*
*viṣṇur avyaya īśvaraḥ*

*tvaṁ mahān prakṛtiḥ sūkṣmā*
*rajaḥ-sattva-tamomayī*
*tvam eva puruṣo 'dhyakṣaḥ*
*sarva-kṣetra-vikāra-vit*

*tvam*—Your Lordship; *ekaḥ*—one; *sarva-bhūtānām*—of all living entities; *deha*—of the body; *asu*—of the life force; *ātma*—of the soul; *indriya*—of the senses; *īśvaraḥ*—the Supersoul, the controller; *tvam*—Your Lordship; *eva*—indeed; *kālaḥ*—the time factor; *bhagavān*—the Supreme Personality of Godhead; *viṣṇuḥ*—all-pervading; *avyayaḥ*—imperishable; *īśvaraḥ*—controller; *tvam*—Your Lordship; *mahān*—the greatest; *prakṛtiḥ*—the cosmic manifestation; *sūkṣmā*—subtle; *rajaḥ-sattva-tamaḥ-mayī*—consisting of three modes of nature (passion, goodness and ignorance); *tvam eva*—Your Lordship is indeed; *puruṣaḥ*—the

Supreme Person; *adhyakṣaḥ*—the proprietor; *sarva-kṣetra*—in all living entities; *vikāra-vit*—knowing the restless mind.

## TRANSLATION

**You are the Supreme Personality of Godhead, the controller of everything. The body, life, ego and senses of every living entity are Your own self. You are the Supreme Person, Viṣṇu, the imperishable controller. You are the time factor, the immediate cause, and You are material nature, consisting of the three modes passion, goodness and ignorance. You are the original cause of this material manifestation. You are the Supersoul, and therefore You know everything within the core of the heart of every living entity.**

## PURPORT

Śrīpāda Madhvācārya has quoted from the *Vāmana Purāṇa* as follows:

*rūpyatvāt tu jagad rūpaṁ*
*viṣṇoḥ sākṣāt sukhātmakam*
*nitya-pūrṇaṁ samuddiṣṭaṁ*
*svarūpaṁ paramātmanaḥ*

## TEXT 32

गृह्यमाणैस्त्वमग्राह्यो विकारैः प्राकृतैर्गुणैः ।
को न्विहार्हति विज्ञातुं प्राक्सिद्धं गुणसंवृतः ॥३२॥

*gṛhyamāṇais tvam agrāhyo*
*vikāraiḥ prākṛtair guṇaiḥ*
*ko nv ihārhati vijñātuṁ*
*prāk siddhaṁ guṇa-saṁvṛtaḥ*

*gṛhyamāṇaiḥ*—accepting the body made of material nature as existing at the present moment because of being visible; *tvam*—You; *agrāhyaḥ*—not confined in a body made of material nature; *vikāraiḥ*—

agitated by the mind; *prākṛtaiḥ guṇaiḥ*—by the material modes of nature (*sattva-guṇa*, *rajo-guṇa* and *tamo-guṇa*); *kaḥ*—who is there; *nu*—after that; *iha*—in this material world; *arhati*—who deserves; *vijñātum*—to know; *prāk siddham*—that which existed before the creation; *guṇa-saṁvṛtaḥ*—because of being covered by the material qualities.

## TRANSLATION

**O Lord, You exist before the creation. Therefore, who, trapped by a body of material qualities in this material world, can understand You?**

## PURPORT

As it is said:

*ataḥ śrī-kṛṣṇa-nāmādi*
*na bhaved grāhyam indriyaiḥ*
*sevonmukhe hi jihvādau*
*svayam eva sphuraty adaḥ*
(*Bhakti-rasāmṛta-sindhu* 1.2.234)

Kṛṣṇa's name, attributes and form are Absolute Truth, existing before the creation. Therefore, how can those who are created—that is, those entrapped in bodies created of material elements—understand Kṛṣṇa perfectly? This is not possible. But, *sevonmukhe hi jihvādau svayam eva sphuraty adaḥ:* Kṛṣṇa reveals Himself to those engaged in devotional service. This is also confirmed in *Bhagavad-gītā* (18.15) by the Lord Himself: *bhaktyā mām abhijānāti.* Even the descriptions of Kṛṣṇa in *Śrīmad-Bhāgavatam* are sometimes misunderstood by less intelligent men with a poor fund of knowledge. Therefore, the best course by which to know Him is to engage oneself in pure devotional activities. The more one advances in devotional activities, the more one can understand Him as He is. If from the material platform one could understand Kṛṣṇa, then, since Kṛṣṇa is everything (*sarvaṁ khalv idaṁ brahma*), one could understand Kṛṣṇa by seeing anything within this material world. But that is not possible.

*mayā tatam idaṁ sarvaṁ*
*jagad avyakta-mūrtinā*
*mat-sthāni sarva-bhūtāni*
*na cāhaṁ teṣv avasthitaḥ*
(Bg. 9.4)

Everything is resting on Kṛṣṇa, and everything is Kṛṣṇa, but this is not to be realized by persons on the material platform.

## TEXT 33

तस्मै तुभ्यं भगवते वासुदेवाय वेधसे ।
आत्मद्योतगुणैश्छन्नमहिम्ने ब्रह्मणे नमः ॥३३॥

*tasmai tubhyaṁ bhagavate*
*vāsudevāya vedhase*
*ātma-dyota-guṇaiś channa-*
*mahimne brahmaṇe namaḥ*

*tasmai*—(because You are not to be understood from the material platform, we simply offer obeisances) unto Him; *tubhyam*—unto You; *bhagavate*—unto the Supreme Personality of Godhead; *vāsudevāya*—unto Vāsudeva, the origin of Saṅkarṣaṇa, Pradyumna and Aniruddha; *vedhase*—unto the origin of creation; *ātma-dyota-guṇaiḥ channa-mahimne*—unto You whose glories are covered by Your personal energy; *brahmaṇe*—unto the Supreme Brahman; *namaḥ*—our respectful obeisances.

## TRANSLATION

**O Lord, whose glories are covered by Your own energy, You are the Supreme Personality of Godhead. You are Saṅkarṣaṇa, the origin of creation, and You are Vāsudeva, the origin of the catur-vyūha. Because You are everything and are therefore the Supreme Brahman, we simply offer our respectful obeisances unto You.**

## PURPORT

Instead of trying to understand Kṛṣṇa in detail, it is better to offer our respectful obeisances unto Him, for He is the origin of everything and

He is everything. Because we are covered by the material modes of nature, He is very difficult for us to understand unless He reveals Himself to us. Therefore it is better for us to acknowledge that He is everything and offer obeisances unto His lotus feet.

## TEXTS 34–35

यस्यावतारा ज्ञायन्ते शरीरेष्वशरीरिणः ।
तैस्तैरतुल्यातिशयैर्वीर्यैर्देहिष्वसंगतैः ॥३४॥
स भवान् सर्वलोकस्य भवाय विभवाय च ।
अवतीर्णोऽंशभागेन साम्प्रतं पतिराशिषाम् ॥३५॥

*yasyāvatārā jñāyante*
*śarīreṣv aśarīriṇaḥ*
*tais tair atulyātiśayair*
*vīryair dehiṣv asaṅgataiḥ*

*sa bhavān sarva-lokasya*
*bhavāya vibhavāya ca*
*avatīrṇo 'ṁśa-bhāgena*
*sāmpratam patir āśiṣām*

*yasya*—of whom; *avatārāḥ*—the different incarnations, like Matsya, Kūrma and Varāha; *jñāyante*—are speculated; *śarīreṣu*—in different bodies, differently visible; *aśarīriṇaḥ*—they are not ordinary material bodies, but are all transcendental; *taiḥ taiḥ*—by such bodily activities; *atulya*—incomparable; *ati-śayaiḥ*—unlimited; *vīryaiḥ*—by strength and power; *dehiṣu*—by those who actually have material bodies; *asaṅgataiḥ*—which activities, enacted in different incarnations, are impossible to be performed; *saḥ*—the same Supreme; *bhavān*—Your Lordship; *sarva-lokasya*—of everyone; *bhavāya*—for the elevation; *vibhavāya*—for the liberation; *ca*—and; *avatīrṇaḥ*—have now appeared; *aṁśa-bhāgena*—in full potency, with different parts and parcels; *sāmpratam*—at the present moment; *patiḥ āśiṣām*—You are the Supreme Personality of Godhead, the master of all auspiciousness.

## TRANSLATION

**Appearing in bodies like those of an ordinary fish, tortoise and hog, You exhibit activities impossible for such creatures to perform—extraordinary, incomparable, transcendental activities of unlimited power and strength. These bodies of Yours, therefore, are not made of material elements, but are incarnations of Your Supreme Personality. You are the same Supreme Personality of Godhead, who have now appeared, with full potency, for the benefit of all living entities within this material world.**

## PURPORT

As stated in *Bhagavad-gītā* (4.7–8):

*yadā yadā hi dharmasya*
*glānir bhavati bhārata*
*abhyutthānam adharmasya*
*tadātmānaṁ sṛjāmy aham*

*paritrāṇāya sādhūnāṁ*
*vināśāya ca duṣkṛtām*
*dharma-saṁsthāpanārthāya*
*sambhavāmi yuge yuge*

Kṛṣṇa appears as an incarnation when real spiritual life declines and when rogues and thieves increase to disturb the situation of the world. Unfortunate, less intelligent persons, bereft of devotional service, cannot understand the Lord's activities, and therefore such persons describe these activities as *kalpanā*—mythology or imagination—because they are rascals and the lowest of men (*na māṁ duṣkṛtino mūḍhāḥ prapadyante narādhamāḥ*). Such men cannot understand that the events described by Vyāsadeva in the *Purāṇas* and other *śāstras* are not fictitious or imaginary, but factual.

Kṛṣṇa, in His full, unlimited potency, here shows that He is the Supreme Personality of Godhead, for although the two trees were so large and sturdy that even many elephants could not move them, Kṛṣṇa, as a child, exhibited such extraordinary strength that they fell down with a great sound. From the very beginning, by killing Pūtanā, Śakaṭāsura and Tṛṇāvartāsura, by causing the trees to fall, and by showing the entire universe within His mouth, Kṛṣṇa proved that He is the Supreme Personality of Godhead. The lowest of men (*mūḍhas*), because of sinful activities, cannot understand this, but devotees can accept it without a doubt. Thus the position of a devotee is different from that of a nondevotee.

## TEXT 36

नमः परमकल्याण नमः परममङ्गल ।
वासुदेवाय शान्ताय यदूनां पतये नमः ॥३६॥

*namaḥ parama-kalyāṇa*
*namaḥ parama-maṅgala*
*vāsudevāya śāntāya*
*yadūnāṁ pataye namaḥ*

*namaḥ*—we therefore offer our respectful obeisances; *parama-kalyāṇa*—You are the supreme auspiciousness; *namaḥ*—our respectful obeisances unto You; *parama-maṅgala*—whatever You do is good; *vāsudevāya*—unto the original Personality of Godhead, Vāsudeva; *śāntāya*—unto the most peaceful; *yadūnām*—of the Yadu dynasty; *pataye*—unto the controller; *namaḥ*—our respectful obeisances unto You.

## TRANSLATION

**O supremely auspicious, we offer our respectful obeisances unto You, who are the supreme good. O most famous descendant and controller of the Yadu dynasty, O son of Vasudeva, O most peaceful, let us offer our obeisances unto Your lotus feet.**

## PURPORT

The word *parama-kalyāṇa* is significant because Kṛṣṇa, in any of His incarnations, appears in order to protect the *sādhus* (*paritrāṇāya sādhūnām*). The *sādhus*, saintly persons or devotees, are always harassed by nondevotees, and Kṛṣṇa appears in His incarnations to give them relief. This is His first concern. If we study the history of Kṛṣṇa's life, we shall find that for most of His life He predominantly engaged in killing demons one after another.

## TEXT 37

अनुजानीहि नौ भूमंस्तवानुचरकिङ्करौ ।
दर्शनं नौ भगवत ऋषेरासीदनुग्रहात् ॥३७॥

*anujānīhi nau bhūmaṁs*
*tavānucara-kiṅkarau*
*darśanaṁ nau bhagavata*
*ṛṣer āsīd anugrahāt*

*anujānīhi*—may we have permission; *nau*—we; *bhūman*—O greatest universal form; *tava anucara-kiṅkarau*—because of being servants of Your most confidential devotee Nārada Muni; *darśanam*—to see personally; *nau*—of us; *bhagavataḥ*—of You, the Supreme Personality of Godhead; *ṛṣeḥ*—of the great saint Nārada; *āsīt*—there was (in the form of a curse); *anugrahāt*—from the mercy.

## TRANSLATION

**O supreme form, we are always servants of Your servants, especially of Nārada Muni. Now give us permission to leave for our home. It is by the grace and mercy of Nārada Muni that we have been able to see You face to face.**

## PURPORT

Unless delivered or blessed by a devotee, one cannot realize that Kṛṣṇa is the Supreme Personality of Godhead. *Manuṣyāṇāṁ sahasreṣu kaścid yatati siddhaye.* According to this verse of *Bhagavad-gītā* (7.3), there are so many *siddhas* or *yogīs* who cannot understand Kṛṣṇa; instead, they misunderstand Him. But if one takes shelter of a devotee descending from the *paramparā* system of Nārada (*svayambhūr nāradaḥ śambhuḥ*), one can then understand who is an incarnation of the Supreme Personality of Godhead. In this age, many pseudo incarnations are advertised simply for having exhibited some magical performances, but except for persons who are servants of Nārada and other servants of Kṛṣṇa, no one can understand who is God and who is not. This is confirmed by Narottama dāsa Ṭhākura. *Chāḍiyā vaiṣṇava-sevā nistāra pāyeche kebā:* no one is delivered from the material conception of life unless favored by a Vaiṣṇava. Others can never understand, neither by speculation nor by any other bodily or mental gymnastics.

## TEXT 38

वाणी गुणानुकथने श्रवणौ कथायां
हस्तौ च कर्मसु मनस्तव पादयोर्नः ।
स्मृत्यां शिरस्तव निवासजगत्प्रणामे
दृष्टिः सतां दर्शनेऽस्तु भवत्तनूनाम् ॥३८॥

*vāṇī guṇānukathane śravaṇau kathāyāṁ*
*hastau ca karmasu manas tava pādayor naḥ*
*smṛtyāṁ śiras tava nivāsa-jagat-praṇāme*
*dṛṣṭiḥ satāṁ darśane 'stu bhavat-tanūnām*

*vāṇī*—words, the power of speech; *guṇa-anukathane*—always engaged in talking about Your pastimes; *śravaṇau*—the ear, or aural reception; *kathāyām*—in talks about You and Your pastimes; *hastau*—hands and legs and other senses; *ca*—also; *karmasu*—engaging them in executing Your mission; *manaḥ*—the mind; *tava*—Your; *pādayoḥ*—of Your lotus feet; *naḥ*—our; *smṛtyām*—in remembrance always engaged in meditation; *śiraḥ*—the head; *tava*—Your; *nivāsa-jagat-praṇāme*—because You are all-pervading, You are everything, and our heads should bow down, not looking for enjoyment; *dṛṣṭiḥ*—the power of sight; *satām*—of the Vaiṣṇavas; *darśane*—in seeing; *astu*—let all of them be engaged in this way; *bhavat-tanūnām*—who are nondifferent from You.

## TRANSLATION

**Henceforward, may all our words describe Your pastimes, may our ears engage in aural reception of Your glories, may our hands, legs and other senses engage in actions pleasing to You, and may**

**our minds always think of Your lotus feet. May our heads offer our obeisances to everything within this world, because all things are also Your different forms, and may our eyes see the forms of Vaiṣṇavas, who are nondifferent from You.**

## PURPORT

Here the process of understanding the Supreme Personality of Godhead is given. This process is *bhakti.*

*śravaṇaṁ kīrtanaṁ viṣṇoḥ*
*smaraṇaṁ pāda-sevanam*
*arcanaṁ vandanaṁ dāsyaṁ*
*sakhyam ātma-nivedanam*
(*Bhāg.* 7.5.23)

Everything should be engaged in the service of the Lord. *Hṛṣīkeṇa hṛṣīkeśa-sevanaṁ bhaktir ucyate* (*Nārada-pañcarātra*). Everything—the mind, the body and all the sense organs—should be engaged in Kṛṣṇa's service. This is to be learned from expert devotees like Nārada, Svayambhū and Śambhu. This is the process. We cannot manufacture our own way of understanding the Supreme Personality of Godhead, for it is not that everything one manufactures or concocts will lead to understanding God. Such a proposition—*yata mata, tata patha*—is foolish. Kṛṣṇa says, *bhaktyāham ekayā grāhyaḥ:* "Only by executing the activities of *bhakti* can one understand Me." (*Bhāg.* 11.14.21) This is called *ānukūlyena kṛṣṇānuśīlanam*, remaining engaged favorably in the service of the Lord.

## TEXT 39

श्रीशुक उवाच
इत्थं संकीर्तितस्ताभ्यां भगवान् गोकुलेश्वरः ।
दाम्ना चोलूखले बद्धः प्रहसन्नाह गुह्यकौ ॥३९॥

*śrī-śuka uvāca*
*itthaṁ saṅkīrtitas tābhyām*
*bhagavān gokuleśvaraḥ*

*dāmnā colūkhale baddhaḥ*
*prahasann āha guhyakau*

*śrī-śukaḥ uvāca*—Śrī Śukadeva Gosvāmī continued to speak; *ittham*—in this way, as aforesaid; *saṅkīrtitaḥ*—being glorified and praised; *tābhyām*—by the two young demigods; *bhagavān*—the Supreme Personality of Godhead; *gokula-īśvaraḥ*—the master of Gokula (because He is *sarva-loka-maheśvara*); *dāmnā*—by the rope; *ca*—also; *ulūkhale*—on the wooden mortar; *baddhaḥ*—bound; *prahasan*—smiling; *āha*—said; *guhyakau*—unto the two young demigods.

## TRANSLATION

**Śukadeva Gosvāmī continued: The two young demigods thus offered prayers to the Supreme Personality of Godhead. Although Śrī Kṛṣṇa, the Supreme Godhead, is the master of all and was certainly Gokuleśvara, the master of Gokula, He was bound to the wooden mortar by the ropes of the gopīs, and therefore, smiling widely, He spoke to the sons of Kuvera the following words.**

## PURPORT

Kṛṣṇa was smiling because He was thinking to Himself, "These two young demigods fell from the higher planetary system to this planet, and I have delivered them from the bondage of standing for a long time as trees, but as for Me, I am bound by the ropes of the *gopīs* and am subject to their chastisements." In other words, Kṛṣṇa submits to being chastised and bound by the *gopīs* because of pure love and affection worthy of being praised by a devotee in so many ways.

## TEXT 40

श्रीभगवानुवाच
ज्ञातं मम पुरैवैतदृषिणा करुणात्मना ।
यच्छ्रीमदान्धयोर्वाग्भिर्विभ्रंशोऽनुग्रहः कृतः ॥४०॥

*śrī-bhagavān uvāca*
*jñātaṁ mama puraivaitad*
*ṛṣiṇā karuṇātmanā*

*yac chrī-madāndhayor vāgbhir*
*vibhraṁśo 'nugrahaḥ kṛtaḥ*

*śrī-bhagavān uvāca*—the Supreme Personality of Godhead said; *jñātam*—everything is known; *mama*—to Me; *purā*—in the past; *eva*—indeed; *etat*—this incident; *ṛṣiṇā*—by the great sage Nārada; *karuṇā-ātmanā*—because he was very, very kind to you; *yat*—which; *śrī-mada-andhayoḥ*—who had become mad after material opulence and had thus become blind; *vāgbhiḥ*—by words or by cursing; *vibhraṁśaḥ*—falling down from the heavenly planet to become *arjuna* trees here; *anugrahaḥ kṛtaḥ*—this was a great favor done by him to you.

## TRANSLATION

**The Supreme Personality of Godhead said: The great saint Nārada Muni is very merciful. By his curse, he showed the greatest favor to both of you, who were mad after material opulence and who had thus become blind. Although you fell from the higher planet Svargaloka and became trees, you were most favored by him. I knew of all these incidents from the very beginning.**

## PURPORT

It is now confirmed by the Supreme Personality of Godhead that the curse of a devotee is also to be regarded as mercy. As Kṛṣṇa, God, is all-good, a Vaiṣṇava is also all-good. Whatever he does is good for everyone. This is explained in the following verse.

## TEXT 41

साधूनां समचित्तानां सुतरां मत्कृतात्मनाम् ।
दर्शनान्नो भवेद् बन्धः पुंसोऽक्ष्णोः सवितुर्यथा ॥४१॥

*sādhūnāṁ sama-cittānāṁ*
*sutarāṁ mat-kṛtātmanām*
*darśanān no bhaved bandhaḥ*
*puṁso 'kṣṇoḥ savitur yathā*

*sādhūnām*—of devotees; *sama-cittānām*—who are equally disposed toward everyone; *sutarām*—excessively, completely; *mat-kṛta-ātmanām*—of persons who are fully surrendered, determined to render service unto Me; *darśanāt*—simply by the audience; *no bhavet bandhaḥ*—freedom from all material bondage; *puṁsaḥ*—of a person; *akṣṇoḥ*—of the eyes; *savituḥ yathā*—as by being face to face with the sun.

## TRANSLATION

**When one is face to face with the sun, there is no longer darkness for one's eyes. Similarly, when one is face to face with a sādhu, a devotee, who is fully determined and surrendered to the Supreme Personality of Godhead, one will no longer be subject to material bondage.**

## PURPORT

As stated by Caitanya Mahāprabhu (Cc. *Madhya* 22.54):

*'sādhu-saṅga,' 'sādhu-saṅga'—sarva-śāstre kaya*
*lava-mātra sādhu-saṅge sarva-siddhi haya*

If by chance one meets a *sādhu*, a devotee, one's life is immediately successful, and one is freed from material bondage. It may be argued that whereas someone may receive a *sādhu* with great respect, someone else may not receive a *sādhu* with such respect. A *sādhu*, however, is always equipoised toward everyone. Because of being a pure devotee, a *sādhu* is always ready to deliver Kṛṣṇa consciousness without discrimination. As soon as one sees a *sādhu*, one naturally becomes free. Nonetheless, persons who are too much offensive, who commit *vaiṣṇava-aparādhas*, or offenses to a *sādhu*, will have to take some time before being rectified. This is also indicated herein.

## TEXT 42

**तद् गच्छतं मत्परमौ नलकूवर सादनम् ।**
**सञ्जातो मयि भावो वामीप्सितः परमोऽभवः ॥४२॥**

*tad gacchataṁ mat-paramau*
*nalakūvara sādanam*
*sañjāto mayi bhāvo vām*
*īpsitaḥ paramo 'bhavaḥ*

*tat gacchatam*—now both of you may return; *mat-paramau*—accepting Me as the supreme destination of life; *nalakūvara*—O Nalakūvara and Maṇigrīva; *sādanam*—to your home; *sañjātaḥ*—being saturated with; *mayi*—unto Me; *bhāvaḥ*—devotional service; *vām*—by you; *īpsitaḥ*—which was desired; *paramaḥ*—supreme, highest, always engaged with all senses; *abhavaḥ*—from which there is no falldown into material existence.

## TRANSLATION

**O Nalakūvara and Maṇigrīva, now you may both return home. Since you desire to be always absorbed in My devotional service, your desire to develop love and affection for Me will be fulfilled, and now you will never fall from that platform.**

## PURPORT

The highest perfection of life is to come to the platform of devotional service and always engage in devotional activities. Understanding this, Nalakūvara and Maṇigrīva desired to attain that platform, and the Supreme Personality of Godhead blessed them with the fulfillment of their transcendental desire.

## TEXT 43

श्रीशुक उवाच
इत्युक्तौ तौ परिक्रम्य प्रणम्य च पुनः पुनः ।
बद्धोलूखलमामन्त्र्य जग्मतुर्दिशमुत्तराम् ॥४३॥

*śrī-śuka uvāca*
*ity uktau tau parikramya*
*praṇamya ca punaḥ punaḥ*
*baddholūkhalam āmantrya*
*jagmatur diśam uttarām*

*śrī-śukaḥ uvāca*—Śrī Śukadeva Gosvāmī said; *iti uktau*—having been ordered by the Supreme Personality of Godhead in this way; *tau*—Nalakūvara and Maṇigrīva; *parikramya*—circumambulating; *praṇamya*—offering obeisances; *ca*—also; *punaḥ punaḥ*—again and again; *baddha-ulūkhalam āmantrya*—taking the permission of the Supreme Personality of Godhead, who was bound to the wooden mortar; *jagmatuḥ*—departed; *diśam uttarām*—to their respective destinations.

## TRANSLATION

**Śukadeva Gosvāmī said: The Supreme Personality of Godhead having spoken to the two demigods in this way, they circumambulated the Lord, who was bound to the wooden mortar, and offered obeisances to Him. After taking the permission of Lord Kṛṣṇa, they returned to their respective homes.**

*Thus end the Bhaktivedanta purports of the Tenth Canto, Tenth Chapter, of the* Śrīmad-Bhāgavatam, *entitled "Deliverance of the Yamala-arjuna Trees."*

## CHAPTER ELEVEN

# The Childhood Pastimes of Kṛṣṇa

This chapter describes how the inhabitants of Gokula left Gokula and went to Vṛndāvana and how Kṛṣṇa killed Vatsāsura and Bakāsura.

When the *yamala-arjuna* trees fell, they made a tremendous sound, like that of falling thunderbolts. Being surprised, Kṛṣṇa's father, Nanda, and the other elderly inhabitants of Gokula went to the spot, where they saw the fallen trees and Kṛṣṇa standing between them, bound to the *ulūkhala*, the wooden mortar. They could find no cause for the trees' having fallen and Kṛṣṇa's being there. They thought this might be the work of some other *asura* who had met Kṛṣṇa on this spot, and they inquired from the playmates of Kṛṣṇa about how the whole incident had taken place. The children properly described how everything had happened, but the elderly persons could not believe the story. Some of them, however, thought that it might be true, since they had already seen many wonderful incidents in connection with Kṛṣṇa. Anyway, Nanda Mahārāja immediately released Kṛṣṇa from the ropes.

In this way, Kṛṣṇa, at every day and every moment, displayed wonderful incidents to increase the parental affection of Nanda Mahārāja and Yaśodā, who thus felt both surprise and joy. The breaking of the *yamala-arjunas* was one of these wonderful pastimes.

One day a fruit vendor approached Nanda Mahārāja's house, and Kṛṣṇa gathered some food grains with His little palms and went to the vendor to exchange the grains for fruit. On the way, almost all the grains fell from His palms, only one or two grains remaining, but the fruit vendor, out of full affection, accepted these grains in exchange for as much fruit as Kṛṣṇa could take. As soon as she did this, her basket became filled with gold and jewels.

Thereafter, all the elderly *gopas* decided to leave Gokula because they saw that in Gokula there was always some disturbance. They decided to go to Vṛndāvana, Vraja-dhāma, and the next day they all departed. In Vṛndāvana, both Kṛṣṇa and Balarāma, after finishing Their childhood pastimes, began to take charge of the calves and send them to the pasturing grounds (*go-caraṇa*). During this time, a demon named Vatsāsura entered among the calves and was killed, and another *asura*, in the shape of a big duck, was also killed. The playmates of Kṛṣṇa narrated all these stories to their mothers. The mothers could not believe their children, Kṛṣṇa's playmates, but because of full affection they enjoyed these narrations of Kṛṣṇa's activities.

## TEXT 1

श्रीशुक उवाच
गोपा नन्दादयः श्रुत्वा द्रुमयोः पततोरवम् ।
तत्राजग्मुः कुरुश्रेष्ठ निर्घातभयशङ्किताः ॥ १ ॥

*śrī-śuka uvāca*
*gopā nandādayaḥ śrutvā*
*drumayoḥ patato ravam*
*tatrājagmuḥ kuru-śreṣṭha*
*nirghāta-bhaya-śaṅkitāḥ*

*śrī-śukaḥ uvāca*—Śrī Śukadeva Gosvāmī said; *gopāḥ*—all the cowherd men; *nanda-ādayaḥ*—headed by Nanda Mahārāja; *śrutvā*—hearing; *drumayoḥ*—of the two trees; *patatoḥ*—falling down; *ravam*—the high sound, as terrible as a thunderbolt; *tatra*—there, on the spot; *ājagmuḥ*—went; *kuru-śreṣṭha*—O Mahārāja Parīkṣit; *nirghāta-bhaya-śaṅkitāḥ*—who were afraid of falling thunderbolts.

## TRANSLATION

**Śukadeva Gosvāmī continued: O Mahārāja Parīkṣit, when the yamala-arjuna trees fell, all the cowherd men in the neighborhood, hearing the fierce sound and fearing thunderbolts, went to the spot.**

## TEXT 2

भूम्यां निपतितौ तत्र ददृशुर्यमलार्जुनौ ।
बभ्रमुस्तदविज्ञाय लक्ष्यं पतनकारणम् ॥ २ ॥

*bhūmyāṁ nipatitau tatra*
*dadṛśur yamalārjunau*

*babhramus tad avijñāya*
*lakṣyaṁ patana-kāraṇam*

*bhūmyām*—on the ground; *nipatitau*—which had fallen; *tatra*—there; *dadṛśuḥ*—all of them saw; *yamala-arjunau*—the twin *arjuna* trees; *babhramuḥ*—they became bewildered; *tat*—that; *avijñāya*—but they could not trace out; *lakṣyam*—although they could directly perceive that the trees had fallen; *patana-kāraṇam*—the cause of their falling (how could it have happened all of a sudden?).

## TRANSLATION

**There they saw the fallen yamala-arjuna trees on the ground, but they were bewildered because even though they could directly perceive that the trees had fallen, they could not trace out the cause for their having done so.**

## PURPORT

Considering all the circumstances, had this been done by Kṛṣṇa? He was standing on the spot, and His playmates described that this had been done by Him. Had Kṛṣṇa actually done this, or were these merely stories? This was a cause of bewilderment.

## TEXT 3

उलूखलं विकर्षन्तं दाम्ना बद्धं च बालकम् ।
कस्येदं कुत आश्चर्यमुत्पात इति कातराः ॥ ३ ॥

*ulūkhalaṁ vikarṣantaṁ*
*dāmnā baddhaṁ ca bālakam*
*kasyedaṁ kuta āścaryam*
*utpāta iti kātarāḥ*

*ulūkhalam*—the wooden mortar; *vikarṣantam*—dragging; *dāmnā*—with the rope; *baddham ca*—and bound by the belly; *bālakam*—Kṛṣṇa; *kasya*—of whom; *idam*—this; *kutaḥ*—wherefrom; *āścaryam*—these wonderful happenings; *utpātaḥ*—disturbance; *iti*—thus; *kātarāḥ*—they were very much agitated.

### TRANSLATION

**Kṛṣṇa was bound by the rope to the ulūkhala, the mortar, which He was dragging. But how could He have pulled down the trees? Who had actually done it? Where was the source for this incident? Considering all these astounding things, the cowherd men were doubtful and bewildered.**

### PURPORT

The cowherd men were very much agitated because the child Kṛṣṇa, after all, had been standing between the two trees, and if by chance the trees had fallen upon Him, He would have been smashed. But He was standing as He was, and still the things had happened, so who had done all this? How could these events have happened in such a wonderful way? These considerations were some of the reasons they were agitated and bewildered. They thought, however, that by chance Kṛṣṇa had been saved by God so that nothing had happened to Him.

### TEXT 4

**बाला ऊचुरनेनेति तिर्यग्गतमुलूखलम् ।**
**विकर्षता मध्यगेन पुरुषावप्यचक्ष्महि ॥ ४ ॥**

*bālā ūcur aneneti*
*tiryag-gatam ulūkhalam*
*vikarṣatā madhya-gena*
*puruṣāv apy acakṣmahi*

*bālāḥ*—all the other boys; *ūcuḥ*—said; *anena*—by Him (Kṛṣṇa); *iti*—thus; *tiryak*—crosswise; *gatam*—which had become; *ulūkhalam*—the wooden mortar; *vikarṣatā*—by Kṛṣṇa, who was dragging; *madhya-gena*—going between the two trees; *puruṣau*—two beautiful persons; *api*—also; *acakṣmahi*—we have seen with our own eyes.

### TRANSLATION

**Then all the cowherd boys said: It is Kṛṣṇa who has done this. When He was in between the two trees, the mortar fell crosswise. Kṛṣṇa dragged the mortar, and the two trees fell down. After that,**

**two beautiful men came out of the trees. We have seen this with our own eyes.**

## PURPORT

Kṛṣṇa's playmates wanted to inform Kṛṣṇa's father of the exact situation by explaining that not only did the trees break, but out of the broken trees came two beautiful men. "All these things happened," they said. "We have seen them with our own eyes."

## TEXT 5

न ते तदुक्तं जगृहुर्न घटेतेति तस्य तत् ।
बालस्योत्पाटनं तर्वोः केचित् सन्दिग्धचेतसः ॥ ५ ॥

*na te tad-uktaṁ jagṛhur*
*na ghaṭeteti tasya tat*
*bālasyotpāṭanaṁ tarvoḥ*
*kecit sandigdha-cetasaḥ*

*na*—not; *te*—all the *gopas; tat-uktam*—being spoken by the boys; *jagṛhuḥ*—would accept; *na ghaṭeta*—it cannot be; *iti*—thus; *tasya*—of Kṛṣṇa; *tat*—the activity; *bālasya*—of a small boy like Kṛṣṇa; *utpāṭanam*—the uprooting; *tarvoḥ*—of the two trees; *kecit*—some of them; *sandigdha-cetasaḥ*—became doubtful about what could be done (because Gargamuni had predicted that this child would be equal to Nārāyaṇa).

## TRANSLATION

**Because of intense paternal affection, the cowherd men, headed by Nanda, could not believe that Kṛṣṇa could have uprooted the trees in such a wonderful way. Therefore they could not put their faith in the words of the boys. Some of the men, however, were in doubt. "Since Kṛṣṇa was predicted to equal Nārāyaṇa," they thought, "it might be that He could have done it."**

## PURPORT

One view was that it was impossible for a small boy like this to have done such a thing as pulling down the trees. But there were doubts because Kṛṣṇa had been predicted to equal Nārāyaṇa. Therefore the cowherd men were in a dilemma.

### TEXT 6

उलूखलं विकर्षन्तं दाम्ना बद्धं स्वमात्मजम् ।
विलोक्य नन्दः प्रहसद्वदनो विमुमोच ह ॥ ६ ॥

*ulūkhalaṁ vikarṣantaṁ*
*dāmnā baddhaṁ svam ātmajam*
*vilokya nandaḥ prahasad-*
*vadano vimumoca ha*

*ulūkhalam*—the wooden mortar; *vikarṣantam*—dragging; *dāmnā*—by the rope; *baddham*—bound; *svam ātmajam*—his own son Kṛṣṇa; *vilokya*—by seeing; *nandaḥ*—Mahārāja Nanda; *prahasat-vadanaḥ*—whose face began to smile when he saw the wonderful child; *vimumoca ha*—released Him from the bonds.

### TRANSLATION

**When Nanda Mahārāja saw his own son bound with ropes to the wooden mortar and dragging it, he smiled and released Kṛṣṇa from His bonds.**

### PURPORT

Nanda Mahārāja was surprised that Yaśodā, Kṛṣṇa's mother, could have bound her beloved child in such a way. Kṛṣṇa was exchanging love with her. How then could she have been so cruel as to bind Him to the wooden mortar? Nanda Mahārāja understood this exchange of love, and therefore he smiled and released Kṛṣṇa. In other words, as Kṛṣṇa, the Supreme Personality of Godhead, binds a living entity in fruitive activities, He binds mother Yaśodā and Nanda Mahārāja in parental affection. This is His pastime.

### TEXT 7

गोपीभिः स्तोभितोऽनृत्यद् भगवान् बालवत् क्वचित् ।
उद्गायति क्वचिन्मुग्धस्तद्वशो दारुयन्त्रवत् ॥ ७ ॥

*gopībhiḥ stobhito 'nṛtyad*
*bhagavān bālavat kvacit*
*udgāyati kvacin mugdhas*
*tad-vaśo dāru-yantravat*

*gopībhiḥ*—by the *gopīs* (by flattery and offers of prizes); *stobhitaḥ*—encouraged, induced; *anṛtyat*—the small Kṛṣṇa danced; *bhagavān*—although He was the Supreme Personality of Godhead; *bāla-vat*—exactly like a human child; *kvacit*—sometimes; *udgāyati*—He would sing very loudly; *kvacit*—sometimes; *mugdhaḥ*—being amazed; *tat-vaśaḥ*—under their control; *dāru-yantra-vat*—like a wooden doll.

## TRANSLATION

**The gopīs would say, "If You dance, my dear Kṛṣṇa, then I shall give You half a sweetmeat." By saying these words or by clapping their hands, all the gopīs encouraged Kṛṣṇa in different ways. At such times, although He was the supremely powerful Personality of Godhead, He would smile and dance according to their desire, as if He were a wooden doll in their hands. Sometimes He would sing very loudly, at their bidding. In this way, Kṛṣṇa came completely under the control of the gopīs.**

## TEXT 8

बिभर्ति क्वचिदाज्ञप्तः पीठकोन्मानपादुकम् ।
बाहुक्षेपं च कुरुते स्वानां च प्रीतिमावहन् ॥ ८ ॥

*bibharti kvacid ājñaptaḥ*
*pīṭhakonmāna-pādukam*
*bāhu-kṣepaṁ ca kurute*
*svānāṁ ca prītim āvahan*

*bibharti*—Kṛṣṇa would simply stand and touch articles as if unable to raise them; *kvacit*—sometimes; *ājñaptaḥ*—being ordered; *pīṭhaka-unmāna*—the wooden seat and wooden measuring pot; *pādukam*—bringing the wooden shoes; *bāhu-kṣepam ca*—striking the arms on the body; *kurute*—does; *svānām ca*—of His own relatives, the *gopīs* and other intimate friends; *prītim*—the pleasure; *āvahan*—inviting.

## TRANSLATION

**Sometimes mother Yaśodā and her gopī friends would tell Kṛṣṇa, "Bring this article" or "Bring that article." Sometimes they would order Him to bring a wooden plank, wooden shoes or a wooden measuring pot, and Kṛṣṇa, when thus ordered by the mothers, would try to bring them. Sometimes, however, as if unable to raise these things, He would touch them and stand there. Just to invite the pleasure of His relatives, He would strike His body with His arms to show that He had sufficient strength.**

## TEXT 9

दर्शयंस्तद्विदां लोक आत्मनो भृत्यवश्यताम् ।
व्रजस्योवाह वै हर्षं भगवान् बालचेष्टितैः ॥ ९ ॥

*darśayaṁs tad-vidāṁ loka*
*ātmano bhṛtya-vaśyatām*
*vrajasyovāha vai harṣaṁ*
*bhagavān bāla-ceṣṭitaiḥ*

*darśayan*—exhibiting; *tat-vidām*—unto persons who can understand Kṛṣṇa's activities; *loke*—throughout the whole world; *ātmanaḥ*—of Himself; *bhṛtya-vaśyatām*—how He is agreeable to carrying out the orders of His servants, His devotees; *vrajasya*—of Vrajabhūmi; *uvāha*—executed; *vai*—indeed; *harṣam*—pleasure; *bhagavān*—the Supreme Personality of Godhead; *bāla-ceṣṭitaiḥ*—by His activities like those of a child trying to do so many things.

## TRANSLATION

**To pure devotees throughout the world who could understand His activities, the Supreme Personality of Godhead, Kṛṣṇa, exhibited how much He can be subdued by His devotees, His servants. In this way He increased the pleasure of the Vrajavāsīs by His childhood activities.**

## PURPORT

That Kṛṣṇa performed childhood activities to increase the pleasure of His devotees was another transcendental humor. He exhibited these activities not only to the inhabitants of Vrajabhūmi, but also to others, who were captivated by His external potency and opulence. Both the internal devotees, who were simply absorbed in love of Kṛṣṇa, and the external devotees, who were captivated by His unlimited potency, were informed of Kṛṣṇa's desire to be submissive to His servants.

## TEXT 10

क्रीणीहि भोः फलानीति श्रुत्वा सत्वरमच्युतः ।
फलार्थी धान्यमादाय ययौ सर्वफलप्रदः ॥१०॥

*krīṇīhi bhoḥ phalānīti*
*śrutvā satvaram acyutaḥ*
*phalārthī dhānyam ādāya*
*yayau sarva-phala-pradaḥ*

*krīṇīhi*—please come and purchase; *bhoḥ*—O neighborhood residents; *phalāni*—ripe fruits; *iti*—thus; *śrutvā*—hearing; *satvaram*—very soon; *acyutaḥ*—Kṛṣṇa; *phala-arthī*—as if He wanted some fruits; *dhānyam ādāya*—capturing some grains of paddy; *yayau*—went to the fruit vendor; *sarva-phala-pradaḥ*—the Supreme Personality of Godhead, who can give all kinds of fruit to everyone, had now become in need of fruits.

## TRANSLATION

**Once a woman selling fruit was calling, "O inhabitants of Vrajabhūmi, if you want to purchase some fruits, come here!" Upon hearing this, Kṛṣṇa immediately took some grains and went to barter as if He needed some fruits.**

## PURPORT

Aborigines generally go to the villagers to sell fruits. How much the aborigines were attached to Kṛṣṇa is here described. Kṛṣṇa, to show His favor to the aborigines, would immediately go purchase fruits, bartering with paddy in His hand as He had seen others do.

## TEXT 11

फलविक्रयिणी तस्य च्युतधान्यकरद्वयम् ।
फलैरपूरयद् रत्नैः फलभाण्डमपूरि च ॥११॥

*phala-vikrayiṇī tasya*
*cyuta-dhānya-kara-dvayam*
*phalair apūrayad ratnaiḥ*
*phala-bhāṇḍam apūri ca*

*phala-vikrayiṇī*—the aborigine fruit vendor, who was an elderly woman; *tasya*—of Kṛṣṇa; *cyuta-dhānya*—the paddy He brought to barter having mostly fallen; *kara-dvayam*—palms of the hands; *phalaiḥ apūrayat*—the fruit vendor filled His small palms with fruits; *ratnaiḥ*—in exchange for jewels and gold; *phala-bhāṇḍam*—the basket of fruit; *apūri ca*—filled.

## TRANSLATION

**While Kṛṣṇa was going to the fruit vendor very hastily, most of the grains He was holding fell. Nonetheless, the fruit vendor filled Kṛṣṇa's hands with fruits, and her fruit basket was immediately filled with jewels and gold.**

## PURPORT

In *Bhagavad-gītā* (9.26) Kṛṣṇa says:

*patraṁ puṣpaṁ phalaṁ toyaṁ*
*yo me bhaktyā prayacchati*
*tad ahaṁ bhakty-upahṛtam*
*aśnāmi prayatātmanaḥ*

Kṛṣṇa is so kind that if anyone offers Him a leaf, a fruit, a flower or some water, He will immediately accept it. The only condition is that these things should be offered with *bhakti* (*yo me bhaktyā prayacchati*).

Otherwise, if one is puffed up with false prestige, thinking, "I have so much opulence, and I am giving something to Kṛṣṇa," one's offering will not be accepted by Kṛṣṇa. The fruit vendor, although a woman belonging to the poor aborigine class, dealt with Kṛṣṇa with great affection, saying, "Kṛṣṇa, You have come to me to take some fruit in exchange for grains. All the grains have fallen, but still You may take whatever You like." Thus she filled Kṛṣṇa's palms with whatever fruits He could carry. In exchange, Kṛṣṇa filled her whole basket with jewels and gold.

From this incident one should learn that for anything offered to Kṛṣṇa with love and affection, Kṛṣṇa can reciprocate many millions of times over, both materially and spiritually. The basic principle involved is an exchange of love. Therefore Kṛṣṇa teaches in *Bhagavad-gītā* (9.27):

*yat karoṣi yad aśnāsi*
*yaj juhoṣi dadāsi yat*
*yat tapasyasi kaunteya*
*tat kuruṣva mad-arpaṇam*

"O son of Kuntī, all that you do, all that you eat, all that you offer and give away, as well as all austerities that you may perform, should be done as an offering unto Me." With love and affection, one should try to give something to Kṛṣṇa from one's source of income. Then one's life will be successful. Kṛṣṇa is full in all opulences; He does not need anything from anyone. But if one is prepared to give something to Kṛṣṇa, that is for one's own benefit. The example given in this connection is that when one's real face is decorated, the reflection of one's face is automatically decorated. Similarly, if we try to serve Kṛṣṇa with all our opulences, we, as parts and parcels or reflections of Kṛṣṇa, will become happy in exchange. Kṛṣṇa is always happy, for He is *ātmārāma*, fully satisfied with His own opulence.

## TEXT 12

सरित्तीरगतं कृष्णं भग्नार्जुनमथाह्वयत् ।
रामं च रोहिणी देवी क्रीडन्तं बालकैर्भृशम् ॥१२॥

*sarit-tīra-gataṁ kṛṣṇaṁ*
*bhagnārjunam athāhvayat*

*rāmaṁ ca rohiṇī devī*
*krīḍantaṁ bālakair bhṛśam*

*sarit-tīra*—to the riverside; *gatam*—who had gone; *kṛṣṇam*—unto Kṛṣṇa; *bhagna-arjunam*—after the pastime of breaking the *yamala-arjuna* trees; *atha*—then; *āhvayat*—called; *rāmam ca*—as well as Balarāma; *rohiṇī*—the mother of Balarāma; *devī*—the goddess of fortune; *krīḍantam*—who were engaged in playing; *bālakaiḥ*—with many other boys; *bhṛśam*—with deep attention.

## TRANSLATION

**Once, after the uprooting of the yamala-arjuna trees, Rohiṇīdevī went to call Rāma and Kṛṣṇa, who had both gone to the riverside and were playing with the other boys with deep attention.**

## PURPORT

Mother Yaśodā was more attached to Kṛṣṇa and Balarāma than Rohiṇīdevī was, although Rohiṇīdevī was the mother of Balarāma. Mother Yaśodā sent Rohiṇīdevī to call Rāma and Kṛṣṇa from Their play, since it was the right time for lunch. Therefore Rohiṇīdevī went to call Them, breaking Their engagement in play.

## TEXT 13

**नोपेयातां यदाहूतौ क्रीडासङ्गेन पुत्रकौ ।**
**यशोदां प्रेषयामास रोहिणी पुत्रवत्सलाम् ॥१३॥**

*nopeyātāṁ yadāhūtau*
*krīḍā-saṅgena putrakau*
*yaśodāṁ preṣayām āsa*
*rohiṇī putra-vatsalām*

*na upeyātām*—would not return home; *yadā*—when; *āhūtau*—They were called back from playing; *krīḍā-saṅgena*—because of so much attachment to playing with other boys; *putrakau*—the two sons (Kṛṣṇa and Balarāma); *yaśodām preṣayām āsa*—sent mother Yaśodā to call Them;

*rohiṇī*—mother Rohiṇī; *putra-vatsalām*—because mother Yaśodā was a more affectionate mother to Kṛṣṇa and Balarāma.

## TRANSLATION

**Because of being too attached to playing with the other boys, Kṛṣṇa and Balarāma did not return upon being called by Rohiṇī. Therefore Rohiṇī sent mother Yaśodā to call Them back, because mother Yaśodā was more affectionate to Kṛṣṇa and Balarāma.**

## PURPORT

*Yaśodāṁ preṣayām āsa.* These very words show that since Kṛṣṇa and Balarāma did not care to return in response to the order of Rohiṇī, Rohiṇī thought that if Yaśodā called They would have to return, for Yaśodā was more affectionate to Kṛṣṇa and Balarāma.

## TEXT 14

क्रीडन्तं सा सुतं बालैरतिवेलं सहाग्रजम् ।
यशोदाजोहवीत् कृष्णं पुत्रस्नेहस्नुतस्तनी ॥१४॥

*krīḍantaṁ sā sutaṁ bālair*
*atívelaṁ sahāgrajam*
*yaśodājohavīt kṛṣṇaṁ*
*putra-sneha-snuta-stanī*

*krīḍantam*—engaged in playing; *sā*—mother Yaśodā; *sutam*—her son; *bālaiḥ*—with the other boys; *ati-velam*—although it was too late; *saha-agrajam*—who was playing with His elder brother, Balarāma; *yaśodā*—mother Yaśodā; *ajohavīt*—called ("Kṛṣṇa and Balarāma, come here!"); *kṛṣṇam*—unto Kṛṣṇa; *putra-sneha-snuta-stanī*—while she was calling Them, milk flowed from her breast because of her ecstatic love and affection.

## TRANSLATION

**Kṛṣṇa and Balarāma, being attached to Their play, were playing with the other boys although it was very late. Therefore mother Yaśodā called Them back for lunch. Because of her ecstatic love**

**and affection for Kṛṣṇa and Balarāma, milk flowed from her breasts.**

## PURPORT

The word *ajohavīt* means "calling them again and again." "Kṛṣṇa and Balarāma," she called, "please come back. You are late for Your lunch. You have played sufficiently. Come back."

## TEXT 15

कृष्ण कृष्णारविन्दाक्ष तात एहि स्तनं पिब ।
अलं विहारैः क्षुत्क्षान्तः क्रीडाश्रान्तोऽसि पुत्रक ॥१५॥

*kṛṣṇa kṛṣṇāravindākṣa*
*tāta ehi stanaṁ piba*
*alaṁ vihāraiḥ kṣut-kṣāntaḥ*
*krīḍā-śrānto 'si putraka*

*kṛṣṇa kṛṣṇa aravinda-akṣa*—O Kṛṣṇa, my son, lotus-eyed Kṛṣṇa; *tāta*—O darling; *ehi*—come here; *stanam*—the milk of my breast; *piba*—drink; *alam vihāraiḥ*—after this there is no necessity of playing; *kṣut-kṣāntaḥ*—tired because of hunger; *krīḍā-śrāntaḥ*—fatigued from playing; *asi*—You must be; *putraka*—O my son.

## TRANSLATION

**Mother Yaśodā said: My dear son Kṛṣṇa, lotus-eyed Kṛṣṇa, come here and drink the milk of my breast. My dear darling, You must be very tired because of hunger and the fatigue of playing so long. There is no need to play any more.**

## TEXT 16

हे रामागच्छ ताताशु सानुजः कुलनन्दन ।
प्रातरेव कृताहारस्तद् भवान् भोक्तुमर्हति ॥१६॥

*he rāmāgaccha tātāśu*
*sānujaḥ kula-nandana*

*prātar eva kṛtāhāras*
*tad bhavān bhoktum arhati*

*he rāma*—my dear son Balarāma; *āgaccha*—please come here; *tāta*—my dear darling; *āśu*—immediately; *sa-anujaḥ*—with Your younger brother; *kula-nandana*—the great hope of our family; *prātaḥ eva*—certainly in the morning; *kṛta-āhāraḥ*—have taken Your breakfast; *tat*—therefore; *bhavān*—You; *bhoktum*—to eat something more; *arhati*—deserve.

## TRANSLATION

**My dear Baladeva, best of our family, please come immediately with Your younger brother, Kṛṣṇa. You both ate in the morning, and now You ought to eat something more.**

## TEXT 17

प्रतीक्षते त्वां दाशार्ह भोक्ष्यमाणो व्रजाधिपः ।
एह्यावयोः प्रियं धेहि स्वगृहान् यात बालकाः ॥१७॥

*pratīkṣate tvāṁ dāśārha*
*bhokṣyamāṇo vrajādhipaḥ*
*ehy āvayoḥ priyaṁ dhehi*
*sva-gṛhān yāta bālakāḥ*

*pratīkṣate*—is waiting; *tvām*—for both of You (Kṛṣṇa and Balarāma); *dāśārha*—O Balarāma; *bhokṣyamāṇaḥ*—desiring to eat; *vraja-adhipaḥ*—the King of Vraja, Nanda Mahārāja; *ehi*—come here; *āvayoḥ*—our; *priyam*—pleasure; *dhehi*—just consider; *sva-gṛhān*—to their respective homes; *yāta*—let them go; *bālakāḥ*—the other boys.

## TRANSLATION

**Nanda Mahārāja, the King of Vraja, is now waiting to eat. O my dear son Balarāma, he is waiting for You. Therefore, come back to please us. All the boys playing with You and Kṛṣṇa should now go to their homes.**

## PURPORT

It appears that Nanda Mahārāja regularly took his food with his two sons, Kṛṣṇa and Balarāma. Yaśodā told the other boys, "Now you should go to your homes." Father and son generally sit together, so mother Yaśodā requested Kṛṣṇa and Balarāma to return, and she advised the other boys to go home so that their parents would not have to wait for them.

## TEXT 18

धूलिधूसरिताङ्गस्त्वं पुत्र मज्जनमावह ।
जन्मर्क्षं तेऽद्य भवति विप्रेभ्यो देहि गाः शुचिः ॥१८॥

*dhūli-dhūsaritāṅgas tvaṁ*
*putra majjanam āvaha*
*janmarkṣaṁ te 'dya bhavati*
*viprebhyo dehi gāḥ śuciḥ*

*dhūli-dhūsarita-aṅgaḥ tvam*—You have become covered with dust and sand all over Your body; *putra*—my dear son; *majjanam āvaha*—now come here, take Your bath and cleanse Yourself; *janma-ṛkṣam*—the auspicious star of Your birth; *te*—of You; *adya*—today; *bhavati*—it is; *viprebhyaḥ*—unto the pure *brāhmaṇas; dehi*—give in charity; *gāḥ*—cows; *śuciḥ*—being purified.

## TRANSLATION

**Mother Yaśodā further told Kṛṣṇa: My dear son, because of playing all day, Your body has become covered with dust and sand. Therefore, come back, take Your bath and cleanse Yourself. Today the moon is conjoined with the auspicious star of Your birth. Therefore, be pure and give cows in charity to the brāhmaṇas.**

## PURPORT

It is a custom of Vedic culture that whenever there is any auspicious ceremony, one should give valuable cows in charity to the *brāhmaṇas.* Therefore mother Yaśodā requested Kṛṣṇa, "Instead of being enthusiastic in playing, now please come and be enthusiastic in charity."

*Yajña-dāna-tapaḥ-karma na tyājyaṁ kāryam eva tat.* As advised in *Bhagavad-gītā* (18.5), sacrifice, charity and austerity should never be given up. *Yajño dānaṁ tapaś caiva pāvanāni manīṣiṇām:* even if one is very much advanced in spiritual life, one should not give up these three duties. To observe one's birthday ceremony, one should do something in terms of one of these three items (*yajña, dāna* or *tapaḥ*), or all of them together.

## TEXT 19

पश्य पश्य वयस्यांस्ते मातृमृष्टान् स्वलङ्कृतान् ।
त्वं च स्नातः कृताहारो विहरस्व स्वलङ्कृतः ॥१९॥

*paśya paśya vayasyāṁs te*
*mātṛ-mṛṣṭān svalaṅkṛtān*
*tvaṁ ca snātaḥ kṛtāhāro*
*viharasva svalaṅkṛtaḥ*

*paśya paśya*—just see, just see; *vayasyān*—boys of Your age; *te*—Your; *mātṛ-mṛṣṭān*—cleansed by their mothers; *su-alaṅkṛtān*—decorated with nice ornaments; *tvam ca*—You also; *snātaḥ*—after taking a bath; *kṛta-āhāraḥ*—and eating Your lunch; *viharasva*—enjoy with them; *su-alaṅkṛtaḥ*—fully decorated like them.

## TRANSLATION

**Just see how all Your playmates of Your own age have been cleansed and decorated with beautiful ornaments by their mothers. You should come here, and after You have taken Your bath, eaten Your lunch and been decorated with ornaments, You may play with Your friends again.**

## PURPORT

Generally young boys are competitive. If one friend has done something, another friend also wants to do something. Therefore mother Yaśodā pointed out how Kṛṣṇa's playmates were decorated, so that Kṛṣṇa might be induced to decorate Himself like them.

## TEXT 20

इत्थं यशोदा तमशेषशेखरं
मत्वा सुतं स्नेहनिबद्धधीर्नृप ।
हस्ते गृहीत्वा सहराममच्युतं
नीत्वा स्ववाटं कृतवत्यथोदयम् ॥२०॥

*ittharh yaśodā tam aśeṣa-śekharaṁ*
*matvā sutaṁ sneha-nibaddha-dhīr nṛpa*
*haste gṛhītvā saha-rāmam acyutaṁ*
*nītvā sva-vāṭaṁ kṛtavaty athodayam*

*ittham*—in this way; *yaśodā*—mother Yaśodā; *tam aśeṣa-śekharam*—unto Kṛṣṇa, who was on the peak of everything auspicious, with no question of dirtiness or uncleanliness; *matvā*—considering; *sutam*—as her son; *sneha-nibaddha-dhīḥ*—because of an intense spirit of love; *nṛpa*—O King (Mahārāja Parīkṣit); *haste*—in the hand; *gṛhītvā*—taking; *saha-rāmam*—with Balarāma; *acyutam*—Kṛṣṇa, the infallible; *nītvā*—bringing; *sva-vāṭam*—at home; *kṛtavatī*—performed; *atha*—now; *udayam*—brilliancy by bathing Him, dressing Him and decorating Him with ornaments.

## TRANSLATION

**My dear Mahārāja Parīkṣit, because of intense love and affection, mother Yaśodā, Kṛṣṇa's mother, considered Kṛṣṇa, who was at the peak of all opulences, to be her own son. Thus she took Kṛṣṇa by the hand, along with Balarāma, and brought Them home, where she performed her duties by fully bathing Them, dressing Them and feeding Them.**

## PURPORT

Kṛṣṇa is always neat, clean and opulent and does not need to be washed, bathed or dressed, yet mother Yaśodā, because of affection, considered Him her ordinary child and did her duties to keep her son brilliant.

## TEXT 21

श्रीशुक उवाच
गोपवृद्धा महोत्पाताननुभूय बृहद्वने ।
नन्दादयः समागम्य व्रजकार्यममन्त्रयन् ॥२१॥

*śrī-śuka uvāca*
*gopa-vṛddhā mahotpātān*
*anubhūya bṛhadvane*
*nandādayaḥ samāgamya*
*vraja-kāryam amantrayan*

*śrī-śukaḥ uvāca*—Śrī Śukadeva Gosvāmī said; *gopa-vṛddhāḥ*—the elderly persons among the cowherd men; *mahā-utpātān*—very great disturbances; *anubhūya*—after experiencing; *bṛhadvane*—in the place known as Bṛhadvana; *nanda-ādayaḥ*—the cowherd men, headed by Nanda Mahārāja; *samāgamya*—assembled, came together; *vraja-kāryam*—the business of Vrajabhūmi; *amantrayan*—deliberated on how to stop the continuous disturbances in Mahāvana.

## TRANSLATION

**Śrī Śukadeva Gosvāmī continued: Then one time, having seen the great disturbances in Bṛhadvana, all the elderly persons among the cowherd men, headed by Nanda Mahārāja, assembled and began to consider what to do to stop the continuous disturbing situations in Vraja.**

## TEXT 22

तत्रोपानन्दनामाह गोपो ज्ञानवयोऽधिकः ।
देशकालार्थतत्त्वज्ञः प्रियकृद् रामकृष्णयोः ॥२२॥

*tatropānanda-nāmāha*
*gopo jñāna-vayo-'dhikaḥ*
*deśa-kālārtha-tattva-jñaḥ*
*priya-kṛd rāma-kṛṣṇayoḥ*

*tatra*—in the assembly; *upānanda-nāmā*—by the name Upānanda (the elder brother of Nanda Mahārāja); *āha*—said; *gopaḥ*—the cowherd man; *jñāna-vayaḥ-adhikaḥ*—who by knowledge and by age was the eldest of all; *deśa-kāla-artha-tattva-jñaḥ*—very experienced according to time, place and circumstances; *priya-kṛt*—just for the benefit; *rāma-kṛṣṇayoḥ*—of Balarāma and Kṛṣṇa, the Supreme Personalities of Godhead.

## TRANSLATION

**At this meeting of all the inhabitants of Gokula, a cowherd man named Upānanda, who was the most mature in age and knowledge and was very experienced according to time, circumstances and country, made this suggestion for the benefit of Rāma and Kṛṣṇa.**

## TEXT 23

उत्थातव्यमितोऽस्माभिर्गोकुलस्य हितैषिभिः ।
आयान्त्यत्र महोत्पाता बालानां नाशहेतवः ॥२३॥

*utthātavyam ito 'smābhir*
*gokulasya hitaiṣibhiḥ*
*āyānty atra mahotpātā*
*bālānāṁ nāśa-hetavaḥ*

*utthātavyam*—now this place should be left; *itaḥ*—from here, from Gokula; *asmābhiḥ*—by all of us; *gokulasya*—of this place, Gokula; *hita-eṣibhiḥ*—by persons who desire good for this place; *āyānti*—are happening; *atra*—here; *mahā-utpātāḥ*—many great disturbances; *bālānām*—for the boys like Rāma and Kṛṣṇa; *nāśa-hetavaḥ*—having the definite purpose of killing Them.

## TRANSLATION

**He said: My dear friends the cowherd men, in order to do good to this place, Gokula, we should leave it, because so many disturbances are always occurring here, just for the purpose of killing Rāma and Kṛṣṇa.**

## TEXT 24

मुक्तः कथञ्चिद् राक्षस्या बालघ्न्या बालको ह्यसौ ।
हरेरनुग्रहान्नूनमनश्चोपरि नापतत् ॥२४॥

*muktaḥ kathañcid rākṣasyā*
*bāla-ghnyā bālako hy asau*
*harer anugrahān nūnam*
*anaś copari nāpatat*

*muktaḥ*—was delivered; *kathañcit*—somehow or other; *rākṣasyāḥ*—from the hands of the Rākṣasī Pūtanā; *bāla-ghnyāḥ*—who was determined to kill small children; *bālakaḥ*—especially the child Kṛṣṇa; *hi*—because; *asau*—He; *hareḥ anugrahāt*—by the mercy of the Supreme Personality of Godhead; *nūnam*—indeed; *anaḥ ca*—and the handcart; *upari*—on top of the child; *na*—not; *apatat*—did fall down.

## TRANSLATION

**The child Kṛṣṇa, simply by the mercy of the Supreme Personality of Godhead, was somehow or other rescued from the hands of the Rākṣasī Pūtanā, who was determined to kill Him. Then, again by the mercy of the Supreme Godhead, the handcart missed falling upon the child.**

## TEXT 25

चक्रवातेन नीतोऽयं दैत्येन विपदं वियत् ।
शिलायां पतितस्तत्र परित्रातः सुरेश्वरैः ॥२५॥

*cakra-vātena nīto 'yaṁ*
*daityena vipadaṁ viyat*
*śilāyāṁ patitas tatra*
*paritrātaḥ sureśvaraiḥ*

*cakra-vātena*—by the demon in the shape of a whirlwind (Tṛṇāvarta); *nītaḥ ayam*—Kṛṣṇa was taken away; *daityena*—by the demon; *vipadam*—dangerous; *viyat*—to the sky; *śilāyām*—on a slab of stone; *patitaḥ*—fallen; *tatra*—there; *paritrātaḥ*—was saved; *sura-īśvaraiḥ*—by the mercy of Lord Viṣṇu or His associates.

## TRANSLATION

**Then again, the demon Tṛṇāvarta, in the form of a whirlwind, took the child away into the dangerous sky to kill Him, but the**

**demon fell down onto a slab of stone. In that case also, by the mercy of Lord Viṣṇu or His associates, the child was saved.**

## TEXT 26

यन्न म्रियेत द्रुमयोरन्तरं प्राप्य बालकः ।
असावन्यतमो वापि तदप्यच्युतरक्षणम् ॥२६॥

*yan na mriyeta drumayor*
*antaraṁ prāpya bālakaḥ*
*asāv anyatamo vāpi*
*tad apy acyuta-rakṣaṇam*

*yat*—then again; *na mriyeta*—did not die; *drumayoḥ antaram*—between the two trees; *prāpya*—although He was between; *bālakaḥ asau*—that child, Kṛṣṇa; *anyatamaḥ*—another child; *vā api*—or; *tat api acyuta-rakṣaṇam*—in that case also, He was saved by the Supreme Personality of Godhead.

## TRANSLATION

**Even the other day, neither Kṛṣṇa nor any of His playmates died from the falling of the two trees, although the children were near the trees or even between them. This also is to be considered the mercy of the Supreme Personality of Godhead.**

## TEXT 27

यावदौत्पातिकोऽरिष्टो व्रजं नाभिभवेदितः ।
तावद् बालानुपादाय यास्यामोऽन्यत्र सानुगाः॥२७॥

*yāvad autpātiko 'riṣṭo*
*vrajaṁ nābhibhaved itaḥ*
*tāvad bālān upādāya*
*yāsyāmo 'nyatra sānugāḥ*

*yāvat*—so long; *autpātikaḥ*—disturbing; *ariṣṭaḥ*—the demon; *vrajam*—this Gokula Vrajabhūmi; *na*—not; *abhibhavet itaḥ*—go away from this place; *tāvat*—so long; *bālān upādāya*—for the benefit of the boys; *yāsyāmaḥ*—we shall go; *anyatra*—somewhere else; *sa-anugāḥ*—with our followers.

## TRANSLATION

**All these incidents are being caused by some unknown demon. Before he comes here to create another disturbance, it is our duty to go somewhere else with the boys until there are no more disturbances.**

## PURPORT

Upānanda suggested, "By the mercy of Lord Viṣṇu, Kṛṣṇa has always been saved from so many dangerous incidents. Now let us leave this place and go someplace where we may worship Lord Viṣṇu undisturbed, before there is another cause of death from some demon who may attack us." A devotee desires only that he may execute devotional service undisturbed. Actually we see, however, that even during the presence of Kṛṣṇa, when Nanda Mahārāja and the other cowherd men had the Supreme Personality of Godhead in their presence, there were disturbances. Of course, in every case, Kṛṣṇa came out victorious. The instruction we may derive from this is that we should not be disturbed by so-called disturbances. There have been so many disturbances to our Kṛṣṇa consciousness movement, but we cannot give up our forward march. On the contrary, people are receiving this movement very enthusiastically all over the world, and they are purchasing literature about Kṛṣṇa consciousness with redoubled energy. Thus there are both encouragements and disturbances. This was so even in Kṛṣṇa's time.

## TEXT 28

वनं वृन्दावनं नाम पशव्यं नवकाननम् ।
गोपगोपीगवां सेव्यं पुण्याद्रितृणवीरुधम् ॥२८॥

*vanaṁ vṛndāvanaṁ nāma*
*paśavyaṁ nava-kānanam*
*gopa-gopī-gavāṁ sevyaṁ*
*puṇyādri-tṛṇa-vīrudham*

*vanam*—another forest; *vṛndāvanam nāma*—named Vṛndāvana; *paśavyam*—a very suitable place for maintenance of the cows and other animals; *nava-kānanam*—there are many new gardenlike places; *gopa-gopī-gavām*—for all the cowherd men, the members of their families, and the cows; *sevyam*—a very happy, very suitable place; *puṇya-adri*—there are nice mountains; *tṛṇa*—plants; *vīrudham*—and creepers.

## TRANSLATION

**Between Nandeśvara and Mahāvana is a place named Vṛndāvana. This place is very suitable because it is lush with grass, plants and creepers for the cows and other animals. It has nice gardens and tall mountains and is full of facilities for the happiness of all the gopas and gopīs and our animals.**

## PURPORT

Vṛndāvana is situated between Nandeśvara and Mahāvana. Formerly the cowherd men had shifted to Mahāvana, but still there were disturbances. Therefore the cowherd men selected Vṛndāvana, which was between the two villages, and decided to go there.

## TEXT 29

तत्तत्राद्यैव यास्यामः शकटान् युङ्क्त मा चिरम् ।
गोधनान्यग्रतो यान्तु भवतां यदि रोचते ॥२९॥

*tat tatrādyaiva yāsyāmaḥ*
*śakaṭān yuṅkta mā ciram*
*godhanāny agrato yāntu*
*bhavatāṁ yadi rocate*

*tat*—therefore; *tatra*—there; *adya eva*—just today; *yāsyāmaḥ*—let us go; *śakaṭān*—all the carts; *yuṅkta*—make ready; *mā ciram*—without delay; *go-dhanāni*—all the cows; *agrataḥ*—in front; *yāntu*—let them go; *bhavatām*—of all of you; *yadi*—if; *rocate*—it is pleasing to accept it.

## TRANSLATION

**Therefore, let us immediately go today. There is no need to wait any further. If you agree to my proposal, let us prepare all the bullock carts and put the cows in front of us, and let us go there.**

## TEXT 30

तच्छ्रुत्वैकधियो गोपाः साधु साध्विति वादिनः ।
व्रजान् स्वान् स्वान् समायुज्य ययू रूढपरिच्छदाः ॥३०॥

*tac chrutvaika-dhiyo gopāḥ*
*sādhu sādhv iti vādinaḥ*
*vrajān svān svān samāyujya*
*yayū rūḍha-paricchadāḥ*

*tat śrutvā*—hearing this advice of Upānanda's; *eka-dhiyaḥ*—voting unanimously; *gopāḥ*—all the cowherd men; *sādhu sādhu*—very nice, very nice; *iti*—thus; *vādinaḥ*—speaking, declaring; *vrajān*—cows; *svān svān*—own respective; *samāyujya*—assembling; *yayuḥ*—started; *rūḍha-paricchadāḥ*—all the dresses and paraphernalia having been kept on the carts.

## TRANSLATION

**Upon hearing this advice from Upānanda, the cowherd men unanimously agreed. "Very nice," they said. "Very nice." Thus they sorted out their household affairs, placed their clothing and other paraphernalia on the carts, and immediately started for Vṛndāvana.**

## TEXTS 31–32

वृद्धान् बालान् स्त्रियो राजन् सर्वोपकरणानि च ।
अनःस्वारोप्य गोपाला यत्ता आत्तशरासनाः ॥३१॥
गोधनानि पुरस्कृत्य शृङ्गाण्यापूर्य सर्वतः ।
तूर्यघोषेण महता ययुः सहपुरोहिताः ॥३२॥

*vṛddhān bālān striyo rājan*
*sarvopakaraṇāni ca*
*anaḥsv āropya gopālā*
*yattā ātta-śarāsanāḥ*

*godhanāni puraskṛtya*
*śṛṅgāṇy āpūrya sarvataḥ*

*tūrya-ghoṣeṇa mahatā*
*yayuḥ saha-purohitāḥ*

*vṛddhān*—first all the old men; *bālān*—children; *striyaḥ*—women; *rājan*—O King Parīkṣit; *sarva-upakaraṇāni ca*—then all sorts of necessities and whatever belongings they had; *anaḥsu*—on the bullock carts; *āropya*—keeping; *gopālāḥ*—all the cowherd men; *yattāḥ*—with great care; *ātta-śara-asanāḥ*—fully equipped with arrows and bows; *go-dhanāni*—all the cows; *puraskṛtya*—keeping in front; *śṛṅgāṇi*—bugles or horns; *āpūrya*—vibrating; *sarvataḥ*—all around; *tūrya-ghoṣeṇa*—with the resounding of the bugles; *mahatā*—loud; *yayuḥ*—started; *saha-purohitāḥ*—with the priests.

## TRANSLATION

**Keeping all the old men, women, children and household paraphernalia on the bullock carts and keeping all the cows in front, the cowherd men picked up their bows and arrows with great care and sounded bugles made of horn. O King Parīkṣit, in this way, with bugles vibrating all around, the cowherd men, accompanied by their priests, began their journey.**

## PURPORT

In this connection it is to be noted that although the inhabitants of Gokula were mostly cowherd men and cultivators, they knew how to defend themselves from danger and how to give protection to the women, the old men, the cows and the children, as well as to the brahminical *purohitas.*

## TEXT 33

गोप्यो रूढरथा नूत्नकुचकुङ्कुमकान्तयः ।
कृष्णलीला जगुः प्रीत्या निष्ककण्ठ्यः सुवाससः ॥३३॥

*gopyo rūḍha-rathā nūtna-*
*kuca-kuṅkuma-kāntayaḥ*
*kṛṣṇa-līlā jaguḥ prītyā*
*niṣka-kaṇṭhyaḥ suvāsasaḥ*

*gopyaḥ*—all the cowherd women; *rūḍha-rathāḥ*—while riding on the bullock carts; *nūtna-kuca-kuṅkuma-kāntayaḥ*—their bodies, especially their breasts, were decorated with fresh *kuṅkuma*; *kṛṣṇa-līlāḥ*—the pastimes of Kṛṣṇa; *jaguḥ*—they chanted; *prītyā*—with great pleasure; *niṣka-kaṇṭhyaḥ*—decorated with lockets on their necks; *su-vāsasaḥ*—very well dressed.

## TRANSLATION

**The cowherd women, riding on the bullock carts, were dressed very nicely with excellent garments, and their bodies, especially their breasts, were decorated with fresh kuṅkuma powder. As they rode, they began to chant with great pleasure the pastimes of Kṛṣṇa.**

## TEXT 34

तथा यशोदारोहिण्यावेकं शकटमास्थिते ।
रेजतुः कृष्णरामाभ्यां तत्कथाश्रवणोत्सुके ॥३४॥

*tathā yaśodā-rohiṇyāv*
*ekaṁ śakaṭam āsthite*
*rejatuḥ kṛṣṇa-rāmābhyāṁ*
*tat-kathā-śravaṇotsuke*

*tathā*—as well as; *yaśodā-rohiṇyau*—both mother Yaśodā and mother Rohiṇī; *ekam śakaṭam*—on one bullock cart; *āsthite*—seated; *rejatuḥ*—very beautiful; *kṛṣṇa-rāmābhyām*—Kṛṣṇa and Balarāma, along with Their mothers; *tat-kathā*—of the pastimes of Kṛṣṇa and Balarāma; *śravaṇa-utsuke*—being situated in hearing with great transcendental pleasure.

## TRANSLATION

**Thus hearing about the pastimes of Kṛṣṇa and Balarāma with great pleasure, mother Yaśodā and Rohiṇīdevī, so as not to be separated from Kṛṣṇa and Balarāma for even a moment, got up with Them on one bullock cart. In this situation, they all looked very beautiful.**

## PURPORT

It appears that mother Yaśodā and Rohiṇī could not be separated from Kṛṣṇa and Balarāma even for a moment. They used to pass their time either by taking care of Kṛṣṇa and Balarāma or by chanting about Their pastimes. Thus mother Yaśodā and Rohiṇī looked very beautiful.

## TEXT 35

वृन्दावनं संप्रविश्य सर्वकालसुखावहम् ।
तत्र चक्रुर्व्रजावासं शकटैरर्धचन्द्रवत् ॥३५॥

*vṛndāvanaṁ sampraviśya*
*sarva-kāla-sukhāvaham*
*tatra cakrur vrajāvāsaṁ*
*śakaṭair ardha-candravat*

*vṛndāvanam*—the sacred place by the name Vṛndāvana; *sampraviśya*—after entering; *sarva-kāla-sukha-āvaham*—where in all seasons it is pleasing to live; *tatra*—there; *cakruḥ*—they made; *vraja-āvāsam*—inhabitation of Vraja; *śakaṭaiḥ*—by the bullock carts; *ardha-candra-vat*—making a semicircle like a half moon.

## TRANSLATION

**In this way they entered Vṛndāvana, where it is always pleasing to live in all seasons. They made a temporary place to inhabit by placing their bullock carts around them in the shape of a half moon.**

## PURPORT

As stated in the *Viṣṇu Purāṇa:*

*śakaṭī-vāṭa-paryantaś*
*candrārdha-kāra-saṁsthite*

And as stated in the *Hari-vaṁśa:*

*kaṇṭakībhiḥ pravṛddhābhis*
*tathā kaṇṭakībhir drumaiḥ*

*nikhātocchrita-śākhābhir*
*abhiguptaṁ samantataḥ*

There was no need to make fences all around. One side was already defended by thorn trees, and thus the thorn trees, the bullock carts and the animals encircled the inhabitants in their temporary residence.

## TEXT 36

वृन्दावनं गोवर्धनं यमुनापुलिनानि च ।
वीक्ष्यासीदुत्तमा प्रीती राममाधवयोर्नृप ॥३६॥

*vṛndāvanaṁ govardhanaṁ*
*yamunā-pulināni ca*
*vīkṣyāsīd uttamā prītī*
*rāma-mādhavayor nṛpa*

*vṛndāvanam*—the place known as Vṛndāvana; *govardhanam*—along with Govardhana Hill; *yamunā-pulināni ca*—and the banks of the River Yamunā; *vīkṣya*—seeing this situation; *āsīt*—remained or was enjoyed; *uttamā prītī*—first-class pleasure; *rāma-mādhavayoḥ*—of Kṛṣṇa and Balarāma; *nṛpa*—O King Parīkṣit.

## TRANSLATION

**O King Parīkṣit, when Rāma and Kṛṣṇa saw Vṛndāvana, Govardhana and the banks of the River Yamunā, They both enjoyed great pleasure.**

## TEXT 37

एवं व्रजौकसां प्रीतिं यच्छन्तौ बालचेष्टितैः ।
कलवाक्यैः स्वकालेन वत्सपालौ बभूवतुः ॥३७॥

*evaṁ vrajaukasāṁ prītiṁ*
*yacchantau bāla-ceṣṭitaiḥ*
*kala-vākyaiḥ sva-kālena*
*vatsa-pālau babhūvatuḥ*

*evam*—in this way; *vraja-okasām*—to all the inhabitants of Vraja; *prītim*—pleasure; *yacchantau*—giving; *bāla-ceṣṭitaiḥ*—by the activities and pastimes of childhood; *kala-vākyaiḥ*—and by very sweet broken language; *sva-kālena*—in due course of time; *vatsa-pālau*—to take care of the calves; *babhūvatuḥ*—were grown up.

## TRANSLATION

**In this way, Kṛṣṇa and Balarāma, acting like small boys and talking in half-broken language, gave transcendental pleasure to all the inhabitants of Vraja. In due course of time, They became old enough to take care of the calves.**

## PURPORT

As soon as Kṛṣṇa and Balarāma were a little grown up, They were meant for taking care of the calves. Although born of a very well-to-do family, They still had to take care of the calves. This was the system of education. Those who were not born in *brāhmaṇa* families were not meant for academic education. The *brāhmaṇas* were trained in a literary, academic education, the *kṣatriyas* were trained to take care of the state, and the *vaiśyas* learned how to cultivate the land and take care of the cows and calves. There was no need to waste time going to school to be falsely educated and later increase the numbers of the unemployed. Kṛṣṇa and Balarāma taught us by Their personal behavior. Kṛṣṇa took care of the cows and played His flute, and Balarāma took care of agricultural activities with a plow in His hand.

## TEXT 38

अविदूरे व्रजभुवः सह गोपालदारकैः ।
चारयामासतुर्वत्सान् नानाक्रीडापरिच्छदौ ॥३८॥

*avidūre vraja-bhuvaḥ*
*saha gopāla-dārakaiḥ*
*cārayām āsatur vatsān*
*nānā-krīḍā-paricchadau*

*avidūre*—not very far from the residential quarters of the Vrajavāsīs; *vraja-bhuvaḥ*—from the land known as Vraja; *saha gopāla-dārakaiḥ*—

with other boys of the same profession (cowherd boys); *cārayām āsatuḥ*—tended; *vatsān*—the small calves; *nānā*—various; *krīḍā*—sporting; *paricchadau*—dressed very nicely in different ways and equipped with implements.

### TRANSLATION

**Not far away from Their residential quarters, both Kṛṣṇa and Balarāma, equipped with all kinds of playthings, played with other cowherd boys and began to tend the small calves.**

### TEXTS 39–40

क्वचिद् वादयतो वेणुं क्षेपणैः क्षिपतः क्वचित् ।
क्वचित् पादैः किङ्किणीभिः क्वचित् कृत्रिमगोवृषैः ॥३९॥
वृषायमाणौ नर्दन्तौ युयुधाते परस्परम् ।
अनुकृत्य रुतैर्जन्तूंश्चेरतुः प्राकृतौ यथा ॥४०॥

*kvacid vādayato veṇuṁ*
*kṣepaṇaiḥ kṣipataḥ kvacit*
*kvacit pādaiḥ kiṅkiṇībhiḥ*
*kvacit kṛtrima-go-vṛṣaiḥ*

*vṛṣāyamāṇau nardantau*
*yuyudhāte parasparam*
*anukṛtya rutair jantūṁś*
*ceratuḥ prākṛtau yathā*

*kvacit*—sometimes; *vādayataḥ*—blowing; *veṇum*—on the flute; *kṣepaṇaiḥ*—with a device of rope for throwing; *kṣipataḥ*—throwing stones to get fruit; *kvacit*—sometimes; *kvacit pādaiḥ*—sometimes with the legs; *kiṅkiṇībhiḥ*—with the sound of ankle bells; *kvacit*—sometimes; *kṛtrima-go-vṛṣaiḥ*—by becoming artificial cows and bulls; *vṛṣāyamāṇau*—imitating the animals; *nardantau*—roaring loudly; *yuyudhāte*—They both used to fight; *parasparam*—with one another; *anukṛtya*—imitating; *rutaiḥ*—by resounding; *jantūn*—all the animals; *ceratuḥ*—They used to wander; *prākṛtau*—two ordinary human children; *yathā*—like.

### TRANSLATION

**Sometimes Kṛṣṇa and Balarāma would play on Their flutes, sometimes They would throw ropes and stones devised for getting fruits from the trees, sometimes They would throw only stones, and sometimes, Their ankle bells tinkling, They would play football with fruits like bael and āmalakī. Sometimes They would cover Themselves with blankets and imitate cows and bulls and fight with one another, roaring loudly, and sometimes They would imitate the voices of the animals. In this way They enjoyed sporting, exactly like two ordinary human children.**

### PURPORT

Vṛndāvana is full of peacocks. *Kūjat-kokila-haṁsa-sārasa-gaṇākīrṇe mayūrākule.* The Vṛndāvana forest is always full of cuckoos, ducks, swans, peacocks, cranes and also monkeys, bulls and cows. So Kṛṣṇa and Balarāma used to imitate the sounds of these animals and enjoy sporting.

### TEXT 41

कदाचिद् यमुनातीरे वत्सांश्चारयतोः स्वकैः ।
वयस्यैः कृष्णबलयोर्जिघांसुर्दैत्य आगमत् ॥४१॥

*kadācid yamunā-tīre*
*vatsāṁś cārayatoḥ svakaiḥ*
*vayasyaiḥ kṛṣṇa-balayor*
*jighāṁsur daitya āgamat*

*kadācit*—sometimes; *yamunā-tīre*—on the bank of the Yamunā; *vatsān*—the calves; *cārayatoḥ*—when They were tending; *svakaiḥ*—Their own; *vayasyaiḥ*—with other playmates; *kṛṣṇa-balayoḥ*—both Kṛṣṇa and Balarāma; *jighāṁsuḥ*—desiring to kill Them; *daityaḥ*—another demon; *āgamat*—reached there.

### TRANSLATION

**One day while Rāma and Kṛṣṇa, along with Their playmates, were tending the calves on the bank of the River Yamunā, another demon arrived there, desiring to kill Them.**

## TEXT 42

तं वत्सरूपिणं वीक्ष्य वत्सयूथगतं हरिः ।
दर्शयन् बलदेवाय शनैर्मुग्ध इवासदत् ॥४२॥

*taṁ vatsa-rūpiṇaṁ vīkṣya*
*vatsa-yūtha-gataṁ hariḥ*
*darśayan baladevāya*
*śanair mugdha ivāsadat*

*tam*—unto the demon; *vatsa-rūpiṇam*—assuming the form of a calf; *vīkṣya*—seeing; *vatsa-yūtha-gatam*—when the demon entered the group of all the other calves; *hariḥ*—the Supreme Personality of Godhead, Kṛṣṇa; *darśayan*—indicating; *baladevāya*—unto Baladeva; *śanaiḥ*—very slowly; *mugdhaḥ iva*—as if He did not understand anything; *āsadat*—came near the demon.

## TRANSLATION

**When the Supreme Personality of Godhead saw that the demon had assumed the form of a calf and entered among the groups of other calves, He pointed out to Baladeva, "Here is another demon." Then He very slowly approached the demon, as if He did not understand the demon's intentions.**

## PURPORT

The import of the words *mugdha iva* is that although Kṛṣṇa knows everything, here He pretended that He did not understand why the demon had entered among the calves, and He informed Baladeva by a sign.

## TEXT 43

गृहीत्वापरपादाभ्यां सहलाङ्गूलमच्युतः ।
भ्रामयित्वा कपित्थाग्रे प्राहिणोद् गतजीवितम् ।
स कपित्थैर्महाकायः पात्यमानैः पपात ह ॥४३॥

*gṛhītvāpara-pādābhyāṁ*
*saha-lāṅgūlam acyutaḥ*

*bhrāmayitvā kapitthāgre*
*prāhiṇod gata-jīvitam*
*sa kapitthair mahā-kāyaḥ*
*pātyamānaiḥ papāta ha*

*gṛhītvā*—capturing; *apara-pādābhyām*—with the hind legs; *saha*—along with; *lāṅgūlam*—the tail; *acyutaḥ*—Kṛṣṇa, the Supreme Personality of Godhead; *bhrāmayitvā*—twirling around very severely; *kapittha-agre*—on the top of a *kapittha* tree; *prāhiṇot*—threw him; *gata-jīvitam*—lifeless body; *saḥ*—that demon; *kapitthaiḥ*—with the *kapittha* trees; *mahā-kāyaḥ*—assumed a great body; *pātyamānaiḥ*—and while the tree fell down; *papāta ha*—he fell dead on the ground.

## TRANSLATION

**Thereafter, Śrī Kṛṣṇa caught the demon by the hind legs and tail, twirled the demon's whole body very strongly until the demon was dead, and threw him into the top of a kapittha tree, which then fell down, along with the body of the demon, who had assumed a great form.**

## PURPORT

Kṛṣṇa killed the demon in such a way as to get the *kapittha* fruits to fall so that He and Balarāma and the other boys could take advantage of the opportunity to eat them. The *kapittha* is sometimes called *kṣatbel-phala.* The pulp of this fruit is very palatable. It is sweet and sour, and everyone likes it.

## TEXT 44

तं वीक्ष्य विस्मिता बालाः शशंसुः साधु साध्विति ।
देवाश्च परिसन्तुष्टा बभूवुः पुष्पवर्षिणः ॥४४॥

*taṁ vīkṣya vismitā bālāḥ*
*śaśaṁsuḥ sādhu sādhv iti*
*devāś ca parisantuṣṭā*
*babhūvuḥ puṣpa-varṣiṇaḥ*

*tam*—this incident; *vīkṣya*—observing; *vismitāḥ*—very much astonished; *bālāḥ*—all the other boys; *śaśaṁsuḥ*—praised highly; *sādhu*

*sādhu iti*—exclaiming, "Very good, very good"; *devāḥ ca*—and all the demigods from the heavenly planets; *parisantuṣṭāḥ*—being very much satisfied; *babhūvuḥ*—became; *puṣpa-varṣiṇaḥ*—showered flowers on Kṛṣṇa.

## TRANSLATION

**Upon seeing the dead body of the demon, all the cowherd boys exclaimed, "Well done, Kṛṣṇa! Very good, very good! Thank You." In the upper planetary system, all the demigods were pleased, and therefore they showered flowers on the Supreme Personality of Godhead.**

## TEXT 45

तौ वत्सपालकौ भूत्वा सर्वलोकैकपालकौ ।
सप्रातराशौ गोवत्सांश्चारयन्तौ विचेरतुः ॥४५॥

*tau vatsa-pālakau bhūtvā*
*sarva-lokaika-pālakau*
*saprātar-āśau go-vatsāṁś*
*cārayantau viceratuḥ*

*tau*—Kṛṣṇa and Balarāma; *vatsa-pālakau*—as if taking care of the calves; *bhūtvā*—so becoming; *sarva-loka-eka-pālakau*—although They are the maintainers of all living beings throughout the whole universe; *sa-prātaḥ-āśau*—finishing breakfast in the morning; *go-vatsān*—all the calves; *cārayantau*—tending; *viceratuh*—wandered here and there.

## TRANSLATION

**After the killing of the demon, Kṛṣṇa and Balarāma finished Their breakfast in the morning, and while continuing to take care of the calves, They wandered here and there. Kṛṣṇa and Balarāma, the Supreme Personalities of Godhead, who maintain the entire creation, now took charge of the calves as if cowherd boys.**

## PURPORT

*Paritrāṇāya sādhūnāṁ vināśāya ca duṣkṛtām.* Kṛṣṇa's daily business here in this material world was to kill the *duṣkṛtīs.* This did not hamper

His daily affairs, for it was routine work. While He tended the calves on the bank of the River Yamunā, two or three incidents took place every day, and although these were serious, killing the demons one after another appeared to be His daily routine work.

### TEXT 46

स्वं स्वं वत्सकुलं सर्वे पाययिष्यन्त एकदा ।
गत्वा जलाशयाभ्याशं पाययित्वा पपुर्जलम् ॥४६॥

*svaṁ svaṁ vatsa-kulaṁ sarve*
*pāyayiṣyanta ekadā*
*gatvā jalāśayābhyāśaṁ*
*pāyayitvā papur jalam*

*svam svam*—own respective; *vatsa-kulam*—the group of calves; *sarve*—all the boys and Kṛṣṇa and Balarāma; *pāyayiṣyantaḥ*—desiring to have them drink water; *ekadā*—one day; *gatvā*—going; *jala-āśaya-abhyāśam*—near the water tank; *pāyayitvā*—after allowing the animals to drink water; *papuḥ jalam*—they also drank water.

### TRANSLATION

**One day all the boys, including Kṛṣṇa and Balarāma, each boy taking his own group of calves, brought the calves to a reservoir of water, desiring to allow them to drink. After the animals drank water, the boys drank water there also.**

### TEXT 47

ते तत्र ददृशुर्बाला महासत्त्वमवस्थितम् ।
तत्रसुर्वज्रनिर्भिन्नं गिरेः शृङ्गमिव च्युतम् ॥४७॥

*te tatra dadṛśur bālā*
*mahā-sattvam avasthitam*
*tatrasur vajra-nirbhinnaṁ*
*gireḥ śṛṅgam iva cyutam*

*te*—they; *tatra*—there; *dadṛśuḥ*—observed; *bālāḥ*—all the boys; *mahā-sattvam*—a gigantic body; *avasthitam*—situated; *tatrasuḥ*—became afraid; *vajra-nirbhinnam*—broken by a thunderbolt; *gireḥ śṛṅgam*—the peak of a mountain; *iva*—like; *cyutam*—fallen there.

## TRANSLATION

**Right by the reservoir, the boys saw a gigantic body resembling a mountain peak broken and struck down by a thunderbolt. They were afraid even to see such a huge living being.**

## TEXT 48

स वै बको नाम महानसुरो बकरूपधृक् ।
आगत्य सहसा कृष्णं तीक्ष्णतुण्डोऽग्रसद् बली ॥४८॥

*sa vai bako nāma mahān*
*asuro baka-rūpa-dhṛk*
*āgatya sahasā kṛṣṇaṁ*
*tīkṣṇa-tuṇḍo 'grasad balī*

*saḥ*—that creature; *vai*—indeed; *bakaḥ nāma*—by the name Bakāsura; *mahān asuraḥ*—a great, gigantic demon; *baka-rūpa-dhṛk*—assumed the bodily shape of a big duck; *āgatya*—coming there; *sahasā*—all of a sudden; *kṛṣṇam*—Kṛṣṇa; *tīkṣṇa-tuṇḍaḥ*—sharp beak; *agrasat*—swallowed; *balī*—very powerful.

## TRANSLATION

**That great-bodied demon was named Bakāsura. He had assumed the body of a duck with a very sharp beak. Having come there, he immediately swallowed Kṛṣṇa.**

## TEXT 49

कृष्णं महाबकग्रस्तं दृष्ट्वा रामादयोऽर्भकाः ।
बभूवुरिन्द्रियाणीव विना प्राणं विचेतसः ॥४९॥

*kṛṣṇaṁ mahā-baka-grastaṁ*
*dṛṣṭvā rāmādayo 'rbhakāḥ*

*babhūvur indriyāṇīva*
*vinā prāṇaṁ vicetasaḥ*

*kṛṣṇam*—unto Kṛṣṇa; *mahā-baka-grastam*—swallowed by the great duck; *dṛṣṭvā*—seeing this incident; *rāma-ādayaḥ arbhakāḥ*—all the other boys, headed by Balarāma; *babhūvuḥ*—became overwhelmed; *indriyāṇi*—senses; *iva*—like; *vinā*—without; *prāṇam*—life; *vicetasaḥ*—very much bewildered, almost unconscious.

## TRANSLATION

**When Balarāma and the other boys saw that Kṛṣṇa had been devoured by the gigantic duck, they became almost unconscious, like senses without life.**

## PURPORT

Although Balarāma can do everything, because of intense affection for His brother He was momentarily bewildered. A similar thing is stated to have happened in connection with *rukmiṇī-haraṇa*, the kidnapping of Rukmiṇī. When Kṛṣṇa, after kidnapping Rukmiṇī, was attacked by all the kings, Rukmiṇī was momentarily bewildered, until the Lord took the proper steps.

## TEXT 50

तं तालुमूलं प्रदहन्तमग्निवद्
गोपालसूनुं पितरं जगद्गुरोः ।
चच्छर्द सद्योऽतिरुषाक्षतं बक-
स्तुण्डेन हन्तुं पुनरभ्यपद्यत ॥५०॥

*taṁ tālu-mūlaṁ pradahantam agnivad*
*gopāla-sūnuṁ pitaraṁ jagad-guroḥ*
*caccharda sadyo 'tiruṣākṣataṁ bakas*
*tuṇḍena hantuṁ punar abhyapadyata*

*tam*—Kṛṣṇa; *tālu-mūlam*—the root of the throat; *pradahantam*—burning; *agni-vat*—like fire; *gopāla-sūnum*—Kṛṣṇa, the son of a cowherd man; *pitaram*—the father; *jagat-guroḥ*—of Lord Brahmā;

*caccharda*—got out of his mouth; *sadyaḥ*—immediately; *ati-ruṣā*—with great anger; *akṣatam*—without being hurt; *bakaḥ*—Bakāsura; *tuṇḍena*—with his sharp beak; *hantum*—to kill; *punaḥ*—again; *abhyapadyata*—endeavored.

## TRANSLATION

**Kṛṣṇa, who was the father of Lord Brahmā but who was acting as the son of a cowherd man, became like fire, burning the root of the demon's throat, and the demon Bakāsura immediately disgorged Him. When the demon saw that Kṛṣṇa, although having been swallowed, was unharmed, he immediately attacked Kṛṣṇa again with his sharp beak.**

## PURPORT

Although Kṛṣṇa is always as soft as a lotus, within the throat of Bakāsura He created a burning sensation of being hotter than fire. Although Kṛṣṇa's whole body is sweeter than sugar candy, Bakāsura tasted bitterness and therefore immediately vomited Kṛṣṇa up. As stated in *Bhagavad-gītā* (4.11), *ye yathā māṁ prapadyante tāṁs tathaiva bhajāmy aham.* When Kṛṣṇa is accepted as an enemy, He becomes the most intolerable object for the nondevotee, who cannot tolerate Kṛṣṇa within or without. Here this is shown by the example of Bakāsura.

## TEXT 51

तमापतन्तं स निगृह्य तुण्डयो-
दोर्भ्यां बकं कंससखं सतां पतिः ।
पश्यत्सु बालेषु ददार लीलया
मुदावहो वीरणवद् दिवौकसाम् ॥५१॥

*tam āpatantaṁ sa nigṛhya tuṇḍayor*
*dorbhyāṁ bakaṁ kaṁsa-sakhaṁ satāṁ patiḥ*
*paśyatsu bāleṣu dadāra līlayā*
*mudāvaho vīraṇavad divaukasām*

*tam*—unto Bakāsura; *āpatantam*—again endeavoring to attack Him; *saḥ*—Lord Kṛṣṇa; *nigṛhya*—capturing; *tuṇḍayoḥ*—by the beak;

*dorbhyām*—with His arms; *bakam*—Bakāsura; *kaṁsa-sakham*—who was the friend and associate of Kaṁsa; *satām patiḥ*—Lord Kṛṣṇa, the master of the Vaiṣṇavas; *paśyatsu*—while observing; *bāleṣu*—all the cowherd boys; *dadāra*—bifurcated; *līlayā*—very easily; *mudā-āvahaḥ*—this action was very much pleasing; *vīraṇa-vat*—like the grass called *vīraṇa* (as it is bifurcated); *divaukasām*—to all the denizens of heaven.

## TRANSLATION

**When Kṛṣṇa, the leader of the Vaiṣṇavas, saw that the demon Bakāsura, the friend of Kaṁsa, was endeavoring to attack Him, with His arms He captured the demon by the two halves of the beak, and in the presence of all the cowherd boys Kṛṣṇa very easily bifurcated Him, as a child splits a blade of vīraṇa grass. By thus killing the demon, Kṛṣṇa very much pleased the denizens of heaven.**

## TEXT 52

तदा बकारिं सुरलोकवासिनः
समाकिरन् नन्दनमल्लिकादिभिः ।
समीडिरे चानकशङ्खसंस्तवै-
स्तद् वीक्ष्य गोपालसुता विसिस्मिरे ॥५२॥

*tadā bakāriṁ sura-loka-vāsinaḥ*
*samākiran nandana-mallikādibhiḥ*
*samīḍire cānaka-śaṅkha-saṁstavais*
*tad vīkṣya gopāla-sutā visismire*

*tadā*—at that time; *baka-arim*—unto the enemy of Bakāsura; *sura-loka-vāsinaḥ*—the celestial denizens of the higher planets; *samākiran*—showered flowers; *nandana-mallikā-ādibhiḥ*—with such flowers as *mallikā*, which are grown in Nandana-kānana; *samīḍire*—also congratulated Him; *ca*—and; *ānaka-śaṅkha-saṁstavaiḥ*—by celestial kettledrums and conchshells, accompanied with prayers; *tat vīkṣya*—by seeing this; *gopāla-sutāḥ*—the cowherd boys; *visismire*—were struck with wonder.

### TRANSLATION

**At that time, the celestial denizens of the higher planetary system showered mallikā-puṣpa, flowers grown in Nandana-kānana, upon Kṛṣṇa, the enemy of Bakāsura. They also congratulated Him by sounding celestial kettledrums and conchshells and by offering prayers. Seeing this, the cowherd boys were struck with wonder.**

### TEXT 53

मुक्तं बकास्यादुपलभ्य बालका
रामादयः प्राणमिवेन्द्रियो गणः ।
स्थानागतं तं परिरभ्य निर्वृताः
प्रणीय वत्सान् व्रजमेत्य तज्जगुः ॥५३॥

*muktaṁ bakāsyād upalabhya bālakā*
*rāmādayaḥ prāṇam ivendriyo gaṇaḥ*
*sthānāgataṁ taṁ parirabhya nirvṛtāḥ*
*praṇīya vatsān vrajam etya taj jaguḥ*

*muktam*—thus released; *baka-āsyāt*—from the mouth of Bakāsura; *upalabhya*—getting back; *bālakāḥ*—all the boys, the playmates; *rāma-ādayaḥ*—headed by Balarāma; *prāṇam*—life; *iva*—like; *indriyaḥ*—senses; *gaṇaḥ*—all of them; *sthāna-āgatam*—going to their own place; *tam*—unto Kṛṣṇa; *parirabhya*—embracing; *nirvṛtāḥ*—being freed from the danger; *praṇīya*—after collecting; *vatsān*—all the calves; *vrajam etya*—returning to Vrajabhūmi; *tat jaguḥ*—loudly declared the incident.

### TRANSLATION

**Just as the senses are pacified when consciousness and life return, so when Kṛṣṇa was freed from this danger, all the boys, including Balarāma, thought that their life had been restored. They embraced Kṛṣṇa in good consciousness, and then they collected their own calves and returned to Vrajabhūmi, where they declared the incident loudly.**

## PURPORT

It was the practice of the inhabitants of Vrajabhūmi to compose poetry about the incidents that occurred in the forest when Kṛṣṇa performed His different activities of killing the *asuras.* They would compose all the stories in poetry or have this done by professional poets, and then they would sing about these incidents. Thus it is written here that the boys sang very loudly.

## TEXT 54

श्रुत्वा तद् विस्मिता गोपा गोप्यश्चातिप्रियादृताः ।
प्रेत्यागतमिवोत्सुक्यादैक्षन्त तृषितेक्षणाः ॥५४॥

*śrutvā tad vismitā gopā*
*gopyaś cātipriyādṛtāḥ*
*pretyāgatam ivotsukyād*
*aikṣanta tṛṣitekṣaṇāḥ*

*śrutvā*—after hearing; *tat*—these incidents; *vismitāḥ*—being struck with wonder; *gopāḥ*—the cowherd men; *gopyaḥ ca*—and their respective wives; *ati-priya-ādṛtāḥ*—received the news with great transcendental pleasure; *pretya āgatam iva*—thought that it was as if the boys had returned from death; *utsukyāt*—with great eagerness; *aikṣanta*—began to look upon the boys; *tṛṣita-īkṣaṇāḥ*—with full satisfaction, they did not want to turn their eyes from Kṛṣṇa and the boys.

## TRANSLATION

**When the cowherd men and women heard about the killing of Bakāsura in the forest, they were very much astonished. Upon seeing Kṛṣṇa and hearing the story, they received Kṛṣṇa very eagerly, thinking that Kṛṣṇa and the other boys had returned from the mouth of death. Thus they looked upon Kṛṣṇa and the boys with silent eyes, not wanting to turn their eyes aside now that the boys were safe.**

## PURPORT

Because of intense love for Kṛṣṇa, the cowherd men and women simply remained silent, thinking of how Kṛṣṇa and the boys had been saved. The cowherd men and women looked upon Kṛṣṇa and the boys and did not desire to turn their eyes aside.

## TEXT 55

अहो बतास्य बालस्य बहवो मृत्यवोऽभवन् ।
अप्यासीद् विप्रियं तेषां कृतं पूर्वं यतो भयम् ॥५५॥

*aho batāsya bālasya*
*bahavo mṛtyavo 'bhavan*
*apy āsīd vipriyaṁ teṣāṁ*
*kṛtaṁ pūrvaṁ yato bhayam*

*aho bata*—it is very astonishing; *asya*—of this; *bālasya*—Kṛṣṇa; *bahavaḥ*—many, many; *mṛtyavaḥ*—causes of death; *abhavan*—appeared; *api*—still; *āsīt*—there was; *vipriyam*—the cause of death; *teṣām*—of them; *kṛtam*—done; *pūrvam*—formerly; *yataḥ*—from which; *bhayam*—there was fear of death.

## TRANSLATION

**The cowherd men, headed by Nanda Mahārāja, began to contemplate: It is very astonishing that although this boy Kṛṣṇa has many times faced many varied causes of death, by the grace of the Supreme Personality of Godhead it was these causes of fear that were killed, instead of Him.**

## PURPORT

The cowherd men innocently thought, "Because our Kṛṣṇa is innocent, the causes of death that appeared before Him were themselves killed instead of Kṛṣṇa. This is the greatest grace of the Supreme Personality of Godhead."

## TEXT 56

अथाप्यभिभवन्त्येनं नैव ते घोरदर्शनाः ।
जिघांसयैनमासाद्य नश्यन्त्यग्नौ पतङ्गवत् ॥५६॥

*athāpy abhibhavanty enaṁ*
*naiva te ghora-darśanāḥ*

*jighāṁsayainam āsādya*
*naśyanty agnau pataṅgavat*

*atha api*—although they come to attack; *abhibhavanti*—they are able to kill; *enam*—this boy; *na*—not; *eva*—certainly; *te*—all of them; *ghora-darśanāḥ*—very fierce looking; *jighāṁsayā*—because of envy; *enam*—unto Kṛṣṇa; *āsādya*—approaching; *naśyanti*—are vanquished (death occurs to the aggressor); *agnau*—in fire; *pataṅga-vat*—like flies.

## TRANSLATION

**Although the causes of death, the daityas, were very fierce, they could not kill this boy Kṛṣṇa. Rather, because they came to kill innocent boys, as soon as they approached they themselves were killed, exactly like flies attacking a fire.**

## PURPORT

Nanda Mahārāja innocently thought, "Perhaps this boy Kṛṣṇa formerly killed all these demons, and therefore in this life they are envious and are attacking Him. But Kṛṣṇa is a fire, and they are flies, and in a fight between fire and flies, the fire is always victorious." Fighting is always taking place between the demons and the power of the Supreme Personality. *Paritrāṇāya sādhūnāṁ vināśāya ca duṣkṛtām* (Bg. 4.8). Anyone who is against the control of the Supreme Personality of Godhead must be killed, life after life. Ordinary living beings are subject to *karma*, but the Supreme Personality of Godhead is always victorious over the demons.

## TEXT 57

अहो ब्रह्मविदां वाचो नासत्याः सन्ति कर्हिचित् ।
गर्गो यदाह भगवानन्वभावि तथैव तत् ॥५७॥

*aho brahma-vidāṁ vāco*
*nāsatyāḥ santi karhicit*
*gargo yad āha bhagavān*
*anvabhāvi tathaiva tat*

*aho*—how wonderful it is; *brahma-vidām*—of persons who have full knowledge of Brahman, transcendence; *vācaḥ*—the words; *na*—never;

*asatyāḥ*—untruth; *santi*—become; *karhicit*—at any time; *gargaḥ*—Gargamuni; *yat*—whatever; *āha*—predicted; *bhagavān*—Gargamuni, the most powerful; *anvabhāvi*—is exactly happening; *tathā eva*—as; *tat*—that.

## TRANSLATION

**The words of persons in full knowledge of Brahman never become untrue. It is very wonderful that whatever Gargamuni predicted we are now actually experiencing in all detail.**

## PURPORT

The purpose of human life is indicated in the *Brahma-sūtra: athāto brahma-jijñāsā.* To make one's life perfect—in the past, present and future—one must learn about Brahman. Because of intense affection, Nanda Mahārāja could not understand Kṛṣṇa as He is. Gargamuni was able to know everything, past, present and future, by studying the *Vedas,* but Nanda Mahārāja could not understand Kṛṣṇa directly. Because of his intense love for Kṛṣṇa, he forgot who Kṛṣṇa was and could not understand Kṛṣṇa's potency. Although Kṛṣṇa is Nārāyaṇa Himself, Gargamuni did not disclose this. Thus Nanda Mahārāja appreciated the words of Gargamuni, but because of his deep affection he could not understand who Kṛṣṇa was, although Gargamuni had said that Kṛṣṇa's qualities would be exactly like those of Nārāyaṇa.

## TEXT 58

इति नन्दादयो गोपाः कृष्णरामकथां मुदा ।
कुर्वन्तो रममाणाश्च नाविन्दन् भववेदनाम् ।।५८।।

*iti nandādayo gopāḥ*
*kṛṣṇa-rāma-kathāṁ mudā*
*kurvanto ramamāṇāś ca*
*nāvindan bhava-vedanām*

*iti*—in this way; *nanda-ādayaḥ*—all the cowherd men, headed by Nanda Mahārāja; *gopāḥ*—cowherd men; *kṛṣṇa-rāma-katham*—narration of incidents in connection with Bhagavān Kṛṣṇa and Rāma; *mudā*—in great transcendental pleasure; *kurvantaḥ*—doing that; *ramamāṇāḥ ca*—enjoyed life and increased their affection for Kṛṣṇa; *na*—not; *avindan*—perceived; *bhava-vedanām*—the tribulations of material existence.

## TRANSLATION

**In this way all the cowherd men, headed by Nanda Mahārāja, enjoyed topics about the pastimes of Kṛṣṇa and Balarāma with great transcendental pleasure, and they could not even perceive material tribulations.**

## PURPORT

Here is an instruction about the result of studying or discussing the *kṛṣṇa-līlās* that appear in *Śrīmad-Bhāgavatam. Sadyo hṛdy avarudhyate 'tra kṛtibhiḥ śuśrūṣubhis tat-kṣaṇāt* (*Bhāg.* 1.1.2). Nanda Mahārāja and Yaśodā in Vṛndāvana appeared like ordinary persons of this material world, but they never felt the tribulations of this world, although they sometimes met many dangerous situations created by the demons. This is a practical example. If we follow in the footsteps of Nanda Mahārāja and the *gopas*, we can all be happy simply by discussing the activities of Kṛṣṇa.

*anarthopaśamaṁ sākṣād*
*bhakti-yogam adhokṣaje*
*lokasyājānato vidvāṁś*
*cakre sātvata-saṁhitām*
(*Bhāg.* 1.7.6)

Vyāsadeva has given this literature so that everyone may understand one's transcendental position simply by discussing *bhāgavata-kathā*. Even at the present moment, everyone everywhere can be happy and free from material tribulations by following *Śrīmad-Bhāgavatam*. There is no need of austerities and penances, which in this age are very difficult to perform. Śrī Caitanya Mahāprabhu has therefore declared, *sarvātma-snapanaṁ paraṁ vijayate śrī-kṛṣṇa-saṅkīrtanam*. By our Kṛṣṇa consciousness movement, we are trying to distribute *Śrīmad-Bhāgavatam* so that anyone in any part of the world can be absorbed in the Kṛṣṇa consciousness movement by chanting and hearing about the activities of Kṛṣṇa and be free from all material tribulations.

### TEXT 59

एवं विहारैः कौमारैः कौमारं जहतुर्व्रजे ।
निलायनैः सेतुबन्धैर्मर्कटोत्प्लवनादिभिः ॥५९॥

*evaṁ vihāraiḥ kaumāraiḥ*
*kaumāraṁ jahatur vraje*
*nilāyanaiḥ setu-bandhair*
*markaṭotplavanādibhiḥ*

*evam*—in this way; *vihāraiḥ*—by different pastimes; *kaumāraiḥ*—childish; *kaumāram*—the age of childhood; *jahatuḥ*—(Kṛṣṇa and Balarāma) passed; *vraje*—in Vrajabhūmi; *nilāyanaiḥ*—by playing hide-and-seek; *setu-bandhaiḥ*—by constructing an artificial bridge on the ocean; *markaṭa*—like the monkeys; *utplavana-ādibhiḥ*—by jumping here and there, etc.

### TRANSLATION

**In this way Kṛṣṇa and Balarāma passed Their childhood age in Vrajabhūmi by engaging in activities of childish play, such as playing hide-and-seek, constructing a make-believe bridge on the ocean, and jumping here and there like monkeys.**

*Thus end the Bhaktivedanta purports of the Tenth Canto, Eleventh Chapter, of the* Śrīmad-Bhāgavatam, *entitled "The Childhood Pastimes of Kṛṣṇa."*

## CHAPTER TWELVE

# The Killing of the Demon Aghāsura

This chapter describes in detail Kṛṣṇa's pastime of killing Aghāsura.

One day Kṛṣṇa wanted to enjoy a picnic lunch within the forest, and therefore He went out early into the forest with the other cowherd boys, accompanied by their respective groups of calves. While they were enjoying their picnic, Aghāsura, the younger brother of Pūtanā and Bakāsura, appeared there, desiring to kill Kṛṣṇa and His companions. The demon, who had been sent by Kaṁsa, assumed the form of a python, expanding himself to a length of eight miles and the height of a mountain, his mouth seeming to extend from the surface of the earth to the heavenly planets. Having assumed this feature, Aghāsura lay on the road. Kṛṣṇa's friends, the cowherd boys, thought that the demon's form was one of the beautiful spots of Vṛndāvana. Thus they wanted to enter within the mouth of this gigantic python. The gigantic figure of the python became a subject for their sporting pleasure, and they began to laugh, confident that even if this figure were dangerous, Kṛṣṇa was there to protect them. In this way, they proceeded toward the mouth of the gigantic figure.

Kṛṣṇa knew everything about Aghāsura, and therefore He wanted to forbid His friends to enter the demon's mouth, but in the meantime all the cowherd boys, along with their groups of calves, entered the mouth of that gigantic figure. Kṛṣṇa was waiting outside, and Aghāsura was waiting for Kṛṣṇa, thinking that as soon as Kṛṣṇa entered he would close his mouth so that everyone would die. While waiting for Kṛṣṇa, he refrained from swallowing the boys. In the meantime, Kṛṣṇa was thinking of how to save the boys and kill Aghāsura. Thus He entered the mouth of the gigantic *asura*, and when He was within the demon's mouth along with His friends, He expanded His body to such an extent that the *asura* suffocated and died. After this, Kṛṣṇa, by casting His nectarean glance upon His friends, brought them back to life, and with pleasure they all came out unhurt. Thus Kṛṣṇa encouraged all the demigods, and they expressed their pleasure and happiness. For a crooked, sinful person there is no scope for *sāyujya-mukti*, or becoming one with the effulgence of Kṛṣṇa, but because the Supreme Personality of Godhead entered the body of Aghāsura, by His touch this demon got the opportunity to merge into the existence of the Brahman effulgence and thus attain *sāyujya-mukti.*

When this pastime was performed, Kṛṣṇa was only five years old. One year later, when He was six years old and He stepped into the *paugaṇḍa* age, this pastime was disclosed to the inhabitants of Vraja. Parīkṣit Mahārāja inquired, "Why is it that this pastime was disclosed only after one year and yet the inhabitants of Vraja thought that it had been performed that very day?" With this question, the Twelfth Chapter ends.

## TEXT 1

श्रीशुक उवाच
क्वचिद् वनाशाय मनो दधद् व्रजात्
प्रातः समुत्थाय वयस्यवत्सपान् ।
प्रबोधयञ्छृङ्गरवेण चारुणा
विनिर्गतो वत्सपुरःसरो हरिः ॥ १ ॥

*śrī-śuka uvāca*
*kvacid vanāśāya mano dadhad vrajāt*
*prātaḥ samutthāya vayasya-vatsapān*
*prabodhayañ chṛṅga-raveṇa cāruṇā*
*vinirgato vatsa-puraḥsaro hariḥ*

*śrī-śukaḥ uvāca*—Śrī Śukadeva Gosvāmī said; *kvacit*—one day; *vana-āśāya*—just to enjoy a picnic in the forest; *manaḥ*—mind; *dadhat*—gave attention; *vrajāt*—and went out of Vrajabhūmi; *prātaḥ*—early in the morning; *samutthāya*—waking up; *vayasya-vatsa-pān*—the cowherd boys and the calves; *prabodhayan*—to get everyone to rise, waking up and informing them; *śṛṅga-raveṇa*—by sounding the bugle made of horn; *cāruṇā*—very beautiful; *vinirgataḥ*—came out of Vrajabhūmi; *vatsa-puraḥsaraḥ*—keeping the respective groups of calves in front; *hariḥ*—the Supreme Personality of Godhead.

## TRANSLATION

**Śukadeva Gosvāmī continued: O King, one day Kṛṣṇa decided to take His breakfast as a picnic in the forest. Having risen early in**

**the morning, He blew His bugle made of horn and woke all the cowherd boys and calves with its beautiful sound. Then Kṛṣṇa and the boys, keeping their respective groups of calves before them, proceeded from Vrajabhūmi to the forest.**

## TEXT 2

तेनैव साकं पृथुकाः सहस्रशः
स्निग्धाः सुशिग्वेत्रविषाणवेणवः ।
स्वान् स्वान् सहस्रोपरिसंख्ययान्वितान्
वत्सान् पुरस्कृत्य विनिर्ययुर्मुदा ॥ २ ॥

*tenaiva sākaṁ pṛthukāḥ sahasraśaḥ*
*snigdhāḥ suśig-vetra-viṣāṇa-veṇavaḥ*
*svān svān sahasropari-saṅkhyayānvitān*
*vatsān puraskṛtya viniryayur mudā*

*tena*—Him; *eva*—indeed; *sākam*—accompanied by; *pṛthukāḥ*—the boys; *sahasraśaḥ*—by the thousands; *snigdhāḥ*—very attractive; *su*—beautiful; *śik*—lunch bags; *vetra*—sticks for controlling the calves; *viṣāṇa*—horn bugles; *veṇavaḥ*—flutes; *svān svān*—their own respective; *sahasra-upari-saṅkhyayā anvitān*—numbering over a thousand; *vatsān*—the calves; *puraḥ-kṛtya*—keeping in front; *viniryayuḥ*—they came out; *mudā*—with great pleasure.

## TRANSLATION

**At that time, hundreds and thousands of cowherd boys came out of their respective homes in Vrajabhūmi and joined Kṛṣṇa, keeping before them their hundreds and thousands of groups of calves. The boys were very beautiful, and they were equipped with lunch bags, bugles, flutes, and sticks for controlling the calves.**

## TEXT 3

कृष्णवत्सैरसंख्यातैर्यूथीकृत्य स्ववत्सकान् ।
चारयन्तोऽर्भलीलाभिर्विजहुस्तत्र तत्र ह ॥ ३ ॥

*kṛṣṇa-vatsair asaṅkhyātair*
*yūthī-kṛtya sva-vatsakān*
*cārayanto 'rbha-līlābhir*
*vijahrus tatra tatra ha*

*kṛṣṇa*—of Lord Kṛṣṇa; *vatsaiḥ*—along with the calves; *asaṅkhyātaiḥ*—unlimited; *yūthī-kṛtya*—assembled them; *sva-vatsakān*—personal calves; *cārayantaḥ*—executing; *arbha-līlābhiḥ*—by boyhood pastimes; *vijahruḥ*—enjoyed; *tatra tatra*—here and there; *ha*—indeed.

## TRANSLATION

**Along with the cowherd boys and their own groups of calves, Kṛṣṇa came out with an unlimited number of calves assembled. Then all the boys began to sport in the forest in a greatly playful spirit.**

## PURPORT

In this verse the words *kṛṣṇa-vatsair asaṅkhyātaiḥ* are significant. The word *asaṅkhyāta* means "unlimited." Kṛṣṇa's calves were unlimited. We may speak of hundreds, thousands, tens of thousands, hundreds of thousands, millions, billions, trillions, tens of trillions, and so on, but when we go further to speak of numbers impossible for us to count, we are speaking of unlimited numbers. Such unlimited numbers are indicated here by the word *asaṅkhyātaiḥ*. Kṛṣṇa is unlimited, His potency is unlimited, His cows and calves are unlimited, and His space is unlimited. Therefore He is described in *Bhagavad-gītā* as Parabrahman. The word *brahman* means "unlimited," and Kṛṣṇa is the Supreme Unlimited, Parabrahman. Therefore, we should not consider the statements of this verse to be mythological. They are factual, but inconceivable. Kṛṣṇa can accommodate an unlimited number of calves and an unlimited measurement of space. This is neither mythological nor false, but if we study Kṛṣṇa's potency with our limited knowledge, that potency will never be possible to understand. *Ataḥ śrī-kṛṣṇa-nāmādi na bhaved grāhyam indriyaiḥ* (*Bhakti-rasāmṛta-sindhu* 1.2.109). Our senses cannot perceive how He could keep an unlimited number of calves and cows and have unlimited space in which to do so. But this is answered in the *Bṛhad-bhāgavatāmṛta:*

*evaṁ prabhoḥ priyāṇāṁ ca*
*dhāmnaś ca samayasya ca*
*avicintya-prabhāvatvād*
*atra kiñcin na durghaṭam*

Śrī Sanātana Gosvāmī, in the *Bṛhad-bhāgavatāmṛta*, states that since everything about Kṛṣṇa is unlimited, nothing is impossible for Him. It is in this sense that we have to understand this verse.

## TEXT 4

फलप्रबालस्तवकसुमनःपिच्छधातुभिः ।
काचगुञ्जामणिस्वर्णभूषिता अप्यभूषयन् ॥ ४ ॥

*phala-prabāla-stavaka-*
*sumanaḥ-piccha-dhātubhiḥ*
*kāca-guñjā-maṇi-svarṇa-*
*bhūṣitā apy abhūṣayan*

*phala*—fruits from the forest; *prabāla*—green leaves; *stavaka*—bunches; *sumanaḥ*—beautiful flowers; *piccha*—peacock feathers; *dhātubhiḥ*—very soft and colorful minerals; *kāca*—a kind of gem; *guñjā*—small conchshells; *maṇi*—pearls; *svarṇa*—gold; *bhūṣitāḥ*—although decorated; *api abhūṣayan*—in spite of being decorated by their mothers, the boys decorated themselves still more with the above-mentioned articles.

## TRANSLATION

**Although all these boys were already decorated by their mothers with ornaments of kāca, guñjā, pearls and gold, when they went into the forest they further decorated themselves with fruits, green leaves, bunches of flowers, peacock feathers and soft minerals.**

## TEXT 5

मुष्णन्तोऽन्योन्यशिक्यादीन् ज्ञातानाराच्च चिक्षिपुः ।
तत्रत्याश्च पुनर्दूराद्धसन्तश्च पुनर्ददुः ॥ ५ ॥

*muṣṇanto 'nyonya-śikyādīn*
*jñātān ārāc ca cikṣipuḥ*
*tatratyāś ca punar dūrād*
*dhasantaś ca punar daduḥ*

*muṣṇantaḥ*—stealing; *anyonya*—from one another; *śikya-ādīn*—lunch bags and other belongings; *jñātān*—having been understood by the proprietor of the bag; *ārāt ca*—to a distant place; *cikṣipuḥ*—threw away; *tatratyāḥ ca*—those who were in that place also; *punaḥ dūrāt*—then again threw farther away; *hasantaḥ ca punaḥ daduḥ*—when they saw the proprietor, they threw it farther away and enjoyed laughing, and when the owner sometimes cried, his bag was given to him again.

## TRANSLATION

**All the cowherd boys used to steal one another's lunch bags. When a boy came to understand that his bag had been taken away, the other boys would throw it farther away, to a more distant place, and those standing there would throw it still farther. When the proprietor of the bag became disappointed, the other boys would laugh, the proprietor would cry, and then the bag would be returned.**

## PURPORT

This kind of playing and stealing among boys still exists even in the material world because this kind of sporting pleasure is present in the spiritual world, from which this idea of enjoyment emanates. *Janmādy asya yataḥ* (*Vedānta-sūtra* 1.1.2). This same enjoyment is displayed by Kṛṣṇa and His associates in the spiritual world, but there the enjoyment is eternal, whereas here, on the material platform, it is temporary; there the enjoyment is Brahman, whereas here the enjoyment is *jaḍa.* The Kṛṣṇa consciousness movement is meant to train one how to transfer oneself from the *jaḍa* to the Brahman, because human life is meant for this purpose. *Athāto brahma-jijñāsā* (*Vedānta-sūtra* 1.1.1). Kṛṣṇa comes down to teach us how we can enjoy with Him on the spiritual platform, in the spiritual world. Not only does He come, but He personally displays His pastimes in Vṛndāvana and attracts people to spiritual enjoyment.

## TEXT 6

यदि दूरं गतः कृष्णो वनशोभेक्षणाय तम् ।
अहं पूर्वमहं पूर्वमिति संस्पृश्य रेमिरे ॥ ६ ॥

*yadi dūraṁ gataḥ kṛṣṇo*
*vana-śobhekṣaṇāya tam*
*ahaṁ pūrvam ahaṁ pūrvam*
*iti saṁspṛśya remire*

*yadi*—if; *dūram*—to a distant place; *gataḥ*—went; *kṛṣṇaḥ*—the Supreme Personality of Godhead; *vana-śobha*—the beauty of the forest; *īkṣaṇāya*—for visiting and enjoying; *tam*—unto Kṛṣṇa; *aham*—I; *pūrvam*—first; *aham*—I; *pūrvam*—first; *iti*—in this way; *saṁspṛśya*—by touching Him; *remire*—they enjoyed life.

## TRANSLATION

**Sometimes Kṛṣṇa would go to a somewhat distant place to see the beauty of the forest. Then all the other boys would run to accompany Him, each one saying, "I shall be the first to run and touch Kṛṣṇa! I shall touch Kṛṣṇa first!" In this way they enjoyed life by repeatedly touching Kṛṣṇa.**

## TEXTS 7–11

केचिद् वेणून् वादयन्तो ध्मान्तः शृङ्गाणि केचन ।
केचिद् भृङ्गैः प्रगायन्तः कूजन्तः कोकिलैः परे ॥७॥
विच्छायाभिः प्रधावन्तो गच्छन्तः साधु हंसकैः ।
बकैरुपविशन्तश्च नृत्यन्तश्च कलापिभिः ॥ ८ ॥
विकर्षन्तः कीशबालानारोहन्तश्च तैर्द्रुमान् ।
विकुर्वन्तश्च तैः साकं प्लवन्तश्च पलाशिषु ॥ ९ ॥
साकं भेकैर्विलङ्घन्तः सरितः स्रवसम्प्लुताः ।
विहसन्तः प्रतिच्छायाः शपन्तश्च प्रतिस्वनान् ॥१०॥

इत्थं सतां ब्रह्मसुखानुभूत्या
दास्यं गतानां परदैवतेन ।
मायाश्रितानां नरदारकेण
साकं विजह्रुः कृतपुण्यपुञ्जाः ॥११॥

*kecid veṇūn vādayanto*
*dhmāntaḥ śṛṅgāṇi kecana*
*kecid bhṛṅgaiḥ pragāyantaḥ*
*kūjantaḥ kokilaiḥ pare*

*vicchāyābhiḥ pradhāvanto*
*gacchantaḥ sādhu-haṁsakaiḥ*
*bakair upaviśantaś ca*
*nṛtyantaś ca kalāpibhiḥ*

*vikarṣantaḥ kīśa-bālān*
*ārohantaś ca tair drumān*
*vikurvantaś ca taiḥ sākaṁ*
*plavantaś ca palāśiṣu*

*sākaṁ bhekair vilaṅghantaḥ*
*saritaḥ srava-samplutāḥ*
*vihasantaḥ praticchāyāḥ*
*śapantaś ca pratisvanān*

*itthaṁ satāṁ brahma-sukhānubhūtyā*
*dāsyaṁ gatānāṁ para-daivatena*
*māyāśritānāṁ nara-dārakeṇa*
*sākaṁ vijahruḥ kṛta-puṇya-puñjāḥ*

*kecit*—some of them; *veṇūn*—flutes; *vādayantaḥ*—blowing; *dhmāntaḥ*—bugling; *śṛṅgāṇi*—the horn bugles; *kecana*—someone else; *kecit*—someone; *bhṛṅgaiḥ*—with the bumblebees; *pragāyantaḥ*—singing along with; *kūjantaḥ*—imitating the sound of; *kokilaiḥ*—with the cuckoos; *pare*—others; *vicchāyābhiḥ*—with running shadows; *pradhāvantaḥ*—someone running on the ground after the birds; *gacchantaḥ*—going along; *sādhu*—beautiful; *haṁsakaiḥ*—with the swans; *bakaiḥ*—with the ducks sitting in one place; *upaviśantaḥ ca*—sitting silently like them; *nṛtyantaḥ ca*—and dancing with; *kalāpibhiḥ*—with the peacocks; *vikarṣantaḥ*—attracting; *kīśa-bālān*—the young monkeys; *ārohantaḥ ca*—gliding over; *taiḥ*—with the monkeys; *drumān*—the trees; *vikurvantaḥ ca*—exactly imitating them; *taiḥ*—with the monkeys; *sākam*—along with; *plavantaḥ ca*—gliding over; *palāśiṣu*—on the trees; *sākam*—along with; *bhekaiḥ*—with the frogs; *vilaṅghantaḥ*—jumping like them; *saritaḥ*—the water; *srava-samplutāḥ*—became wet in the water of the river; *vihasantaḥ*—laughing; *praticchāyāḥ*—at the shadows; *śapantaḥ ca*—condemned; *pratisvanān*—the sound of their echoes; *ittham*—in this way; *satām*—of the transcendentalists; *brahma-sukha-anubhūtyā*—with Kṛṣṇa, the source of *brahma-sukha* (Kṛṣṇa is Parabrahman, and from Him originates His personal effulgence); *dāsyam*—servitorship; *gatānām*—of the devotees who have accepted; *para-daivatena*—with the Supreme Personality of Godhead; *māyā-āśritānām*—for those in the clutches of material energy; *nara-dārakeṇa*—with Him who is like an ordinary child; *sākam*—along with; *vijahruḥ*—enjoyed; *kṛta-puṇya-puñjāḥ*—all these boys, who had accumulated the results of life after life of pious activities.

## TRANSLATION

**All the boys would be differently engaged. Some boys blew their flutes, and others blew bugles made of horn. Some imitated the buzzing of the bumblebees, and others imitated the voice of the cuckoo. Some boys imitated flying birds by running after the birds' shadows on the ground, some imitated the beautiful movements and attractive postures of the swans, some sat down with the ducks, sitting silently, and others imitated the dancing of the peacocks. Some boys attracted young monkeys in the trees, some jumped into the trees, imitating the monkeys, some made faces as the monkeys were accustomed to do, and others jumped from one branch to another. Some boys went to the waterfalls and crossed over the river, jumping with the frogs, and when they saw their own reflections on the water they would laugh. They would also condemn the sounds of their own echoes. In this way, all the cowherd boys used to play with Kṛṣṇa, who is the source of the Brahman effulgence for jñānīs desiring to merge into that effulgence, who is the Supreme Personality of Godhead for**

**devotees who have accepted eternal servitorship, and who for ordinary persons is but another ordinary child. The cowherd boys, having accumulated the results of pious activities for many lives, were able to associate in this way with the Supreme Personality of Godhead. How can one explain their great fortune?**

## PURPORT

As recommended by Śrīla Rūpa Gosvāmī, *tasmāt kenāpy upāyena manaḥ kṛṣṇe niveśayet* (*Bhakti-rasāmṛta-sindhu* 1.2.4). Somehow or other, whether one thinks of Kṛṣṇa as an ordinary human child, as the source of the Brahman effulgence, as the origin of Paramātmā, or as the Supreme Personality of Godhead, one should concentrate one's full attention upon the lotus feet of Kṛṣṇa. That is also the instruction of *Bhagavad-gītā* (18.66): *sarva-dharmān parityajya mām ekaṁ śaraṇaṁ vraja*. *Śrīmad-Bhāgavatam* is the easiest way of directly approaching Kṛṣṇa. *Īśvaraḥ sadyo hṛdy avarudhyate 'tra kṛtibhiḥ śuśrūṣubhis tat-kṣaṇāt* (*Bhāg.* 1.1.2). Diverting even a little of one's attention toward Kṛṣṇa and activities in Kṛṣṇa consciousness immediately enables one to achieve the highest perfection of life. This is the purpose of the Kṛṣṇa consciousness movement. *Lokasyājānato vidvāṁś cakre sātvata-saṁhitām* (*Bhāg.* 1.7.6). The secret of success is unknown to people in general, and therefore Śrīla Vyāsadeva, being compassionate toward the poor souls in this material world, especially in this age of Kali, has given us the *Śrīmad-Bhāgavatam*. *Śrīmad-bhāgavataṁ purāṇam amalaṁ yad vaiṣṇavānāṁ priyam* (*Bhāg.* 12.13.18). For Vaiṣṇavas who are somewhat advanced, or who are fully aware of the glories and potencies of the Lord, *Śrīmad-Bhāgavatam* is a beloved Vedic literature. After all, we have to change this body (*tathā dehāntara-prāptiḥ*). If we do not care about *Bhagavad-gītā* and *Śrīmad-Bhāgavatam*, we do not know what the next body will be. But if one adheres to these two books—*Bhagavad-gītā* and *Śrīmad-Bhāgavatam*—one is sure to obtain the association of Kṛṣṇa in the next life (*tyaktvā dehaṁ punar janma naiti mām eti so 'rjuna*). Therefore, distribution of *Śrīmad-Bhāgavatam* all over the world is a great welfare activity for theologians, philosophers, transcendentalists and *yogīs* (*yogināṁ api sarveṣām*), as well as for people in general. *Janma-lābhaḥ paraḥ puṁsāṁ ante nārāyaṇa-smṛtiḥ* (*Bhāg.* 2.1.6): if we can somehow or other remember Kṛṣṇa, Nārāyaṇa, at the end of life, our life will be successful.

## TEXT 12

यत्पादपांसुर्बहुजन्मकृच्छ्रतो
धृतात्मभिर्योगिभिरप्यलभ्यः ।
स एव यद्दृग्विषयः स्वयं स्थितः
किं वर्ण्यते दिष्टमतो व्रजौकसाम् ॥१२॥

*yat-pāda-pāṁsur bahu-janma-kṛcchrato*
*dhṛtātmabhir yogibhir apy alabhyaḥ*
*sa eva yad-dṛg-viṣayaḥ svayaṁ sthitaḥ*
*kiṁ varṇyate diṣṭam ato vrajaukasām*

*yat*—whose; *pāda-pāṁsuḥ*—dust of the lotus feet; *bahu-janma*—in many births; *kṛcchrataḥ*—from undergoing severe austerities and penances as a way of practicing *yoga*, meditation, etc.; *dhṛta-ātmabhiḥ*—by persons able to control the mind; *yogibhiḥ*—by such *yogīs* (*jñāna-yogīs, rāja-yogīs, dhyāna-yogīs,* etc.); *api*—indeed; *alabhyaḥ*—cannot be achieved; *saḥ*—the Supreme Personality of Godhead; *eva*—indeed; *yat-dṛk-viṣayaḥ*—has become the object of direct vision, face to face; *svayam*—personally; *sthitaḥ*—present in front of them; *kim*—what; *varṇyate*—can be described; *diṣṭam*—about the fortune; *ataḥ*—therefore; *vraja-okasām*—of the inhabitants of Vrajabhūmi, Vṛndāvana.

## TRANSLATION

**Yogīs may undergo severe austerities and penances for many births by practicing yama, niyama, āsana and prāṇāyāma, none of which are easily performed. Yet in due course of time, when these yogīs attain the perfection of controlling the mind, they will still be unable to taste even a particle of dust from the lotus feet of the Supreme Personality of Godhead. What then can we describe about the great fortune of the inhabitants of Vrajabhūmi, Vṛndāvana, with whom the Supreme Personality of Godhead personally lived and who saw the Lord face to face?**

## PURPORT

We can simply imagine the great fortune of the inhabitants of Vṛndāvana. It is impossible to describe how, after many, many births of pious activities, they have become so fortunate.

## TEXT 13

अथाघनामाभ्यपतन्महासुर-
स्तेषां सुखक्रीडनवीक्षणाक्षमः ।
नित्यं यदन्तर्निजजीवितेप्सुभिः
पीतामृतैरप्यमरैः प्रतीक्ष्यते ॥१३॥

*athāgha-nāmābhyapatan mahāsuras*
*teṣāṁ sukha-krīḍana-vīkṣaṇākṣamaḥ*
*nityaṁ yad-antar nija-jīvitepsubhiḥ*
*pītāmṛtair apy amaraiḥ pratīkṣyate*

*atha*—thereafter; *agha-nāma*—a very powerful demon by the name Agha; *abhyapatat*—appeared on the spot; *mahā-asuraḥ*—a great, extremely powerful demon; *teṣām*—of the cowherd boys; *sukha-krīḍana*—the enjoyment of their transcendental pastimes; *vīkṣaṇa-akṣamaḥ*—being unable to see, he could not tolerate the transcendental happiness of the cowherd boys; *nityam*—perpetually; *yat-antaḥ*—the end of the life of Aghāsura; *nija-jīvita-īpsubhiḥ*—just to live undisturbed by Aghāsura; *pīta-amṛtaiḥ api*—although they drank nectar every day; *amaraiḥ*—by such demigods; *pratīkṣyate*—was also being awaited (the demigods were also awaiting the death of the great demon Aghāsura).

## TRANSLATION

**My dear King Parīkṣit, thereafter there appeared a great demon named Aghāsura, whose death was being awaited even by the demigods. The demigods drank nectar every day, but still they feared this great demon and awaited his death. This demon could not tolerate the transcendental pleasure being enjoyed in the forest by the cowherd boys.**

## PURPORT

One may ask how Kṛṣṇa's pastimes could be interrupted by a demon. Śrīla Viśvanātha Cakravartī Ṭhākura answers this question by saying that although the transcendental pleasure being enjoyed by the cowherd boys could not be stopped, unless they stopped the transcendental pleasure of their various activities they could not eat their lunch. Therefore at lunchtime Aghāsura appeared by the arrangement of *yogamāyā*, so that for the time being they could stop their activities and take lunch. Changing varieties are the mother of enjoyment. The cowherd boys would continuously play, then stop, and then again enjoy in a different way. Therefore every day a demon would come and interrupt their sporting pastimes. The demon would be killed, and then the boys would engage again in their transcendental pastimes.

## TEXT 14

दृष्ट्वार्भकान् कृष्णमुखानघासुरः
कंसानुशिष्टः स बकीबकानुजः ।
अयं तु मे सोदरनाशकृत्तयो-
र्द्वयोर्ममैनं सबलं हनिष्ये ॥१४॥

*dṛṣṭvārbhakān kṛṣṇa-mukhān aghāsuraḥ*
*kaṁsānuśiṣṭaḥ sa bakī-bakānujaḥ*
*ayaṁ tu me sodara-nāśa-kṛt tayor*
*dvayor mamainaṁ sa-balaṁ haniṣye*

*dṛṣṭvā*—after seeing; *arbhakān*—all the cowherd boys; *kṛṣṇa-mukhān*—headed by Kṛṣṇa; *aghāsuraḥ*—the demon by the name Aghāsura; *kaṁsa-anuśiṣṭaḥ*—sent by Kaṁsa; *saḥ*—he (Aghāsura); *bakī-baka-anujaḥ*—the younger brother of Pūtanā and Bakāsura; *ayam*—this Kṛṣṇa; *tu*—indeed; *me*—my; *sodara-nāśa-kṛt*—the killer of my brother and sister; *tayoḥ*—for my brother and sister; *dvayoḥ*—for those two; *mama*—my; *enam*—Kṛṣṇa; *sa-balam*—along with His assistants, the cowherd boys; *haniṣye*—I shall kill.

### TRANSLATION

**Aghāsura, who had been sent by Kaṁsa, was the younger brother of Pūtanā and Bakāsura. Therefore when he came and saw Kṛṣṇa at the head of all the cowherd boys, he thought, "This Kṛṣṇa has killed my sister and brother, Pūtanā and Bakāsura. Therefore, in order to please them both, I shall kill this Kṛṣṇa, along with His assistants, the other cowherd boys."**

## TEXT 15

एते यदा मत्सुहृदोस्तिलापः
कृतास्तदा नष्टसमा व्रजौकसः ।
प्राणे गते वर्ष्मसु का नु चिन्ता
प्रजासवः प्राणभृतो हि ये ते ॥१५॥

*ete yadā mat-suhṛdos tilāpaḥ*
*kṛtās tadā naṣṭa-samā vrajaukasaḥ*
*prāṇe gate varṣmasu kā nu cintā*
*prajāsavaḥ prāṇa-bhṛto hi ye te*

*ete*—this Kṛṣṇa and His associates, the cowherd boys; *yadā*—when; *mat-suhṛdoḥ*—of my brother and sister; *tila-āpaḥ kṛtāḥ*—become the last ritualistic ceremonial offering of sesame and water; *tadā*—at that time; *naṣṭa-samāḥ*—without life; *vraja-okasaḥ*—all the inhabitants of Vrajabhūmi, Vṛndāvana; *prāṇe*—when the vital force; *gate*—has been thrown out of the body; *varṣmasu*—as far as the body is concerned; *kā*—what; *nu*—indeed; *cintā*—consideration; *prajā-asavaḥ*—those whose love for their children is the same as their love for their own life; *prāṇa-bhṛtaḥ*—those living beings; *hi*—indeed; *ye te*—all the inhabitants of Vrajabhūmi.

## TRANSLATION

**Aghāsura thought: If somehow or other I can make Kṛṣṇa and His associates serve as the last offering of sesame and water for the departed souls of my brother and sister, then the inhabitants of Vrajabhūmi, for whom these boys are the life and soul, will automatically die. If there is no life, there is no need for the body; consequently, when their sons are dead, naturally all the inhabitants of Vraja will die.**

## TEXT 16

इति व्यवस्याजगरं बृहद् वपुः
स योजनायाममहाद्रिपीवरम् ।

धृत्वाद्भुतं व्यात्तगुहाननं तदा
पथि व्यशेत ग्रसनाशया खलः ॥१६॥

*iti vyavasyājagaraṁ bṛhad vapuḥ*
*sa yojanāyāma-mahādri-pīvaram*
*dhṛtvādbhutaṁ vyātta-guhānanaṁ tadā*
*pathi vyaśeta grasanāśayā khalaḥ*

*iti*—in this way; *vyavasya*—deciding; *ājagaram*—python; *bṛhat vapuḥ*—a very, very large body; *saḥ*—Aghāsura; *yojana-āyāma*—occupying eight miles of land; *mahā-adri-pīvaram*—as thick as a great mountain; *dhṛtvā*—assuming this form; *adbhutam*—wonderful; *vyātta*—spread; *guhā-ānanam*—having a mouth resembling a big cave in a mountain; *tadā*—at that time; *pathi*—on the road; *vyaśeta*—occupied; *grasana-āśayā*—expecting to swallow all the cowherd boys; *khalaḥ*—the most crooked.

## TRANSLATION

**After thus deciding, that crooked Aghāsura assumed the form of a huge python, as thick as a big mountain and as long as eight miles. Having assumed this wonderful python's body, he spread his mouth like a big cave in the mountains and lay down on the road, expecting to swallow Kṛṣṇa and His associates the cowherd boys.**

## TEXT 17

धराधरोष्ठो जलदोत्तरोष्ठो
दर्याननान्तो गिरिशृङ्गदंष्ट्रः ।
ध्वान्तान्तरास्यो विततध्वजिह्वः
परुषानिलश्वासदवेक्षणोष्णः ॥१७॥

*dharādharoṣṭho jaladottaroṣṭho*
*dary-ānanānto giri-śṛṅga-daṁṣṭraḥ*
*dhvāntāntar-āsyo vitatādhva-jihvaḥ*
*paruṣānila-śvāsa-davekṣaṇoṣṇaḥ*

*dharā*—on the surface of the globe; *adhara-oṣṭhaḥ*—whose lower lip; *jalada-uttara-oṣṭhaḥ*—whose upper lip was touching the clouds; *darī-ānana-antaḥ*—whose mouth was expanded very widely like a mountain cave; *giri-śṛṅga*—like a mountain peak; *daṁṣṭraḥ*—whose teeth; *dhvānta-antaḥ-āsyaḥ*—within whose mouth the atmosphere was as dark as possible; *vitata-adhva-jihvaḥ*—whose tongue was like a broad way; *paruṣa-anila-śvāsa*—whose breath was like a warm wind; *dava-īkṣaṇa-uṣṇaḥ*—and whose glance was like flames of fire.

## TRANSLATION

**His lower lip rested on the surface of the earth, and his upper lip was touching the clouds in the sky. The borders of his mouth resembled the sides of a big cave in a mountain, and the middle of his mouth was as dark as possible. His tongue resembled a broad trafficway, his breath was like a warm wind, and his eyes blazed like fire.**

## TEXT 18

**दृष्ट्वा तं तादृशं सर्वे मत्वा वृन्दावनश्रियम् ।**
**व्यात्ताजगरतुण्डेन ह्युत्प्रेक्षन्ते स्म लीलया ॥१८॥**

*dṛṣṭvā taṁ tādṛśaṁ sarve*
*matvā vṛndāvana-śriyam*
*vyāttājagara-tuṇḍena*
*hy utprekṣante sma līlayā*

*dṛṣṭvā*—seeing; *tam*—that Aghāsura; *tādṛśam*—in that posture; *sarve*—Kṛṣṇa and all the cowherd boys; *matvā*—thought it; *vṛndāvana-śriyam*—a beautiful statue of Vṛndāvana; *vyātta*—spread; *ajagara-tuṇḍena*—with the form of a python's mouth; *hi*—indeed; *utprekṣante*—as if observing; *sma*—in the past; *līlayā*—as a matter of pastimes.

## TRANSLATION

**Upon seeing this demon's wonderful form, which resembled a great python, the boys thought that it must be a beautiful scenic**

**spot of Vṛndāvana. Thereafter, they imagined it to be similar to the mouth of a great python. In other words, the boys, unafraid, thought that it was a statue made in the shape of a great python for the enjoyment of their pastimes.**

## PURPORT

Some of the boys, upon seeing this wonderful phenomenon, thought that it was in fact a python, and they were fleeing from the spot. But others said, "Why are you fleeing? It is not possible that a python like this is staying here. This is a spot of beauty for sporting." This is what they imagined.

## TEXT 19

अहो मित्राणि गदत सत्त्वकूटं पुरः स्थितम् ।
अस्मत्संग्रसनव्यात्तव्यालतुण्डायते न वा ॥१९॥

*aho mitrāṇi gadata*
*sattva-kūṭaṁ puraḥ sthitam*
*asmat-saṅgrasana-vyātta-*
*vyāla-tuṇḍāyate na vā*

*aho*—oh; *mitrāṇi*—friends; *gadata*—just let us know; *sattva-kūṭam*—dead python; *puraḥ sthitam*—as it is just before us all; *asmat*—all of us; *saṅgrasana*—to devour us altogether; *vyātta-vyāla-tuṇḍāyate*—the python has spread its mouth; *na vā*—whether it is a fact or not.

## TRANSLATION

**The boys said: Dear friends, is this creature dead, or is it actually a living python with its mouth spread wide just to swallow us all? Kindly clear up this doubt.**

## PURPORT

The friends began to discuss among themselves the reality of the wonderful creature laying before them. Was it dead, or was it actually a living python trying to swallow them up?

## TEXT 20

सत्यमर्ककरारक्तमुत्तराहनुवद् घनम् ।
अधराहनुवद् रोधस्तत्प्रतिच्छाययारुणम् ॥२०॥

*satyam arka-karāraktam*
*uttarā-hanuvad ghanam*
*adharā-hanuvad rodhas*
*tat-praticchāyayāruṇam*

*satyam*—now the boys decided that it was in fact a living python; *arka-kara-āraktam*—appearing like the sunshine; *uttarā-hanuvat ghanam*—on the cloud resembling the upper lips; *adharā-hanuvat*—resembling the lower lips; *rodhaḥ*—big bank; *tat-praticchāyayā*—by the reflection of sunshine; *aruṇam*—reddish.

## TRANSLATION

**Thereafter they decided: Dear friends, this is certainly an animal sitting here to swallow us all. Its upper lip resembles a cloud reddened by the sunshine, and its lower lip resembles the reddish shadows of a cloud.**

## TEXT 21

प्रतिस्पर्धेते सृक्कभ्यां सव्यासव्ये नगोदरे ।
तुङ्गशृङ्गालयोऽप्येतास्तद्दंष्ट्राभिश्च पश्यत ॥२१॥

*pratispardhete sṛkkabhyāṁ*
*savyāsavye nagodare*
*tuṅga-śṛṅgālayo 'py etās*
*tad-daṁṣṭrābhiś ca paśyata*

*pratispardhete*—just resembling; *sṛkkabhyām*—with the corners of the mouth; *savya-asavye*—left and right; *naga-udare*—caves of a mountain; *tuṅga-śṛṅga-ālayaḥ*—the high mountain peaks; *api*—although it is so; *etāḥ tat-daṁṣṭrābhiḥ*—they resemble the teeth of the animal; *ca*—and; *paśyata*—just see.

## TRANSLATION

**On the left and right, the two depressions resembling mountain caves are the corners of its mouth, and the high mountain peaks are its teeth.**

## TEXT 22

आस्तृतायाममार्गोऽयं रसनां प्रतिगर्जति ।
एषामन्तर्गतं ध्वान्तमेतदप्यन्तराननम् ॥२२॥

*āstṛtāyāma-mārgo 'yaṁ*
*rasanāṁ pratigarjati*
*eṣām antar-gataṁ dhvāntam*
*etad apy antar-ānanam*

*āstṛta-āyāma*—the length and breadth; *mārgaḥ ayam*—a broad way; *rasanām*—the tongue; *pratigarjati*—resembles; *eṣām antaḥ-gatam*—on the inside of the mountains; *dhvāntam*—darkness; *etat*—this; *api*—indeed; *antaḥ-ānanam*—the inside of the mouth.

## TRANSLATION

**In length and breadth the animal's tongue resembles a broad trafficway, and the inside of its mouth is very, very dark, like a cave in a mountain.**

## TEXT 23

दावोष्णखरवातोऽयं श्वासवद् भाति पश्यत ।
तद्दग्धसत्त्वदुर्गन्धोऽप्यन्तरामिषगन्धवत् ॥२३॥

*dāvoṣṇa-khara-vāto 'yaṁ*
*śvāsavad bhāti paśyata*
*tad-dagdha-sattva-durgandho*
*'py antar-āmiṣa-gandhavat*

*dāva-uṣṇa-khara-vātaḥ ayam*—hot breath coming out exactly like fire; *śvāsa-vat bhāti paśyata*—just see how it resembles his breath;

*tat-dagdha-sattva*—of burning corpses; *durgandhaḥ*—the bad smell; *api*—indeed; *antaḥ-āmiṣa-gandha-vat*—is like the fleshy smell coming out from within.

## TRANSLATION

**The hot fiery wind is the breath coming out of his mouth, which is giving off the bad smell of burning flesh because of all the dead bodies he has eaten.**

## TEXT 24

अस्मान् किमत्र ग्रसिता निविष्टा-
नयं तथा चेद् बकवद् विनङ्क्ष्यति ।
क्षणादनेनेति बकार्युशन्मुखं
वीक्ष्योद्धसन्तः करताडनैर्ययुः ॥२४॥

*asmān kim atra grasitā niviṣṭān*
*ayaṁ tathā ced bakavad vinaṅkṣyati*
*kṣaṇād aneneti bakāry-uśan-mukhaṁ*
*vīkṣyoddhasantaḥ kara-tāḍanair yayuḥ*

*asmān*—all of us; *kim*—whether; *atra*—here; *grasitā*—will swallow; *niviṣṭān*—who have attempted to enter; *ayam*—this animal; *tathā*—so; *cet*—if; *baka-vat*—like Bakāsura; *vinaṅkṣyati*—he will be vanquished; *kṣaṇāt*—immediately; *anena*—by this Kṛṣṇa; *iti*—in this way; *baka-ari-uśat-mukham*—the beautiful face of Kṛṣṇa, the enemy of Bakāsura; *vīkṣya*—observing, looking at; *uddhasantaḥ*—loudly laughing; *kara-tāḍanaiḥ*—with clapping of hands; *yayuḥ*—entered the mouth.

## TRANSLATION

**Then the boys said, "Has this living creature come to swallow us? If he does so, he will immediately be killed like Bakāsura, without delay." Thus they looked at the beautiful face of Kṛṣṇa, the enemy of Bakāsura, and, laughing loudly and clapping their hands, they entered the mouth of the python.**

## PURPORT

After talking about the terrible animal this way and that way, they decided to enter the demon's mouth. They had full faith in Kṛṣṇa because they had experienced how Kṛṣṇa had saved them from the mouth of Bakāsura. Now, here was another *asura,* Aghāsura. Therefore, they wanted to enjoy the sport of entering the demon's mouth and being saved by Kṛṣṇa, the enemy of Bakāsura.

## TEXT 25

इत्थं मिथोऽतथ्यमतज्ज्ञभाषितं
श्रुत्वा विचिन्त्येत्यमृषा मृषायते ।
रक्षो विदित्वाखिलभूतहृत्स्थितः
स्वानां निरोद्धुं भगवान् मनो दधे ॥२५॥

*ittham mitho 'tathyam ataj-jña-bhāṣitam*
*śrutvā vicintyety amṛṣā mṛṣāyate*
*rakṣo viditvākhila-bhūta-hṛt-sthitaḥ*
*svānāṁ niroddhuṁ bhagavān mano dadhe*

*ittham*—in this way; *mithaḥ*—or another; *atathyam*—a subject matter that is not a fact; *a-tat-jña*—without knowledge; *bhāṣitam*—while they were talking; *śrutvā*—Kṛṣṇa hearing them; *vicintya*—thinking; *iti*—thus; *amṛṣā*—actually, truly; *mṛṣāyate*—who is trying to appear as a false thing (actually the animal was Aghāsura, but because of poor knowledge they were thinking him to be a dead python); *rakṣaḥ*—(Kṛṣṇa, however, could understand that) he was a demon; *viditvā*—knowing it; *akhila-bhūta-hṛt-sthitaḥ*—because He is *antaryāmī,* situated everywhere, in the core of everyone's heart; *svānām*—of His own associates; *niroddhum*—just to forbid them; *bhagavān*—the Supreme Personality of Godhead; *manaḥ dadhe*—made up His mind.

## TRANSLATION

**The Supreme Personality of Godhead, Śrī Kṛṣṇa, who is situated as antaryāmī, the Supersoul, in the core of everyone's heart, heard the boys talking among themselves about the artificial python.**

**Unknown to them, it was actually Aghāsura, a demon who had appeared as a python. Kṛṣṇa, knowing this, wanted to forbid His associates to enter the demon's mouth.**

### TEXT 26

तावत् प्रविष्टास्त्वसुरोदरान्तरं
परं न गीर्णाः शिशवः सवत्साः ।
प्रतीक्षमाणेन बकारिवेशनं
हतस्वकान्तस्मरणेन रक्षसा ॥२६॥

*tāvat praviṣṭās tv asurodarāntaraṁ*
*paraṁ na gīrṇāḥ śiśavaḥ sa-vatsāḥ*
*pratīkṣamāṇena bakāri-veśanaṁ*
*hata-sva-kānta-smaraṇena rakṣasā*

*tāvat*—in the meantime; *praviṣṭāḥ*—all entered; *tu*—indeed; *asura-udara-antaram*—within the belly of the great demon; *param*—but; *na gīrṇāḥ*—they were not swallowed; *śiśavaḥ*—all the boys; *sa-vatsāḥ*—along with their calves; *pratīkṣamāṇena*—who was just waiting for; *baka-ari*—of the enemy of Bakāsura; *veśanam*—the entering; *hata-sva-kānta-smaraṇena*—the *asura* was thinking of his own dead relatives, who would not be satisfied unless Kṛṣṇa were dead; *rakṣasā*—by the demon.

### TRANSLATION

**In the meantime, while Kṛṣṇa was considering how to stop them, all the cowherd boys entered the mouth of the demon. The demon, however, did not swallow them, for he was thinking of his own relatives who had been killed by Kṛṣṇa and was just waiting for Kṛṣṇa to enter his mouth.**

### TEXT 27

तान् वीक्ष्य कृष्णः सकलाभयप्रदो
ह्यनन्यनाथान् स्वकरादवच्युतान् ।
दीनांश्च मृत्योर्जठराग्निघासान्
घृणार्दितो दिष्टकृतेन विस्मितः ॥२७॥

*tān vīkṣya kṛṣṇaḥ sakalābhaya-prado*
*hy ananya-nāthān sva-karād avacyutān*
*dīnāṁś ca mṛtyor jaṭharāgni-ghāsān*
*ghṛṇārdito diṣṭa-kṛtena vismitaḥ*

*tān*—all those boys; *vīkṣya*—seeing; *kṛṣṇaḥ*—the Supreme Personality of Godhead, Kṛṣṇa; *sakala-abhaya-pradaḥ*—who is the source of fearlessness for everyone; *hi*—indeed; *ananya-nāthān*—especially for the cowherd boys, who did not know anyone except Kṛṣṇa; *sva-karāt*—from the control of His hand; *avacyutān*—now gone out; *dīnān ca*—helpless; *mṛtyoḥ jaṭhara-agni-ghāsān*—who had all entered like straws into the fire of the abdomen of Aghāsura, who was very bold and hungry, like death personified (because the *asura* had assumed a big body, he must have had a very strong appetite); *ghṛṇā-arditaḥ*—therefore, being compassionate due to causeless mercy; *diṣṭa-kṛtena*—by things arranged by His internal potency; *vismitaḥ*—He also, for the time being, was astonished.

## TRANSLATION

**Kṛṣṇa saw that all the cowherd boys, who did not know anyone but Him as their Lord, had now gone out of His hand and were helpless, having entered like straws into the fire of the abdomen of Aghāsura, who was death personified. It was intolerable for Kṛṣṇa to be separated from His friends the cowherd boys. Therefore, as if seeing that this had been arranged by His internal potency, Kṛṣṇa was momentarily struck with wonder and unsure of what to do.**

## TEXT 28

कृत्यं किमत्रास्य खलस्य जीवनं
न वा अमीषां च सतां विहिंसनम् ।
द्वयं कथं स्यादिति संविचिन्त्य
ज्ञात्वाविशत्तुण्डमशेषदृग्घरिः ॥२८॥

*kṛtyaṁ kim atrāsya khalasya jīvanaṁ*
*na vā amīṣāṁ ca satāṁ vihiṁsanam*

*dvayaṁ kathaṁ syād iti saṁvicintya*
*jñātvāviśat tuṇḍam aśeṣa-dṛgghariḥ*

*kṛtyam kim*—what to do; *atra*—in this situation; *asya khalasya*—of this envious demon; *jīvanam*—the existence of life; *na*—there should not be; *vā*—either; *amīṣām ca*—and of those who are innocent; *satām*—of the devotees; *vihiṁsanam*—the death; *dvayam*—both actions (killing the demon and saving the boys); *katham*—how; *syāt*—can be possible; *iti saṁvicintya*—very perfectly thinking about the subject matter; *jñātvā*—and deciding what to do; *aviśat*—entered; *tuṇḍam*—within the mouth of the demon; *aśeṣa-dṛk hariḥ*—Kṛṣṇa, who has unlimited potency, could understand past, future and present.

## TRANSLATION

**Now, what was to be done? How could both the killing of this demon and the saving of the devotees be performed simultaneously? Kṛṣṇa, being unlimitedly potent, decided to wait for an intelligent means by which He could simultaneously save the boys and kill the demon. Then He entered the mouth of Aghāsura.**

## PURPORT

Kṛṣṇa is known as *ananta-vīrya-sarvajña* because everything is known to Him. Because He knows everything perfectly well, it was not difficult for Him to find a means by which He could save the boys and at the same time kill the demon. Thus He also decided to enter the demon's mouth.

## TEXT 29

तदा घनच्छदा देवा भयाद्धाहेति चुक्रुशुः ।
जहृषुर्ये च कंसाद्याः कौणपास्त्वघबान्धवाः ॥२९॥

*tadā ghana-cchadā devā*
*bhayād dhā-heti cukruśuḥ*
*jahṛṣur ye ca kaṁsādyāḥ*
*kauṇapās tv agha-bāndhavāḥ*

*tadā*—at that time; *ghana-chadāḥ*—behind the clouds; *devāḥ*—all the demigods; *bhayāt*—on account of feeling danger because Kṛṣṇa had entered the mouth of the demon; *hā-hā*—alas, alas; *iti*—in this way; *cukruśuḥ*—they exclaimed; *jahṛṣuḥ*—became jubilant; *ye*—those; *ca*—also; *kaṁsa-ādyāḥ*—Kaṁsa and others; *kauṇapāḥ*—the demons; *tu*—indeed; *agha-bāndhavāḥ*—the friends of Aghāsura.

## TRANSLATION

**When Kṛṣṇa entered the mouth of Aghāsura, the demigods hidden behind the clouds exclaimed, "Alas! Alas!" But the friends of Aghāsura, like Kaṁsa and other demons, were jubilant.**

## TEXT 30

तच्छ्रुत्वा भगवान् कृष्णस्त्वव्ययः सार्भवत्सकम् ।
चूर्णीचिकीर्षोरात्मानं तरसा ववृधे गले ॥३०॥

*tac chrutvā bhagavān kṛṣṇas*
*tv avyayaḥ sārbha-vatsakam*
*cūrṇī-cikīrṣor ātmānaṁ*
*tarasā vavṛdhe gale*

*tat*—that exclamation of *hā-hā; śrutvā*—hearing; *bhagavān*—the Supreme Personality of Godhead; *kṛṣṇaḥ*—Lord Kṛṣṇa; *tu*—indeed; *avyayaḥ*—never vanquishable; *sa-arbha-vatsakam*—along with the cowherd boys and the calves; *cūrṇī-cikīrṣoḥ*—of that demon, who desired to smash within the abdomen; *ātmānam*—personally, Himself; *tarasā*—very soon; *vavṛdhe*—enlarged; *gale*—within the throat.

## TRANSLATION

**When the invincible Supreme Personality of Godhead, Kṛṣṇa, heard the demigods crying "Alas! Alas!" from behind the clouds, He immediately enlarged Himself within the demon's throat, just to save Himself and the cowherd boys, His own associates, from the demon who wished to smash them.**

## PURPORT

Such are the acts of Kṛṣṇa. *Paritrāṇāya sādhūnāṁ vināśāya ca duṣkṛtām* (Bg. 4.8). By enlarging Himself within the throat of the demon, Kṛṣṇa suffocated and killed him and at the same time saved Himself and His associates from imminent death and also saved the demigods from lamentation.

## TEXT 31

ततोऽतिकायस्य निरुद्धमार्गिणो
ह्युद्गीर्णदृष्टेर्भ्रमतस्त्वितस्ततः ।
पूर्णोऽन्तरङ्गे पवनो निरुद्धो
मूर्धन् विनिर्भिद्य विनिर्गतो बहिः ॥३१॥

*tato 'tikāyasya niruddha-mārgiṇo*
*hy udgīrṇa-dṛṣṭer bhramatas tv itas tataḥ*
*pūrṇo 'ntar-aṅge pavano niruddho*
*mūrdhan vinirbhidya vinirgato bahiḥ*

*tataḥ*—after Kṛṣṇa took action to kill the demon's body from within the mouth; *ati-kāyasya*—of that great demon, who had expanded his body to a very large size; *niruddha-mārgiṇaḥ*—because of suffocating, all outlets being stopped up; *hi udgīrṇa-dṛṣṭeḥ*—whose eyes had popped out; *bhramataḥ tu itaḥ tataḥ*—the eyeballs, or the life air, moving here and there; *pūrṇaḥ*—completely filled; *antaḥ-aṅge*—within the body; *pavanaḥ*—the life air; *niruddhaḥ*—being stopped; *mūrdhan*—the hole in the top of the head; *vinirbhidya*—breaking; *vinirgataḥ*—went out; *bahiḥ*—externally.

## TRANSLATION

**Then, because Kṛṣṇa had increased the size of His body, the demon extended his own body to a very large size. Nonetheless, his breathing stopped, he suffocated, and his eyes rolled here and there and popped out. The demon's life air, however, could not pass through any outlet, and therefore it finally burst out through a hole in the top of the demon's head.**

## TEXT 32

तेनैव सर्वेषु बहिर्गतेषु
प्राणेषु वत्सान् सुहृदः परेतान् ।
दृष्ट्या स्वयोत्थाप्य तदन्वितः पुन-
र्वक्त्रान्मुकुन्दो भगवान् विनिर्ययौ ॥३२॥

*tenaiva sarveṣu bahir gateṣu*
*prāṇeṣu vatsān suhṛdaḥ paretān*
*dṛṣṭyā svayotthāpya tad-anvitaḥ punar*
*vaktrān mukundo bhagavān viniryayau*

*tena eva*—through that *brahma-randhra*, or the hole in the top of the head; *sarveṣu*—all the air within the body; *bahiḥ gateṣu*—having gone out; *prāṇeṣu*—the life airs, along with the vital force; *vatsān*—the calves; *suhṛdaḥ*—the cowherd boy friends; *paretān*—who were all dead within; *dṛṣṭyā svayā*—by Kṛṣṇa's glancing over; *utthāpya*—brought them back to life; *tat-anvitaḥ*—thus accompanied by them; *punaḥ*—again; *vaktrāt*—from the mouth; *mukundaḥ*—the Supreme Personality of Godhead; *bhagavān*—Kṛṣṇa; *viniryayau*—came out.

## TRANSLATION

**When all the demon's life air had passed away through that hole in the top of his head, Kṛṣṇa glanced over the dead calves and cowherd boys and brought them back to life. Then Mukunda, who can give one liberation, came out from the demon's mouth with His friends and the calves.**

## TEXT 33

पीनाहिभोगोत्थितमद्भुतं महद्-
ज्ज्योतिः स्वधाम्ना ज्वलयद् दिशो दश ।
प्रतीक्ष्य खेऽवस्थितमीशनिर्गमं
विवेश तस्मिन् मिषतां दिवौकसाम् ॥३३॥

*pīnāhi-bhogotthitam adbhutaṁ mahaj*
*jyotiḥ sva-dhāmnā jvalayad diśo daśa*
*pratīkṣya khe 'vasthitam īśa-nirgamaṁ*
*viveśa tasmin miṣatāṁ divaukasām*

*pīna*—very great; *ahi-bhoga-utthitam*—issuing from the serpent's body, which was meant for material enjoyment; *adbhutam*—very wonderful; *mahat*—great; *jyotiḥ*—effulgence; *sva-dhāmnā*—by his own illumination; *jvalayat*—making glaring; *diśaḥ daśa*—all the ten directions; *pratīkṣya*—waiting; *khe*—in the sky; *avasthitam*—individually staying; *īśa-nirgamam*—until the Supreme Personality of Godhead, Kṛṣṇa, came out; *viveśa*—entered; *tasmin*—in the body of Kṛṣṇa; *miṣatām*—while observing; *divaukasām*—all the demigods.

## TRANSLATION

**From the body of the gigantic python, a glaring effulgence came out, illuminating all directions, and stayed individually in the sky until Kṛṣṇa came out from the corpse's mouth. Then, as all the demigods looked on, this effulgence entered into Kṛṣṇa's body.**

## PURPORT

Apparently the serpent named Aghāsura, because of having received association with Kṛṣṇa, attained *mukti* by entering Kṛṣṇa's body. Entering the body of Kṛṣṇa is called *sāyujya-mukti*, but later verses prove that Aghāsura, like Dantavakra and others, received *sārūpya-mukti*. This has been broadly described by Śrīla Viśvanātha Cakravartī Ṭhākura with references from the *Vaiṣṇava-toṣaṇī* of Śrīla Jīva Gosvāmī. Aghāsura attained *sārūpya-mukti*, being promoted to the Vaikuṇṭha planets to live with the same four-armed bodily features as Viṣṇu. The explanation of how this is so may be summarized as follows.

The effulgence came out from the python's body and became purified, attaining spiritual *śuddha-sattva*, freedom from material contamination, because Kṛṣṇa had stayed within the serpent's body, even after the serpent's death. One may doubt that such a demon, full of mischievous activities, could attain the liberation of *sārūpya* or *sāyujya*, and one may be astonished about this. But Kṛṣṇa is so kind that in order to drive away such doubts, He had the effulgence, the individual life of the python, wait for some time in its individuality, in the presence of all the demigods.

Kṛṣṇa is the full effulgence, and every living being is part and parcel of that effulgence. As proved here, the effulgence in every living being is individual. For some time, the effulgence remained outside the demon's body, individually, and did not mix with the whole effulgence, the *brahmajyoti.* The Brahman effulgence is not visible to material eyes, but to prove that every living being is individual, Kṛṣṇa had this individual effulgence stay outside the demon's body for some time, for everyone to see. Then Kṛṣṇa proved that anyone killed by Him attains liberation, whether *sāyujya, sārūpya, sāmīpya* or whatever.

But the liberation of those who are on the transcendental platform of love and affection is *vimukti,* special liberation. Thus the serpent first entered the body of Kṛṣṇa personally and mixed with the Brahman effulgence. This merging is called *sāyujya-mukti.* But from later verses we find that Aghāsura attained *sārūpya-mukti.* Text 38 explains that Aghāsura attained a body exactly like that of Viṣṇu, and the verse after that also clearly states that he attained a completely spiritual body like that of Nārāyaṇa. Therefore in two or three places the *Bhāgavatam* has confirmed that Aghāsura attained *sārūpya-mukti.* One may then argue, How is it that he mixed with the Brahman effulgence? The answer is that as Jaya and Vijaya, after three births, again attained *sārūpya-mukti* and association with the Lord, Aghāsura received a similar liberation.

## TEXT 34

ततोऽतिहृष्टाः स्वकृतोऽकृतार्हणं
पुष्पैः सुगा अप्सरसश्च नर्तनैः ।
गीतैः सुरा वाद्यधराश्च वाद्यकैः
स्तवैश्च विप्रा जयनिःस्वनैर्गणाः ॥३४॥

*tato 'tihṛṣṭāḥ sva-kṛto 'kṛtārhaṇaṁ*
*puṣpaiḥ sugā apsarasaś ca nartanaiḥ*
*gītaiḥ surā vādya-dharāś ca vādyakaiḥ*
*stavaiś ca viprā jaya-niḥsvanair gaṇāḥ*

*tataḥ*—thereafter; *ati-hṛṣṭāḥ*—everyone becoming very much pleased; *sva-kṛtaḥ*—own respective duty; *akṛta*—executed; *arhaṇam*—

in the shape of worshiping the Supreme Personality of Godhead; *puṣpaiḥ*—by showering flowers grown in Nandana-kānana from the heavens; *su-gāḥ*—the celestial singers; *apsarasaḥ ca*—and the celestial dancing girls; *nartanaiḥ*—by dancing; *gītaiḥ*—by singing celestial songs; *surāḥ*—all the demigods; *vādya-dharāḥ ca*—those who played on musical drums; *vādyakaiḥ*—by playing respectively; *stavaiḥ ca*—and by offering prayers; *viprāḥ*—the *brāhmaṇas; jaya-niḥsvanaiḥ*—simply by glorifying the Supreme Personality of Godhead; *gaṇāḥ*—everyone.

## TRANSLATION

**Thereafter, everyone being pleased, the demigods began to shower flowers from Nandana-kānana, the celestial dancing girls began to dance, and the Gandharvas, who are famous for singing, offered songs of prayer. The drummers began to beat their ket-tledrums, and the brāhmaṇas offered Vedic hymns. In this way, both in the heavens and on earth, everyone began to perform his own duties, glorifying the Lord.**

## PURPORT

Everyone has some particular duty. The *śāstra* has concluded (*nirūpitaḥ*) that everyone should glorify the Supreme Personality of Godhead by his own qualifications. If you are a singer, always glorify the Supreme Lord by singing very nicely. If you are a musician, glorify the Supreme Lord by playing musical instruments. *Svanuṣṭhitasya dharmasya saṁsiddhir hari-toṣaṇam* (*Bhāg.* 1.2.13). The perfection of life is to satisfy the Personality of Godhead. Therefore, beginning from this earth up to the celestial kingdom, everyone engaged in glorifying the Supreme Personality of Godhead. The decision of all great saintly persons is that whatever qualifications one has acquired should be utilized to glorify the Supreme Lord.

*idaṁ hi puṁsas tapasaḥ śrutasya vā*
*sviṣṭasya sūktasya ca buddhi-dattayoḥ*
*avicyuto 'rthaḥ kavibhir nirūpito*
*yad uttamaśloka-guṇānuvarṇanam*

"Learned sages have definitely concluded that the infallible purpose of the advancement of knowledge, austerity, Vedic study, sacrifice, the chanting of hymns, and charity is found in the transcendental descriptions of the qualities of the Lord, who is defined in choice poetry." (*Bhāg.* 1.5.22) This is the perfection of life. One should be trained how to glorify the Supreme Personality of Godhead by one's respective qualities. Education, austerity, penance or, in the modern world, business, industry, education and so on—all should be engaged in glorifying the Lord. Then everyone in the world will be happy.

Kṛṣṇa comes, therefore, to exhibit His transcendental activities so that people may have the chance to glorify Him in every respect. To understand how to glorify the Lord is actual research work. It is not that everything should be understood without God. That is condemned.

*bhagavad-bhakti-hīnasya*
*jātiḥ śāstraṁ japas tapaḥ*
*aprāṇasyaiva dehasya*
*maṇḍanaṁ loka-rañjanam*
(*Hari-bhakti-sudhodaya* 3.11)

Without *bhagavad-bhakti*, without glorification of the Supreme Lord, whatever we have is simply a decoration of the dead body.

## TEXT 35

तदद्भुतस्तोत्रसुवाद्यगीतिका-
जयादिनैकोत्सवमङ्गलस्वनान् ।
श्रुत्वा स्वधाम्नोऽन्त्यज आगतोऽचिराद्
दृष्ट्वा महीशस्य जगाम विस्मयम् ॥३५॥

*tad-adbhuta-stotra-suvādya-gītikā-*
*jayādi-naikotsava-maṅgala-svanān*
*śrutvā sva-dhāmno 'nty aja āgato 'cirād*
*dṛṣṭvā mahīśasya jagāma vismayam*

*tat*—that celebration performed by the demigods in the upper planetary system; *adbhuta*—wonderful; *stotra*—prayers; *su-vādya*—glorious musical sounds of drums and other instruments; *gītikā*—celestial songs; *jaya-ādi*—sounds of *jaya*, etc.; *na-eka-utsava*—

celebrations simply for glorifying the Supreme Personality of Godhead; *maṅgala-svanān*—transcendental sounds auspicious for everyone; *śrutvā*—hearing such sounds; *sva-dhāmnaḥ*—from his abode; *anti*—nearby; *ajaḥ*—Lord Brahmā; *āgataḥ*—coming there; *acirāt*—very soon; *dṛṣṭvā*—seeing; *mahi*—the glorification; *īśasya*—of Lord Kṛṣṇa; *jagāma vismayam*—became astonished.

## TRANSLATION

**When Lord Brahmā heard the wonderful ceremony going on near his planet, accompanied by music and songs and sounds of "Jaya! Jaya!" he immediately came down to see the function. Upon seeing so much glorification of Lord Kṛṣṇa, he was completely astonished.**

## PURPORT

Here the word *anti* means "near," indicating that even in the higher planetary systems near Brahmaloka, like Maharloka, Janaloka and Tapoloka, the festival of glorification of Lord Kṛṣṇa was going on.

## TEXT 36

राजन्नाजगरं चर्म शुष्कं वृन्दावनेऽद्भुतम् ।
व्रजौकसां बहुतिथं बभूवाक्रीडगह्वरम् ॥३६॥

*rājann ājagaraṁ carma*
*śuṣkaṁ vṛndāvane 'dbhutam*
*vrajaukasāṁ bahu-tithaṁ*
*babhūvākrīḍa-gahvaram*

*rājan*—O Mahārāja Parīkṣit; *ājagaram carma*—the dry body of Aghāsura, which remained only a big skin; *śuṣkam*—when it completely dried up; *vṛndāvane adbhutam*—like a wonderful museum piece in Vṛndāvana; *vraja-okasām*—for the inhabitants of Vrajabhūmi, Vṛndāvana; *bahu-titham*—for many days, or for a long time; *babhūva*—became; *ākrīḍa*—sporting place; *gahvaram*—a cave.

## TRANSLATION

**O King Parīkṣit, when the python-shaped body of Aghāsura dried up into merely a big skin, it became a wonderful place for**

**the inhabitants of Vṛndāvana to visit, and it remained so for a long, long time.**

## TEXT 37

एतत् कौमारजं कर्म हरेरात्माहिमोक्षणम् ।
मृत्योः पौगण्डके बाला दृष्ट्वोचुर्विस्मिता व्रजे ॥३७॥

*etat kaumārajaṁ karma*
*harer ātmāhi-mokṣaṇam*
*mṛtyoḥ paugaṇḍake bālā*
*dṛṣṭvocur vismitā vraje*

*etat*—this incident of delivering both Aghāsura and Kṛṣṇa's associates from death; *kaumāra-jam karma*—performed during their *kaumāra* age (the age of five years); *hareḥ*—of the Supreme Personality of Godhead; *ātma*—the devotees are the Lord's heart and soul; *ahi-mokṣaṇam*—their deliverance and the deliverance of the python; *mṛtyoḥ*—from the path of repeated birth and death; *paugaṇḍake*—at the age of *paugaṇḍa*, beginning with the sixth year (one year later); *bālāḥ*—all the boys; *dṛṣṭvā ūcuḥ*—disclosed the fact after one year; *vismitāḥ*—as if it had happened on that very day; *vraje*—in Vṛndāvana.

## TRANSLATION

**This incident of Kṛṣṇa's saving Himself and His associates from death and of giving deliverance to Aghāsura, who had assumed the form of a python, took place when Kṛṣṇa was five years old. It was disclosed in Vrajabhūmi after one year, as if it had taken place on that very day.**

## PURPORT

The word *mokṣaṇam* means "liberation." For the associates of Kṛṣṇa and for Kṛṣṇa Himself, there is no question about liberation; they are already liberated, being in the spiritual world. In the material world there are birth, death, old age and disease, but in the spiritual world there are no such things because everything is eternal. As for the python, however, by the association of Kṛṣṇa and His devotees, Aghāsura also achieved the same facility of eternal life. Therefore, as indicated here by the word *ātmāhi-mokṣaṇam*, if the python Aghāsura could receive eternal association with the Supreme Personality of Godhead, what is to be said of those who are already associates of the Lord? *Sākaṁ vijahruḥ kṛta-puṇya-puñjāḥ* (*Bhāg.* 10.12.11). Here is proof that God is good for everyone. Even when He kills someone, the one who is killed attains liberation. What then is to be said of those who are already in the association of the Lord?

## TEXT 38

नैतद् विचित्रं मनुजार्भमायिनः
परावराणां परमस्य वेधसः ।
अघोऽपि यत्स्पर्शनधौतपातकः
प्रापात्मसाम्यं त्वसतां सुदुर्लभम् ॥३८॥

*naitad vicitraṁ manujārbha-māyinaḥ*
*parāvarāṇāṁ paramasya vedhasaḥ*
*agho 'pi yat-sparśana-dhauta-pātakaḥ*
*prāpātma-sāmyaṁ tv asatāṁ sudurlabham*

*na*—not; *etat*—this; *vicitram*—is wonderful; *manuja-arbha-māyinaḥ*—of Kṛṣṇa, who appeared as the son of Nanda Mahārāja and Yaśodā, being compassionate upon them; *para-avarāṇām*—of all causes and effects; *paramasya vedhasaḥ*—of the supreme creator; *aghaḥ api*—Aghāsura also; *yat-sparśana*—simply by the slight association of whom; *dhauta-pātakaḥ*—became freed from all contamination of material existence; *prāpa*—became elevated; *ātma-sāmyam*—to a body exactly resembling that of Nārāyaṇa; *tu*—but; *asatām sudurlabham*—which is not at all possible to be obtained by contaminated souls (but everything can be possible by the mercy of the Supreme Lord).

## TRANSLATION

**Kṛṣṇa is the cause of all causes. The causes and effects of the material world, both higher and lower, are all created by the Supreme Lord, the original controller. When Kṛṣṇa appeared as the son of Nanda Mahārāja and Yaśodā, He did so by His causeless mercy. Consequently, for Him to exhibit His unlimited opulence was not**

**at all wonderful. Indeed, He showed such great mercy that even Aghāsura, the most sinful miscreant, was elevated to being one of His associates and achieving sārūpya-mukti, which is actually impossible for materially contaminated persons to attain.**

## PURPORT

The word *māyā* is also used in connection with love. Out of *māyā*, love, a father has affection for his child. Therefore the word *māyinaḥ* indicates that Kṛṣṇa, out of love, appeared as the son of Nanda Mahārāja and assumed the form of a human child (*manujārbha*). Kṛṣṇa is the cause of all causes. He is the creator of cause and effect, and He is the supreme controller. Nothing is impossible for Him. Therefore, that He enabled even a living being like Aghāsura to attain the salvation of *sārūpya-mukti* was not at all wonderful for Kṛṣṇa. Kṛṣṇa took pleasure in entering the mouth of Aghāsura in a sporting spirit along with His associates. Therefore, when Aghāsura, by that sporting association, as maintained in the spiritual world, was purified of all contamination, he attained *sārūpya-mukti* and *vimukti* by the grace of Kṛṣṇa. For Kṛṣṇa this was not at all wonderful.

## TEXT 39

सकृद् यदङ्गप्रतिमान्तराहिता
मनोमयी भागवतीं ददौ गतिम् ।
स एव नित्यात्मसुखानुभूत्यभि-
व्युदस्तमायोऽन्तर्गतो हि किं पुनः ॥३९॥

*sakṛd yad-aṅga-pratimāntar-āhitā*
*manomayī bhāgavatīṁ dadau gatim*
*sa eva nityātma-sukhānubhūty-abhi-*
*vyudasta-māyo 'ntar-gato hi kiṁ punaḥ*

*sakṛt*—once only; *yat*—whose; *aṅga-pratimā*—the form of the Supreme Lord (there are many forms, but Kṛṣṇa is the original form); *antaḥ-āhitā*—placing within the core of the heart, somehow or other; *manaḥ-mayī*—thinking of Him even by force; *bhāgavatīm*—which is competent to offer devotional service to the Lord; *dadau*—Kṛṣṇa gave; *gatim*—the best destination; *saḥ*—He (the Supreme Personality of Godhead); *eva*—indeed; *nitya*—always; *ātma*—of all living entities; *sukha-anubhūti*—anyone thinking of Him immediately enjoys transcendental pleasure; *abhivyudasta-māyaḥ*—because all illusion is completely removed by Him; *antaḥ-gataḥ*—He is always present within the core of the heart; *hi*—indeed; *kim punaḥ*—what to speak.

## TRANSLATION

**If even only once or even by force one brings the form of the Supreme Personality of Godhead into one's mind, one can attain the supreme salvation by the mercy of Kṛṣṇa, as did Aghāsura. What then is to be said of those whose hearts the Supreme Personality of Godhead enters when He appears as an incarnation, or those who always think of the lotus feet of the Lord, who is the source of transcendental bliss for all living entities and by whom all illusion is completely removed?**

## PURPORT

The process for receiving the favor of the Supreme Personality of Godhead is described here. *Yat-pāda-paṅkaja-palāśa-vilāsa-bhaktyā* (*Bhāg.* 4.22.39). Simply by thinking of Kṛṣṇa, one can attain Him very easily. Kṛṣṇa is also described as having His lotus feet always within the hearts of His devotees (*bhagavān bhakta-hṛdi sthitaḥ*). In the case of Aghāsura, one may argue that he was not a devotee. The answer to this is that he thought of Kṛṣṇa for a moment with devotion. *Bhaktyāham ekayā grāhyaḥ.* Without devotion, one cannot think of Kṛṣṇa; and, conversely, whenever one thinks of Kṛṣṇa, one undoubtedly has devotion. Although Aghāsura's purpose was to kill Kṛṣṇa, for a moment Aghāsura thought of Kṛṣṇa with devotion, and Kṛṣṇa and His associates wanted to sport within Aghāsura's mouth. Similarly, Pūtanā wanted to kill Kṛṣṇa by poisoning Him, but Kṛṣṇa took her as His mother because He had accepted the milk of her breast. *Svalpam apy asya dharmasya trāyate mahato bhayāt* (Bg. 2.40). Especially when Kṛṣṇa appears as an *avatāra*, anyone who thinks of Kṛṣṇa in His different incarnations (*rāmādi-mūrtiṣu kalā-niyamena tiṣṭhan*), and especially in His original form as

Kṛṣṇa, attains salvation. There are many instances of this, and among them is Aghāsura, who attained the salvation of *sārūpya-mukti.* Therefore the process is *satataṁ kīrtayanto māṁ yatantaś ca dṛḍha-vratāḥ* (Bg. 9.14). Those who are devotees always engage in glorifying Kṛṣṇa. *Advaitam acyutam anādim ananta-rūpam:* when we speak of Kṛṣṇa, we refer to all His *avatāras,* such as Kṛṣṇa, Govinda, Nārāyaṇa, Viṣṇu, Lord Caitanya, Kṛṣṇa-Balarāma and Śyāmasundara. One who always thinks of Kṛṣṇa must attain *vimukti,* special salvation as the Lord's personal associate, not necessarily in Vṛndāvana, but at least in Vaikuṇṭha. This is called *sārūpya-mukti.*

## TEXT 40

श्रीसूत उवाच
इत्थं द्विजा यादवदेवदत्तः
श्रुत्वा स्वरातुश्चरितं विचित्रम् ।
पप्रच्छ भूयोऽपि तदेव पुण्यं
वैयासकिं यन्निगृहीतचेताः ॥४०॥

*śrī-sūta uvāca*
*itthaṁ dvijā yādavadeva-dattaḥ*
*śrutvā sva-rātuś caritaṁ vicitram*
*papraccha bhūyo 'pi tad eva puṇyaṁ*
*vaiyāsakiṁ yan nigṛhīta-cetāḥ*

*śrī-sūtaḥ uvāca*—Śrī Sūta Gosvāmī spoke to the assembled saints at Naimiṣāraṇya; *ittham*—in this way; *dvijāḥ*—O learned *brāhmaṇas; yādava-deva-dattaḥ*—Mahārāja Parīkṣit (or Mahārāja Yudhiṣṭhira), who was protected by Yādavadeva, Kṛṣṇa; *śrutvā*—hearing; *sva-rātuḥ*—of Kṛṣṇa, who was his savior within the womb of his mother, Uttarā; *caritam*—the activities; *vicitram*—all wonderful; *papraccha*—inquired; *bhūyaḥ api*—even again; *tat eva*—such activities; *puṇyam*—which are always full of pious activities (*śṛṇvatāṁ sva-kathāḥ kṛṣṇaḥ puṇya-śravaṇa-kīrtanaḥ:* to hear about Kṛṣṇa is always pious); *vaiyāsakim*—unto Śukadeva Gosvāmī; *yat*—because; *nigṛhīta-cetāḥ*—Parīkṣit Mahārāja had already become steady in hearing about Kṛṣṇa.

## TRANSLATION

**Śrī Sūta Gosvāmī said: O learned saints, the childhood pastimes of Śrī Kṛṣṇa are very wonderful. Mahārāja Parīkṣit, after hearing about those pastimes of Kṛṣṇa, who had saved him in the womb of his mother, became steady in his mind and again inquired from Śukadeva Gosvāmī to hear about those pious activities.**

## TEXT 41

श्रीराजोवाच

ब्रह्मन् कालान्तरकृतं तत्कालीनं कथं भवेत् ।
यत् कौमारे हरिकृतं जगुः पौगण्डकेऽर्भकाः ॥४१॥

*śrī-rājovāca*
*brahman kālāntara-kṛtaṁ*
*tat-kālīnaṁ kathaṁ bhavet*
*yat kaumāre hari-kṛtaṁ*
*jaguḥ paugaṇḍake 'rbhakāḥ*

*śrī-rājā uvāca*—Mahārāja Parīkṣit inquired; *brahman*—O learned *brāhmaṇa* (Śukadeva Gosvāmī); *kāla-antara-kṛtam*—things done in the past, at a different time (in the *kaumāra* age); *tat-kālīnam*—described as happening now (in the *paugaṇḍa* age); *katham bhavet*—how could it be so; *yat*—which pastime; *kaumāre*—in the *kaumāra* age; *hari-kṛtam*—was done by Kṛṣṇa; *jaguḥ*—they described; *paugaṇḍake*—in the *paugaṇḍa* age (after one year); *arbhakāḥ*—all the boys.

## TRANSLATION

**Mahārāja Parīkṣit inquired: O great sage, how could things done in the past have been described as being done at the present? Lord Śrī Kṛṣṇa performed this pastime of killing Aghāsura during His kaumāra age. How then, during His paugaṇḍa age, could the boys have described this incident as having happened recently?**

## TEXT 42

तद् ब्रूहि मे महायोगिन् परं कौतूहलं गुरो ।
नूनमेतद्धरेरेव माया भवति नान्यथा ॥४२॥

*tad brūhi me mahā-yogin*
*paraṁ kautūhalaṁ guro*
*nūnam etad dharer eva*
*māyā bhavati nānyathā*

*tat brūhi*—therefore please explain that; *me*—unto me; *mahā-yogin*—O great *yogī; param*—very much; *kautūhalam*—curiosity; *guro*—O my lord, my spiritual master; *nūnam*—otherwise; *etat*—this incident; *hareḥ*—of the Supreme Personality of Godhead; *eva*—indeed; *māyā*—the illusion; *bhavati*—becomes; *na anyathā*—nothing more.

## TRANSLATION

**O greatest yogī, my spiritual master, kindly describe why this happened. I am very much curious to know about it. I think that it was nothing but another illusion due to Kṛṣṇa.**

## PURPORT

Kṛṣṇa has many potencies: *parāsya śaktir vividhaiva śrūyate* (*Śvetāśvatara Upaniṣad* 6.8). The description of Aghāsura was disclosed after one year. Some act of Kṛṣṇa's potency must have been involved. Therefore Mahārāja Parīkṣit was very curious to know about this, and he requested Śukadeva Gosvāmī to explain it.

## TEXT 43

वयं धन्यतमा लोके गुरोऽपि क्षत्रबन्धवः ।
यत् पिबामो मुहुस्त्वत्तः पुण्यं कृष्णकथामृतम् ॥४३॥

*vayaṁ dhanyatamā loke*
*guro 'pi kṣatra-bandhavaḥ*
*vayaṁ pibāmo muhus tvattaḥ*
*puṇyaṁ kṛṣṇa-kathāmṛtam*

*vayam*—we are; *dhanya-tamāḥ*—most glorified; *loke*—in this world; *guro*—O my lord, my spiritual master; *api*—although; *kṣatra-bandhavaḥ*—the lowest of the *kṣatriyas* (because we did not act like *kṣatriyas*); *vayam*—we are; *pibāmaḥ*—drinking; *muhuḥ*—always; *tvattaḥ*—from you; *puṇyam*—pious; *kṛṣṇa-kathā-amṛtam*—the nectar of *kṛṣṇa-kathā*.

## TRANSLATION

**O my lord, my spiritual master, although we are the lowest of kṣatriyas, we are glorified and benefited because we have the opportunity of always hearing from you the nectar of the pious activities of the Supreme Personality of Godhead.**

## PURPORT

The pious activities of the Supreme Personality of Godhead are very confidential. It is not ordinarily possible to hear such activities unless one is very, very fortunate. Parīkṣit Mahārāja placed himself as *kṣatra-bandhavaḥ,* which means "the lowest of the *kṣatriyas.*" The qualities of the *kṣatriya* are described in *Bhagavad-gītā,* and although the general quality of the *kṣatriya* is *īśvara-bhāva,* the tendency to rule, a *kṣatriya* is not supposed to rule over a *brāhmaṇa.* Thus Mahārāja Parīkṣit regretted that he had wanted to rule over the *brāhmaṇas* and had therefore been cursed. He considered himself the lowest of the *kṣatriyas. Dānam īśvara-bhāvaś ca kṣātraṁ karma svabhāvajam* (Bg. 18.43). There was no doubt that Mahārāja Parīkṣit had the good qualities of a *kṣatriya,* but as a devotee he presented himself, with submissiveness and humility, as the lowest of the *kṣatriyas,* remembering his act of wrapping a dead serpent around the neck of a *brāhmaṇa.* A student and disciple has the right to ask the *guru* about any confidential service, and it is the duty of the *guru* to explain these confidential matters to his disciple.

## TEXT 44

श्रीसूत उवाच
इत्थं स्म पृष्टः स तु बादरायणि-
स्तत्स्मारितानन्तहृताखिलेन्द्रियः ।
कृच्छ्रात् पुनर्लब्धबहिर्दृशिः शनैः
प्रत्याह तं भागवतोत्तमोत्तम ॥४४॥

*śrī-sūta uvāca*
*itthaṁ sma pṛṣṭaḥ sa tu bādarāyaṇis*
*tat-smāritānanta-hṛtākhilendriyaḥ*
*kṛcchrāt punar labdha-bahir-dṛśiḥ śanaiḥ*
*pratyāha taṁ bhāgavatottamottama*

*śrī-sūtaḥ uvāca*—Śrī Sūta Gosvāmī said; *ittham*—in this way; *sma*—in the past; *pṛṣṭaḥ*—being inquired from; *saḥ*—he; *tu*—indeed; *bādarāyaṇiḥ*—Śukadeva Gosvāmī; *tat*—by him (Śukadeva Gosvāmī); *smārita-ananta*—as soon as Lord Kṛṣṇa was remembered; *hṛta*—lost in ecstasy; *akhila-indriyaḥ*—all actions of the external senses; *kṛcchrāt*—with great difficulty; *punaḥ*—again; *labdha-bahiḥ-dṛśiḥ*—having revived his external sensory perception; *śanaiḥ*—slowly; *pratyāha*—replied; *tam*—unto Mahārāja Parīkṣit; *bhāgavata-uttama-uttama*—O great saintly person, greatest of all devotees (Śaunaka).

## TRANSLATION

**Sūta Gosvāmī said: O Śaunaka, greatest of saints and devotees, when Mahārāja Parīkṣit inquired from Śukadeva Gosvāmī in this way, Śukadeva Gosvāmī, immediately remembering subject matters about Kṛṣṇa within the core of his heart, externally lost contact with the actions of his senses. Thereafter, with great difficulty, he revived his external sensory perception and began to speak to Mahārāja Parīkṣit about kṛṣṇa-kathā.**

*Thus end the Bhaktivedanta purports of the Tenth Canto, Twelfth Chapter, of the* Śrīmad-Bhāgavatam, *entitled, "The Killing of the Demon Aghāsura."*

# CHAPTER THIRTEEN

# The Stealing of the Boys and Calves by Brahmā

This chapter describes Lord Brahmā's attempt to take away the calves and cowherd boys, and it also describes the bewilderment of Lord Brahmā and finally the clearance of his illusion.

Although the incident concerning Aghāsura had been performed one year before, when the cowherd boys were five years old, when they were six years old they said, "It happened today." What happened was this. After killing Aghāsura, Kṛṣṇa, along with His associates the cowherd boys, went for a picnic within the forest. The calves, being allured by green grasses, gradually went far away, and therefore Kṛṣṇa's associates became a little agitated and wanted to bring back the calves. Kṛṣṇa, however, encouraged the boys by saying, "You take your tiffin without being agitated. I shall go find the calves." And thus the Lord departed. Then, just to examine the potency of Kṛṣṇa, Lord Brahmā took away all the calves and cowherd boys and kept them in a secluded place.

When Kṛṣṇa was unable to find the calves and boys, He could understand that this was a trick performed by Brahmā. Then the Supreme Personality of Godhead, the cause of all causes, in order to please Lord Brahmā, as well as His own associates and their mothers, expanded Himself to become the calves and boys, exactly as they were before. In this way, He discovered another pastime. A special feature of this pastime was that the mothers of the cowherd boys thus became more attached to their respective sons, and the cows became more attached to their calves. After nearly a year, Baladeva observed that all the cowherd boys and calves were expansions of Kṛṣṇa. Thus He inquired from Kṛṣṇa and was informed of what had happened.

When one full year had passed, Brahmā returned and saw that Kṛṣṇa was still engaged as usual with His friends and the calves and cows. Then Kṛṣṇa exhibited all the calves and cowherd boys as four-armed forms of Nārāyaṇa. Brahmā could then understand Kṛṣṇa's potency, and he was astonished by the pastimes of Kṛṣṇa, his worshipable Lord. Kṛṣṇa, however, bestowed His causeless mercy upon Brahmā and released him from illusion. Thus Brahmā began to offer prayers to glorify the Supreme Personality of Godhead.

## TEXT 1

श्रीशुक उवाच

साधु पृष्टं महाभाग त्वया भागवतोत्तम।
यन्नूतनयसीशस्य शृण्वन्नपि कथां मुहुः ॥ १ ॥

*śrī-śuka uvāca*
*sādhu pṛṣṭaṁ mahā-bhāga*
*tvayā bhāgavatottama*
*yan nūtanayasīśasya*
*śṛṇvann api kathāṁ muhuḥ*

*śrī-śukaḥ uvāca*—Śukadeva Gosvāmī said; *sādhu pṛṣṭam*—I have been very much honored by your inquiry; *mahā-bhāga*—you are a greatly fortunate personality; *tvayā*—by you; *bhāgavata-uttama*—O best of devotees; *yat*—because; *nūtanayasi*—you are making newer and newer; *īśasya*—of the Supreme Personality of Godhead; *śṛṇvan api*—although you are continuously hearing; *kathām*—the pastimes; *muhuḥ*—again and again.

## TRANSLATION

**Śrīla Śukadeva Gosvāmī said: O best of devotees, most fortunate Parīkṣit, you have inquired very nicely, for although constantly hearing the pastimes of the Lord, you are perceiving His activities to be newer and newer.**

## PURPORT

Unless one is very advanced in Kṛṣṇa consciousness, one cannot stick to hearing the pastimes of the Lord constantly. *Nityaṁ nava-navāya-mānam:* even though advanced devotees hear continually about the Lord for years, they still feel that these topics are coming to them as newer and fresher. Therefore such devotees cannot give up hearing of the pastimes of Lord Kṛṣṇa. *Premāñjana-cchurita-bhakti-vilocanena santaḥ sadaiva hṛdayeṣu vilokayanti.* The word *santaḥ* is used to refer to persons who have developed love for Kṛṣṇa. *Yaṁ śyāmasundaram acintya-guṇa-svarūpaṁ govindam ādi-puruṣaṁ tam ahaṁ bhajāmi* (*Brahma-saṁhitā* 5.38). Parīkṣit Mahārāja, therefore, is addressed as *bhāgavatottama*, the best of devotees, because unless one is very much elevated in devotional service, one cannot feel ecstasy from hearing more and more and appreciate the topics as ever fresher and newer.

## TEXT 2

सतामयं सारभृतां निसर्गो
यदर्थवाणीश्रुतिचेतसामपि ।
प्रतिक्षणं नव्यवदच्युतस्य यत्
स्त्रिया विटानामिव साधुवार्ता ॥ २ ॥

*satām ayaṁ sāra-bhṛtāṁ nisargo*
*yad-artha-vāṇī-śruti-cetasām api*
*prati-kṣaṇaṁ navya-vad acyutasya yat*
*striyā viṭānām iva sādhu vārtā*

*satām*—of the devotees; *ayam*—this; *sāra-bhṛtām*—those who are *paramahaṁsas*, who have accepted the essence of life; *nisargaḥ*—feature or symptom; *yat*—which; *artha-vāṇī*—the aim of life, the aim of profit; *śruti*—the aim of understanding; *cetasām api*—who have decided to accept the bliss of transcendental subjects as the aim and object of life; *prati-kṣaṇam*—every moment; *navya-vat*—as if newer and newer; *acyutasya*—of Lord Kṛṣṇa; *yat*—because; *striyāḥ*—(topics) of woman or sex; *viṭānām*—of debauchees, who are attached to women; *iva*—exactly like; *sādhu vārtā*—actual conversation.

## TRANSLATION

**Paramahaṁsas, devotees who have accepted the essence of life, are attached to Kṛṣṇa in the core of their hearts, and He is the aim of their lives. It is their nature to talk only of Kṛṣṇa at every**

**moment, as if such topics were newer and newer. They are attached to such topics, just as materialists are attached to topics of women and sex.**

## PURPORT

The word *sāra-bhṛtām* means *paramahaṁsas.* The *haṁsa,* or swan, accepts milk from a mixture of milk and water and rejects the water. Similarly, the nature of persons who have taken to spiritual life and Kṛṣṇa consciousness, understanding Kṛṣṇa to be the life and soul of everyone, is that they cannot give up *kṛṣṇa-kathā,* or topics about Kṛṣṇa, at any moment. Such *paramahaṁsas* always see Kṛṣṇa within the core of the heart (*santaḥ sadaiva hṛdayeṣu vilokayanti*). *Kāma* (desires), *krodha* (anger) and *bhaya* (fear) are always present in the material world, but in the spiritual, or transcendental, world one can use them for Kṛṣṇa. *Kāmaṁ kṛṣṇa-karmārpaṇe.* The desire of the *paramahaṁsas,* therefore, is to act always for Kṛṣṇa. *Krodhaṁ bhakta-dveṣi jane.* They use anger against the nondevotees and transform *bhaya,* or fear, into fear of being deviated from Kṛṣṇa consciousness. In this way, the life of a *paramahaṁsa* devotee is used entirely for Kṛṣṇa, just as the life of a person attached to the material world is used simply for women and money. What is day for the materialistic person is night for the spiritualist. What is very sweet for the materialist—namely women and money—is regarded as poison by the spiritualist.

*sandarśanaṁ viṣayiṇām atha yoṣitāṁ ca*
*ha hanta hanta viṣa-bhakṣaṇato 'py asādhu*

This is the instruction of Caitanya Mahāprabhu. For the *paramahaṁsa,* Kṛṣṇa is everything, but for the materialist, women and money are everything.

## TEXT 3

शृणुष्वावहितो राजन्नपि गुह्यं वदामि ते ।
ब्रूयुः स्निग्धस्य शिष्यस्य गुरवो गुह्यमप्युत ॥ ३ ॥

*śṛṇuṣvāvahito rājann*
*api guhyaṁ vadāmi te*

*brūyuḥ snigdhasya śiṣyasya*
*guravo guhyam apy uta*

*śṛṇuṣva*—please hear; *avahitaḥ*—with great attention; *rājan*—O King (Mahārāja Parīkṣit); *api*—although; *guhyam*—very confidential (because ordinary men cannot understand the activities of Kṛṣṇa); *vadāmi*—I shall explain; *te*—unto you; *brūyuḥ*—explain; *snigdhasya*—submissive; *śiṣyasya*—of a disciple; *guravaḥ*—spiritual masters; *guhyam*—very confidential; *api uta*—even so.

## TRANSLATION

**O King, kindly hear me with great attention. Although the activities of the Supreme Lord are very confidential, no ordinary man being able to understand them, I shall speak about them to you, for spiritual masters explain to a submissive disciple even subject matters that are very confidential and difficult to understand.**

## TEXT 4

तथाघवदनान्मृत्यो रक्षित्वा वत्सपालकान् ।
सरित्पुलिनमानीय भगवानिदमब्रवीत् ॥ ४ ॥

*tathāgha-vadanān mṛtyo*
*rakṣitvā vatsa-pālakān*
*sarit-pulinam ānīya*
*bhagavān idam abravīt*

*tathā*—thereafter; *agha-vadanāt*—from the mouth of Aghāsura; *mṛtyoḥ*—death personified; *rakṣitvā*—after saving; *vatsa-pālakān*—all the cowherd boys and calves; *sarit-pulinam*—to the bank of the river; *ānīya*—bringing them; *bhagavān*—the Supreme Personality of Godhead, Kṛṣṇa; *idam*—these words; *abravīt*—spoke.

## TRANSLATION

**Then, after saving the boys and calves from the mouth of Aghāsura, who was death personified, Lord Kṛṣṇa, the Supreme**

**Personality of Godhead, brought them all to the bank of the river and spoke the following words.**

## TEXT 5

अहोऽतिरम्यं पुलिनं वयस्याः
स्वकेलिसम्पन्मृदुलाच्छबालुकम् ।
स्फुटत्सरोगन्धहृतालिपत्रिक-
ध्वनिप्रतिध्वानलसद्द्रुमाकुलम् ॥ ५ ॥

*aho 'tiramyaṁ pulinaṁ vayasyāḥ*
*sva-keli-sampan mṛdulāccha-bālukam*
*sphuṭat-saro-gandha-hṛtāli-patrika-*
*dhvani-pratidhvāna-lasad-drumākulam*

*aho*—oh; *ati-ramyam*—very, very beautiful; *pulinam*—the bank of the river; *vayasyāḥ*—My dear friends; *sva-keli-sampat*—full with all paraphernalia for pastimes of play; *mṛdula-accha-bālukam*—the very soft and clean sandy bank; *sphuṭat*—in full bloom; *saraḥ-gandha*—by the aroma of the lotus flower; *hṛta*—attracted; *ali*—of the bumblebees; *patrika*—and of the birds; *dhvani-pratidhvāna*—the sounds of their chirping and moving and the echoes of these sounds; *lasat*—moving all over; *druma-ākulam*—full of nice trees.

## TRANSLATION

**My dear friends, just see how this riverbank is extremely beautiful because of its pleasing atmosphere. And just see how the blooming lotuses are attracting bees and birds by their aroma. The humming and chirping of the bees and birds is echoing throughout the beautiful trees in the forest. Also, here the sands are clean and soft. Therefore, this must be considered the best place for our sporting and pastimes.**

## PURPORT

The description of Vṛndāvana forest as given herewith was spoken by Kṛṣṇa five thousand years ago, and the same condition prevailed during the time of the Vaiṣṇava *ācāryas* three or four hundred years ago. *Kūjat-kokila-haṁsa-sārasa-gaṇākīrṇe mayūrākule.* Vṛndāvana forest is always filled with the chirping and cooing of birds like cuckoos (*kokila*), ducks (*haṁsa*) and cranes (*sārasa*), and it is also full of peacocks (*mayūrākule*). The same sounds and atmosphere still prevail in the area where our Kṛṣṇa-Balarāma temple is situated. Everyone who visits this temple is pleased to hear the chirping of the birds as described here (*kū-jat-kokila-haṁsa-sārasa*).

## TEXT 6

अत्र भोक्तव्यमस्माभिर्दिवारूढं क्षुधार्दिताः ।
वत्साः समीपेऽपः पीत्वा चरन्तु शनकैस्तृणम् ॥६॥

*atra bhoktavyam asmābhir*
*divārūḍhaṁ kṣudhārditāḥ*
*vatsāḥ samīpe 'paḥ pītvā*
*carantu śanakais tṛṇam*

*atra*—here, on this spot; *bhoktavyam*—our lunch should be eaten; *asmābhiḥ*—by us; *diva-ārūḍham*—it is very late now; *kṣudhā arditāḥ*—we are fatigued with hunger; *vatsāḥ*—the calves; *samīpe*—nearby; *apaḥ*—water; *pītvā*—after drinking; *carantu*—let them eat; *śanakaiḥ*—slowly; *tṛṇam*—the grasses.

## TRANSLATION

**I think we should take our lunch here, since we are already hungry because the time is very late. Here the calves may drink water and go slowly here and there and eat the grass.**

## TEXT 7

तथेति पाययित्वार्भा वत्सानारुध्य शाद्वले ।
मुक्त्वा शिक्यानि बुभुजुः समं भगवता मुदा ॥ ७ ॥

*tatheti pāyayitvārbhā*
*vatsān ārudhya śādvale*

*muktvā śikyāni bubhujuḥ*
*samaṁ bhagavatā mudā*

*tathā iti*—as Kṛṣṇa proposed, the other cowherd boys agreed; *pāyayitvā arbhāḥ*—they allowed to drink water; *vatsān*—the calves; *ārudhya*—tying them to the trees, allowed them to eat; *śādvale*—in a place of green, tender grasses; *muktvā*—opening; *śikyāni*—their bags of eatables and other paraphernalia; *bubhujuḥ*—went and enjoyed; *samam*—equally; *bhagavatā*—with the Supreme Personality of Godhead; *mudā*—in transcendental pleasure.

## TRANSLATION

**Accepting Lord Kṛṣṇa's proposal, the cowherd boys allowed the calves to drink water from the river and then tied them to trees where there was green, tender grass. Then the boys opened their baskets of food and began eating with Kṛṣṇa in great transcendental pleasure.**

## TEXT 8

कृष्णस्य विष्वक् पुरुराजिमण्डलै-
रम्याननाः फुल्लदृशो व्रजार्भकाः ।
सहोपविष्टा विपिने विरेजु-
श्छदा यथाम्भोरुहकर्णिकायाः ॥ ८ ॥

*kṛṣṇasya viṣvak puru-rāji-maṇḍalair*
*abhyānanāḥ phulla-dṛśo vrajārbhakāḥ*
*sahopaviṣṭā vipine virejuś*
*chadā yathāmbhoruha-karṇikāyāḥ*

*kṛṣṇasya viṣvak*—surrounding Kṛṣṇa; *puru-rāji-maṇḍalaiḥ*—by different encirclements of associates; *abhyānanāḥ*—everyone looking forward to the center, where Kṛṣṇa was sitting; *phulla-dṛśaḥ*—their faces looking very bright because of transcendental pleasure; *vraja-arbhakāḥ*—all the cowherd boys of Vrajabhūmi; *saha-upaviṣṭāḥ*—sitting with Kṛṣṇa; *vipine*—in the forest; *virejuḥ*—so nicely and beautifully made; *chadāḥ*—petals and leaves; *yathā*—just as; *ambho-ruha*—of a lotus flower; *karṇikāyāḥ*—of the whorl.

## TRANSLATION

**Like the whorl of a lotus flower surrounded by its petals and leaves, Kṛṣṇa sat in the center, encircled by lines of His friends, who all looked very beautiful. Every one of them was trying to look forward toward Kṛṣṇa, thinking that Kṛṣṇa might look toward him. In this way they all enjoyed their lunch in the forest.**

## PURPORT

To a pure devotee, Kṛṣṇa is always visible, as stated in the *Brahma-saṁhitā* (*santaḥ sadaiva hṛdayeṣu vilokayanti*) and as indicated by Kṛṣṇa Himself in *Bhagavad-gītā* (*sarvataḥ pāṇi-pādaṁ tat sarvato 'kṣi-śiro-mukham*). If by accumulating pious activities (*kṛta-puṇya-puñjāḥ*) one is raised to the platform of pure devotional service, Kṛṣṇa is always visible in the core of one's heart. One who has attained such perfection is all-beautiful in transcendental bliss. The present Kṛṣṇa consciousness movement is an attempt to keep Kṛṣṇa in the center, for if this is done all activities will automatically become beautiful and blissful.

## TEXT 9

केचित् पुष्पैर्दलैः केचित् पल्लवैरङ्कुरैः फलैः ।
शिग्भिस्त्वग्भिर्दृषद्भिश्च बुभुजुः कृतभाजनाः ॥ ९ ॥

*kecit puṣpair dalaiḥ kecit*
*pallavair aṅkuraiḥ phalaiḥ*
*śigbhis tvagbhir dṛṣadbhiś ca*
*bubhujuḥ kṛta-bhājanāḥ*

*kecit*—someone; *puṣpaiḥ*—by flowers; *dalaiḥ*—by nice leaves of flowers; *kecit*—someone; *pallavaiḥ*—on the surface of bunches of leaves; *aṅkuraiḥ*—on the sprouts of flowers; *phalaiḥ*—and some on fruits; *śigbhiḥ*—some actually in the basket or packet; *tvagbhiḥ*—by the bark of trees; *dṛṣadbhiḥ*—on rocks; *ca*—and; *bubhujuḥ*—enjoyed; *kṛta-bhājanāḥ*—as if they had made their plates for eating.

### TRANSLATION

**Among the cowherd boys, some placed their lunch on flowers, some on leaves, fruits, or bunches of leaves, some actually in their baskets, some on the bark of trees and some on rocks. This is what the children imagined to be their plates as they ate their lunch.**

### TEXT 10

सर्वे मिथो दर्शयन्तः स्वस्वभोज्यरुचिं पृथक् ।
हसन्तो हासयन्तश्चाभ्यवजह्रुः सहेश्वराः ॥१०॥

*sarve mitho darśayantaḥ*
*sva-sva-bhojya-rucim̐ pṛthak*
*hasanto hāsayantaś cā-*
*bhyavajahruḥ saheśvarāḥ*

*sarve*—all the cowherd boys; *mithaḥ*—to one another; *darśayantaḥ*—showing; *sva-sva-bhojya-rucim pṛthak*—different varieties of foodstuffs brought from home, with their separate and different tastes; *hasantaḥ*—after tasting, they were all laughing; *hāsayantaḥ ca*—and making others laugh; *abhyavajahruḥ*—enjoyed lunch; *saha-īśvarāḥ*—along with Kṛṣṇa.

### TRANSLATION

**All the cowherd boys enjoyed their lunch with Kṛṣṇa, showing one another the different tastes of the different varieties of preparations they had brought from home. Tasting one another's preparations, they began to laugh and make one another laugh.**

### PURPORT

Sometimes one friend would say, "Kṛṣṇa, see how my food is relishable," and Kṛṣṇa would take some and laugh. Similarly, Balarāma, Sudāmā and other friends would taste one another's food and laugh. In this way, the friends very jubilantly began to eat their respective preparations brought from home.

## TEXT 11

बिभ्रद् वेणुं जठरपटयोः शृङ्गवेत्रे च कक्षे
वामे पाणौ मसृणकवलं तत्फलान्यङ्गुलीषु ।
तिष्ठन् मध्ये स्वपरिसुहृदो हासयन् नर्मभिः स्वैः
स्वर्गे लोके मिषति बुभुजे यज्ञभुग् बालकेलिः ॥११॥

*bibhrad veṇuṁ jaṭhara-paṭayoḥ śṛṅga-vetre ca kakṣe*
*vāme pāṇau masṛṇa-kavalaṁ tat-phalāny aṅguliṣu*
*tiṣṭhan madhye sva-parisuhṛdo hāsayan narmabhiḥ svaiḥ*
*svarge loke miṣati bubhuje yajña-bhug bāla-keliḥ*

*bibhrat veṇum*—keeping the flute; *jaṭhara-paṭayoḥ*—between the tight clothing and the abdomen; *śṛṅga-vetre*—both the horn bugle and the cow-driving stick; *ca*—also; *kakṣe*—on the waist; *vāme*—on the left-hand side; *pāṇau*—taking in hand; *masṛṇa-kavalam*—very nice food prepared with rice and first-class curd; *tat-phalāni*—suitable pieces of fruit like bael; *aṅguliṣu*—between the fingers; *tiṣṭhan*—staying in this way; *madhye*—in the middle; *sva-pari-suhṛdaḥ*—His own personal associates; *hāsayan*—making them laugh; *narmabhiḥ*—with joking words; *svaiḥ*—His own; *svarge loke miṣati*—while the inhabitants of the heavenly planets, Svargaloka, were watching this wonderful scene; *bubhuje*—Kṛṣṇa enjoyed; *yajña-bhuk bāla-keliḥ*—although He accepts offerings in *yajña*, for the sake of childhood pastimes He was enjoying foodstuffs very jubilantly with His cowherd boyfriends.

## TRANSLATION

**Kṛṣṇa is yajña-bhuk—that is, He eats only offerings of yajña—but to exhibit His childhood pastimes, He now sat with His flute tucked between His waist and His tight cloth on His right side and with His horn bugle and cow-driving stick on His left. Holding in His hand a very nice preparation of yogurt and rice, with pieces of suitable fruit between His fingers, He sat like the whorl of a lotus flower, looking forward toward all His friends, personally joking with them and creating jubilant laughter among them as He ate. At**

**that time, the denizens of heaven were watching, struck with wonder at how the Personality of Godhead, who eats only in yajña, was now eating with His friends in the forest.**

## PURPORT

When Kṛṣṇa was eating with His cowherd boyfriends, a certain bumblebee came there to take part in the eating. Thus Kṛṣṇa joked, "Why have you come to disturb My *brāhmaṇa* friend Madhumaṅgala? You want to kill a *brāhmaṇa.* This is not good." All the boys would laugh and enjoy, speaking such joking words while eating. Thus the inhabitants of the higher planets were astonished at how the Supreme Personality of Godhead, who eats only when *yajña* is offered, was now eating like an ordinary child with His friends in the forest.

## TEXT 12

भारतैवं वत्सपेषु भुञ्जानेष्वच्युतात्मसु ।
वत्सास्त्वन्तर्वने दूरं विविशुस्तृणलोभिताः ॥१२॥

*bhārataivaṁ vatsa-peṣu*
*bhuñjāneṣv acyutātmasu*
*vatsās tv antar-vane dūraṁ*
*viviśus tṛṇa-lobhitāḥ*

*bhārata*—O Mahārāja Parīkṣit; *evam*—in this way (while they were enjoying their lunch); *vatsa-peṣu*—along with all the boys tending the calves; *bhuñjāneṣu*—engaged in taking their food; *acyuta-ātmasu*—all of them being very near and dear to Acyuta, Kṛṣṇa; *vatsāḥ*—the calves; *tu*—however; *antaḥ-vane*—within the deep forest; *dūram*—far away; *viviśuḥ*—entered; *tṛṇa-lobhitāḥ*—being allured by green grass.

## TRANSLATION

**O Mahārāja Parīkṣit, while the cowherd boys, who knew nothing within the core of their hearts but Kṛṣṇa, were thus engaged in eating their lunch in the forest, the calves went far away, deep into the forest, being allured by green grass.**

## TEXT 13

तान् दृष्ट्वा भयसंत्रस्तानूचे कृष्णोऽस्य भीभयम् ।
मित्राण्याशान्मा विरमतेहानेष्ये वत्सकानहम् ॥१३॥

*tān dṛṣṭvā bhaya-santrastān*
*ūce kṛṣṇo 'sya bhī-bhayam*
*mitrāṇy āśān mā viramate-*
*hāneṣye vatsakān aham*

*tān*—that those calves were going away; *dṛṣṭvā*—seeing; *bhaya-santrastān*—to the cowherd boys, who were disturbed by fear that within the dense forest the calves would be attacked by some ferocious animals; *ūce*—Kṛṣṇa said; *kṛṣṇaḥ asya bhī-bhayam*—Kṛṣṇa, who is Himself the fearful element of all kinds of fear (when Kṛṣṇa is present, there is no fear); *mitrāṇi*—My dear friends; *āśāt*—from your enjoyment of eating; *mā viramata*—do not stop; *iha*—in this place, in this spot; *āneṣye*—I shall bring back; *vatsakān*—the calves; *aham*—I.

## TRANSLATION

**When Kṛṣṇa saw that His friends the cowherd boys were frightened, He, the fierce controller even of fear itself, said, just to mitigate their fear, "My dear friends, do not stop eating. I shall bring your calves back to this spot by personally going after them Myself."**

## PURPORT

In the presence of Kṛṣṇa's friendship, a devotee cannot have any fear. Kṛṣṇa is the supreme controller, the controller of even death, which is supposed to be the ultimate fear in this material world. *Bhayaṁ dvitīyābhiniveśataḥ syāt* (*Bhāg.* 11.2.37). This fear arises because of lack of Kṛṣṇa consciousness; otherwise there cannot be any fear. For one who has taken shelter of the lotus feet of Kṛṣṇa, this material world of fear becomes hardly dangerous at all.

*bhavāmbudhir vatsa-padaṁ paraṁ padaṁ*
*padaṁ padaṁ yad vipadāṁ na teṣām*

*Bhavāmbudhiḥ*, the material ocean of fear, becomes very easy to cross by the mercy of the supreme controller. This material world, in which there is fear and danger at every step (*padaṁ padaṁ yad vipadām*), is not meant for those who have taken shelter at Kṛṣṇa's lotus feet. Such persons are delivered from this fearful world.

*samāśritā ye pada-pallava-plavaṁ*
*mahat-padaṁ puṇya-yaśo murāreḥ*
*bhavāmbudhir vatsa-padaṁ paraṁ padaṁ*
*padaṁ padaṁ yad vipadāṁ na teṣām*
(*Bhāg.* 10.14.58)

Everyone, therefore, should take shelter of the Supreme Person, who is the source of fearlessness, and thus be secure.

### TEXT 14

इत्युक्त्वाद्रिदरीकुञ्जगह्वरेष्वात्मवत्सकान् ।
विचिन्वन् भगवान् कृष्णः सपाणिकवलो ययौ ॥१४॥

*ity uktvādri-darī-kuñja-*
*gahvareṣv ātma-vatsakān*
*vicinvan bhagavān kṛṣṇaḥ*
*sapāṇi-kavalo yayau*

*iti uktvā*—saying this ("Let Me bring your calves personally"); *adri-darī-kuñja-gahvareṣu*—everywhere in the mountains, the mountain caves, the bushes and narrow places; *ātma-vatsakān*—the calves belonging to His own personal friends; *vicinvan*—searching out; *bhagavān*—the Supreme Personality of Godhead; *kṛṣṇaḥ*—Lord Kṛṣṇa; *sa-pāṇi-kavalaḥ*—carrying His yogurt and rice in His hand; *yayau*—started out.

### TRANSLATION

**"Let Me go and search for the calves," Kṛṣṇa said. "Don't disturb your enjoyment." Then, carrying His yogurt and rice in His hand, the Supreme Personality of Godhead, Kṛṣṇa, immediately went out to search for the calves of His friends. To please His**

**friends, He began searching in all the mountains, mountain caves, bushes and narrow passages.**

## PURPORT

The *Vedas* (*Śvetāśvatara Up.* 6.8) assert that the Supreme Personality of Godhead has nothing to do personally (*na tasya kāryaṁ karaṇaṁ ca vidyate*) because He is doing everything through His energies and potencies (*parāsya śaktir vividhaiva śrūyate*). Nonetheless, here we see that He took personal care to find the calves of His friends. This was Kṛṣṇa's causeless mercy. *Mayādhyakṣeṇa prakṛtiḥ sūyate sa-carācaram:* all the affairs of the entire world and the entire cosmic manifestation are working under His direction, through His different energies. Still, when there is a need to take care of His friends, He does this personally. Kṛṣṇa assured His friends, "Don't be afraid. I am going personally to search for your calves." This was Kṛṣṇa's causeless mercy.

## TEXT 15

अम्भोजन्मजनिस्तदन्तरगतो मायार्भकस्येशितु-
र्द्रष्टुं मञ्जु महित्वमन्यदपि तद्वत्सानितो वत्सपान् ।
नीत्वान्यत्र कुरूद्वहान्तरदधात् खेऽवस्थितो यः पुरा
दृष्ट्वाघासुरमोक्षणं प्रभवतः प्राप्तः परं विस्मयम्॥१५॥

*ambhojanma-janis tad-antara-gato māyārbhakasyeśitur*
*draṣṭuṁ mañju mahitvam anyad api tad-vatsān ito vatsapān*
*nītvānyatra kurūdvahāntaradadhāt khe 'vasthito yaḥ purā*
*dṛṣṭvāghāsura-mokṣaṇaṁ prabhavataḥ prāptaḥ paraṁ vismayam*

*ambhojanma-janiḥ*—Lord Brahmā, who was born from a lotus flower; *tat-antara-gataḥ*—now became entangled with the affairs of Kṛṣṇa, who was enjoying luncheon pastimes with His cowherd boys; *māyā-arbhakasya*—of the boys made by Kṛṣṇa's *māyā; īśituḥ*—of the supreme controller; *draṣṭum*—just to see; *mañju*—very pleasing; *mahitvam anyat api*—other glories of the Lord also; *tat-vatsān*—their calves; *itaḥ*—than that place where they were; *vatsa-pān*—and the cowherd boys taking care of the calves; *nītvā*—bringing them; *anyatra*—to a different place; *kurūdvaha*—O Mahārāja Parīkṣit; *antaradadhāt*—kept hidden and invisible for some time; *khe avasthitaḥ yaḥ*—this person Brahmā, who was situated in the higher planetary system in the sky; *purā*—formerly; *dṛṣṭvā*—was observing; *aghāsura-mokṣaṇam*—the wonderful killing and deliverance of Aghāsura from material tribulation; *prabhavataḥ*—of the all-potent Supreme Person; *prāptaḥ param vismayam*—had become extremely astonished.

## TRANSLATION

**O Mahārāja Parīkṣit, Brahmā, who resides in the higher planetary system in the sky, had observed the activities of the most powerful Kṛṣṇa in killing and delivering Aghāsura, and he was astonished. Now that same Brahmā wanted to show some of his own power and see the power of Kṛṣṇa, who was engaged in His childhood pastimes, playing as if with ordinary cowherd boys. Therefore, in Kṛṣṇa's absence, Brahmā took all the boys and calves to another place. Thus he became entangled, for in the very near future he would see how powerful Kṛṣṇa was.**

## PURPORT

When Aghāsura was being killed by Kṛṣṇa, who was accompanied by His associates, Brahmā was astonished, but when he saw that Kṛṣṇa was very much enjoying His pastimes of lunch, he was even more astonished and wanted to test whether Kṛṣṇa was actually there. Thus he became entangled in Kṛṣṇa's *māyā*. After all, Brahmā was born materially. As mentioned here, *ambhojanma-janiḥ:* he was born of *ambhoja*, a lotus flower. It does not matter that he was born of a lotus and not of any man, animal or material father. A lotus is also material, and anyone born through the material energy must be subject to the four material deficiencies: *bhrama* (the tendency to commit mistakes), *pramāda* (the tendency to be illusioned), *vipralipsā* (the tendency to cheat) and *karaṇāpāṭava* (imperfect senses). Thus Brahmā also became entangled.

Brahmā, with his *māyā*, wanted to test whether Kṛṣṇa was actually present. These cowherd boys were but expansions of Kṛṣṇa's personal self (*ānanda-cinmaya-rasa-pratibhāvitābhiḥ*). Later Kṛṣṇa would show Brahmā how He expands Himself into everything as His personal pleasure, *ānanda-cinmaya-rasa. Hlādinī śaktir asmāt:* Kṛṣṇa has a transcendental potency called *hlādinī śakti.* He does not enjoy anything that is a product of the material energy. Brahmā, therefore, would see Lord Kṛṣṇa expand His energy.

Brahmā wanted to take away Kṛṣṇa's associates, but instead he took away some other boys and calves. Rāvaṇa wanted to take away Sītā, but that was impossible, and instead he took away a *māyā* Sītā. Similarly, Brahmā took away *māyārbhakāḥ:* boys manifested by Kṛṣṇa's *māyā.* Brahmā could show some extraordinary opulence to the *māyārbhakāḥ;* but he could not show any extraordinary potency to Kṛṣṇa's associates. That he would see in the very near future. *Māyārbhakasya īśituḥ.* This bewilderment, this *māyā,* was caused by the supreme controller, *prabhavataḥ*—the all-potent Supreme Person, Kṛṣṇa—and we shall see the result. Anyone materially born is subject to bewilderment. This pastime is therefore called *brahma-vimohana-līlā,* the pastime of bewildering Brahmā. *Mohitaṁ nābhijānāti mām ebhyaḥ param avyayam* (Bg. 7.13). Materially born persons cannot fully understand Kṛṣṇa. Even the demigods cannot understand Him (*muhyanti yat sūrayaḥ*). *Tene brahmā hṛdā ya ādi-kavaye* (*Bhāg.* 1.1.1). Everyone, from Brahmā down to the small insect, must take lessons from Kṛṣṇa.

## TEXT 16

ततो वत्सानदृष्ट्वैत्य पुलिनेऽपि च वत्सपान् ।
उभावपि वने कृष्णो विचिकाय समन्ततः ॥१६॥

*tato vatsān adṛṣṭvaitya*
*puline 'pi ca vatsapān*
*ubhāv api vane kṛṣṇo*
*vicikāya samantataḥ*

*tataḥ*—thereafter; *vatsān*—the calves; *adṛṣṭvā*—not seeing there within the forest; *etya*—after; *puline api*—to the bank of the Yamunā; *ca*—also; *vatsapān*—could not see the cowherd boys; *ubhau api*—both of them (the calves and the cowherd boys); *vane*—within the forest; *kṛṣṇaḥ*—Lord Kṛṣṇa; *vicikāya*—searched all over; *samantataḥ*—here and there.

## TRANSLATION

**Thereafter, when Kṛṣṇa was unable to find the calves, He returned to the bank of the river, but there He was also unable to see the cowherd boys. Thus He began to search for both the calves and the boys, as if He could not understand what had happened.**

## PURPORT

Kṛṣṇa could immediately understand that Brahmā had taken away both the calves and the boys, but as an innocent child He searched here and there so that Brahmā could not understand Kṛṣṇa's *māyā*. This was all a dramatic performance. A player knows everything, but still he plays on the stage in such a way that others do not understand him.

## TEXT 17

क्वाप्यदृष्ट्वान्तर्विपिने वत्सान् पालांश्च विश्ववित् ।
सर्वं विधिकृतं कृष्णः सहसावजगाम ह ॥१७॥

*kvāpy adṛṣṭvāntar-vipine*
*vatsān pālāṁś ca viśva-vit*
*sarvaṁ vidhi-kṛtaṁ kṛṣṇaḥ*
*sahasāvajagāma ha*

*kva api*—anywhere; *adṛṣṭvā*—not seeing at all; *antaḥ-vipine*—within the forest; *vatsān*—the calves; *pālān ca*—and their caretakers, the cowherd boys; *viśva-vit*—Kṛṣṇa, who is aware of everything going on throughout the whole cosmic manifestation; *sarvam*—everything; *vidhi-kṛtam*—was executed by Brahmā; *kṛṣṇaḥ*—Lord Kṛṣṇa; *sahasā*—immediately; *avajagāma ha*—could understand.

## TRANSLATION

**When Kṛṣṇa was unable to find the calves and their caretakers, the cowherd boys, anywhere in the forest, He could suddenly understand that this was the work of Lord Brahmā.**

## PURPORT

Although Kṛṣṇa is *viśva-vit*, the knower of everything happening in the entire cosmic manifestation, as an innocent child He showed ignorance of Brahmā's actions, although He could immediately understand that these were the doings of Brahmā. This pastime is called *brahma-vimohana*, the bewilderment of Brahmā. Brahmā was already bewildered by Kṛṣṇa's activities as an innocent child, and now he would be further bewildered.

## TEXT 18

ततः कृष्णो मुदं कर्तुं तन्मातॄणां च कस्य च ।
उभयायितमात्मानं चक्रे विश्वकृदीश्वरः ॥१८॥

*tataḥ kṛṣṇo mudaṁ kartuṁ*
*tan-mātṝṇāṁ ca kasya ca*
*ubhayāyitam ātmānaṁ*
*cakre viśva-kṛd īśvaraḥ*

*tataḥ*—thereafter; *kṛṣṇaḥ*—the Supreme Personality of Godhead; *mudam*—pleasure; *kartum*—to create; *tat-mātṝṇām ca*—of the mothers of the cowherd boys and calves; *kasya ca*—and (the pleasure) of Brahmā; *ubhayāyitam*—expansion, both as the calves and as the cowherd boys; *ātmānam*—Himself; *cakre*—did; *viśva-kṛt īśvaraḥ*—it was not difficult for Him, for He is the creator of the whole cosmic manifestation.

## TRANSLATION

**Thereafter, just to create pleasure both for Brahmā and for the mothers of the calves and cowherd boys, Kṛṣṇa, the creator of the entire cosmic manifestation, expanded Himself as calves and boys.**

## PURPORT

Although Brahmā was already entangled in bewilderment, he wanted to show his power to the cowherd boys; but after he took away the boys and their calves and returned to his abode, Kṛṣṇa created further astonishment for Brahmā, and for the mothers of the boys, by establishing the lunch pastimes in the forest again and replacing all the calves and boys, just as they had appeared before. According to the *Vedas, ekaṁ bahu syām:* the Personality of Godhead can become many, many millions upon millions of calves and cowherd boys, as He did to bewilder Brahmā more and more.

## TEXT 19

यावद् वत्सपवत्सकाल्पकवपुर्यावत् कराङ्घ्र्यादिकं
यावद् यष्टिविषाणवेणुदलशिग् यावद् विभूषाम्बरम् ।
यावच्छीलगुणाभिधाकृतिवयो यावद् विहारादिकं
सर्वं विष्णुमयं गिरोऽङ्गवदजः सर्वस्वरूपो बभौ ॥१९॥

*yāvad vatsapa-vatsakālpaka-vapur yāvat karāṅghry-ādikaṁ*
*yāvad yaṣṭi-viṣāṇa-veṇu-dala-śig yāvad vibhūṣāmbaram*
*yāvac chīla-guṇābhidhākṛti-vayo yāvad vihārādikaṁ*
*sarvaṁ viṣṇumayaṁ giro 'ṅga-vad ajaḥ sarva-svarūpo babhau*

*yāvat vatsapa*—exactly like the cowherd boys; *vatsaka-alpaka-vapuḥ*—and exactly like the tender bodies of the calves; *yāvat kara-aṅghri-ādikam*—exactly to the measurement of their particular varieties of legs and hands; *yāvat yaṣṭi-viṣāṇa-veṇu-dala-śik*—not only like their bodies but exactly like their bugles, flutes, sticks, lunch bags and so on; *yāvat vibhūṣā-ambaram*—exactly like their ornaments and dress in all their varied particulars; *yāvat śīla-guṇa-abhidhā-ākṛti-vayaḥ*—their exact character, habits, features, attributes and explicit bodily features; *yāvat vihāra-ādikam*—exactly according to their tastes or amusements; *sarvam*—everything in detail; *viṣṇu-mayam*—expansions of Vāsudeva, Viṣṇu; *giraḥ aṅga-vat*—voices exactly like theirs; *ajaḥ*—Kṛṣṇa; *sarva-svarūpaḥ babhau*—created everything in detail as Himself, without any change.

## TRANSLATION

**By His Vāsudeva feature, Kṛṣṇa simultaneously expanded Himself into the exact number of missing cowherd boys and calves,**

**with their exact bodily features, their particular types of hands, legs and other limbs, their sticks, bugles and flutes, their lunch bags, their particular types of dress and ornaments placed in various ways, their names, ages and forms, and their special activities and characteristics. By expanding Himself in this way, beautiful Kṛṣṇa proved the statement samagra-jagad viṣṇumayam: "Lord Viṣṇu is all-pervading."**

## PURPORT

As stated in the *Brahma-saṁhitā* (5.33):

*advaitam acyutam anādim ananta-rūpam*
*ādyam purāṇa-puruṣaṁ nava-yauvanaṁ ca*

Kṛṣṇa, *paraṁ brahma,* the Supreme Personality of Godhead, is *ādyam,* the beginning of everything; He is *ādi-puruṣam,* the ever-youthful original person. He can expand Himself in more forms than one can imagine, yet He does not fall down from His original form as Kṛṣṇa; therefore He is called Acyuta. This is the Supreme Personality of Godhead. *Sarvaṁ viṣṇumayaṁ jagat. Sarvaṁ khalv idaṁ brahma.* Kṛṣṇa thus proved that He is everything, that He can become everything, but that still He is personally different from everything (*mat-sthāni sarva-bhūtāni na cāhaṁ teṣv avasthitaḥ*). This is Kṛṣṇa, who is understood by *acintya-bhedābheda-tattva* philosophy. *Pūrṇasya pūrṇam ādāya pūrṇam evāvaśiṣyate:* Kṛṣṇa is always complete, and although He can create millions of universes, all of them full in all opulences, He remains as opulent as ever, without any change (*advaitam*). This is explained by different Vaiṣṇava *ācāryas* through philosophies such as *viśuddhādvaita, viśiṣṭādvaita* and *dvaitādvaita.* Therefore one must learn about Kṛṣṇa from the *ācāryas. Ācāryavān puruṣo veda:* one who follows the path of the *ācāryas* knows things as they are. Such a person can know Kṛṣṇa as He is, at least to some extent, and as soon as one understands Kṛṣṇa (*janma karma ca me divyam evaṁ yo vetti tattvataḥ*), one is liberated from material bondage (*tyaktvā dehaṁ punar janma naiti mām eti so 'rjuna*).

## TEXT 20

स्वयमात्मात्मगोवत्सान् प्रतिवार्यात्मवत्सपैः ।
क्रीडन्नात्मविहारैश्च सर्वात्मा प्राविशद् व्रजम् ॥२०॥

*svayam ātmātma-govatsān*
*prativāryātma-vatsapaiḥ*
*krīḍann ātma-vihāraiś ca*
*sarvātmā prāviśad vrajam*

*svayam ātmā*—Kṛṣṇa, who is personally the Supreme Soul, the Supersoul; *ātma-go-vatsān*—now expanded into calves that were also He Himself; *prativārya ātma-vatsapaiḥ*—again He Himself was represented as the cowherd boys controlling and commanding the calves; *krīḍan*—thus Himself constituting everything in these transcendental pastimes; *ātma-vihāraiḥ ca*—enjoying Himself by Himself in different ways; *sarva-ātmā*—the Supersoul, Kṛṣṇa; *prāviśat*—entered; *vrajam*—Vrajabhūmi, the land of Mahārāja Nanda and Yaśodā.

## TRANSLATION

**Now expanding Himself so as to appear as all the calves and cowherd boys, all of them as they were, and at the same time appear as their leader, Kṛṣṇa entered Vrajabhūmi, the land of His father, Nanda Mahārāja, just as He usually did while enjoying their company.**

## PURPORT

Kṛṣṇa usually stayed in the forest and pasturing ground, taking care of the calves and cows with His associates the cowherd boys. Now that the original group had been taken away by Brahmā, Kṛṣṇa Himself assumed the forms of every member of the group, without anyone's knowledge, even the knowledge of Baladeva, and continued the usual program. He was ordering His friends to do this and that, and He was controlling the calves and going into the forest to search for them when they went astray, allured by new grass, but these calves and boys were He Himself. This was Kṛṣṇa's inconceivable potency. As explained by Śrīla Jīva Gosvāmī, *rādhā kṛṣṇa-praṇaya-vikṛtir hlādinī śaktir asmāt.* Rādhā and

Kṛṣṇa are the same. Kṛṣṇa, by expanding His pleasure potency, becomes Rādhārāṇī. The same pleasure potency (*ānanda-cinmaya-rasa*) was expanded by Kṛṣṇa when He Himself became all the calves and boys and enjoyed transcendental bliss in Vrajabhūmi. This was done by the *yogamāyā* potency and was inconceivable to persons under the potency of *mahāmāyā*.

### TEXT 21

तत्तद्वत्सान् पृथङ् नीत्वा तत्तद् गोष्ठे निवेश्य सः ।
तत्तदात्माभवद् राजंस्तत्तत्सद्म प्रविष्टवान् ॥२१॥

*tat-tad-vatsān pṛthaṅ nītvā*
*tat-tad-goṣṭhe niveśya saḥ*
*tat-tad-ātmābhavad rājaṁs*
*tat-tat-sadma praviṣṭavān*

*tat-tat-vatsān*—the calves, which belonged to different cows; *pṛthak*—separately; *nītvā*—bringing; *tat-tat-goṣṭhe*—to their respective cow sheds; *niveśya*—entering; *saḥ*—Kṛṣṇa; *tat-tat-ātmā*—as originally different individual souls; *abhavat*—He expanded Himself in that way; *rājan*—O King Parīkṣit; *tat-tat-sadma*—their respective houses; *praviṣṭavān*—entered (Kṛṣṇa thus entered everywhere).

### TRANSLATION

**O Mahārāja Parīkṣit, Kṛṣṇa, who had divided Himself as different calves and also as different cowherd boys, entered different cow sheds as the calves and then different homes as different boys.**

### PURPORT

Kṛṣṇa had many, many friends, of whom Śrīdāmā, Sudāmā and Subala were prominent. Thus Kṛṣṇa Himself became Śrīdāmā, Sudāmā and Subala and entered their respective houses with their respective calves.

### TEXT 22

तन्मातरो वेणुरवत्वरोत्थिता
उत्थाप्य दोर्भिः परिरभ्य निर्भरम् ।

स्नेहस्नुतस्तन्यपयःसुधासवं
मत्वा परं ब्रह्म सुतानपाययन् ॥२२॥

*tan-mātaro veṇu-rava-tvarotthitā*
*utthāpya dorbhiḥ parirabhya nirbharam*
*sneha-snuta-stanya-payaḥ-sudhāsavaṁ*
*matvā paraṁ brahma sutān apāyayan*

*tat-mātaraḥ*—the mothers of the respective cowherd boys; *veṇu-rava*—because of the sounds played on flutes and bugles by the cowherd boys; *tvara*—immediately; *utthitāḥ*—awakened from their respective household duties; *utthāpya*—immediately lifted their respective sons; *dorbhiḥ*—with their two arms; *parirabhya*—embracing; *nirbharam*—without feeling any weight; *sneha-snuta*—which was flowing because of intense love; *stanya-payaḥ*—their breast milk; *sudhā-āsavam*—tasting just like a nectarean beverage; *matvā*—accepting the milk like that; *param*—the Supreme; *brahma*—Kṛṣṇa; *sutān apāyayan*—began to feed their respective sons.

## TRANSLATION

**The mothers of the boys, upon hearing the sounds of the flutes and bugles being played by their sons, immediately rose from their household tasks, lifted their boys onto their laps, embraced them with both arms and began to feed them with their breast milk, which flowed forth because of extreme love specifically for Kṛṣṇa. Actually Kṛṣṇa is everything, but at that time, expressing extreme love and affection, they took special pleasure in feeding Kṛṣṇa, the Parabrahman, and Kṛṣṇa drank the milk from His respective mothers as if it were a nectarean beverage.**

## PURPORT

Although all the elderly *gopīs* knew that Kṛṣṇa was the son of mother Yaśodā, they still desired, "If Kṛṣṇa had become my son, I would also have taken care of Him like mother Yaśodā." This was their inner ambition. Now, in order to please them, Kṛṣṇa personally took the role of their sons and fulfilled their desire. They enhanced their special love for

Kṛṣṇa by embracing Him and feeding Him, and Kṛṣṇa tasted their breast milk to be just like a nectarean beverage. While thus bewildering Brahmā, He enjoyed the special transcendental pleasure created by *yogamāyā* between all the other mothers and Himself.

## TEXT 23

ततो नृपोन्मर्दनमज्जलेपना-
लङ्कारक्षातिलकाशनादिभिः ।
संलालितः स्वाचरितैः प्रहर्षयन्
सायं गतो यामयमेन माधवः ॥२३॥

*tato nṛponmardana-majja-lepanā-*
*laṅkāra-rakṣā-tilakāśanādibhiḥ*
*saṁlālitaḥ svācaritaiḥ praharṣayan*
*sāyaṁ gato yāma-yamena mādhavaḥ*

*tataḥ*—thereafter; *nṛpa*—O King (Mahārāja Parīkṣit); *unmardana*—by massaging them with oil; *majja*—by bathing; *lepana*—by smearing the body with oil and sandalwood pulp; *alaṅkāra*—by decorating with ornaments; *rakṣā*—by chanting protective *mantras; tilaka*—by decorating the body with *tilaka* marks in twelve places; *aśana-ādibhiḥ*—and by feeding them sumptuously; *saṁlālitaḥ*—in this way cared for by the mothers; *sva-ācaritaiḥ*—by their characteristic behavior; *praharṣayan*—making the mothers very much pleased; *sāyam*—evening; *gataḥ*—arrived; *yāma-yamena*—as the time of each activity passed; *mādhavaḥ*—Lord Kṛṣṇa.

## TRANSLATION

**Thereafter, O Mahārāja Parīkṣit, as required according to the scheduled round of His pastimes, Kṛṣṇa returned in the evening, entered the house of each of the cowherd boys, and engaged exactly like the former boys, thus enlivening their mothers with transcendental pleasure. The mothers took care of the boys by massaging them with oil, bathing them, smearing their bodies with sandalwood pulp, decorating them with ornaments, chanting**

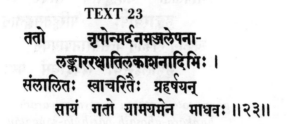

**protective mantras, decorating their bodies with tilaka and giving them food. In this way, the mothers served Kṛṣṇa personally.**

### TEXT 24

गावस्ततो गोष्ठमुपेत्य सत्वरं
हुङ्कारघोषैः परिहूतसङ्गतान् ।
स्वकान् स्वकान् वत्सतराननपाययन्
मुहुर्लिहन्त्यः स्रवदौधसं पयः ॥२४॥

*gāvas tato goṣṭham upetya satvaraṁ*
*huṅkāra-ghoṣaiḥ parihūta-saṅgatān*
*svakān svakān vatsatarān apāyayan*
*muhur lihantyaḥ sravad audhasaṁ payaḥ*

*gāvaḥ*—the calves; *tataḥ*—thereafter; *goṣṭham*—to the cow sheds; *upetya*—reaching; *satvaram*—very soon; *huṅkāra-ghoṣaiḥ*—by making jubilant mooing sounds; *parihūta-saṅgatān*—to call the cows; *svakān svakān*—following their respective mothers; *vatsatarān*—the respective calves; *apāyayan*—feeding them; *muhuḥ*—again and again; *lihantyaḥ*—licking the calves; *sravat audhasam payaḥ*—abundant milk flowing from their milk bags.

### TRANSLATION

**Thereafter, all the cows entered their different sheds and began mooing loudly, calling for their respective calves. When the calves arrived, the mothers began licking the calves' bodies again and again and profusely feeding them with the milk flowing from their milk bags.**

### PURPORT

All the dealings between the calves and their respective mothers taking care of them were enacted by Kṛṣṇa Himself.

### TEXT 25

गोगोपीनां मातृतास्मिन्नासीत् स्नेहर्धिकां विना ।
पुरोवदास्वपि हरेस्तोकता मायया विना ॥२५॥

*go-gopīnāṁ mātṛtāsminn*
*āsīt snehardhikāṁ vinā*
*purovad āsv api hares*
*tokatā māyayā vinā*

*go-gopīnām*—for both the cows and the *gopīs*, the elderly cowherd women; *mātṛtā*—motherly affection; *asmin*—unto Kṛṣṇa; *āsīt*—there ordinarily was; *sneha*—of affection; *ṛdhikām*—any increase; *vinā*—without; *puraḥ-vat*—like before; *āsu*—there was among the cows and *gopīs; api*—although; *hareḥ*—of Kṛṣṇa; *tokatā*—Kṛṣṇa is my son; *māyayā vinā*—without *māyā.*

## TRANSLATION

**Previously, from the very beginning, the gopīs had motherly affection for Kṛṣṇa. Indeed, their affection for Kṛṣṇa exceeded even their affection for their own sons. In displaying their affection, they had thus distinguished between Kṛṣṇa and their sons, but now that distinction disappeared.**

## PURPORT

The distinction between one's own son and another's son is not unnatural. Many elderly women have motherly affection for the sons of others. They observe distinctions, however, between those other sons and their own. But now the elderly *gopīs* could not distinguish between their own sons and Kṛṣṇa, for since their own sons had been taken by Brahmā, Kṛṣṇa had expanded as their sons. Therefore, their extra affection for their sons, who were now Kṛṣṇa Himself, was due to bewilderment resembling that of Brahmā. Previously, the mothers of Śrīdāmā, Sudāmā, Subala and Kṛṣṇa's other friends did not have the same affection for one another's sons, but now the *gopīs* treated all the boys as their own. Śukadeva Gosvāmī, therefore, wanted to explain this increment of affection in terms of Kṛṣṇa's bewilderment of Brahmā, the *gopīs*, the cows and everyone else.

## TEXT 26

व्रजौकसां स्वतोकेषु स्नेहवल्ल्याब्दमन्वहम् ।
शनैर्निःसीम ववृधे यथा कृष्णे त्वपूर्ववत् ॥२६॥

*vrajaukasāṁ sva-tokeṣu*
*sneha-vally ābdaṁ anvaham*
*śanair niḥsīma vavṛdhe*
*yathā kṛṣṇe tv apūrvavat*

*vraja-okasām*—of all the inhabitants of Vraja, Vṛndāvana; *sva-tokeṣu*—for their own sons; *sneha-vallī*—the creeper of affection; *ā-abdam*—for one year; *anu-aham*—every day; *śanaiḥ*—gradually; *niḥsīma*—without limit; *vavṛdhe*—increased; *yathā kṛṣṇe*—exactly accepting Kṛṣṇa as their son; *tu*—indeed; *apūrva-vat*—as it had not been previously.

## TRANSLATION

**Although the inhabitants of Vrajabhūmi, the cowherd men and cowherd women, previously had more affection for Kṛṣṇa than for their own children, now, for one year, their affection for their own sons continuously increased, for Kṛṣṇa had now become their sons. There was no limit to the increment of their affection for their sons, who were now Kṛṣṇa. Every day they found new inspiration for loving their children as much as they loved Kṛṣṇa.**

## TEXT 27

इत्थमात्मात्मनात्मानं वत्सपालमिषेण सः ।
पालयन् वत्सपो वर्षं चिक्रीडे वनगोष्ठयोः ॥२७॥

*ittham ātmātmanātmānaṁ*
*vatsa-pāla-miṣeṇa saḥ*
*pālayan vatsapo varṣaṁ*
*cikrīḍe vana-goṣṭhayoḥ*

*ittham*—in this way; *ātmā*—the Supreme Soul, Kṛṣṇa; *ātmanā*—by Himself; *ātmānam*—Himself again; *vatsa-pāla-miṣeṇa*—with the forms of cowherd boys and calves; *saḥ*—Kṛṣṇa Himself; *pālayan*—maintaining; *vatsa-paḥ*—tending the calves; *varṣam*—continuously for one year; *cikrīḍe*—enjoyed the pastimes; *vana-goṣṭhayoḥ*—both in Vṛndāvana and in the forest.

## TRANSLATION

**In this way, Lord Śrī Kṛṣṇa, having Himself become the cowherd boys and groups of calves, maintained Himself by Himself. Thus He continued His pastimes, both in Vṛndāvana and in the forest, for one year.**

## PURPORT

Everything was Kṛṣṇa. The calves, the cowherd boys and their maintainer Himself were all Kṛṣṇa. In other words, Kṛṣṇa expanded Himself in varieties of calves and cowherd boys and continued His pastimes uninterrupted for one year. As stated in *Bhagavad-gītā*, Kṛṣṇa's expansion is situated in everyone's heart as the Supersoul. Similarly, instead of expanding Himself as the Supersoul, He expanded Himself as a portion of calves and cowherd boys for one continuous year.

## TEXT 28

एकदा चारयन् वत्सान् सरामो वनमाविशत् ।
पञ्चषासु त्रियामासु हायनापूरणीष्वजः ॥२८॥

*ekadā cārayan vatsān*
*sa-rāmo vanam āviśat*
*pañca-ṣāsu tri-yāmāsu*
*hāyanāpūraṇīṣv ajaḥ*

*ekadā*—one day; *cārayan vatsān*—while taking care of all the calves; *sa-rāmaḥ*—along with Balarāma; *vanam*—within the forest; *āviśat*—entered; *pañca-ṣāsu*—five or six; *tri-yāmāsu*—nights; *hāyana*—a whole year; *apūraṇiṣu*—not being fulfilled (five or six days before the completion of one year); *ajaḥ*—Lord Śrī Kṛṣṇa.

## TRANSLATION

**One day, five or six nights before the completion of the year, Kṛṣṇa, tending the calves, entered the forest along with Balarāma.**

## PURPORT

Up to this time, even Balarāma was captivated by the bewilderment that covered Brahmā. Even Balarāma did not know that all the calves and cowherd boys were expansions of Kṛṣṇa or that He Himself was also an expansion of Kṛṣṇa. This was disclosed to Balarāma just five or six days before the completion of the year.

## TEXT 29

ततो विदूराच्चरतो गावो वत्सानुपव्रजम् ।
गोवर्धनाद्रिशिरसि चरन्त्यो ददृशुस्तृणम् ॥२९॥

*tato vidūrāc carato*
*gāvo vatsān upavrajam*
*govardhanādri-śirasi*
*carantyo dadṛśus tṛṇam*

*tataḥ*—thereafter; *vidūrāt*—from a not-distant place; *carataḥ*—while pasturing; *gāvaḥ*—all the cows; *vatsān*—and their respective calves; *upavrajam*—also pasturing near Vṛndāvana; *govardhana-adri-śirasi*—on the top of Govardhana Hill; *carantyaḥ*—while pasturing to find; *dadṛśuḥ*—saw; *tṛṇam*—tender grass nearby.

## TRANSLATION

**Thereafter, while pasturing atop Govardhana Hill, the cows looked down to find some green grass and saw their calves pasturing near Vṛndāvana, not very far away.**

## TEXT 30

दृष्ट्वाथ तत्स्नेहवशोऽस्मृतात्मा
स गोव्रजोऽत्यात्मपदुर्गमार्गः ।
द्विपात् ककुद्ग्रीव उदास्यपुच्छो-
ऽगाद्धुङ्कृतैरास्रुपया जवेन ॥३०॥

*dṛṣṭvātha tat-sneha-vaśo 'smṛtātmā*
*sa go-vrajo 'tyātmapa-durga-mārgaḥ*
*dvi-pāt kukud-grīva udāsya-puccho*
*'gād dhuṅkṛtair āsru-payā javena*

*dṛṣṭvā*—when the cows saw their calves below: *atha*—thereafter; *tat-sneha-vaśaḥ*—because of increased love for the calves: *asmṛta-ātmā*—as if they had forgotten themselves; *saḥ*—that: *go-vrajaḥ*—herd of cows; *ati-ātma-pa-durga-mārgaḥ*—escaping their caretakers because of increased affection for the calves, although the way was very rough and hard; *dvi-pāt*—pairs of legs together; *kakut-grīvaḥ*—their humps moving with their necks; *udāsya-pucchaḥ*—raising their heads and tails; *agāt*—came; *huṅkṛtaiḥ*—lowing very loudly; *āsru-payāḥ*—with milk flowing from the nipples; *javena*—very forcibly.

## TRANSLATION

**When the cows saw their own calves from the top of Govardhana Hill, they forgot themselves and their caretakers because of increased affection, and although the path was very rough, they ran toward their calves with great anxiety, each running as if with one pair of legs. Their milk bags full and flowing with milk, their heads and tails raised, and their humps moving with their necks, they ran forcefully until they reached their calves to feed them.**

## PURPORT

Generally the calves and cows are pastured separately. The elderly men take care of the cows, and the small children see to the calves. This time, however, the cows immediately forgot their position as soon as they saw the calves below Govardhana Hill, and they ran with great force, their tails erect and their front and hind legs joined, until they reached their calves.

## TEXT 31

समेत्य गावोऽधो वत्सान् वत्सवत्योऽप्यपाययन् ।
गिलन्त्य इव चाङ्गानि लिहन्त्यः स्वौधसं पयः ॥३१॥

*sametya gāvo 'dho vatsān*
*vatsavatyo 'py apāyayan*
*gilantya iva cāṅgāni*
*lihantyaḥ svaudhasaṁ payaḥ*

*sametya*—assembling; *gāvaḥ*—all the cows; *adhaḥ*—down at the foot of Govardhana Hill; *vatsān*—all their calves; *vatsa-vatyaḥ*—as if new calves had been born from them; *api*—even though new calves were present; *apāyayan*—fed them; *gilantyaḥ*—swallowing them; *iva*—as if; *ca*—also; *aṅgāni*—their bodies; *lihantyaḥ*—licking as they do when newborn calves are present; *sva-odhasam payaḥ*—their own milk flowing from the milk bags.

## TRANSLATION

**The cows had given birth to new calves, but while coming down from Govardhana Hill, the cows, because of increased affection for the older calves, allowed the older calves to drink milk from their milk bags and then began licking the calves' bodies in anxiety, as if wanting to swallow them.**

## TEXT 32

गोपास्तद्रोधनायासमौघ्यलज्जोरुमन्युना ।
दुर्गाध्वकृच्छ्रतोऽभ्येत्य गोवत्सैर्ददृशुः सुतान् ॥३२॥

*gopās tad-rodhanāyāsa-*
*maughya-lajjoru-manyunā*
*durgādhva-kṛcchrato 'bhyetya*
*go-vatsair dadṛśuḥ sutān*

*gopāḥ*—the cowherd men; *tat-rodhana-āyāsa*—of their attempt to stop the cows from going to their calves; *maughya*—on account of the frustration; *lajjā*—being ashamed; *uru-manyunā*—and at the same time becoming very angry; *durga-adhva-kṛcchrataḥ*—although they passed the very rough way with great difficulty; *abhyetya*—after reaching there; *go-vatsaiḥ*—along with the calves; *dadṛśuḥ*—saw; *sutān*—their respective sons.

## TRANSLATION

**The cowherd men, having been unable to check the cows from going to their calves, felt simultaneously ashamed and angry. They**

**crossed the rough road with great difficulty, but when they came down and saw their own sons, they were overwhelmed by great affection.**

## PURPORT

Everyone was increasing in affection for Kṛṣṇa. When the cowherd men coming down from the hill saw their own sons, who were no one else than Kṛṣṇa, their affection increased.

## TEXT 33

तदीक्षणोत्प्रेमरसाप्लुताशया
जातानुरागा गतमन्यवोऽर्भकान् ।
उदुह्य दोर्भिः परिरभ्य मूर्धनि
घ्राणैरवापुः परमां मुदं ते ॥३३॥

*tad-īkṣaṇotprema-rasāplutāśayā*
*jātānurāgā gata-manyavo 'rbhakān*
*uduhya dorbhiḥ parirabhya mūrdhani*
*ghrāṇair avāpuḥ paramāṁ mudaṁ te*

*tat-īkṣaṇa-utprema-rasa-āpluta-āśayāḥ*—all the thoughts of the cowherd men merged in the mellow of paternal love, which was aroused by seeing their sons; *jāta-anurāgāḥ*—experiencing a great longing or attraction; *gata-manyavaḥ*—their anger disappeared; *arbhakān*—their young sons; *uduhya*—lifting; *dorbhiḥ*—with their arms; *parirabhya*—embracing; *mūrdhani*—on the head; *ghrāṇaiḥ*—by smelling; *avāpuḥ*—obtained; *paramām*—the highest; *mudam*—pleasure; *te*—those cowherd men.

## TRANSLATION

**At that time, all the thoughts of the cowherd men merged in the mellow of paternal love, which was aroused by the sight of their sons. Experiencing a great attraction, their anger completely disappearing, they lifted their sons, embraced them in their arms and enjoyed the highest pleasure by smelling their sons' heads.**

## PURPORT

After Brahmā stole the original cowherd boys and calves, Kṛṣṇa expanded Himself to become the boys and calves again. Therefore, because the boys were actually Kṛṣṇa's expansions, the cowherd men were especially attracted to them. At first the cowherd men, who were on top of the hill, were angry, but because of Kṛṣṇa the boys were extremely attractive, and therefore the cowherd men immediately came down from the hill with special affection.

## TEXT 34

ततः प्रवयसो गोपास्तोकाश्लेषसुनिर्वृताः ।
कृच्छ्राच्छनैरपगतास्तदनुस्मृत्युदश्रवः ॥३४॥

*tataḥ pravayaso gopās*
*tokāśleṣa-sunirvṛtāḥ*
*kṛcchrāc chanair apagatās*
*tad-anusmṛty-udaśravaḥ*

*tataḥ*—thereafter; *pravayasaḥ*—elderly; *gopāḥ*—cowherd men; *toka-āśleṣa-sunirvṛtāḥ*—became overjoyed by embracing their sons; *kṛcchrāt*—with difficulty; *śanaiḥ*—gradually; *apagatāḥ*—ceased from that embracing and returned to the forest; *tat-anusmṛti-uda-śravaḥ*—as they remembered their sons, tears began to roll down from their eyes.

## TRANSLATION

**Thereafter the elderly cowherd men, having obtained great feeling from embracing their sons, gradually and with great difficulty and reluctance ceased embracing them and returned to the forest. But as the men remembered their sons, tears began to roll down from their eyes.**

## PURPORT

In the beginning the cowherd men were angry that the cows were being attracted by the calves, but when the men came down from the hill, they themselves were attracted by their sons, and therefore the men embraced them. To embrace one's son and smell his head are symptoms of affection.

## TEXT 35

व्रजस्य रामः प्रेमर्धेर्वीक्ष्यौत्कण्ठ्यमनुक्षणम् ।
मुक्तस्तनेष्वपत्येष्वप्यहेतुविदचिन्तयत् ॥३५॥

*vrajasya rāmaḥ premardher*
*vīkṣyautkaṇṭhyam anukṣaṇam*
*mukta-staneṣv apatyeṣv apy*
*ahetu-vid acintayat*

*vrajasya*—of the herd of cows; *rāmaḥ*—Balarāma; *prema-ṛdheḥ*—because of an increase of affection; *vīkṣya*—after observing; *aut-kaṇṭhyam*—attachment; *anu-kṣaṇam*—constantly; *mukta-staneṣu*—who had grown up and were no longer drawing milk from their mothers; *apatyeṣu*—in regard to those calves; *api*—even; *ahetu-vit*—not understanding the reason; *acintayat*—began to consider as follows.

## TRANSLATION

**Because of an increase of affection, the cows had constant attachment even to those calves that were grown up and had stopped sucking milk from their mothers. When Baladeva saw this attachment, He was unable to understand the reason for it, and thus He began to consider as follows.**

## PURPORT

The cows had younger calves who had started sucking milk from their mothers, and some of the cows had newly given birth, but now, because of love, the cows enthusiastically showed their affection for the older calves, which had left off milking. These calves were grown up, but still the mothers wanted to feed them. Therefore Balarāma was a little surprised, and He wanted to inquire from Kṛṣṇa about the reason for their behavior. The mothers were actually more anxious to feed the older calves, although the new calves were present, because the older calves were expansions of Kṛṣṇa. These surprising events were taking place by the manipulation of *yogamāyā*. There are two *māyās* working under the direction of Kṛṣṇa—*mahāmāyā*, the energy of the material world, and *yogamāyā*, the energy of the spiritual world. These uncommon events were taking place because of the influence of *yogamāyā*. From the very day on which Brahmā stole the calves and boys, *yogamāyā* acted in such a way that the residents of Vṛndāvana, including even Lord Balarāma, could not understand how *yogamāyā* was working and causing such uncommon things to happen. But as *yogamāyā* gradually acted, Balarāma in particular was able to understand what was happening, and therefore He inquired from Kṛṣṇa.

## TEXT 36

किमेतदद्भुतमिव वासुदेवेऽखिलात्मनि ।
व्रजस्य सात्मनस्तोकेष्वपूर्वं प्रेम वर्धते ॥३६॥

*kim etad adbhutam iva*
*vāsudeve 'khilātmani*
*vrajasya sātmanas tokeṣv*
*apūrvaṁ prema vardhate*

*kim*—what; *etat*—this; *adbhutam*—wonderful; *iva*—just as; *vāsudeve*—in Vāsudeva, Lord Śrī Kṛṣṇa; *akhila-ātmani*—the Supersoul of all living entities; *vrajasya*—of all the inhabitants of Vraja; *sa-ātmanaḥ*—along with Me; *tokeṣu*—in these boys; *apūrvam*—unprecedented; *prema*—affection; *vardhate*—is increasing.

## TRANSLATION

**What is this wonderful phenomenon? The affection of all the inhabitants of Vraja, including Me, toward these boys and calves is increasing as never before, just like our affection for Lord Kṛṣṇa, the Supersoul of all living entities.**

## PURPORT

This increase of affection was not *māyā;* rather, because Kṛṣṇa had expanded Himself as everything and because the whole life of everyone in Vṛndāvana was meant for Kṛṣṇa, the cows, because of affection for Kṛṣṇa, had more affection for the older calves than for the new calves, and the men increased in their affection for their sons. Balarāma was astonished to see all the residents of Vṛndāvana so affectionate toward their own children, exactly as they had been for Kṛṣṇa. Similarly, the cows had grown affectionate toward their calves—as much as toward Kṛṣṇa. Balarāma was surprised to see the acts of *yogamāyā*. Therefore He inquired from Kṛṣṇa, "What is happening here? What is this mystery?"

## TEXT 37

केयं वा कुत आयाता दैवी वा नार्युतासुरी ।
प्रायो मायास्तु मे भर्तुर्नान्या मेऽपि विमोहिनी ॥३७॥

*keyaṁ vā kuta āyātā*
*daivī vā nāry utāsurī*
*prāyo māyāstu me bhartur*
*nānyā me 'pi vimohinī*

*kā*—who; *iyam*—this; *vā*—or; *kutaḥ*—from where; *āyātā*—has come; *daivī*—whether demigod; *vā*—or; *nārī*—woman; *uta*—or; *āsurī*—demoness; *prāyaḥ*—in most cases; *māyā*—illusory energy; *astu*—she must be; *me*—My; *bhartuḥ*—of the master, Lord Kṛṣṇa; *na*—not; *anyā*—any other; *me*—My; *api*—certainly; *vimohinī*—bewilderer.

## TRANSLATION

**Who is this mystic power, and where has she come from? Is she a demigod or a demoness? She must be the illusory energy of My master, Lord Kṛṣṇa, for who else can bewilder Me?**

## PURPORT

Balarāma was surprised. This extraordinary show of affection, He thought, was something mystical, performed either by the demigods or some wonderful man. Otherwise, how could this wonderful change take place? "This *māyā* might be some *rākṣasī-māyā*," He thought, "but how can *rākṣasī-māyā* have any influence upon Me? This is not possible. Therefore it must be the *māyā* of Kṛṣṇa." He thus concluded that the mystical change must have been caused by Kṛṣṇa, whom Balarāma considered His worshipable Personality of Godhead. He thought, "It was arranged by Kṛṣṇa, and even I could not check its mystic power." Thus Balarāma understood that all these boys and calves were only expansions of Kṛṣṇa.

## TEXT 38

इति सञ्चिन्त्य दाशार्हो वत्सान् सवयसानपि ।
सर्वानाचष्ट वैकुण्ठं चक्षुषा वयुनेन सः ॥३८॥

*iti sañcintya dāśārho*
*vatsān sa-vayasān api*
*sarvān ācaṣṭa vaikuṇṭhaṁ*
*cakṣuṣā vayunena saḥ*

*iti sañcintya*—thinking in this way; *dāśārhaḥ*—Baladeva; *vatsān*—the calves; *sa-vayasān*—along with His companions; *api*—also; *sarvān*—all; *ācaṣṭa*—saw; *vaikuṇṭham*—as Śrī Kṛṣṇa only; *cakṣuṣā vayunena*—with the eye of transcendental knowledge; *saḥ*—He (Baladeva).

## TRANSLATION

**Thinking in this way, Lord Balarāma was able to see, with the eye of transcendental knowledge, that all these calves and Kṛṣṇa's friends were expansions of the form of Śrī Kṛṣṇa.**

## PURPORT

Every individual is different. There are even differences between twin brothers. Yet when Kṛṣṇa expanded Himself as the boys and calves, each boy and each calf appeared in its own original feature, with the same individual way of acting, the same tendencies, the same color, the same dress, and so on, for Kṛṣṇa manifested Himself with all these differences. This was Kṛṣṇa's opulence.

## TEXT 39

नैते सुरेशा ऋषयो न चैते
त्वमेव भासीश भिदाश्रयेऽपि ।
सर्वं पृथक्त्वं निगमात् कथं वदे-
त्युक्तेन वृत्तं प्रभुणा बलोऽवैत् ॥३९॥

*naite sureśā ṛṣayo na caite*
*tvam eva bhāsīśa bhid-āśraye 'pi*

*sarvaṁ pṛthak tvaṁ nigamāt kathaṁ vadety*
*uktena vṛttaṁ prabhuṇā balo 'vait*

*na*—not; *ete*—these boys; *sura-īśāḥ*—the best of the demigods; *ṛṣayaḥ*—great sages; *na*—not; *ca*—and; *ete*—these calves; *tvam*—You (Kṛṣṇa); *eva*—alone; *bhāsi*—are manifesting; *īśa*—O supreme controller; *bhit-āśraye*—in the existence of varieties of difference; *api*—even; *sarvam*—everything; *pṛthak*—existing; *tvam*—You (Kṛṣṇa); *nigamāt*—briefly; *katham*—how; *vada*—please explain; *iti*—thus; *uktena*—having been requested (by Baladeva); *vṛttam*—the situation; *prabhuṇā*—(having been explained) by Lord Kṛṣṇa; *balaḥ*—Baladeva; *avait*—understood.

## TRANSLATION

**Lord Baladeva said, "O supreme controller! These boys are not great demigods, as I previously thought. Nor are these calves great sages like Nārada. Now I can see that You alone are manifesting Yourself in all varieties of difference. Although one, You are existing in the different forms of the calves and boys. Please briefly explain this to Me." Having thus been requested by Lord Baladeva, Kṛṣṇa explained the whole situation, and Baladeva understood it.**

## PURPORT

Inquiring from Kṛṣṇa about the actual situation, Lord Balarāma said, "My dear Kṛṣṇa, in the beginning I thought that all these cows, calves and cowherd boys were either great sages and saintly persons or demigods, but at the present it appears that they are actually Your expansions. They are all You; You Yourself are playing as the calves and cows and boys. What is the mystery of this situation? Where have those other calves and cows and boys gone? And why are You expanding Yourself as the cows, calves and boys? Will You kindly tell Me what is the cause?" At the request of Balarāma, Kṛṣṇa briefly explained the whole situation: how the calves and boys were stolen by Brahmā and how He was concealing the incident by expanding Himself so that people would not know that the original cows, calves and boys were missing. Balarāma understood, therefore, that this was not *māyā* but Kṛṣṇa's opulence. Kṛṣṇa has all opulences, and this was but another opulence of Kṛṣṇa.

"At first," Lord Balarāma said, "I thought that these boys and calves were a display of the power of great sages like Nārada, but now I see that all these boys and calves are You." After inquiring from Kṛṣṇa, Lord Balarāma understood that Kṛṣṇa Himself had become many. That the Lord can do this is stated in the *Brahma-saṁhitā* (5.33). *Advaitam acyutam anādim ananta-rūpam:* although He is one, He can expand Himself in so many forms. According to the Vedic version, *ekaṁ bahu syām:* He can expand Himself into many thousands and millions but still remain one. In that sense, everything is spiritual because everything is an expansion of Kṛṣṇa; that is, everything is an expansion either of Kṛṣṇa Himself or of His potency. Because the potency is nondifferent from the potent, the potency and the potent are one (*śakti-śaktimator abhedaḥ*). The Māyāvādīs, however, say, *cid-acit-samanvayaḥ:* spirit and matter are one. This is a wrong conception. Spirit (*cit*) is different from matter (*acit*), as explained by Kṛṣṇa Himself in *Bhagavad-gītā* (7.4–5):

*bhūmir āpo 'nalo vāyuḥ*
*khaṁ mano buddhir eva ca*
*ahaṅkāra itīyaṁ me*
*bhinnā prakṛtir aṣṭadhā*

*apareyam itas tv anyāṁ*
*prakṛtiṁ viddhi me parām*
*jīva-bhūtāṁ mahā-bāho*
*yayedaṁ dhāryate jagat*

"Earth, water, fire, air, ether, mind, intelligence and false ego—all together these eight comprise My separated material energies. But besides this inferior nature, O mighty-armed Arjuna, there is a superior energy of Mine, which consists of all living entities who are struggling with material nature and are sustaining the universe." Spirit and matter cannot be made one, for actually they are superior and inferior energies, yet the Māyāvādīs, or Advaita-vādīs, try to make them one. This is wrong. Although spirit and matter ultimately come from the same one source, they cannot be made one. For example, there are many things that come from our bodies, but although they come from the same source, they cannot be made one. We should be careful to note that although the supreme source is one, the emanations from this source should be separately regarded as inferior and superior. The difference between the Māyāvāda and Vaiṣṇava philosophies is that the Vaiṣṇava philosophy recognizes this fact. Śrī Caitanya Mahāprabhu's philosophy, therefore, is called *acintya-bhedābheda*—simultaneous oneness and difference. For example, fire and heat cannot be separated, for where there is fire there is heat and where there is heat there is fire. Nonetheless, although we cannot touch fire, heat we can tolerate. Therefore, although they are one, they are different.

## TEXT 40

तावदेत्यात्मभूरात्ममानेन त्रुट्यनेहसा ।
पुरोवदाब्दं क्रीडन्तं ददृशे सकलं हरिम् ॥४०॥

*tāvad etyātmabhūr ātma-*
*mānena truṭy-anehasā*
*purovad ābdaṁ krīḍantaṁ*
*dadṛśe sa-kalaṁ harim*

*tāvat*—for so long; *etya*—after returning; *ātma-bhūḥ*—Lord Brahmā; *ātma-mānena*—by his (Brahmā's) own measurement; *truṭi-anehasā*—by a moment's time; *puraḥ-vat*—just as previously; *ā-abdam*—for one year (by human measurement of time); *krīḍantam*—playing; *dadṛśe*—he saw; *sa-kalam*—along with His expansions; *harim*—Lord Hari (Śrī Kṛṣṇa).

## TRANSLATION

**When Lord Brahmā returned after a moment of time had passed (according to his own measurement), he saw that although by human measurement a complete year had passed, Lord Kṛṣṇa, after all that time, was engaged just as before in playing with the boys and calves, who were His expansions.**

## PURPORT

Lord Brahmā had gone away for only a moment of his time, but when he returned, a year of human time had passed. On different planets, the calculation of time is different. To give an example, a man-made satellite may orbit the earth in an hour and twenty-five minutes and thus complete one full day, although a day ordinarily takes twenty-four hours for those living on earth. Therefore, what was but a moment for Brahmā was one year on earth. Kṛṣṇa continued to expand Himself in so many forms for one year, but by the arrangement of *yogamāyā* no one could understand this but Balarāma.

After one moment of Brahmā's calculation, Brahmā came back to see the fun caused by his stealing the boys and calves. But he was also afraid that he was playing with fire. Kṛṣṇa was his master, and he had played mischief for fun by taking away Kṛṣṇa's calves and boys. He was really anxious, so he did not stay away very long; he came back after a moment (of his calculation). When Brahmā returned, he saw that all the boys, calves and cows were playing with Kṛṣṇa in the same way as when he had come upon them; by Kṛṣṇa's display of *yogamāyā*, the same pastimes were going on without any change.

On the day when Lord Brahmā had first come, Baladeva could not go with Kṛṣṇa and the cowherd boys, for it was His birthday, and His mother had kept Him back for the proper ceremonial bath, called *śāntika-snāna.* Therefore Lord Baladeva was not taken by Brahmā at that time. Now, one year later, Brahmā returned, and because he returned on exactly the same day, Baladeva was again kept at home for His birthday. Therefore, although this verse mentions that Brahmā saw Kṛṣṇa and all the cowherd boys, Baladeva is not mentioned. It was five or six days earlier that Baladeva had inquired from Kṛṣṇa about the extraordinary affection of the cows and cowherd men, but now, when Brahmā returned, Brahmā saw all the calves and cowherd boys playing with Kṛṣṇa as expansions of Kṛṣṇa, but he did not see Baladeva. As in the previous year, Lord Baladeva did not go to the woods on the day Lord Brahmā appeared there.

## TEXT 41

यावन्तो गोकुले बालाः सवत्साः सर्व एव हि ।
मायाशये शयाना मे नाद्यापि पुनरुत्थिताः ॥४१॥

*yāvanto gokule bālāḥ*
*sa-vatsāḥ sarva eva hi*

*māyāśaye śayānā me*
*nādyāpi punar utthitāḥ*

*yāvantaḥ*—whatsoever, as many as; *gokule*—in Gokula; *bālāḥ*—boys; *sa-vatsāḥ*—along with their calves; *sarve*—all; *eva*—indeed; *hi*—because; *māyā-āśaye*—on the bed of *māyā; śayānāḥ*—are sleeping; *me*—my; *na*—not; *adya*—today; *api*—even; *punaḥ*—again; *utthitāḥ*—have risen.

## TRANSLATION

**Lord Brahmā thought: Whatever boys and calves there were in Gokula, I have kept them sleeping on the bed of my mystic potency, and to this very day they have not yet risen again.**

## PURPORT

For one year Lord Brahmā kept the calves and boys lying down in a cave by his mystic power. Therefore when Brahmā saw Lord Kṛṣṇa still playing with all the cows and calves, he began trying to reason about what was happening. "What is this?" he thought. "Maybe I took those calves and cowherd boys away but now they have been taken from that cave. Is this what has happened? Has Kṛṣṇa brought them back here?" Then, however, Lord Brahmā saw that the calves and boys he had taken were still in the same mystic *māyā* into which he had put them. Thus he concluded that the calves and cowherd boys now playing with Kṛṣṇa were different from the ones in the cave. He could understand that although the original calves and boys were still in the cave where he had put them, Kṛṣṇa had expanded Himself and so the present demonstration of calves and boys consisted of expansions of Kṛṣṇa. They had the same features, the same mentality and the same intentions, but they were all Kṛṣṇa.

## TEXT 42

इत एतेऽत्र कुत्रत्या मन्मायामोहितेतरे ।
तावन्त एव तत्राब्दं क्रीडन्तो विष्णुना समम् ॥४२॥

*ita ete 'tra kutratyā*
*man-māyā-mohitetare*

*tāvanta eva tatrābdaṁ*
*krīḍanto viṣṇunā samam*

*itaḥ*—for this reason; *ete*—these boys with their calves; *atra*—here; *kutratyāḥ*—where have they come from; *mat-māyā-mohita-itare*—different from those who were mystified by my illusory potency; *tāvantaḥ*—the same number of boys; *eva*—indeed; *tatra*—there; *ā-abdam*—for one year; *krīḍantaḥ*—are playing; *viṣṇunā samam*—along with Kṛṣṇa.

## TRANSLATION

**A similar number of boys and calves have been playing with Kṛṣṇa for one whole year, yet they are different from the ones illusioned by my mystic potency. Who are they? Where did they come from?**

## PURPORT

Although appearing like calves, cows and cowherd boys, these were all Viṣṇu. Actually they were *viṣṇu-tattva*, not *jīva-tattva*. Brahmā was surprised. "The original cowherd boys and cows," he thought, "are still where I put them last year. So who is it that is now keeping company with Kṛṣṇa exactly as before? Where have they come from?" Brahmā was surprised that his mystic power had been neglected. Without touching the original cows and cowherd boys kept by Brahmā, Kṛṣṇa had created another assembly of calves and boys, who were all expansions of *viṣṇu-tattva*. Thus Brahmā's mystic power was superseded.

## TEXT 43

एवमेतेषु भेदेषु चिरं ध्यात्वा स आत्मभूः ।
सत्याः के कतरे नेति ज्ञातुं नेष्टे कथञ्चन ॥४३॥

*evam eteṣu bhedeṣu*
*ciraṁ dhyātvā sa ātma-bhūḥ*
*satyāḥ ke katare neti*
*jñātuṁ neṣṭe kathañcana*

*evam*—in this way; *eteṣu bhedeṣu*—between these boys, who were existing separately; *ciram*—for a long time; *dhyātvā*—after thinking; *saḥ*—he; *ātma-bhūḥ*—Lord Brahmā; *satyāḥ*—real; *ke*—who; *katare*—who; *na*—are not; *iti*—thus; *jñātum*—to understand; *na*—not; *iṣṭe*—was able; *kathañcana*—in any way at all.

## TRANSLATION

**Thus Lord Brahmā, thinking and thinking for a long time, tried to distinguish between those two sets of boys, who were each separately existing. He tried to understand who was real and who was not real, but he couldn't understand at all.**

## PURPORT

Brahmā was puzzled. "The original boys and calves are still sleeping as I have kept them," he thought, "but another set is here playing with Kṛṣṇa. How has this happened?" Brahmā could not grasp what was happening. Which boys were real, and which were not real? Brahmā was unable to come to any definite conclusion. He pondered the matter for a long while. "How can there be two sets of calves and boys at the same time? Have the boys and calves here been created by Kṛṣṇa, or has Kṛṣṇa created the ones lying asleep? Or are both merely creations of Kṛṣṇa?" Brahmā thought about the subject in many different ways. "After I go to the cave and see that the boys and calves are still there, does Kṛṣṇa go take them away and put them here so that I come here and see them, and does Kṛṣṇa then take them from here and put them there?" Brahmā could not figure out how there could be two sets of calves and cowherd boys exactly alike. Although thinking and thinking, he could not understand at all.

## TEXT 44

एवं सम्मोहयन् विष्णुं विमोहं विश्वमोहनम् ।
स्वयैव माययाजोऽपि स्वयमेव विमोहितः ॥४४॥

*evaṁ sammohayan viṣṇuṁ*
*vimohaṁ viśva-mohanam*

*svayaiva māyayājo 'pi*
*svayam eva vimohitaḥ*

*evam*—in this way; *sammohayan*—wanting to mystify; *viṣṇum*—the all-pervading Lord Kṛṣṇa; *vimoham*—who can never be mystified; *viśva-mohanam*—but who mystifies the entire universe; *svayā*—by his (Brahmā's) own; *eva*—indeed; *māyayā*—by mystic power; *ajaḥ*—Lord Brahmā; *api*—even; *svayam*—himself; *eva*—certainly; *vimohitaḥ*—was put into bewilderment, became mystified.

## TRANSLATION

**Thus because Lord Brahmā wanted to mystify the all-pervading Lord Kṛṣṇa, who can never be mystified, but who, on the contrary, mystifies the entire universe, he himself was put into bewilderment by his own mystic power.**

## PURPORT

Brahmā wanted to bewilder Kṛṣṇa, who bewilders the entire universe. The whole universe is under Kṛṣṇa's mystic power (*mama māyā duratyayā*), but Brahmā wanted to mystify Him. The result was that Brahmā himself was mystified, just as one who wants to kill another may himself be killed. In other words, Brahmā was defeated by his own attempt. In a similar position are the scientists and philosophers who want to overcome the mystic power of Kṛṣṇa. They challenge Kṛṣṇa, saying, "What is God? We can do this, and we can do that." But the more they challenge Kṛṣṇa in this way, the more they are implicated in suffering. The lesson here is that we should not try to overcome Kṛṣṇa. Rather, instead of endeavoring to surpass Him, we should surrender to Him (*sarva-dharmān parityajya māṁ ekaṁ śaraṇaṁ vraja*).

Instead of defeating Kṛṣṇa, Brahmā himself was defeated, for he could not understand what Kṛṣṇa was doing. Since Brahmā, the chief person within this universe, was so bewildered, what is to be said of so-called scientists and philosophers? *Sarva-dharmān parityajya māṁ ekaṁ śaraṇaṁ vraja.* We should give up all our tiny efforts to defy the arrangement of Kṛṣṇa. Instead, whatever arrangements He proposes, we should accept. This is always better, for this will make us happy. The more we try to defeat the arrangement of Kṛṣṇa, the more we become implicated in Kṛṣṇa's *māyā* (*daivī hy eṣā guṇamayī mama māyā duratyayā*). But one who has reached the point of surrendering to the instructions of Kṛṣṇa (*mām eva ye prapadyante*) is liberated, free from *kṛṣṇa-māyā* (*māyām etāṁ taranti te*). The power of Kṛṣṇa is just like a government that cannot be overcome. First of all there are laws, and then there is police power, and beyond that is military power. Therefore, what is the use of trying to overcome the power of the government? Similarly, what is the use of trying to challenge Kṛṣṇa?

From the next verse it is clear that Kṛṣṇa cannot be defeated by any kind of mystic power. If one gets even a little power of scientific knowledge, one tries to defy God, but actually no one is able to bewilder Kṛṣṇa. When Brahmā, the chief person within the universe, tried to bewilder Kṛṣṇa, he himself was bewildered and astonished. This is the position of the conditioned soul. Brahmā wanted to mystify Kṛṣṇa, but he himself was mystified.

The word *viṣṇum* is significant in this verse. Viṣṇu pervades the entire material world, whereas Brahmā merely occupies one subordinate post.

*yasyaika-niśvasita-kālam athāvalambya*
*jīvanti loma-vila-jā jagadaṇḍa-nāthāḥ*
(*Brahma-saṁhitā* 5.48)

The word *nāthāḥ*, which refers to Lord Brahmā, is plural because there are innumerable universes and innumerable Brahmās. Brahmā is but a tiny force. This was exhibited in Dvārakā when Kṛṣṇa called for Brahmā. One day when Brahmā came to see Kṛṣṇa at Dvārakā, the doorman, at Lord Kṛṣṇa's request, asked, "Which Brahmā are you?" Later, when Brahmā inquired from Kṛṣṇa whether this meant that there was more than one Brahmā, Kṛṣṇa smiled and at once called for many Brahmās from many universes. The four-headed Brahmā of this universe then saw innumerable other Brahmās coming to see Kṛṣṇa and offer their respects. Some of them had ten heads, some had twenty, some had a hundred and some had a million heads. Upon seeing this wonderful exhibition, the four-headed Brahmā became nervous and began to think of himself as no more than a mosquito in the midst of many elephants. Therefore, what can Brahmā do to bewilder Kṛṣṇa?

## TEXT 45

तम्यां तमोवन्नैहारं खद्योतार्चिरिवाहनि ।
महतीतरमायैश्यं निहन्त्यात्मनि युञ्जतः ॥४५॥

*tamyāṁ tamovan naihāraṁ*
*khadyotārcir ivāhani*
*mahatītara-māyaiśyaṁ*
*nihanty ātmani yuñjataḥ*

*tamyām*—on a dark night; *tamaḥ-vat*—just as darkness; *naihāram*—produced by snow; *khadyota-arciḥ*—the light of a glowworm; *iva*—just as; *ahani*—in the daytime, in the sunlight; *mahati*—in a great personality; *itara-māyā*—inferior mystic potency; *aiśyam*—the ability; *nihanti*—destroys; *ātmani*—in his own self; *yuñjataḥ*—of the person who attempts to use.

## TRANSLATION

**As the darkness of snow on a dark night and the light of a glowworm in the light of day have no value, the mystic power of an inferior person who tries to use it against a person of great power is unable to accomplish anything; instead, the power of that inferior person is diminished.**

## PURPORT

When one wants to supersede a superior power, one's own inferior power becomes ludicrous. Just as a glowworm in the daytime and snow at night have no value, Brahmā's mystic power became worthless in the presence of Kṛṣṇa, for greater mystic power condemns inferior mystic power. On a dark night, the darkness produced by snow has no meaning. The glowworm appears very important at night, but in the daytime its glow has no value; whatever little value it has is lost. Similarly, Brahmā became insignificant in the presence of Kṛṣṇa's mystic power. Kṛṣṇa's *māyā* was not diminished in value, but Brahmā's *māyā* was condemned. Therefore, one should not try to exhibit one's insignificant opulence before a greater power.

## TEXT 46

तावत् सर्वे वत्सपालाः पश्यतोऽजस्य तत्क्षणात् ।
व्यदृश्यन्त घनश्यामाः पीतकौशेयवाससः ॥४६॥

*tāvat sarve vatsa-pālāḥ*
*paśyato 'jasya tat-kṣaṇāt*
*vyadṛśyanta ghana-śyāmāḥ*
*pīta-kauśeya-vāsasaḥ*

*tāvat*—so long; *sarve*—all; *vatsa-pālāḥ*—both the calves and the boys tending them; *paśyataḥ*—while he was watching; *ajasya*—of Lord Brahmā; *tat-kṣaṇāt*—immediately; *vyadṛśyanta*—were seen; *ghana-śyāmāḥ*—as having a complexion resembling bluish rainclouds; *pīta-kauśeya-vāsasaḥ*—and dressed in yellow silk garments.

## TRANSLATION

**Then, while Lord Brahmā looked on, all the calves and the boys tending them immediately appeared to have complexions the color of bluish rainclouds and to be dressed in yellow silken garments.**

## PURPORT

While Brahmā was contemplating, all the calves and cowherd boys immediately transformed into *viṣṇu-mūrtis*, having bluish complexions and wearing yellow garments. Brahmā was contemplating his own power and the immense, unlimited power of Kṛṣṇa, but before he could come to a conclusion, he saw this immediate transformation.

## TEXTS 47–48

चतुर्भुजाः शङ्खचक्रगदाराजीवपाणयः ।
किरीटिनः कुण्डलिनो हारिणो वनमालिनः ॥४७॥

श्रीवत्साङ्गददोरत्नकम्बुकङ्कणपाणयः ।
नूपुरैः कटकैर्भाताः कटिसूत्राङ्गुलीयकैः ॥४८॥

*catur-bhujāḥ śaṅkha-cakra-*
*gadā-rājīva-pāṇayaḥ*
*kirīṭinaḥ kuṇḍalino*
*hāriṇo vana-mālinaḥ*

*śrīvatsāṅgada-do-ratna-*
*kambu-kaṅkaṇa-pāṇayaḥ*
*nūpuraiḥ kaṭakair bhātāḥ*
*kaṭi-sūtrāṅgulīyakaiḥ*

*catuḥ-bhujāḥ*—having four arms; *śaṅkha-cakra-gadā-rājīva-pāṇayaḥ*—holding conchshell, disc, club and lotus flower in Their hands; *kirīṭinaḥ*—bearing helmets on Their heads; *kuṇḍalinaḥ*—wearing earrings; *hāriṇaḥ*—wearing pearl necklaces; *vana-mālinaḥ*—wearing garlands of forest flowers; *śrīvatsa-aṅgada-do-ratna-kambu-kaṅkaṇa-pāṇayaḥ*—bearing the emblem of the goddess of fortune on Their chests, armlets on Their arms, the Kaustubha gem on Their necks, which were marked with three lines like a conchshell, and bracelets on Their hands; *nūpuraiḥ*—with ornaments on the feet; *kaṭakaiḥ*—with bangles on Their ankles; *bhātāḥ*—appeared beautiful; *kaṭi-sūtra-aṅgulīyakaiḥ*—with sacred belts around the waist and with rings on the fingers.

## TRANSLATION

**All those personalities had four arms, holding conchshell, disc, mace and lotus flower in Their hands. They wore helmets on Their heads, earrings on Their ears and garlands of forest flowers around Their necks. On the upper portion of the right side of Their chests was the emblem of the goddess of fortune. Furthermore, They wore armlets on Their arms, the Kaustubha gem around Their necks, which were marked with three lines like a conchshell, and bracelets on Their wrists. With bangles on Their ankles, ornaments on Their feet, and sacred belts around Their waists, They all appeared very beautiful.**

## PURPORT

All the Viṣṇu forms had four arms, with conchshell and other articles, but these characteristics are also possessed by those who have attained *sārūpya-mukti* in Vaikuṇṭha and who consequently have forms exactly like the form of the Lord. However, these Viṣṇu forms appearing before Lord Brahmā also possessed the mark of Śrīvatsa and the Kaustubha gem, which are special characteristics possessed only by the Supreme Lord Himself. This proves that all these boys and calves were in fact directly expansions of Viṣṇu, the Personality of Godhead, not merely His associates of Vaikuṇṭha. Viṣṇu Himself is included within Kṛṣṇa. All the opulences of Viṣṇu are already present in Kṛṣṇa, and consequently for Kṛṣṇa to demonstrate so many Viṣṇu forms was actually not very astonishing.

The Śrīvatsa mark is described by the *Vaiṣṇava-toṣaṇī* as being a curl of fine yellow hair on the upper portion of the right side of Lord Viṣṇu's chest. This mark is not for ordinary devotees. It is a special mark of Viṣṇu or Kṛṣṇa.

## TEXT 49

आङ्घ्रिमस्तकमापूर्णास्तुलसीनवदामभिः ।
कोमलैः सर्वगात्रेषु भूरिपुण्यवदर्पितैः ॥४९॥

*āṅghri-mastakam āpūrṇās*
*tulasī-nava-dāmabhiḥ*
*komalaiḥ sarva-gātreṣu*
*bhūri-puṇyavad-arpitaiḥ*

*ā-aṅghri-mastakam*—from the feet up to the top of the head; *āpūrṇāḥ*—fully decorated; *tulasī-nava-dāmabhiḥ*—with garlands of fresh *tulasī* leaves; *komalaiḥ*—tender, soft; *sarva-gātreṣu*—on all the limbs of the body; *bhūri-puṇyavat-arpitaiḥ*—which were offered by devotees engaged in the greatest pious activity, worshiping the Supreme Lord by hearing, chanting and so on.

## TRANSLATION

**Every part of Their bodies, from Their feet to the top of Their heads, was fully decorated with fresh, tender garlands of tulasī leaves offered by devotees engaged in worshiping the Lord by the greatest pious activities, namely hearing and chanting.**

## PURPORT

The word *bhūri-puṇyavad-arpitaiḥ* is significant in this verse. These forms of Viṣṇu were worshiped by those who had performed pious activities (*sukṛtibhiḥ*) for many births and who were constantly engaged in devotional service (*śravaṇaṁ kīrtanaṁ viṣṇoḥ*). *Bhakti*, devotional service, is the engagement of those who have performed highly developed pious activities. The accumulation of pious activities has already been mentioned elsewhere in the *Śrīmad-Bhāgavatam* (10.12.11), where Śukadeva Gosvāmī says,

*itthaṁ satāṁ brahma-sukhānubhūtyā*
*dāsyaṁ gatānāṁ para-daivatena*
*māyāśritānāṁ nara-dārakeṇa*
*sākaṁ vijahruḥ kṛta-puṇya-puñjāḥ*

"Those who are engaged in self-realization, appreciating the Brahman effulgence of the Lord, and those engaged in devotional service, accepting the Supreme Personality of Godhead as master, as well as those who are under the clutches of *māyā*, thinking the Lord an ordinary person, cannot understand that certain exalted personalities—after accumulating volumes of pious activities—are now playing with the Lord in friendship as cowherd boys."

In our Kṛṣṇa-Balarāma Temple in Vṛndāvana, there is a *tamāla* tree that covers an entire corner of the courtyard. Before there was a temple the tree was lying neglected, but now it has developed very luxuriantly, covering the whole corner of the courtyard. This is a sign of *bhūri-puṇya*.

## TEXT 50

चन्द्रिकाविशदस्मेरैः सारुणापाङ्गवीक्षितैः ।
स्वकार्थानामिव रजःसत्त्वाभ्यां स्रष्टृपालकाः ॥५०॥

*candrikā-viśada-smeraiḥ*
*sāruṇāpāṅga-vīkṣitaiḥ*
*svakārthānām iva rajaḥ-*
*sattvābhyāṁ sraṣṭṛ-pālakāḥ*

*candrikā-viśada-smeraiḥ*—by pure smiling like the full, increasing moonlight; *sa-aruṇa-apāṅga-vīkṣitaiḥ*—by the clear glances of Their reddish eyes; *svaka-arthānām*—of the desires of His own devotees; *iva*—just as; *rajaḥ-sattvābhyām*—by the modes of passion and goodness; *sraṣṭṛ-pālakāḥ*—were creators and protectors.

## TRANSLATION

**Those Viṣṇu forms, by Their pure smiling, which resembled the increasing light of the moon, and by the sidelong glances of Their reddish eyes, created and protected the desires of Their own devotees, as if by the modes of passion and goodness.**

## PURPORT

Those Viṣṇu forms blessed the devotees with Their clear glances and smiles, which resembled the increasingly full light of the moon (*śreyaḥ-kairava-candrikā-vitaraṇam*). As maintainers, They glanced upon Their devotees, embracing them and protecting them by smiling. Their smiles resembled the mode of goodness, protecting all the desires of the devotees, and the glancing of Their eyes resembled the mode of passion. Actually, in this verse the word *rajaḥ* means not "passion" but "affection." In the material world, *rajo-guṇa* is passion, but in the spiritual world it is affection. In the material world, affection is contaminated by *rajo-guṇa* and *tamo-guṇa*, but in the *śuddha-sattva* the affection that maintains the devotees is transcendental.

The word *svakārthānām* refers to great desires. As mentioned in this verse, the glance of Lord Viṣṇu creates the desires of the devotees. A pure devotee, however, has no desires. Therefore Sanātana Gosvāmī comments that because the desires of devotees whose attention is fixed on Kṛṣṇa have already been fulfilled, the Lord's sidelong glances create variegated desires in relation to Kṛṣṇa and devotional service. In the material world, desire is a product of *rajo-guṇa* and *tamo-guṇa*, but desire in the spiritual world gives rise to a variety of everlasting transcendental service. Thus the word *svakārthānām* refers to eagerness to serve Kṛṣṇa.

In Vṛndāvana there is a place where there was no temple, but a devotee desired, "Let there be a temple and *sevā*, devotional service." Therefore, what was once an empty corner has now become a place of pilgrimage. Such are the desires of a devotee.

## TEXT 51

आत्मादिस्तम्बपर्यन्तैर्मूर्तिमद्भिश्चराचरैः ।
नृत्यगीताद्यनेकार्हैः पृथक् पृथगुपासिताः ॥५१॥

*ātmādi-stamba-paryantair*
*mūrtimadbhiś carācaraiḥ*
*nṛtya-gītādy-anekārhaiḥ*
*pṛthak pṛthag upāsitāḥ*

*ātma-ādi-stamba-paryantaiḥ*—from Lord Brahmā to the insignificant living entity; *mūrti-madbhiḥ*—assuming some form; *cara-acaraiḥ*—both the moving and the nonmoving; *nṛtya-gīta-ādi-aneka-arhaiḥ*—by many varied means of worship, such as dancing and singing; *pṛthak pṛthak*—differently; *upāsitāḥ*—who were being worshiped.

## TRANSLATION

**All beings, both moving and nonmoving, from the four-headed Lord Brahmā down to the most insignificant living entity, had taken forms and were differently worshiping those viṣṇu-mūrtis, according to their respective capacities, with various means of worship, such as dancing and singing.**

## PURPORT

Innumerable living entities are engaged in different types of worship of the Supreme, according to their abilities and *karma*, but everyone is engaged (*jīvera 'svarūpa' haya—kṛṣṇera 'nitya-dāsa'*); there is no one who is not serving. Therefore the *mahā-bhāgavata*, the topmost devotee, sees everyone as being engaged in the service of Kṛṣṇa; only himself does he see as not engaged. We have to elevate ourselves from a lower position to a higher position, and the topmost position is that of direct service in Vṛndāvana. But everyone is engaged in service. Denial of the service of the Lord is *māyā*.

*ekale īśvara kṛṣṇa, āra saba bhṛtya*
*yāre yaiche nācāya, se taiche kare nṛtya*

"Only Kṛṣṇa is the supreme master, and all others are His servants. As Kṛṣṇa desires, everyone dances according to His tune." (Cc. *Ādi* 5.142)

There are two kinds of living entities—the moving and the nonmoving. Trees, for example, stand in one place, whereas ants move. Brahmā saw that all of them, down to the smallest creatures, had assumed different forms and were accordingly engaged in the service of Lord Viṣṇu.

One receives a form according to the way one worships the Lord. In the material world, the body one receives is guided by the demigods. This is sometimes referred to as the influence of the stars. As indicated in *Bhagavad-gītā* (3.27) by the words *prakṛteḥ kriyamāṇāni*, according to the laws of nature one is controlled by the demigods.

All living entities are serving Kṛṣṇa in different ways, but when they are Kṛṣṇa conscious, their service is fully manifest. As a flower in the bud gradually fructifies and yields its desired aroma and beauty, so when a living entity comes to the platform of Kṛṣṇa consciousness, the beauty of his real form comes into full blossom. That is the ultimate beauty and the ultimate fulfillment of desire.

## TEXT 52

अणिमाद्यैर्महिमभिरजाद्याभिर्विभूतिभिः ।
चतुर्विंशतिभिस्तत्त्वैः परीता महदादिभिः ॥५२॥

*aṇimādyair mahimabhir*
*ajādyābhir vibhūtibhiḥ*
*catur-viṁśatibhis tattvaiḥ*
*parītā mahad-ādibhiḥ*

*aṇimā-ādyaiḥ*—headed by *aṇimā; mahimabhiḥ*—by opulences; *ajā-ādyābhiḥ*—headed by Ajā; *vibhūtibhiḥ*—by potencies; *catuḥ-viṁśatibhiḥ*—twenty-four in number; *tattvaiḥ*—by elements for the creation of the material world; *parītāḥ*—(all the *viṣṇu-mūrtis*) were surrounded; *mahat-ādibhiḥ*—headed by the *mahat-tattva.*

## TRANSLATION

**All the viṣṇu-mūrtis were surrounded by the opulences, headed by aṇimā-siddhi; by the mystic potencies, headed by Ajā; and by**

**the twenty-four elements for the creation of the material world, headed by the mahat-tattva.**

## PURPORT

In this verse the word *mahimabhiḥ* means *aiśvarya*, or opulence. The Supreme Personality of Godhead can do whatever He likes. That is His *aiśvarya*. No one can command Him, but He can command everyone. *Ṣaḍ-aiśvarya-pūrṇam.* The Lord is full in six opulences. The *yoga-siddhis*, the perfections of *yoga*, such as the ability to become smaller than the smallest (*aṇimā-siddhi*) or bigger than the biggest (*mahimā-siddhi*), are present in Lord Viṣṇu. *Ṣaḍ-aiśvaryaiḥ pūrṇo ya iha bhagavān* (Cc. *Ādi* 1.3). The word *ajā* means *māyā*, or mystic power. Everything mysterious is in full existence in Viṣṇu.

The twenty-four elements mentioned are the five working senses (*pañca-karmendriya*), the five senses for obtaining knowledge (*pañca-jñānendriya*), the five gross material elements (*pañca-mahābhūta*), the five sense objects (*pañca-tanmātra*), the mind (*manas*), the false ego (*ahaṅkāra*), the *mahat-tattva*, and material nature (*prakṛti*). All twenty-four of these elements are employed for the manifestation of this material world. The *mahat-tattva* is divided into different subtle categories, but originally it is called the *mahat-tattva.*

## TEXT 53

कालस्वभावसंस्कारकामकर्मगुणादिभिः ।
स्वमहिध्वस्तमहिभिर्मूर्तिमद्भिरुपासिताः ॥५३॥

*kāla-svabhāva-saṁskāra-*
*kāma-karma-guṇādibhiḥ*
*sva-mahi-dhvasta-mahibhir*
*mūrtimadbhir upāsitāḥ*

*kāla*—by the time factor; *svabhāva*—own nature; *saṁskāra*—reformation; *kāma*—desire; *karma*—fruitive action; *guṇa*—the three modes of material nature; *ādibhiḥ*—and by others; *sva-mahi-dhvasta-mahibhiḥ*—whose own independence was subordinate to the potency of the Lord; *mūrti-madbhiḥ*—possessing form; *upāsitāḥ*—were being worshiped.

## TRANSLATION

**Then Lord Brahmā saw that kāla (the time factor), svabhāva (one's own nature by association), saṁskāra (reformation), kāma (desire), karma (fruitive activity) and the guṇas (the three modes of material nature), their own independence being completely subordinate to the potency of the Lord, had all taken forms and were also worshiping those viṣṇu-mūrtis.**

## PURPORT

No one but Viṣṇu has any independence. If we develop consciousness of this fact, then we are in actual Kṛṣṇa consciousness. We should always remember that Kṛṣṇa is the only supreme master and that everyone else is His servant (*ekale īśvara kṛṣṇa, āra saba bhṛtya*). Be one even Nārāyaṇa or Lord Śiva, everyone is subordinate to Kṛṣṇa (*śiva-viriñci-nutam*). Even Baladeva is subordinate to Kṛṣṇa. This is a fact.

*ekale īśvara kṛṣṇa, āra saba bhṛtya*
*yāre yaiche nācāya, se taiche kare nṛtya*
(Cc. *Ādi* 5.142)

One should understand that no one is independent, for everything is part and parcel of Kṛṣṇa and is acting and moving by the supreme desire of Kṛṣṇa. This understanding, this consciousness, is Kṛṣṇa consciousness.

*yas tu nārāyaṇaṁ devaṁ*
*brahma-rudrādi-daivataiḥ*
*samatvenaiva vīkṣeta*
*sa pāṣaṇḍī bhaved dhruvam*

"A person who considers demigods like Brahmā and Śiva to be on an equal level with Nārāyaṇa must certainly be considered an offender." No one can compare to Nārāyaṇa, or Kṛṣṇa. Kṛṣṇa is Nārāyaṇa, and Nārāyaṇa is also Kṛṣṇa, for Kṛṣṇa is the original Nārāyaṇa. Brahmā himself addresses Kṛṣṇa, *nārāyaṇas tvaṁ na hi sarva-dehinām:* "You are also Nārāyaṇa. Indeed, You are the original Nārāyaṇa." (*Bhāg.* 10.14.14)

*Kāla,* or the time factor, has many assistants, such as *svabhāva, saṁskāra, kāma, karma* and *guṇa. Svabhāva,* or one's own nature, is formed according to the association of the material qualities. *Kāraṇaṁ guṇa-saṅgo 'sya sad-asad-yoni-janmasu* (Bg. 13.22). *Sat* and *asat-svabhāva*—one's higher or lower nature—is formed by association with the different qualities, namely *sattva-guṇa, rajo-guṇa* and *tamo-guṇa.* We should gradually come to the *sattva-guṇa*, so that we may avoid the two lower *guṇas.* This can be done if we regularly discuss *Śrīmad-Bhāgavatam* and hear about Kṛṣṇa's activities. *Naṣṭa-prāyeṣv abhadreṣu nityaṁ bhāgavata-sevayā* (*Bhāg.* 1.2.18). All the activities of Kṛṣṇa described in *Śrīmad-Bhāgavatam*, beginning even with the pastimes concerning Pūtanā, are transcendental. Therefore, by hearing and discussing *Śrīmad-Bhāgavatam*, the *rajo-guṇa* and *tamo-guṇa* are subdued, so that only *sattva-guṇa* remains. Then *rajo-guṇa* and *tamo-guṇa* cannot do us any harm.

*Varṇāśrama-dharma*, therefore, is essential, for it can bring people to *sattva-guṇa. Tadā rajas-tamo-bhāvāḥ kāma-lobhādayaś ca ye* (*Bhāg.* 1.2.19). *Tamo-guṇa* and *rajo-guṇa* increase lust and greed, which implicate a living entity in such a way that he must exist in this material world in many, many forms. That is very dangerous. One should therefore be brought to *sattva-guṇa* by the establishment of *varṇāśrama-dharma* and should develop the brahminical qualifications of being very neat and clean, rising early in the morning and seeing *maṅgala-ārātrika*, and so on. In this way, one should stay in *sattva-guṇa*, and then one cannot be influenced by *tamo-guṇa* and *rajo-guṇa.*

*tadā rajas-tamo-bhāvāḥ*
*kāma-lobhādayaś ca ye*
*ceta etair anāviddhaṁ*
*sthitaṁ sattve prasīdati*
(*Bhāg.* 1.2.19)

The opportunity for this purification is the special feature of human life; in other lives, this is not possible. Such purification can be achieved very easily by *rādhā-kṛṣṇa-bhajana*, devotional service rendered to Rādhā and Kṛṣṇa, and therefore Narottama dāsa Ṭhākura sings, *hari hari viphale janama goṅāinu*, indicating that unless one worships Rādhā-Kṛṣṇa, one's human form of life is wasted. *Vāsudeve bhagavati bhakti-yogaḥ prayojitaḥ/ janayaty āśu vairāgyam* (*Bhāg.* 1.2.7). By engagement in the service of Vāsudeva, one very quickly renounces material life. The members of the Kṛṣṇa consciousness movement, for example, being engaged in *vāsudeva-bhakti,* very quickly come to the stage of being nice Vaiṣṇavas, so much so that people are surprised that *mlecchas* and *yavanas* are able to come to this stage. This is possible by *vāsudeva-bhakti.* But if we do not come to the stage of *sattva-guṇa* in this human life, then, as Narottama dāsa Ṭhākura sings, *hari hari viphale janama goṅāinu*—there is no profit in gaining this human form of life.

Śrī Vīrarāghava Ācārya comments that each of the items mentioned in the first half of this verse is a cause for material entanglement. *Kāla,* or the time factor, agitates the modes of material nature, and *svabhāva* is the result of association with these modes. Therefore Narottama dāsa Ṭhākura says, *bhakta-sane vāsa.* If one associates with *bhaktas,* then one's *svabhāva,* or nature, will change. Our Kṛṣṇa consciousness movement is meant to give people good association so that this change may take place, and we actually see that by this method people all over the world are gradually becoming devotees.

As for *saṁskāra,* or reformation, this is possible by good association, for by good association one develops good habits, and habit becomes second nature. Therefore, *bhakta-sane vāsa:* let people have the chance to live with *bhaktas.* Then their habits will change. In the human form of life one has this chance, but as Narottama dāsa Ṭhākura sings, *hari hari viphale janama goṅāinu:* if one fails to take advantage of this opportunity, one's human life is wasted. We are therefore trying to save human society from degradation and actually elevate people to the higher nature.

As for *kāma* and *karma*—desires and activities—if one engages in devotional service, one develops a different nature than if one engages in activities of sense gratification, and of course the result is also different. According to the association of different natures, one receives a particular type of body. *Kāraṇaṁ guṇa-saṅgo 'sya sad-asad-yoni-janmasu* (Bg. 13.22). Therefore we should always seek good association, the association of devotees. Then our life will be successful. A man is known by his company. If one has the chance to live in the good association of devotees, one is able to cultivate knowledge, and naturally one's character or nature will change for one's eternal benefit.

## TEXT 54

सत्यज्ञानानन्तानन्दमात्रैकरसमूर्तयः ।
अस्पृष्टभूरिमाहात्म्या अपि ह्युपनिषद्दृशाम् ॥५४॥

*satya-jñānānantānanda-*
*mātraika-rasa-mūrtayaḥ*
*aspṛṣṭa-bhūri-māhātmyā*
*api hy upaniṣad-dṛśām*

*satya*—eternal; *jñāna*—having full knowledge; *ananta*—unlimited; *ānanda*—fully blissful; *mātra*—only; *eka-rasa*—always existing; *mūrtayaḥ*—forms; *aspṛṣṭa-bhūri-māhātmyāḥ*—whose great glory is not touched; *api*—even; *hi*—because; *upaniṣat-dṛśām*—by those *jñānīs* who are engaged in studying the *Upaniṣads.*

## TRANSLATION

**The viṣṇu-mūrtis all had eternal, unlimited forms, full of knowledge and bliss and existing beyond the influence of time. Their great glory was not even to be touched by the jñānīs engaged in studying the Upaniṣads.**

## PURPORT

Mere *śāstra-jñāna,* or knowledge in the *Vedas,* does not help anyone understand the Personality of Godhead. Only one who is favored or shown mercy by the Lord can understand Him. This is also explained in the *Upaniṣads* (*Muṇḍaka Up.* 3.2.3):

*nāyam ātmā pravacanena labhyo*
*na medhasā na bahunā śrutena*
*yam evaiṣa vṛṇute tena labhyas*
*tasyaiṣa ātmā vivṛṇute tanuṁ svām*

"The Supreme Lord is not obtained by expert explanations, by vast intelligence, or even by much hearing. He is obtained only by one whom He Himself chooses. To such a person, He manifests His own form."

One description given of Brahman is *satyaṁ brahma, ānanda-rūpam:* "Brahman is the Absolute Truth and complete *ānanda,* or bliss." The forms of Viṣṇu, the Supreme Brahman, were one, but They were manifested differently. The followers of the *Upaniṣads,* however, cannot understand the varieties manifested by Brahman. This proves that Brahman and Paramātmā can actually be understood only through devotion, as confirmed by the Lord Himself in *Śrīmad-Bhāgavatam* (*bhaktyāham ekayā grāhyaḥ, Bhāg.* 11.14.21). To establish that Brahman indeed has transcendental form, Śrīla Viśvanātha Cakravartī Ṭhākura gives various quotations from the *śāstras.* In the *Śvetāśvatara Upaniṣad* (3.8), the Supreme is described as *āditya-varṇaṁ tamasaḥ parastāt,* "He whose self-manifest form is luminous like the sun and transcendental to the darkness of ignorance." *Ānanda-mātram ajaraṁ purāṇam ekaṁ santaṁ bahudhā dṛśyamānam:* "The Supreme is blissful, with no tinge of unhappiness. Although He is the oldest, He never ages, and although one, He is experienced in different forms." *Sarve nityāḥ śāśvatāś ca dehās tasya parātmanaḥ:* "All the forms of that Supreme Person are eternal." (*Mahā-varāha Purāṇa*) The Supreme Person has a form, with hands and legs and other personal features, but His hands and legs are not material. *Bhaktas* know that the form of Kṛṣṇa, or Brahman, is not at all material. Rather, Brahman has a transcendental form, and when one is absorbed in it, being fully developed in *bhakti,* one can understand Him (*premāñjana-cchurita-bhakti-vilocanena*). The Māyāvādīs, however, cannot understand this transcendental form, for they think that it is material.

Transcendental forms of the Supreme Personality of Godhead in His person are so great that the impersonal followers of the *Upaniṣads* cannot reach the platform of knowledge to understand them. Particularly, the transcendental forms of the Lord are beyond the reach of the impersonalists, who can only understand, through the studies of the *Upaniṣads,* that the Absolute Truth is not matter and that the Absolute Truth is not materially restricted by limited potency.

Yet although Kṛṣṇa cannot be seen through the *Upaniṣads,* in some places it is said that Kṛṣṇa can in fact be known in this way. *Aupaniṣadaṁ puruṣam:* "He is known by the *Upaniṣads.*" This means that when one is purified by Vedic knowledge, one is then allowed to enter into devotional understanding (*mad-bhaktiṁ labhate parām*).

*tac chraddadhānā munayo*
*jñāna-vairagya-yuktayā*
*paśyanty ātmani cātmānaṁ*
*bhaktyā śruta-gṛhītayā*

"The seriously inquisitive student or sage, well equipped with knowledge and detachment, realizes that Absolute Truth by rendering devotional service in terms of what he has heard from the *Vedānta-śruti.*" (*Bhāg.* 1.2.12) The word *śruta-gṛhītayā* refers to *Vedānta* knowledge, not sentimentality. *Śruta-gṛhīta* is sound knowledge.

Lord Viṣṇu, Brahmā thus realized, is the reservoir of all truth, knowledge and bliss. He is the combination of these three transcendental features, and He is the object of worship for the followers of the *Upaniṣads.* Brahmā realized that all the different forms of cows, boys and calves transformed into Viṣṇu forms were not transformed by mysticism of the type that a *yogī* or demigod can display by specific powers invested in him. The cows, calves and boys transformed into *viṣṇu-mūrtis,* or Viṣṇu forms, were not displays of *viṣṇu-māyā,* or Viṣṇu energy, but were Viṣṇu Himself. The respective qualifications of Viṣṇu and *viṣṇu-māyā* are just like those of fire and heat. In heat there is the qualification of fire, namely warmth; and yet heat is not fire. The manifestation of the Viṣṇu forms of the boys, cows and calves was not like the heat, but rather like the fire—they were all actually Viṣṇu. Factually, the qualification of Viṣṇu is full truth, full knowledge and full bliss. Another example may be given with material objects, which may be reflected in many, many forms. For example, the sun is reflected in many waterpots, but the reflections of the sun in many pots are not actually the sun. There is no actual heat and light from the sun in the pot, although it appears as the sun. But each and every one of the forms Kṛṣṇa assumed was fully Viṣṇu.

We should discuss *Śrīmad-Bhāgavatam* daily as much as possible, and then everything will be clarified, for *Bhāgavatam* is the essence of all Vedic literature (*nigama-kalpataror galitaṁ phalam*). It was written by Vyāsadeva (*mahāmuni-kṛte*) when he was self-realized. Thus the more we read *Śrīmad-Bhāgavatam,* the more its knowledge becomes clear. Each and every verse is transcendental.

## TEXT 55

एवं सकृद् ददर्शाजः परब्रह्मात्मनोऽखिलान् ।
यस्य भासा सर्वमिदं विभाति सचराचरम् ॥५५॥

*evaṁ sakṛd dadarśājaḥ*
*para-brahmātmano 'khilān*
*yasya bhāsā sarvam idaṁ*
*vibhāti sa-carācaram*

*evam*—thus; *sakṛt*—at one time; *dadarśa*—saw; *ajaḥ*—Lord Brahmā; *para-brahma*—of the Supreme Absolute Truth; *ātmanaḥ*—expansions; *akhilān*—all the calves and boys, etc.; *yasya*—of whom; *bhāsā*—by the manifestation; *sarvam*—all; *idam*—this; *vibhāti*—is manifested; *sa-cara-acaram*—whatever is moving and nonmoving.

## TRANSLATION

**Thus Lord Brahmā saw the Supreme Brahman, by whose energy this entire universe, with its moving and nonmoving living beings, is manifested. He also saw at the same time all the calves and boys as the Lord's expansions.**

## PURPORT

By this incident, Lord Brahmā was able to see how Kṛṣṇa maintains the entire universe in different ways. It is because Kṛṣṇa manifests everything that everything is visible.

## TEXT 56

ततोऽतिकुतुकोद्वृत्यस्तिमितैकादशेन्द्रियः ।
तद्धाम्नाभूदजस्तूष्णीं पूर्देव्यन्तीव पुत्रिका ॥५६॥

*tato 'tikutukodvṛtya-*
*stimitaikādaśendriyaḥ*
*tad-dhāmnābhūd ajas tūṣṇīṁ*
*pūr-devy-antīva putrikā*

*tataḥ*—then; *atikutuka-udvṛtya-stimita-ekādaśa-indriyaḥ*—whose eleven senses had all been jolted by great astonishment and then stunned by transcendental bliss; *tad-dhāmnā*—by the effulgence of those *viṣṇu-mūrtis; abhūt*—became; *ajaḥ*—Lord Brahmā; *tūṣṇīm*—silent; *pūḥ-devī-anti*—in the presence of a village deity (*grāmya-devatā*); *iva*—just as; *putrikā*—a clay doll made by a child.

## TRANSLATION

**Then, by the power of the effulgence of those viṣṇu-mūrtis, Lord Brahmā, his eleven senses jolted by astonishment and stunned by transcendental bliss, became silent, just like a child's clay doll in the presence of the village deity.**

## PURPORT

Brahmā was stunned because of transcendental bliss (*muhyanti yat sūrayaḥ*). In his astonishment, all his senses were stunned, and he was unable to say or do anything. Brahmā had considered himself absolute, thinking himself the only powerful deity, but now his pride was subdued, and he again became merely one of the demigods—an important demigod, of course, but a demigod nonetheless. Brahmā, therefore, cannot be compared to God—Kṛṣṇa, or Nārāyaṇa. It is forbidden to compare Nārāyaṇa even to demigods like Brahmā and Śiva, what to speak of others.

*yas tu nārāyaṇaṁ devaṁ*
*brahma-rudrādi-daivataiḥ*
*samatvenaiva vīkṣeta*
*sa pāṣaṇḍī bhaved dhruvam*

"One who considers demigods like Brahmā and Śiva to be on an equal level with Nārāyaṇa must certainly be considered an offender." We should not equate the demigods with Nārāyaṇa, for even Śaṅkarācārya has forbidden this (*nārāyaṇaḥ paro 'vyaktāt*). Also, as mentioned in the *Vedas, eko nārāyaṇa āsīn na brahmā neśānaḥ:* "In the beginning of creation there was only the Supreme Personality, Nārāyaṇa, and there was no existence of Brahmā or Śiva." Therefore, one who at the end of his life remembers Nārāyaṇa attains the perfection of life (*ante nārāyaṇa-smṛtiḥ*).

## TEXT 57

इतीरेशेऽतर्क्ये निजमहिमनि स्वप्रमितिके
परत्राजातोऽतन्निरसनमुखब्रह्मकमितौ ।
अनीशेऽपि द्रष्टुं किमिदमिति वा मुह्यति सति
चच्छादाजो ज्ञात्वा सपदि परमोऽजाजवनिकाम् ॥५७॥

*itīreśe 'tarkye nija-mahimani sva-pramitike*
*paratrājāto 'tan-nirasana-mukha-brahmaka-mitau*
*anīśe 'pi draṣṭuṁ kim idam iti vā muhyati sati*
*cacchādājo jñātvā sapadi paramo 'jā-javanikām*

*iti*—thus; *irā-īśe*—Lord Brahmā, the lord of Sarasvatī (Irā); *atarkye*—beyond; *nija-mahimani*—whose own glory; *sva-pramitike*—self-manifest and blissful; *paratra*—beyond; *ajātaḥ*—the material energy (*prakṛti*); *atat*—irrelevant; *nirasana-mukha*—by the rejection of that which is irrelevant; *brahmaka*—by the crest jewels of the *Vedas*; *mitau*—in whom there is knowledge; *anīśe*—not being able; *api*—even; *draṣṭum*—to see; *kim*—what; *idam*—is this; *iti*—thus; *vā*—or; *muhyati sati*—being mystified; *cacchāda*—removed; *ajaḥ*—Lord Śrī Kṛṣṇa; *jñātvā*—after understanding; *sapadi*—at once; *paramaḥ*—the greatest of all; *ajā-javanikām*—the curtain of *māyā*.

## TRANSLATION

**The Supreme Brahman is beyond mental speculation, He is self-manifest, existing in His own bliss, and He is beyond the material energy. He is known by the crest jewels of the Vedas by refutation of irrelevant knowledge. Thus in relation to that Supreme Brahman, the Personality of Godhead, whose glory had been shown by the manifestation of all the four-armed forms of Viṣṇu, Lord Brahmā, the lord of Sarasvatī, was mystified. "What is this?" he thought, and then he was not even able to see. Lord Kṛṣṇa, understanding Brahmā's position, then at once removed the curtain of His yogamāyā.**

## PURPORT

Brahmā was completely mystified. He could not understand what he was seeing, and then he was not even able to see. Lord Kṛṣṇa, understanding Brahmā's position, then removed that *yogamāyā* covering. In this verse, Brahmā is referred to as *ireśa. Irā* means Sarasvatī, the goddess of learning, and Ireśa is her husband, Lord Brahmā. Brahmā, therefore, is most intelligent. But even Brahmā, the lord of Sarasvatī, was bewildered about Kṛṣṇa. Although he tried, he could not understand Lord Kṛṣṇa. In the beginning the boys, the calves and Kṛṣṇa Himself had been covered by *yogamāyā,* which later displayed the second set of calves and boys, who were Kṛṣṇa's expansions, and which then displayed so many four-armed forms. Now, seeing Brahmā's bewilderment, Lord Kṛṣṇa caused the disappearance of that *yogamāyā.* One may think that the *māyā* taken away by Lord Kṛṣṇa was *mahāmāyā,* but Śrīla Viśvanātha Cakravartī Ṭhākura comments that it was *yogamāyā,* the potency by which Kṛṣṇa is sometimes manifest and sometimes not manifest. The potency which covers the actual reality and displays something unreal is *mahāmāyā,* but the potency by which the Absolute Truth is sometimes manifest and sometimes not is *yogamāyā.* Therefore, in this verse the word *ajā* refers to *yogamāyā.*

Kṛṣṇa's energy—His *māyā-śakti,* or *svarūpa-śakti*—is one, but it is manifested in varieties. *Parāsya śaktir vividhaiva śrūyate* (*Śvetāśvatara Up.* 6.8). The difference between Vaiṣṇavas and Māyāvādīs is that Māyāvādīs say that this *māyā* is one, whereas Vaiṣṇavas recognize its varieties. There is unity in variety. For example, in one tree, there are varieties of leaves, fruits and flowers. Varieties of energy are required for performing the varieties of activity within the creation. To give another example, in a machine all the parts may be iron, but the machine includes varied activities. Although the whole machine is iron, one part works in one way, and other parts work in other ways. One who does not know how the machine is working may say that it is all iron; nonetheless, in spite of its being iron, the machine has different elements, all working differently to accomplish the purpose for which the machine was made. One wheel runs this way, another wheel runs that way, functioning naturally in such a way that the work of the machine goes on. Consequently we give different names to the different parts of the machine, saying, "This is a wheel," "This is a screw," "This is a spindle," "This is the lubrication," and so on. Similarly, as explained in the *Vedas,*

*parāsya śaktir vividhaiva śrūyate*
*svābhāvikī jñāna-bala-kriyā ca*

Kṛṣṇa's power is variegated, and thus the same *śakti,* or potency, works in variegated ways. *Vividhā* means "varieties." There is unity in variety. Thus *yogamāyā* and *mahāmāyā* are among the varied individual parts of the same one potency, and all of these individual potencies work in their own varied ways. The *saṁvit, sandhinī* and *āhlādinī* potencies—Kṛṣṇa's potency for existence, His potency for knowledge and His potency for pleasure—are distinct from *yogamāyā.* Each is an individual potency. The *āhlādinī* potency is Rādhārāṇī. As Svarūpa Dāmodara Gosvāmī has explained, *rādhā kṛṣṇa-praṇaya-vikṛtir hlādinī śaktir asmāt* (Cc. *Ādi* 1.5). The *āhlādinī-śakti* is manifested as Rādhārāṇī, but Kṛṣṇa and Rādhārāṇī are the same, although one is potent and the other is potency.

Brahmā was mystified about Kṛṣṇa's opulence (*nija-mahimani*) because this opulence was *atarkya,* or inconceivable. With one's limited senses, one cannot argue about that which is inconceivable. Therefore the inconceivable is called *acintya,* that which is beyond *cintya,* our thoughts and arguments. *Acintya* refers to that which we cannot contemplate but have to accept. Śrīla Jīva Gosvāmī has said that unless we accept *acintya* in the Supreme, we cannot accommodate the conception of God. This must be understood. Therefore we say that the words of *śāstra* should be taken as they are, without change, since they are beyond our arguments. *Acintyāḥ khalu ye bhāvā na tāṁs tarkeṇa yojayet:* "That which is *acintya* cannot be ascertained by argument." People generally argue, but our process is not to argue but to accept the Vedic knowledge as it is. When Kṛṣṇa says, "This is superior, and this is inferior," we accept what He says. It is not that we argue, "Why is this superior and that inferior?" If one argues, for him the knowledge is lost.

This path of acceptance is called *avaroha-panthā.* The word *avaroha* is related to the word *avatāra,* which means "that which descends." The materialist wants to understand everything by the *āroha-panthā*—by argument and reason—but transcendental matters cannot be understood in this way. Rather, one must follow the *avaroha-panthā,* the process of descending knowledge. Therefore one must accept the *paramparā* system. And the best *paramparā* is that which extends from Kṛṣṇa (*evaṁ paramparā-prāptam*). What Kṛṣṇa says, we should accept (*imaṁ rājarṣayo viduḥ*). This is called the *avaroha-panthā*.

Brahmā, however, adopted the *āroha-panthā*. He wanted to understand Kṛṣṇa's mystic power by his own limited, conceivable power, and therefore he himself was mystified. Everyone wants to take pleasure in his own knowledge, thinking, "I know something." But in the presence of Kṛṣṇa this conception cannot stand, for one cannot bring Kṛṣṇa within the limitations of *prakṛti*. One must submit. There is no alternative. *Na tāṁs tarkeṇa yojayet.* This submission marks the difference between Kṛṣṇa-ites and Māyāvādīs.

The phrase *atan-nirasana* refers to the discarding of that which is irrelevant. (*Atat* means "that which is not a fact.") Brahman is sometimes described as *asthūlam anaṇv ahrasvam adīrgham*, "that which is not large and not small, not short and not long." (*Bṛhad-āraṇyaka Up.* 5.8.8) *Neti neti:* "It is not this, it is not that." But what is it? In describing a pencil, one may say, "It is not this; it is not that," but this does not tell us what it is. This is called definition by negation. In *Bhagavad-gītā*, Kṛṣṇa also explains the soul by giving negative definitions. *Na jāyate mriyate vā:* "It is not born, nor does it die. You can hardly understand more than this." But what is it? It is eternal. *Ajo nityaḥ śāśvato 'yaṁ purāṇo na hanyate hanyamāne śarīre:* "It is unborn, eternal, ever-existing, undying and primeval. It is not slain when the body is slain." (Bg. 2.20) In the beginning the soul is difficult to understand, and therefore Kṛṣṇa has given negative definitions:

*nainaṁ chindanti śastrāṇi*
*nainaṁ dahati pāvakaḥ*
*na cainaṁ kledayanty āpo*
*na śoṣayati mārutaḥ*

"The soul can never be cut into pieces by any weapon, nor can it be burned by fire, nor moistened by water, nor withered by the wind." (Bg. 2.23) Kṛṣṇa says, "It is not burned by fire." Therefore, one has to imagine what it is that is not burned by fire. This is a negative definition.

## TEXT 58

ततोऽर्वाक् प्रतिलब्धाक्षः कः परेतवदुत्थितः ।
कृच्छ्रादुन्मील्य वै दृष्टीराचष्टेदं सहात्मना ॥५८॥

*tato 'rvāk pratilabdhākṣaḥ*
*kaḥ paretavad utthitaḥ*
*kṛcchrād unmīlya vai dṛṣṭīr*
*ācaṣṭedaṁ sahātmanā*

*tataḥ*—then; *arvāk*—externally; *pratilabdha-akṣaḥ*—having revived his consciousness; *kaḥ*—Lord Brahmā; *pareta-vat*—just like a dead man; *utthitaḥ*—stood up; *kṛcchrāt*—with great difficulty; *unmīlya*—opening up; *vai*—indeed; *dṛṣṭīḥ*—his eyes; *ācaṣṭa*—he saw; *idam*—this universe; *saha-ātmanā*—along with himself.

## TRANSLATION

**Lord Brahmā's external consciousness then revived, and he stood up, just like a dead man coming back to life. Opening his eyes with great difficulty, he saw the universe, along with himself.**

## PURPORT

We actually do not die. At death, we are merely kept inert for some time, just as during sleep. At night we sleep, and all our activities stop, but as soon as we arise, our memory immediately returns, and we think, "Oh, where am I? What do I have to do?" This is called *suptotthita-nyāya.* Suppose we die. "Die" means that we become inert for some time and then again begin our activities. This takes place life after life, according to our *karma*, or activities, and *svabhāva*, or nature by association. Now, in the human life, if we prepare ourselves by beginning the activity of our spiritual life, we return to our real life and attain perfection. Otherwise, according to *karma*, *svabhāva*, *prakṛti* and so on, our varieties of life and activity continue, and so also do our birth and death. As explained by Bhaktivinoda Ṭhākura, *māyāra vaśe, yāccha bhese, khāccha hābuḍubu bhāi:* "My dear brothers, why are you being washed away by the waves of *māyā*?" One should come to the spiritual platform, and then one's activities will be permanent. *Kṛta-puṇya-puñjāḥ:* this stage is attained after one accumulates the results of pious activities for many, many lives. *Janma-koṭi-sukṛtair na labhyate* (Cc. *Madhya* 8.70). The Kṛṣṇa consciousness movement wants to stop *koṭi-janma*, repeated birth and death. In one birth, one should rectify everything and come to permanent life. This is Kṛṣṇa consciousness.

## TEXT 59

सपद्येवाभितः पश्यन् दिशोऽपश्यत् पुरः स्थितम् ।
वृन्दावनं जनाजीव्यद्रुमाकीर्णं समाप्रियम् ॥५९॥

*sapady evābhitaḥ paśyan*
*diśo 'paśyat puraḥ-sthitam*
*vṛndāvanaṁ janājīvya-*
*drumākīrṇaṁ samā-priyam*

*sapadi*—immediately; *eva*—indeed; *abhitaḥ*—on all sides; *paśyan*—looking; *diśaḥ*—in the directions; *apaśyat*—Lord Brahmā saw; *puraḥ-sthitam*—situated in front of him; *vṛndāvanam*—Vṛndāvana; *jana-ājīvya-druma-ākīrṇam*—dense with trees, which were the means of living for the inhabitants; *samā-priyam*—and which was equally pleasing in all seasons.

## TRANSLATION

**Then, looking in all directions, Lord Brahmā immediately saw Vṛndāvana before him, filled with trees, which were the means of livelihood for the inhabitants and which were equally pleasing in all seasons.**

## PURPORT

*Janājīvya-drumākīrṇam:* trees and vegetables are essential, and they give happiness all year round, in all seasons. That is the arrangement in Vṛndāvana. It is not that in one season the trees are pleasing and in another season not pleasing; rather, they are equally pleasing throughout the seasonal changes. Trees and vegetables provide the real means of livelihood recommended for everyone. *Sarva-kāma-dughā mahī* (*Bhāg.* 1.10.4). Trees and vegetables, not industry, provide the real means of life.

## TEXT 60

यत्र नैसर्गदुर्वैराः सहासन् नृमृगादयः ।
मित्राणीवाजितावासद्रुतरुट्तर्षकादिकम् ॥६०॥

*yatra naisarga-durvairāḥ*
*sahāsan nṛ-mṛgādayaḥ*
*mitrāṇīvājitāvāsa-*
*druta-ruṭ-tarṣakādikam*

*yatra*—where; *naisarga*—by nature; *durvairāḥ*—living in enmity; *saha āsan*—live together; *nṛ*—human beings; *mṛga-ādayaḥ*—and animals; *mitrāṇi*—friends; *iva*—like; *ajita*—of Lord Śrī Kṛṣṇa; *āvāsa*—residence; *druta*—gone away; *ruṭ*—anger; *tarṣaka-ādikam*—thirst and so on.

## TRANSLATION

**Vṛndāvana is the transcendental abode of the Lord, where there is no hunger, anger or thirst. Though naturally inimical, both human beings and fierce animals live there together in transcendental friendship.**

## PURPORT

The word *vana* means "forest." We are afraid of the forest and do not wish to go there, but in Vṛndāvana the forest animals are as good as demigods, for they have no envy. Even in this material world, in the forest the animals live together, and when they go to drink water they do not attack anyone. Envy develops because of sense gratification, but in Vṛndāvana there is no sense gratification, for the only aim is Kṛṣṇa's satisfaction. Even in this material world, the animals in Vṛndāvana are not envious of the *sādhus* who live there. The *sādhus* keep cows and supply milk to the tigers, saying, "Come here and take a little milk." Thus envy and malice are unknown in Vṛndāvana. That is the difference between Vṛndāvana and the ordinary world. We are horrified to hear the name of *vana*, the forest, but in Vṛndāvana there is no such horror. Everyone there is happy by pleasing Kṛṣṇa. *Kṛṣṇotkīrtana-gāna-nartana-parau.* Whether a *gosvāmī* or a tiger or other ferocious animal, everyone's business is the same—to please Kṛṣṇa. Even the tigers are also devotees. This is the specific qualification of Vṛndāvana. In Vṛndāvana everyone is happy. The calf is happy, the cat is happy, the dog is happy, the man is happy—everyone. Everyone wants to serve Kṛṣṇa in a different capacity, and thus there is no envy. One may sometimes think that the monkeys in Vṛndāvana are envious, because they cause mischief and steal food, but in Vṛndāvana we find that the monkeys are allowed to take butter, which Kṛṣṇa Himself distributes. Kṛṣṇa personally demonstrates that everyone has the right to live. This is Vṛndāvana life. Why should I live and you die? No. That is material life. The inhabitants of Vṛndāvana think, "Whatever is given by Kṛṣṇa, let us divide it as *prasāda* and eat." This mentality cannot appear all of a sudden, but it will gradually develop with Kṛṣṇa consciousness; by *sādhana*, one can come to this platform.

In the material world one may collect funds all over the world in order to distribute food freely, yet those to whom the food is given may not even feel appreciative. The value of Kṛṣṇa consciousness, however, will gradually be very much appreciated. For instance, in an article about the temple of the Hare Kṛṣṇa movement in Durban, South Africa, the *Durban Post* reported, "All the devotees here are very active in the service of Lord Kṛṣṇa, and the results are obvious to see: happiness, good health, peace of mind, and the development of all good qualities." This is the nature of Vṛndāvana. *Harāv abhaktasya kuto mahad-guṇāḥ:* without Kṛṣṇa consciousness, happiness is impossible; one may struggle, but one cannot have happiness. We are therefore trying to give human society the opportunity for a life of happiness, good health, peace of mind and all good qualities through God consciousness.

## TEXT 61

तत्रोद्वहत् पशुपवंशशिशुत्वनाट्यं
ब्रह्माद्वयं परमनन्तमगाधबोधम् ।
वत्सान् सखीनिव पुरा परितो विचिन्व-
देकं सपाणिकवलं परमेष्ठ्यचष्ट ॥६१॥

*tatrodvahat paśupa-vaṁśa-śiśutva-nāṭyaṁ*
*brahmādvayaṁ param anantam agādha-bodham*
*vatsān sakhīn iva purā parito vicinvad*
*ekaṁ sa-pāṇi-kavalaṁ parameṣṭhy acaṣṭa*

*tatra*—there (in Vṛndāvana); *udvahat*—assuming; *paśupa-vaṁśa-śiśutva-nāṭyam*—the play of being a child in a family of cowherd men (another of Kṛṣṇa's names is Gopāla, "He who maintains the cows"); *brahma*—the Absolute Truth; *advayam*—without a second; *param*—the Supreme; *anantam*—unlimited; *agādha-bodham*—possessing unlimited knowledge; *vatsān*—the calves; *sakhīn*—and His friends, the boys; *iva purā*—just as before; *paritaḥ*—everywhere; *vicinvat*—searching; *ekam*—alone, all by Himself; *sa-pāni-kavalam*—with a morsel of food in His hand; *parameṣṭhī*—Lord Brahmā; *acaṣṭa*—saw.

## TRANSLATION

**Then Lord Brahmā saw the Absolute Truth—who is one without a second, who possesses full knowledge and who is unlimited—assuming the role of a child in a family of cowherd men and standing all alone, just as before, with a morsel of food in His hand, searching everywhere for the calves and His cowherd friends.**

## PURPORT

The word *agādha-bodham*, meaning "full of unlimited knowledge," is significant in this verse. The Lord's knowledge is unlimited, and therefore one cannot touch where it ends, just as one cannot measure the ocean. What is the extent of our intelligence in comparison to the vast expanse of water in the ocean? On my passage to America, how insignificant the ship was, like a matchbox in the midst of the ocean. Kṛṣṇa's intelligence resembles the ocean, for one cannot imagine how vast it is. The best course, therefore, is to surrender to Kṛṣṇa. Don't try to measure Kṛṣṇa.

The word *advayam*, meaning "one without a second," is also significant. Because Brahmā was overcast by Kṛṣṇa's *māyā*, he was thinking himself the Supreme. In the material world, everyone thinks, "I am the best man in this world. I know everything." One thinks, "Why should I read *Bhagavad-gītā*? I know everything. I have my own interpretation."

Brahmā, however, was able to understand that the Supreme Personality is Kṛṣṇa. *Īśvaraḥ paramaḥ kṛṣṇaḥ.* Another of Kṛṣṇa's names, therefore, is *parameśvara.*

Now Brahmā saw Kṛṣṇa, the Supreme Personality of Godhead, appearing as a cowherd boy in Vṛndāvana, not demonstrating His opulence but standing just like an innocent boy with some food in His hand, loitering with His cowherd boyfriends, calves and cows. Brahmā did not see Kṛṣṇa as *catur-bhuja,* the opulent Nārāyaṇa; rather, he simply saw an innocent boy. Nonetheless, he could understand that although Kṛṣṇa was not demonstrating His power, He was the same Supreme Person. People generally do not appreciate someone unless he shows something wonderful, but here, although Kṛṣṇa did not manifest anything wonderful, Brahmā could understand that the same wonderful person was present like an ordinary child, although He was the master of the whole creation. Thus Brahmā prayed, *govindam ādi-puruṣaṁ tam ahaṁ bhajāmi:* "You are the original person, the cause of everything. I bow down to You." This was his realization. *Tam ahaṁ bhajāmi.* This is what is wanted. *Vedeṣu durlabham:* one cannot reach Kṛṣṇa merely by Vedic knowledge. *Adurlabham ātma-bhaktau:* but when one becomes a devotee, then one can realize Him. Brahmā, therefore, became a devotee. In the beginning he was proud of being Brahmā, the lord of the universe, but now he understood, "Here is the Lord of the universe. I am simply an insignificant agent. *Govindam ādi-puruṣaṁ tam ahaṁ bhajāmi.*"

Kṛṣṇa was playing like a dramatic actor. Because Brahmā had some false prestige, thinking that he had some power, Kṛṣṇa showed him his real position. A similar incident occurred when Brahmā went to see Kṛṣṇa in Dvārakā. When Kṛṣṇa's doorman informed Lord Kṛṣṇa that Lord Brahmā had arrived, Kṛṣṇa responded, "Which Brahmā? Ask him which Brahmā." The doorman relayed this question, and Brahmā was astonished. "Is there another Brahmā besides me?" he thought. When the doorman informed Lord Kṛṣṇa, "It is four-headed Brahmā," Lord Kṛṣṇa said, "Oh, four-headed. Call others. Show him." This is Kṛṣṇa's position. For Kṛṣṇa the four-headed Brahmā is insignificant, to say nothing of "four-headed scientists." Materialistic scientists think that although this planet earth is full of opulence, all others are vacant. Because they simply speculate, this is their scientific conclusion. But from the *Bhāgavatam* we understand that the entire universe is full of living entities everywhere. Thus it is the folly of the scientists that although they do not know anything, they mislead people by presenting themselves as scientists, philosophers and men of knowledge.

## TEXT 62

दृष्ट्वा त्वरेण निजधोरणतोऽवतीर्य
पृथ्व्यां वपुः कनकदण्डमिवाभिपात्य ।
स्पृष्ट्वा चतुर्मुकुटकोटिभिरङ्घ्रियुग्मं
नत्वा मुदश्रुसुजलैरकृताभिषेकम् ॥६२॥

*dṛṣṭvā tvareṇa nija-dhoraṇato 'vatīrya*
*pṛthvyāṁ vapuḥ kanaka-daṇḍam ivābhipātya*
*spṛṣṭvā catur-mukuṭa-koṭibhir aṅghri-yugmaṁ*
*natvā mud-aśru-sujalair akṛtābhiṣekam*

*dṛṣṭvā*—after seeing; *tvareṇa*—with great speed, hastily; *nija-dhoraṇataḥ*—from his swan carrier; *avatīrya*—descended; *pṛthvyām*—on the ground; *vapuḥ*—his body; *kanaka-daṇḍam iva*—like a golden rod; *abhipātya*—fell down; *spṛṣṭvā*—touching; *catuḥ-mukuṭa-koṭi-bhiḥ*—with the tips of his four crowns; *aṅghri-yugmam*—the two lotus feet; *natvā*—making obeisances; *mut-aśru-su-jalaiḥ*—with the water of his tears of joy; *akṛta*—performed; *abhiṣekam*—the ceremony of bathing His lotus feet.

## TRANSLATION

**After seeing this, Lord Brahmā hastily got down from his swan carrier, fell down like a golden rod and touched the lotus feet of Lord Kṛṣṇa with the tips of the four crowns on his heads. Offering his obeisances, he bathed the feet of Kṛṣṇa with the water of his tears of joy.**

## PURPORT

Lord Brahmā bowed down like a stick, and because Lord Brahmā's complexion is golden, he appeared to be like a golden stick lying down before Lord Kṛṣṇa. When one falls down before a superior just like a stick, one's offering of obeisances is called *daṇḍavat. Daṇḍa* means "stick," and *vat* means "like." It is not that one should simply say, "*daṇḍavat.*" Rather, one must fall down. Thus Brahmā fell down, touching his foreheads to the lotus feet of Kṛṣṇa, and his crying in ecstasy is to be regarded as an *abhiṣeka* bathing ceremony of Kṛṣṇa's lotus feet.

He who appeared before Brahmā as a human child was in fact the Absolute Truth, Parabrahman (*brahmeti paramātmeti bhagavān iti śabdyate*). The Supreme Lord is *narākṛti;* that is, He resembles a human being. It is not that He is four-armed (*catur-bāhu*). Nārāyaṇa is *catur-bāhu*, but the Supreme Person resembles a human being. This is also confirmed in the Bible, where it is said that man was made in the image of God.

Lord Brahmā saw that Kṛṣṇa, in His form as a cowherd boy, was Parabrahman, the root cause of everything, but was now appearing as a human child, loitering in Vṛndāvana with a morsel of food in His hand. Astonished, Lord Brahmā hastily got down from his swan carrier and let his body fall to the earth. Usually, the demigods never touch the ground, but Lord Brahmā, voluntarily giving up his prestige as a demigod, bowed down on the ground before Kṛṣṇa. Although Brahmā has one head in each direction, he voluntarily brought all his heads to the ground and touched Kṛṣṇa's feet with the tips of his four helmets. Although his intelligence works in every direction, he surrendered everything before the boy Kṛṣṇa.

It is mentioned that Brahmā washed the feet of Kṛṣṇa with his tears, and here the word *sujalaiḥ* indicates that his tears were purified. As soon as *bhakti* is present, everything is purified (*sarvopādhi-vinirmuktam*). Therefore Brahmā's crying was a form of *bhakty-anubhāva*, a transformation of transcendental ecstatic love.

## TEXT 63

उत्थायोत्थाय कृष्णस्य चिरस्य पादयोः पतन् ।
आस्ते महित्वं प्राग्दृष्टं स्मृत्वा स्मृत्वा पुनः पुनः ॥६३॥

*utthāyotthāya kṛṣṇasya*
*cirasya pādayoḥ patan*
*āste mahitvaṁ prāg-dṛṣṭam*
*smṛtvā smṛtvā punaḥ punaḥ*

*utthāya utthāya*—rising repeatedly; *kṛṣṇasya*—of Lord Kṛṣṇa; *cirasya*—for a long time; *pādayoḥ*—at the lotus feet; *patan*—falling down; *āste*—remained; *mahitvam*—the greatness; *prāk-dṛṣṭam*—which he had previously seen; *smṛtvā smṛtvā*—remembering and remembering; *punaḥ punaḥ*—again and again.

## TRANSLATION

**Rising and falling again and again at the lotus feet of Lord Kṛṣṇa for a long time, Lord Brahmā remembered over and over the Lord's greatness he had just seen.**

## PURPORT

As stated in one prayer,

*śrutim apare smṛtim itare*
*bhāratam anye bhajantu bhava-bhītāḥ*
*aham iha nandaṁ vande*
*yasyālinde paraṁ brahma*

"Let others study the *Vedas, smṛti* and *Mahābhārata*, fearing material existence, but I shall worship Nanda Mahārāja, in whose courtyard is crawling the Supreme Brahman. Nanda Mahārāja is so great that the Parabrahman is crawling in his yard, and therefore I shall worship him." (*Padyāvali* 126)

Brahmā was falling down in ecstasy. Because of the presence of the Supreme Personality of Godhead, who exactly resembled a human child, Brahmā was naturally astonished. Therefore with a faltering voice he offered prayers, understanding that here was the Supreme Person.

## TEXT 64

शनैरथोत्थाय विमृज्य लोचने
मुकुन्दमुद्वीक्ष्य विनम्रकन्धरः ।
कृताञ्जलिः प्रश्रयवान् समाहितः
सवेपथुर्गद्गदयैलतेलया ॥६४॥

*śanair athotthāya vimṛjya locane*
*mukundam udvīkṣya vinamra-kandharaḥ*
*kṛtāñjaliḥ praśrayavān samāhitaḥ*
*sa-vepathur gadgadayailatelayā*

*śanaiḥ*—gradually; *atha*—then; *utthāya*—rising; *vimṛjya*—wiping; *locane*—his two eyes; *mukundam*—at Mukunda, Lord Śrī Kṛṣṇa; *udvīkṣya*—looking up; *vinamra-kandharaḥ*—his neck bent; *kṛta-añjaliḥ*—with folded hands; *praśraya-vān*—very humble; *samāhitaḥ*—his mind concentrated; *sa-vepathuḥ*—his body trembling; *gadgadayā*—faltering; *ailata*—Brahmā began to offer praise; *īlayā*—with words.

## TRANSLATION

**Then, rising very gradually and wiping his two eyes, Lord Brahmā looked up at Mukunda. Lord Brahmā, his head bent low, his mind concentrated and his body trembling, very humbly began, with faltering words, to offer praises to Lord Kṛṣṇa.**

## PURPORT

Brahmā, being very joyful, began to shed tears, and he washed the lotus feet of Kṛṣṇa with his tears. Repeatedly he fell and rose as he recalled the wonderful activities of the Lord. After repeating obeisances for a long time, Brahmā stood up and smeared his hands over his eyes. Śrīla Viśvanātha Cakravartī Ṭhākura comments that the word *locane* indicates that with his two hands he wiped the two eyes on each of his four faces. Seeing the Lord before him, Brahmā began to offer prayers with great humility, respect and attention.

*Thus end the Bhaktivedanta purports of the Tenth Canto, Thirteenth Chapter, of the* Śrīmad-Bhāgavatam, *entitled "The Stealing of the Boys and Calves by Brahmā."*

# Appendixes

# About the Author

His Divine Grace A.C. Bhaktivedanta Swami Prabhupāda appeared in this world in 1896 in Calcutta, India. He first met his spiritual master, Śrīla Bhaktisiddhānta Sarasvatī Gosvāmī, in Calcutta in 1922. Bhaktisiddhānta Sarasvatī, a prominent religious scholar and the founder of sixty-four Gauḍīya Maṭhas (Vedic institutes), liked this educated young man and convinced him to dedicate his life to teaching Vedic knowledge. Śrīla Prabhupāda became his student, and eleven years later (1933) at Allahabad he became his formally initiated disciple.

At their first meeting, in 1922, Śrīla Bhaktisiddhānta Sarasvatī Ṭhākura requested Śrīla Prabhupāda to broadcast Vedic knowledge through the English language. In the years that followed, Śrīla Prabhupāda wrote a commentary on the *Bhagavad-gītā,* assisted the Gauḍīya Maṭha in its work and, in 1944, started *Back to Godhead,* an English fortnightly magazine. Maintaining the publication was a struggle. Singlehandedly, Śrīla Prabhupāda edited it, typed the manuscripts, checked the galley proofs, and even distributed the individual copies. Once begun, the magazine never stopped; it is now being continued by his disciples in the West and is published in over thirty languages.

Recognizing Śrīla Prabhupāda's philosophical learning and devotion, the Gauḍīya Vaiṣṇava Society honored him in 1947 with the title "Bhaktivedanta." In 1950, at the age of fifty-four, Śrīla Prabhupāda retired from married life, adopting the *vānaprastha* (retired) order to devote more time to his studies and writing. Śrīla Prabhupāda traveled to the holy city of Vṛndāvana, where he lived in very humble circumstances in the historic medieval temple of Rādhā-Dāmodara. There he engaged for several years in deep study and writing. He accepted the renounced order of life (*sannyāsa*) in 1959. At Rādhā-Dāmodara, Śrīla Prabhupāda began work on his life's masterpiece: a multivolume annotated translation of the eighteen-thousand-verse *Śrīmad-Bhāgavatam* (*Bhāgavata Purāṇa*). He also wrote *Easy Journey to Other Planets.*

After publishing three volumes of the *Bhāgavatam,* Śrīla Prabhupāda came to the United States, in September 1965, to fulfill the mission of his spiritual master. Subsequently, His Divine Grace wrote more than sixty volumes of authoritative annotated translations and summary studies of the philosophical and religious classics of India.

When he first arrived by freighter in New York City, Śrīla Prabhupāda was practically penniless. Only after almost a year of great difficulty did he establish the International Society for Krishna Consciousness, in July of 1966. Before his passing away on November 14, 1977, he guided the Society and saw it grow to a worldwide confederation of more than one hundred *āśramas*, schools, temples, institutes and farm communities.

In 1968, Śrīla Prabhupāda created New Vrindaban, an experimental Vedic community in the hills of West Virginia. Inspired by the success of New Vrindaban, now a thriving farm community of more than two thousand acres, his students have since founded several similar communities in the United States and abroad.

In 1972, His Divine Grace introduced the Vedic system of primary and secondary education in the West by founding the Gurukula school in Dallas, Texas. Since then, under his supervision, his disciples have established children's schools throughout the United States and the rest of the world, with the principal educational center now located in Vṛndāvana, India.

Śrīla Prabhupāda also inspired the construction of several large international cultural centers in India. The center at Śrīdhāma Māyāpur in West Bengal is the site for a planned spiritual city, an ambitious project for which construction will extend over many years to come. In Vṛndāvana, India, are the magnificent Kṛṣṇa-Balarāma Temple and International Guesthouse, and Śrīla Prabhupāda Memorial and Museum. There is also a major cultural and educational center in Bombay. Other centers are planned in a dozen important locations on the Indian subcontinent.

Śrīla Prabhupāda's most significant contribution, however, is his books. Highly respected by the academic community for their authority, depth and clarity, they are used as standard textbooks in numerous college courses. His writings have been translated into over fifty languages. The Bhaktivedanta Book Trust, established in 1972 to publish the works of His Divine Grace, has thus become the world's largest publisher of books in the field of Indian religion and philosophy.

In just twelve years, in spite of his advanced age, Śrīla Prabhupāda circled the globe fourteen times on lecture tours that took him to six continents. In spite of such a vigorous schedule, Śrīla Prabhupāda continued to write prolifically. His writings constitute a veritable library of Vedic philosophy, religion, literature and culture.

# References

The purports of *Śrīmad-Bhāgavatam* are all confirmed by standard Vedic authorities. The following authentic scriptures are cited in this volume. For specific page references, consult the general index.

*Āyurveda-śāstra*

*Bhagavad-gītā*

*Bhakti-rasāmṛta-sindhu*

*Brahma-saṁhitā*

*Brahma-sūtra*

*Bṛhad-āraṇyaka Upaniṣad*

*Bṛhad-bhāgavatāmṛta*

*Caitanya-bhāgavata*

*Caitanya-candrāmṛta*

*Caitanya-caritāmṛta*

*Caṇḍī*

*Chāndogya Upaniṣad*

*Gīta-govinda*

*Hari-bhakti-sudhodaya*

*Hari-bhakti-vilāsa*

*Hari-vaṁśa*

*Hitopadeśa*

*Īśopaniṣad*

*Kaṭha Upaniṣad*

*Kṛṣṇa-sandarbha*

*Mahābhārata*

*Mārkaṇḍeya Purāṇa*

*Muṇḍaka Upaniṣad*

*Nārada-pañcarātra*

*Padma Purāṇa*

*Padyāvali*

*Prema-vivarta*

*Rāmāyana*

*Ṣaḍ-gosvāmy-aṣṭaka*

*Śikṣāṣṭaka*

*Śrīmad-Bhāgavatam*

*Śvetāśvatara Upaniṣad*

*Tantra-bhāgavata*

*Vaiṣṇava-toṣaṇī*

*Vāmana Purāṇa*

*Vedānta-sūtra*

*Viṣṇu Purāṇa*

*Viśva-kośa*

# GLOSSARY

## A

**Abhiṣeka**—a bathing ceremony, particularly for the coronation of a king or the installation of the Lord's Deity form.

**Ācārya**—an ideal teacher, who teaches by his personal example; a spiritual master.

**Acintya-bhedābheda-tattva**—Lord Caitanya's doctrine of the "inconceivable oneness and difference" of God and His energies.

**Adhibhautika**—(misery) caused by other living beings.

**Adhidaivika**—(misery) caused by nature.

**Adhokṣaja**—the Supreme Lord, who is beyond material sense perception.

**Adhyātmika**—(misery) caused by one's own body and mind.

**Ādi-puruṣa**—the Supreme Lord, Kṛṣṇa, the original person.

**Advaita-vādīs**—atheistic philosophers who say all distinctions are but material illusions. *See also:* Māyāvādīs.

**Aghāsura**—the python-shaped demon sent by Kaṁsa to kill Kṛṣṇa.

**Ahaṅkāra**—false ego, by which the soul misidentifies with the material body.

**Aja**—the unborn; the Supreme Lord.

**Ajāmila**—a fallen *brāhmaṇa* who was saved from hell by chanting the name of Lord Nārāyaṇa at the time of death.

**Ānakadundubhi**—another name of Vasudeva, the father of Kṛṣṇa.

**Ānanda-cinmaya-rasa-vigraha**—the personal, spiritual form of bliss and knowledge.

**Aṇimā**—the mystic power to become as small as an atom.

**Ārati**—a ceremony for greeting the Lord with chanting and offerings of food, lamps, fans, flowers and incense.

**Arcanā**—the devotional process of Deity worship.

**Arjuna**—one of the five Pāṇḍava brothers. Kṛṣṇa became his chariot driver and spoke the *Bhagavad-gītā* to him.

**Artha**—economic development.

**Āsana**—a sitting posture in *yoga* practice.

**Āśrama**—one of four spiritual orders of life. *See also: Brahmacarya; Gṛhastha; Vānaprastha; Sannyāsa*

**Asura**—an atheistic demon; a gross materialist.

**Ātmārāma**—one who is self-satisfied, free from external, material desires.

**Avaiṣṇava**—a nondevotee.

**Avatāra**—a descent, or incarnation, of the Supreme Lord.

## B

**Bābā**—one who dwells alone in one place in a life of meditation, penance and austerity.

**Bakāsura**—a demon who was shaped like a huge duck and who tried to kill Kṛṣṇa.

**Balarāma (Baladeva)**—a plenary expansion of the Supreme Personality of Godhead appearing as the son of Rohiṇī and elder brother of Lord Kṛṣṇa.

**Bhagavad-gītā**—the discourse between the Supreme Lord, Kṛṣṇa, and His devotee Arjuna expounding devotional service as both the principal means and the ultimate end of spiritual perfection.

**Bhagavān**—the Supreme Lord, who possesses all opulences in full.

**Bhāgavata-saptāha**—a seven-day series of lectures on *Śrīmad-Bhāgavatam* given by professional reciters to a paying audience.

**Bhāgavata-svarūpa**—the personal form of the Lord.

**Bhakta**—a devotee of the Supreme Lord.

**Bhakta-vatsala**—the Supreme Lord, who favors His devotees.

**Bhakti**—devotional service to the Supreme Lord.

**Bhaktisiddhānta Sarasvatī Ṭhākura**—(1874–1937) the spiritual master of the author, His Divine Grace A. C. Bhaktivedanta Swami Prabhupāda, and thus the spiritual grandfather of the present-day Kṛṣṇa consciousness movement. A powerful preacher, he founded sixty-four missions in India.

**Bhaktivinoda Ṭhākura**—(1838–1915) the great-grandfather of the present-day Kṛṣṇa consciousness movement, the spiritual master of Śrīla Gaurakiśora dāsa Bābājī and the father of Śrīla Bhaktisiddhānta Sarasvatī.

**Bhakti-yoga**—linking with the Supreme Lord by devotional service.

**Brahmā**—the first created living being and secondary creator of the material universe.

**Brahmacarya**—celibate student life; the first order of Vedic spiritual life.
**Brahman**—the Absolute Truth; especially the impersonal aspect of the Absolute.
**Brāhmaṇa**—a member of the intellectual, priestly class; the first Vedic social order.
**Brahmāṇḍas**—universes.
**Brahmāstra**—a nuclear weapon produced by chanting *mantras.*

## C

**Caitanya Mahāprabhu**—(1486-1534) the Supreme Lord appearing as His own greatest devotee to teach love of God, especially through the process of *saṅkīrtana.*
**Cakrī**—the Supreme Lord, who carries the disc weapon.
**Catur-bhuja**—four-armed.
**Catur-vyūha**—the Lord's plenary expansions Vāsudeva, Saṅkarṣaṇa, Pradyumna and Aniruddha.

## D

**Daityas**—demons; a race of demons descending from Diti.
**Daivas**—the demigods or godly persons.
**Dāmodara**—Lord Kṛṣṇa in His pastime of being bound by mother Yaśodā.
**Daridra-nārāyaṇa**—"poor Nārāyaṇa," an offensive term used by Māyāvādis to equate poor men with the Supreme Lord.
**Daśa-avatāras**—ten pastime incarnations of the Supreme Lord.
**Dāsya-rasa**—the servitor relationship with the Lord.
**Devakī**—a wife of Vasudeva and the mother of Lord Kṛṣṇa.
**Devamāyā**—the illusory potency of the demigods.
**Devarṣi**—a title meaning "sage among the demigods."
**Dhāma**—abode, place of residence; usually referring to the Lord's abodes.
**Dharā**—the name of mother Yaśodā in a previous birth.
**Dharma**—religion; duty, especially everyone's eternal service nature.
**Dhruva Mahārāja**—a great devotee who as a child performed severe austerities to meet the Lord and get the kingdom denied him, and who thus received an entire planet and God realization as well.

**Droṇa**—the name of Mahārāja Nanda in a previous birth.
**Duṣkṛtī**—a miscreant.

## E

**Ekādaśī**—a special day for increased remembrance of Kṛṣṇa, which comes on the eleventh day after both the full and new moon. Abstinence from grains and beans is prescribed.

## G

**Gadādharī**—the Supreme Lord, the carrier of the club.
**Garbhādhāna-saṁskāra**—the Vedic ceremony of purification to be performed by parents before conceiving a child.
**Gargamuni**—the family priest for the Yadu dynasty.
**Garuḍa**—Lord Viṣṇu's eternal carrier, a great devotee in a birdlike form.
**Gaurasundara**—the beautiful, golden-complexioned Lord, Śrī Caitanya Mahāprabhu.
**Giridhārī**—the Supreme Lord, Kṛṣṇa, the lifter of Govardhana Hill.
**Gokula**—*See:* Vṛndāvana
**Gokuleśvara**—Lord Kṛṣṇa, the master of Gokula.
**Goloka Vṛndāvana (Kṛṣṇaloka)**—the highest spiritual planet, Lord Kṛṣṇa's personal abode.
**Gopa-jāti**—*See: Vaiśyas*
**Gopāla**—the Supreme Lord, Kṛṣṇa, who protects the cows.
**Gopī-jana-vallabha**—the Supreme Lord, Kṛṣṇa, who is dear to the *gopīs.*
**Gopīs**—Kṛṣṇa's cowherd girl friends, who are His most surrendered and confidential devotees.
**Gosvāmī**—a controller of the mind and senses; the title of one in the renounced, or *sannyāsa*, order.
**Govinda**—the Supreme Lord, Kṛṣṇa, who gives pleasure to the land, the cows and the senses.
**Gṛhastha**—regulated householder life; the second order of Vedic spiritual life.
**Guṇa-avatāras**—Viṣṇu, Brahmā and Śiva, the presiding deities of the three modes of nature.
**Guṇas**—the three modes, or qualities, of material nature: goodness, passion and ignorance.
**Guru**—a spiritual master.

## H

**Haladhara**—the Supreme Lord, who, in the form of Balarāma, bears a plow in His hands.

**Hare Kṛṣṇa mantra**—*See: Mahā-mantra*

**Hari**—the Supreme Lord, who removes all obstacles to spiritual progress.

**Haṭha-yoga**—the practice of postures and breathing exercises for achieving purification and sense control.

**Hiraṇyakaśipu**—a demoniac king killed by the Lord's incarnation Nṛsiṁhadeva.

**Hlādinī-śakti**—the Supreme Lord's pleasure potency.

## I

**Indra**—the chief of the administrative demigods and king of the heavenly planets.

**Īśa**—the Supreme Lord, who is the supreme controller.

**Īśitva**—in mystic *yoga,* the perfection of control over others.

**Īśvara**—the Supreme Lord, who is the supreme controller.

## J

**Jaḍa**—dull or material.

**Jaya and Vijaya**—two doorkeepers of Vaikuṇṭha who were cursed for offending the four Kumāra Ṛṣis, but who after three births as demons attained liberation.

**Jīva Gosvāmī**—one of the six Vaiṣṇava spiritual masters who directly followed Lord Śrī Caitanya Mahāprabhu and systematically presented His teachings.

**Jīva-tattva**—the living entities, atomic parts of the Supreme Lord.

**Jñāna-kāṇḍa**—the portions of the *Vedas* containing knowledge of Brahman, or spirit.

**Jñāna-yoga**—the process of approaching the Supreme by the cultivation of knowledge.

**Jñānī**—one who cultivates knowledge by empirical speculation.

## K

**Kāla-cakra**—the wheel of time.

**Kali-yuga (Age of Kali)**—the present age, characterized by quarrel. It is last in the cycle of four ages and began five thousand years ago.

**Kāma**—lust.
**Kāmāvasāyitā**—the mystic ability to do the impossible.
**Kaṁsa**—a demoniac king of the Bhoja dynasty and maternal uncle of Kṛṣṇa.
**Karatālas**—hand cymbals used in *kīrtana*.
**Karma**—material, fruitive activity and its reactions.
**Karma-kāṇḍa-vicāra**—the rituals for material prosperity prescribed in the portion of the *Vedas* known as *karma-kāṇḍa*.
**Karmī**—one engaged in *karma* (fruitive activity); a materialist.
**Kaumāra**—the period of childhood before five years.
**Keśava**—the Supreme Lord, Kṛṣṇa, who has fine, black hair.
**Kīrtana**—the devotional process of chanting the names and glories of the Supreme Lord.
**Kṛṣṇa**—the Supreme Personality of Godhead appearing in His original, two-armed form.
**Kṛṣṇa-kathā**—discussions by or about the Supreme Lord, Kṛṣṇa.
**Kṛṣṇa-līlā**—the transcendental pastimes of Lord Kṛṣṇa.
**Kṛṣṇaloka**—*See:* Goloka Vṛndāvana
**Kṣatriya**—a warrior or administrator; the second Vedic social order.
**Kuntī**—an aunt of Lord Kṛṣṇa and the mother of the Pāṇḍavas.
**Kūrma**—the Supreme Lord's incarnation as a tortoise.
**Kuśa**—an auspicious grass used in Vedic rituals and sacrifices.
**Kuvera**—the treasurer of the demigods; father of Nalakūvara and Maṇigrīva.

## L

**Laghimā**—the mystic perfection of becoming very light.
**Lakṣmī**—the goddess of fortune and eternal consort of the Supreme Lord as Nārāyaṇa.
**Līlā-avatāras**—innumerable incarnations of the Supreme Lord who descend to the material world to display spiritual pastimes.
**Loka**—a planet.

## M

**Mādhurya-rasa**—the spiritual relationship in which the Supreme Lord and His devotee reciprocate as lovers.

**Madhusūdana**—the Supreme Lord, Kṛṣṇa, the killer of the demon Madhu.

**Madhvācārya**—a great thirteenth-century Vaiṣṇava spiritual master who preached the theistic philosophy of pure dualism.

**Mahā-mantra**—the great chant for deliverance:
Hare Kṛṣṇa, Hare Kṛṣṇa, Kṛṣṇa Kṛṣṇa, Hare Hare
Hare Rāma, Hare Rāma, Rāma Rāma, Hare Hare.

**Mahā-roga**—a severe illness.

**Mahābhārata**—Vyāsadeva's epic history of greater India, which includes the events of the Kurukṣetra war and the narration of *Bhagavad-gītā*.

**Mahādeva**—*See:* Śiva

**Mahāmāyā**—the illusory, material energy of the Supreme Lord.

**Mahat-tattva**—the original, undifferentiated form of the total material energy, from which the material world is manifest.

**Mahimā**—the mystic ability to become unlimitedly large.

**Maṅgala-ārati**—the daily predawn worship ceremony honoring the Deity of the Supreme Lord.

**Maṇigrīva**—a son of Kuvera cursed by Nārada Muni to take birth as an *arjuna* tree. He was ultimately liberated by Lord Kṛṣṇa.

**Maṇimān**—the Supreme Lord, who is always ornamented with brilliant jewels.

**Mantra**—a transcendental sound or Vedic hymn, which can deliver the mind from illusion.

**Manvantara-avatāras**—the incarnations of the Supreme Lord who appear during the reign of each Manu.

**Mathurā**—Lord Kṛṣṇa's abode, surrounding Vṛndāvana, where He took birth and to which He later returned after performing His childhood Vṛndāvana pastimes.

**Matsya**—the fish incarnation of the Supreme Lord.

**Māyā**—the inferior, illusory energy of the Supreme Lord, which rules over this material creation; forgetfulness of one's relationship with Kṛṣṇa.

**Māyāvāda**—relating to an impersonal concept of the Absolute and the theory of unqualified oneness of the living entities, nature and God.

**Māyāvādīs**—impersonalist philosophers who conceive of the Absolute as ultimately formless and the living entity as equal to God.

**Mlecchas**—uncivilized humans, outside the Vedic system of society, who are generally meat-eaters.
**Mṛdaṅga**—a clay drum used for congregational chanting.
**Mūḍha**—a foolish, asslike person.
**Mukti**—liberation from material bondage.
**Mukunda**—the Supreme Lord, the giver of liberation.
**Muni**—a sage.

## N

**Nalakūvara**—a son of Kuvera cursed by Nārada Muni to take birth as an *arjuna* tree. He was ultimately liberated by Lord Kṛṣṇa.
**Nāma-karaṇa ceremony**—a name-giving ceremony.
**Namaskāra**—a respectful greeting or address.
**Nanda Mahārāja**—the king of Vraja and foster father of Lord Kṛṣṇa.
**Nandana-kānana**—a celestial garden.
**Nārada Muni**—a pure devotee of the Lord who travels throughout the universes in his eternal body, glorifying devotional service. He is the spiritual master of Vyāsadeva and of many other great devotees.
**Nārāyaṇa**—Lord Kṛṣṇa's expansion as the Supreme Lord, the resting place of all living entities, in His majestic four-armed form; Lord Viṣṇu.
**Narottama dāsa Ṭhākura**—a Vaiṣṇava spiritual master in the disciplic succession from Lord Śrī Caitanya.Mahāprabhu. A disciple of Lokanātha dāsa Gosvāmī, he wrote many Bengali songs glorifying Lord Kṛṣṇa.
**Niyama**—restraint of the senses.
**Nṛsiṁhadeva**—the half-man, half-lion incarnation of the Supreme Lord, who protected Prahlāda and killed the demon Hiraṇyakaśipu.

## P

**Pañca-gavya**—five products from the cow, used in bathing a worshipable person.
**Pañca-ratna**—five gems.
**Pañca-śasya**—five grains.

**Parabrahman**—the Supreme Absolute Truth as the Personality of Godhead—Viṣṇu, or Kṛṣṇa.

**Paraṁ brahma**—*See:* Parabrahman.

**Paramahaṁsa**—a topmost, swanlike devotee of the Supreme Lord; the highest stage of *sannyāsa.*

**Paramātmā**—the Supersoul, a Viṣṇu expansion of the Supreme Lord present in the heart of each embodied living entity and throughout material nature.

**Paramparā**—a disciplic succession of bona fide spiritual masters.

**Parīkṣit Mahārāja**—the emperor of the world who heard *Śrīmad-Bhāgavatam* from Śukadeva Gosvāmī and thus attained perfection.

**Pārvatī**—Satī, Lord Śiva's consort, reborn as the daughter of the king of the Himalaya Mountains.

**Paugaṇḍa**—the period of childhood between ages five and ten.

**Pradhāna**—the total material energy in its unmanifest state.

**Prahlāda Mahārāja**—a devotee persecuted by his demoniac father but protected and saved by the Lord in the form of Nṛsiṁhadeva.

**Prajāpatis**—the demigods in charge of populating the universe.

**Prākāmya**—the mystic ability to fulfill any of one's desires.

**Prakṛti**—material nature, the energy of the Supreme; the enjoyed.

**Prāṇāyāma**—breath control used in the practice of *aṣṭāṅga-yoga.*

**Prāpti**—the mystic ability to immediately obtain any material object.

**Prasādam**—the Lord's mercy; food or other items spiritualized by being first offered to the Supreme Lord.

**Prema-bhakta**—a devotee absorbed in pure love of God.

**Pṛśnigarbha**—the name of Devakī in a previous birth.

**Pṛthā**—Kuntī, the aunt of Lord Kṛṣṇa who was the mother of the Pāṇḍavas.

**Pūtanā**—a witch who was sent by Kaṁsa to appear in the form of a beautiful woman to kill baby Kṛṣṇa but who was killed by Him and granted liberation.

## R

**Rajo-guṇa**—the material mode of passion.

**Rākṣasas**—man-eating demons.

**Rākṣasī**—a female *rākṣasa,* or demoness.

**Rāma**—*See:* Rāmacandra

**Rāmacandra**—an incarnation of the Supreme Lord as the perfect king.

**Rāvaṇa**—a demoniac ruler who was killed by Lord Rāmacandra.

**Rohiṇī**—one of Vasudeva's wives, who later lived under the care of Nanda Mahārāja. She is the mother of Balarāma.

**Ṛṣabhadeva**—an incarnation of the Supreme Lord as a devotee-king who, after instructing His sons in spiritual life, renounced His kingdom for a life of austerity.

**Rukmiṇī**—Lord Kṛṣṇa's principal queen in Dvārakā.

**Rūpa Gosvāmī**—the chief of the six Vaiṣṇava spiritual masters who directly followed Lord Śrī Caitanya Mahāprabhu and systematically presented His teachings.

## S

**Sac-cid-ānanda-vigraha**—the Lord's transcendental form, which is eternal and full of knowledge and bliss.

**Ṣaḍ-aiśvarya-pūrṇa**—the Supreme Lord, who is full in all six opulences: wealth, strength, knowledge, fame, beauty and renunciation.

**Sādhana**—the beginning phase of devotional service as regulated practice.

**Sādhu**—a saintly person.

**Śakaṭāsura**—a ghost who took shelter of a bullock cart with the intention of killing Kṛṣṇa but who instead was killed by the Lord.

**Sakhya-rasa**—the relationship with the Supreme Lord in devotional friendship.

**Śakty-āveśa**—empowered by the Supreme Lord with one or more of the Lord's opulences.

**Sālokya**—the liberation of residing on the same planet as the Supreme Lord.

**Śambhu**—a name of Lord Śiva.

**Sāmīpya**—the liberation of becoming a personal associate of the Supreme Lord.

**Saṁskāra**—one of the Vedic rituals performed one by one from the time of conception until death for purifying a human being.

**Sanātana Gosvāmī**—one of the six Vaiṣṇava spiritual masters who directly followed Lord Śrī Caitanya Mahāprabhu and systematically presented His teachings.

**Śaṅkarācārya**—the incarnation of Lord Śiva as the great philosopher who, on the order of the Supreme Lord, preached impersonalism based on the *Vedas*.

**Saṅkarṣaṇa**—one of the four original expansions of Lord Kṛṣṇa in the spiritual world; also, another name of Balarāma, given by Gargamuni.

**Saṅkīrtana**—congregational or public glorification of the Supreme Lord, Kṛṣṇa, especially through chanting of the Lord's holy names.

**Sannyāsa**—renounced life; the fourth order of Vedic spiritual life.

**Śānta-rasa**—the relationship with the Supreme Lord in neutrality.

**Sārṣṭi**—the liberation of achieving equal opulence with the Lord.

**Sārūpya**—the liberation of attaining a spiritual form like that of the Supreme Lord.

**Śāstra**—revealed scripture, such as the Vedic literature.

**Saunaka Ṛṣi**—the chief of the sages assembled at Naimiṣāraṇya when Sūta Gosvāmī spoke *Śrīmad-Bhāgavatam*.

**Sāyujya**—the liberation of merging into the spiritual effulgence of the Lord.

**Sītā**—the eternal consort of Lord Rāmacandra.

**Śiva**—the special incarnation of the Lord as the demigod in charge of the mode of ignorance and the destruction of the material manifestation.

**Smṛti**—revealed scriptures supplementary to the *śruti*, or original Vedic scriptures, which are the *Vedas* and *Upaniṣads*.

**Śravaṇaṁ kīrtanaṁ viṣṇoḥ**—the devotional process of hearing and chanting about Lord Viṣṇu, or Kṛṣṇa.

**Sudarśana cakra**—the disc weapon of the Supreme Lord.

**Śuddha-sattva**—the spiritual platform of pure goodness.

**Śūdra**—a laborer; the fourth of the Vedic social orders.

**Śukadeva Gosvāmī**—the great devotee-sage who originally spoke *Śrīmad-Bhāgavatam* to King Parīkṣit just prior to the king's death.

**Sūrya**—the demigod of the sun.

**Sūta Gosvāmī**—the great devotee-sage who recounted the discourses between Parīkṣit and Śukadeva to the sages assembled in the forest of Naimiṣāraṇya.

**Sutapā**—the name of Vasudeva in a previous birth.

**Svāmī**—a controller of the mind and senses; the title of one in the renounced, or *sannyāsa*, order.

**Svargaloka**—the heavenly planets of the material world.
**Svarūpa-siddhi**—the perfection of attaining one's original, spiritual form.
**Svayambhū**—the "self-born one," Lord Brahmā.
**Śyāmasundara**—the Supreme Personality of Godhead, Kṛṣṇa, who is blackish and very beautiful.

## T

**Tamo-guṇa**—the material mode of ignorance.
**Tapasvī**—one who performs severe penances and austerities.
**Tapasya**—austerity; accepting some voluntary inconvenience for a higher purpose.
**Tilaka**—auspicious clay markings placed by devotees on the forehead and other parts of the body.
**Tṛṇāvarta**—a whirlwind-shaped demon sent by Kaṁsa to kill Kṛṣṇa.
**Tulasī**—a sacred plant dear to Lord Kṛṣṇa and worshiped by His devotees.

## U

**Uddhava**—a confidential friend of Lord Kṛṣṇa's in Dvārakā.
**Ugra-karma**—evil activities.
**Upananda**—the brother of Nanda Mahārāja and oldest and most knowledgeable of the cowherd men of Gokula Vṛndāvana.
**Upaniṣads**—the most significant philosophical sections of the *Vedas*.
**Upāsanā-kāṇḍa**—the portions of the *Vedas* dealing with ceremonies of worship, especially demigod worship.
**Upendra**—Vāmanadeva, who sometimes appears as the younger brother of Indra.
**Urugāya**—the Supreme Lord, who is worshiped by sublime prayers.
**Urukrama**—the Supreme Lord, who takes wonderful steps (especially as the dwarf-*brāhmaṇa* incarnation, Vāmanadeva).

## V

**Vaikuṇṭha**—the spiritual world, where there is no anxiety.
**Vaiṣṇava**—a devotee of Viṣṇu, or Kṛṣṇa, the Supreme Lord.
**Vaiṣṇava-aparādha**—an offense to a devotee of the Lord.
**Vaiśyas**—farmers and merchants; the third Vedic social order.
**Vānaprastha**—one who has retired from family life; the third order of Vedic spiritual life.

**Varāha**—the incarnation of the Supreme Lord as a boar.

**Varṇa**—one of the four Vedic social-occupational divisions of society, distinguished by quality of work and situation with regard to the modes of nature (*guṇas*). *See also: Brāhmaṇa; Kṣatriya; Vaiśya; Śūdra*

**Varṇāśrama-dharma**—the Vedic social system of four social and four spiritual orders. *See also: Varṇa; Āśrama*

**Vaśitva**—the mystic ability to control others' minds.

**Vasudeva**—the father of Kṛṣṇa, and half-brother of Nanda Mahārāja.

**Vāsudeva**—the Supreme Lord, Kṛṣṇa, son of Vasudeva and proprietor of everything, material and spiritual.

**Vātsalya-rasa**—the relationship with the Supreme Lord, Kṛṣṇa, wherein the devotee loves the Lord with parental affection.

**Vatsāsura**—a demon who came to Vṛndāvana and, in the form of a calf, tried to kill Kṛṣṇa.

**Vedānta**—the philosophy of the *Vedānta-sūtra* of Śrīla Vyāsadeva, containing a conclusive summary of Vedic philosophical knowledge and showing Kṛṣṇa as the goal.

**Vedas**—the original revealed scriptures, first spoken by Lord Kṛṣṇa.

**Vijaya**—*See:* Jaya and Vijaya

**Vijayadhvaja Tīrtha**—a Vaiṣṇava spiritual master in the line of Madhvācārya, and a commentator on *Śrīmad-Bhāgavatam.*

**Vimukta**—a liberated person.

**Viṣṇu**—the Supreme Lord; Lord Kṛṣṇa's expansions in Vaikuṇṭha and for the creation and maintenance of the material universes.

**Viṣṇu-tattva**—the status or category of Godhead. The term applies to primary expansions of the Supreme Lord.

**Viṣṇu-mūrtis**—forms of the Supreme Lord.

**Viśvanātha Cakravartī Ṭhākura**—a great Vaiṣṇava spiritual master in the line of Lord Śrī Caitanya Mahāprabhu, and a commentator on *Śrīmad-Bhāgavatam.*

**Vrajabhūmi**—*See:* Vṛndāvana

**Vṛndāvana**—Kṛṣṇa's eternal abode, where He fully manifests His quality of sweetness; the village on this earth in which He enacted His childhood pastimes five thousand years ago.

**Vṛtrāsura**—a great demon killed by Indra. He was actually the devotee Citraketu, who had been cursed to take a low birth.

**Vyāsadeva**—the incarnation of Lord Kṛṣṇa who gave the *Vedas, Purāṇas, Vedānta-sūtra* and *Mahābhārata* to mankind.

## Y

**Yajña**—a Vedic sacrifice; also, the Supreme Lord, the goal and enjoyer of all sacrifices.

**Yamarāja**—the demigod in charge of death and of punishing the sinful.

**Yaśodā**—the foster mother of Kṛṣṇa; the Queen of Vraja and wife of Mahārāja Nanda.

**Yavana**—a low-class person, generally a meat-eater; a barbarian.

**Yogamāyā**—the internal, spiritual energy of the Supreme Lord; also, its personification as Kṛṣṇa's younger sister.

**Yogī**—a transcendentalist striving for union with the Supreme.

**Yoginī**—a female *yogī*.

**Yugas**—ages in the life of a universe, occurring in a repeated cycle of four.

# Sanskrit Pronunciation Guide

**Throughout the centuries, the Sanskrit language has been written in a variety of alphabets. The mode of writing most widely used throughout India, however, is called *devanāgarī*, which means, literally, the writing used in "the cities of the demigods." The *devanāgarī* alphabet consists of forty-eight characters: thirteen vowels and thirty-five consonants. Ancient Sanskrit grammarians arranged this alphabet according to practical linguistic principles, and this order has been accepted by all Western scholars. The system of transliteration used in this book conforms to a system that scholars in the last fifty years have accepted to indicate the pronunciation of each Sanskrit sound.**

### Vowels

अ a आ ā इ i ई ī उ u ऊ ū ऋ ṛ

ॠ ṝ ऌ ḷ ए e ऐ ai ओ o औ au

### Consonants

| | | | | | |
|---|---|---|---|---|---|
| Gutturals: | क ka | ख kha | ग ga | घ gha | ङ ṅa |
| Palatals: | च ca | छ cha | ज ja | झ jha | ञ ña |
| Cerebrals: | ट ṭa | ठ ṭha | ड ḍa | ढ ḍha | ण ṇa |
| Dentals: | त ta | थ tha | द da | ध dha | न na |
| Labials: | प pa | फ pha | ब ba | भ bha | म ma |
| Semivowels: | य ya | र ra | ल la | व va | |
| Sibilants: | | श śa | ष ṣa | स sa | |
| Aspirate: | ह ha | Anusvāra: ं ṁ | | Visarga: ः ḥ | |

## Numerals

० -0 १-1 २-2 ३-3 ४-4 ५-5 ६-6 ७-7 ८-8 ९-9

The vowels are written as follows after a consonant:

ा ā ि i ी ī ु u ू ū ृ ṛ ॄ ṝ े e ै ai ो o ौ au

For example: क ka का kā कि ki की kī कु ku कू kū

कृ kṛ कॄ kṝ के ke कै kai को ko कौ kau

Generally two or more consonants in conjunction are written together in a special form, as for example: क्ष kṣa त्र tra

The vowel "a" is implied after a consonant with no vowel symbol.

The symbol virāma ( ् ) indicates that there is no final vowel: क्

## The vowels are pronounced as follows:

a — as in but
ā — as in far but held twice as long as a
ai — as in aisle
au — as in how
e — as in they
i — as in pin
ī — as in pique but held twice as long as i
ḷ — as in lree
o — as in go
ṛ — as in rim
ṝ — as in reed but held twice as long as ṛ
u — as in push
ū — as in rule but held twice as long as u

## The consonants are pronounced as follows:

**Gutturals**
**(pronounced from the throat)**

k — as in kite
kh — as in Eckhart
g — as in give
gh — as in dig-hard
ṅ — as in sing

**Labials**
**(pronounced with the lips)**

p — as in pine
ph — as in up-hill (not f)
b — as in bird
bh — as in rub-hard
m — as in mother

**Cerebrals**
**(pronounced with tip of tongue against roof of mouth)**

ṭ — as in tub
ṭh — as in light-heart
ḍ — as in dove
ḍh — as in red-hot
ṇ — as in sing

**Dentals**
**(pronounced as cerebrals but with tongue against teeth)**

t — as in tub
th — as in light-heart
d — as in dove
dh — as in red-hot
n — as in nut

**Aspirate**

h — as in home

**Anusvāra**

ṁ — a resonant nasal sound like in the French word *bon*

**Palatals**
**(pronounced with middle of tongue against palate)**

c — as in chair
ch — as in staunch-heart
j — as in joy
jh — as in hedgehog
ñ — as in canyon

**Semivowels**

y — as in yes
r — as in run
l — as in light
v — as in vine, except when preceded in the same syllable by a consonant, then like in swan

**Sibilants**

ś — as in the German word *sprechen*
ṣ — as in shine
s — as in sun

**Visarga**

ḥ — a final h-sound: aḥ is pronounced like aha; iḥ like ihi

There is no strong accentuation of syllables in Sanskrit, or pausing between words in a line, only a flowing of short and long (twice as long as the short) syllables. A long syllable is one whose vowel is long (ā, ai, au, e, ī, o, ṝ, ū) or whose short vowel is followed by more than one consonant (including ḥ and ṁ). Aspirated consonants (consonants followed by an h) count as single consonants.

# Index of Sanskrit Verses

This index constitutes a complete listing of the first and third lines of each of the Sanskrit poetry verses of this volume of *Śrīmad-Bhāgavatam*, arranged in English alphabetical order. The first column gives the Sanskrit transliteration; the second, the chapter-verse reference. Apostrophes are alphabetized as *a*'s.

## B

# C



# D

## O



## P

## R

## T

## U

# Index of Verses Quoted

This index lists the verses quoted in the purports and footnotes of this volume of *Śrīmad-Bhāgavatam*. Numerals in boldface type refer to the first or third lines of verses quoted in full; numerals in roman type refer to partially quoted verses.

# General Index

Numerals in boldface type indicate references to translations of the verses of *Śrīmad-Bhāgavatam*.


## A

*Abhaya* defined, 196
*Abhidheya* defined, 479
*Abhiṣeka* bathing ceremony by Brahmā for Kṛṣṇa, 732
Aborigines selling fruits, Kṛṣṇa's favor to, 575-77
Absolute Truth
  Brahmā saw, **729**
  devotional service reveals, 156, 718
  impersonalist's understanding of, 717
  Kṛṣṇa as, 34, **156**, 158, 160, 465, 553, 732
  manifest & unmanifest, 722
  realization of, 480-81
    personal & impersonal, 75
  *See also:* Cause, ultimate; Kṛṣṇa; Supreme Lord
*Abudhaḥ* defined, 223
*Ācamana* purification, 367
*Ācāryas. See:* Spiritual master(s)
*Acintya-bhedābheda* philosophy, 128, 236, 677, 697
*Acintya* defined, 723
Activities
  of God. *See:* Kṛṣṇa, pastimes of; Supreme Lord, activities of
  of irresponsible persons, 318
  of Kṛṣṇa. *See:* Kṛṣṇa, pastimes of
  in Kṛṣṇa consciousness, 192, 665
  material compared with spiritual, 725-26
  pious, devotional service preceded by, 665, 708, 726
  sinful. *See:* Sinful activities
  *See also:* Endeavor; Fruitive activities; *Karma;* Sinful activities
*Ādi-kavi* defined, 513
Aditi, Devakī was, **261**
Administrators. *See:* King(s); *Kṣatriya(s);* Government(s), leader(s); Politician(s)
Advaita-vādis. *See:* Impersonalist(s)
Advancement, spiritual
  fitness for, 537
  hearing about Lord constantly as sign of, 658-59
  *See also:* Goal of life; Perfection; Success
Affection. *See:* Love
Age of Kali. *See:* Kali-yuga
Aghāsura, **119**, **661**, **672**
  advent of, arrangement of, 627
  compared to mountain, **629**, **630**, **633**
  compared with Jaya & Vijaya, 643
  cowherd boys considering, **631-34**
  cowherd boys entered mouth of, **634-**35, **636**
  demigods feared, **626**
  Kṛṣṇa liberated, **642-**43, 647-48, **649**, **650-**51
  Kṛṣṇa vs., **627-29**, **634-42**
  in python form, **629-34**, **636**, **642**, 643, **646**, **647**
  quoted on killing Kṛṣṇa & His associates, **627**, **628**
  relatives of, **627**
Agriculture. *See:* Cow(s), protection of; *Vaiśya(s)*
*Aguru* scent, **377**, 378
*Ahaṅkāra* (false ego). *See:* Bodily concept
*Āhlādinī* potency, 723
*Aiśvarya* defined, 712
*Ajā* defined, 712
Ajāmila history, Yamarāja & Kṛṣṇa's devotees in, 504
*Ajñāna* defined, 512

Birth (*continued*)
of Kṛṣṇa. *See:* Kṛṣṇa, advent of
of living entity compared with Lord's advent, **194–95,** 196, 205, 210, 212
modes of nature determine, 72
name-giving ceremony after, 88
process of, 70
*See also:* Birth-death cycle; Childbirth; Transmigration of soul(s)
Birth-death cycle
education for avoiding, 252
faithless persons return to, 173
Kṛṣṇa consciousness vs., 76, 279, 726
*kṛṣṇa-kathā* stops, **21,** 25, 35
Lord saves devotee from, 165
purification stops, 73
*See also:* Birth; Death; Transmigration of soul(s)
Birthright, education more important than, 437
Bkaktivinoda Ṭhākura quoted
on knowing Kṛṣṇa via following devotee, 547
on renouncing sin & remaining in Kṛṣṇa's family, 383
on seeking shelter of Hare Kṛṣṇa *mantra,* 352
Bliss, transcendental
Brahmā in, **720**
via chanting Lord's names, 105
devotees in, 418, 489
Kṛṣṇa bestows, 448, 449
Kṛṣṇa in, 399, 411, 514
seeing Kṛṣṇa as, 665
*See also:* Enjoyment; Happiness; Pleasure
Boat
Lord's lotus feet compared to, **168,** 169, 172
mind compared to, 71
Bodily concept of life
attachment to, **293–94**
Brahmā and Śiva &, 516
as ignorance, 179, 297, **300–**301
Kṛṣṇa inaccessible via, **515**
via modes of nature, 51, 74
sinful activities via, 149, 150
suffering due to, 294, **297**
*See also:* Attachment; Body, material; Desires, material; False ego; Illusion; *Māyā*
Body, material
before birth & after death, **532–**33
by-products of, example of, 696
changes of, 292
compared to
dress, 64
tree, **161–62,** 163
demigods award, 711
desire determines, 287, 292
elements in, **64, 162,** 222, 292
evil spirits trouble, **372**
fate of, **530, 531**
formation of, 70
ghosts haunt, 399
happiness from, **161–62**
identification with. *See:* Bodily concept of life
living force in, 146, 162–63
as materialist's reality, **223,** 225
mind develops, 68–70, **71,** 72, 101, 102
via modes of nature, 715
nature awards, 64–65, 72, 279
in next life, 624
as perishable, **528**
protection for, 373
as punishment or reward, 528
soul
basis of, **223**
changes, **64–**76, 317–18
contrasted to, 292, 293
within, 435, 515
suffering due to, 65, 76, **77,** 149–50, 390, 435, 475
Supersoul in, 163
true but temporary, 224–25
*See also:* Senses; Subtle body
Body, spiritual
of pure devotee, 103
of spiritual master, 295
Body of Lord. *See:* Kṛṣṇa, body of; Supreme Lord, body of
Bombay
Dīpāvali Day festival in, 493
Durgā worship in, 287
Hare Kṛṣṇa center in, 232
Bondage, material
liberation from, **563,** 677
*See also:* Birth-death cycle; Material life; *Māyā*

## C

## E

"Gods." *See:* Demigod(s)
Gokula Vṛndāvana. *See:* Vṛndāvana
Golden stick & Brahmā bowing down, analogy of, **731–32**
Goloka Vṛndāvana, 49, 108, 111
  Pūtanā promoted to, 381
  *See also:* Spiritual world; Vṛndāvana
Goodness, mode of
  absent in nondevotee, 534
  for cosmic maintenance, **227**
  elevation to, 714
  higher planets via, 72
  human life for, 527
  pure. *See: Śuddha-sattva*
  Viṣṇus' smiles resembled, **709**
*Gopas.* *See:* Cowherd men
*Gopī(s)*
  cart collapsing around Kṛṣṇa perplexed, **398,** 399, **400**
  devotional ecstasy of, 489
  enjoyed Kṛṣṇa defying Yaśodā's ropes, **509,** 510
  happy after Kṛṣṇa survived whirlwind demon, **419**
  Kṛṣṇa
    bound by, **561**
    charmed, **464,** 465
    did bidding of, **573, 574**
    loved by, 379, **382,** 383
    missed by, after dust storm, **414**
    protected by, **365–67, 369–71, 374**
    received by, after Bakāsura pastime, **608–9**
    served by, 451
    as "sons" of, 680-81, **683, 684**
    thought of by, always, 193
  at Kṛṣṇa's "birth" festival, **327, 329, 330**
  Kṛṣṇa's childhood pastimes enjoyed by, **456–57**
  Lord's lotus feet enchanted, 193
  missed Kṛṣṇa after dust storm, **414**
  moved to Vṛndāvana, **592–94**
  perfection achieved by, 379, 383
  Yaśodā informed by, of Kṛṣṇa's mischief, **460, 461, 463, 464**
Gosvāmis, six. *See:* Jiva Gosvāmi; Rūpa Gosvāmi; Sanātana Gosvāmi
Govardhana Hill, **595**
  cows ran from, to calves, **686–88**
  Kṛṣṇa lifted, 188
Government(s)
  demoniac leaders ruin, 40-41
  leader(s)
    blind, 311-12
    demoniac, endanger world, **40–41,** 47, 230
    duty of, 41
    Hare Kṛṣṇa movement opposed by, 230-32
    *kṛṣṇa-kathā* essential for, 38
    *See also:* King(s); *Kṣatriya(s);* Politician(s)
  power of, Kṛṣṇa's power compared to, 703
Grains, Kṛṣṇa traded, for fruit, **575, 576,** 577
  *See also:* Food
*Grāmya-dharma* defined, 259
Grasses, flavorful, Yaśodā's cows ate, 493
Greed, 714
*Gṛhastha(s)*
  devotees instruct, **432,** 433
  training vital for, 433
  *See also:* Father(s); Mother(s); Parent(s)
*Guṇa-avatāras,* 516
  *See also:* Incarnation(s) of Supreme Lord
*Guṇas.* *See:* Modes of nature; *specific modes*
*Guru.* *See:* Spiritual master(s)

## H

*Haṁsa* defined, 660, 663
Happiness
  from body, **161–62**
  via cow protection, 342
  of cows in Vedic times, 325
  demoniac leaders disrupt, 311-12
  of devotee, 153
  via devotional service, 577
  via glorifying Lord, 645
  via hearing Kṛṣṇa's pastimes, 612
  in Kali-yuga, 180
  via Kṛṣṇa consciousness, 152, 254, 702-3, 728

*Hitopadeśa* quoted on fool angered by good instructions, 282
*Hlādinī* potency, 514
Holy men. *See:* Devotee(s); Pure devotee(s); Saintly person(s); Spiritual master(s)
Holy names of God. *See:* Chanting holy names of Lord; Hare Kṛṣṇa *mantra*
Holy places. *See: Dhāma;* Dvārakā; Mathurā; Navadvipa; Vṛndāvana; *specific holy places*
Householder(s). *See: Gṛhastha(s)*
*Hṛta-jñāna* defined, 522
Human being(s)
  animals compared with, 434
  *Bhagavad-gītā* for, 180
  cow protection for, 342
  demigods less fortunate than, 391
  duty neglected by, 146
  food for, 529
  Kṛṣṇa in role of, 29, **32–**33, 106-8, 263, **265,** 266, **391**
  Lord resembles, 732
  love of Lord for, 479-80
  as part of Lord, 445
  purification for, 714
  spiritual life for, 725-26
  types of, 104, 154
  Vedic knowledge for, 163
  *See also:* Conditioned soul(s); Life, human; Living entities; Society, human; *specific humans*
Hunters of animals, 105-6

# I

"I-&-mine" misconception, 476-77
Identity. *See:* Kṛṣṇa consciousness; Soul(s)
Ignorance
  bodily concept as, 179, 297, **300–**301
  civilization in, 163
  irresponsible persons in, 318
  Lord's form as imagined in, 183
  Western leaders in, 66
Ignorance, mode of
  abatement of, 714
  bad body from, 65
  condemned, 527, 528, 531
  for cosmic annihilation, **227–**28
  devotees free of, 542
  hell via, 72
Illusion
  material life as, 383, 390
  *See also:* Bodily concept; Ignorance; *Mahāmāyā; Māyā;* Yogamāyā
Imagination, Lord not known via, 182, 183, **185,** 250
Immortality. *See:* Eternality
Impersonal Brahman, 235, 236
Impersonalist(s)
  devotee compared with, 75, 696-97, 722, 724
  hearing from, forbidden, 191
  labor of, 75, 174
  Lord's form misunderstood by, 183, 184, 186, 717
  *māyā* as seen by, 722
  merging with Brahman desired by, 152
  philosophy of, 696-97
  quoted on spirit & matter, 696
  *See also: Jñānī(s);* Philosopher(s)
Incarnation(s) of Supreme Lord
  in animal forms, **556**
  Caitanya (Gaurasundara) as, 445-46
  devotees understand, 199
  false, 416, 558-59
  *guṇa-*, 516
  Hare Kṛṣṇa movement as, 230
  as innumerable, 445
  Kṛṣṇa as, 390, 391, 397, **444,** 445-46, 650-51
  Kṛṣṇa as origin of, 46-47, 160
  Kṛṣṇa's name as, 230
  as limitless, 199
  Lord's names according to, 183-84
  via Lord's pleasure potency, 195
  philosophers disbelieve in, 195
  protect world, **197**
  purpose of, **167**
  Śeṣa as, 127, 129
  for time & place, 391

## K


Kailāsa Hill, **521**
*Kaivalya* defined, 453
*Kāla* defined, 107, 239, **278–79**, **713**, 715
Kālanemi
  Kaṁsa was, **99**, 112, 113, 123
  sons of, 112-13
*Kalā-viśeṣa* defined, 19
Kali-yuga
  Āryans powerless in, 281
  *brāhmaṇas* in, 404, 436
  Caitanya's program for, 95, 96, 180
  human society in, 393, 537
  *kṛṣṇa-kathā* counteracts, 20, **36**, 37
  Lord's incarnation for, 445
  people in, 441
  Rākṣasas (man-eaters) in, 289
*Kalpanā* defined, 556
*Kāma* defined, 660, **713**, 715
Kaṁsa, **438**, **439**, **627**, **639**
  Akrūra with, 122
  associates of, as demigods, **93**, 94
  as Bhoja king, 62
  as charioteer for Vasudeva & Devakī, **56**, **59**, 60
  as cruel, 282, **283**
  deliberated on Devakī pregnant with Kṛṣṇa, **147**, 148, 149, **151**
  as demon, 76, **79**, 86, 89, 99, 154, **231**, 292, **315–16**
  demoniac ministers advised, **304–16**
  destiny ordained killings by, **281**, 282, **295**, 296, 299-300
  Devakī
    attacked by, **60**
    feared, on Kṛṣṇa's account, 128-29, **233**, 236, 242, **243–44**, **245–46**
    imprisoned by, **97**
    pleaded with, on baby daughter's behalf, **280–83**
    sister of, **56**, **62**, **147**, 148
  Devakī's sons killed by, **97**, 113, **122**, 123
  forgiven by Vasudeva & Devakī, **299–**300
  as Kālanemi in past birth, **99**, 112, 113, 123
Kaṁsa (*continued*)
  in knowledge of self, 292, 297
  Kṛṣṇa
    killed, **31**, 32, 97
    saved, 29, 99, 107
  as Kṛṣṇa conscious unfavorably, **152**, 153, 154
  lamented Devakī's "miscarriage," 137
  *māyā* influenced, 110, 280
  Nanda paid taxes to, **336–37**
  Nārada's death-warning to, **95**, **97**, 114
  omen of doom for, **59**, 60
  politicians as baser than, 292
  quoted. *See:* Kaṁsa quoted
  repented atrocities to Vasudeva & Devakī, **288–99**
  soul's transmigration known to, 147, 149
  symbolizes fear, 129
  as Ugrasena's son, **100**, 243
  Vasudeva
    advises, about life & death, **62–64**, 65, **66**, **67**, **71**, **74**, 76, **77**
    dissuaded, from killing Devakī, **78**, **79**, 80, **81–86**, **88**, 89, 112
    equanimity of, pleased, **90**, **91**
    feared, on Kṛṣṇa's account, **231**, 232, 233
    imprisoned by, **97**
  watchmen of, slept due to Yogamāyā, **269**, 277
  Yadus persecuted by, **119**, 120
  Yogamāyā outwitted, **284–86**, 303-4
Kaṁsa quoted
  on bodily concept of life, **293–94**, **297**
  on embodied living entities, **292**
  on living entities under Supreme control, **291**, **295**
*Kapittha* fruits, Kṛṣṇa obtained, 600
*Karaṇāpāṭava* defined, 672
Kāraṇodakaśāyī Viṣṇu (Mahā-Viṣṇu), 19, 108, 217, 221
*Karma*
  defined, **713**, 715
  life according to, 725
  living entities subject to, 524
  separates everyone in time, **341**
  *See also:* Destiny

Kṛṣṇa
advent of (*continued*)
as perpetual pastime, 48
purposes of, 556, 643
teaches spiritual enjoyment, 620
time of, **204,** 205, 206
as transcendental, 97-98, 485-86
transformation at, **265,** 266-67
Vasudeva beheld, **211, 213, 214**
in Viṣṇu form, **208,** 209, **211,** 212
as wonderful, **211,** 212, 213
*See also:* Incarnation(s) of Supreme Lord
affection for. *See:* Love, for Lord
Aghāsura
killed by, **672**
liberated by, **642–**43, 647-48, **649, 650–**51
vs., **627–29, 634–42**
above all, 673
as all-
attractive, 465
good, 562, 648
pervading, **506**
pervading & aloof, 677
arguing with, 723
Arjuna &. *See:* Arjuna, Kṛṣṇa &...
*arjuna* trees uprooted by, **546–49,** 556-57
associates of, 484, 647-48, 651
*avatāras* of. *See:* Incarnation(s) of Supreme Lord
Bakāsura vs., **603–6**
Balarāma &. *See:* Balarāma, Kṛṣṇa &...
bewilders the materially born, 672, 673
beyond
bewilderment, 702, 703
commands, 712
description, 19
liberation, 647
material energy, 673
material world, 216
time & space, **506**
via *Bhagavad-gītā*, 624
"birth" of. *See:* Kṛṣṇa, advent of
in bliss, 399, 411, 514
bliss bestowed by, 448, 449
body of, 399, 605
color of, 107

Kṛṣṇa
body of (*continued*)
as transcendental, 180
*See also:* Supreme Lord, body of
boys & calves saved by, from Aghāsura, **661**
Brahmā &. *See:* Brahmā, Kṛṣṇa &...
as *brahmajyoti's* basis, 235
Brahmā mystified by, as boys & calves, **697–702,** 703, **719–21,** 722-24
*brāhmaṇas'* ceremony for safety of, **401–3**
*brāhmaṇas* favored by, 448-49
Brahman effulgence from, 502-4, **623,** 624, 643
as butter thief, **461,** 462, **463,** 493, **498–500**
Caitanya as, 55, 144, 445-46, 486
calf demon killed by, **599, 600**
calves & cowherd boys revived by, **641**
calves tended by, **596–98, 601, 602, 617, 618**
cart demon (Śakaṭāsura) kicked by, 395, **396,** 397, **398–99**
catching calves' tails, **456–57**
as cause of all, 730, 732
as cause of all causes, **473,** 474, **506,** 507, **648,** 649
challenge to, futility of, 702-3
chanting about, 377-78
colors of, for incarnations, **444,** 445-46
compared
to dramatic player, 674
to fire, **355, 605,** 610
to Nārāyaṇa, **450–51, 571–**72, 611
to snake, **356,** 357
competitors of, 415, 416
complete & changeless, 677
consciousness of. *See:* Kṛṣṇa consciousness
as controller, **669–**70
as cowherd boy, **729,** 730, 732
cowherd friends of. *See:* Cowherd boys
cowherd men & women loved, **608–**9
cowherd men bewildered about, after *yamala-arjuna* trees' fall, **569–71,** 572

Kṛṣṇa (*continued*)
killing demons, 95, 228, **229**, 230, 245, **355**–56, 426, **449**, 558, 601-2, 610, **672**
known
via His mercy, 716
via spiritual masters, 677
knows everything, 638, 675, 729
in Kṛṣṇa consciousness movement, 41, 47, 146
on Kurukṣetra battlefield, 184, 186
liberation given by, **382**, 383, 643, 648, 651
liberation via knowing, 677
as limitless, 618, 619
living entities &. *See:* Living entities, Kṛṣṇa &...
Lord's mercy "saved," **587, 588**, 589, **609**
lotus feet of, as shelter, 669-70, 710-11
love for. *See:* Love, for Lord
lunching with cowherd boys, **663–71**
man in image of, 732
as master of all, 513, 711, 713
materialists can't know, 553-54
mercy of, Lord known via, 716
mischief done by, **461–65**
mission of, 432-33
mother of. *See:* Devakī; Yaśodā
as Mukunda, 447
mystic power of, 415
Brahmā baffled by, **693, 699, 700, 702**, 703, 704, 705, 722-24
Nalakūvara & Maṇigrīva delivered by, 551, 561, **564**
Nalakūvara & Maṇigrīva prayed to, **550, 552–54, 556–60**
name(s) of
as Kṛṣṇa Himself, 47
as Kṛṣṇa's incarnation, 230
meaning of, 34, 183, 444, 447, 448, 465
other, **446–47**, 451
name-giving ceremony for, **444, 446–51**
Nanda &. *See:* Nanda, Kṛṣṇa &...
Nārada's words fulfilled by, **546, 547**
via Nārada we can know, 558-59
Nārāyaṇa under, 713

Kṛṣṇa (*continued*)
nature controlled by, 471
nondevotee vs., 605
offerings for, 576-77
as one & different, 677, **695**, 696-97
opened mouth wide, **469, 471**
opulence of, **469**, 577, **584**, 694, 695, 707, 712, 723
as original person, 677
as origin of all, 19, 44, 47, 235, **409**, 471, **552, 554**
other names of, **446, 447**, 451
owns everything, 476, 477
Pāṇḍavas saved by, **27–28**, 29
as Parabrahman, 618, 732
*paramahaṁsas* devoted to, **659–60**
parents of, 484-86, 488
*See also:* Devakī; Nanda; Vasudeva; Yaśodā
Parīkṣit saved by, **28**, 29
pastimes of
as absolute, 465
Balarāma in, **50**
bewildering Brahmā, 672-73, 675
childhood, **389**, 390, **391**, 453, 483, **489–90, 493, 574–75, 613, 652**
as confidential & confounding, **661**
as contradictory, 512
cowherd ladies enjoyed, **456–57**
*dāmodara-līla*, 549
demigods in, **93**, 94
demons interrupted, 626-27
devotee promoted to, 48-49, 70, 94
elevate less intelligent, 186-87
as eternal, 48, 484
hearing about, 377, **386, 389**, 390-91, 395, 396, 399-400, 612
via His energies, 671
mischievous, **461–65**
misunderstanding as mythology, 556
names of Kṛṣṇa according to, **447**, 448
Parīkṣit attracted to, **389**, 390, **391**
remembrance about, 493-94
Śukadeva summarized, 16
as transcendental, 458, 714
Vrajabhūmi's inhabitants sang, 608
women of heaven in, 49

## N

## Q



## R

Senses (*continued*)
Kṛṣṇa's potency beyond perception of, 618
in Kṛṣṇa's service, 69, 73, 377, 378, 560
*See also:* Body, material
Servant(s) of God. *See:* Devotee(s); Pure devotee(s); Spiritual master(s)
Service
to devotees, 103-4
devotional. *See:* Devotional service
everyone engaged in, 710-11
material, compared with spiritual, 68
*See also:* Devotional service
Śeṣa-nāga. *See:* Ananta
Sex life
material desire for, 259
materialist attached to, **660**
spiritual principles for, 251-52
*See also:* Desire, material; Lust; Sense gratification
Ship in ocean, example of, 729
Shower of flowers by demigods for Kṛṣṇa, **601, 607, 644**
Siddhas, **207, 285-86**
*Siddhas* defined, 558
*Siddhis* (mystic perfections) listed, 415
*Śikṣāṣṭaka* quoted
on desiring devotional service, 190-91, 258
on purifying materialistic heart, 539
Sinful activities
animal slaughter among, 150, 342, **530, 532**
bad body by, 65, **77**
bodily concept causes, 149, 150
as condemned, 63
four listed, 171
Ganges River &, 523
Kṛṣṇa consciousness stops, 95-96
*prasāda* dispels reactions to, 529
punishment for, 528-29
suffering due to, **530**, 531
Vasudeva warned Kaṁsa about, 62, 65, 76, **77**
Sītā, Rāvaṇa took *māyā* form of, 673
Śiva, Lord, **418**
as annihilator, 42, 228, 229
as authority, 169
Śiva (*continued*)
in bodily concept, 516
chants Lord's holy name, 154
color of, 228
devotees of, 522
Kṛṣṇa compared with, 164, 165, 713, 720
Kuvera's sons devoted to, **521**
at Lord's advent, **154**, 158
quoted on Viṣṇu worship, 480
worships Lord, 504
Yaśodā compared with, **513-14**
Slaughter of animals
Sleep, death compared to, 725
Snake
corpse of, burning of, 376-77
cruel person compared with, 282
Kṛṣṇa compared to, **356**, 357
Snow's darkness & inferior's power, analogy of, **704**
Society, human
animalistic, 179, 180
in chaos, 311-12
elevation of, 715
fallen condition of, 146
food supply for, 405-6
God-consciousness opportunity for, 728
godly, compared with godless, **313-14**
in Kali-yuga, 393, 537
Kṛṣṇa consciousness movement guides, 436, 437
occupational divisions of, 41, 179
past & present, 441
purification of, 440-41
social orders in, 404, 436-37
in Western countries, 328
*See also:* Civilization, modern; *Varṇāśrama-dharma;* Vedic culture
Soldier(s). *See: Kṣatriya(s)*
*Soma-vaṁśa. See:* Yadu dynasty
Son(s)
mother's affection for, 683
Soul(s)
atheists deny, 532
body based on, **223**
body contrasted to, 292, 293
changes bodies, **64-76**, 317-18, 434-35
conditioned. *See:* Conditioned soul(s)
consciousness symptomizes, 68

## T



## U